KREINDLER

International Arbitration in Sweden

International Arbitration in Sweden

A Practitioner's Guide

Editors

Ulf Franke

Annette Magnusson

Jakob Ragnwaldh

Martin Wallin

Assistant Editor

Björn Rundblom Andersson

Wolters Kluwer

Law & Business

Published by:
Kluwer Law International
PO Box 316
2400 AH Alphen aan den Rijn
The Netherlands
Website: www.kluwerlaw.com

Sold and distributed in North, Central and South America by:
Aspen Publishers, Inc.
7201 McKinney Circle
Frederick, MD 21704
United States of America
Email: customer.service@aspenpublishers.com

Sold and distributed in all other countries by:
Turpin Distribution Services Ltd
Stratton Business Park
Pegasus Drive, Biggleswade
Bedfordshire SG18 8TQ
United Kingdom
Email: kluwerlaw@turpin-distribution.com

Printed on acid-free paper.

ISBN 978-90-411-3795-1

Printed and Bound by CPI Group (UK) Ltd, Croydon, CR0 4YY.

Summary of Contents

Table of Contents

List of Editors

Ulf Franke is Chairman of the Arbitration Institute of the Stockholm Chamber of Commerce (SCC); Past Secretary General, SCC; Past Secretary General, International Council for Commercial Arbitration (ICCA); Past President, International Federation of Commercial Arbitration Institutions (IFCAI).

Annette Magnusson is Secretary General of the Arbitration Institute of the Stockholm Chamber of Commerce. She joined the SCC from Mannheimer Swartling in 2010, and before that Baker & McKenzie in Stockholm. Annette Magnusson is the author of several publications on international arbitration and a frequent lecturer.

Jakob Ragnwaldh is a partner with Mannheimer Swartling. He has represented clients in arbitrations under the auspices of most major arbitral institutions (including the SCC, the ICC, ICSID, HKIAC and the Arbitral Centre of the Austrian Federal Economic Chamber) as well as under the UNCITRAL Rules. He also represents investors and States in investment treaty arbitrations under bilateral investment treaties and the Energy Charter Treaty. Jakob Ragnwaldh sits as an arbitrator in institutional and ad hoc arbitrations. He is a board member of the Arbitration Institute of the Stockholm Chamber of Commerce and teaches investment treaty arbitration at Stockholm University.

Martin Wallin is a partner with Hannes Snellman in Stockholm and head of the dispute resolution group. He has been practicing arbitration and litigation for more than twenty years both as a counsel and as an arbitrator in Swedish and international proceedings. He is a board member of the Arbitration Institute of the Stockholm Chamber of Commerce and the Swedish Bar Association. He regularly lectures on arbitration and procedural law.

List of Contributors

Stefan Brocker is a partner with Mannheimer Swartling and specializes in commercial litigation and arbitration. He has acted as counsel in a large number of Swedish and international proceedings conducted under *inter alia* the SCC Rules, the ICC Rules and the UNCITRAL Rules as well as domestic arbitrations.

Christer Danielsson is a partner with Frank Advokatbyrå in Stockholm. Previously he was for many years a partner with Gernandt & Danielsson. Mr Danielsson's practice is focused on arbitration and litigation. In addition to representing a number of large corporations on a regular basis, he is a frequently appointed arbitrator, both in domestic and international arbitration proceedings.

Dr Nils Eliasson is a partner with Mannheimer Swartling specializing in international commercial arbitration and investment treaty arbitration. Based in Hong Kong, Nils is responsible for Mannheimer Swartling's Asian dispute resolution practice. Nils has experience in conducting arbitrations under the auspices of most major arbitration institutions (including, *inter alia*, the ICSID, HKIAC, ICC, SIAC, LCIA, DIS and SCC) as well as ad hoc proceedings under the UNCITRAL arbitration rules. He has also acted as counsel for investors and States in a number of investment arbitrations under bilateral investment treaties as well as under the Energy Charter Treaty.

Pontus Ewerlöf specializes in arbitration and civil litigation. He is partner with, and head of, MAQS Law Firm's Dispute Resolution Group in Stockholm. Pontus has vast experience as counsel in arbitrations under the SCC, the ICC, UNCITRAL and other rules in both Sweden and abroad. He also sits as arbitrator and has been appointed as sole arbitrator by the SCC and the Finnish Chamber of Commerce. He is a member of the Board of Young Arbitrators Sweden, and of the Executive committee of the Swedish Arbitration Association.

Dr. Gisela Knuts is a partner with Roschier specialized in commercial dispute resolution and continuously involved in disputes in areas such as distribution, energy, M&A, construction and anti-trust damages. She frequently acts as counsel and arbitrator, and she is a member of the Executive Committee of the Swedish Arbitration Association.

Kristoffer Löf is partner with Mannheimer Swartling, specialising in arbitration with an emphasis on oil & gas and construction disputes. He has acted in arbitrations conducted under a variety of rules, including the SCC, ICC, ICDR and UNCITRAL Rules.

He is a member of the Board of Young Arbitrators Sweden and of the Global Advisory Board of the ICDR Y&I.

Bo G.H. Nilsson is a dispute resolution partner with Advokatfirman Lindahl. He has more than thirty years of experience in dispute resolution, both arbitration and litigation, internationally and domestically, largely also as arbitrator or chairman of arbitral tribunals. He has been active in over 300 cases. He is the immediate past President of Swedish Arbitration Association, the current Swedish member of ICC International Court of Arbitration, a member of the Board of the Stockholm Center of Commercial Law, Section for Dispute Resolution at Stockholm University.

Ola Nilsson is counsel at White & Case in Stockholm and focuses on arbitration and commercial litigation. He has represented parties in several Swedish and international arbitrations and has acted as arbitrator. Ola Nilsson has published several articles on arbitration in international legal publications and he lectures regularly at Stockholm University

Anders Reldén is a partner with White & Case in Stockholm and specializes in arbitration and commercial litigation. He has represented Swedish and foreign corporations and state entities in complex Swedish and international arbitration matters. He also regularly serves as arbitrator and is a member of the executive committee of the Swedish Arbitration Association.

Björn Rundblom Andersson is an associate with Advokatfirman Lindahl, where he practices exclusively in the field of dispute resolution, internationally as well as domestically. He has previously been a legal counsel with the SCC.

Dr. Patrik Schöldström is a Judge at the Svea Court of Appeal in Stockholm, serving in the division of the Court that handles arbitration cases. He was previously a member of the Swedish bar; his practice included appearing as counsel in arbitrations and sitting as an arbitrator. He has written a doctoral dissertation in arbitration law: '*The Arbitrator's Mandate*' (1998). He regularly lectures and writes articles and case notes on arbitration and procedural law.

Dr. Patricia Shaughnessy directs the Master of International Commercial Arbitration Law programme at Stockholm University and is a vice-chairperson of the Board of the Arbitration Institute of the Stockholm Chamber of Commerce. She is on the Board of Directors of the Stockholm Centre for Commercial Law and heads the Section on Arbitration and Other Dispute Resolution. She also acts as a consultant in arbitration and commercial law projects and activities in a number of countries.

Marie Öhrström is a senior associate with Setterwalls' dispute resolution team, focusing on domestic and international commercial arbitration. Previously she was the deputy secretary general of the Arbitration Institute of the Stockholm Chamber of Commerce (SCC). Ms. Öhrström is also the author of an extensive handbook and commentary to SCC arbitration.

Foreword: An Introduction from an Outside Perspective – Reflections on International Arbitration with a Particular Focus on Sweden

Swedes have favoured arbitration for a very long time, and so in particular have the Swedish Parliament and the Swedish courts – as can be verified by contemplating the Swedish Arbitration Act of 1929 and the decided cases throughout the twentieth century. Swedish business contracts so routinely include arbitration clauses that one suspects that a party putting forward a draft in which that clause was missing would be looked at with something akin to suspicion. The old Act was drafted with the plain objective of giving broad effect to agreements to arbitrate, and courts applied it in a straight-forward, no-nonsense way. In sum, the national tradition is that business disputes *mean* arbitration.

What could be more natural, one might have thought, for Sweden therefore to become a haven for *international* arbitration? Indeed so it has, but therein lies a paradox, because the context of international arbitration in Sweden contrasts vividly with that of the domestic variety.

The latter has for generations operated in an environment which ensures its effectiveness: a small, homogenous society with strong institutions, a culture of voluntary compliance with established obligations, and a judicial system respectful of the authority of arbitrators and consistent in its deference to arbitration agreements and the enforcement of arbitral awards.

The international environment cannot, in a broad perspective, be said to mirror this idyll. There have been some notorious instances (isolated, but no less famous for that) of international arbitrations that found their seat in Sweden and gave rise to distressing stories of obstreperousness, chicanery, corruption, and even threats of violence. The ordinary run of the international mill is of course less dramatic, but still of a dimension quite different from the purely national process.

An important part of the narrative some decades ago was Sweden's attraction to parties who above all valued the perception of national geopolitical neutrality. For example, as the USSR, and later the PRC, began to expand their economic relations with the West, Sweden's historic and doggedly preserved neutrality gave it ready credibility as an acceptable venue for the resolution of disputes. (The famous exchange of letters between the American Arbitration Association and the USSR Chamber of Commerce and Industry in 1976 remains the iconic illustration of this development; it was countered by a simultaneous letter form the Stockholm Camber of Commerce setting out the manner in which arbitrations could be conducted in accordance with an 'optional clause' endorsed by the US and USSR entities.). As a result it became acceptable for trading entities of the Eastern command economies to agree routinely to arbitration in Sweden; a practice which remains habitual in the contract practices of a number of ex-East Block parties notwithstanding the disappearance of the political tension of that age.

The same factors that led to Sweden's prominence as a venue for East-West arbitration doubtless explain the subsequent emergence of Sweden as a leading venue for investment treaty arbitrations; the Stockholm Chamber of Commerce is the most frequently chosen of all arbitral institutions in this context save ICSID, which of course is an international organisation in the strict sense of that term and does not insert itself into the legal orders of any national 'seat' of arbitration.

All these international arbitrations did not look much like Swedish ones. Often neither party was Swedish. It became commonplace that none of the members of the arbitral tribunal was Swedish. The courts asked to defer to arbitration in Sweden, or to enforce awards rendered those, were located elsewhere – leaving only the task of examining annulment applications for the Swedish courts. Nor were the arbitrants especially devoted to the process, or respectful of its outcome; the Swedish venue was the least bad alternative, and the result quite likely to be repudiated by the losing party. Examples of truculence during the arbitration, and acrimonious objections in the aftermath, of a nature unknown in Sweden, came to the fore.

'Your system', Kant might have lectured the Swedes, using his famous expression, 'can no longer count on the same obedience as that of your equable population; justice will not be effective until it is designed to work for a Nation of Devils'.

Against this background, the reader does well to reflect on the first word in the title of this book. Through its pages, practitioners can verify how Swedish law and practice has evolved as it confronts not only model cases where parties placidly resolve the inevitable controversies which arise form business transactions, but also politicized conflicts involving obdurate parties who resent all attempts to subject them to adjudication in a foreign forum, and could not care less what damage may be done to the process using all means to make it ineffective.

Such difficulties are an inherent part of international arbitration, and this book deals with them amply. It is nothing less than remarkable to consider the difference of the experience of non-Swedish lawyers contemplating arbitration in Sweden thirty years ago, when their opportunity to make themselves conversant with the process by reading about it in English was essentially limited to the book *Arbitration in Sweden* which came out in 1977 (reedited and expanded in 1984). Excellent as it was, that book essentially comprised an analysis of the law as illuminated by a series of mainly domestic cases which were (i) unfamiliar to foreigners and (ii) inaccessible otherwise than in Swedish. To the extent that one wished to imagine how Swedish law would have dealt with thorny questions that are the staple of international arbitration, such as the effect of competing procedures abroad, of foreign acts of states purporting to curtail the options of the arbitrators, or of the endless varieties of peculiar initiatives that are the staple of the folklore of international arbitration but are simply not part of the culture of Swedish arbitrants and therefore does not occur to them, there was nothing for it but to use one's imagination, or at best extrapolate.

Foreign readers of this book, on the other hand, will be exposed to a trove of pertinent references to important international cases with which they are already largely familiar, because these are well-known international cases and available in English. Equally, like other legal systems which have been favoured by foreign arbitration as venues of choice, Sweden, has on occasion generated practices or decisions which have caused foreigners to lift their eyebrows. In many instances, the questions were ones of first impression and have been satisfactorily put to rest – although foreigner readers may remember the first surprise rather than the conventional correction. An instance of this type is the matter of confidentiality as illuminated in the *Bulgarian Foreign Trade Bank ('Bulbank')* case, with respect to which the unremarkable and sensible outcome is straightforwardly explained in Chapter 8 (Section VI). Other topics should be recognized as part of the specifics which international practitioners must deal with, and must continue to do so, as long as we do not have global uniformity. An example of this is the availability of judicial recourse against the establishment of the fees of the arbitrator even if they have been set by an arbitral institution (see Chapter 9, Section III) and the importance of the formal request for relief in terms of establishing the scope of the arbitral mission, with the effect that the common formula 'and such other relief as the arbitral tribunal considers appropriate' is meaningless, as it could not be granted without committing the error of *ultra petita* (Chapter [illegible]).

These cases have been widely discussed not only by Swedish commentators but in studies generated by the broader international arbitral community. Time and again, one turns the page and is referred once more to dispositions made by Swedish courts of important issues that have in recent decades been generated by the stream of major international cases heard in Sweden. It is worth stressing, in this connection, that although Sweden is properly characterized as a civil law country its courts and scholars give unusual weight to precedents, in a manner that makes the common lawyer feel at home – as if engaged in a conversation with cousins, if not quite siblings.[1]

Sweden is now one of a handful of countries where the international arbitral process has reached a stage where the jurisprudence is replete with instances involving

1. If the third sentence of this book is to be believed (which one expects is so), there is no room in Sweden for the anti-arbitration sentiment openly expressed in England and the United States by those who fear that "the law" will atrophy if important legal issues are withheld from binding judicial determination: "the State has no interest in whether or not all private law disputes between private entities are resolved by state courts insofar as those disputes do not involve public interests".

no local parties at all. This is a context of especially credible neutrality, where one may expect that the richness of the body of decided cases makes it likely to be echoed and relied upon elsewhere in the converging world of international arbitration. This book goes a long way to making that body accessible and understandable, as a premium to be added to the achievement of its primary aim of satisfying the international community's interest in knowing what will happen when its disputes are brought to Sweden.

Jan Paulsson
February 2013

President, International Council for Commercial Arbitration
Centennial Professor, London School of Economics
Professor of Law, University of Miami

Preface

The first book on arbitration in Sweden written in English was published in 1977. It was issued following the conclusion of the USA-USSR Optional Clause Agreement, which provided for arbitration in Sweden, and marked the start of a development that over the next few decades would bring Sweden into a leading position in international arbitration. This achievement was facilitated by the fact that arbitration was widely used in Sweden and had been so for several hundred years.

In 1999, a new arbitration act was adopted. By this time the Arbitration Institute of the Stockholm Chamber of Commerce (SCC) had already revised its rules and practices to an international standard prompted by the rapid increase of the SCC's international caseload.

The Swedish arbitration community, which in the mid-1970s consisted of a handful of specialists, today includes hundreds of legal professionals dedicated to the practice of international arbitration. They have established the Swedish Arbitration Association (SAA) open to members from both Sweden and other countries. In addition, a number of very active associations for young arbitrators and practitioners will ensure a high standard also for the future.

Recognizing the strong interest for Swedish case law in matters of arbitration in the international arbitration community, the SCC has launched an arbitration portal, which provides free access to English translations of Swedish court decisions of relevance to arbitration. Due to the longstanding practice of arbitration in Sweden, the Swedish judiciary is very familiar with and supportive of arbitration as a means of settling disputes.

Sweden also offers a successful Master's programme in International Commercial Arbitration, through Stockholm University. For more than ten years, the Master's programme of Stockholm University has attracted applications from thousands of students from across the globe. Beginning in 2013, Uppsala University will offer a Master's programme in Investment Treaty Arbitration.

The purpose of the present book, written by thirteen eminent practitioners, is to provide a practical guide to international arbitration in Sweden, whether *ad hoc* or institutional. It is our hope that this book will further add to the dissemination of knowledge of international arbitration in Sweden, and also serve as a reliable source for anyone who is called upon to act as arbitrator or counsel, or in any other capacity, in an international arbitration in Sweden.

We take this opportunity to thank the authors for their excellent contributions. A special thanks also to assistant editor Björn Rundblom Andersson, and language editor Christopher Goddard.

Although the group of editors consists of three Members of the SCC Board and the Secretary General of the SCC, this book is not intended to be an official commentary to the SCC Rules, nor are the views expressed therein necessarily representative of those of the SCC.

Ulf Franke
Annette Magnusson
Jakob Ragnwaldh
Martin Wallin
Stockholm, March 2013

CHAPTER 1

Fundamental Principles of International Arbitration in Sweden

Bo G.H. Nilsson & Björn Rundblom Andersson

I. INTRODUCTION

A. Brief Historical Overview of Swedish Arbitration

1. Arbitration has a long tradition as the preferred method of solving commercial disputes in Sweden. Reference to arbitration can already be found in legislation from the fourteenth century. The Swedish State has long recognized the legitimacy of allowing parties to decide on how to settle their own disputes, as the State has no interest in whether or not all private law disputes between private entities are resolved by state courts insofar as those disputes do not involve public interests.[1] Upholding arbitration as a legitimate means of resolving disputes, the State has instructed state organs to enforce arbitral awards. The first statutory provision on enforcement of arbitral awards was adopted in the seventeenth century.

2. In the early days of Swedish arbitration law, the procedure was unregulated. Testimonies from the nineteenth century suggest that it was not uncommon for arbitration to be obstructed by respondents and that the law did not provide a claimant with sufficient means of obtaining an arbitral award in those cases.[2] By adoption of the first Swedish Arbitration Act in 1887, the legislator sought to ensure that arbitration proceedings could also be conducted efficiently against recalcitrant respondents.[3]

1. NJA II 1929 p. 5.
2. NJA II 1887 No. 4 p. 13 et seq.
3. *Ibid*.

3. The 1887 Arbitration Act remained in force for some forty years before being replaced by the 1929 Arbitration Act. The latter Act was generally regarded as an efficient basis for arbitration proceedings which catered well to the needs of the arbitration community. It would remain in force for seventy years, when it was replaced.

B. Development of Sweden as a Venue for International Arbitration

4. Due to continuing cooperation to ensure a functioning legal framework for international commercial arbitration, the twentieth century saw the conclusion of a number of multilateral treaties on arbitration. Sweden, which is a country heavily dependent on international trade, recognized the advantages that international arbitration offered and therefore participated in international cooperation. During the 1920s, Sweden ratified the Protocol on Arbitration Clauses made in Geneva on 24 September 1923, and the Convention on the Execution of Foreign Arbitral Awards made in Geneva on 26 September 1927. The need to comply with obligations arising from those treaties led to adoption of the 1929 Foreign Arbitration Agreements and Arbitral Awards Act.[4]

5. During the 1950s Sweden participated in drafting the highly successful Convention on the Recognition and Enforcement of Foreign Arbitral Awards, 1958 (New York Convention) made in New York on 10 June 1958. Sweden ratified the New York Convention on 28 January 1972.

6. The 1960s saw conclusion of two multilateral treaties: the European Convention on International Commercial Arbitration made in Geneva on 21 April 1961, and the Convention on the Settlement of Investment Disputes between States and Nationals of Other States (ICSID Convention) made in Washington on 18 March 1965. Sweden ratified the ICSID Convention on 16 December 1966 but has not signed the 1961 European Convention.

7. Diplomatic efforts to create a functioning legal framework for international arbitration were successful. While Sweden's participation in these efforts may have been a factor, Sweden's status as one of the foremost venues for international arbitration does not directly owe its inception to creation of a legal framework. An important reason why Sweden became a frequently used forum for international arbitration lies in the political climate of the second half of the twentieth century. When the peace finally achieved at the end of the Second World War turned into a cold war between East and West, trade between East and West by no means ended. Through special purpose state organs, foreign trade organizations or FTOs, the States of the Eastern bloc traded with Western commercial parties. The political animosity between East and West complicated resolution of disputes arising from those transactions. For reasons that are easily understood, Western parties were reluctant to bring their contract claims against organs of an Eastern State before the courts of the same State or before arbitral institutions under state control. Equally, FTOs were reluctant to bring actions before

4. *(Sw: Lag (1929:147) om utländska skiljeavtal och skiljedomar)*.

Western courts or before arbitral institutions perceived as having a pro-western bias. The middle road available was to have disputes resolved in neutral jurisdictions. Therefore Sweden, which has pursued a policy of neutrality and non-alignment in foreign affairs since the nineteenth century, came to see a significant increase in international arbitration.

8. Endeavours undertaken by Eastern trade organizations and Western commercial interests in the 1970s to agree on a means of dispute resolution acceptable to both Western and Eastern parties are often cited as one of the reasons for Sweden's popularity as a venue for international arbitration. These endeavours resulted in the agreement on the Optional Clause for Use in Contracts in USA-USSR Trade 1977 (hereinafter the 'Optional Clause Agreement'), by the American Arbitration Association (hereinafter the 'AAA'), the USSR Chamber of Commerce and Industry (hereinafter the 'USSR Chamber') and the Stockholm Chamber of Commerce (SCC).

9. The Optional Clause Agreement provided for a model arbitration clause (hereinafter the 'Optional Clause') which both the AAA and the USSR Chamber considered acceptable and recommended for inclusion in contracts for East-West trade. The Optional Clause provided for ad hoc arbitration in Sweden under the 1976 UNCITRAL Arbitration Rules, with the SCC acting as appointing authority. The Optional Clause Agreement created a pool of presiding arbitrators, comprising six Eastern arbitrators (none from the USSR), six Western arbitrators (none from the USA) and six Swedish arbitrators, from which the parties could agree on the chairman of the arbitral tribunal and from which the SCC would normally appoint the chairman where the parties failed to do so.[5]

10. The Optional Clause Agreement was preceded by a thorough review of Swedish arbitration law in an international context by Swedish lawyers under the auspices of the SCC. The outcome of the review led foreign parties to conclude that Sweden was a jurisdiction favourable for resolution of international disputes. The result of the review was published by the SCC as the first edition of *Arbitration in Sweden* in 1977.[6] Some legislative changes to Swedish arbitration law were undertaken in connection with the review in order to better accommodate international arbitration.

11. Following the Optional Clause Agreement, other countries came to see Sweden as the preferred neutral forum for international dispute resolution. Most prominent among these countries is undoubtedly China. Contacts between the China Council for the Promotion of International Trade ('CCPIT', the parent body of today's CIETAC) and the SCC began in 1973 and the SCC's contacts with Chinese arbitration interests have since continued.[7] On 30 October 1984, the SCC and CCPIT signed a Cooperation Agreement, providing for regular exchange and cooperation between the Chinese and

5. After the fall of the USSR, in 1992, a new Optional Clause Agreement was made with the Chamber of Commerce and Industry of the Russian Federation. This agreement was subsequently updated in 2005.
6. (Stockholm: Norstedts, 1977).
7. M. Moser, *Ulf Franke, Stockholm Arbitration, and the Bridge to China*, in *Between East and West: Essays in Honour of Ulf Franke* 344 (K. Hobér et al. eds., Juris 2010).

Swedish arbitration communities.[8] The Agreement was subsequently amended and expanded.

12. Following these contacts, arbitration in Stockholm under the Rules of Arbitration of the Arbitration Institute of the SCC Rules became the only politically accepted alternative to arbitration in China for Chinese parties to international transactions. In fact the Chinese Ministry of Foreign Economic Relations and Trade published a Foreign Negotiation Handbook in which readers were instructed to insist on arbitration in China by CIETAC when entering into a contract with foreigners. In some special cases, however, it was permissible to agree to arbitration in Stockholm under the SCC Rules.[9]

13. In the late 1980s and thereafter, another development took place which would further fuel international arbitration in Sweden, namely conclusion of a number of Bilateral Investment Treaties (BIT) between the then socialist countries of Eastern Europe and Western countries. These treaties often designated arbitration under the auspices of the SCC as one option for investor-State dispute resolution. Additionally, the ECT provides for arbitration under the SCC Rules as an alternative available to investors. This development has led the SCC to become the world's second most popular institution for investment arbitration, after ICSID.[10]

14. Since the late 1970s, the number of international arbitrations conducted in Sweden has increased steadily. The caseload of the SCC may serve as a benchmark in this regard. While in 1989 the SCC handled 22 arbitrations in total,[11] the number of cases filed with the SCC in 2009 was 215, out of which 96 cases were international.[12] The number of international cases filed with the SCC in 2009 was thus more than four times the total caseload twenty years earlier. Most cases concern parties from Europe and Asia, but arbitration involving parties from Africa and North or South America is not uncommon.[13]

15. The inflow of international disputes has prompted a number of changes to the Swedish arbitration landscape. International arbitration cases have brought about the entry of foreign lawyers, acting both as arbitrators and as counsel, onto the Swedish scene. Today most of the world's prominent arbitration lawyers have acted in Swedish arbitrations. Some of them serve or have served as Board Members with the SCC.

16. Internationalism has not been a one-way street, however. The Swedish arbitration scene has undoubtedly benefited from the inflow of international disputes, but at the same time Swedish arbitration practitioners have contributed heavily to the evolution

8. Moser, *Ulf Franke, Stockholm Arbitration, and the Bridge to China*, in *Between East and West: Essays in Honour of Ulf Franke*, 346.
9. Moser, *Ulf Franke, Stockholm Arbitration, and the Bridge to China*, in *Between East and West: Essays in Honour of Ulf Franke*, 348.
10. UNCTAD *report Latest Developments in Investor-State Dispute Settlement* (IIA Issues Note No. 1 for 2011).
11. J. Gernandt, *Ulf Franke – Thirty-five Years and Afterwards* in *Between East and West: Essays in Honour of Ulf Franke*, 171 (K. Hobér et al. eds., Juris 2010).
12. See statistics published at the SCC website, http://www.sccinstitute.com.
13. *Ibid.*

of a truly international approach to arbitration. For example, Sweden had a substantial number of arbitrators that ventured beyond Sweden's borders at an early stage and took with them their experiences of Swedish arbitration law. Many of these arbitrators became prominent actors on the international scene. In this vein, two of the neutral arbitrators appointed when the Iran-United States Claims Tribunal was set up following the Algiers Declarations, were of Swedish nationality; the late Gunnar Lagergren was in fact the Tribunal's first President and responsible for organizing its operation.

17. As will be further discussed in the following, the legal framework for Swedish arbitration is just that, a framework. This affords parties and arbitrators considerable freedom to vary or supplement the relevant statutory provisions and arbitration rules. International arbitration in Sweden can accordingly be conducted very differently depending on the nationality and identity of the members of the tribunal and of the parties' counsel. In particular, the chairman's style and the expectations of counsel influence proceedings considerably. Over time lawyers exposed to international arbitration, in Sweden as elsewhere, are inevitably inspired by practices observed with others, resulting in a convergence towards best, or at least generally accepted, practices in international arbitration.

18. While thirty years ago a Swedish lawyer would have been minded to look primarily to the Swedish Code of Judicial Procedure for guidance on most procedural issues arising, the Code's influence has decreased over time. In international arbitration conducted in Sweden today, international rules, guidelines and practices are the preferred sources for guidance on procedural issues.

19. In parallel with this development, the SCC has become a truly internationally minded institution. Its former Secretary General, Ulf Franke, was for many years also the Secretary General of ICCA. In appointing a chairman of a particular arbitral tribunal, the SCC today looks worldwide for the individual best suited to the task.

II. LEGAL FRAMEWORK

A. The 1999 Arbitration Act

20. In the early 1990s, the Swedish legislator recognized that the realities of the Swedish arbitration environment had changed since 1929, when the arbitration act then in force was adopted. The government thus appointed an arbitration committee which was charged with the task of preparing a new arbitration act. In 1994, the committee presented an official report containing a draft arbitration act.[14] The draft was then reviewed and revised by the Ministry of Justice. In 1998, the Government submitted a Government bill[15] proposing adoption of a new arbitration act to the parliament, which approved the Government bill. On 1 April 1999, the Swedish Arbitration Act (Sw: *Lag (1999:116) om skiljeförfarande*) (the Act) entered into force.

14. SOU 1994:81.
15. Govt. bill 1998/99:35.

The Government bill is an important source of information when it comes to proper interpretation of the Act.

21. Unlike its predecessors, the Act applies to international as well as to domestic arbitration. The legislative history of the Act demonstrates that the legislator wanted to maintain and strengthen Sweden's role as a venue for international arbitration. In this endeavour, the legislator turned its attention to the UNCITRAL Model Law on International Commercial Arbitration 1985, which came to exert substantial influence on the legislative process. The principles underlying the Act are thus largely identical to those of the Model Law. Some differences exist between the Model Law and the Act but these are rarely substantial; an overview of some of the most notable differences appears below.

B. Fundamental Principles of Swedish Arbitration Law

1. Party Autonomy

22. In drafting the Act, the Swedish legislator recognized party autonomy as a 'central ingredient' of Swedish arbitration legislation.[16] The Act is generally non-mandatory.[17] The Act does not contain any general provision on the extent to which parties are free to deviate from the Act, although some of its provisions expressly provide that they apply only unless otherwise agreed by the parties. Ultimately the extent of party autonomy is dependent on such circumstances as, for example, the nature of the provision in question, the significance of the deviation and its timing.[18]

23. The party autonomy principle allows the parties to adapt the procedure to the practicalities of their dispute. An arbitral tribunal is, under section 21 of the Act, required to follow the parties' joint instructions insofar as those instructions are not unlawful (or wholly impractical in which case the arbitrators may be entitled to resign). However, it is fairly rare that parties to arbitration are able to reach full agreement on the procedure once a dispute has arisen. Detailed provisions on the arbitration procedure in arbitration agreements are even rarer. It has therefore been submitted that the main significance of party autonomy may be that the arbitral tribunal should consult the parties before making important decisions on procedure.[19]

2. Confidentiality and Its Limits

24. One factor often named as an advantage of arbitration compared with litigation before State courts, is that the procedure is confidential. The Act contains no provisions on confidentiality. It is nevertheless clear that Swedish arbitrations are confidential in the sense that they are private. This entails that non-parties in general have no right to

16. Govt. bill 1998/99:35 p. 43.
17. Govt. bill 1998/99:35 p. 44.
18. *Ibid.*
19. L. Heuman, *Arbitration Law of Sweden: Practice and Procedure*, 250 (Juris 2003).

obtain information about arbitration proceedings or to attend hearings. Whether the principle of confidentiality creates obligations for the parties not to disclose information about the arbitration to third parties has been the subject of some debate. The Supreme Court judgment in *Bulgarian Foreign Trade Bank Ltd v. A.I. Trade Finance Inc* (the 'Bulbank' case),[20] settled this debate. In its judgment the Court held that unless the parties have assumed such an obligation by agreement, there is no obligation on them not to disclose information about a pending arbitration.

25. It is generally accepted that arbitrators may not disclose information received in the performance of their mandate. This confidentiality obligation, which also applies to the SCC as an institution, appears expressly from its Rules.

3. *Due Process*

26. Insofar as the merits of the dispute are concerned, the State assumes no responsibility for the administration of justice in arbitral proceedings.[21] However, as a condition for upholding and enforcing the agreement to arbitrate the State does require that the arbitral procedure satisfy fundamental principles of due process, such as equality of arms and the independence and impartiality of the arbitral tribunal.[22] Section 34, and in graver cases section 33, of the Act provide for remedies against arbitrations conducted in violation of due process standards.

4. *Finality of Arbitral Awards*

27. One of the essential features of arbitration is that the arbitral tribunal's award cannot be appealed on the merits. Swedish arbitration law upholds this principle. Under Swedish law an arbitral award can only be set aside in a few situations, largely corresponding to the Model Law and the grounds for refusal of recognition and enforcement under Article 5 of the New York Convention. In certain jurisdictions, for example England, it is possible to appeal an arbitral award on points of law.[23] No such recourse is available against a Swedish arbitral award. Quite the contrary, the Supreme Court has been firm in its reluctance to examine challenges where requests to set aside would open the back door for re-examination of the merits of the case.[24]

20. *Bulgarian Foreign Trade Bank Ltd v. A.I. Trade Finance Inc*, judgment by the Supreme Court made on 27 Oct. 2000 in case no T 1881-99, NJA 2000 p. 538.
21. For example, NJA II 1929 p. 5 and Govt. bill 1998/99:35 p. 35.
22. NJA II 1929 p. 6, cf. Govt. bill 1998/99:35 p. 43 et seq.
23. See for example s. 69 of the English Arbitration Act 1996.
24. E.g. *Soyak International Construction & Investment Inc v. Hochtief AG*, judgment of the Supreme Court on 31 Mar. 2009 in case no T 4387-07, NJA 2009 p. 128, in which the Supreme Court was called upon to examine whether insufficient reasons in the award could be grounds for setting it aside. The Court expressly cited the interest of finality as relevant in the context and emphasized that a qualitative review of the reasons for an award would give rise to serious issues as to the scope of such review, since arbitral awards cannot be re-examined on the merits.

28. The Act does, however, allow appeal against arbitral awards in one particular case, and that is where an arbitral tribunal by its award has declined jurisdiction, held a dispute inadmissible or otherwise terminated the proceedings without ruling on the merits of the dispute. The Act provides that the award can in that case be appealed to the courts which may hold e.g., that the arbitral tribunal had jurisdiction. However, the court may not remit the case back to the arbitral tribunal. Instead, a new arbitration may be initiated. The remedy under section 36 expresses the principle that the courts always have the last word insofar as concerns the existence, scope and validity of an arbitration agreement.

29. An arbitral award is enforceable immediately upon being rendered and a request to set aside or invalidate the award does not bar its enforcement. The only means of preventing enforcement of a Swedish arbitral award while an action to set it aside is pending is to convince the court to stay enforcement of the award. In order to obtain an order for stay of enforcement, the applicant must show probable cause for the request to set aside the award and that enforcement would cause the applicant irreparable or serious harm. A stay is rarely granted.

5. *Non-Intervention of the Courts*

30. No provisions of Swedish law would allow the courts to compel or forbid arbitration or to interfere with the manner in which arbitral proceedings are conducted. Although the Act does not contain any provision similar to Article 5 of the Model Law, which provides that State courts may only intervene in arbitral proceedings where the Model Law so provides, the position of Swedish law is the same.

C. Use of International Arbitration Authorities in Swedish Arbitration

31. Since the beginning of the twentieth century, adoption of private law legislation of importance has in Sweden often been preceded by a review of how the relevant questions have been addressed by foreign legal systems. A prominent example of this practice is found in official reports produced by the important Committee on the Law of Obligations, which sat during the early twentieth century. This comparative approach has allowed the Swedish legislator the benefit of evaluating the pros and cons of solutions to problems found in foreign laws.

32. However, preparation of the Arbitration Act 1929[25] does not seem to have been much influenced by this practice. Presumably, it was felt that issues of procedure were intrinsically more domestic in character than issues of substantive law. An illustrative example is that the list of authorities (contained in Appendix 4) of the first edition of *Arbitration in Sweden* comprised almost exclusively Swedish materials.

25. (*Sw: Lag (1929:145) om skiljemän*).

33. However, adoption of the Act was preceded by reviews of foreign arbitration laws. The Government bill refers to specific aspects of Belgian, Dutch, Finnish, French, German, Spanish and Swiss arbitration law.

34. The international authority which was given the most consideration during preparation of the Act was the Model Law. As explained above, Sweden ultimately did not formally adopt the Model Law but the legislator decided that it should be considered to what extent each provision would conform to the Model Law.[26]

35. In the same vein, modern Swedish arbitration literature contains extensive references to international materials. The arbitration library of a Swedish law firm will today contain a majority of English language titles.

36. The sources of Swedish arbitration law should therefore largely be familiar to an international arbitration law practitioner, and international material is certainly familiar to Swedish lawyers. This includes Sweden's Supreme Court justices, several of whom have practiced extensively as arbitrators before, and some after, taking office.

37. Nevertheless, explicit references to international authorities are relatively scarce in judgments from the Swedish Supreme Court dealing with arbitration issues. The explanation is probably that in most cases the Court has felt no need to look for international authorities in order to determine the issues in dispute. However, when confronted with issues of principal importance the Court has seen reason to look beyond Swedish borders even in domestic arbitration:

> In *MS "Emja" Braack Schiffahrts KG v. Wärtsilä Diesel AB*[27], the Supreme Court referred to prevailing opinions under Dutch and German arbitration law, in arriving at its conclusion that, as a matter of Swedish arbitration law, an assignee is normally bound by an arbitration clause contained in the agreement assigned.
>
> In *Bulbank*[28], the Supreme Court turned its attention to certain foreign jurisdictions, namely England, France and Australia and found that these jurisdictions had taken different positions on the issue of confidentiality in arbitration. Ultimately the Court held that parties to a Swedish arbitration agreement are under no obligation to keep information on arbitration proceedings confidential.
>
> In *Anders Jilkén v. Ericsson AB*[29] the Supreme Court concluded that, whilst it is true that the question whether an arbitrator has been impartial or independent is to be answered with reference to the provisions of the Act, there is often reason to consider institutional rules and international guidelines. The Court held that the arbitrator had not been independent and confirmed this conclusion by referring to the IBA Guidelines on Conflict of Interest in International Arbitration (IBA Guidelines). The Supreme Court made a passing reference to these Guidelines also

26. E.g. Govt. bill 1998/99:35 p. 46.
27. *MS 'Emja' Braack Schiffahrts KG v. Wärtsilä Diesel AB*, decision by the Supreme Court made on 15 Oct. 1997 in case no Ö 3174-95, NJA 1997 p. 866. The assignee was a German company, the assignors were Dutch companies and the *debitor cessus* was a Swedish company.
28. *Bulgarian Foreign Trade Bank Ltd v. A.I. Trade Finance Inc*, judgment by the Supreme Court made on 27 Oct. 2000 in case no T 1881-99, NJA 2000 p. 538.
29. *Anders Jilkén v. Ericsson AB*, judgment by the Supreme Court made on 19 Nov. 2007 in case no T 2448-06, NJA 2007 p. 841.

in *Korsnäs AB v. AB Fortum Värme samägt med Stockholms stad.*[30] These cases show that the Supreme Court is inclined to consider international authorities also in strictly domestic cases.

In *Soyak International Construction & Investment Inc*[31] an arbitral award was challenged for having insufficiently clear reasons. The Supreme Court rejected the request to set aside the award with reference to Swedish law authorities. The Court confirmed its conclusion by referring to the position of Danish and Norwegian arbitration law.

38. It is impossible to ascertain the full extent to which Swedish arbitrators and counsel use international authorities in domestic arbitrations as well. It seems safe to assume, however, that this is becoming increasingly common. When confronted with issues of conflict of interest most Swedish lawyers would today look to the IBA Guidelines.

D. A brief Comparison of the Act and the Model Law

1. *Introduction*

39. This section provides a comparison between the Act and the Model Law where that comparison is relevant. The Model Law was a source of inspiration for the Swedish legislator and most differences between the two relate to form rather than substance; these differences will not be examined in this comparison.[32]

2. *Scope*

40. Unlike the Model Law, the scope of the Act is not limited to international commercial disputes. The Act thus applies to both domestic and international arbitrations alike, whether or not they relate to a commercial relationship.

3. *Notices Provisions*

41. Article 3 of the Model Law provides a rule on written communication, under which written communication is considered to be received when delivered in accordance with the Article. Article 3 also establishes that parties may agree on the manner of valid notice. The Act is silent as to how to serve notice in Swedish arbitration proceedings.

30. *Korsnäs AB v. AB Fortum Värme samägt med Stockholms stad*, judgment by the Supreme Court made on 9 Jun. 2010 in case no T 156-09, NJA 2010 p. 317.
31. *Soyak International Construction & Investment Inc v. Hochtief AG*, judgment of the Supreme Court on 31 Mar. 2009 in case no T 4387-07, NJA 2009 p. 128.
32. For a more detailed comparison between the Act and the Model Law, please refer to J. Sekolec & N. Eliasson, *The UNCITRAL Model Law on Arbitration and the Swedish Arbitration Act: A Comparison*, in *The Swedish Arbitration Act of 1999, Five Years On – A Critical Review of Strengths and Weaknesses* (L. Heuman & S. Jarvin eds., Juris 2006).

In its judgment in *Lenmorniiproekt OAO v. Arne Larsson & Partners AB*,[33] the Supreme Court found that, at least insofar as valid notice of the request for arbitration is concerned, actual receipt of the document is required as a matter of Swedish law.

4. *Form of the Arbitration Agreement*

42. Article 7 of the Model Law, like the New York Convention and most national arbitration laws, requires that an arbitration agreement be in writing.[34] Swedish law has never required written form. An arbitration agreement can be made orally or tacitly. Parties have been considered bound to arbitrate under practices established between them.[35] The vast majority of arbitration agreements are nevertheless made in writing. The absence of a required form, however, allows flexibility in determining whether an arbitration agreement has been concluded.

5. *The Arbitral Tribunal*

43. Unlike the Model law, the Act sets out formal requirements which all arbitrators must meet. Essentially, section 7 of the Act bars anyone who is not vested with full legal capacity in relation to his or her actions or property.

44. The procedure for appointing the arbitral tribunal is the same under the Act and the Model Law, but a difference occurs if an arbitrator resigns or is discharged. Under the Act, the party which appointed that arbitrator may appoint a replacement arbitrator only where the reason for the first arbitrator's resignation or discharge arose subsequent to the appointment. The reason is to stop a party from obstructing arbitration proceedings by appointing a series of arbitrators who resign or are disqualified.[36]

6. *The Concept of an Arbitral Award*

45. Article 32 of the Model Law provides that arbitral proceedings may be terminated by an award or an order. The Model Law is silent as to what awards other than a final award may be issued by an arbitral tribunal.

46. The Act goes further than the Model Law in setting out the awards which an arbitral tribunal may issue. The Act also provides that a decision whereby the arbitral tribunal resolves matters referred to it or otherwise terminates the proceedings must be made in the form of an arbitral award. This also applies to termination of a case which has been withdrawn.

33. *Lenmorniiproekt OAO v. Arne Larsson & Partners AB*, decision of the Supreme Court on 16 Apr. 2010 in case no Ö 13-09, NJA 2010 p. 219.
34. The 2006 amendments to the Model Law provide two alternative options for Art. 7. The second option does not require that an arbitration agreement be made in writing.
35. *Värmeledningsaktiebolaget Radiator v. Skanska AB*, decision by the Svea Court of Appeal made on 15 Nov. 1988 in case no Ö 2840-87, RH 1989:83.
36. Govt. bill 1998/99:35 p. 93 et seq.

47. It is not entirely uncommon for international tribunals sitting in Sweden to style as an award what under Swedish arbitration law is an order or vice versa.

E. Some Further Swedish Arbitration Law Issues

48. It is not possible to determine all procedural requirements that an arbitral tribunal must comply with by merely consulting the Act. The provisions contained in sections 33, 34 and 36 of the Act seemingly give the courts rather broad discretion to set aside an arbitral award. In practice, the courts have used this discretion quite restrictively. Many deviations from what is perceived as normal practice will not result in the award being set aside. It is nevertheless clear from the *travaux préparatoires* and case law that fundamental principles of Swedish procedure should be complied with in arbitration. Some of these principles are more stringent than in certain other jurisdictions. In particular, requests for relief and facts invoked as the basis for relief set the outer limits of the arbitral tribunal's mandate.

1. Importance of the Request for Relief

49. A principle generally considered as fundamental is that a tribunal has the power to grant relief only as requested by a party. The principle is expressed in Chapter 17, section 3 of the Swedish Code of Judicial Procedure, which provides that a judgment may not go beyond the relief sought. Under section 34(1) item 2 of the Act, an arbitral award will be set aside if the arbitral tribunal has exceeded its mandate.[37] The legislator assumed that this would be the case if a tribunal grants a party relief beyond what is requested.[38]

50. It is not uncommon in international arbitrations held in Sweden that parties, particularly when represented by English counsel, request the arbitral tribunal to award them such other relief as the arbitral tribunal considers appropriate. These requests are meaningless, as granting relief outside the specific request would under Swedish law be regarded as *ultra petita*.[39]

2. Importance of the Grounds of the Request for Relief

51. Another fundamental principle of Swedish procedural law is that the mandate of a court or arbitral tribunal is limited by the facts invoked by the parties as the basis for their claims. This principle is also expressed in Chapter 17, section 3 of the Swedish Code of Judicial Procedure. A fact is not considered as invoked in this sense merely

37. Govt. bill 1998/99:35 p. 143.
38. Govt. bill 1998/99:35 p. 142.
39. Chapter 17, s. 3 of the Code of Judicial Procedure (*Sw: Rättegångsbalk (1942:740)*) (available in English at http://www.regeringen.se/content/1/c4/15/40/472970fc.pdf) (accessed 18 Jan. 2013) and Govt. bill 1998/99:35 p. 142.

because it is mentioned somewhere in possibly extensive submissions.[40] Only if it is clear that the party mentioning the fact wishes the arbitral tribunal to base its award on that fact is it invoked as a basis for a claim.[41]

52. On the face of it, this principle seems fairly simple to apply and it serves the useful purpose of making the other side aware of the case brought against it. However, in large complex arbitration cases it can be difficult to determine whether or not a fact has been formally invoked. In a judgment setting aside a domestic arbitral award, the Svea Court of Appeal seemingly placed a strict burden on each party to be very clear in presenting the grounds on which it wishes the arbitral tribunal to rule.[42] The extent to which this principle would be applied in relation to international arbitration cases is presently unsettled. The Supreme Court has yet to rule on the issue. However, the legislator was well aware that application of the principle requires caution.[43]

3. *Iura Novit Arbiter?*

53. Under Swedish procedural law, a court is in principle free to apply whatever rule of law it considers applicable to the facts invoked by the parties. In accordance with the principle of *iura novit curia*, it is clear that a domestic arbitral award cannot be set aside where the arbitral tribunal applied law or authorities not invoked by the parties.[44] It is unsettled whether the principle applies in international disputes. In any event, it is good practice in both domestic and international arbitration that a tribunal invite the parties to comment before applying statutory provisions or case law not invoked by them.

4. *The Doctrine of Assertion*

54. The doctrine of assertion provides that the existence of a circumstance which is relevant both for jurisdiction and the merits of a case should be examined only on the merits. The circumstance is thus assumed to exist for the purpose of jurisdiction. The doctrine has traditionally been relied upon by the Supreme Court in order to determine jurisdictional conflicts between the courts of general jurisdiction and specialized courts.[45] The doctrine of assertion has also been considered applicable in arbitration since the 1960s but its application has rarely given rise to problems.[46] In essence, where a claimant asserts a right under a substantive agreement containing an arbitration

40. *NCC Nordic Construction Company AB v. IDRILLA AB(bankruptcy estate)*, judgment by the Supreme Court made on 12 Feb. 1996 in case no T 2390-94, NJA 1996 p. 52.
41. R. Nordh, *Processens ram i tvistemål* (IUSTUS, 2006), 38.
42. *Systembolaget AB v. V&S Vin & Sprit AB*, judgment by Svea Court of Appeal on 1 Dec. 2009 in case no T 4348-08.
43. Govt. bill 1998/99:35 p. 145.
44. *Ibid.*
45. P. Schöldström, *Påståendedoktrinen och skiljeförfarande*, JT 2008/09, 138–142, at. 140
46. See L. Welamson, review of P-O. Bolding, *Skiljedom*, in Svensk Juristtidning 1964, 278 et seq.

clause, the arbitral tribunal must not examine whether the asserted right in fact exists as an issue relating to jurisdiction.

55. In its judgment in *Petrobart Limited v. The Kyrgyz Republic*,[47] the Supreme Court set aside an arbitral award where an international arbitral tribunal had declined jurisdiction. The Court held that the arbitral tribunal had failed to apply this doctrine of assertion. The Court explained the essence of the doctrine, namely that examination of an assertion of a right under a substantive agreement must be reserved for the merits of a dispute. The Court further explained that application of the doctrine of assertion assumes the existence of an arbitration agreement covering the dispute over the alleged circumstance in question. If the existence or scope of the arbitration agreement is contentious, the arbitral tribunal must determine these issues as a jurisdictional matter.

56. A significant advantage of the doctrine appears if the tribunal ultimately finds that the circumstance alleged in fact does not exist. By applying the doctrine the tribunal will then at the jurisdictional phase have accepted jurisdiction over the claim, but in its final award reject that claim. If the jurisdictional issue has been joined to the merits the tribunal should nevertheless not dismiss for lack of jurisdiction but instead reject the claim. This determination normally cannot then be reviewed in challenge proceedings. Had the tribunal instead refused jurisdiction, that decision could have been reviewed by the courts and reversed. If so, the situation in a second arbitration where the same circumstance was to be tried at the merits phase could lead to an outcome incompatible with the courts' jurisdictional determination.

57. *Petrobart* is controversial because of the particular facts of that case, but application of the doctrine as such is uncontroversial as a matter of Swedish arbitration law.

III. INSTITUTIONAL ARBITRATION IN SWEDEN

58. A statistical survey of the number of arbitrations conducted in Sweden was commissioned in connection with the legislator's preparation of the Act. The survey, conducted by the State Statistical Agency, came to the conclusion that each year during the period 1993–1997 approximately 300–400 arbitrations were conducted in Sweden.[48] Of these, approximately 100 arbitrations yearly were conducted under the SCC Rules. During the period covered by the survey, the majority of arbitrations conducted in Sweden were thus ad hoc arbitrations. No similar survey has been conducted since and it is therefore impossible to say whether or not ad hoc arbitration is still the preferred regime in Sweden. The number of arbitrations administered by the SCC has doubled since the survey was conducted and it may very well be that institutional arbitration has become more popular than it was during the period 1993–1997.

59. The SCC is an internationally renowned arbitration institution and the majority of institutional arbitrations conducted in Sweden are administered by the SCC. However,

47. *Petrobart Limited v. The Kyrgyz Republic*, judgment by the Supreme Court made on 28 Mar. 2008 in case no T 2113-06,NJA 2008 p. 408.
48. Govt. bill 1998/99:35 p. 35.

there is no obstacle to arbitration being conducted in Sweden under the auspices of non-Swedish institutions. This frequently happens under e.g., the Rules of Arbitration of the International Chamber of Commerce (ICC Rules).

60. The SCC consists of a board of directors (hereinafter the 'Board') and a secretariat (hereinafter the 'Secretariat'). Under the 2010 SCC Rules, the Board is composed of both Swedish and foreign nationals and the maximum number of Board Members is sixteen. The Board determines matters such as SCC jurisdiction, advances on costs, appointment of arbitrators, challenges to and removal of arbitrators and fixing arbitration costs. Before the SCC refers a dispute to an arbitral tribunal, the Secretariat is responsible for the everyday case administration.

61. The SCC acts under a number of rules, namely the Arbitration Rules, the Rules for Expedited Arbitrations and Procedures and Services under the UNCITRAL Rules. Under its Arbitration Rules, SCC involvement is limited once the dispute is referred to the arbitral tribunal. There is no scrutiny of the arbitral award but the SCC follows the progress of the proceedings to ensure that awards are rendered within the time limits prescribed.

IV. A BRIEF COMPARISON BETWEEN THE ACT AND THE SCC RULES

A. Jurisdiction

62. Arbitration is a product of consent. The jurisdiction of arbitrators always rests on an agreement between the parties to the dispute. This fundamental feature of arbitration is expressed in section 1 of the Act. An arbitration agreement may be concluded in the form of a submission agreement or, more commonly, by inclusion of an arbitration clause in a contract.

63. The ad hoc regime under the Act will govern the arbitration proceedings if the parties have not specified anything to the contrary in the arbitration agreement. An arbitration agreement must somehow designate the SCC as competent to entertain disputes arising under the arbitration agreement in order for the SCC to have jurisdiction.

B. Procedures Prior to Constitution of the Arbitral Tribunal

1. *Initiation of Arbitration*

64. If the parties have not agreed otherwise, arbitration is, as provided by section 19 of the Act, initiated upon the respondent's receipt of the request for arbitration. Under that section, a request for arbitration must contain an explicit and unconditional request for an arbitral award, set out the issue to be resolved and information on the arbitrator appointed by the claimant.

65. By contrast, Article 4 of the SCC Rules provides that arbitration is commenced when the SCC receives a request for arbitration. Article 2 of the SCC Rules sets out the information which a request for arbitration should include. Upon filing a request for arbitration with the SCC, the claimant pays the registration fee laid down in Appendix III to the SCC Rules. If the registration fee is not paid on filing a request for arbitration, the Secretariat fixes a deadline for payment of the fee. If the fee is not paid within that time, the request for arbitration is dismissed.

66. Besides the respondent's notice of its appointment of an arbitrator, the Act contemplates no further written communication prior to constitution of the arbitral tribunal.

67. In an SCC arbitration, the Secretariat will communicate the request for arbitration to the party or parties named as respondent(s) and fix a deadline for the respondent(s) to file an Answer with the SCC. Formal requirements on an Answer are provided by Article 5. The respondent's failure to file an answer will not prevent the matter from proceeding. Under Swedish arbitration law, it is not possible to make a default award against a respondent who neglects to participate in the proceedings. Instead the tribunal proceeds to determine the case on the basis of the materials before it.

68. After the Answer, and – where applicable – further correspondence, the SCC will fix the advance on costs. Payment of the advance on costs is a prerequisite to the case being referred to the arbitral tribunal.

2. *Prima Facie Examination of Jurisdiction*

69. Under Article 2 of the SCC Rules, the claimant should provide a copy of the arbitration agreement by virtue of which the dispute is referred to arbitration. A respondent should, under Article 5 of the SCC Rules, raise any objections on the existence, applicability or validity of the arbitration agreement in its answer to the request for arbitration.

70. A jurisdictional objection raised by the respondent will normally be ruled upon by an arbitral tribunal. However, the Board may, under Article 10(i) of the Rules, dismiss a case where the SCC manifestly lacks jurisdiction over the dispute. The Board will, as provided by Article 9 of the Rules, review whether a case is to be dismissed 'when necessary'. In view of the SCC duty to make every reasonable effort to ensure that an award is enforceable, the Board may be justified in conducting a review of its own motion in ex parte proceedings.[49] Normally, however, the Board will only consider dismissal of a case where a party so requests.

---

49. M. Öhrström, *Stockholms Handelskammares Skiljedomsinstitut: En handbok och kommentar för skiljeförfaranden* (Norstedts Juridik, 2009), 139 et seq.

71. Published SCC practice indicates that the SCC rarely dismisses a dispute under Article 10 of the SCC Rules.[50] If the arbitration agreement provides for arbitration in Sweden and suggests that institutional arbitration was intended, then this will usually be enough unless some institution other than the SCC is identified.

3. *Pre-arbitral Relief*

72. The Act does not provide for any means of obtaining interim relief before an arbitral tribunal is empanelled. Under section 4(3) of the Act, the arbitration agreement does not bar a court from entertaining a request for interim relief.

73. The SCC may not grant interim relief. Before the SCC has referred a case to the arbitral tribunal, a party seeking provisional measures could thus be forced to take recourse to national courts. The SCC has recognized that this action might not always be appealing to a party. Therefore a revision of the SCC Rules which entered into force on 1 January 2010 now enables parties to initiate emergency arbitrator proceedings under the auspices of the SCC.

74. The provisions on the procedure before an emergency arbitrator are found in Appendix II to the 2010 SCC Rules (hereinafter the 'Emergency Rules'). The procedure before the emergency arbitrator could be described as a miniature arbitration within the arbitration. The determination by the emergency arbitrator is provisional only and will be reviewed once an arbitral tribunal is constituted.

4. *Constitution of the Arbitral Tribunal*

75. The default regime under the Act is that an arbitral tribunal is composed of three arbitrators. The parties are free to vary the default regime by agreement. The claimant should notify the respondent of the arbitrator appointed in the request for arbitration. The respondent then has thirty days from receipt of the request for arbitration to appoint an arbitrator

76. The SCC Rules likewise provide for a tribunal of three arbitrators by default. However, the Board may decide that the dispute is to be resolved by a sole arbitrator. In making its decision, the Board should take the complexity of the dispute and the amount involved into consideration. If the parties have agreed on the number of arbitrators, that agreement will of course prevail.

77. Where the parties have agreed that the dispute is to be resolved by a sole arbitrator, or the Board has so decided under Article 12, the parties are given ten days to jointly appoint the sole arbitrator, failing which the SCC will appoint the arbitrator. If the arbitral tribunal is to consist of multiple arbitrators the parties appoint an equal number

---

50. A. Magnusson, *Prima Facie Decisions on Jurisdiction*, 2 Stockholm Arbitration Report 1–11 (2000) and A. Magnusson & H. Larsson, *Recent Practice of the Arbitration Institute of the Stockholm Chamber of Commerce*, Stockholm Arbitration Report 49–62 (2004).

of arbitrators each and the SCC appoints the chairman. If a party fails to appoint an arbitrator in due time, the Board will make the appointment.

78. The position of Swedish law on the constitution of the arbitral tribunal in multiparty arbitration has not yet been settled. Some authorities assume that Swedish arbitration law upholds the so-called *Dutco* principle, i.e., that it is unfair if one side gets to choose an arbitrator but not the other.[51] The Act provides an opt-in mechanism for appointing the arbitral tribunal in multiparty situations. The competent district court will, under section 12(3) of the Act, appoint arbitrators on the application of a party, if the parties have agreed to vest the court with the power to do so. The SCC Rules on the other hand have been drafted with the *Dutco* principle in mind.[52] Hence, if an arbitral tribunal is to consist of multiple arbitrators and there are multiple claimants or multiple respondents, the multiple parties should make a joint appointment but if they are unable to agree on the appointment the SCC will appoint the entire arbitral tribunal.

79. If an arbitrator resigns or is released from his or her appointment, section 16 of the Act vests the competent district court with the power to appoint a new arbitrator in that person's stead. If, however, the reason for resignation or release arose subsequent to appointment, the new arbitrator should be appointed by whoever appointed the former arbitrator. The ratio behind this rule is to stop respondents from obstructing the procedure by appointing one or several arbitrators who subsequently resign or are released. In SCC arbitration the main rule, as provided in Article 17 of the SCC Rules, is that a replacement arbitrator is appointed by the party that appointed the replaced arbitrator unless the Board considers it appropriate to appoint the replacement arbitrator itself, a possibility which can be used to counter delaying tactics. If the Board appointed the replaced arbitrator, it will also appoint the replacement arbitrator.

5. *Required Qualifications and Challenges to Arbitrators*

80. Section 7 of the Act bars anyone not vested with full legal capacity in relation to his or her actions and property from acting as arbitrator. The provision is mandatory and thus applies to all arbitrations conducted in Sweden. Under section 8 of the Act, all arbitrators must be impartial. The concept of impartiality under the Act also encompasses independence. Section 8 of the Act provides that an arbitrator will be released from their appointment where circumstances may diminish confidence in the arbitrator's impartiality. The section proceeds to list four situations where confidence in the arbitrator's confidence is always diminished, so that the arbitrator should be released. The list is not exhaustive. Under section 9 of the Act, arbitrators are required to disclose all circumstances which may diminish confidence in their impartiality.

51. E.g. L. Heuman, *Arbitration Law of Sweden: Practice and Procedure*, 186.
52. A. Magnusson & P. Shaughnessy, *The 2007 Arbitration Rules of the Arbitration Institute of the Stockholm Chamber of Commerce*, 3 Stockholm Intl. Arbitration Rev. 41 (2006).

81. An arbitrator must, under section 10, be challenged at the latest fifteen days after the party bringing the challenge became aware of both the arbitrator's appointment and the circumstances giving rise to challenge. Under the Act, it is for the arbitral tribunal to examine a request to disqualify an arbitrator. If the request is sustained, that decision is final. If, however, the request is denied, it may be brought before the competent district court.

82. Arbitrators acting under the SCC Rules are required by Article 14 to be impartial and independent. These standards conform to international practice. Published SCC practice on challenges to arbitrators demonstrates that challenges to arbitrators acting under the SCC Rules rarely succeed.[53]

83. A party must bring before the SCC a challenge to an arbitrator at the latest fifteen days after becoming aware of the circumstance giving rise to the challenge. Failure to do so constitutes a waiver of the right to challenge the arbitrator on that ground. Any challenge must be communicated to the other party and the arbitrator challenged, who must be given an opportunity to comment.

6. *Advance on Costs*

84. Under the Act, it is for the arbitrators to fix their own fees. However, the arbitrators' discretion is limited by section 37 of the Act, which requires that fees be reasonable. Section 38 of the Act empowers an arbitral tribunal to require security for arbitrators' fees and expenses and to terminate the proceedings where the required security is not furnished. Under the SCC Rules, arbitration costs, i.e., the arbitrators' remuneration and the administrative fee of the SCC, are based on the amount in dispute. Under Article 45, the Board sets an amount which the parties must pay as an advance on costs, an amount which should correspond to the estimated final arbitration costs. Each party should normally pay half of the amount determined by the Board. If counterclaims or set-off claims have been raised, the Board may apportion payment of the advance so as to correspond to the different claims in dispute. The Board may order the parties to pay additional advances while the arbitration is pending.

85. Failing full satisfaction of the advance on costs, the SCC will dismiss the case. If a party fails to pay its part of the advance, the other party will have the option to pay the outstanding advance on behalf of the defaulting party. A party which chooses to pay

53. N. Lindström, *Challenges to Arbitrators – Decisions by the SCC Board during 2008–2010*, available at http://www.sccinstitute.se/filearchive/4/40158/Challenges%20to%20Arbitrators%20%E2%80%93%20Decisions%20by%20the%20SCC%20Board%20during%202008.pdf (accessed 15 Jan. 2013). For an overview of SCC Board decisions regarding challenges to arbitrators during previous years, see Marie Öhrström, *Decisions by the SCC Institute regarding Challenge of Arbitrators*, 1 Stockholm Arbitration Report 35–37 (2002); Annette Magnusson & Hanna Larsson, *Recent Practice of the Arbitration Institute of the Stockholm Chamber of Commerce: Prima Facie Decisions on Jurisdiction and Challenges of Arbitrators*, 2 Stockholm Arbitration Report 77–84 (2004); and Helena Jung, *SCC Practice: Challenges to Arbitrators, SCC Board Decisions 2005–2007*, 1 Stockholm Intl. Arbitration Rev. 1–18 (2008).

the other party's share of the advance may then seek an award from the arbitral tribunal, ordering the defaulting party to reimburse the other party for the defaulting party's share of the advance.

7. *Seat of the Arbitration*

86. If no seat has been agreed by the parties, section 22 of the Act leaves it to the arbitral tribunal to determine the seat. In SCC arbitration, however, it is for the Board to determine a seat of the arbitration where no agreement on the issue has been made. The award is considered made at the seat irrespective of whether the arbitral tribunal under Article 20 of the SCC Rules elects to conduct parts or all of the procedure somewhere else.

8. *Consolidation of Cases*

87. The Act provides no mechanism under which multiple arbitrations can be consolidated. The legislator expressly left it to the parties to agree on these mechanisms. Perhaps the most common means of reaching agreement is to refer to institutional rules containing provisions on consolidation, such as Article 11 of the SCC Rules. Under Article 11, a party may request the Board to consolidate two arbitrations pending under the SCC Rules. The Board may grant the request where arbitration pertaining to a certain legal relationship is brought at a time when another arbitration relating to the same legal relationship is already pending. Before deciding on the request, the Board must consult the parties and the arbitral tribunal.

88. By use of the term 'legal relationship', the SCC Rules allow disputes relating to different contracts to be consolidated where a connection exists between these contracts. There is, as yet, no published practice on SCC application of Article 11 of the Arbitration Rules, so it is presently not possible to analyse in what circumstances the SCC considers one and the same legal relationship to exist outside of a specific contractual relation.

C. Procedure before the Arbitral Tribunal

1. *Referral to the Arbitral Tribunal and Time Limits*

89. Under the Act, arbitration is pending before the arbitral tribunal immediately upon its constitution and the tribunal is not required to render its final award within any specific period. In SCC arbitration, a case is pending before the SCC until it is referred to the arbitral tribunal, which occurs when the arbitral tribunal is constituted and the advance on costs is paid in full. The arbitral tribunal then, as provided by Article 37, makes its final award at the latest six months after the day on which the case was referred to it. However, the Board may extend this time limit upon a reasoned request from the arbitral tribunal or if otherwise deemed necessary. However, many cases are in fact concluded within this time limit.

2. *Conduct of Proceedings*

90. Neither the Act nor the SCC Rules regulate the conduct of arbitration in any detail. Instead both procedural regimes set forth general standards which the arbitral tribunal must observe in every aspect of the proceedings. Thus section 21 of the Act requires the arbitral tribunal to conduct the proceedings in an impartial, practical, and speedy manner. A corresponding provision is found in Article 19(2) of the SCC Rules. Inside the broad limits laid down by these provisions, the arbitral tribunal has discretion to conduct arbitration as it considers appropriate, provided that the parties have not reached specific procedural agreement. Article 19(1) of the SCC Rules explicitly confirms the arbitral tribunal's power in this regard, whereas power is implied in the Act. As specific procedural agreements are rare, the arbitral tribunal is vested with considerable freedom to determine how the proceedings should be conducted under both the Act and the SCC Rules. A party who fails to object in due time to any failure to comply with the rules applicable to the arbitration is, according to section 34(2) of the Act and Article 32 of the SCC Rules, taken to have waived the right to object to that failure.

91. Section 23 of the Act provides that the party requesting arbitration should submit a statement of the relief sought and an elaboration of the facts which in that party's opinion motivate the grant of that relief. It is for the arbitral tribunal to fix the time for filing the statement of claim. Thereafter, within a period fixed by the Tribunal, the respondent should submit a statement specifying its position in relation to the claimant's request for relief and an elaboration of the facts upon which the respondent bases its position. The SCC Rules contemplate the claimant filing a statement of claim and the respondent a statement of defence. These submissions are subject to formal requirements under Article 24 of the SCC Rules.

92. Both the Act and the SCC Rules leave it to the discretion of the arbitral tribunal to determine whether any further exchange of written submissions should take place. It is not entirely unusual to treat an extensive request for arbitration as also constituting the statement of claim.

93. Under section 23(2) of the Act as well as Article 25 of the SCC Rules, the parties are in principle free to amend their cases at any stage of the procedure. However, the arbitral tribunal may hold these amendments inadmissible, for example for being raised at too late a stage of the proceedings.

94. The arbitral tribunal may order interim relief. Under section 25(3) of the Act and Article 32 of the SCC Rules, the arbitral tribunal has power to grant such interim relief as it considers appropriate and to order the party seeking that relief to furnish appropriate security.

95. The arbitral tribunal is free to determine the relevance, materiality and significance of evidence. This follows from section 25 of the Act as well as Article 26 of the SCC Rules. The latter provisions differ from the statutory provision in one aspect, leaving the arbitral tribunal to determine the admissibility of evidence. The arbitral tribunal also has power to order a party to identify the evidence which that party intends to rely upon and to specify the facts which that party intends to prove with that evidence. Moreover, the arbitral tribunal may order a party to produce documents or other evidence which may be relevant to the outcome of the case but the tribunal has no means of coercion.

96. Section 24 of the Act vests each party to arbitration proceedings with the right to a hearing on the merits. If a party requests a hearing, this request must, under Article 26 of the SCC Rules, be complied with. No mandatory right to a hearing on procedural issues, such as jurisdiction, exists under the Act. It lies in the arbitral tribunal's discretionary power to order that a hearing be held when it considers that to be appropriate. Hearings are held *in camera* if the parties have not agreed otherwise.

97. The Act is, with one notable exception, silent on the issue of by what means parties may prove their claims. Under section 25 of the Act, an arbitral tribunal may not administer oaths or truth affirmations. The SCC Rules, Article 28 (2), expressly allow witness testimonies, including testimony of experts, to be submitted in the form of signed statements. However, if a party wishes to rely on such evidence, the witness or expert must still attend a hearing for examination if the parties have not agreed otherwise. The arbitral tribunal may, after having consulted the parties, appoint an expert of its own. The report of that expert must be submitted to the parties who must be given opportunity to comment on the report. An expert appointed by the arbitral tribunal must be available for examination at a hearing if a party so requests. The silence of the Act should not be understood as disallowing use of written witness statements in arbitrations conducted under the Act. Provided that the use of such statements is combined with the opportunity to cross-examine witnesses at a hearing, no objection can be raised against the practice.

98. When the arbitral tribunal is satisfied that the parties have had reasonable opportunity to present their cases it will, under Article of Article 34 of the SCC Rules, declare the proceedings closed. In exceptional cases, the proceedings may be reopened. No similar mechanism exists under the Act.

D. The Award

99. As mentioned above, the concept of an arbitral award is defined in section 27 of the Act. Basically, any decision by which the proceedings are terminated must be made in the form of an award. Under section 31 of the Act, an arbitral award must be in writing and signed by each member of the arbitral tribunal. If one arbitrator refuses to participate in deliberations or to sign the award the others may nevertheless decide the case and sign. The reason why a signature is missing must be explained in the award.

The Act does not require that an award state the reasons on which it is based. However, under Article 36(1) of the SCC Rules an arbitral award must be reasoned.

100. If there is reason to correct, interpret or supplement an award, this may be done upon request by a party within thirty days from receipt of the award or by the tribunal of its own motion within thirty days from the date of the award.

CHAPTER 2

Stockholm as a Forum for Investment Arbitration

Nils Eliasson

I. INTRODUCTION

1. For many years, investment treaty arbitration was the 'hot new thing' in the world of international arbitration. Today, investment treaty arbitration no longer qualifies as the 'new thing'. It has entered the 'main stream' of international arbitration. The same can be said about Stockholm as a forum for investment treaty arbitration. Building on its reputation as a neutral seat for East-West arbitration, Stockholm has also established itself as a preferred seat of arbitration when it comes to investment treaty cases. The Arbitration Institute of the Stockholm Chamber of Commerce (SCC) is the second most frequently chosen arbitration institution in investment treaty cases. Only the International Centre for Settlement of Investment Disputes (ICSID) handles more investment arbitrations.

2. The purpose of this chapter is to provide a broad overview of issues relating to Stockholm and the SCC as a forum for investment arbitration. The focus will be on issues related to the choice of Stockholm as the seat and the SCC as arbitration institution in investment treaty cases. Procedural issues that may arise when Stockholm is chosen as the seat, e.g., applicable law, challenge of investment treaty awards and enforcement, will also be addressed.

II. INVESTMENT TREATIES AND INVESTMENT ARBITRATION

3. Provisions on investment protection, including investor-state arbitration, are most commonly found in Bilateral Investment Treaties (BIT). BITs are treaties between two states for the reciprocal encouragement, promotion and protection of investments in each other's territories by individuals or companies based in either country. To date, more than 2,700 BITs are in force between different states. Investment protection standards and investor-state arbitration are also provided for by certain Free Trade Agreements (FTAs), e.g., the North American Free Trade Agreement (NAFTA). An industry-specific multilateral investment treaty (MIT) is the Energy Charter Treaty (ECT), which protects foreign investments in the Energy Sector.[1] The ECT is of particular importance for Stockholm, since it designates arbitration proceedings under the SCC as one of the dispute resolution methods available to foreign investors protected by the ECT.[2]

4. With more than 2,700 BITs and other investment treaties, it is only natural that there will be differences between the various treaties. Different states have different model BITs and there is no uniform approach. That being said, however, in terms of substantive investment protection standards BITs and other investment treaties often include a similar set of protection standards. These treaties frequently include obligations on behalf of the host state:

- to ensure that protected investments are accorded fair and equitable treatment;
- to ensure that protected investments enjoy full security and protection;
- not to impair the management, use or enjoyment of investments by unreasonable or discriminatory measures;
- not to expropriate investments unless such expropriation is carried out under due process of law, is in the public interest, on a non-discriminatory basis, and accompanied by compensation;
- to ensure investment treatment no less favourable than that accorded to investments of nationals of the host state (national treatment);
- to ensure investment treatment no less favourable than that accorded to investors or investments of any other state (most favoured nation treatment);
- to ensure the observation of obligations assumed by the host state *vis-à-vis* the investor (umbrella clause); and
- to ensure the right to repatriate earnings from an investment to the investor's home state or a third country.

5. One of the most important provisions in investment treaties is the investor's right to settle disputes against the host state under the treaty by international arbitration. The introduction of these investor-state arbitration clauses in BITs and other investment treaties, thus, effectively 'delegating' enforcement of the substantive protection standard to individual investors, has proved the key to the success of the modern investment protection system. By including in these treaties a right for the investor to bring disputes with the host state concerning alleged breaches of protection standards in the treaty to international arbitration, investors were given an effective remedy which does not depend on the support of their home state. In most cases, the absence

1. See e.g., N. Eliasson, *10 years of Energy Charter Treaty Arbitration*, Conference Report presented at the joint ICSID, SCC and ECT Secretariat Conference *10 years of Energy Charter Treaty Arbitration* (6 June 2011), available at http://www.sccinstitute.se. See also K. Hobér, *The Energy Charter Treaty: An Overview*, 8 J. World Inv. & Trade 323-356 (June 2007).
2. See Art. 26(4)(c) of the ECT.

of an effective investor-state arbitration clause in an investment treaty would render substantive protection under those treaties meaningless. To submit claims to a judicial or administrative body of the host state is normally not a viable option. Nor is it, in most cases, possible for the investor to rely on its home state to extend diplomatic protection and to bring claims on its behalf. In the absence of an efficient arbitration clause in the investment treaty, the investor will, therefore, have no effective and realistic means to enforce its substantive rights under the treaty.

III. ICSID, UNCITRAL OR THE SCC?

6. States concluding investment treaties may in their treaties provide for any form of dispute resolution mechanism for investor-state disputes that they deem fit. Unsurprisingly, investment treaties demonstrate great diversity in this respect. There are treaties providing for ICSID arbitration, ad hoc arbitration under the UNCITRAL Arbitration Rules (UNCITRAL Rules), pure ad hoc arbitration, SCC arbitration or ICC arbitration. Some treaties even offer the investor the right to choose between different dispute-resolution mechanisms.

7. Based on available statistics on publicly disclosed investment arbitrations, ICSID arbitration is the most frequently used dispute settlement mechanism in investment arbitration. By 31 December 2012, 369 arbitration cases had been registered under the Convention on the Settlement of Investment Disputes between States and Nationals of Other States, 1965 (the ICSID Convention) (also known as the Washington Convention) and 41 ICSID Additional Facility arbitration cases.[3] In comparison, 135 known cases had been filed under the UNCITRAL Rules and 57 cases had been filed under the Rules of Arbitration of the Arbitration Institute of the Stockholm Chamber of Commerce (SCC Rules). To date, only eight investment arbitrations have been filed under the Rules of Arbitration of the International Chamber of Commerce (ICC Rules).[4] It should be noted, however, that 8[illegible] of the ICSID cases and five of the SCC cases are cases based on so-called *investment contracts* concluded directly between the investor and the host state, rather than treaty-based cases. It should also be noted that whereas most ad hoc arbitrations under investment treaties are conducted pursuant to the UNCITRAL Rules, there are also some pure ad hoc cases, e.g., the first ever investment treaty claim brought against the Russian Federation, *Sedelmayer v. Russian Federation*. This case had its seat of arbitration in Stockholm. Unlike the ICSID cases, some of the UNCITRAL cases and other non-ICSID cases are not in the public domain. There are therefore likely more ad hoc investment arbitration cases than is reflected in the above-referenced statistics.

A. ICSID

8. ICSID is an autonomous international institution established under the Convention on the Settlement of Investment Disputes between States and Nationals of Other States

3. The ICSID Caseload – Statistics, Issue 2013-1, http://www.icsid.worldbank.org.
4. UNCTAD, Latest Developments in Investor-State Dispute Settlement, IIA No 1 Mar. 2013, http://www.unctad.org/diae.

(ICSID Convention). The ICSID Convention entered into force in 1966 and has, to date, 147 Member States.

9. The ICSID Convention sets forth the ICSID mandate, organization and core functions. In accordance with the provisions of the ICSID Convention, ICSID provides facilities for conciliation and arbitration of investment disputes between Contracting States and nationals of other Contracting States. Thus, the ICSID Convention establishes a special institutional and procedural framework for conciliation and arbitration of investment disputes. It should be noted, however, that the ICSID Convention does not contain any substantive investment protection regime. It merely provides the institutional and procedural framework for settlement of investment disputes between investors from one Contracting State to the ICSID Convention and another Contracting State to the Convention.

10. Consent by the host State to submit a particular dispute to settlement under the ICSID Convention may be expressed in an investment treaty (BIT or MIT), in the foreign investment law of the host state or in an investment contract concluded directly between the investor and the host state.[5]

11. Arbitration proceedings are normally governed by the arbitration law (the *lex arbitri*) at the seat of arbitration agreed by the parties. Such seat of arbitration should not be confused with the actual physical location where the hearing may be held, a place which may very well be elsewhere than at the chosen seat. Arbitrations under the ICSID Convention do not, however, have a seat of arbitration. The ICSID Convention provides for a 'delocalized' or 'transnational' arbitral procedure, in the sense that the arbitral procedure is not subject to the laws of any national jurisdiction. Instead, ICSID arbitration is governed solely by the provisions of the ICSID Convention and by the Rules and Regulations adopted by the Administrative Council of the ICSID. This also means that ICSID awards may not be challenged before any national courts and that enforcement is governed by the ICSID Convention rather than by the Convention on the Recognition and Enforcement of Foreign Arbitral Awards, 1958 (New York Convention) (see sections VI and VII below).

B. UNCITRAL Rules

12. After ICSID, arbitration under the UNCITRAL Rules is the second most frequently used dispute resolution method in investment treaty arbitration. Being ad hoc arbitration, UNCITRAL investment cases are generally not conducted under the auspices of any particular arbitration institution. One notable exception is the Permanent Court of Arbitration (PCA), which more and more frequently is designated to administer

5. To date, 63% of all ICSID cases have been conducted on the basis of a BIT, 20% on the basis of investment contracts concluded directly between the investor and the host state, 6% on the basis of the investment law of the host state, 4% on the basis of the Energy Charter Treaty, 4% on the basis of the NAFTA, 1% on the basis of the Treaty of Amity and Cooperation in Southeast Asia (ASEAN), and 1% on the basis of the Dominican Republic-United States-Central American Free Trade Agreement.

investment treaty arbitrations under the UNCITRAL Rules by agreement between the investor and the host state after the dispute has arisen.

13. Investment treaties providing for UNCITRAL arbitration rarely specify the seat of arbitration. The seat of arbitration in these cases is therefore generally decided on an ad hoc basis by agreement between the parties or decision by the arbitral tribunal.[6] As far as the author is aware, there are no comprehensive statistics on the seat of arbitration in UNCITRAL cases. However, seats that have been chosen in publicly known investment arbitration cases include Brussels, Geneva, Frankfurt, The Hague, London, Montreal, New York, Ottawa, Paris, Stockholm, Toronto, Vancouver, Vienna, Washington D.C. and Zurich.

C. Stockholm and the SCC

14. The SCC Rules are the third most frequently used arbitration rules in investment treaty cases and the SCC is the second most frequently employed arbitration institution. As of September 2011, the SCC had registered 57 investment arbitration cases since its first investment treaty case in 1993. Nine of these cases were claims brought under the ECT, whereas 43 cases were brought under different BITs. The remaining five cases were arbitrations based on investment contracts.[7] The involvement of the SCC in those disputes ranges from administering the case applying the SCC Rules (40 cases) to acting as an appointing authority and rendering decisions on challenge to arbitrator applications (17 cases).[8]

15. Considering that there have also been UNCITRAL cases in Stockholm, in which the services of the SCC as appointing authority were not required, it would be reasonable to estimate that the total number of investment arbitrations having had their seat in Stockholm is at least 60. In total, approximately 220 known investment arbitrations were not conducted under the ICSID Convention (as mentioned above, ICSID Convention cases do not have a seat). Sixty cases in Stockholm therefore constitute approximately 27% of the total number of non-ICSID cases. This figure clearly demonstrates the significance of the SCC and Stockholm as a forum for non-ICSID investment treaty arbitrations. Few other seats, if any, can boast such a high number of investment treaty cases.

D. Some Differences between Investment Arbitration under the SCC Rules and the ICSID Convention

16. Since the focus of this chapter is investment treaty arbitration in Sweden, a brief overview of some of the differences between ICSID arbitration and investment treaty arbitration conducted under the SCC Rules may be of interest.

6. Article 16 of the 1976 UNCITRAL Rules and Art. 18 of the 2010 UNCITRAL Rules.
7. Information from the SCC Secretariat.
8. Information from the SCC Secretariat and SCC website, http://www.sccinstitute.com/hem-3/statistik-2.aspx (accessed 19 Apr. 2013).

17. As mentioned in section III.A above, a significant difference between arbitral proceedings pursued under the SCC Rules (or any other set of institutional rules) and ICSID arbitration is that ICSID arbitration is 'delocalized' or 'transnational', whereas arbitral proceedings pursued under the SCC Rules (or any other set of institutional rules) always have their seat in a particular jurisdiction.

18. Another example of the way in which investment arbitration under the SCC Rules and the ICSID Convention differs is the procedure and standard for challenging arbitrators. Under the SCC Rules, an arbitrator may be challenged if circumstances exist which give rise to *'justifiable doubts as to the arbitrator's impartiality or independence'*.[9] In comparison, under the ICSID Convention,[10] a party may propose the disqualification of an arbitrator on the ground that there is an indication of a *'manifest lack of the qualities required'* of an arbitrator pursuant to the Convention. The standard for challenge of arbitrators under ICSID has been interpreted in various ways,[11] but is generally considered to be high,[12] and the burden of proof on the party seeking to have an arbitrator removed is arguably heavier under the ICSID Convention than under the *'justifiable doubts'* standard under the SCC Rules.[13]

19. Pursuant to the SCC Rules, a challenge to an arbitrator is to be determined by the Board of the SCC.[14] Under the ICSID Convention, a challenge is to be decided by the coarbitrators.[15] Concerns have been raised by some commentators that it may be too difficult to pursue a successful challenge of an arbitrator under the ICSID Convention both because of the high standard required for a challenge and because the other tribunal members may be reluctant to disqualify a coarbitrator.[16] Since the early 1980s and up to 2011 there were forty-one challenges in arbitrations under the ICSID Rules of Procedure for Arbitration Proceedings (ICSID Rules). In nine of these challenges, the arbitrator resigned voluntarily. Out of the thirty-two challenges that were adjudicated, only one challenge was successful.[17] This can be compared with statistics from the SCC. During the period 1995–2007, the SCC Board issued ninety-three[18] decisions on challenges presented under either the SCC Rules, the SCC Rules for Expedited

9. Article 15(1) of the SCC Rules. An arbitrator may also be challenged if not possessing qualifications agreed by the parties.
10. Article 57 of the ICSID Convention.
11. See K. Daele, *The Challenge and Disqualification of International Arbitrators* 218ff (Kluwer L. Intl. 2012).
12. L. Reed, J. Paulsson & N. Blackaby, *Guide to ICSID Arbitration* 134 (2d ed., Kluwer L. Intl. 2011).
13. See also C. Schreuer et al., *The ICSID Convention – A Commentary* 1202 (Cambridge U. Press 2009).
14. Article 15(4) of the SCC Rules.
15. Article 58 of the ICSID Convention.
16. See e.g., K. Daele, *The Challenge and Disqualification of International Arbitrators* 169ff (Kluwer L. Intl. 2012) and A. Sheppard, *Arbitrator Independence in ICSID Arbitration* in *International Investment Law for the 21st Century* 131ff (Oxford U. Press 2009).
17. Interview with K. Daele by IAReporter, 8 Jun. 2011, http://www.iareporter.com/articles/20110608.
18. This number does not include challenges where no decision was taken by the SCC Board, such as cases where the arbitrator voluntarily resigned.

Arbitrations or the UNCITRAL Rules.[19] In twenty-nine of those decisions, the challenged arbitrator was subsequently discharged from his or her duties.[20] There, thus, seems to be some merit to the argument that the threshold for having an arbitrator disqualified under the ICSID Convention is higher than under the SCC Rules or other rules providing a similar standard.

20. As from 1 January 2010, the SCC Rules contain provisions on emergency arbitrators which apply to investment treaty arbitration as well as regular commercial arbitration. These rules offer the parties (generally the claimant) the option of requesting the appointment of an Emergency Arbitrator with authority to order interim measures *before* the case is referred to the arbitral tribunal. There is no such possibility under the ICSID Rules (although the parties to an ICSID arbitration may request the arbitral tribunal – after it has been constituted – to recommend provisional measures[21]).

21. As far as the author is aware, the emergency arbitrator provisions in the SCC Rules have not yet been applied in any investment treaty arbitration. They have, however, been applied in a contract arbitration involving a state-party, *viz. OAO Gazprom v. Ministry of Energy of the Republic of Lithuania*. In this case, Gazprom unsuccessfully sought an order to stay court proceedings which – in its view – were brought in violation of an arbitration agreement between the parties by means of the SCC's emergency arbitrator procedure.[22]

22. A feature of the ICSID Arbitration Rules, to which there is no corresponding provision under the SCC Rules, is the possibility to request a summary determination of whether a claim is '*manifestly without legal merit*'. Pursuant to Rule 41(5) of the ICSID Arbitration Rules, a party may file an objection to this effect no later than thirty days after the constitution of the tribunal. After having given the parties an opportunity to present their observations on the objection, the tribunal is to decide promptly if the objection is well founded. If so, the tribunal is to issue an award dismissing the case, in part or in its entirety. The possibility to request a summary determination of the merits of a claim was included in the ICSID Arbitration Rules of 2006.[23]

19. Although we have not come across any statistics exclusively for challenges under the SCC Rules, the statistics for challenges under the UNCITRAL Rules are also of relevance as the standard for a challenge in the UNCITRAL Rules is very similar to the standard under the SCC Rules.
20. M. Johansson, *Decisions by the Arbitration Institute of the Stockholm Chamber of Commerce regarding Challenge of Arbitrators*, Stockholm Arbitration Report 2 (1999); M. Öhrström, *Decisions by the SCC Institute regarding Challenge of Arbitrators*, Stockholm Arbitration Report 1 (2002); A. Magnusson & H. Larsson, *Recent Practice of the Arbitration Institute of the Stockholm Chamber of Commerce: Prima Facie Decisions on Jurisdiction and Challenges of Arbitrators*, Stockholm Arbitration Report 2 (2004); and H. Jung, *SCC Practice: Challenges to Arbitrators, SCC Board Decisions 2005-2007*, Stockholm Intl. Arbitration Rev. 1 (2008), http://www.sccinstitute.se/?id=11666&newsid=40160.
21. Article 47 of the ICSID Convention and Rule 39 of the ICSID Arbitration Rules.
22. Global Arbitration Rev., 13 Aug. 2012 (http://www.globalarbitrationreview.com/news/article/3075[illegible]/gazprom-lithuania-award-online/) and *OAO Gazprom v. Ministry of Energy of the Republic of Lithuania*, SCC Case No. 125/2011, Final Award, 31 Jul. 2012.
23. As far as the author is aware, five ICSID tribunals have so far issued decisions on objections under Art. 41(5). In two of these cases, *Global Trading Resource Corp. and Globex International,*

23. Finally, as regards time taken for arbitrations, statistics suggest that investment proceedings under the SCC Rules tend to take less time than arbitrations pursued under the ICSID Convention. The average time for an ICSID proceeding, from the date of filing the request for arbitration to the date of a final award, has been calculated at approximately 3.6 years,[24] while the average time for investment disputes pursued under the SCC Rules has been 1.75 years.[25]

E. The ECT

24. Analysing figures relating to investment treaty arbitrations it may also be of interest to take a closer look at the ECT.[26] One of the distinguishing features of the ECT is that it offers the investor the right to choose between ICSID, UNCITRAL Rules and the SCC.[27] Most investment treaties do not offer such a wide selection. The investor's choice of arbitration institution in ECT cases may therefore serve as a *litmus test* for the preferences of investors. The table below sets out the choices made by investors in the thirty-five cases that have so far been commenced under the ECT:

ARBITRATION INSTITUTE/RULES	NUMBER OF ECT CASES	TOTAL NUMBER OF KNOWN INVESTMENT TREATY CASES
ICSID or ICSID Additional Facility	20	303[28]
UNCITRAL Rules	6	135
SCC Rules	9	40
ICC	N/A	8

Inc. v. Ukraine, ICSID Case No. ARB/09/11, 1 Dec. 2010 and *RSM Production Corporation and others v. Grenada*, ICSID Case No. ARB/10/6, 10 Dec. 2010, the tribunals ruled to dismiss the alleged claims as being manifestly without legal merit.

24. A. Sinclair, *ICSID Arbitration: How Long Does It Take?*, 4 Global Arbitration Rev. (26 Oct. 2009).
25. Information from the SCC website, http://www.sccinstitute.com/hem-3/statistik-2.aspx, last accessed on 15 Aug. 2012.
26. See further N. Eliasson, *10 Years of Energy Charter Treaty Arbitration*, Conference Report presented at the joint ICSID, SCC and ECT Secretariat Conference *10 years of Energy Charter Treaty Arbitration*, available at http://www.sccinstitute.se.
27. See Art. 26 of the ECT. On arbitration under the ECT see e.g., K. Hobér, *Investment Arbitration and the Energy Charter Treaty*, 1 J. Intl. Dispute Settle. 153–190 (2010); and T. Wälde, *Investment Arbitration under the Energy Charter Treaty – From Dispute Settlement to Treaty Implementation*, 12 Arbitration Intl. 437 (1996).
28. This figure only includes treaty-based investment arbitration cases. The total number of cases under the ICSID Convention and ICSID Additional Facility (including conciliation cases and arbitration cases under investment contracts entered into directly between the investor and the host State and arbitrations under the investment law of the host State) was 410 by 31 Dec. 2012 (The ICSID Caseload – Statistics, Issue 2013-1, www.icsid.worldbank.org). ICSID also administers non-ICSID cases, including State-State cases. These non-ICSID cases administrated by ICSID have ranged between 3 and 12 a year during the last ten years.

25. The above figures show a clear preference for ICSID arbitration when it comes to ECT arbitrations. ICSID or the ICSID Additional Facility was chosen in twenty out of thirty-five cases (approximately 57%). This is marginally lower than for investment claims in general. The total number of ICSID cases represents approximately 63% of all investment treaty cases. This percentage, however, must be viewed with some caution since a number of unreported UNCITRAL cases do not appear in any statistics.

26. The UNCITRAL Rules (six cases, 17%) and the SCC (nine cases, 26%) were chosen less frequently than ICSID in ECT arbitration. It should be noted, however, that in all instances where the investors chose not to go to ICSID, they did so despite the fact that ICSID or the ICSID Additional Facility would have been available, thus expressing a preference for the SCC or the UNCITRAL Rules in these cases.

27. The choices made by investors in ECT cases also express a strong preference for *institutional arbitration*. ICSID and SCC together represent 83% of cases. Moreover, four of the cases heard under the UNCITRAL Rules are administrated by the PCA.[29]

28. It is interesting to note the strong position the SCC maintains also with regard to ECT cases. The fact that the SCC was chosen in seven ECT cases where the investor could have chosen ICSID, the ICSID additional facility or the UNCITRAL Rules shows that the SCC represents a viable option for administrated investment arbitration.

IV. STOCKHOLM AS THE SEAT IN INVESTMENT ARBITRATION

A. Does the Seat of Arbitration Matter in Investment Treaty Cases?

29. For obvious reasons, public international law plays a significant role in investment treaty arbitration. The issues in dispute are normally decided in accordance with the applicable investment treaty supplemented by rules and principles of customary public international law. The rules and principles of public international law relating to the interpretation of treaties and the law of state responsibility will often be decisive.[30] The dispute resolution provisions in investment treaties are part of the applicable investment treaty and, as such, are interpreted in accordance with the rules and principles of public international law relating to the interpretation of treaties.

30. The significance of public international law notwithstanding, in non-ICSID investment arbitration, the arbitral procedure is ultimately anchored in a national jurisdiction. To date, arbitration under the ICSID Convention is the only form of settlement of investment disputes that provides for a completely 'delocalized' arbitral procedure, in the sense that the arbitral procedure is not subject to the laws of any national

29. Three of these four cases, i.e., the *Yukos* cases (*Yukos Universal Ltd. (UK – Isle of Man) v. Russian Federation*, PCA Case No. AA 227, 30 Nov. 2009, *Hulley Enterprises Ltd. (Cyprus) v. Russian Federation*, PCA Case No. AA 226, 30 Nov. 2009 and *Veteran Petroleum Trust (Cyprus) v. Russian Federation*, PCA Case No. AA 228, 30 Nov. 2009) are heard by a joint tribunal. The fourth case is *EDF v. the Republic of Hungary*.
30. See e.g., K. Hobér, *State Responsibility and Attribution*, in *The Oxford Handbook of International Investment Law* (Muchlinski et al. eds., Oxford U. Press 2008).

jurisdiction. As explained above in section III.A, ICSID arbitration is governed by the ICSID Convention and its self-contained system for annulment of arbitral awards and for their recognition and enforcement.

31. In non-ICSID arbitration, such as arbitration under the SCC Rules or the UNCITRAL Rules, the arbitral procedure is ultimately subject to the law applicable at the seat of the arbitration and the normal way to challenge an investment treaty award is through municipal courts. Thus, in non-ICSID investment arbitration, the seat of arbitration plays a significant role.

B. How Is Stockholm Chosen as the Seat of Arbitration in Investment Treaty Cases?

1. Treaties Providing for SCC Arbitration

32. There are several ways in which Stockholm may become the seat of arbitration in investment arbitrations. The most frequent reason for the seat to be in Stockholm is, unsurprisingly, that the applicable investment treaty provides that disputes between the investor and the host State under the treaty are to be resolved by arbitration under the auspices of the SCC. As mentioned in section III.E above, the ECT provides for '*arbitral proceedings under the Arbitration Institute of the Stockholm Chamber of Commerce*' as one of the options for investor-state dispute settlement.[31] Similarly, around 139 BITs provide for arbitration under the SCC Rules, arbitration with the seat in Sweden, or the SCC as appointing authority. In particular BITs concluded by Russia, other former Soviet Republics as well as Chinese first generation BITs[32] often provide for SCC arbitration. For instance, Article 8(3) of the Agreement between the Government of the United Kingdom and the Government of the USSR for the Promotion and Reciprocal Protection of Investments (1989) provides that:

> Where the dispute is referred to arbitration, the investor concerned in the dispute shall have the right to refer the dispute either to:
>
> (a) the Institute of Arbitration of the Chamber of Commerce of Stockholm; or
> (b) an international arbitrator or *ad hoc* arbitration tribunal appointed by a special agreement or under the Arbitration Rules of the United Nations Commission on International Trade Law, the arbitration shall be conducted under these rules unless the parties agree in writing to modify them.

33. There are also BITs, for instance the BITs China has concluded with several former Soviet Republics, including Armenia, Belarus, Kazakhstan, Kyrgyzstan, Tajikistan,

31. Article 26(4)(c) of the ECT.
32. On Chinese first generation BITs see further e.g., N. Eliasson, *Investor-State Arbitration and Chinese Investors*, 2 Contemporary Asia Arbitration J. (November 2009); N. Eliasson, *Investment Arbitration and Hong Kong*, in *Arbitration in Hong Kong: A Practical Guide* (2d ed., Sweet & Maxwell 2011); and N. Eliasson, *Chinese Investment Treaties: Jurisdictional Aspects*, in *Foreign Investment and Dispute Resolution Law and Practice in Asia* 90 (V. Bath & L. Nottage eds., Routledge 2011).

Ukraine and Uzbekistan, that provide for ad hoc arbitration using the SCC Rules as reference. These BITs are important from the perspective of Chinese investors, since all of these countries have been specifically targeted for Chinese overseas natural resources investments by the Ministry of Commerce, the National Development and Reform Commission, and the Ministry of Foreign Affairs.[33] Moreover, Kazakhstan, Kyrgyzstan, Tajikistan, and Uzbekistan are already among the main recipients of Chinese natural resources investments globally. For instance, Tajikistan and Uzbekistan are major suppliers of natural gas to China. We are, therefore, likely to see disputes under these BITs in the future. Given the reference to use of the SCC Rules 'as reference' in these BITs, the seat of arbitration will likely be decided to be Stockholm if disputes under these BITs should go to arbitration.

2. *The Seat of Arbitration May Be Stockholm in UNCITRAL Cases*

34. BITs providing for investor-State arbitration under the UNCITRAL Rules generally do not specify the seat of arbitration. In investment arbitrations under the UNCITRAL Rules the seat of arbitration will therefore be fixed either by agreement between the parties after the dispute has arisen or by decision of the arbitral tribunal.[34] Some BITs providing for UNCITRAL arbitration designate the SCC or the Secretary-General of the SCC as appointing authority. The SCC has so far handled around ten applications to act as appointing authority under the UNCITRAL Rules. Where the BIT designates the SCC as appointing authority, it would also often be appropriate to designate Stockholm as the seat of arbitration. This was done for instance in *CME v. Czech Republic.*[35] Article 8(4) of the BIT between the Czech Republic and the Netherlands, which was applicable in this arbitration, provides that:

> If the appointments have not been made in the above mentioned periods, either party to the dispute may invite the President of the Arbitration Institute of the Chamber of Commerce of Stockholm to make the necessary appointments.

C. The Statutory Framework Applicable to an Investment Arbitration Having the Seat of Arbitration in Stockholm

35. The first question that arises in connection with any discussion of Stockholm as the seat of arbitration is whether the Swedish Arbitration Act (Sw: *Lag (1999:116) om skiljeförfarande*) (the Act) applies to an investment arbitration with its seat in Stockholm (or elsewhere in Sweden).

36. Pursuant to section 46, the Act applies to arbitral proceedings which take place in Sweden, notwithstanding the fact that the dispute has an international connection.

---

33. N. Eliasson, *Investment Treaty Protection of Chinese Natural Resources Investments*, 7 Transnatl. Dispute Mgt. (Dec. 2010).
34. Article 16 of the 1976 UNCITRAL Rules and Art. 18 of the 2010 UNCITRAL Rules.
35. *CME Czech Republic BV v. Czech Republic*, Partial Award and Separate Opinion, Ad hoc – UNCITRAL Arbitration Rules, adopted 2010 (UNCITRAL Rules), 13 Sep. 2001, para. 16.

Although investment arbitration is arbitration based on an international treaty, both under the SCC Rules and the UNCITRAL Rules the designated form of dispute settlement is that of international commercial arbitration. The applicability of the Act is not affected by the fact that the arbitration agreement, or rather the host state's 'offer to arbitrate' and the terms for such offer, is set out in an international treaty rather than in a normal contract.

37. In most investment arbitrations with their seat in Stockholm, be it under the SCC Rules or the UNCITRAL Rules, the applicability of the Act has not been questioned. As far as the author is aware, the only 'Stockholm case' where issues related to the applicability of the Act (or rather the Arbitration Act 1929[36] which was still in force at that time) arose was *Sedelmayer v. Russian Federation*.[37]

38. Following an award in favour of Mr Sedelmayer in the arbitration, the Russian Federation brought challenge proceedings against the award before the Stockholm District Court.[38] In the challenge proceedings, Mr Sedelmayer claimed that the courts of Sweden lacked jurisdiction to hear the challenge. He argued that the arbitral proceedings as well as the award were governed by public international law and that the award therefore could not be challenged under the 1929 Arbitration Act. In the alternative, Mr Sedelmayer argued that, despite the fact that the seat of arbitration was Stockholm, the arbitral award should be equated with a foreign arbitral award and therefore not be subject to court review under the 1929 Arbitration Act. Finally, Mr Sedelmayer argued that it was implied in the German-Soviet BIT that the Contracting Parties to the BIT had agreed that an arbitral award issued under the BIT could not be challenged in municipal courts.

39. The Stockholm District Court dealt very briefly with Mr Sedelmayer's objections to its jurisdiction. The Court emphasized that it was a well-established principle of Swedish arbitration law that an arbitral award issued in proceedings having their seat in Sweden can be challenged before the Swedish courts, even if the parties have no connection to Sweden. Since the seat of arbitration in the present case was Stockholm, the proceedings – unless otherwise agreed between the parties – were governed by the Arbitration Act 1929 and the award must be regarded as a Swedish arbitral award that can be challenged in accordance with the provisions of the 1929 Arbitration Act. In the view of the Court, Mr Sedelmayer had not established that the parties had agreed that any of the provisions of the Arbitration Act 1929 should not apply to the proceedings, or to the award. The Court concluded that, at least where one of the parties to the arbitration was a subject of municipal law, and not a sovereign State, the fact that the

36. (*Sw: Lag (1929:145) om skiljemän*).
37. *Sedelmayer v. Russian Federation*, Award 7 Jul. 1998, Ad hoc arbitration. This case was governed by the Swedish Arbitration Act of 1929, which was replaced by the Act in 1999. The entry into force of the Act in 1999 did not, however, bring about any significant changes with respect to the issues that arose in the Sedelmayer case.
38. *Sedelmayer v. Russian Federation*, judgment by the Stockholm District Court made on 12 Dec. 2002 in case no T6-583-98. For an English translation of the judgment by the Stockholm District Court, see Stockholm Intl. Arbitration Rev. 2005:2.

arbitration was based on a treaty concluded between two sovereign States did not cause it to conclude that the Arbitration Act 1929 did not apply.[39]

40. Similar conclusions have been reached in other jurisdictions where investment treaty awards have been challenged.[40] In England, for instance, the supervisory jurisdiction of the English courts over investment treaty awards, and, thus, the applicability of the English Arbitration Act of 1996 in investment treaty arbitration, was ruled upon by the High Court in *Ecuador v. Occidental Exploration and Production Company*.[41]

D. ICSID Arbitration in Stockholm

41. Proceedings under the ICSID Convention may also be held in Stockholm. However, as mentioned above in section III.A, arbitration under the ICSID Convention provides for a 'delocalized' arbitral procedure, in the sense that the arbitral procedure is not subject to the laws of any national jurisdiction. Instead, ICSID arbitration is governed solely by the ICSID Convention and by the Rules and Regulations adopted by the Administrative Council of the ICSID. Thus, the jurisdiction of ICSID, the arbitration procedure, annulment of arbitral awards as well as recognition and enforcement of ICSID awards are governed solely by the Convention. Since the ICSID Convention establishes a self-contained system for the arbitration of investment disputes, including challenge and enforcement of awards, the Convention precludes the supervisory jurisdiction of the courts at the place of proceedings under the Convention. In fact, as explained above, ICSID arbitration does not require a formal seat or place of arbitration within the meaning of the New York Convention or national arbitration laws.[42]

42. The default position under the ICSID Convention is that proceedings be held at the seat of ICSID in Washington. Proceedings may also be held at the PCA in The Hague, at other institutions with which ICSID makes arrangements, or at a place agreed between the parties and approved by the arbitral tribunal. Again, however, this does not mean that the proceedings will be covered by the law of the country where the proceedings are held.

---

39. In subsequent challenge proceedings against investment treaty awards rendered in Sweden the applicability of the Act, as such, has not been questioned. See e.g., the *Czech Republic v. CME Czech Republic B.V.*, judgment of the Svea Court of Appeal on 15 May 2003 in case no T-8735-01, RH 2003:55; *Petrobart Limited v. Kyrgyz Republic*, judgment of the Svea Court of Appeal on 13 Apr. 2006 in case no T 3739-03 and judgment of the Supreme Court on 28 Mar. 2008 in case no T 2113-06, NJA 2008 p. 406; and *Kyrgyz Republic v. Petrobart Limited*, Judgment of the Svea Court of Appeal of 19 Jan. 2007, Case No. T 5208-05.

40. See further in K. Hobér & N. Eliasson, *Review of Investment Treaty Awards by Municipal Courts*, in *Arbitration under International Investment Agreements* (K. Small ed., Oxford U. Press 2010).

41. *Ecuador v. Occidental Exploration and Production Company* (non-justiciability), Judgment, [2005] EWHC 774 (Comm), 29 Apr. 2005.

42. As regards the physical place of the proceedings, the ICSID Convention simply provides that proceedings shall be held at the seat of the ICSID centre (Art. 62), at the seat of the PCA or of any other appropriate institution or at any other place approved by the relevant conciliation commission or tribunal after consultation with the ICSID Secretary General (Art. 63).

43. Prudent parties would only agree, and arbitral tribunals should only accept, to conduct ICSID proceedings in a jurisdiction which is a member of the ICSID Convention. The reason is that unless the state in question has ratified the ICSID Convention, it would not be obliged to treat the arbitral proceedings as ICSID proceedings. Thus, if ICSID proceedings were to be held in a non-ICSID Member State, there is a risk that those proceedings would be treated as regular arbitral proceedings, and, thus, be subject to the supervisory jurisdiction of the local courts.

44. Sweden ratified the ICSID Convention in 1966. Thus, the ICSID Convention applies in Sweden. This means that if arbitration proceedings under the ICSID Convention are conducted in Sweden, the Act will not apply to those proceedings, and the proceedings will not be subject to the supervisory jurisdiction of the Courts of Sweden.

45. As far as the author is aware, however, so far there have been no arbitration proceedings under the ICSID Convention in Stockholm. Moreover, ICSID has no institutional arrangement with the SCC.[43] To conclude such an arrangement would facilitate the conduct of ICSID proceedings in Stockholm, as parties pursuant to the ICSID Convention[44] are free to agree that the hearing be held at one of the venues with which arrangements have been made. In the absence of such arrangements, the tribunal's approval of the venue is required, and the tribunal may only give approval after having consulted the ICSID Secretary-General.[45]

46. ICSID also administers certain investment arbitration proceedings where the ICSID Convention does not apply, *viz.*, under the so-called ICSID Additional Facility. The ICSID Additional Facility Rules authorize the ICSID Secretariat to administer certain categories of proceedings between states and nationals of other states that fall outside the scope of the ICSID Convention, including: (i) arbitration proceedings for the settlement of investment disputes between parties one of which is not a Contracting State or a national of a Contracting State; and (ii) arbitration proceedings between parties at least one of which is a Contracting State or a national of a Contracting State for the settlement of disputes that do not arise directly out of an investment, provided that the underlying transaction is not an ordinary commercial transaction.

47. Arbitration proceedings under the ICSID Additional Facility constitute *regular* arbitration proceedings in the sense that such proceedings, just like arbitration proceedings under the UNCITRAL Rules or the SCC Rules, are governed by the national

43. ICSID has to date concluded such arrangements with the: Permanent Court of Arbitration at The Hague; Regional Arbitration Centres of the Asian-African Legal Consultative Committee in Cairo, in Kuala Lumpur and in Lagos; Australian Commercial Disputes Centre in Sydney; Australian Centre for International Commercial Arbitration in Melbourne; Singapore International Arbitration Centre; Gulf Cooperation Council Commercial Arbitration Centre in Bahrain; German Institution of Arbitration; Maxwell Chambers, Singapore; and Hong Kong International Arbitration Centre.
44. Article 63 of the ICSID Convention.
45. Article 63(b) of the ICSID Convention.

arbitration law at the seat of arbitration.[46] Proceedings under the ICSID Additional Facility are, thus, another instance where the seat of arbitration could be in Stockholm.

V. APPLICABLE LAW

48. Turning next to the question of applicable law in investment treaty cases seated in Sweden. It is a well established principle within the Swedish legal system that the principle of party autonomy applies to the choice of law by the parties.[47] Moreover, the SCC Rules expressly recognize the freedom of the parties to agree on the 'rules of law' applicable to the substance of the dispute.

49. Article 22 (1) of the SCC Rules provides that '*the Arbitral Tribunal shall decide the merits of the dispute on the basis of the law or rules of law agreed upon by the parties*' and that in the absence of such agreement '*the Arbitral Tribunal shall apply the law or rules of law which it considers to be most appropriate.*' Other arbitration rules, which are generally applied in investment disputes, also recognize this fundamental principle, e.g., the ICSID Convention, the ICSID Additional Facility Arbitration Rules and the UNCITRAL Rules.

50. The reference to 'rules of law' in the SCC Rules clarifies that the parties are not limited to the choice of a particular national jurisdiction. The parties may, for instance, designate a particular international treaty, e.g., an investment treaty, or public international law. The same principle also applies under Swedish arbitration law.[48]

51. With respect to investor-state disputes under BITs, '*the rules of law*...*agreed by the parties*', if any, would typically not be found in an agreement between the parties to the dispute, i.e., the investor and the host state, but rather in the applicable investment treaty. However, investment treaties do not display any uniform practice in this regard.

52. Governing law clauses in BITs often refer to the BIT itself, customary international law and the law of the respondent state to the arbitration. Although the interplay between international law and municipal law in investment disputes may sometimes raise difficult questions, as a rule of thumb, questions such as the jurisdiction of the arbitral tribunal under the BIT, the liability of the host State for alleged treaty breaches as well as remedies available to the investor as a result of such breaches are governed by the provisions of the BIT as supplemented by customary public international law. Municipal law, on the other hand, may be relevant for determining many of the preliminary questions which must be addressed in order to rule on the above-mentioned issues of public international law. Such questions may include, whether, and at what time, the investor acquired certain assets allegedly constituting an 'investment' under the BIT, what rights the investor possessed in the legal system of

46. Article 19 of the ICSID Additional Facility Arbitration Rules provides that '*Arbitration proceedings shall be held only in States that are parties to the 1958 UN Convention on the Recognition and Enforcement of Foreign Arbitral Awards*'.
47. K. Hobér, *International Commercial Arbitration in Sweden* 39ff (Oxford U. Press 2011).
48. K. Hobér, *International Commercial Arbitration in Sweden* 42 (Oxford U. Press, 2011).

the host state prior to the allegedly wrongful acts committed by the host state, and what remains of those rights thereafter, as well as the legal nature and effect of various acts undertaken by the host state.

53. As was held by the arbitral tribunal in *RosInvestCo v. Russian Federation* in an investment treaty arbitration in Stockholm under the SCC Rules:

> *the Tribunal finds that the law applicable to the claim under the [treaty] is the [treaty] itself and international law. Russian law comes into play only in so far as it is relevant in determining whether the Respondent acted in breach of an international obligation.*[49]

54. As regards applicable rules of public international law, the rules and principles relating to the *interpretation of treaties*, i.e., the Vienna Convention on the Law of Treaties, often play an important role.

55. Another set of public international law rules and principles which often plays an important role in investment arbitration are the rules and principles relating to *state responsibility*.[50] The law of state responsibility is, to a large part, reflected in the work of the International Law Commission (ILC) of the United Nations. The ILC Articles on Responsibility of States for Internationally Wrongful Acts is currently the most authoritative document on the law of state responsibility.

56. In investment arbitration, one particular aspect of the law of state responsibility has become increasingly important, *viz.*, the attribution of conduct to states. Pursuant to the principles of attribution, if an entity acts on behalf of a state or exercises governmental authority, such conduct is attributable to the state, even if the entity is a separate legal person.[51] Similarly, even if such separate legal entity is not state-owned, its actions may nevertheless be attributable to the state, if such acts have been carried out '*under the direction or control of*' the state.[52]

VI. CHALLENGE OF INVESTMENT TREATY AWARDS

A. Introduction

57. In investment arbitration, just as in commercial arbitration between two private parties, the final award of the arbitral tribunal is not always the end of the matter. It is not uncommon that the final award is merely the starting signal for challenge and/or enforcement proceedings that may take as long as, or even longer than, the arbitral

49. *RosInvestCo UK Ltd. v. The Russian Federation*, SCC Case No.V(079/2005), Final Award of 12 Sep. 2010, para. 249. Available at http://italaw.com/cases/923.
50. See e.g., K. Hobér, *State Responsibility and Attribution*, in *The Oxford Handbook of International Investment Law* (Muchlinski et al. eds., Oxford U. Press 2008).
51. See Art. 5 of the ILC Articles.
52. See Art. 8 of the ILC Articles.

proceedings leading up to the final award. Challenge proceedings are relatively common in investor-state arbitration.[53]

58. In non-ICSID Convention investment arbitration proceedings in Stockholm, be it under the SCC Rules, the UNCITRAL Rules or the ICSID Additional Facility, the arbitral procedure is ultimately subject to the law at the seat of the arbitration. This means that in all such investment arbitrations, the normal way to challenge an investment treaty award is through the municipal courts. There have to date been five concluded challenge proceedings concerning investment treaty awards issued in Sweden.[54]

59. In Sweden the Act regulates the grounds for invalidity and setting aside of investment treaty awards as well as other arbitral awards.[55] The following sections will only discuss issues related to challenges to investment treaty awards.

B. Lack of Jurisdiction Is the Most Frequent Challenge Ground in Investment Treaty Cases and Often Requires a Determination of Complex Issues of Fact and Law

60. The most frequently invoked ground in actions to set aside investment treaty awards before the Courts of Sweden is *lack of jurisdiction*. The same applies to challenges to investment treaty awards issued in other jurisdictions.[56] Challenges to investment treaty awards appear to involve challenges to the jurisdiction of the arbitral tribunal more frequently than challenges to awards in traditional international commercial arbitration. This is not surprising given the relative complexity of arbitration

53. No statistics are available of the total number of challenged investment arbitration awards. I have identified twenty-seven cases before municipal courts in eight different jurisdictions (Belgium, Canada, England, France, Germany, Sweden, Switzerland, and United States), but additional unreported cases might exist. The statistics of ICSID awards do, however, indicate that challenges to investment arbitration awards are common. Out of the 150 awards rendered under the ICSID Convention during the period 1971–2011, 42 (i.e., 28%) resulted in an application for annulment. See The ICSID Caseload – Statistics, Issue 2012-2, http://www.icsid.worldbank.org.

54. *The Russian Federation v. Sedelmayer*, judgment of the Stockholm District Court made on 12 Dec. 2002 in case no T6-583-98; *The Czech Republic v. CME Czech Republic B.V.*, judgment by the Svea Court of Appeal made on 15 May 2003 in case no T-8735-01, RH 2003:55; *Mr. Nagel v. The Czech Republic*, decision by the Svea Court of Appeal made on 30 May 2005 in case no T 9059-03; *Petrobart Limited v. Kyrgyz Republic*, judgment by the Svea Court of Appeal made in 13 Apr. 2006 in case no T 3739-03 and judgment by the Supreme Court made in 28 Mar. 2008 in case no T 2113-06, NJA 2008 p. 406; *Kyrgyz Republic v. Petrobart Limited*, judgment by the Svea Court of Appeal made on 19 Jan. 2007 in case no T 5208-05; *RosInvestCo UK Ltd v. The Russian Federation*, decision by the Supreme Court made on 12 Nov. 2010 in case no Ö 2301-09, NJA 2010 p. 508; and currently pending challenge; *The Russian Federation v. RovimeInversiones SICAV SA et al.*

55. See e.g., K. Hobér, *International Commercial Arbitration in Sweden* 294f. (Oxford U. Press 2011); J. Seablec & N. Eliasson, *The UNCITRAL Model Law on Arbitration and the Swedish Arbitration Act: A Comparison*, in *The Swedish Arbitration Act of 1999, Five Years On: A Critical Review of Strengths and Weaknesses* 236 (L. Heuman & S. Jarvin eds. JurisNet 2006).

56. K. Hobér & N. Eliasson, *Review of Investment Treaty Awards by Municipal Courts*, in *Arbitration under International Investment Agreements* 635 (K. Yannaca-Small ed., Oxford U. Press 2010).

clauses in investment treaties compared to standard arbitration clauses in commercial contracts.

61. Rulings on jurisdiction in international commercial arbitration are often limited to determining whether the dispute 'arose out of or in connection with' the contract containing the arbitration clause. Arbitral tribunals in investment treaty arbitration, on the other hand, frequently must rule on issues of public international law, including treaty interpretation, such as whether the claimant qualifies as an 'investor' as defined in the treaty, whether the claimant has made an 'investment' as defined in the treaty, whether the dispute is covered by the dispute resolution clause of the treaty, and so on. Ruling conclusively on these issues often requires the arbitral tribunal to determine complex issues of fact and law. In addition, such issues are often closely connected to the merits of the case.

C. What Standard Is to Be Applied by the Court when Reviewing the Arbitral Tribunal's Jurisdictional Decision?

1. Introduction

62. The complexity of jurisdictional issues in many investment treaty cases also raises the question of what standard of review is to be applied by the courts when reviewing the arbitral tribunal's jurisdictional decision. At first glance, the answer might seem straightforward: the host state's consent to arbitration does not extend beyond the limits of the arbitration clause in the applicable investment treaty. This would call for a full hearing *de novo* of all issues of fact and law that form part of the arbitral tribunal's decision on jurisdiction. The standard of review would be correctness, in the sense that the arbitral award should be set aside if the court finds that the decision of the arbitral tribunal was incorrect.

63. However, given the fact that jurisdictional determinations in investment arbitration involve mixed questions of fact and law which are often closely connected to the merits of the case, it may prove difficult for the reviewing court – in particular if the arbitral tribunal's ruling on jurisdiction was merged with the merits – to maintain a clear distinction between jurisdiction and merits when determining the challenge to the jurisdiction of the tribunal.

64. Considering the close connection between jurisdiction and merits in investment treaty arbitrations, it is not surprising that courts in different jurisdictions have taken different approaches concerning the standard of review.[57] In sections VI.C.2 and VI.C.3 below, I will address the approach taken by Swedish courts.

57. Hobér & Eliasson, *Review of Investment Treaty Awards by Municipal Courts*, 665–668.

2. *Court of Appeal Decisions in Petrobart I and II: The de novo Approach*

65. One of the longest running investment disputes with its seat of arbitration in Sweden was the dispute between Petrobart Ltd (Petrobart) and the Kyrgyz Republic. This dispute gave rise to two separate investment arbitrations, both with the seat of arbitration in Sweden, and two separate challenge proceedings before the courts of Sweden: *Petrobart Limited v. Kyrgyz Republic* (*Petrobart I*)[58] and *Kyrgyz Republic v. Petrobart Limited* (*Petrobart II*).[59] As will be explained in more detail below, in both these cases the Court of Appeal made a *de novo* determination of the jurisdictional issues that had been before the arbitral tribunals.

a. *Court of Appeal Decision in Petrobart I*

66. Petrobart, a company registered in Gibraltar, entered into a contract with the Kyrgyz state-owned joint stock company Kyrgyzgazmunaizat (KGM) regarding the supply of stable gas condensate. Petrobart delivered five shipments of gas but was only paid for the first two. At the same time as Petrobart turned to the domestic courts for recourse, the Kyrgyz authorities – as part of a reform of the system for supply of oil and gas in the Kyrgyz Republic and to deal with the critical financial situation of KGM – took certain measures that made it impossible for Petrobart to enforce its rights under the contract. Petrobart initiated arbitral proceedings against the Kyrgyz Republic under the Law on Foreign Investments in the Kyrgyz Republic. The arbitral proceedings were conducted under the UNCITRAL Rules. The seat of arbitration was Stockholm. The arbitral tribunal found that it lacked jurisdiction to determine Petrobart's claim, since Petrobart had not made an investment in the Kyrgyz Republic that qualified as an 'investment' under the Foreign Investment Law. The tribunal therefore dismissed the dispute in its entirety without any determination of the merits.

67. Petrobart challenged the arbitral award before the Svea Court of Appeal in Stockholm under section 36 of the Act.[60] Parallel to the challenge proceedings, Petrobart commenced new arbitral proceedings under the ECT (*Petrobart II*). In the challenge proceedings, Petrobart argued that, in order for an arbitral tribunal to have jurisdiction to rule on the merits of a claim, it is generally sufficient that the claimant has invoked circumstances (whether true or not) that – if they were true – would establish jurisdiction (the so-called doctrine of assertion). Applied to the present case, Petrobart argued that this doctrine meant that it was sufficient that Petrobart claimed to have made an 'investment' under the Foreign Investment Law in order to establish jurisdiction for the arbitral tribunal to determine the merits of the claim. The question whether Petrobart had actually made such an investment would be a substantive

58. *Petrobart Limited v. Kyrgyz Republic*, judgment by the Svea Court of Appeal made on 13 Apr. 2006 in case no T 3739-03.
59. *Kyrgyz Republic v. Petrobart Limited*, judgment by the Svea Court of Appeal made on 19 Jan. 2007 in case no T 5208-05.
60. *Petrobart Limited v. Kyrgyz Republic*, judgment by the Svea Court of Appeal made on 13 Apr. 2006 in case no T 3739-03.

matter which (unlike matters of jurisdiction) could not be reviewed by national courts. Petrobart also argued that the tribunal in any event had erred in finding that Petrobart was not an 'investor' under the Foreign Investment Law, which according to Petrobart, *inter alia*, was evidenced by the fact that the ECT Tribunal in Petrobart II had found that Petrobart's investment qualified as an 'investment' under the ECT.

68. The Court of Appeal agreed with the UNCITRAL Tribunal that the question whether Petrobart had made an 'investment' in accordance with the Foreign Investment Law was a matter of jurisdiction. It also found that, in order for the tribunal to have jurisdiction, it had to be established that the investor had actually made an 'investment' in accordance with the Foreign Investment Law. Thus, according to the Court, it was not sufficient that the investor claimed that it had made such an investment. The Court, furthermore, did not consider it persuasive that the ECT Tribunal had found that Petrobart had made an investment, given that the ECT Tribunal had relied on the definition of 'investment' in the ECT and not in the Foreign Investment Law of the Kyrgyz Republic. Thus, the Court fully upheld the tribunal's decision on jurisdiction.

69. Despite the fact, that Petrobart's claim in the meantime had been partially granted by the ECT Tribunal in *Petrobart II*, Petrobart appealed the decision of the Court of Appeal to the Swedish Supreme Court. As will be explained in further detail in section VI.C.3 below, the Supreme Court found that the arbitral tribunal had been wrong in finding that it did not have jurisdiction.[61]

b. Court of Appeal Decision in Petrobart II

70. As mentioned above, subsequent to the negative jurisdictional ruling in *Petrobart I*, Petrobart initiated new arbitral proceedings against the Kyrgyz Republic, this time under the ECT.[62] The circumstances invoked by Petrobart were essentially the same as in Petrobart I. The proceedings were conducted under the auspices of the SCC. The seat of arbitration was Stockholm. Again, in these proceedings the Kyrgyz Republic disputed the jurisdiction of the ECT Tribunal, *inter alia*, on the ground that Petrobart had not made an 'investment' within the meaning of the ECT. The ECT Tribunal, however, disagreed and found that Petrobart had made an 'investment' within the meaning of the ECT.

71. The Kyrgyz Republic also argued that the previous decision of the arbitral tribunal in Petrobart I was a bar to Petrobart's claim under the ECT on the grounds of res judicata. The arbitral tribunal, however, rejected the res judicata defence as the two arbitrations were based on different arbitration clauses, *viz.*, the first arbitration was

61. *Petrobart Limited v. The Kyrgyz Republic*, judgment by the Supreme Court made on 28 Mar. 2008 in case no T 2113-06, NJA 2008 p. 406.
62. *Petrobart Ltd v. Kyrgyzstan*, Award, SCC Case No 126/2003, 29 Mar. 2005. The Petrobart Case is also discussed in greater detail in K. Hobér, *The Energy Charter Treaty – Awards rendered* [2007] Dispute Res. Intl., 1–22 and in K. Hobér, *Investment Arbitration in Eastern Europe: In Search for a Definition of Expropriation* 209–220 (JurisNet 2007).

based on a clause in the Foreign Investment Law of the Kyrgyz Republic and the other arbitration on a clause in the ECT, and also since the first arbitration dealt with alleged violations of Kyrgyz law, whereas the other dealt with alleged violations of the ECT.[63]

72. As to the merits of the case, the arbitral tribunal found that the Kyrgyz Government had failed to provide fair and equitable treatment to Petrobart by transferring assets from KGM to a newly established company to the detriment of KGM's creditors, including Petrobart, and by intervening in court proceedings regarding execution of a judgment against KGM to the detriment of Petrobart.[64]

73. It was now the Kyrgyz Republic's turn to challenge the ECT award before the Svea Court of Appeal.[65] The Kyrgyz Republic argued that there was no valid arbitration agreement between Petrobart and the Kyrgyz Republic, since the ECT was not applicable with respect to investors from Gibraltar. While Gibraltar had been included in the United Kingdom's declaration of provisional application upon signature of the ECT, it was not listed in its subsequent instrument of ratification which, the Kyrgyz Republic argued, had the effect of terminating the provisional application. The Kyrgyz Republic also argued that there was no valid arbitration agreement in this case since delivery of gas did not constitute an 'investment' under the ECT.

74. In its determination of whether the ECT applied to investors from Gibraltar, the Court turned to Article 45 of the ECT, which governs the treaty's provisional application in relation to signatory states that have not yet ratified the treaty.[66] Article 45(3)(a)[67] stipulates that a signatory state may terminate its provisional application of the ECT by special notification to the depository declaring its intention not to become a contracting party to the treaty. The provisional application of the ECT also ends when a signatory state ratifies the treaty. The Court noted that the ECT does not expressly regulate the situation in the present case where the provisional application of the treaty and the final ratification do not have the same territorial scope. The Court found that, had the intention been to terminate the provisional application with regard to Gibraltar, the United Kingdom should have explicitly declared this when ratifying the treaty. The non-inclusion of Gibraltar in the United Kingdom's instrument of ratification meant that Gibraltar was still covered by the provisional application of the ECT and,

---

63. *Petrobart Ltd. v. Kyrgyzstan*, Award, SCC Case No 126/2003, 29 Mar. 2005, pp. 65–66.
64. *Petrobart Ltd. v. Kyrgyzstan*, Award, SCC Case No 126/2003, 29 Mar. 2005, p. 76.
65. *Kyrgyz Republic v. Petrobart Limited*, judgment by the Svea Court of Appeal made on 19 Jan. 2007 in case no T 5208-05.
66. The provisional application of the ECT – in particular in relation to the Russian Federation – is dealt with in greater detail in K. Hobér, *The Energy Charter Treaty - An Overview*, 8 J. World Inv. & Trade 323–356 (2007). Moreover, the provisional application of the ECT in relation to the Russian Federation is also subject to arbitral proceedings in two of the Yukos Cases, *viz.*, *Yukos Universal Ltd. (UK – Isle of Man) v. Russian Federation*, PCA Case No. AA 227, 30 Nov. 2009, Ad hoc UNCITRAL Rules; *Hulley Enterprises Ltd. (Cyprus) v. Russian Federation*, PCA Case No. AA 226, 30 Nov. 2009, Ad hoc UNCITRAL Rules.
67. Article 45(3)(a) of the ECT reads as follows: '*Any signatory may terminate its provisional application of this Treaty by written notification to the Depository of its intention not to become a Contracting Party to the Treaty. Termination of provisional application for any signatory shall take effect upon the expiration of 60 days from the date on which such signatory's written notification is received by the Depository.*'

accordingly, a valid arbitration agreement was in effect between the parties when Petrobart made its investment as well as when Petrobart initiated arbitral proceedings against the Kyrgyz Republic under the ECT.

75. As to the Kyrgyz Republic's second objection, i.e., that Petrobart had not made an 'investment' within the meaning of the ECT, the Court simply stated that the term 'investment' in the ECT should be given a broad interpretation and agreed with the conclusion of the arbitral tribunal that Article 1(5)[68] and 1(6)[69] of the ECT must be interpreted such that Petrobart must be deemed to have made an 'investment'. The request to set aside the award was denied.

76. The Court of Appeal thus made a *de novo* determination both in *Petrobart I* and *Petrobart II*. In particular, the judgment in *Petrobart II* involved a full review of complex issues of treaty interpretation with regard to the provisional application of the ECT in relation to Gibraltar as well as factual issues with regard to the United Kingdom's ratification of the ECT.

3. *Supreme Court Decision in Petrobart I and Sedelmayer: The Doctrine of Assertion*

77. A slightly different approach was taken by the Stockholm District Court, as confirmed by the Svea Court of Appeal, in *Russian Federation v. Sedelmayer* and, as mentioned in section VI.C.2.a above, by the Swedish Supreme Court in *Petrobart I* (reversing the above-mentioned decision of the Court of Appeal) based on the so-called 'doctrine of assertion'.[70] According to the doctrine of assertion, arbitrators, when ruling on their jurisdiction, should not examine the existence of any facts which the claimant alleges establish a legal relationship that is covered by the arbitration agreement. To establish jurisdiction for the arbitral tribunal, it is thus sufficient that the claimant asserts that the facts that allegedly create jurisdiction exist.

---

68. Article 1(5) of the ECT reads as follows: '*"Economic Activity in the Energy Sector" means an economic activity concerning the exploration, extraction, refining, production, storage, land transport, transmission, distribution, trade, marketing, or sale of Energy Materials and Products except those included in Annex NI, or concerning the distribution of heat to multiple premises.*'
69. Article 1(6) of the ECT reads in relevant parts as follows: '*"Investment" means every kind of asset, owned or controlled directly or indirectly by an Investor and includes: (a) tangible and intangible, and movable and immovable, property, and any property rights such as leases, mortgages, liens, and pledges; (b) a company or business enterprise, or shares, stock, or other forms of equity participation in a company or business enterprise, and bonds and other debt of a company or business enterprise; (c) claims to money and claims to performance pursuant to contract having an economic value and associated with an Investment; (d) Intellectual Property; (e) Returns; (f) any right conferred by law or contract or by virtue of any licences and permits granted pursuant to law to undertake any Economic Activity in the Energy Sector. [...]*'.
70. See further discussion of these cases below.

a. *Supreme Court Decision in Petrobart I*

78. As mentioned above, Petrobart appealed the decision of the Court of Appeal in Petrobart I to the Swedish Supreme Court, which found that the arbitral tribunal had been wrong in concluding that it did not have jurisdiction.[71] The Supreme Court took the view that, in deciding that it did not have jurisdiction, the arbitral tribunal had made a substantive determination that Petrobart had not made a foreign investment within the meaning of the Foreign Investment Law. The Supreme Court held that, when deciding on its jurisdiction, the arbitral tribunal should have assumed that the factual circumstances referred to by the claimant were present. If this had been done, the arbitral tribunal would – in the opinion of the Supreme Court – have found that it had jurisdiction.[72]

b. *Sedelmayer*

79. The dispute between Mr Sedelmayer and the Russian Federation arose out of a forced transfer of certain premises in St. Petersburg belonging to Mr Sedelmayer's Russian investment, a local joint venture company in which Mr Sedelmayer had invested through SGC International, incorporated in the United States. Mr Sedelmayer, as the ultimate investor controlling SGC International, commenced arbitral proceedings under the German-Soviet BIT, claiming expropriation of his investment. The BIT provided for ad hoc arbitration with the Chairman of the SCC as appointing authority. The seat of arbitration was Stockholm.

80. The arbitral tribunal ruled in favour of Mr Sedelmayer.[73] However, one of the arbitrators filed a dissenting opinion to the effect that the arbitral tribunal did not have jurisdiction under the German-Soviet BIT, since the investments in question had been made by a U.S. corporation and not by Mr Sedelmayer, and since there is no BIT in force between the United States and the Russian Federation.

81. The Russian Federation challenged the arbitral award before the Stockholm District Court on the ground that the arbitral tribunal had no jurisdiction.[74]

82. The Russian Federation argued that the tribunal lacked jurisdiction for three reasons. First, indirect investments, such as Mr Sedelmayer's, fell outside the scope of the arbitration clause in the German-Soviet BIT. Second, Mr Sedelmayer could not be regarded as an 'investor' under the German-Soviet BIT, since he did not have his

---

71. *Petrobart Limited v. The Kyrgyz Republic*, judgment by the Supreme Court made on 28 Mar. 2008 in case no T 2113-06, NJA 2008 p. 406.
72. *Petrobart Limited v. The Kyrgyz Republic*, judgment by the Supreme Court made on 28 Mar. 2008 in case no T 2113-06, NJA 2008 p. 406, 6–7.
73. The Sedelmayer case is discussed in greater detail in K. Hobér, *Investment Arbitration in Eastern Europe: In Search for a Definition of Expropriation* 46–60 (JurisNet 2007).
74. *Sedelmayer v. Russian Federation*, judgment by the Stockholm District Court made on 12 Dec. 2002 in case no T6-583-98. For an English translation of the judgment by the Stockholm District Court, see Stockholm International Arbitration Review 2005:2.

'permanent place of residence' in Germany.[75] Third, the request for arbitration had been directed to the Procurement Department of the Russian Federation and not to the Russian Federation, and no arbitration agreement existed between the Procurement Department and Mr Sedelmayer; accordingly, the decision by the arbitrators to issue its award against the Russian Federation had no legal effect between the parties.

83. The District Court found that the first two grounds relied on by the Russian Federation should be resolved applying the so-called 'doctrine of assertion.[76] This meant that Mr Sedelmayer's assertion that he was an 'investor' with a 'permanent place of residence' in Germany, thus being assured of investment protection under the German-Soviet BIT, was sufficient to establish jurisdiction for the arbitral tribunal.[77]

84. The District Court also explained, however, that application of the doctrine of assertion did not mean that the arbitral tribunal subsequently, when ruling on the merits of the dispute, would be bound by the determination of these issues for the purpose of jurisdiction. Whether or not Mr Sedelmayer in fact was an 'investor' who had made an 'investment' in Russia would still have to be determined by the arbitral tribunal as part of the merits. Such determination, however, could not be subject to court review in challenge proceedings, since it is part of the merits of the dispute.[78]

85. Regarding the argument by the Russian Federation that the request for arbitration had been directed to the Procurement Department of the Russian Federation and not to the Russian Federation, the District Court noted that under the German-Soviet BIT, it was the Russian Federation – as a party to the BIT – that was the proper Respondent regarding claims under the BIT. The court found that since the Procurement Department was the State organ directly involved in the forced transfer of the premises, the Russian Federation was properly represented in the arbitration through the Procurement Department.

86. The Russian Federation appealed the judgment of the Stockholm District Court to the Svea Court of Appeal. The Court of Appeal upheld the District Court's decision on the grounds given by the District Court.[79]

---

75. Article 1(c) of the German-Soviet BIT provides that '"*investor" means an individual having a permanent place of residence in the area covered by this Agreement, or a body corporate having its registered office therein, authorized to make investments.*'
76. *Sedelmayer v. Russian Federation*, judgment by the Stockholm District Court made on 12 Dec. 2002 in case no T6-583-98, 17. For an English translation of the judgment by the Stockholm District Court, see Stockholm International Arbitration Review 2005:2. See also L. Heuman, *Arbitration Law of Sweden: Practice and Procedure* 56–63 (Juris Publg. 2003).
77. *Sedelmayer v. Russian Federation*, judgment by the Stockholm District Court made on 12 Dec. 2002 in case no T6-583-98. For an English translation of the judgment by the Stockholm District Court, see Stockholm International Arbitration Review 2005:2.
78. *Sedelmayer v. Russian Federation*, judgment by the Stockholm District Court made on 12 Dec. 2002 in case no T6-583-98. For an English translation of the judgment by the Stockholm District Court, see Stockholm International Arbitration Review 2005:2.
79. *The Russian Federation v. Sedelmayer*, judgment by the Svea Court of Appeal made on 15 May 2003 in case no T8735-01, 3. For an English translation of the judgment by the Svea Court of Appeal, see Stockholm International Arbitration Review 2005:2.

4. *Standard of Review: Concluding Remarks*

87. One of the most difficult questions for domestic courts hearing challenges of investment treaty awards is arguably to strike the right balance between the exercise of the court's supervisory jurisdiction over the conduct of the arbitration and deference to the knowledge and experience of the appointed arbitrators to determine complex jurisdictional issues in investment treaty cases. In *Petrobart I* and *Petrobart II*, the Court of Appeal made a full *de novo* review of the jurisdiction of the arbitral tribunals, whereas the Supreme Court in *Petrobart I* (reversing the decision of the Court of Appeal) and the Stockholm District Court (confirmed by the Court of Appeal) in *Sedelmayer* declined to review factual determinations by the arbitral tribunals that formed part of the determination of the jurisdiction of the respective tribunals.

88. In England the High Court applied a standard similar to that of the Court of Appeal in *Petrobart I* and *Petrobart II*. As clearly stated by the High Court in *Ecuador v. Occidental*[80] and repeated in *Czech Republic v. EMV*,[81] a challenge to the jurisdiction of the arbitral tribunal proceeds by way of a rehearing by the court of the matters that had been before the arbitrators, i.e., a hearing *de novo* of the host state's jurisdictional objection. The test for the court was, in the view of the High Court, whether the arbitral tribunal was *correct* in its decision on jurisdiction.[82]

89. A different approach, however, was taken by the Ontario Superior Court in *Bayview Irrigation District #11 and ors v. Mexico*.[83] In this case, the Ontario Superior Court emphasized that its role in judicial review was *not* to conduct a hearing *de novo* of the merits of the arbitral tribunal's decision on jurisdiction. The Court further stated that:

> while decisions by arbitral tribunals are not immune from challenge, any challenge is confronted with the 'powerful presumption' that the tribunal acted within its authority. An arbitral decision is not invalid because it wrongly decided a point of fact or law.[84]

90. A similar position has been taken by BG Group Plc in its application to the U.S. Supreme Court to hear an appeal of a judgment by the D.C. Court of Appeal setting aside an investment treaty award against Argentina.[85] The BG Group, supported by several groups of amicus curiae (friends of the court), argues that the D.C. Court of Appeal ruling, which held that the U.S. Courts should determine *de novo* threshold

---

80. *Ecuador v. Occidental Exploration and Production Company*, Judgment, [2006] EWHC 345 (Comm), 2 Mar. 2006.
81. *Czech Republic v. European Media Ventures SA*, Judgment, [2007] EWHC 285 (Comm), 5 Dec. 2007.
82. *Ecuador v. Occidental Exploration and Production Company*, Judgment, [2006] EWHC 345 (Comm), 2 Mar. 2006, para. 7.
83. *Bayview Irrigation District #11 and ors v. Mexico*, Ontario Superior Court, Judicial Review 07-CV-340139-PD2, Judgment of 5 May 2008.
84. *Bayview Irrigation District #11 and ors v. Mexico*, Ontario Superior Court, Judicial Review 07-CV-340139-PD2, Judgment of 5 May 2008, para. 63.
85. *Republic of Argentina v. BG Group Plc*, U.S. Court of Appeals for the District of Columbia Circuit, 17 Jan. 2012.

questions under the investor-state arbitration provision of the applicable treaty, shows insufficient deference to the views of arbitrators, which are best suited to decide whether conditions precedent to arbitration have been met. The petitioners further argue that the approach by the Court of Appeal, substituting its own *de novo* interpretation of a treaty between two sovereign states for that of the arbitrators could seriously disrupt the system of investment treaty arbitration.[86] BG Group's petition for a Writ of Certiorari is still pending before the Supreme Court.

VII. ENFORCEMENT

91. Sweden is a signatory to the New York Convention and the ICSID Convention (also known as the Washington Convention), which means that, as a matter of principle, both ICSID awards and non-ICSID awards are enforceable in Sweden. Similarly, investment arbitration awards resulting from an investment arbitration with its seat in Sweden are enforceable in countries which have ratified the New York Convention. ICSID awards are enforced pursuant to the special enforcement regime of the ICSID Convention in countries which have ratified it.

92. Article 54 of the ICSID Convention governs the enforcement of ICSID awards. Article 54 provides that ICSID awards are to be recognized as binding and their pecuniary obligations are to be enforced like final domestic judgments in the territories of all States parties to the Convention. The competent court or other authority charged with applications for recognition and enforcement is not entitled to review the award in any respect. Enforcement of investment treaty awards under the ICSID Convention is therefore often deemed to offer advantages compared to enforcement under the New York Convention.

93. When it comes to enforcement in Sweden of non-ICSID awards, the Act distinguishes between domestic and foreign arbitral awards. The provisions regulating recognition and enforcement of foreign awards are found in Articles 52–60 of the Act, which incorporate the provisions of the New York Convention. It should also be noted that Sweden has ratified the New York Convention without exercising any of the available standard reservations, i.e., that the Convention will only apply: (i) to recognition and enforcement of awards made in the territory of another Contracting State and (ii) to differences arising out of legal relationships, whether contractual or not, that are considered commercial under the national law. Consequently, the Act applies to any foreign arbitral award without distinction as to its nature or origin.[87]As far as the author is aware, however, there have not yet been any attempts to enforce a *foreign investment treaty award* in Sweden.

86. See e.g., the Petition by BG Group before the U.S. Supreme Court in the matter of *BG Group PLC v. Argentine Republic*, 27 Jul. 2012 and Amicus brief of practitioners and academics in *BG Group PLC v. Argentine Republic*, 29 Aug. 2012.
87. K. Hobér, *International Commercial Arbitration in Sweden* 357 (Oxford U. Press 2011).

94. Investment treaty awards *issued in Sweden* will for the purposes of enforcement *in Sweden* be treated as domestic Swedish awards. That means that these awards are immediately enforceable in Sweden through a simple application to the Enforcement Authority. As far as the author is aware, only one investment treaty award issued in Sweden has given rise to enforcement proceedings in Sweden, *viz.*, *Sedelmayer v. The Russian Federation*.

95. The enforcement of investment treaty awards, whether ICSID or non-ICSID awards, has in practice often proved to be far more difficult than enforcement of an arbitral award made in regular transnational disputes involving private parties. The reason is the participation of a sovereign state as the respondent party, which raises issues relating to sovereign immunity. For example, in the above-mentioned *Sedelmayer* case, not only did Mr Sedelmayer have to defend the award in challenge proceedings brought by the Russian Federation, but attempts to enforce his award are still on-going. The great majority of his enforcement attempts in various jurisdictions were blocked by objections that the Russian assets which he had traced were sovereign assets that could not be subject to execution.

96. Sweden has adopted the restrictive approach on state immunity. Sweden has also ratified the UN Convention on Jurisdictional Immunities of States and Their Properties[88] on 23 December 2009 (the Immunities Convention). The Immunities Convention has yet to come into force due to the low number of ratifications,[89] but Sweden ratifying the Convention is, nevertheless, a confirmation of Sweden's adherence to the principles of restrictive immunity.

97. Sweden's adherence to the doctrine of restrictive state immunity is also confirmed in recent court practice. As part of Mr Sedelmayer's attempts to recover some of the damages awarded to him as well as his litigation costs in the challenge proceedings, he initiated several enforcement proceedings in Sweden. On 1 July 2011, the Swedish Supreme Court rendered its decision in one of these proceedings.[90]

98. The question before the Supreme Court was whether certain real estate and rental income from offices and apartments located in the building in question, which was owned by the Russian Trade Delegation in Stockholm, were protected from enforcement due to immunity from execution.

99. In its decision, the Supreme Court first noted that the principle of state immunity had evolved from a previous absolute immunity of states towards a more and more restrictive approach to state immunity. The Court confirmed that with respect to immunity from suit the state's immunity only extended to sovereign acts and did not

88. United Nations Convention on Jurisdictional Immunities of States and Their Property, New York, 2 Dec. 2004.
89. Out of 28 signatories, only 12 States have ratified the Convention. According to Art. 30, the Convention needs 30 ratifications to enter into force.
90. *Sedelmayer v. The Russian Federation*, judgment by the Supreme Court made on 1 Jul. 2011 in case no Ö170-10, NJA 2011 p. 475. For English translations of the judgment of the Supreme Court of Sweden, see the Swedish Arbitration Law Portal: http://www.arbitration.scc institute.com/Swedish-Arbitration-Portal/ (last accessed 8 Aug. 2012).

extend to commercial acts. With respect to immunity from execution, on the other hand, the Court noted that it has been viewed as a greater intrusion in a state's sovereignty to subject its property to execution, than to subject the state to the jurisdiction of foreign courts. That being said, relying on the Immunities Convention as an expression of the standard currently accepted by many states, the Court found that enforcement may be granted even in the absence of any waiver of immunity against enforcement and execution, at least with respect to some state property, *viz.*, property used for other purposes than governmental non-commercial purposes.

100. With respect to the question of what should be considered 'property used for governmental non-commercial purposes', the Court found that it would generally cover property used for a state's sovereign or official functions. This must be assessed on a case-by-case basis with reference to the actual use of the property. The building in the present case had forty-eight apartments. Diplomatic staff used fifteen of these apartments, but the remaining apartments were used for other non-official purposes. The Court, with reference to the above-mentioned facts, concluded that the property was not to a substantial extent used for the official purposes of the Russian Federation. The Supreme Court further held that the nature of the use had not otherwise been of such specific nature as to grant the property immunity from enforcement in the present enforcement matter. The enforcement application was therefore granted.

CHAPTER 3
The Arbitration Agreement

Anders Reldén & Ola Nilsson

I. INTRODUCTION

1. Submitting disputes between commercial parties to arbitration presupposes that they have entered into a valid and binding arbitration agreement. This forms the basis for the jurisdiction of an arbitral tribunal to settle disputes covered by the arbitration agreement and render an enforceable arbitral award. Without a valid arbitration agreement there can be no arbitration and a future arbitral award may be set aside or its enforcement may be refused.[1]

2. Another effect of an arbitration agreement is that it bars disputes falling within the scope of the arbitration agreement from being litigated in an ordinary court (if this is duly invoked by the respondent).[2] An arbitration agreement means that the parties derogate dispute resolution from the courts and from the procedural safeguards inherent in ordinary judicial proceedings, including the right to appeal a judgment of a court on the merits. The agreement therefore has to make it clear that the parties intend to refer their disputes to resolution by arbitrators and not to any other type of dispute resolution.[3] Further, the agreement must provide that disputes will be referred to a person or persons as arbitrators and not in any other capacity, e.g., as mediator, valuation expert or any other type of expert.[4] However, it is sufficient that the parties

1. Hobér, *International Commercial Arbitration in Sweden* 90 (Oxford U. Press 2011).
2. Sections 4 and 49 of the Swedish Arbitration Act (Sw: *Lag (1999:116) om skiljeförfarande*) (the Act).
3. *Rita Urhelyi v. Arbetsmarkandens Försäkringsaktiebolag*, NJA 1974 p. 573 and Heuman, 2003, 27.
4. *Bojan Andersson et. al., v. Handelstjänstemannaförbundet*, NJA 1958 p. 654 and *Byggnadsfirman J. Karlsson v. Svenska Byggnadsträarbetareförbundets avdelning nr 89* et al., AD 1931 no. 64 and Andersson et al., 2011, 35. See also *O. Hane v. A.V. Rosenkvist and H.J. Rosenquist*, NJA 1925 p. 29.

have agreed that disputes will be settled in accordance with the Swedish Arbitration Act (Sw: *Lag (1999:116) om skiljeförfarande*) (the Arbitration Act). Parties need not in the arbitration agreement identify the arbitrators, how they are to be appointed and the number of arbitrators.[5]

3. An agreement to simply derogate resolution of disputes from the court, i.e., providing that disputes will not be decided by the courts, without providing for arbitration does not constitute an arbitration agreement.

4. The Act defines an arbitration agreement as an agreement between two or more parties to refer disputes arising from an identified legal relationship to resolution by one or more arbitrators.[6] The definition in the Arbitration Act covers both so-called submission agreements, i.e., an agreement to submit an existing dispute to arbitration, and arbitration clauses in main contracts referring future disputes under the main contract to arbitration. With respect to arbitration agreements referring future disputes to arbitration, the Arbitration Act requires that such disputes must concern an identified legal relationship for the arbitration agreement to be valid.[7] This will be dealt with more closely in section III below regarding the scope of the arbitration agreement.

5. An arbitration agreement may also include provisions to the effect that the parties should first try to settle their disputes by mediation or any other ADR measure before referring the dispute to arbitration (so-called multi-tier arbitration clauses). An agreement containing such provisions is enforceable as an arbitration agreement under the Arbitration Act. It is uncertain whether non-fulfilment of any previous tiers (which are sufficiently clear and possible to determine objectively) may make an action inadmissible.[8]

II. THE FORMATION OF ARBITRATION AGREEMENTS

A. Introduction

6. If the place of arbitration is in Sweden, Swedish law is applicable on formation of the arbitration agreement, unless the parties have agreed otherwise.

---

5. Heuman, 2003, 27.
6. Section 1(1). See also Heuman, 2003, 27 and Andersson et al., 2011, 34.
7. Section 1 of the Act, SOU 1994:81: p. 257, Prop. 1998/99:35 p. 212, Heuman, 2003, 28–29, Andersson et al., 2011, 36.
8. Söderlund, JT 2005/06, 187–197. *Christer J. et al. v. Svenska Kommunalarbetarförbundet*, NJA 1982 p. 853 seems to indicate that the Swedish courts would be prepared to enforce such tiers. However, in Govt. bill 2010/11:128 the Swedish legislator expressed the view that such tiers should not bar commencement of arbitration proceedings. Cf. also *Poiré v. Tripier*, Cour de Cassation, mixed chamber, 11 Feb. 2003 reprinted in 19(3) Arbitration International 368 (2003), ICC Case No. 9977 (final award 22 Jun. 1999), ICC Case No. 7422 (interim award 28 Jun. 1996), ICC Case No. 6276 (partial award 29 Jan. 1990) and *Cable & Wireless plc v. IBM United Kingdom Ltd.* [2002] E.W.H.C. 2059 (comm); [2002] 2 All ER (comm) 1041.

7. An arbitration agreement is generally concluded in the same way as any other agreement. First, we will therefore provide a brief description of the basic principles of the Swedish Contracts Act[9] and analyse whether formation of arbitration agreements may require special considerations. Thereafter, we will briefly deal with passivity and the incorporation of standard terms and conditions containing arbitration clauses.

8. Under Swedish law, there are no formal requirements for conclusion of an arbitration agreement (e.g., under seal, notarized, stamped) and it need not be in writing.[10] An arbitration agreement is entered into when the parties' intentions converge. Moreover, a party may also become bound by an arbitration agreement as a result of its passivity or conduct.

B. Formation of Contracts under the Contracts Act

1. *Agreement is Formed by Consent*

9. Formation of contracts under Swedish law is governed by the Contracts Act. The Act sets out a model for entering into contracts, based on the parties' exchange of written (or oral) offers and counter offers, which are binding and irrevocable during an acceptance period. An agreement is entered into when an offer is accepted.

10. What in fact constitutes a binding contract under Swedish law is the mutual assent of the parties and usually the exchange of some kind of expression of that willingness to be bound.[11] A party's intention and willingness to be bound may be expressed in writing, orally or by conduct.

11. The parties may also agree upon the mechanism for forming a contract as the provisions in the Contracts Act on formation of contracts are non-mandatory. The provisions of the Act may also be set aside by commercial practice and other well-established usage, if such practice or usage can be proved.

12. Although normally an agreement is to be formed by corresponding offer and acceptance, an agreement may occasionally be concluded even if no meeting of minds occurs. Such conclusion is usually based on the principle of trust, i.e., a party's trust in (and justified expectation of) the content of an expression of the other party's intention, even if that expression for some reason deviates from a true intention.[12] Such

---

9. (*Sw: Lag (1915:218) om avtal och andra rättshandlingar på förmögenhetsrättens område*).
10. In Jan. 2011, France adopted a new act on arbitration under which, as regards international arbitrations, there is no longer a requirement that an arbitration agreement should be in writing. (*Fr. Décret no 2011-48 du 13 Janvier 2011 portant réforme de l'arbitrage*). In Sweden, this was not a requirement under the previous Arbitration Act of 1929 nor is it under the current 1999 Arbitration Act.
11. See for example, Grönfors, *Avtalslagen*, 3rd edn Norstedts Juridik, Stockholm 1995, 52 and Jan Ramberg & Christina Ramberg, *Allmän avtalsrätt* 33 and 79 (7th edn Norstedts Juridik 2007).
12. Lehrberg, *Avtalsrättens grundelement* 2nd edn I.B.A. Institutet för Bank- och Affärsjuridik, Stockholm 2006, 235 and 237; Adlercreutz, *Avtalsrätt I*, 37 (12th edn Juristförlaget i Lund 2002).

trust or justified expectations may also be based on the other party's passivity or conduct.

2. *Passivity*

13. In general, a party has no obligation to reply to offers made by other parties and a party will therefore not be bound by its own passivity. However, a party who should realize that the other party believes or assumes that a binding agreement has been concluded, has an obligation to inform the other party that no such agreement has been formed. A party that fails to give such notice without unreasonable delay may be deemed bound to the agreement.[13] If a party is aware of the other party's misunderstanding but neglects to notify the other party, the first party may be bound by its passivity.

3. *Incorporation of Standard Terms*

14. Standard terms are incorporated into an individual contract if they form part of the individual contract or if they are annexed to the contract as an attachment or an appendix. Usually a reference clause, a provision in the individual contract indicating that certain standard terms apply, would be sufficient for the terms to be incorporated. However, one condition is that the standard terms are easily accessible.[14]

C. Formation of Arbitration Agreements

1. *The Law Applicable to the Arbitration Agreement*

15. As noted above, Swedish substantive law applies to all arbitration agreements regarding arbitrations which take place in Sweden, unless otherwise agreed by the parties.[15] This includes how an arbitration agreement is formed (with the exception of the authority and power of the person or persons representing the party entering into

13. See Supreme Court cases *Svenska Musikerförbundet* et al. *v. Yngve S.*, NJA 1962 p. 276; where a party was bound by analogy of s. 9, and to a certain extent, also s. 6 of the Contracts Act and *C.A. MD AB v. the County of Stockholm*, NJA 2006 p. 638.
14. Ulf Bernitz stresses that the standard agreement must be kept available in such a way that the opposite party can without difficulty review the standard terms before the agreement is concluded. Bernitz, *Standardavtalsrätt* (7th edn Norstedts Juridik, Stockholm 2008) 60. According to Jan and Christina Ramberg, standard terms are easily accessible if they are available on a company's webpage or at its business premises – if the agreement is concluded there. Jan Ramberg and Christina Ramberg, *Allmän avtalsrätt* 142–143 (7th edn Norstedts Juridik, Stockholm 2007).
15. Section 48 of the Act. In this respect, the Swedish Arbitration Act differs from the Model law. While s. 48 of the Act gives an answer to the question the Model law does not regulate what is the applicable law of the arbitration agreement (see Zettermarck & Reldén, 'Bör lagen om skiljeförfarande internationaliseras', in *Vänbok till Bertil Södermark* (Lars Göthlin et al. eds., Norstedts Juridik 2009), 84. According to the Arbitration Act ss. 46

the agreement and interpreted, as well as invalidity of and adjustments of unfair arbitration agreements.

2. *Entering into Arbitration Agreements*

16. General contract law principles apply to the formation of arbitration agreements. It has been argued that the conditions for an arbitration agreement to be concluded are more rigid compared to the entering into agreements in general.[16] The rationale for this approach is that an arbitration clause is of particular importance since a party waives its right to settle disputes in court by entering into an arbitration agreement.[17] However, there is no express support in case law that stricter requirements should apply with respect to the entering into arbitration agreements.[18]

3. *Forming Arbitration Agreements in Other Ways than in Writing*

17. An arbitration agreement may also be established by party usage and the parties' previous course of dealings.[19] Such usage is, however, usually hard to prove.

18. An arbitration agreement may also be concluded by subsequent conduct.[20] Such conduct of the party or parties would then reasonably have to indicate a clear expression of the party's intention to be bound by the arbitration agreement.[21]

---

and 48, the law of different countries may be applicable to the arbitration proceedings and the arbitration agreement. Regarding the proceedings, Swedish law is applicable to all arbitrations that take place in Sweden.

16. Lindskog, 2005, 103–105, Hassler & Cars, *Skiljeförfarande*, 2nd ed., 1989, 34, Adlercreutz, *Avtalsrätt II*, 5th ed., 2001, 67.
17. Cf. Lindskog, 104, Heuman, 2003, 32 and Reldén & Nilsson, *Incorporation and Passivity: Entering into Arbitration Agreements under Swedish Law*, in *Between East and West: Essays in Honour of Ulf Franke* 433–434 (Hobér et al. eds., JurisNet 2010).
18. Hobér, *International Commercial Arbitration in Sweden*, 2011, 91; Heuman, 2003, 33; Dillén, *Bidrag till läran om skiljeavtalet*, 1933, 138-139; and Andersson et al., 2011, 41.
19. *Värmeledningsaktiebolaget Radiator v. Skanska AB*, RH 1989:83 and for example Runesson, *The Arbitration Agreement as a matter of Swedish Contract Law*, in *The Swedish Arbitration Act of 1999, Five years on: A Critical Review of Strengths and Weaknesses* 6–7 (Lars Heuman and Sigvard Jarvin eds., JurisNet 2006) and Ramberg, *The Arbitration Agreement*, 1 Stockholm Arbitration Report 25 (1999).
20. As an example of an arbitration agreement constituted by subsequent conduct see *Final Arbitration Award Rendered in 2000 in Case 108/1997: Majority Award one Arbitrator Dissenting in Part* including Observations by Michael S. Walker, 1 Stockholm Arbitration Report 57–73 (2001). See also Madsen, *Skiljeförfarande i Sverige – En kommentar till lagen (1999:116) om skiljeförfarande och till reglerna för Stockholms Handelskammares Skiljedomsinstitut* (2nd edn, Jure Förlag, Stockholm 2009), 70, and Lindskog, 2005, 101-102.
21. A party who takes part in arbitration without objecting to the tribunal's authority is considered to have accepted that an arbitration agreement has been concluded (even if that was not originally the case). This is a special kind of conclusion of agreements through subsequent conduct.

19. During arbitral proceedings, the parties may agree that claims not actually covered by an arbitration agreement shall be tried by the arbitrators.[22]

4. *Concluding Arbitration Agreements by Passivity*

20. It has been questioned in the legal doctrine whether arbitration agreements can be formed through passivity.[23] However, cases from the Court of Appeals indicate that general contract law principles on formation of contracts also apply to the entering into arbitration agreements.[24] In a rather recent unpublished case of 2007, the Svea Court of Appeal seems, in principle, to accept the conclusion of an arbitration agreement by passivity.[25]

5. *Incorporation of Arbitration Clauses*

21. Incorporation of arbitration clauses in standard terms and conditions is accepted internationally, both in the UNCITRAL Model Law and in the New York Convention.[26]

22. The same is the case in Sweden. An arbitration agreement may be concluded through a reference clause[27] provided that the standard terms are easily accessible to the parties, although possible exceptions may exist. For example, arbitration clauses in standard terms may still be considered to be unexpected or burdensome to inexperienced commercial parties who are not familiar with the standard terms in

22. Heuman, 2003, 41–42.
23. Heuman, 2003, 33 and 39.
24. *Lindvall & Helmer in Gothenburg v. Axel Edgrens Eftr in Arvika*, SvJT 1917, 41 and *The State of Ukraine v. Norsk Hydro*, judgment by the Svea Court of Appeal made on 17 Dec. 2007 in case no T 3108-06. See also Hobér, *International Commercial Arbitration in Sweden*, 2011, 100 et seq. and Dillén, *Bidrag till läran om skiljeavtalet*, 1933, 140-141.
25. In *the State of Ukraine v. Norsk Hydro*,(see footnote 24 above) the following contract formation issue arose. At a meeting the representatives of several parties agreed in principle to conclude a contract, and all the parties except two signed a contract. The contract was thereafter sent to persons authorized to sign for the two other parties. Subsequently the contract was signed by one further party and thereafter sent to the ultimate party. This party never did sign the contract. Svea Court of Appeal held that it could be argued that the party not signing the contract had an obligation to inform the other parties when it decided not to sign the contract. The party did, however, inform the other party (approximately three months after receiving the contract). Therefore the party not signing the contract had not been bound by its passivity, according to the court.
26. According to Art. 7(6) of the Model Law (option I), a reference in a contract to any document containing an arbitration clause constitutes an arbitration agreement in writing, provided that the reference is such as to make that clause part of the contract. The New York Convention (Art. II.2) considers an arbitral clause in a contract as an arbitration agreement in writing.
27. *Tureberg - Sollentuna Lastbilcentral ekonomisk förening v. Byggnadsfirman Rudolf Asplund AB*, NJA 1980 p. 46 and confirmed in *DHL Express AB v. Nordic Logistic Service Oy's (bankruptcy estate)*, NJA 2005, N. 8. See also Olsson & Kvart, *Lagen om skiljeförfarande – En kommentar*, 1st edn, Norstedts Juridik, Stockholm 2000 33; and Heuman, 2003, 33–34.

question.[28] The requirement for incorporation of one-sidedly drafted standard terms and conditions may be higher than that for agreed documents.[29]

23. One-sidedly drafted standard terms should, under normal circumstances, be attached to the contract or sent to the other party, either in connection with the main contract being negotiated or at another appropriate instance in order to be considered binding. One may also consider the possibility whereby the party introducing the standard terms indicates that they are easily accessible on the web site of the party relying on them or in that party's catalogues and brochures. An additional circumstance to be considered is when one or all parties are non-Swedish.[30] A prerequisite for incorporation should normally be that the standard terms containing the arbitral clause are in a language comprehensible to the party to be bound or in a language with a connection to the language in which the parties have communicated during negotiations and used for drafting the individual contract. In addition, slightly higher requirements ought to be put on the agreement being made accessible if it is not sent directly to the other party. Hence, both the reference to any standard terms and conditions and their content should in these cases be comprehensible for both parties (including any non-Swedish party) for them to become bound by those terms and conditions.

6. *Burden of Proof*

24. A party alleging that an arbitration agreement has been formed has the burden of proving the facts and circumstances from which the arbitral tribunal or the court should draw the conclusion that a valid arbitration agreement has been formed.[31] The burden of proof is the same whether the matter is tried by an arbitral tribunal or a court, as a jurisdictional issue in an arbitration matter or after challenging an arbitral award.[32]

25. There is one exception to this rule. If a party does not appoint an arbitrator, the other party may request a competent district court to appoint an arbitrator. In this case, the

28. *Taisto L. v. F. E. Wahlgren Ingenjörsbyrå AB*, RH 1989:1, *Lööve Trailer AB v. Kerstin Hörnfeldt*, RH 2012:8 and Andersson et al., 2011, 44.
29. Compare to Grönfors, *Avtalslagen*, 3rd edn, Norstedts Juridik, Stockholm 1995, 67-68; Bernitz, *Standardavtalsrätt*, 7th edn, Norstedts Juridik, Stockholm 2008, 18; and Adlercreutz, *Avtalsrätt II*, 5th edn, Juristförlaget i Lund, Lund 2001, 64. See also UNIDROIT Principles 2.1.19-2.1.22.
30. Heuman, *Current Issues in Swedish Arbitration* 24 (Kluwer Juristförlaget 1990); and Heuman, 2003, 37: 'When foreign parties are involved, it is possible that an ordinary reference clause will not always have the intended effect.'
31. As Stefan Lindskog stresses, the prerequisite for a valid arbitral agreement may consist of several different matters in dispute and different parties may have the burden of proof regarding different matters. Lindskog, 2005, 103 n. 35.
32. Lindskog, 2005, 103, 340 and 923. Compare regarding challenging the award, Heuman, 2003, 591–592. Further, when it comes to enforcement under the New York Convention, the party asserting that an arbitral award is based on a valid arbitration agreement bears the burden of proof. This burden can often be fulfilled by referring to the tribunal's ruling in the award, unless the opposite party makes specific remarks and objections. See *Société Planavergne S.A. v. K.B. i Stockholm AB*, 2003, NJA 2003 p. 379.

court may only reject the request if it is manifest that there is no legal basis for arbitration. In this situation, a party which asserts that no valid arbitration agreement has been entered into bears the burden of proof that an arbitration agreement does not exist.[33]

26. Besides, where parties, during the course of arbitration proceedings, agree to extend the arbitral tribunal's jurisdiction to issues not covered by the arbitration agreement, the burden of proof for that agreement rests with the party relying on it. Evidence about a supplementary oral arbitration agreement entered into before an arbitral tribunal may be included in a protocol together with a declaration by the arbitrators that they also have jurisdiction over these new claims.

27. It is well advised to confirm arbitration agreements in writing, not least from an enforcement point of view. The New York Convention provides that arbitration agreements must be in writing. Hence, contracting states are not required to recognize arbitration agreements entered into orally or by conduct. An award rendered in Sweden based on an oral agreement, party usage or conduct may therefore be difficult, or impossible, to enforce in states which have acceded to the New York Convention and which have not waived the Convention requirement that arbitration agreements must be in writing. On a practical note, a party seldom requests arbitration based on an oral agreement simply because the existence of such agreements is difficult to prove. It is much more common that parties have different opinions about the scope of a written arbitration agreement.

III. THE SCOPE OF ARBITRATION AGREEMENTS

A. Contract Interpretation of Arbitration Agreements

28. As noted in the introduction the arbitrators' powers to settle a dispute are based on the arbitration agreement. The jurisdiction of an arbitral tribunal only covers issues which fall under the arbitration agreement. If an arbitration agreement does not cover a specific dispute the arbitrators have no jurisdiction. To ascertain the scope of an arbitration agreement is therefore of great importance.

29. Issues of interpretation are decided under the law governing the arbitration agreement. If Swedish law is applicable to the arbitration agreement, general principles of Swedish contract law on contract interpretation apply when defining the scope of an arbitration agreement. The basic principle in Swedish contract law is that in case of ambiguity the parties' intentions prevail over the wording.[34] There is no support in Supreme Court case law for restrictive interpretation of arbitration agreements, as has

33. Heuman, 2003, 219.
34. Andersson et al., 2011, 65.

been suggested by certain legal authors.[35] On the contrary, the Supreme Court has recently held that it should be assumed that the parties to an arbitration agreement normally want all disputes arising out of a specific legal relationship to be decided by the arbitrators (and to the extent allowed by the Arbitration Act).[36] The trend in international arbitration is also to construe arbitration agreements extensively.[37]

30. In some countries, the exact wording of an arbitration agreement can be of crucial importance when determining the scope of an arbitration agreement and the arbitral tribunal's jurisdiction.[38] The exact wording is, however, of less importance under Swedish law. The Swedish law presumption that the parties want all their disputes relating to a specific legal relationship to be arbitrated has meant that imprecise or incomplete wording of an arbitration agreement is considered by the courts to be simply imperfect drafting.[39] For example, although the wording of an arbitration clause only referred to 'interpretation' of the main agreement, the Swedish Supreme Court nonetheless found that such a clause was applicable to the issue of whether a party is obligated to pay a certain amount to the other party.[40] The arbitrators were therefore deemed competent to issue enforceable performance awards in such cases. Another example in case law concerned an arbitration clause where the wording referred to 'interpretation and performance' of the main agreement. The Supreme Court found that this clause also covered a dispute regarding validity of the main contract.[41]

31. An arbitration agreement may be phrased so that it is given a very wide scope. It may for example provide that not only disputes arising out of the contract should be referred to arbitration but also disputes 'relating to the contract' or having arisen 'in connection with the contract'. The arbitration agreement would in these cases also seem to cover other legal relationships than the main contract. The scope of such an arbitration agreement is, however, limited by the requirement in the Arbitration Act that disputes must concern an identified legal relationship (see section B below).[42]

32. Common issues of contract interpretation concern the questions whether the parties have actually agreed to arbitrate, in what form (e.g., ad hoc or institutional) and where. Under Article 9(1)(i) of the SCC Rules, the board of directors of the SCC will, if necessary, decide whether the SCC *manifestly* lacks jurisdiction over the dispute pursuant to Article 10(i) of the SCC Rules. This is only a prima facie test: if the board

35. Hassler & Cars, *Skiljeförfarande*, 2nd ed., 1989, 40.
36. *Tupperware Nordic A/S v. The Bankruptcy Estate of Fact Distribution AB*, NJA 2010 p. 734.
37. Heuman, 2003, 53; Craig, Park & Paulsson, *International Chamber of Commerce Arbitration* 87 (3d ed., 2000) and Fouchard, Gaillard & Goldman, *International Commercial Arbitration* 260–261 (1999).
38. Heuman, 2003, 74 and the references in n. 143.
39. Andersson et al., 2011 49 and Lindskog, 2005, 202–205 and footnote 378 on 203.
40. *H.V. Hanzon v. J.P. Pettersson* et al., NJA 1913 p. 415, *Lotsstyrelsen v. Bergsunds mekaniska verkstadsaktiebolag*, NJA 1919 p. 396 and *J. Larsson v. AB Nya Järnhandeln i Sandviken*, NJA 1919 p. 497.
41. *H. Hermansson v. AB Asfaltbeläggningar*, NJA 1976 p. 125.
42. Section 1(1) of the Act and Andersson et al., 2011, 48–49.

finds the SCC to be in manifest want of jurisdiction, the dispute is dismissed; if not, a preliminary objection may still be raised before the arbitral tribunal.

33. Based on published decisions on jurisdiction by the SCC a number of principles for contract interpretation can be distinguished.[43] For example, if the parties have indicated that the arbitration is to be administered by a certain institution in Stockholm or Sweden it is presumed that the parties were referring to the SCC.[44] The same presumption – that SCC arbitration was intended – applies if no institution is named but it is clear that the arbitration is to be administered by institutional rules of some kind.[45] However, the presumption is that the parties agreed on ad hoc arbitration if the arbitration clause states that the dispute is to be decided by 'an arbitration court' or similar.[46] Since the SCC will decide whether it 'manifestly' lacks jurisdiction, non-dismissal by the SCC does not necessarily mean that the SCC actually was of the opinion that the parties had agreed to refer a dispute for arbitration under the SCC Rules.[47]

B. Limiting the Scope to an Identified Legal Relationship

34. As mentioned above the scope of an arbitration agreement referring future disputes to arbitration is limited to an identified legal relationship.[48] This provision in the Arbitration Act is mandatory. An arbitration agreement is not valid if the scope is wider than this.[49] Hence, parties cannot refer all their future disputes to arbitration regardless of the basis for such disputes or all disputes arising between the parties during a certain period.[50] The legal relationship may be contractual or non-contractual and need not exist at the time of the arbitration agreement.[51] However, it may be difficult in practice to identify a future non-contractual legal relationship.

35. In certain cases, it can be difficult to assess whether one or several different legal relationships exist. An arbitration clause in a main contract usually also covers disputes relating to amendments and supplements which only modify the main contract, e.g., by changing the price[52] or the time for performing certain work.[53] However, if the

43. Andersson et al., 2011, 65. Clearly, decisions by the SCC do not have the same authoritative value as a Supreme Court or Court of Appeal ruling but they may have a persuasive value in a Swedish court.
44. Andersson et al., 2011, 65 and the examples listed on the same page where SCC considered it had no reason to decline jurisdiction.
45. '... by a neutral arbitration court in Sweden, Stockholm in accordance with the regulations of said Arbitration ...'(SCC 121/1998).
46. Andersson et al., 2011, 66.
47. Andersson et al., 2011, 66.
48. Section 1(1) of the Act.
49. Andersson et al., 2011, 48 and 50.
50. Andersson et al., 2011, 50.
51. Andersson et al., 2011, 50.
52. *C.A. Lundborg v. K. I. Gustafsson*, NJA 1922 p. 37.
53. *J. Larsson v. AB Nya Järnhandeln i Sandviken*, NJA 1919 p. 497 and *Axel H. Dahlin v. Uddevalla Stuveriförening*, SvJT 1966 ref. 47. But see also *Persson v. AB Sana*, SvJT 1936 ref. 75 and *G. & L. Beijer v. J. Ringborg*, NJA 1910 p. 227.

parties intended to make a new contract to replace the original main contract it is presumed that the arbitration clause does not cover disputes under the new contract unless this is expressly stated.[54] If the contracts are perceived by the parties as independent and separate from each other, a new legal relationship exists.[55]

36. If a settlement agreement has replaced the main contract in its entirety, the settlement agreement itself should include a separate arbitration clause. In that case, an arbitration clause in the main contract cannot, as a core rule, be implied to cover the settlement agreement as well.[56] Nevertheless, settlement agreements which only *partly* change the rights and obligations of a main contract (and lacking an arbitration clause) should in our view *in dubio* be covered by the arbitration clause in the main contract.[57] The result in an individual case depends on the intention of the parties and the wording of the settlement agreement.

37. Parties sometimes enter into relatively brief high-level framework agreements. The purpose of these agreements is often to, at a later stage, sign detailed agreements which include all the terms and conditions for, e.g., a specific purchase. These underlying agreements, though emanating from the framework agreement, are considered to constitute separate legal relationships. An arbitration clause in the framework agreement will therefore, as a main rule, not apply to the sub-agreements if these do not contain arbitration clauses.[58] The opposite may apply if the framework agreement is highly detailed and the sub-agreements are merely brief purchase orders made out under the framework agreement.[59] Disputes regarding sub-orders made under a detailed supply agreement – though being separate agreements from a contractual point of view – may thus be covered by an arbitration clause in such a supply agreement.

C. The Connection between the Legal Relationship and the Dispute Itself

38. A dispute referred to arbitration must normally arise from the legal relationship to which the arbitration agreement refers.[60] Where this is not the case, the dispute is not covered by the arbitration agreement and thus the arbitrators have no jurisdiction over that dispute. In case law, however, promissory notes and bills of exchange issued

54. See e.g., *Niclas Persson v. Onetwocom AB*, judgment by the Svea Court of Appeal made on 21 Feb. 2007 in case no T 6726-05.
55. Heuman, 2003, 66 and Andersson et al., 2011, 51.
56. Andersson et al., 2011, 52. For a different view, see Heuman, 2003, 68.
57. Cf. *Försäkringsaktiebolaget Atlantica v. Nike AB*, RH 1994:116; Heuman, 2003, 68–69 and Andersson et al., 2011, 52
58. *Göran Holmqvist v. Fritidsbolaget M.C.B. AB*, AD 1977:12 and *Alexis W v. Ritva Kredit AB*, in case, NJA 1977 C 15 Cf. *GE Capital Nordic AB v. Belkos System AB*, judgment by the Svea Court of Appeal made on 10 Nov. 1995 in case no Ö 3156-95.
59. See *SAAB Automobile v. Sörman Information & Media AB*, judgment by the Court of Appeal for Western Sweden made on 2 Feb. 2005 in case no Ö 4202-04.
60. Andersson et al., 2011, 53.

under a contract including an arbitration clause – though arguably constituting a separate legal relationship – have been deemed to pertain to the legal relationship (the main contract) referred to in the arbitration clause.[61]

39. If the material circumstances invoked constitute a non-contractual claim which is connected to a contract, subject to arbitration, it follows from Supreme Court case law that arbitrators have jurisdiction over the non-contractual claim only in special circumstances.[62]

40. If a party invokes material circumstances or defences in court proceedings covered by an arbitration clause, the court cannot try those grounds or defences if the opposite party contends that the court lacks jurisdiction due to the arbitration clause. Those material circumstances or defences have to be arbitrated separately. This could, in rare instances, mean that a dispute is fragmentized so that different but connected material circumstances or defences have to be tried partly by a court and partly by an arbitral tribunal.[63] This is further discussed in paragraph 86 of this Chapter.

D. The Doctrine of Assertion

41. An arbitration agreement covers a dispute whether or not the material circumstances[64] alleged by a party exist as long as they, and the legal label[65] attached to them, are based on the legal relationship referred to in the arbitration agreement. The opposite party has to accept arbitration even though the material circumstances invoked may not be true or proven. This is called the *doctrine of assertion* and is applied when, e.g., a claimant alleges that material circumstances are based on a contract with an arbitration clause but the respondent denies that this is the case.[66] If, however, it is

61. *Hans Schröder AB v. Svenska AB Legam*, NJA 1964 p. 2 and *Byggnadsaktiebolaget Lennart Hultenberger v. Bostadsrättsföreningen Hytten*, NJA 1972 p. 458.
62. *Tupperware Nordic A/S v. The Bankrupctcy Estate of Fact Distribution AB*, NJA 2010 p. 734. Such circumstances were present in *Birger Perjos v. Gatu och Väg AB*, NJA 2007 p. 475.
63. *Nykvarn Skyltaktiebolag v. Esselte Dymo AB*, NJA 1982 p. 738, *Ö. Forsman v. A. Inovius*, NJA 1973 p. 480 and *G. Wrande and I. Wrande v. S. Wrande*, NJA 2005 p. 276. But see also the appeal court ruling in *AB Visby Plastindustri (bankruptcy estate) v. AB Express Finans* et al., RH 1987:66. It is submitted that this appeal court case is not good law and that it has no precedential value. See also Heuman, 2003, 60–61 and Andersson et al., 2011, 54.
64. *Nykvarn Skyltaktiebolag v. Esselte Dymo AB*, NJA 1982 p. 738, *PLS Rambøll Management A/S v. A.S.*, NJA 2005 p. 586 and *Petrobart Limited v. The Kyrgyz Republic*, NJA 2008 p. 406.
65. *Sundby egnahemsförening v. AB Ingenjörsfirman Hjalmar Unander*, NJA 1948 p. 590, *The Kingdom of Sweden and The Municipality of Danderyd v. H. Engelsen* et al., NJA 1973 p. 1 I, *The Municipality of Stockholm v. K. Berggren*, NJA 1973 p. 1 II and *Sävedalens Fabriksaktiebolag v. AB Björnverken*, NJA 1973 p. 527.
66. Heuman, 2003, 57–63, Lindskog, 2005, 199 and Andersson et al., 2011, 56.

manifestly unfounded that the material circumstances referred to fall under the legal relationship referred to in the arbitration agreement, the arbitrators have no jurisdiction provided that the opposite party objects. The material circumstances invoked may be relevant both for the issue of jurisdiction and when trying the merits of the case.[67]

42. Further, the doctrine of assertion also applies when a respondent invokes the arbitration agreement as a bar to proceedings in ordinary courts. It is the alleged material circumstances and the legal label attached to them by the claimant that is relevant when determining whether the arbitration agreement bars an action initiated by the claimant. The doctrine of assertion may also apply if the respondent raises defences based on a contract containing an arbitration clause.[68]

43. However, it is not enough to assert that an arbitration agreement exists that covers the material circumstances invoked. If the existence of the arbitration agreement itself is in dispute, the claimant has to prove its existence and validity.[69] The doctrine of assertion cannot itself create a valid arbitration agreement. The doctrine of assertion presupposes a valid arbitration agreement. The same applies if the claimant alleges that the respondent is bound to the arbitration agreement by succession. If this is denied, the claimant has to prove that the respondent has succeeded to the arbitration agreement.[70]

E. Multi-party and Multi-contract Issues

44. Disputes may often involve more than two parties and business contracts may bind three or more parties, e.g., shareholders' agreements. In other cases, several contracts between two or more parties may be closely connected. This can lead to one or several arbitral proceedings with two or more parties. Such proceedings are called multi-party or multi-contract arbitration. Under section 12(3) of the Arbitration Act, the parties may, e.g., agree that the local district court should appoint all arbitrators in the arbitral tribunal if so requested by one party. Apart from this, the Arbitration Act contains no other provisions on multi-party arbitration. However, the arbitration rules of different arbitration institutes such as SCC and ICC usually provide rules aimed at solving multi-party issues when appointing the arbitral tribunal (see e.g., Article 13(4) of the SCC Rules and Article 12(6) of the ICC Rules). There are, however, no model arbitration clauses for multi-party arbitration. Such clauses must be drafted by the parties to cover each individual situation. Drafting multi-party arbitration clauses is a difficult task. Parties drafting arbitration clauses for multi-party arbitration may consider, *inter alia*, the following.

67. See e.g., *Petrobart Limited v. The Kyrgyz Republic*, NJA 2008 p. 406.
68. *Nykvarn Skogsaktiebolag v. Esselte Dymo AB*, NJA 1982 p. 738 and Andersson et al., 2011, 57.
69. *Petrobart Limited v. The Kyrgyz Republic*, NJA 2008 p. 406 and Lindskog, 2005, 199 and Andersson et al., 2011, 56–57.
70. Andersson et al., 2011, 57.

45. With respect to the multiplicity of parties, the IBA Guidelines on Drafting International Arbitration Clauses offer the following advice on drafting arbitration clauses in these cases. The parties should first address how multiplicity may affect the appointment procedure of the tribunal. If the parties are content with a sole arbitrator the clause may provide that the arbitrator is to be appointed jointly by the parties or, failing that, by an arbitral institution or another appointing authority. The same technique could be used when the arbitral tribunal is to consist of three arbitrators. Alternatively, the arbitration clause can require that the parties on each 'side' make joint appointments. This option is available when it can be anticipated at the drafting stage that certain contracting parties will have aligned interests.[71]

46. Second, the parties may then address the issues of joinder and intervention due to the multiplicity of parties. An arbitration clause would be workable even without addressing these complexities. Such a clause would, however, leave open the possibility of overlapping proceedings, conflicting decisions and associated delays, costs and uncertainty.[72] One must bear in mind when addressing these complexities that the clause should provide that notice of any proceedings commenced under the clause should be given to each contracting party. It should also contain a clear time line after the notice for each contracting party to intervene or join other contracting parties in the proceedings. Alternatively, the parties can opt to arbitrate under institutional rules that provide for intervention and joinder.[73]

47. One business transaction may include several contracts. The IBA Guidelines on Drafting International Arbitration Clauses offer the following advice with respect to multiplicity of contracts when drafting arbitration clauses. First, arbitration clauses in related contracts should be compatible. Parties usually want consistent decisions and wish to avoid parallel proceedings. By establishing a stand-alone dispute resolution protocol which has been signed and incorporated, the parties can create a straightforward solution. If it is impractical to conclude such a protocol, the parties should ensure that the arbitration clauses in the related contract are identical or complementary. It is especially important that the arbitration clauses specify the same set of rules and substantive law, language, place of arbitration and number of arbitrators.[74] Second, the parties should address the question of consolidating arbitral proceedings arising from related contracts. Different arbitrations may be commenced under related contracts at different times. It may, or may not, be in the parties' interest to have these arbitrations dealt with in a single consolidated arbitration. If the parties wish to permit consolidation of related arbitrations, they should say so in the arbitration clause. The applicable arbitration rules and the law of the place of arbitration should be reviewed carefully, as they may constrain the parties' ability to consolidate arbitral proceedings.[75] If the place of arbitration is in Sweden, the parties should be aware that Swedish courts have no

71. IBA Guidelines for Drafting International Arbitration Clauses adopted by a resolution of the IBA Council 7 Oct. 2010 (IBA Guidelines on Drafting International Arbitration Clauses), p. 35.
72. Page 36 of IBA Guidelines on Drafting International Arbitration Clauses.
73. Page 36 of IBA Guidelines on Drafting International Arbitration Clauses.
74. Page 39 of IBA Guidelines on Drafting International Arbitration Clauses.
75. Page 40 of IBA Guidelines on Drafting International Arbitration Clauses.

competence to order consolidation of related arbitral proceedings. In 2007, the SCC Rules were amended to empower the SCC to consolidate arbitration proceedings. The SCC may in arbitrations conducted under the SCC Rules and at the request of a party, consolidate two arbitration proceedings between the same parties concerning the same legal relationship.[76]

48. It is a general principle under Swedish contract law that a contract is only binding on the parties. This also applies to arbitration agreements. Third parties cannot invoke an arbitration agreement or intervene in arbitration proceedings.[77] Moreover, a party to an arbitration agreement cannot force third parties into arbitration proceedings on the basis that the main contract affects a third party. The res judicata effect of an arbitral award only applies between the parties as a main rule.[78] The fact that the binding effect of an arbitration agreement requires a contractual undertaking also follows from the fundamental principle that physical and legal entities are entitled to have their civil rights tried in a court of law.[79] A commitment to submit disputes to arbitration – thereby derogating such disputes from being tried in a court of law – must therefore, as noted above, be clear and unequivocal.[80]

49. Since there is no requirement in the Arbitration Act, in case law or otherwise that an arbitration agreement must be in writing, a non-signatory might be considered as a contracting party if it can be proved that the non-signatory has become bound by an arbitration agreement, e.g., by its conduct.[81] Typical examples of arbitration agreements being entered into by conduct might be where a party participates in arbitration proceedings without protesting and contending that the arbitral tribunal lacks jurisdiction. Another example is where a party files a claim in arbitration proceedings not covered by the arbitration agreement without the opposite party objecting. In that case, the arbitration agreement is considered to cover the new claim as well.[82]

50. There is no 'Group of Companies' doctrine in Swedish law according to which affiliates in a company group may be bound by an arbitration agreement entered into by another company in the same corporate group (originally emanating from the *Dow Chemical* case).[83] However, such affiliate companies may in some instances be bound by conduct under general principles of Swedish contract law. In *Concorp Scandinavia*

76. Article 11 of the SCC Rules.
77. A contract may also constitute rights for non-parties (third-party beneficiaries). In the event of a dispute between a party and the third-party beneficiary the latter is bound by an arbitration clause in the contract between the parties (see Lindskog, 2005, 196 and the Swedish Labour Court ruling in *Göran Holmqvist v. Fritidsbolaget M.C.B. AB*, AD 1977:12).
78. Heuman, 2003, 77 and Lindskog, 2005, 158.
79. Lindskog, 2005, 158.
80. *Rita Urhelyi v. Arbetsmarkandens Försäkringsaktiebolag*, NJA 1974 p. 573.
81. That contracts in general can be concluded by conduct have been confirmed by the Supreme Court, *inter alia*, in *AB Håkanssons industrier v. The Municipality of Grästorp*, NJA 1961 p. 658 and *Rockwool AB and Gullfiber AB v. Byggma Syd AB (bankruptcy estate)*, NJA 1982 p. 244.
82. Hobér, *International Commercial Arbitration in Sweden*, 2011, 96.
83. *Dow Chemical v. Isover Saint Gobain*, Interim Award No. 4113 of 23 Sep. 23, 1982, Andersson et al., 2011, 75-76 and Hobér, *International Commercial Arbitration in Sweden*, 2011, 135.

AB v. Xcaret Confectionary Sales AB[84] the Court of Appeals considered that a non-signatory was entitled to invoke an arbitration agreement entered into between two signatory contracting parties as a bar to court proceedings. However, the Supreme Court overruled the Court of Appeals finding and decided the case in accordance with the doctrine of assertion (see section III.D above). The Supreme Court found that the plaintiff had not actually alleged that its claim was based on contracts containing arbitration clauses. Instead, it had alleged that its claim arose from a separate loan agreement (not containing an arbitration clause). For this reason the Supreme Court held that the District Court had jurisdiction to try the plaintiff's claim.

IV. ARBITRABILITY

51. Only disputes concerning matters in respect of which the parties *may reach a settlement*, may be referred to one or several arbitrators for resolution under the Arbitration Act. Hence, only disputes which are amenable to out-of-court settlement may be subject to arbitration, i.e., arbitrable disputes. Disputes which are not amenable to out-of-court settlement are not arbitrable. Applicable substantive law determines whether a dispute can be settled by agreement between the parties.

52. The question of whether a dispute is arbitrable is examined by the arbitrators ex officio. If the arbitrators find that a dispute is non-arbitrable they should decline jurisdiction over the matter. If the arbitrators render an award although the dispute is non-arbitrable, the award is invalid.[85]

53. If Swedish substantive law applies, it follows from the above that disputes concerning rights in rem are not arbitrable. An example from case law is the *Five Seasons* case where a bankruptcy estate was not considered to be bound by an arbitration agreement regarding a dispute with a creditor on illegal distribution of dividends.[86] The reason for this, according to the Supreme Court, was that the debtor and the creditor could not enter into a settlement agreement regarding illegal dividends with binding effect on the bankruptcy estate. Furthermore, in a claw-back dispute (*Sw. återvinning*) regarding payments under an agreement, the bankruptcy estate is not bound by an arbitration clause included in that agreement. The trustee of a bankruptcy estate is entitled to reach a settlement with the counterparty in a claw-back dispute and therefore may conclude an arbitration agreement with respect to such a dispute.[87]

54. Mandatory provisions do not per se make a dispute non-arbitrable.[88] Most mandatory rights under Swedish substantive law could be waived by the parties after the dispute has arisen. A dispute over such rights (e.g., in the consumer and labour law

84. *Concorp Scandinavia AB v. Xcaret Confectionery Sales AB*, NJA 2012 s. 183.
85. Section 33(1) point 1 of the Arbitration Act.
86. *Five Seasons Fritidsaktiebolag (bankruptcy estate) v. Five Seasons Försäljningsaktiebolag*, NJA 1993 p. 641.
87. Lindskog, 2005, 246.
88. *Moscow City Golf Club OOO v. Nordea Bank AB*, NJA 2012 p. 790.

areas) may be settled out-of-court. If this is the case, the dispute is arbitrable. For example, in *G. Wrande and I. Wrande v. S. Wrande*[89] one of the partners in a partnership applied for the appointment of a liquidator with the district court. The basis for the application was that certain mandatory grounds for liquidating a partnership under the Act on Partnership and Non-registered Partnership (*Sw:* (*lag* (*1980:1102*) *om handelsbolag och enkla bolag*) were present. The other partners denied that there was any ground for liquidation and requested, *inter alia*, that the court in any event should reject the application since the partnership agreement contained an arbitration clause. The Supreme Court held that the dispute was arbitrable even though the grounds for liquidation in the Act on Partnership and Non-Registered Partnership were mandatory. The reason was that, when these liquidation grounds arise, the partners may waive those grounds for liquidation by express agreement or by conduct. The Supreme Court concluded that the arbitration clause in the partnership agreement meant that the alleged grounds for liquidation could not be tried by the district court. However, the arbitration clause did not mean that an application for appointment of a liquidator could not per se be filed with the district court. It lay upon the district court to decide whether the application should remain pending while the issue of liquidation was tried in arbitration proceedings or whether the district court should try the application at once.

55. In some instances, the parties may not enter into a binding settlement without the consent of or approval by a third party or without decisions by persons, courts or public authorities. Third party and/or public interests could mean that a dispute is considered non-arbitrable by the arbitrators.[90] Such a contractual dispute may, however, be amenable to settlement if these interests can be safeguarded by a separate action or by a different procedure.[91] For example, two parties may want to cancel an agreement to avoid unfavourable tax consequences. This might be done by arbitral proceedings – the dispute is arbitrable.[92] However, the subsequent award is not binding on the tax authorities and the fiscal interest is safeguarded through separate tax proceedings.

56. There are third party and public interests which may be taken into account both in arbitral and court proceedings.[93] The legal literature mentions disputes that are improper (*lat. pactum turpe*) or which may involve criminal liability.[94] Swedish courts will not enforce contractual rights which contravene public morality, *pactum turpe*. A settlement agreement regarding such rights is not enforceable and therefore not arbitrable. Arbitrators sitting in Sweden must therefore dismiss a dispute which is based on a *pactum turpe*. Agreements on, e.g., bribery, trafficking, smuggling of

---

89. *G. Wrande and I. Wrande v. S. Wrande*, NJA 2005 p. 276.
90. SOU 1994:81 pp. 78–9.
91. SOU 1994:81 pp. 78–9.
92. *Britta N.* et al. *v. Snapphanen i Kristianstad Handelsbolag*, judgment by the Supreme Court made on 24 Jun. 1993 in case no T373-91, *Five Seasons Fritidsaktiebolag (bankruptcy estate) v. Five Seasons Försäljningsaktiebolag*, NJA 1993 p. 319 and Heuman, 2003, 143.
93. SOU 1994:81 p. 79.
94. Heuman, 2003, 144. and Andersson et al. 2011, 60.

contraband and illegal gambling constitute *pactum turpe*.[95] A practical example of where the issue of *pactum turpe* arises is where one party claims that payments made under an agreement are bribes and that the agreement constitutes a *pactum turpe* while the opposite party contends that the payments are commission for services rendered.

57. Further, arbitrators cannot rule on issues regarding penalties constituting punishment for wrongdoing under public law in contrast to contractual penalties under a contract.[96] Disputes regarding the legal status of persons and companies, the existence and validity of patents, declaration of bankruptcy and taxation are also noted in the legal literature as examples of disputes which are not arbitrable.[97] Disputes regarding sanctions which can only be issued by public authorities – such as fines[98] – are non-arbitrable.

A. At What Point in Time Should a Dispute Be Arbitrable?

58. The question of arbitrability relates to the issue whether the arbitration agreement is valid and enforceable. Thus, the relevant time for testing arbitrability would be when the arbitration agreement was concluded. Hence, if a dispute which arose at that time was not amenable to out-of-court settlement, the dispute is not arbitrable.[99] This applies although the dispute becomes arbitrable later but before the award is rendered. If the arbitrators render an award in the last mentioned case, the award is not invalid (see comment on section 33 (1) point 1 of the Arbitration Act in Chapter [ ])[100] but may be successfully challenged on the ground that no valid arbitration agreement was concluded (see section 34(1) point 1 of the Arbitration Act).

B. If Foreign Law Is Applicable to the Dispute

59. If Swedish law is the governing law of the dispute, the question whether the dispute is arbitrable, i.e., amenable to out-of-court settlement, is decided under Swedish law. However, if foreign law is the governing law the question whether the dispute is amenable to settlement should be decided under the foreign *lex causae*.[101] If this is so, the dispute is arbitrable under the Arbitration Act. The applicable law is determined in accordance with international private law rules or in accordance with the *la voie directe* principle.[102]

95. Andersson et al., 2011, 62.
96. Andersson et al., 2011, 63.
97. Andersson et al., 2011, 63.
98. Andersson et al., 2011, 63.
99. Lindskog, 2005, 241 and Andersson et al., 2011, 61.
100. *Moscow City Golf Club OOO v. Nordea Bank AB*, NJA 2012 p. 790.
101. Lindskog, 2005, 245 and Andersson et al., 2011, 58-59.
102. Heuman, 2003, 694 and Art. 28(2) of the Model Law.

C. Civil Law Effects of Competition Law

60. Two parties may not agree on restraints of trade or competition with binding effect if their agreement violates competition law. It follows that disputes regarding competition law are as a main rule not arbitrable.[103] However, section 1(3) of the Arbitration Act provides that arbitrators may rule on the *civil law* effects of competition law as between the parties. Hence, if a party seeks declaratory relief that an agreement is void under a competition law provision or seeks damages due to violations of competition law these disputes are arbitrable. But arbitrators may not deal with the *public law* effects of competition law. Thus, arbitrators may not impose fines, issue exemptions, order a party to cease and desist unlawful activities or grant clearance for asset or company purchases.[104] Disputes on such issues may not be subject to arbitration.

61. Arbitrators should not monitor competition law rules and raise such issues ex officio. They are bound by the reliefs sought and the facts invoked by the parties. Arbitrators may only rule on the civil law effects of competition law upon motion by a party. In the exceptional cases where arbitrators perceive that a future award would be void under the public policy exception in the Arbitration Act – since it violates competition law[105] it is suggested that the arbitrators may terminate the proceedings and resign from their assignment.[106] It is further suggested that the arbitrators may also in such a case raise the competition law issue on their own motion and afford the parties an opportunity to argue the issue.[107] Competition laws outside the EU are most likely not considered to be part of Swedish public policy.[108]

62. An arbitral tribunal is not bound by the competition law assessment of a competition authority. At the same time, a competition authority is not bound by an award which includes a ruling on competition law. Hence, if an award is incompatible with competition law a competition authority may 'correct' the award by issuing public law sanctions. As pointed out by Andersson et al. a party that 'failed' in arbitral proceedings to show that a counterparty's actions violate competition law may get a second bite at the apple by initiating proceedings for administrative sanctions.[109]

---

103. Lindskog, 2005, 250.
104. Andersson et al., 2011, 63.
105. It is not clear to what extent an award which is incompatible with competition law also violates Swedish public policy. An award which contravenes Art. 81 of the Treaty of Rome violates public policy in all EU Member States, including Sweden (*Eco Swiss China Time v. Benetton International* ruling by European Court of Justice in case no C-126/97, 1999, ECR I-3055) and Andersson et al., 2011, 64.
106. SOU 1994:81 p. 85 and Prop. 1998/99:35 p. 59.
107. SOU 1994:81 p. 85 and Prop. 1998/99:35 pp. 58–59 and Heuman, 2003, 151.
108. Andersson et al., 2011, 64.
109. Andersson et al., 2011, 64.

V. DOCTRINE OF SEPARABILITY

63. The doctrine of separability is recognized in Sweden and codified in the Arbitration Act.[110] The doctrine is also widely known and recognized internationally.

64. Where the main contract includes an arbitration clause, the doctrine of separability provides that any objections as to the validity of the arbitration agreement and/or the main contract should be heard separately. When hearing such objections the purchase contract and the arbitration clause in the main contract should be considered to be two separate agreements. Hence, the fact that the purchase contract is considered void does not mean that the arbitration agreement is automatically void and vice versa.

65. The doctrine of separability is based on the presumption that the parties want all their disputes to be decided by arbitrators, including those regarding the validity of the main contract.[111]

66. The doctrine of separability applies when a party alleges that the main contract never came into force (e.g., the signatories lacked authority or the signatures were forged), the main contract was originally invalid (*ab initio*) under Chapter 3 of the Contracts Act (e.g., due to fraud),[112] later became invalid or has been cancelled or terminated, whether for cause or not.[113]

67. In many of the examples in the last mentioned paragraph the objections affect both the arbitration agreement and the main contract. However, objections may only strike at the main contract and not necessarily at the arbitration agreement. One of the parties may contend that the term of the main contract has elapsed or that any party has cancelled or terminated the main contract, or that a contractual right under the main contract is time barred or that statutory matters of forms are not fulfilled for the main contract.

68. Section 3 of the Arbitration Act expressly provides that arbitrators should rely on the doctrine of separability when they try their own jurisdiction. However, the question whether an arbitration agreement is invalid may arise in many different situations. It might come into play in challenge proceedings where a party contends that the award should be set aside on the basis that there was no valid arbitration agreement. Further, it may be referred to in enforcement proceedings where a party contests enforcement on the basis that there was no valid arbitration agreement. In such cases the doctrine of separability should also be recognized by the courts. As pointed out by Heuman, the doctrine of separability would be of no value if it only gave *arbitrators* jurisdiction which would not be recognized by the courts. Hence, a court cannot set aside an award on the basis that the arbitrators have found that the main agreement is null and void.[114]

110. Section 3 of the Arbitration Act.
111. Heuman, 2003, 44.
112. SOU 1994:81 pp. 103–104 and Prop. 1998/99:35 pp. 76 and 215.
113. Andersson et al., 2011, 39–40.
114. Heuman, 2003, 69.

69. The doctrine of separability does not provide an answer to the question whether a dispute concerning alleged invalidity of the main contract is covered by the arbitration agreement – correctly interpreted. Nor does it provide an answer to the question whether the arbitration agreement is valid or not.

VI. PARTY SUCCESSION

70. As any other contract, an arbitration agreement is only binding between the parties (*inter partes*). A third party has no right to intervene in arbitration proceedings even though it may have a legitimate interest to do so. Furthermore, an award only has res judicata effect between the parties. However, there are exceptions to this rule. The most important exception concerns the case when contractual rights or obligations subject to an arbitration agreement are assigned to a third party.

A. Singular Succession

1. Assignments

71. Under Swedish law, an arbitration clause may be assigned, unless the main contract prohibits such assignments.[115] If the assigning party was not entitled to assign its rights under a contract due to a prohibition in the contract or if the procedure laid down in the contract has not been followed, the other contract party is not bound by the assignment of the arbitration clause and, hence, not bound by the arbitration clause vis-à-vis the assignee.[116] According to Andersson et al. contractual requirements for assignments should, *in dubio*, apply to assignment of the arbitration clause as well.[117]

72. With respect to an assignment of claims or rights under a contract subject to an arbitration agreement, it is established case law (the *Emja* case) that an *assignee* is bound by the arbitration agreement although he did not have knowledge of or ought to have known about the arbitration agreement.[118] One purpose of the '*Emja rule*' is to maintain the debtor's right of having its obligations tried in arbitral proceedings.[119] It is also in line with the Swedish civil law principle that an assignee of rights under non-negotiable instruments should not attain a better legal position than the assignor vis-à-vis the remaining party (the debtor).[120] The *Emja* case concerned the situation where only rights had been transferred. Contractual rights are as a main rule freely

115. Andersson et al., 2011, 73.
116. *Regular Capital Incorporated v. AB Custos*, judgment by the Svea Court of Appeal made on 10 Jan. 2003 in case no T 8032-00.
117. Andersson et al., 2011 73 and n. 130.
118. *MS 'Emja' Braack Schiffahrts KG v. Wärtsilä Diesel AB*, NJA 1997 p. 866. Cf. Reldén, Krav på denuntiation för bundenhet av skiljeklausul vid singularsuccession, Juridisk Tidskrift 2003/04, no. 4, 930.
119. Lindskog, 2005, 161.
120. Cf. s. 27 of the Debts Instruments Act (*Sw. lag (1936:81) om skuldebrev*).

transferable under Swedish law, i.e., no consent or knowledge is required. Transfer of obligations requires the consent of the remaining party (the debtor).

73. In the *Emja* case, the Supreme Court also stated - *obiter dicta* - that the remaining party (the debtor) is bound to the arbitration agreement vis-à-vis the assignee unless special circumstances exist.[121] Special circumstances might be a strong personal connection between the original parties and a risk that the assignee could not pay the costs of the arbitration. There is no requirement that the remaining party is notified about the assignment unless this is specifically provided in the contract.[122]

74. When both *rights and obligations* are assigned under a contract subject to an arbitration agreement the remaining party must, as noted above, give its consent for the transfer to be effective. In that case, the assignee and the remaining party are bound by the arbitration agreement.

2. *Subrogation of Claims and Rights*

75. Where e.g., a guarantor pays a debtor's debt to a creditor, the guarantor is subrogated to the creditor's former claims and remedies against the debtor. In that case, the guarantor would probably be bound by any arbitration agreement between the debtor and the creditor in the same manner as set out above with respect to assignment of claims and rights.[123]

B. Universal Succession

76. Universal succession is legal succession where a person or a company succeeds to all rights and obligations (including assets and liabilities) of another person or entity when the latter ceases to exist. The core rule is that the successor is bound by an arbitration agreement entered into between the original parties. Examples of universal succession are the estate of a deceased person and mergers of companies. Additionally, bankruptcy is a form of universal succession. However, under Swedish law the *bankrupcty estate* (*Sw. konkursboet*) does not succeed to the obligations of the debtor but merely to its assets.

121. See *MS 'Emja' Braack Schiffahrts KG v. Wärtsilä Diesel AB*, NJA 1997 p. 866. A different view has been argued amongst some scholars: see Lindskog, 2005, 166-167.
122. However, under the Swedish law of obligations notification may be necessary to ensure, e.g., that a debtor is discharged from liability by paying the assignee and not the assignor (the remaining party). In order to charge a debtor to make payment to the assignee a notice of the assignment to the debtor is required.
123. Lindskog, 2005, 169.

1. *Bankruptcy*

77. Under Swedish law, the bankruptcy estate is, as a core rule, bound by an arbitration agreement entered into by the debtor with respect to contractual rights succeeded to by the bankruptcy estate.[124] Hence, the bankruptcy estate may request arbitration against a creditor based on an arbitration agreement entered into between the creditor and the debtor. On the other hand, the bankruptcy estate must also accept an arbitration initiated by a creditor regarding contractual claims covered by an arbitration agreement concluded by the debtor.

78. The bankruptcy estate is only bound by arbitration agreements covering issues which the debtor and the other party may settle with binding effect vis-à-vis the bankruptcy estate.[125] Issues regarding, e.g., priority rights (*Sw. förmånsrätt*) in a bankruptcy are non-arbitrable since they cannot be subject to a settlement agreement between a debtor and a creditor.[126] The same applies to perfection of pledges,[127] repossession of property where title has been retained,[128] other rights in rem, claw-back claims (*Sw. återvinning*)[129] and claims directly against the bankruptcy estate.[130]

79. In certain bankruptcies under the Swedish Bankruptcy Act (*Sw. konkurslagen*), the creditors have to file proof of their claims, and, if the claims are disputed, the bankruptcy court has to rule upon them – the so-called proof of debt procedure (*Sw. bevakningskonkurs*). All creditors and the bankruptcy estate have standing in this procedure. The Supreme Court has held that the bankruptcy estate and all creditors in the bankruptcy are bound by an arbitration agreement between a creditor and the debtor when deciding if and to what extent a creditor has a valid claim in the bankruptcy.[131]

---

124. Lindskog, 2005, 171.
125. *P. Palén v. C. Theorin and E. Malmberg*, NJA 1913 p. 191 and *Svenska Kreditförsäkringsaktiebolaget (bankruptcy estate) v. certain (41) reinsurer*, NJA 2003 p. 3.
126. *P.F. von Celsing v. F. Lundwalls Hellefors styckebruks verkstäder*, NJA 1902 p. 282, *R. Svensson v. AB Svensk Import (bankruptcy estate)*, NJA 1922 p. 285, *E. Olsson v. Lantbrukarnas andelsexportslakteriförening i Landskrona (bancruptcy estate)u.p.a.*, NJA 1926 p. 109 and *R. E. Westerblad v. Byggnadsfirman Oscarsson & Söderberg*, NJA 1931 p. 647 and Andersson et al., 2011, 71.
127. *Aktiebolaget Baggå ångsåg (bankruptcy estate)v. Norsa ångsåg intressenter*, NJA 1925 p. 557 I and Andersson et al., 2011, 71.
128. *R.E. Westerblad v. Byggnadsfirman Oscarsson & Söderberg*, NJA 1931 p. 647 and Andersson et al., 2011, 71
129. *K. Karlsson (bankruptcy estate) v. Norrköpingsortens Slakteriförening* (SvJT 1945 ref. 31), *AB Visby Plastindustri (bankruptcy estate)v. AB Express Finans et al.*, RH 1987:66 and Andersson et al., 2011, 71.
130. *Svenska Kreditförsäkringsaktiebolaget (bankruptcy estate)v. certain (41) reinsurer*, decision by the Supreme Court made on 2 Jan. 2003 in case no Ö 3504-01, NJA 2003 p. 3 and Andersson et al., 2011, 71
131. *Svenska Kreditförsäkringsaktiebolaget (bankruptcy estate)v. certain (41) reinsurer*, NJA 2003 p. 3.

VII. THE ARBITRATION AGREEMENT AS A BAR TO JUDICIAL PROCEEDINGS

80. Under Swedish law, an arbitration agreement constitutes a bar to proceedings in ordinary courts. This principle is codified in section 4 of the Arbitration Act.

81. The arbitration agreement is an *optional* bar to court proceedings and must be invoked by the opposite party for the court to consider it. Without an objection by a party, the court cannot refuse to accept jurisdiction by referring to an arbitration agreement. If the arbitration agreement is invoked by a defendant and the plaintiff's action is covered by the arbitration agreement, the court should reject the action.

82. Section 4 of the Arbitration Act applies even though the arbitration agreement is governed by foreign law. Section 49 of the Arbitration Act provides that section 4 applies to international arbitration agreements.

83. A request to decline jurisdiction based on the arbitration agreement being a bar to court proceedings must be made on the first occasion when a party pleads its case on the merits in the court. The wording in section 4 of the Arbitration Act refers to the point in time when the party is to plead its case for the first time, not when it is actually done.[132] The request to decline jurisdiction is normally made when the defendant files a statement of defence. There is no duty on a party to inform the opposite party beforehand whether it will invoke the arbitration agreement or not.[133]A party that files a request to decline jurisdiction and invokes the arbitration agreement too late has forfeited the right to invoke the arbitration agreement as a bar to court proceedings with respect to the action initiated by the plaintiff. If the defendant has been granted an extension of time for filing a statement of defence, the right to invoke the arbitration agreement is also extended on the condition that the defendant was not in delay when the request for extension was granted.[134] Further, a party that has a legal excuse[135] for any delay might maintain the right to invoke the arbitration agreement as a bar if this is done as soon as the delay ceases.[136]

84. The court may only reject the plaintiff's action if it is proven that the scope of the arbitration agreement covers the action in question. The party invoking the arbitration agreement has the burden of proof for the scope and existence of the arbitration agreement. A plaintiff who contends that the arbitration agreement is invalid has the burden of proving that the arbitration agreement is invalid. When assessing the scope

132. Lindskog, 2005, 333.
133. *AB Po-Bo Byggtjänst v. Britt and Tord L* NJA, NJA 1982 p. 711, *Västskog Sågråvaru Aktiebolag v. Judit H and Jacob H*, RH 1999:56 and Lindskog, 2005, 332.
134. *MS 'Emja' Braack Schiffahrts KG v. Wärtsilä Diesel AB*, NJA 1997 p.866.
135. Legal excuse is defined in Ch. 32, s. 8 of the Code of Judicial Procedure *(Sw: Rättegångsbalk (1942:740))*.
136. SOU 1994:81 p. 262 and Prop. 1998/99:35 p. 216.

and any objection as to the validity of the arbitration agreement the court is bound by the facts and grounds referred to by the parties.

85. If the defendant during the court proceedings asserts that it is entitled to set off the sums of the claimant's claim against a counter-claim, an arbitration agreement covering the counter-claim needs to be invoked by the plaintiff to bar the counter-claim. This should happen on the first occasion when the plaintiff must comment on the counter-claim. If the plaintiff fails to do so, it forfeits the right to invoke the arbitration agreement as a bar for the court to try the counter-claim.[137] The same applies to defences by the defendant which are covered by an arbitration agreement.[138] There is no time limit stipulated for asserting objections against a party's submission that the opposite party is bound by an arbitration agreement that covers the dispute in question.[139]

86. It may occasionally be the case that only a part of the dispute or certain issues are covered by an arbitration agreement. An arbitration agreement may constitute a bar to court proceedings only partially.[140] If a prejudicial issue which is being disputed is covered by an arbitration agreement, the court cannot rule on the issue if the arbitration agreement is invoked. There are different ways a court may choose to handle this situation. In the event of a declaratory action, the court may choose to render a conditional judgment – a judgment which is conditional upon the outcome of any arbitration proceedings.[141] The court may also choose to stay the proceedings until an award has been rendered on the prejudicial issue. The court will then try the case based on the outcome of the prejudicial issue in the arbitration proceedings.[142]

87. In *Lars S. v. Försäkringsaktiebolaget Skandia,*[143] the terms and conditions of an insurance policy provided that the value of damaged goods had to be determined by arbitrators. A performance claim by the insured for compensation was therefore not per se covered by the arbitration clause and could not be rejected for lack of jurisdiction. According to the Supreme Court, the district court should have stayed the proceedings until an award was rendered on the value of the property and the district court had no jurisdiction to make a valuation of the damaged property.

88. Another example is where the plaintiff's grounds are non-contractual but the defendant's defences are contractual and covered by an arbitration agreement. The Supreme Court has held that a court may stay the proceedings in such a case until an

137. SOU 1994:81 p. 96, Prop. 1998/99:35 p. 216 and Lindskog, 2005, 335.
138. Lindskog, 2005, 335.
139. Lindskog, 2005, 336.
140. *Östen F. v. Allan I.*, NJA 1973 p. 480, Lindskog, 2005, 337, Andersson et al., 2011, 54.
141. *Östen F. v. Allan I.*, NJA 1973 p. 480. The Supreme Court held that a court could rule that A had better title than B on the condition that an award was not rendered according to which B had acquired title by a separate agreement that included an arbitration clause.
142. Compare *G. Wrande and I. Wrande v. S. Wrande,* NJA 2005 p. 276.
143. *Lars S. v. Försäkringsaktiebolaget Skandia,* NJA 1984 p. 229.

award is rendered (assuming the arbitration agreement is invoked by the plaintiff) on the contractual defences raised by the defendant – at least if the defences raised by the defendant are not clearly without merit.[144]

89. If a competent court rejects an action because an arbitration agreement constitutes a bar to court proceedings, that decision gains legal force (res judicata) and will probably bind an arbitral tribunal in the arbitration to follow or in a challenge action under section 34 of the Arbitration Act.[145] If a court, however, denies a request to reject a claim because the arbitration agreement invoked does not constitute a bar to court proceedings, the res judicata effect is limited to the pending court proceedings.[146] The decision is not binding on an arbitral tribunal.[147] Should a party request arbitration in the same matter before the court has ruled on the merits (but after the decision to deny the request to reject), the arbitral tribunal should, however, reject the request for arbitration due to *lis pendens*.[148] However, the action is not subject to *lis pendens* if the party invoking the arbitration agreement as a bar to court proceedings also requests arbitration in the same matter before the court has tried the request to reject for lack of jurisdiction.[149]

90. Finally, it follows from section 4(2) of the Arbitration Act that an arbitration agreement is no hindrance for a creditor to initiate an expedited debt collection proceeding with the Debt Enforcement Authority (*Sw: Kronofogden*). The same applies to other expedited procedures with the Debt Enforcement Authority such as restitution of movable property or eviction of tenants.[150] Further, as set out in section 4(3) of the Act, the arbitration agreement does not prevent a party from seeking interim security measures with a court, prior, during or after the arbitration proceedings have been concluded.

VIII. WAIVER

91. Section 5 of the Arbitration Act provides that a party can no longer rely on the arbitration agreement as a bar to court proceedings if it has opposed a request for arbitration, failed to appoint an arbitrator in due time or fails, within due time, to provide its share of the requested security for compensation to the arbitrators. A party may in addition lose its right to rely on the arbitration agreement if it is considered to have waived its rights under the arbitration agreement based on general contract law principles. As a main rule, a party that initiates court proceedings waives its right to

144. *Nykvarn Skyltaktiebolag v. Esselte Dymo AB*, NJA 1982 p. 738.
145. *C. Lindhoff v. M. Nilsson*, NJA 1923 p. 206, Lindskog, 2005, 343, Heuman, 2003, 168 and Andersson et al., 2011, 154.
146. Lindskog, 2005, 205, 342.
147. Andersson et al., 2011, 154.
148. Andersson et al., 2011, 154 footnote 311 and Lindskog, 2005, 342 n. 58.
149. SOU 1994:81 p. 137, Prop. 1998/99:35 p. 105 and Lindskog, 2005, 345.
150. *G. Paijkull v. G. V. Söderberg*, NJA 1923 p. 460.

invoke the arbitration agreement with respect to the disputed issue (assuming such an agreement covers the plaintiff's action).[151] In a situation where a party has failed to provide its share of the requested security for compensation to the arbitrators, the party may still be able to rely on the arbitration agreement as a bar to court proceedings in a *new* dispute between the parties. The loss of the right to rely on the arbitration agreement under section 5 of the Arbitration Act thus applies only to the subject matter of the first dispute.[152]

151. Heuman, 2003, 144–145, Andersson et al., 2011, 77, Lindskog, 2005, 363 and Hobér, *International Commercial Arbitration in Sweden*, 2011, 124–125. There are exceptions to this rule. In *OAO Arkhangelskoe Geologodobychnoe Predpriyatie v. Archangel Diamond Corporation*, judgment by the Svea Court of Appeal made on 15 Nov. 2005 in case no T 2277-04, the Svea Court of Appeal found that a party had not waived its right to invoke the arbitration agreement by initiating court proceedings. It seems clear from the circumstances of that case that the party in question had not voluntarily chosen litigation instead of arbitration.
152. *Systherm Inc v. Kordab*, NJA 2008 p. 476.

CHAPTER 4

Jurisdiction of the Arbitral Tribunal

Marie Öhrström

I. INTRODUCTION

1. Under Swedish law, a valid arbitral award requires that the arbitral tribunal has jurisdiction to decide the issue referred to it. The parties are entitled to object to the arbitration by raising jurisdictional objections.

2. If the respondent files a jurisdictional objection the claimant may opt to withdraw its case and bring an action in the state courts instead.[1] However, in international disputes it is exceptionally rare that the claimant decides to terminate the arbitration and initiate court proceedings. Typically, the claimant maintains its request for arbitration, whereupon the respondent requests that the arbitral tribunal dismiss the case due to lack of jurisdiction.

3. Under Swedish law, the arbitrators may examine and rule on their own jurisdiction to decide the dispute. This principle of *Kompetenz-Kompetenz* is accepted not only in Sweden but in many other countries, as it enhances the efficiency of the arbitral proceedings. This structure is also enacted in the UNCITRAL Model Law on International Commercial Arbitration 1985. With amendments as adopted in 2006 (Model Law).[2]

4. Nevertheless, the final decision on jurisdiction lies with the state courts. This position is set out in section 2 of the Swedish Arbitration Act (Sw: *Lag (1999:116) om skiljeförfarande*) (the Act).[3] Consequently, if the arbitral tribunal dismisses the request for arbitration, that award can be appealed, and if the arbitral tribunal finds itself to

1. In such a case, the respondent cannot claim that the arbitration agreement constitutes a bar to court proceedings. See s. 5 of the Act.
2. See Art. 16 of the Model law.
3. See s. 2(1) second sentence of the Act.

have jurisdiction a party opposing that decision may challenge the arbitral award. In addition, the parties can request a court to decide the question of jurisdiction in a declaratory judgment prior to or parallel to the arbitral proceedings.[4]

II. THE ARBITRATION AGREEMENT FORMS THE BASIS OF JURISDICTION

5. The foundation of the jurisdiction of the arbitral tribunal and the basis for the arbitral proceedings is the arbitration agreement.[5] Thus, the arbitral tribunal must base their authority on the arbitration agreement. This is laid down in the opening section of the Act.[6]

6. This means that the arbitral tribunal does not have power to go outside of the boundaries set up by the arbitration agreement.[7] Hence, the parties decide the scope of the proceedings and the mandate of the arbitral tribunal when designing the arbitration agreement. However, it is not only the original arbitration agreement which defines the mandate of the tribunal. Additional agreements, instructions and conduct among the parties may affect the mandate and the jurisdiction of the arbitral tribunal.

7. In principle, the general provisions in Chapter 3 of the Contracts Act[8] on invalidity of contracts are applicable to arbitration agreements.[9] When interpreting the arbitration agreement the ordinary principles under Swedish law for interpreting contract provisions are applied.[10]

III. THE ARBITRAL TRIBUNAL'S EXAMINATION OF ITS JURISDICTION

A. The Doctrine of Separability

8. The arbitration agreement is normally included as a dispute resolution clause in a business contract stipulating that any future disputes between the parties will be resolved by arbitration. The doctrine of separability means that this arbitration clause

4. See Heuman, *Skiljemannarätt*, Norstedts Juridik, 1999, 367 and Lindskog, *Skiljeförfarande – En kommentar*, Norstedts Juridik, 2005, 283.
5. See Heuman, 46; Lindskog, 229 and Hobér, *International Commercial Arbitration in Sweden*, 90 and 183 (Oxford U. Press 2011).
6. See s. 1(1) of the Act.
7. If the arbitral tribunal exceeds this mandate the arbitral award may be set aside in a challenge procedure under s. 34 item 1 of the Act.
8. *Sw: Lag (1915:218) om avtal och andra rättshandlingar på förmögenhetsrättens område.*
9. See more about invalidity of arbitration agreements in Lindskog, 117 and Heuman, 133.
10. See Lindskog, 122. More about interpretation of arbitration clauses under the Rules of Arbitration of the Arbitration Institute of the Stockholm Chamber of Commerce (SCC Rules) in Magnusson SAR 2000:2, 171, Magnusson & Larsson SAR 2004:2, 47 and Ramsjö & Strömberg SIAR 2009:2, 55.

is regarded as an independent agreement separate from the general contract.[11] This important rule is codified in section 3 of the Act.

9. The purpose of the doctrine of separability is to enable the arbitral tribunal to hear objections as regards the general contract – and maybe ending up by declaring the contract, or part of it, invalid – without that examination affecting the tribunal's own jurisdiction.[12]

B. The Principle of *Kompetenz-Kompetenz*

10. The arbitral tribunal's competence to examine its own jurisdiction is referred to as the principle of *Kompetenz-Kompetenz.*[13] Under Swedish law, the arbitral tribunal, as a general rule, does not have a duty to examine its own jurisdiction without a party requesting it to do so. However, the tribunal must on its own motion examine the invalidity grounds set forth in section 33 of the Act.

11. If a party raises a jurisdictional objection, the arbitral tribunal must afford both parties a reasonable opportunity to present their views in this respect. Complex jurisdictional issues may require written and oral evidence at a separate hearing.

C. The Timing of Jurisdictional Objection

12. There is no express provision in the Act saying at what time a jurisdictional objection regarding the existence, validity or applicability of the arbitration agreement should be put forward to the tribunal. The objection should, however, be included in the respondent's first submission to the arbitral tribunal, or as soon as the circumstances are known to the respondent,[14] in order not to be barred under section 34(2) first sentence of the Act.

13. In Stockholm Chamber of Commerce (SCC) proceedings, any jurisdictional objections should be included in the respondent's answer to the request for arbitration. However, failure to raise such objections does not preclude the respondent from raising objections in this regard at any time up to and including submission of the statement of defence.[15]

---

11. Govt. bill 1998/99:35 p. 75, Lindskog, 305, Madsen, *Commercial Arbitration in Sweden* 93 (3d ed., Oxford U. Press, 2007) and Heuman, 62. Relevant case law is e.g., *E. A. v. AB Ferrolegeringar,* judgment by the Supreme Court made on 28 May 1936, NJA 1936 p. 521 and *H. Hermansson v. AB Asfaltbeläggningar,* decision by the Supreme Court made on 24 Mar. 1975, NJA 1976 p. 125.
12. See Heuman, 367.
13. See more about the arbitral tribunal's ruling on jurisdiction in Lindskog, 281, Heuman, 363, Hobér, 186 and Madsen, 85. Further, see Smit's commentary to an SCC award in an investment arbitration dealing *inter alia* with '*the Competence-Competence doctrine*' in SIAR 2005:1, 123 and a commentary to a Latvian judgment about *Kompetenz-Kompetenz,* Udris and Kacevska in International Arbitration Court Decisions, 637.
14. See SOU 1994:81, p. 292.
15. Art. 5 (1) (i) and Art. 24 (2) (i) of the SCC Rules.

14. It may be noted that in order not to forfeit its right to challenge the arbitral award a dissatisfied party should take the precaution to object to a decision where the arbitral tribunal establishes that it is vested with jurisdiction. This rule is often referred to as the requirement for 'dual protests' in Swedish arbitration law doctrine.[16]

D. Mandatory and Facultative Circumstances Affecting the Arbitral Tribunal's Jurisdiction

15. The circumstances which may lead to the arbitral award being considered invalid or being set aside are specified in sections 33 and 34 of the Act. These circumstances may even exist before the arbitration commenced, or may occur in the course of the arbitral proceedings.

16. Some obstacles to arbitration are so severe that they are mandatory, i.e., they cannot be opted out of by the parties. These obstacles are non-arbitrability[17] and public policy, which will cause the arbitral award to be invalid under section 33 of the Act. These obstacles should therefore be examined by the arbitral tribunal on its own motion (ex officio), and if any such obstacles exist, the tribunal must dismiss the request for arbitration, even if this has not been requested by the respondent.[18]

17. Other circumstances are disposed by the parties and can, as such, be waived by the parties. These circumstances do not make the arbitral award invalid, but they can result in the award being set aside in a challenge proceeding under section 34 of the Act.[19] Whether a dispute is covered by a valid arbitration agreement between the parties does not have to be heard by the arbitral tribunal on its own motion; rather it should be considered after an objection to that effect has been put forward by a party to the arbitration.

E. The Form of the Arbitral Tribunal's Jurisdictional Decision

18. The arbitral tribunal determines whether it wants to rule upon its jurisdiction as a preliminary issue or in the final arbitral award. The jurisdictional assessment either ends up in the form of an order or in the form of an arbitral award.[20]

1. Decision in the Form of an Order

19. When the arbitral tribunal finds itself to have jurisdiction to decide the case the examination leads to an order. In this determination, the tribunal establishes that it has

16. See Heuman, 293.
17. See s. 1 of the Act.
18. See Lindskog, 289 and Hobér, 184.
19. See more about challenge of arbitral awards in paras 39–42 below.
20. See s. 27 of the Act and Hobér, 261.

jurisdiction and continues the conduct of the proceedings in order to decide the subject matter.[21]

20. A decision in which the arbitral tribunal finds that it has jurisdiction is not final. It can be set aside by the state courts and it does not gain legal force.[22] A party which is dissatisfied with the decision does not have to bring an action in the courts within a specific time frame to maintain the possibility of challenging the subsequent award due to lack of jurisdiction. This Swedish approach differs from the one stipulated in the Model Law.[23]

21. However, a party continuing to participate in the arbitral proceedings without protesting risks losing its right to challenge the arbitral award on that ground. Section 34 of the Act sets out that a party cannot rely upon a circumstance which the party may be considered to have waived.[24]

22. Once the arbitral award on the merits has been rendered, a challenge action must be brought within three months from the date upon which the party received the award.[25]

23. It should be noted, however, that a party can never waive its right to claim that the subject matter was non-arbitrable and that, for this reason, the award is invalid under section 33 of the Act.

24. The arbitral tribunal is not bound by its affirmative jurisdictional decision.[26] Accordingly, the arbitral tribunal may make a new ruling on the jurisdictional issue at a later stage of the proceedings.[27] Of course, this non-binding character of a decision on jurisdiction does not change even if the decision is incorrectly labelled an 'award'.

25. A dissatisfied party can ask the arbitral tribunal to revise its decision or – as highlighted above in paragraph 14 – continue to participate in the proceedings under protest[28] and subsequently challenge the final award. A third option is to bring an action before a court requesting the court to establish that the arbitration agreement is invalid or inapplicable.

2. *Decision in the Form of an Arbitral Award*

26. If the arbitral tribunal finds that it lacks jurisdiction to determine the dispute, it dismisses the request for arbitration in the form of an arbitral award. As a consequence, the dispute is terminated without the tribunal deciding the merits of the case. Under

21. See SOU 1994:81 p. 107 and Govt. bill 1998/99:35 p. 214.
22. See Heuman, 368, Lindskog, 295, Hobér, 187 and Madsen, 91.
23. See Art. 16 (3) of the Model Law which stipulates a thirty-day period for a party to bring such an action to the courts.
24. See s. 34(2) of the Act. Further, see Govt. bill 1998/99:35 p. 77, Hobér, 187 and Heuman, 293.
25. See s. 34(3) of the Act.
26. See s. 2(2) of the Act.
27. SOU 1994:81 p. 259, Govt. bill 1998/99:35 p. 215, Lindskog, 296, Heuman, 359 and Madsen, 91.
28. See Heuman, 293.

section 27 of the Act, an arbitral tribunal must always conclude its assignment by rendering an award.[29]

27. An award declining jurisdiction gains legal force if it is not appealed within three months. This is set out in section 36 of the Act.

28. Thus, a dissatisfied party may bring an action with the competent Court of Appeal[30] and the Court can, if it finds it appropriate, replace the arbitral tribunal's award declining jurisdiction with a binding judgment establishing the jurisdiction of the tribunal. This is in line with the general principle under Swedish law that jurisdictional issues are finally decided by the state courts.

IV. EXAMINATION BY STATE COURTS OF THE ARBITRAL TRIBUNAL'S JURISDICTION

A. Determining Jurisdiction in a Declaratory Judgment

29. A declaratory action concerning the jurisdiction of an arbitral tribunal can be brought with a court prior to or parallel to a pending arbitration.[31] This action can seek to establish either the absence or existence of jurisdiction.[32]

30. However, an action before a court regarding establishment of the validity and applicability of an arbitration agreement prior to any arbitration is commenced is rare.[33] If an action is brought parallel to ongoing arbitral proceedings, the action may be brought before or after the arbitral tribunal has made its decision on jurisdiction. In practice, however, such actions are commonly brought by the respondent after the tribunal has decided that it has jurisdiction.[34]

31. The declaratory action is tried by the District Court. The judgment can be appealed to the Court of Appeal and to the Supreme Court if leave to appeal is granted. When the judgment gains legal force it finally determines the validity and applicability of the arbitration agreement and the arbitral tribunal's jurisdiction.

32. The court's examination of jurisdiction is fully independent of the arbitration. The court deciding the arbitral tribunal's jurisdiction does not have power to stay the arbitral proceedings. Nor can the court in any other way stop or affect the conduct of the arbitration. The arbitral tribunal is free to continue the arbitration notwithstanding the court procedure regarding its jurisdiction.[35] This is expressly stated in section 2(1)

29. See Madsen, 27.
30. See s. 43 of the Act.
31. See SOU 1994:81 p. 258, Govt. bill 1998/99:35 p. 214; Heuman, 367; Lindskog, 283 and Hobér, 187.
32. See Lindskog, 297.
33. See Madsen, 87.
34. See Lindskog, 299 and Hobér, 187.
35. See Lindskog, 301; Hobér, 184 and Madsen, 90.

third sentence of the Act, and the purpose is to avoid a delay pending the court's decision.

33. Even if the jurisdictional issue appears complicated, an arbitral tribunal rarely stays the proceedings.[36] However, the tribunal can stay the proceedings at the request of a party, but even in these cases it is very unusual for the arbitration to be stayed.

34. Should a court find that an arbitral tribunal lacks jurisdiction, the arbitration should be terminated. If the arbitral tribunal, notwithstanding the declaratory judgment, continues the arbitration, the arbitral award can be set aside in later challenge proceedings.[37]

1. *Jurisdiction of the Swedish Courts*

35. The Swedish Supreme Court ruled upon the issue of jurisdiction of Swedish courts in conjunction with international arbitration in *RosInvest v. Russian Federation*.[38]

36. In *RosInvest v. Russian Federation*, an SCC arbitral tribunal having its seat in Stockholm rendered an affirmative decision on jurisdiction. Subsequently, the Russian Federation initiated legal action in the District Court claiming that the tribunal lacked jurisdiction to decide the matter. RosInvest requested dismissal of the Russian Federation's lawsuit arguing that the action lacked Swedish judicial interest since neither of the parties nor any of the facts had a connection to Sweden.

37. The Supreme Court held that the Act applies to any arbitral proceedings that take place in Sweden notwithstanding that the only connection to Sweden is that the seat of arbitration is in Sweden.[39]

38. Furthermore, the issue of timing for an action to obtain a declaratory judgment on jurisdiction was addressed in the *RosInvest v. Russian Federation* decision. In this regard, the Supreme Court held that a party is permitted to have such an action adjudicated if there are good reasons to assume that the arbitral award on the merits is not going to be rendered in the near future.

36. See Heumann 366.
37. See s. 34 item 1, 2 and 6 of the Act.
38. *RosInvestCO UK Ltd v. The Russian Federation*, decision by the Supreme Court made on 12 Nov. 2010 in case no Ö 2301-09, NJA 2010 p. 508.
39. Thus the Supreme Court effectively removed any uncertainty caused by the Svea Court of Appeal's decision in the *Titan Corporation v. Alcatel CIT SA*, decision by the Svea Court of Appeal made on 28 Feb. 2008 in case no T 1038-05, RH 2005:1, where the Court of Appeal dismissed a challenge action due to lack of Swedish judicial interest – despite the fact that the parties' arbitration agreement and the arbitral award stated that Stockholm was the seat of arbitration. The *Titan v. Alcatel* decision was heavily criticized by the Swedish arbitration community. See comments by Shaughnessy and Söderlund, SIAR 2005:2, 259 and Reldén and Nilsson, JT 2005-06, 913.

2. *Requirements for a Declaratory Judgment*

39. In addition to establishing the jurisdiction of the Swedish courts, a party which wishes to attack arbitral proceedings through a declaratory action must satisfy the court that the action meets the requirement laid down in the Swedish Procedural Code for a declaratory judgment – i.e., there must be uncertainty as to whether or not a certain legal relationship exists and that the uncertainty will expose the plaintiff to detriment.[40] The relevant legal relationship in this context is the existence of a valid and applicable arbitration agreement.[41]

B. Examination of the Arbitral Tribunal's Jurisdiction in Challenge Proceedings

40. In addition to a declaratory judgment as described above, the validity and applicability of the arbitration agreement can be examined in a challenge procedure under section 34 of the Act once the arbitral award has been rendered.

41. A party which has taken part in the arbitration without objecting is, as a general rule, prevented from challenging the award since it is considered to have accepted the arbitration agreement and its validity.[42] As described above in paragraph 14, a party may lose its right to challenge the award invoking lack of jurisdiction if the party has not fulfilled the standard of 'dual protests'.[43]

42. According to Swedish law several grounds may lead to an arbitral award being set aside – although this is exceptionally rare – e.g., if the dispute is not covered by a valid arbitration agreement between the parties.[44] As explained above in paragraph 17, the absence of a valid arbitration agreement does not render the award invalid, only challengeable.[45]

43. Under Swedish law the parties are, under certain conditions, allowed to agree to refrain from challenging an arbitral award, a so-called exclusion agreement.[46] In these cases the jurisdiction of the arbitral tribunal cannot be examined in a subsequent challenge proceeding. However, an award subject to such agreement will be recognized and enforced in Sweden in accordance with the rules applicable to a foreign award.[47]

---

40. Chapter 13, s. 2 of the Swedish Procedural Code. See Madsen, 87.
41. See Hobér, 192.
42. See s. 34(2) of the Act and corresponding stipulations in Art. 31 of the SCC Rules. Further, see Madsen, 88.
43. See Heuman, 293.
44. See s. 34 item 1 of the Act.
45. See SOU 1994:81 p. 174 and Govt. bill 1998/99:35 p. 142.
46. See s. 51 of the Act.
47. See ss. 54 and 55 of the Act.

V. THE SCC'S EXAMINATION OF ITS JURISDICTION

44. When choosing institutional arbitration, the institute referred to in the arbitration agreement normally makes a jurisdictional assessment at an early stage of the process. The institution primarily examines whether there is an arbitration agreement between the parties as regards the subject matter, and decides whether it appears as if the parties were in agreement to refer any disputes to settlement under the rules of the institution.[48]

45. In arbitration administered under the SCC Rules, the SCC Board initially examines whether the SCC manifestly lacks jurisdiction. This power of the Board follows from Articles 9 and 10 of the SCC Rules.[49]

A. Prima Facie Decision

46. A jurisdictional objection from the respondent is determined by the SCC Board based on the parties' written submissions.[50] Once the parties' initial exchange of briefs is concluded, the case is reported at the SCC Board meeting.[51] If the respondent's answer includes a jurisdictional objection, the claimant is given an opportunity to provide its views regarding the objection before the case is reported at the Board meeting.

47. As mentioned above, the SCC Board rarely makes decisions on its own motion concerning its jurisdiction. However, in exceptional cases this can be done when the dispute concerns a non-arbitrable issue or if the respondent has failed to file an answer. The reason for making prima facie decisions in these circumstances is that the SCC strives to create the best conditions for an arbitral award to be enforceable and to reduce any risk of the award being challenged.[52]

B. Dismissal If the SCC Manifestly Lacks Jurisdiction

48. As expressly stated in Articles 9 and 10 of the SCC Rules, the SCC must manifestly lack jurisdiction in order for the Board to dismiss a request for arbitration. This means that it must be clear and obvious that the SCC does not have jurisdiction to administer the arbitration.[53] Otherwise, the SCC should accept the case.

---

48. See Lindskog, 279.
49. Corresponding provisions are included in the SCC Rules for Expedited Arbitrations.
50. See Öhrström, *Stockholms Handelskammares Skiljedomsinstitut – En handbok och regelkommentar för skiljeförfaranden*, Norstedts Juridik, 2009, 138. The same type of examination is carried out by the ICC under Art. 6.4 of the Rules of Arbitration of the International Chamber of Commerce (ICC Rules).
51. In urgent cases, prima facie decisions regarding the SCC's jurisdiction can be made by the SCC Board chairperson or vice chairperson on behalf of the Board. More information about the SCC Board and its decision making is found in Appendix I of the SCC Rules.
52. See Art. 47 of the SCC Rules.
53. See Hobér, 1[illegible]5.

49. A request for arbitration can be dismissed in whole or in part by the SCC.[54] If the respondent files a counterclaim which manifestly does not fall within the scope of the arbitration agreement, the respondent's counterclaim can be dismissed. However, insofar as the claimant's request for relief falls within the scope of the arbitration agreement, the case continues with the claimant's claims only. Partial dismissal may also apply when the claimant relies on a number of contracts in its request for arbitration but only one, or some, of them refer(s) to the SCC Rules.

C. Referral of the Dispute to the Arbitral Tribunal

50. If the SCC Board finds that the SCC does not manifestly lack jurisdiction, the dispute is referred to the arbitral tribunal.[55] If the respondent maintains its jurisdictional objection, the tribunal may rule on its jurisdiction pursuant to the principle of *Kompetenz-Kompetenz.*

51. Of course, the arbitral tribunal is free to make a different assessment to that of the SCC when deciding the jurisdictional issue. Before the tribunal the parties generally submit additional briefs and evidence concerning the tribunal's jurisdiction. If the matter is complicated, the arbitral tribunal might schedule a separate hearing for the jurisdictional issue.

D. SCC Case Law

52. Below is a discussion relating to SCC cases and some of the most commonly invoked grounds in support of a request for dismissal before the SCC.[56]

53. A jurisdictional ground which the SCC is confronted with quite often is that the arbitration agreement referred to includes an ad hoc arbitration agreement and, thus, the dispute should be settled by arbitration under the Act and not under the SCC Rules. This argument was put forth in SCC arbitration[57] where the clause read:

> All disputes arising in connection with the validity, interpretation and performance of this agreement, which cannot directly be settled in an amicable way between the parties to this agreement, shall be decided without recourse to the ordinary courts by a court of arbitration in Stockholm...

54. The SCC found that it manifestly lacked jurisdiction. The SCC does not provide reason for its decisions but probably attention was paid to the fact the arbitration clause did not refer to any set of arbitration rules or any specific arbitration body. The wording

54. This provision was introduced in the 2007 SCC Rules. See Magnusson & Shaughnessy, SIAR 2006:3, 46.
55. See Art. 18 of the SCC Rules.
56. For an in depth case study of the prima facie decisions with the SCC Board see Magnusson SAR 2000:2, 171, Magnusson & Larsson SIAR 2004:2, 47 and Ramsjö & Strömberg, SIAR 2009:2, 55.
57. SCC Case No 2/2005, SIAR 2009:2, 59.

merely referred to the submission of any disputes to 'a' court of arbitration. Moreover, there were no other circumstances connecting the dispute with the SCC.

55. Another SCC case that involved objection on the ground that the parties had agreed to ad hoc arbitration included the following arbitration clause:[58]

> Arbitration. Any disputes and differences arising out of or in connection with the present Contract are to be settled, without recourse to Courts of Law, by the Arbitration Court of Stockholm (Sweden) in accordance to the procedure and regulations of said Court.

56. In this case the SCC found that it did not manifestly lack jurisdiction. In contrast to the case mentioned above, this arbitration clause did refer to 'the procedure and regulations' of the arbitration court. In the final award, the arbitral tribunal noted that it is common practice to look beyond the actual wording of an arbitration clause if the true intention of the parties was to refer to a particular arbitral body. The arbitral tribunal also addressed whether a reasonable person of the same kind as the respondent would have understood the clause to mean the SCC. The answer to that question was yes.

57. Another jurisdictional objection appearing in the SCC caseload on a regular basis is that the arbitration agreement does not include the full and correct name of the SCC. An illustrative example in this regard is the following arbitration clause:[59]

> All disputes in connection with this Contract of execution thereof shall be settled friendly through negotiations. In case no settlement can be reached, the case may then be submitted for arbitration to the Arbitration Committee of Sweden and accepted by both parties in accordance with its arbitrage rules of procedure. ...

58. The SCC found that it did not manifestly lack jurisdiction and referred the case to the arbitral tribunal, which decided on jurisdiction in the affirmative. Here one can imagine that the SCC placed emphasis on the fact that the clause said 'the' Arbitration Committee of Sweden – i.e., the intention of the parties seems to have been to point to a specific arbitration centre in Sweden and to have the dispute settled under that centre's 'arbitrage rules of procedure'. According to the tribunal the only international arbitration institution in Sweden was the SCC. To conclude, it is not necessary to state the accurate name of the SCC. Rather, it is essential to assess the probable intention of the parties when entering into the arbitration agreement.[60]

59. Sometimes the respondent argues that the parties have not properly conducted friendly negotiations as stipulated in their arbitration agreement. This was the case in the above-mentioned arbitration.[61] The respondent's position was that the parties had

58. SCC Case 04[illegible]/2006, SIAR 2009:2, 63.
59. SCC case No 10/2005, SIAR 2009:2, 61.
60. See Hobér, 1[illegible]5.
61. I.e., SCC case No 10/2005. Capper has commented the case in SCC Arbitral Awards, Juris, 2011, p. 392. In addition, see commentary by O'Connor, Gatenby and Menin in SIAR 2004:2, 165 regarding an SCC award in which the arbitration agreement stipulated 'mutual consultations' before referral to arbitration.

not attempted to settle the dispute as required and, consequently, the request for arbitration was premature. The arbitral tribunal pointed out that there were 'no detailed rules on a procedure to be followed, nor a clear lapse of time or such like' in the clause and stated that it was clear that there had been contacts off and on between the parties over several years concerning the deficient nature of the goods. Thus, the tribunal found that the parties had done what could reasonably be required under the arbitration clause in question and established that it had jurisdiction.

60. Occasionally, it may be uncertain whether the arbitration agreement refers to the SCC or to another arbitral institution. This was the case in an arbitration with the following clause:[62]

> In case of disputes ... will be submitted to the International Commercial Arbitration Court in Stockholm, Sweden

61. The SCC found that it did not manifestly lack jurisdiction and referred the dispute to the arbitral tribunal, which held that it was sufficiently clear that the reference in the arbitration clause should be understood as a reference to the SCC.[63] It may be noted that there is no 'International Commercial Arbitration Court' in Stockholm, or elsewhere in Sweden, although there is the International Chamber of Commerce (ICC) national committee for Sweden, which fulfils certain duties in relation to the ICC International Court of Arbitration. The national committee, however, does not administer any cases.

62. In another SCC arbitration, where the respondent also argued that the parties had agreed to arbitration with another institution than the SCC, the arbitration clause read:[64]

> Any difference or dispute arising out of or in connection with this contract shall be settled by arbitration at the Stockholm Chamber of Commerce in Stockholm, Sweden, according to its expedited arbitration rules. Their rules to be final and binding.

Next to the arbitration clause, however, the following was handwritten on the respondent's version of the agreement:

> Beijing, China International Econo. and Trade Arbitration Commission.

63. The SCC found that it did not manifestly lack jurisdiction over the dispute. It can be noted that the arbitral tribunal considered it unconvincing that the parties should have made handwritten modifications in the agreement and that both parties should have signed such a poorly modified text.

64. Another argument sometimes put forward is that the respondent (or the claimant) is not a party to the arbitration agreement. This was the case in a dispute where the respondent held that the party that the respondent had entered into an agreement with

62. SCC case No 7/2005, SCC Arbitral Awards p. 339.
63. Schöldström has commented the case in SIAR 2007:1, 155.
64. SCC case No 37/2007, SIAR 2009:2, 65.

had only transferred an outstanding claim for damages and that the claimant had not succeeded to other rights and obligations. Thus, the claimant had not become a party to the agreement and could not invoke the arbitration agreement. The SCC found that it did not manifestly lack jurisdiction, which is in line with SCC practice to assume prima facie jurisdiction rather than deny it.[65]

65. Furthermore, respondents on occasion argue that the dispute does not fall within the scope of the arbitration agreement, that the signature of the contract is falsified or is made by a person not authorized to represent the company. The latter, for instance, was argued in an SCC case where the respondent asserted that it had not been represented by an authorized agency.[66] The SCC held that it did not manifestly lack jurisdiction. The arbitral tribunal, however, found that the companies that had signed the agreement could not be regarded as agents for the parties. Thus the arbitral tribunal held that the arbitration clause was not applicable to the parties and that the tribunal did not have jurisdiction to decide on the claimant's claims against the respondent.

66. It may be argued that the subject matter is non-arbitrable or against public policy. The issue of subject matter being against public policy was debated in an SCC arbitration[67] in which the respondent argued that a certain contract was, according to Egyptian public policy, non-arbitrable and therefore should be non-arbitrable under Swedish law which governed the arbitration. The arbitral tribunal found that mandatory rules or public interest in foreign jurisdictions should not influence arbitrability under Swedish law. Accordingly, the arbitral tribunal found that it did have jurisdiction over the dispute.[68]

67. Another situation may be that there are multiple contracts with conflicting arbitration clauses. In a SCC case, the parties had entered into two contracts where the first contract contained an arbitration clause, referring the dispute to the SCC, and the second contract which was a settlement contract, referred disputes to the courts of the State of Iowa.[69] The claimant commenced arbitration proceedings based on the first

65. SCC case No 123/2009, SIAR 2009:2, 71. What conclusion the arbitral tribunal came to is, unfortunately, unknown to the author since the SCC has not published the decision of the arbitral tribunal. See also a commentary to a separate award about jurisdiction from 2001 and the Svea Court of Appeal. judgment from 2004 (case No T 1361-01) by Moholitny and Åhman, International Arbitration Court Decisions. 903 as well as Smit's commentary to an SCC award in an investment arbitration dispute against Kazakhstan, in SIAR 2005:1, 123. See SCC case No 74/2000 regarding assignment of an arbitration agreement in SCC Arbitral Awards, p. 25. The case is commented by Puhakka and Pråhl as well as by Dhunér. See SCC case No 12/2002 regarding transfer of an arbitration agreement in SCC Arbitral Awards p. 73. The case is commented by Zykin and by Landrove. See SCC case No 143/2003 regarding, *inter alia*, the 'piercing the corporate veil' of one entity, SCC Arbitral Awards p. 283. The case is commented by Goldberg and Blanke. See the above-mentioned SCC case No 10/2005 regarding whether the claimant and the second respondent were parties to the arbitration agreement, SCC Arbitral Awards p. 369.

66. SCC case No 30/2003, SCC Arbitral Awards, p. 227. The case is commented by Farren.

67. See above-mentioned SCC case No 10/2005, SCC Arbitral Awards p. 369. The case is commented by Capper.

68. See SCC case No 53/2005 regarding the law to apply in determining the non-arbitrability issue. The case is commented by Wallgren-Lindholm and Antila as well as by Runesson.

69. SCC case No 098/2007, SIAR 2009:22, 69.

contract and the respondent argued, *inter alia*, that the court in Iowa had found that arbitration was not warranted and that in any case, the settlement agreement explicitly superseded the first contract. The SCC found that it manifestly lacked jurisdiction over the dispute arising out of the second contract but that it did not manifestly lack jurisdiction over the dispute arising out of the first contract. The arbitral tribunal also found that they lacked jurisdiction over matters covered by the second contract and, hence, dismissed three out of four of the claimant's claims due to lack of jurisdiction.

68. Finally, parties may argue that the dispute has been decided previously (res judicata) or is being tried in an ongoing legal procedure (lis pendens). The Act contains no provisions on res judicata or lis pendens. However, these legal principles, as a general rule, apply in arbitral proceedings as well.[70]

70. See SOU 1994:81 p. 136 and Govt. bill 1998/99:35 p. 104. See Lindskog 345 and 590, Heuman 373 and 710 as well as JT 1992-93, 930. See a commentary to a judgment from the Svea Court of Appeal from 1998 (case No 925-98-80) regarding whether an arbitral award involved a subject matter already decided in a previous award, by Schöldström in International Arbitration Court Decisions, 1177. In addition see a commentary to a judgment from Svea Court of Appeal from 2002 (case No Ö 7192-01) regarding whether enforcement should be refused due to lack of jurisdiction with the arbitral tribunal because of lis pendens by Liebscher in International Arbitration Court Decisions, 1065. See a commentary to a judgment from Svea Court of Appeal from 2003 (case No T 8735-01) concerning whether the arbitral tribunal lacked jurisdiction due to lis pendens and res judicata by Rubins, Stoltysinski and Olechowski, Bagner as well as Wiwen-Nilsson in International Arbitration Court Decisions, 979. See a commentary to an ad hoc arbitral award against the Russian Federation concerning lis pendens by di Pietro in SIAR 2005:2, 37.

CHAPTER 5

Interim Measures

Patricia Shaughnessy

I. INTRODUCTION

1. Parties may sometimes need to obtain immediate relief prior to or during arbitral proceedings rather than awaiting the final outcome of the dispute. For example, a party may want to ensure that performance under a contract continues during the resolution of a dispute or may have serious concerns about the dissipation of assets or destruction of evidence. There can be many reasons why a party may need to obtain some relief before the final arbitral award will be rendered. Sometimes the failure to obtain such relief may render the arbitral proceedings less effective or in some cases even a futile exercise. Parties in these and other circumstances may need to obtain urgent measures to ensure that the situation will not significantly deteriorate and to ensure that the arbitral process will be effective. This type of relief is commonly referred to as interim measures.[1]

2. Foreign or domestic parties arbitrating in Sweden can obtain interim measures from either arbitrators or courts, unless the parties have agreed otherwise. The Swedish arbitration legal framework and practice provides for availability of a range of interim

1. Interim measures may also be referred to as interim measures of protection, provisional measures, or conservatory measures. The UNCITRAL Model Law on International Commercial Arbitration 1985 (Model Law) uses the term 'interim measures', but makes a distinction for ex parte measures which are termed 'preliminary orders', Art. 17 of the Model Law. Some commentators and legal systems may make some distinctions regarding the linguistic label and the type of relief sought. See e.g., Gary Born, *International Commercial Arbitration*, 1944–45 (2009).

measures. Parties arbitrating in ad hoc proceedings or under the administration of an arbitral institution have access to interim measures. The Swedish Arbitration Act (Sw: *Lag (1999:116) om skiljeförfarande*) (the Act) specifically empowers arbitrators to issue decisions on interim measures upon the request of a party unless the parties have agreed otherwise[2] and also provides that a court may issue decisions on interim measures in disputes subject to arbitration.[3] Similarly, the Rules of Arbitration of the Arbitration Institute of the Stockholm Chamber of Commerce (SCC Rules)provide that parties may request interim measures from arbitral tribunals or courts[4] and these Rules also provide for the early availability of emergency interim measures from a so-called emergency arbitrator.[5] Other rules that may be applied in arbitrations seated in Sweden, such as the UNCITRAL Arbitration Rules, adopted 2010 (UNCITRAL Rules) and the Rules of Arbitration of the International Chamber of Commerce (ICC Rules), also provide for access to interim measures from arbitral tribunals or courts.[6] The ICC Rules, adopted in 2010 introduced a new 'opt-out' provision that allows for the appointment of an emergency arbitrator,[7] while the 1998 ICC Rules contained an 'opt-in' procedure for the appointment of a 'pre-arbitral referee'.

3. This chapter will present the Swedish legal framework and practice relating to interim measures in arbitration. This presentation will focus on the Swedish Arbitration Act, the SCC Rules, and practice in courts and in arbitral proceedings conducted under this framework. While the UNCITRAL Rules and the ICC Rules may be applied in arbitrations seated in Sweden, this chapter does not attempt to comprehensively analyse and discuss the UNCITRAL Rules or the ICC Rules and practice under these rules. The scope of this chapter is limited to interim measures in arbitral proceedings seated in Sweden. When arbitral proceedings take place in Sweden, a party may sometimes need to seek interim measures from a court outside of Sweden, for example to compel someone located outside of Sweden to do something. This discussion will not address interim measures brought to courts outside of Sweden in support of arbitrations seated in Sweden. Generally, such relief will need to be sought under the applicable legal framework in the country where the foreign court is located.

4. This chapter will first provide an overview of the legal framework of interim measures in Sweden, followed by a discussion of the type of measures that might be obtained and the procedures for obtaining them.

2. Section 25(4) of the Act.
3. Section 4(3) of the Act.
4. Article 32 of the SCC Rules.
5. Article 32 of the SCC Rules.
6. Article 28 under both the 1998 and 2012 versions of the ICC Rules, provides for Interim Measures. All references to the ICC Rules in this chapter refer to the 2012 version of the ICC Rules, unless otherwise indicated.
7. Article 28 of the ICC Rules.

II. OVERVIEW OF THE STATUTORY PROVISIONS FOR INTERIM MEASURES

5. The Act provides a modern approach to interim measures by specifically providing that parties who are bound to arbitrate their dispute may obtain interim measures from either courts or arbitrators. This concurrent jurisdiction for interim measures allows parties the choice of selecting the forum that best suits their particular needs. There can be a number of reasons why a party may prefer to seek measures from either a court or from arbitrators; these reasons are explored in more detail below. There are also important distinctions between obtaining measures from either a court or from a tribunal and parties should carefully consider which forum will provide the most effective relief under the circumstances of their situation. Generally, seeking relief from arbitrators will retain the flexibility that earmarks arbitration, while seeking relief from courts will introduce a national court procedure. These distinctions will be discussed more fully below.

A. Statutory Provisions Empowering Swedish Courts to Order Interim Measures

1. *Court-Ordered Interim Measures Are Not Contrary to the Agreement to Arbitrate*

6. The Act specifically empowers Swedish courts to consider requests from parties to obtain interim measures in disputes subject to arbitration.[8] Such requests for interim measures may be sought from a Swedish court prior to or during the pendency of arbitral proceedings.[9] The statutory provision clarifies that seeking interim measures from a court during or prior to arbitral proceedings is not contrary to an agreement to arbitrate.[10] This provision only applies to interim measures sought from a court and does not allow a court to make a final ruling on a substantive issue that is encompassed by the parties' agreement to arbitrate.[11] A court will nonetheless need to make a determination of the likelihood of success of the claim relating to the interim measures

8. Section 4(3) of the Act provides as follows: 'During the pendency of a dispute before arbitrators or prior thereto, a court may, irrespective of the arbitration agreement, issue such decisions in respect of security measures as the court has jurisdiction to issue.'This unofficial translation of the Act is found at the SCC website: http://www.sccinstitute.com/?id=23746 (last visited 3 Oct. 2012).
9. There may be some limited opportunities to obtain interim measures following the rendering of the award when there is a serious risk of sabotage of the award, although the Swedish Enforcement Code includes procedures for provisional enforcement. See, Lars Heuman, *Arbitration Law in Sweden: Practice and Procedure* 330 (Juris Publg. Inc. 2003).
10. Govt. bill1998/99:35, pp. 73–74.
11. Section 4(1) of the Act provides: 'A court may not, over an objection of a party, rule on an issue which, pursuant to an arbitration agreement, shall be decided by arbitrators.'

when it is assessing the request for interim measures, as is further discussed below.[12] However, this determination is not binding on the arbitrators.

7. It should be noted that the Act specifically provides that a court may only order such measures as it 'has jurisdiction to issue'. The jurisdiction of the court is determined by Swedish procedural law and not by the Act. Generally, Swedish courts will have jurisdiction over people and entities domiciled in Sweden, as well as over property located in Sweden. The District Court where the person is domiciled or the property is located would be competent to consider requests for interim measures. In international contexts, a Swedish court may have jurisdiction when there is a 'Swedish interest in the administration of justice with respect to the issue in question'.[13] The mere fact that an arbitration is seated in Sweden will not necessarily provide a sufficient basis for a court to have jurisdiction to issue an interim order, particularly when the requested measure is aimed at persons, entities or property not subject to Swedish court jurisdiction.[14]

8. As Sweden is a member of the European Union, the Brussels I Regulation and Lugano Convention apply when considering jurisdiction of the courts.[15] The main jurisdictional principle of this Regulation provides that persons should be sued in the courts of the Member State where they are domiciled, regardless of their nationality.[16] When a defendant is not domiciled in a Member State of the European Union, the forum court may apply the jurisdictional rules of the forum court state.[17] The national rules may provide that a court may assert jurisdiction if the defendant's assets are located in the forum and may allow a foreigner domiciled in the forum state to bring suit in the forum court. These national rules vary within the European Union. Parties to commercial contracts may enter into forum selection agreements that may deviate

12. Swedish Code of Judicial Procedure (SFS, Ch. 15, ss 1 and 2. See, Stefan Lindskog, *Skiljeförfarande, En kommentar* (2nd ed. 2012), footnote 85, 325.
13. Kaj Hobér, *International Commercial Arbitration in Sweden* 240 (Oxford U. Press 2011).
14. *Ibid.* See also, *Sveriges Pälsdjursuppfödares Riksförbund v. Dansk Pelsdyravlerförening*, decision by the Supreme Court made on 29 Jun. 1994 in case no SÖ 171, NJA 1994 C48. When the seat of international arbitration is in Sweden, there is a Swedish interest in the administration of justice in the arbitration and Swedish courts may provide judicial assistance as provided in the Act, such as proceedings to set aside an award or challenge jurisdiction. See, *RosInvestCO UK Ltd v. The Russian Federation*, decision by the Supreme Court made on 12 Nov. 2010 in case no Ö 2301-09, NJA 2010 p. 508, 4–5; see also, *Joint Stock Company Acron v. Yara International ASA*, decision by the Svea Court of Appeal made on 12 Apr. 2010 in case no Ö 9250-09, RH 2010:75, 2–3. However, this may not be sufficient to provide the courts with jurisdiction to issue orders of interim measures against people or entities or property not subject to Swedish court jurisdiction.
15. Council Regulation (EC) No 44/2001 of 22 Dec. 2000 on jurisdiction and the recognition and enforcement of judgments in civil and commercial matters, OJ 2001 L 12 p.1 (Brussels I Regulation) as recently 'recast'. See *infra* n. 21. The Lugano Convention on Jurisdiction and Enforcement of Judgments in Civil and Commercial Matters, OJ 1988 L 319 p. 9, (Lugano Convention) will apply with regard to members of the European Free Trade Association (EFTA), which includes Iceland, Norway and Switzerland. The Lugano Convention basically follows the Brussels I Regulation, providing essentially the same rules despite some minor textual differences.
16. Articles 2 and 3 of the Brussels I Regulation. See, Michael Bogdan, *Concise Introduction to EU Private International Law*, 43 (Europa Law Publishing, 2006).
17. Article 4 of the Brussels I Regulation.Bogdan, *supra* n. 19, at 44.

from the general rules and provide for other courts to have jurisdiction. Interim measures can be applied for in other Member State courts pursuant to the national law of that state, including when the dispute is subject to arbitration.[18] There are exceptions to the general principles of jurisdiction and the Regulation also contains a specific exception for arbitration.[19] This so-called arbitration exception has been the subject of case law,[20] commentary, and calls for revision. After considerable controversy, the arbitration exception was generally left intact in the newly "recast" Regulation.[21]

9. The Brussels I Regulation and Lugano Convention create obligations for courts to recognize and enforce civil judgments made by courts of the states subject to these instruments, including orders for interim measures.[22] Consequently, interim measures obtained from courts of these states are generally enforceable throughout the European Union and EFTA countries. What constitutes a jurisdictional basis for a national court to issue an interim measure under the Brussels I Regulation is subject to the Regulation and the case law of the Court of Justice of the European Union interpreting the relevant provisions. The conditions under which such measures may be granted by a Member State court are subject to the relevant provisions of the national law of the court.[23] This area of law is complex and a comprehensive presentation of private international law rules and practice under the Brussels I Regulation and Lugano Convention is beyond the scope of this discussion.

10. When a request for interim measures is brought to a Swedish court, the court procedure will be subject to the Swedish Code of Judicial Procedure,[24] Chapter 15. These provisions set out the procedures and standards that apply when seeking interim measures from a court. This includes the standards that the court should apply in assessing the application, as well as the type of measures that a court may order. A court must apply these provisions regardless of whether the main dispute is subject to arbitration or to regular court proceedings. These provisions are briefly addressed below.

18. Article 31 of the Brussels I Regulation. *Ibid.*, at 72–73. The interim measure exception to the general jurisdictional approach of the Brussels I Regulation has been interpreted restrictively and has been the subject of case law from the Court of Justice of the European Union.
19. Article 1.2 (d) of the Brussels I Regulation.
20. See, *Allianz SpA et al., v. West Tankers, Inc.*, ruling by European Court of Justice in case no C-185/07, 2009, ECRI-00663, (the court of a Member State may not issue an anti-suit injunction to restrain a party from pursuing judicial proceedings in another Member State to enforce an arbitration agreement).
21. Regulation (EU) No 1215/2012 of the European Parliament and of the Council of 12 Dec. 2012 on jurisdiction and the recognition and enforcement of judgments in civil and commercial matters (recast), OJ 2012 L 351/1. The 'recast' regulation shall apply from 15 Jan. 2015, except for Articles 75 and 76, which shall apply from 10 January 2014.
22. Article 32 of the Brussels I Regulation.
23. Bogdan, *supra* n. 19 at 73.
24. (*Sw: Rättegångsbalk* (*1942:740*)).

2. *Requests for Interim Measures Prior to the Commencement of Arbitration*

11. Parties whose dispute is subject to an arbitration agreement may bring requests for interim measures to a Swedish court prior to commencing arbitration, subject to the provisions of the Code of Judicial Procedure, Chapter 15. When a request for interim measures is brought to a Swedish court prior to the commencement of arbitration, the requesting party must commence the arbitration within one month of the issuance of an interim order.[25] The order will lapse upon failure to commence arbitration within one month. Generally, to prevent the interim order from lapsing, the requested relief in the commenced arbitration should include a request to order or prohibit some performance rather than merely requesting declaratory relief.[26] The party who obtained the interim measure should commence arbitration in accordance with section 19 of the Act,[27] which provides the requirements for a Request for Arbitration, unless the parties have agreed otherwise.[28] When parties have agreed to arbitrate pursuant to arbitration rules such as the SCC Rules, then the agreed-upon rules will provide the procedure for commencing the arbitration.[29] Although the Act provides that arbitration is commenced upon the opposing party receiving the Request for Arbitration,[30] in an arbitration conducted pursuant to the SCC Rules, the arbitration is commenced when the SCC receives the Request for Arbitration.[31]

12. Should the arbitration be started within the month but the proceedings are terminated without a decision on the merits, the Act provides an opportunity for the party to bring new proceedings within thirty days of the termination. For example, the arbitration may be dismissed due to lack of jurisdiction. Section 45 of the Act provides that if the arbitration was brought within the required month, but was terminated without a legal determination of an issue submitted to the arbitrators, then the proceedings will be deemed instituted in due time if the party initiates arbitration or court proceedings within thirty days of receipt of the award dismissing the case.[32]

---

25. Chapter 15, s. 7 of the Code of Judicial Procedure.
26. Chapter 15 of the Code of Judicial Procedure. See e.g., *Lena Hallberg v. Seth-RolandArnérs (bankruptcy estate)*, et al., decision by the Svea Court of Appeal made on 10 Oct. 2006 in case no Ö 6866-06. See also, Lars Heuman, *Skiljemannarätt*, 347–348 (1999).
27. It is possible that the party responding to the requested measure commences arbitration relating to the dispute, thus eliminating the need for the requesting party to commence arbitration.
28. Section 19 of the Act provides that unless the parties have agreed otherwise, a request for arbitration must be in writing and include: (1) an express and unconditional request for arbitration; (2) a statement of the issue which is covered by the arbitration agreement and which is to be resolved by the arbitrators; and (3) a statement of the party's choice of arbitrator where the party is required to appoint an arbitrator. SCC Rules,
29. Articles 2, 3 and 4 of the SCC Rules relate to the commencement of proceedings.
30. Section 19 of the Act.
31. Article 4 of the SCC Rules.
32. Section 45 of the Act provides as follows: 'Where, according to law or by agreement, an action by a party must be brought within a certain period, but the action is covered by an arbitration agreement, the party must request arbitration in accordance with s. 19 within the stated period. Where arbitration has been requested in due time but the arbitral proceedings are terminated without a legal determination of the issue which was submitted to the arbitrators, and this is

However, section 45 will only provide the additional time when the dismissal of the case is not due to the 'negligence' of the party.[33]

13. The effect of this provision is to prevent the lapse of the court-ordered interim measure by giving the party a new thirty-day period to commence new proceedings either in court, or if appropriate, a new arbitration. However, the additional time will not apply when the party who obtained the interim measures has contributed to the dismissal of the arbitration. For example, if a party initiated arbitration within thirty days of obtaining court-ordered interim measures and then failed to pay its share of the security for costs thus causing the arbitral proceedings to be dismissed, the court-ordered interim measure would lapse as the party neglected to pursue the arbitration.

3. *Requests for Court-Ordered Measures in Support of Foreign Arbitration*

14. Swedish courts may also issue interim measures in support of arbitrations seated outside of Sweden. As noted above, if such a request is brought prior to the commencement of arbitration, any granted measure will expire if arbitral proceedings are not brought within a month.[34] Swedish law considers that such proceedings have been commenced if the commenced foreign arbitral proceedings might result in an award enforceable in Sweden.[35] As Sweden did not make a reciprocity reservation under the Convention on the Recognition and Enforcement of Foreign Arbitral Awards, 1958(New York Convention), foreign arbitral awards are generally potentially enforceable in Sweden and thus this 'enforceable award' condition will seldom raise an issue.[36] Consequently, a Swedish District Court considering issuing an interim measure in support of a foreign arbitration will not usually need to consider the enforceability of the foreign award that may result from the arbitration.[37]

not due to the negligence of the party, the action shall be deemed to have been instituted in due time where a party requests arbitration or institutes court proceedings within thirty days of receipt of the award, or where the award has been set aside or declared invalid or an action against the award in accordance with s. 36 has been dismissed, from the time that this decision becomes final.'

33. *Ibid.*
34. Chapter 15, s. 7 of the Code of Judicial Procedure.
35. Section 60 of the Act provides: 'Where an interim measure has been granted in accordance with Ch. 15 of the Code of Procedure, in conjunction with the application of s. 7 of the same Ch., a request for arbitration abroad which might result in an award which is recognized and may be enforced in Sweden shall be equated with the commencement of an action.' See also, SOU 1994:81, p. 242 and Govt. bill 1998/99:35 pp. 204–05.
36. Lars Heuman, *supra* n. 9, 700; '[A] timely request for arbitration abroad will always meet the enforceability requirement for sustaining an order of provisional measures made by a Swedish court.' *Ibid.*
37. *Ibid.* According to Professor Heuman, if a Respondent can prove that the alleged arbitration agreement is invalid and that requested relief may only be sought from a foreign court whose judgments are not enforceable in Sweden, the Swedish District Court may deny the requested relief. *Ibid.* at 700-701. However, generally objections to arbitral jurisdiction should be brought to the courts at the seat of arbitration, or raised in enforcement proceedings under the New York Convention, and this issue should not be litigated in Swedish courts in the context of a request for interim relief in support of foreign arbitral proceedings.

15. In the unusual case where interim measures in connection with a foreign arbitration are sought after enforcement proceedings of the final award have been commenced at the Svea Court of Appeal, this court would be the appropriate forum for seeking such measures. Similarly, when enforcement proceedings are pending at the Svea Court of Appeal, any request to discontinue or set aside interim measures that were earlier obtained from a Swedish district court should be addressed by the Svea Court of Appeal.[38]

4. *The Type of Interim Measures Which Courts May Order*

16. Swedish courts are limited to issuing interim orders as provided for pursuant to Chapter 15 of the Code of Judicial Procedure. This chapter provides for the types of measures and the conditions under which they may be obtained. Chapter 15 provides for measures in four main situations:[39] attachment to secure creditor claims,[40] attachment to secure movable property when a party appears to have a stronger claim of ownership,[41] appropriate measures to secure other claims,[42] and orders to return control of property.[43] One of the requirements for obtaining interim relief pursuant to Chapter 15 is that the requested measure is capable of enforcement.[44] In other words, the requested measure should require some performance that can be enforced, such as returning property, making deliveries, attaching assets, etc. Consequently, as a general rule a request for a declaratory judgment as an interim measure would not be an interim measure that a court would grant under Chapter 15.

17. Chapter 15 does not provide for securing or preserving evidence. Chapter 41 of the Code of Judicial Procedure provides for the early taking of evidence when there is a serious risk that the evidence will be lost or may only be obtained later with substantial difficulty. This however is not an interim measure and the Act does not specifically refer to such a measure being available in disputes subject to arbitration.

18. Because the Act does provide for court assistance in taking evidence when a party's request is approved by the arbitrators,[45] allowing a party to obtain evidence through a court-ordered interim measure without the arbitrators' approval could be considered contrary to the Act's approach. However, one leading commentator has noted that 'in cases of extreme urgency ... it is possible that a District Court would

38. Section 60(2) of the Act provides: 'Where an application for enforcement of a foreign award has been lodged, the Court of Appeal shall examine a request for an interim measure or a request to set aside such decision.' See also, Govt. bill 1998/99:35 p. 205.
39. Peter Westberg, *Det Provisoriska Rättsskyddet i Tvistemål, Bok 1* (Skrifter utgivna vid Juridiska Fakulteten i Lund, nr 153) (2004), 56.
40. Chapter 15, s. 1 of the Code of Judicial Procedure (fordringsanspråk).
41. Chapter 15, s. 2 of the Code of Judicial Procedure (bättre rätt till viss egendom).
42. Chapter 15, s. 3 of the Code of Judicial Procedure (annat anspråk).
43. Chapter 15, s. 4 of the Code of Judicial Procedure (återställande av rubbad besittning).
44. There are some limited exceptions.
45. Section 26 of the Act.

assist in taking evidence'.[46] This conclusion could be justified when a party would be left without a remedy during the period needed to constitute an arbitral tribunal. It would seem particularly justified if the other party was delaying the referral of the case to the arbitral tribunal by not appointing an arbitrator or paying its share of the advance on costs. Challenges to the appointment of an arbitrator and jurisdictional objections might also cause delays which could make it difficult to obtain orders from the arbitral tribunal. However, according to another leading commentator, the agreement to arbitrate a dispute should not be an obstacle to seeking court assistance to preserve evidence when needed.[47] He notes that a court should not order evidence taking when there is an on-going arbitration, as it would circumvent section 25 of the Act, which provides for court assistance upon the approval of the arbitrators. This provision seeks to ensure the effectiveness of an on-going arbitration. However, he notes this reasoning loses force with regard to preservation of evidence for the future when an arbitration is not underway.[48]

19. The SCC Rules providing for the appointment of an Emergency Arbitrator might create a remedy that resolves the gap in securing and preserving evidence prior to the appointment of the arbitral tribunal. However, there may remain a need to obtain a court order despite the possibility to obtain relief from an Emergency Arbitrator. The evidence to be secured and preserved may be under the control or in the custody of a third party to whom the Emergency Arbitrator could not issue orders. There may also be situations where a party refuses to cooperate and the party seeking to secure and preserve the evidence might not be satisfied with limited sanctions available to arbitrators for the failure of a party to abide by their orders. To obtain an enforceable order to compel a party to secure and preserve evidence it is probably necessary to seek such relief from a court.[49]

20. A distinction should be made between obtaining or taking of evidence and preserving evidence for the future. If a party seeks to obtain potential evidence to use in arbitral proceedings, the party may request the arbitrators to order the other party to produce the evidence. If the evidence is under the control or in the custody of third parties, or there is a need to obtain an enforceable order to compel a non-cooperative party to produce the evidence, the party seeking the evidence can request the arbitrators to allow it to seek assistance from the courts.[50] Preservation of evidence is a method to secure evidence to ensure its availability for future use, while taking or obtaining evidenceis a method for a party to gain possession or presentation of desired evidence in an on-going proceeding.

46. Heuman, *supra* n. 9, at 332. Heuman notes the neither the provisions of the Code of Judicial Procedure for interim measures (Chapter 15) nor for securing evidence (Chapter 41) are applicable to seeking court assistance to preserve evidence for arbitral proceedings. *Ibid.* Thus, he opines that such assistance would be exceptional.
47. Stefan Lindskog, *Skiljeförfarande, En kommentar*, 327 (2d ed., 2012).
48. *Ibid.*, noting also that it is doubtful if a party should start arbitration in order to preserve evidence which may be needed in the future.
49. The SCC Emergency Arbitrator Rules allow an Emergency Arbitrator to issue a decision in the form of an order or an award.
50. Section 26 of the Act.

5. *Procedures and Standards for Obtaining Interim Measures*

21. When considering whether to grant interim measures, a Swedish Court will need to ensure that the requesting party has fulfilled the requirements of the Code of Judicial Procedure that apply to such requests.[51] These requirements include that the requesting party is likely to succeed on the merits of its claim, that the claim is or can be assumed to be the subject of legal proceedings, and that there is cause to fear that the responding party is acting or will act in a manner that will obstruct enforcement of a judgment in favour of the requesting party or in another manner diminish the value of a future judgment or right.[52]

22. A leading commentator has noted that these requirements lead to three main questions which the court must determine.[53] First, does the requesting party have an actual need for the interim legal protection? Second, is it possible to order some form of protection which is adapted to the circumstances in the actual case? Third, is the potential measure justified with consideration to what has to be protected and in light of the effects that the measure may cause the responding party? These questions lead to a number of issues, which will not be addressed in detail here as they concern Swedish procedural law generally rather than arbitration law specifically.

23. Generally, in order to obtain interim measures a requesting party will bear the burden of proof to establish a need for such measures. An interim measure by its nature is granted prior to the determination of the legal rights of the parties and as such it should only provisionally affect the legal rights and situation between the parties when needed. The Swedish Supreme Court has noted that such measures should not be granted without strong reasons and that the parties' respective rights must be weighed against each other.[54] This requires that some urgency can be shown to justify not awaiting the final outcome of the dispute. The requesting party must also demonstrate that unless the measure is granted, the potential harm to the requesting party will be greater than the potential harm that the measure may cause the responding party; a balancing of potential harm that is often referred to as a proportionality test. To protect a responding party, a court may order the requesting party to post security as a condition to obtaining the measure.[55] The security should cover the entire potential damage that the responding party might reasonably incur as a result of the measure.[56]

51. Code of Judicial Procedure, Ch. 15.
52. Peter Westberg, *supra* n. 39, at 56.
53. *Ibid.*, at 58.
54. *Hydraulkranar Sverige Aktiebolag v. Crane Building Sweden AB*, decision by the Supreme Court made on 18 Dec. 2003 in case no Ö 4190-03, 5, citing Govt. bill1980/81:84 p. 230. In a dispute regarding the repair of a truck, the Court allowed grant of an interim order requiring the company that did the repair to return the truck pending the outcome of the dispute regarding the repair and payment for it.
55. Chapter 15 s. 6 of the Code of Procedure.
56. Peter Westberg, *supra* n. 39, at 61.

24. In considering the requirements for granting relief under Chapter 15, section 3, the Swedish Supreme Court noted that the requesting party must show that it probably[57] has a claim against the responding party, which is or can be assumed to be litigated in court or another forum, and that there is reason to fear that the other party will take action or fail to take action or in some other way will hinder or make difficult the exercise of the other party's rights or substantially reduce the value of those rights.[58] Besides proving the probability of prevailing in its claim and the likelihood that its rights will be 'sabotaged', the requesting party must also provide security for the potential harm to the other party.[59] The Court interpreted the provision to provide that the requesting party could through an interim measure gain immediate performance by the responding party (in this case the return of a truck), which was the object of the claim in the litigation, provided that the requirements for relief were met.[60]

25. Usually Swedish courts will require that a responding party is given notice of the requested measures and afforded an opportunity to respond. However, in cases of exceptional urgency it is possible for a requesting party to seek an ex parte interim order.[61]

26. The legal costs connected with requests for interim relief from a court should be determined only in connection with the final determination of the claims in dispute.[62] Consequently, parties may seek legal costs associated with requests for court-ordered interim relief from the arbitrators when the main dispute is decided. If the arbitrators do not grant relief on the claim upon which a court-ordered interim measure was granted, a party can request the court to terminate the measure.[63]

27. A court may order interim measures in a matter that has been the subject of a request to the arbitrators for interim measures.[64] In addition, the determinations of the arbitrators may be relevant for the court when considering whether the requirements for granting interim measures have been met.[65] However, if a court has ordered an interim measure there would usually not be any need for the arbitrators to order an equivalent measure.[66] As discussed below, arbitrators have greater flexibility than a court to order interim measures and consequently a party might seek measures from arbitrators which were either not awarded or not requested from a court.

28. Some of the advantages of seeking interim measures from a court rather than an arbitral tribunal include the fact that the courts are permanent institutions that are readily and inexpensively available, courts can make enforceable orders to compel

---

57. The Swedish term is 'sannolika skäl', which implies a fairly high degree of likelihood.
58. *Hydraulkranar Sverige Aktiebolag v. Crane Building Sweden AB*, decision by the Supreme Court made on 18 Dec. 2003 in case no Ö 4190-03, *supra* n. 56, at 3.
59. *Ibid.*
60. *Ibid.*
61. Chapter 15 s. 5(3) of the Code of Judicial Procedure.
62. Chapter 15 s. 6(4) of the Code of Judicial Procedure.
63. Stefan Lindskog, *supra* n. 47, at 325.
64. *Ibid.*, at 347
65. *Ibid.*
66. *Ibid.*, at 738

both parties and third parties to take or to refrain from taking the ordered action subject to penalty or fines, and courts can in exceptional circumstances make ex parte orders. Some of the disadvantages of seeking interim measures from courts rather than an arbitral tribunal include the need to conduct the proceedings in Swedish and pursuant to the Swedish Code of Procedure, the potential public disclosure of the proceedings, the need to establish jurisdiction, the limitations on the type of measures a court may grant, and the potentially stricter requirements for obtaining the measures. There may be some advantage or disadvantage in having arbitrators consider the interim measures rather than a court as the arbitrators will make the final determinations on the claims and defences in the case.

29. The enforceability of an order for interim measures can be a matter of great importance when determining whether to seek relief from either a court or arbitrators. As noted above, only courts can make orders against third parties (people and entities not party to the arbitration). Generally, in Sweden an interim order made by arbitrators is not enforceable as arbitrators lack the power of compulsion. When a party needs to compel immediate actual performance, a court order may be preferable because of its enforceability. A court order made by a Swedish court will generally be enforceable in Sweden, as well as in the European Union and EFTA area, as noted above. The enforceability of a court order outside of these areas will depend on the law and practice of the enforcing court and matters of international judicial comity.

B. Statutory Provisions Empowering Arbitrators to Order Interim Measures

30. Swedish law empowers arbitrators to make decisions on interim measures upon the request of parties.[67] Section 25 of the Act respects the principle of party autonomy by making such power subject to a request by a party and subject to any agreement of the parties to limit such power. Consequently, parties may preclude the possibility to obtain interim relief from arbitrators, but this is seldom done in practice. Many commentators and practitioners report that parties increasingly want and request interim measures. An agreement to exclude access to arbitrator assistance to obtain interim measures must be clear and unambiguous.[68] In most cases, the parties will have retained the opportunity to seek measures from both courts and arbitrators. By

67. Section 25(4) of the Act provides:

> Unless the parties have agreed otherwise, the arbitrators may, at the request of a party, decide that, during the proceedings, the opposing party must undertake a certain interim measure to secure the claim which is to be adjudicated by the arbitrators. The arbitrators may prescribe that the party requesting the interim measure must provide reasonable security for the damage which may be incurred by the opposing party as a result of the interim measure.

68. Born notes that '(g)iven the likely expectations of reasonable business parties, and the benefits in terms of fairness and efficiency, no agreement to exclude the arbitrators' powers to order provisional measures should otherwise be presumed or implied, save in unusual circumstances.' Gary B. Born, *International Commercial Arbitration*, 1974.

agreeing to arbitrate under the SCC Rules,[69] as well as under the UNCITRAL Rules[70] and ICC Rules,[71] the parties have agreed to empower arbitrators to make interim orders unless they have specifically agreed otherwise.

31. Swedish law does not provide for enforcing interim orders made by arbitrators. The legislative history to the Act indicates that interim measures made by arbitrators are unenforceable orders and that only a court can make enforceable orders.[72],[73] However, an interim measure order made by an arbitral tribunal seated in Sweden may be enforced in a country that provides for the enforcement of interim orders issued by arbitrators.

32. The SCC Rules provide that arbitrators may make interim measures in the form of an order or an award.[74] It can be discussed whether it might be possible for a Swedish court to enforce arbitrators' interim decisions that are made in the form of an award or that constitute an award despite the designation of the decision. Naming the decision an order or an award is not decisive; rather it is the final and binding nature of the decision that determines the legal character of the decision. As one commentator has noted, even if an interim order is termed an 'award' it will not be enforced in Sweden.[75] While another commentator has noted that the main rule is that arbitrator decisions on interim measures are not enforceable, he also noted that an interim measure could be enforceable if 'designated as a provisional award with regard to content'.[76] This would require that such a decision was actually final and binding in nature and with respect to the subject matter.[77] Such an 'interim decision' could in principle constitute a separate award. If such a decision constitutes an award such that it would qualify for enforcement under the New York Convention, then it theoretically could be enforced.[78] If such a decision were deemed an award, it should comply with the form requirements of an award. It should be borne in mind that an interim measure should not be a

69. Article 32 of the SCC Rules.
70. Aricle 26 of the UNCITRAL Rules.
71. Article 28 of the ICC Arbitration Rules, (2012 version).
72. Govt. bill1998/99:35, pp. 72–75. 'The government considers, against the background noted above, that the current regulation giving courts exclusive competence to make enforceable decisions on interim measures should be retained.' *Ibid.* at 73. (unofficial translation by the author). The report notes that during the preparation of the new arbitration act, the drafting committee considered giving arbitrators authority to make enforceable orders on interim measures but recommended against it because of difficulties that would arise; a position that the government concurred with. The reasons include the following. Arbitrators should not be able to make enforceable orders without possible court control, particularly when arbitrators need not be lawyers. Making arbitrators' orders enforceable would require creating an opportunity to challenge the award similar to procedures to annul an award. The report also notes that the New York Convention does not encompass such decisions on interim measures. *Ibid.*, at 73.
73. This can be contrasted with Art. 17 H of the Model Law provision which was amended in 2006 to allow for court recognition and enforcement of interim measures issued by arbitrators.
74. Article 32(3) of the SCC Rules.
75. Kaj Hobér, *International Commercial Arbitration in Sweden*, 2011, 249.
76. Lars Heuman, *supra* n. 9, at 333.
77. *Ibid.*
78. Lars Heuman, *supra* n. 9, at 333.

'short-cut' to the final decision on the merits,[79] but provides provisional relief when it is urgently needed while awaiting the decision on the merits. Consequently, in most situations an interim measure decision would not constitute a final and binding decision as regards the subject matter of the decision.

33. Although the Act does not provide for enforcing arbitrators' orders for interim measures, such measures may nonetheless be helpful as parties usually do not want to appear uncooperative to the arbitrators who will decide the merits of the case and thus may voluntarily comply with such orders. Furthermore, arbitrators may draw negative inferences from a party's conduct and may also consider such conduct when assessing the costs of arbitration.[80] Although arbitrator orders on interim measures may not be enforced by the official enforcement authority in Sweden, they may be enforceable between the parties as a contractual obligation based upon the arbitration agreement when the agreement subjects the parties to arbitrator orders on interim measures, as is provided for in the SCC, UNCITRAL, and ICC Rules.[81]

34. Arbitrators sitting in Swedish arbitrations may enjoy greater powers to issue interim measures than do Swedish courts as they are not limited by the provisions of the Swedish Judicial Code of Procedure.[82] This greater power may be attributed to the fact that such orders are generally not enforceable by Swedish courts under Swedish law, thus allowing for greater discretion to issue interim measures both as regards the type of measures and the conditions for granting them.

C. The SCC Rules on Interim Measures

1. The SCC Approach to Interim Measures

35. The SCC Rules provide for a flexible and modern approach to interim measures. Article 32 of the SCC Rules provides that interim measures may be sought from a court, the arbitral tribunal, or from a so-called emergency arbitrator. It provides that the Arbitral Tribunal may, upon the request of a party, grant any interim measure that it finds appropriate. The drafters of the SCC Rules considered and rejected providing a non-exclusive 'laundry list' of potential interim measures that could be sought, electing to adopt a less detailed approach to regulating interim measures.[83] The SCC Rules take a 'minimalist' approach which provides the arbitrators with considerable discretion,

79. *Ibid.*, at 334.
80. Bo Nilsson, *Negative Inferences: An Arbitral Tribunal's Power to Draw Adverse Conclusions from a Party's Failure to Comply with the Tribunal's Orders*, in *Between East and West: Essays in Honour of Ulf Franke* (Hobér et al. eds., JurisNet 2010). See also, Lars Heuman, *supra* n. 9, at 404-05.
81. See, Stefan Lindskog, *supra* n. 47 at 690 - 93.
82. Lars Heuman, *supra* n. 9, at 334. '(I)f a determination refers to a specific issue severable and independent from the substantive issue to be later decided, and the arbitrators have resolved in a final and binding manner that separate issue, then such a determination should presumably be enforceable under the New York Convention even if it is not termed an award.'
83. See Magnusson & Shaughnessy, *The 2007 Arbitration Rules of the Arbitration Institute of the Stockholm Chamber of Commerce*, 3 Stockholm Intl. Arbitration Rev. 33-66 and 59-60 (2006).

rather than follow a detailed regulated approach.[84] Under both the SCC Rules and the Swedish Arbitration Act, the arbitrators have more flexibility to order interim measures than does a Swedish court.[85] As noted above, this may be justified by the lack of enforceability of arbitrator-ordered measures.[86]

36. Article 32 of the SCC Rules does not set out the standards that should be applied in assessing requests for interim measures, leaving this entirely to the arbitrators' discretion.[87] However, this does not mean that arbitrators may act arbitrarily;[88] they should apply some standards when assessing a request for interim measures.[89] International arbitration calls for an international approach adapted to arbitration,[90] and the appropriate standards may pose a choice-of-law issue for the tribunal to determine.[91] Additionally, different types of measures may call for different types of standards to be applied.[92] The standards applied in national court proceedings should not be imported into arbitral proceedings, although arbitrators and counsel may be informed or inspired by their national court proceedings.[93]

37. The standards used in court proceedings may be stricter than the standards used in arbitration and thus should not automatically be applied in arbitration. For example, the Code of Judicial Procedure requires that the requesting party show that it is likely to succeed on the merits of its claim. This can be compared to the UNCITRAL Rules which require the requesting party to show that there is 'a reasonable possibility that it will succeed on the merits'.[94] The lower burden may in part be justified by a concern that the arbitral tribunal does not give the impression of pre-judging the merits of the case.

38. The standards adopted in the UNCITRAL Arbitration Rules, adopted in 2010, (UNCITRAL Rules) might provide guidance to an arbitral tribunal, as they may reflect

84. This can be compared to the Model Law and UNCITRAL Rules approach. See, Patricia Shaughnessy, *The New SCC Emergency Arbitrator Rules*, Between East and West, Essays in Honour of Ulf Franke (2010).
85. Lars Heuman, *supra* n. 9, at 334, 'the power of (arbitrator) decision-making may concern measures upon which a Swedish court has no competence to decide.'
86. Govt. bill 1998/99:35 pp. 73–74.
87. This can be compared with the extensive regulation provided for in the 2006 amendments to the Art. 17 of the Model Law provisions on interim relief and in the proposed revisions to the Art. 26 of the UNCITRAL Rules.
88. Lars Heuman, *supra* n. 9, at 335.
89. Patricia Shaughnessy, *Pre-Arbitral Urgent Relief, The New SCC Emergency Arbitrator Rules*, 27 J. Intl. Arbitration 343–44 (2010).
90. The standards included in Art. 17 of the Model Law and Art. 26 of the UNCITRAL Rules, arguably provide an international approach based on international consensus and best practices.
91. Gary B. Born *supra* n. 42, 1976–1980 (2009).
92. *Ibid.*, at 1991–95.
93. The lack of explicit standards might cause arbitrators to consider their national procedural law for guidance. Finn Madsen, *Interim Measures – the Frontier of International Arbitration*, Festskrift till Lars Heuman, 354–355 (2008).
94. Article 26 (3) (b) of the UNCITRAL Rules. See, *UNCITRAL Report of Working Group II (Arbitration and Conciliation) on the Work of its Fiftieth Session New York, 9 – 13 February, 2009*, A/CN.9/669, para. 97, 22 (9 Mar. 2009).

an international approach. However, the SCC Rules have elected a less regulated approach thus allowing the arbitral tribunal discretion in its determination. In exercising this discretion, the arbitral tribunal should find that the requesting party has a claim that it may prevail upon in the arbitration. Importantly the arbitral tribunal should consider whether there is actually a need for issuing the requested interim measures in the particular circumstances of the case. The requirement that there is some need for the requested measures is often equated with a requirement of urgency. The requesting party may need to demonstrate that it will suffer some irreparable harm if the measure is not granted. This fact-based determination will involve some proportionality assessment as to the respective harm likely to be suffered by the requesting and responding parties.[95] Article 32 specifically provides that the tribunal may require the requesting party to provide appropriate security to ensure that that the responding party might be compensated for losses incurred as a result of the measure.[96]

39. The arbitral tribunal may issue an interim measure in the form of an order or an award.[97] If the decision takes the form of an award, then it must fulfil the form requirement contained in Article 36 of the SCC Rules and will have the final and binding effects provided for in Article 40 of the SCC Rules. The SCC Rules do not expressly provide for ex parte interim measures. A distinction should be made for ex parte orders made upon the request of a party to obtain relief without notice to the other party and interim relief requests made when the opposing party is not participating in an arbitration although it has had the opportunity to participate. In the latter case, the opposing party has received notice of the arbitration and the request for the interim measure, but has elected not to respond. In such cases, the arbitrators may proceed with considering the request and issuing orders.[98]

2. The SCC Emergency Arbitrator Rules

40. In 2010, the SCC launched its new Emergency Arbitrator Rules (EA Rules) which provide opportunities for parties to obtain urgent interim measures prior to commencing arbitration, or if already commenced, prior to the constitution of the arbitral tribunal. A party may need urgent relief and may prefer not to seek such relief from a court. It can take time for an arbitral tribunal to be constituted and thus able even to consider issuing interim measures. The EA Rules provide for expedited procedures to ensure that parties have an opportunity to obtain quick and effective relief for an urgent situation, before the passage of time renders any measures practically ineffective. The SCC EA Rules have been applied in several cases and practice indicates that the EA Rules work efficiently and effectively.[99] In all cases, the SCC has appointed the

95. See, Lars Heuman, *supra* n. 9, at 335–36.
96. Article 32(2) of the SCC Rules.
97. Article 32(3) of the SCC Rules.
98. See, Article 30(2) and (3) of the SCC Rules.
99. See Johan Lundstedt, *SCC Practice: Emergency Arbitrator Decisions Rendered in 2010*, available at http://www.sccinstitute.com/filearchive/4/41504/Emergency%20arbitration%20final.pdf (last visited 13 Nov. 2011).

Emergency Arbitrator within twenty-four hours and the proceedings have been handled expeditiously. As can be seen from a report on the first four cases, published on the SCC website, in all of the reported cases except one the requested measure(s) was not granted, usually because the requesting party has not demonstrated the urgency of the request.[100] The first Emergency Arbitrator request asked for prohibitive orders relating to disposing of shares in a company, including asking for a prohibition on state authorities, which was beyond the mandate of the emergency arbitrator as it would require issuing an order against a non-party. The emergency arbitrator found that the urgency and harm requirements had not been met and did not grant the requested relief.[101] In the second Emergency Arbitrator case, the responding party objected to jurisdiction and the emergency arbitrator determined he had jurisdiction on a prima facie basis but denied the requested relief, which was sought to prevent the responding party from collecting on a guarantee, because the claimant had not proved the urgency of the measure and the risk of irreparable loss.[102] In the third case, the claimant sought an interim order for continued deliveries and maintenance, which the emergency arbitrator denied because the requested order did not secure a future claim but sought the final relief requested.[103] In the fourth case the emergency arbitrator granted the requested relief to prohibit the transfer or other disposition of shares in a company.[104]

41. The SCCEA Rules are provided for in Article 32(4) as part of the provisions on interim measures. The general provisions of Article 32 are applicable, although the more specific provisions governing the EA procedures are set out in Appendix II of the SCC Rules. The EA Rules apply to parties who have agreed to arbitrate under the SCC Rules unless the parties specifically 'opt-out' of the EA Rules. The EA Rules are available regardless of when the arbitration agreement was entered into, meaning that the EA Rules are applied retroactively to arbitration agreements entered into prior to the effective date of the EA Rules.[105] Generally, the EA Rules empower an emergency arbitrator to make decisions on urgent requests for interim measures prior to the commencement of arbitral proceedings, or prior to the constitution of the arbitral tribunal if arbitral proceedings have already been commenced at the SCC.[106]

42. A party seeking to obtain relief from an emergency arbitrator must file a request for an emergency arbitrator with the SCC Secretariat. Upon receipt of a request for the appointment of an emergency arbitrator,[107] the SCC Secretariat should notify the

100. *Ibid.*
101. *Ibid.*
102. *Ibid.*
103. *Ibid.*
104. *Ibid.*
105. Patricia Shaughnessy, *supra* n. 89, at 350–52.
106. SCC Rules, Appendix II, Art. 1 (1).
107. SCC Rules, Art. 32 (4), Appendix II, Art. 2 provides that:
An application for the appointment of an Emergency Arbitrator shall include:

(i) a statement of the names and addresses, telephone and facsimile numbers and e-mail addresses of the parties and their counsel;

targeted party of the application.[108] Ex parte decisions are not allowed.[109] The notification should be made in accordance with Article 8 of the SCC Rules, which provides for delivery to the last known address by a means that provides a record of the sending. In practice, the SCC Secretariat usually uses a courier service to deliver notices. The time periods for appointing the emergency arbitrator and for rendering the decision are determined from when the request was filed and when the emergency arbitrator was appointed.

43. Pursuant to the EA Rules, the SCC Board will seek to appoint an emergency arbitrator, which is a sole arbitrator, within twenty-four hours of receiving a request for such an appointment.[110] The language 'will seek to appoint' provides some flexibility to depart from the twenty-four hour time limit when needed in complex cases or when there is difficulty obtaining a suitable emergency arbitrator. However, based upon the practice to date it can be expected that the SCC will nearly always make appointments within the twenty-four hour period. Once appointed as an emergency arbitrator, the appointee may not act as an arbitrator in any future proceedings relating to the dispute, unless otherwise agreed by the parties.[111]

44. The emergency arbitrator should issue a decision within five days of the date when the application was referred to the emergency arbitrator, unless granted additional time by the SCC Board after considering a reasoned request from the emergency arbitrator for an extension of time to issue the decision.[112] Granting additional time is exceptional as the intent of the new EA Rules is to ensure that parties have access to speedy relief when they urgently need it. The emergency proceedings may take place and a decision may be rendered even if the responding party fails to respond or appear at a scheduled hearing.[113]

45. Challenges to the emergency arbitrator must be brought within twenty-four hours of when the circumstances giving rise to the challenge became known to the party.[114] The Rules do not indicate the time period and process for dealing with a challenge, but

---

(ii) a summary of the dispute;
(iii) a statement of the interim relief sought and the reasons therefore;
(iv) a copy or description of the arbitration agreement or clause on the basis of which the dispute is to be settled;
(v) comments on the seat of the emergency proceedings, the applicable law(s) and the language(s) of the proceedings; and
(vi) proof of payment of the costs for the emergency proceedings pursuant to Art. 10 (1)-(2) of this Appendix.

108. SCC Rules, Art. 32 (4), Appendix II, Art. 3 provides: 'As soon as an application for the appointment of an Emergency Arbitrator has been received, the Secretariat shall send the application to the other party.'
109. *Ibid.*
110. SCC Rules, Art. 32(4), Appendix II, Art. 4(1).
111. SCC Rules, Appendix II, Art. 4(4).
112. SCC Rules, Art. 32(4), Appendix II, Art. 8 (1).
113. SCC Rules, Art. 30(2). It should be borne in mind that even if a party has difficulty in physically appearing for a hearing on short notice, modern technology can be used to provide an opportunity for parties to participate in a hearing via other means.
114. SCC Rules, Art. 32(4), Appendix II, Art. 4(3).

refer generally to SCC Rules, Article 15. It can be expected that the SCC Board will act swiftly in deciding challenges. While due process guarantees of equal treatment and the right to be heard must be observed in the emergency proceedings, the expedited nature of the proceedings must be borne in mind.[115] The SCC Board may also make prima facie jurisdiction decisions[116] and if the parties have not agreed on the seat of the arbitration, the Board may determine the seat of the emergency proceedings.[117] In determining the seat it will be important to ensure that the law of the seat is compatible with such emergency proceedings.

46. An emergency arbitrator enjoys the same broad powers to issue interim measures as an ordinary arbitrator enjoys pursuant to Article 32(1)–(3) of the SCC Rules. This invests an Emergency Arbitrator with considerable discretion to make orders or awards which he or she deems appropriate.

47. The EA Rules provide that the decision of the emergency arbitrator must be in writing, reasoned, dated, and signed.[118] It should be delivered to the parties and, according to the Rules, the parties 'undertake to carry out any emergency decision without delay'.[119] Upon delivery to the parties, the decision becomes binding on the parties, but not on the subsequent arbitral tribunal. The decision will lapse upon one of the following events: the emergency arbitrator decides otherwise, a Request for Arbitration is not filed within thirty days from the day when the emergency decision was made, if the case is not referred to an Arbitral Tribunal within ninety days from that day, or when a final award has been made.[120]

48. The costs of the emergency arbitrator proceedings are fixed by a set amount.[121] The party requesting appointment of an emergency arbitrator pays the fees and costs relating to it.[122] Upon the request of the emergency arbitrator or if otherwise required, the Board may increase or decrease the fees taking into account the nature of the case, the work performed by the emergency arbitrator and the SCC, and other relevant circumstances.[123] If payment is not made, the SCC Secretariat may dismiss the application and the case will not be referred to the emergency arbitrator.[124] The Rules specifically provide that a party can request that the costs of the emergency proceedings be apportioned between the parties by the arbitral tribunal in the final award.[125]

115. SCC Rules, Art. 32(4), Appendix II, Art. 7 provides: 'Art. 19 of the Arbitration Rules shall apply to the emergency proceedings, taking into account the urgency inherent in such proceedings.'
116. SCC Rules, Art. 32(4), Appendix II, Art. 4(2).
117. SCC Rules, Art. 32(4), Appendix II, Art. 5.
118. SCC Rules, Appendix II, Art. 8(2).
119. SCC Rules, Appendix II, Art. 9(1).
120. SCC Rules, Appendix II, Art. 9(4).
121. SCC Art. 32(4), Appendix II, Art. 10(2).
122. SCC Art. 32(4), Appendix II, Art. 10 (1), which provides: 'The party applying for the appointment of an Emergency Arbitrator shall pay the costs of the emergency proceedings upon filing the application.'
123. SCC Rules, Art. 32(4), Appendix II, Art. 10(3).
124. SCC Rules, Art. 32(4), Appendix II, Art. 10(4).
125. SCC Rules, Art. 10(5), Appendix II.

III. CONCLUSION

49. Parties who choose to arbitrate in Sweden have broad access to obtaining interim measures from courts or arbitral tribunals. The SCC Rules provide a flexible and modern approach which invests arbitrators with wide discretion to efficiently and effectively provide needed relief in appropriate circumstances. In urgent situations prior to the commencement of arbitral proceedings or before the arbitral tribunal is constituted, parties may request urgent relief in SCC arbitrations from an emergency arbitrator or from a court.

CHAPTER 6

The Arbitrators

Patrik Schöldström

I. INTRODUCTION

1. This chapter should be read together with the Swedish Arbitration Act (Sw: *Lag (1999:116) om skiljeförfarande*) (the Act) and the Rules of Arbitration of the Arbitration Institute of the Stockholm Chamber of Commerce (SCC Rules). Not every detail of the provisions of the Act or the SCC Rules is covered. The ambition is to address fundamental and practically important issues, rather than to comment in full on the complete wording of all provisions.

II. QUALIFICATIONS OF ARBITRATOR

A. General Qualifications: Impartiality and Independence

2. Any adult person in charge of their faculties and property may under Swedish law serve as an arbitrator. This requirement is expressed in section 7: 'Any person who possesses full legal capacity in regard to his actions and his property may act as an arbitrator.' This means that any such person, regardless of for example nationality or profession, may as an arbitrator render a valid and enforceable arbitral award. The personal law of the individual in question determines whether that individual 'possesses full legal capacity'. Swedes, for example, lack full legal capacity if they are under the age of 18 or have by a court of law been placed into legal guardianship or bankruptcy.

3. Section 8 lays down further requirements. Section 8(1) states the fundamental rule: 'An arbitrator shall be impartial.' The word 'impartial' is intended[1] – and is in Swedish arbitration law understood[2] – to include the concept of 'independence' as laid down, for example, in Article 12 of the UNCITRAL Model Law on International Commercial Arbitration 1985, with amendments adopted in 2006 (Model Law). In what follows, only 'impartiality' is used, but should thus be read as 'impartiality and independence'.

4. Section 8(2) provides that an arbitrator shall be 'discharged' (removed) at the request of a party if any circumstance exists that may diminish confidence in the arbitrator's impartiality. Section 8(2) then says that such a circumstance is always considered to exist in the following four cases:

(a) The arbitrator or a person closely associated to the arbitrator is a party, or otherwise may expect benefit or detriment worth attention, as a result of the outcome of the dispute.
(b) The arbitrator or a person closely associated to the arbitrator is the director of a company or other association which is a party, or otherwise represents a party or other person who may expect benefit or detriment worth attention as a result of the outcome of the dispute.
(c) The arbitrator has taken a position in the dispute, as an expert or otherwise, or has assisted a party in the preparation or conduct of their case in the dispute.
(d) The arbitrator has received or demanded compensation in violation of section 39(2).

5. For practical purposes, the following three points may be noted, even if this follows from the wording of section 8(2).

6. The first point is that the four cases are not exhaustive. Other circumstances may also cause lack of impartiality in the arbitrator. A clear illustration is the case of *Anders Jilkén v. Ericsson AB*.[3] In this case the arbitral award was set aside because the chair of the arbitral tribunal was considered to have lacked impartiality. The situation producing the lack of impartiality was that during the arbitration he had had an 'of counsel' arrangement with a law firm where, in effect, one of the parties in the arbitration was and had been a major client for a number of years.

7. This case also deserves attention for the Supreme Court's willingness to take into account international standards of arbitrator impartiality and independence. Thus the Supreme Court by way of introduction stated: 'Even if the case is to be assessed on the basis of the provisions in the Act, it may, in view of the similar rules and the often recurring international elements in [arbitration], be appropriate to look also at the

1. Govt. bill 1998/99:35 p. 83.
2. For example Andersson, F. et al., *Arbitration in Sweden* 84 (Jure Förlag AB 2011) and Hobér, K., *International Commercial Arbitration in Sweden* 162 (Oxford U. Press 2011).
3. *Anders Jilkén v. Ericsson AB*, judgment by the Supreme Court made on 19 Nov. 2007 in case no T 2448-06, NJA 2007 p. 841. Case commentaries by Fellas, J. and by Schöldström, P., SIAR 2007:3.

application of rules and guidelines' such as the Rules of Arbitration of the International Chamber of Commerce (ICC Rules), the SCC Rules and the IBA Guidelines on Conflicts of Interest in International Arbitration (IBA Guidelines). The Court finally observed that to find that the arbitrator in question lacked requisite impartiality under the Act would be supported by the IBA Guidelines and by previous determinations by the SCC. A legitimate conclusion is that the IBA Guidelines play a rather important role in assessing arbitrator impartiality under Swedish law.

8. Another case deserves particular mention, namely *Korsnäs AB v. AB Fortum Värme samägt med Stockholms stad*,[4] where the arbitral award was challenged on the ground that the chair of the arbitral tribunal lacked impartiality for having several times been appointed as arbitrator by one of the law firms representing a party to the arbitration. The Supreme Court, noting that these appointments were only about 10% of the chair's total number of appointments as arbitrator during the previous ten years, found that the several appointments by the relevant law firm had not caused lack of impartiality. The Court thus did not set aside the award.

9. Several other determinations on arbitrator impartiality have been made over the years. From case law the following two may be mentioned.

10. In *Ingela C. v. Kommunernas Försäkringsaktiebolag*,[5] a substitute member of the board of directors was held to have lacked requisite impartiality as arbitrator in an arbitration where the company was party; the arbitral award was set aside.

11. *Altinel v. Saudoimport* was a case where an arbitrator was considered biased for having previously been a director and shareholder of one of the parties to the arbitration. However, the Supreme Court held that the right to have the award set aside on that ground had been waived.[6]

12. The second point that may be noted is that in circumstances corresponding to (one of) the four cases, it cannot be argued that the arbitrator does not lack impartiality. It is of course possible for the parties to argue and to adduce evidence about whether such circumstances do exist, but if it is found (by the body determining the removal issue: see below) that they do exist, then the arbitrator does as a matter of law lack the requisite impartiality.

13. The third point that should be noted is that in practice it is often common ground between the parties that those facts exist that one party claims to amount to a lack of impartiality – for example that the challenged arbitrator has or has had a certain relationship to a certain law firm or group of companies – but the parties disagree about whether those facts amount in law to lack of impartiality.

---

4. *Korsnäs AB v. AB Fortum Värme samägt med Stockholms stad*, judgment by the Supreme Court made on 9 Jun. 2010 in case no T 156-09, NJA 2010 p. 317.
5. *Ingela C. v. Kommunernas Försäkringsaktiebolag*, judgment by the Supreme Court made on 17 Dec. 1981 in case no T 303-81, NJA 1981 p. 1205.
6. *Altinel v. Saudoimport*, judgment by Svea Court of Appeal made on 27 Nov. 1990 in case no T 1157-89, RH 1991:15.

B. Qualifications Agreed by Parties

14. Though this is not expressly dealt with in the Act, it is clear that the parties are free to agree that the arbitrators must have certain qualifications in addition to the general requirements in sections 7 and 8.[7] Swedish arbitration agreements sometime provide that the chair of a three-member arbitral tribunal must be an acting or former judge. Acting Swedish judges are not forbidden to serve as arbitrators and some regularly do so, but judges usually do not accept party appointment.[8]

15. Some advantages may well attach to agreeing that the arbitrators should have certain qualifications. A dispute may be arbitrated more quickly and more competently if the arbitrators are experienced in the industry or trade concerned. For example, arbitration clauses in insurance contracts may require arbitrators to have a certain number of years of particular experience in the insurance industry. Language skills are other examples of qualifications that may be required of arbitrators. However, such requirements in arbitration clauses may also have disadvantages. Two main disadvantages deserve to be mentioned. The first is that the qualification can be such that it may not be easy to determine whether a particular individual is qualified. For instance, a requirement that an arbitrator should have '15 years of experience as a senior executive in the insurance business', may present difficulties both as to 'senior executive' and to 'insurance business'. Requirements referring to such items as university degrees or authorizations (past or present) are much more easily determined. The second disadvantage is that the issues in the arbitration may not, or at least not mainly, be about the subject matter of the contract; an eminent construction lawyer may be in the position as arbitrator of having to decide fine points of private international law.

C. SCC Arbitration

16. Article 14(1) states the familiar and fundamental requirement that every arbitrator 'must be impartial and independent'. No other requirement is expressly set out. The Act's requirements in section 7 (stating in effect the same thing as Article 14(1)) and section 8 also apply in SCC arbitration.

7. See, for example, Govt. bill 1998/99:35 p. 217, where it is said that s. 7 'only states minimum requirements and does not prevent the parties from demanding additional requirements of the arbitrators.'
8. Judges may thus be expected to accept appointments by parties jointly, by party-appointed arbitrators and by arbitral institutions.

17. The SCC has a number of times made determinations on arbitrator impartiality where the arbitrator has been challenged for alleged lack of impartiality.[9] The following are a few examples.[10]

18. The SCC removed a challenged arbitrator for lack of impartiality in the following situations. The law firm of the chair of the arbitral tribunal, but not the chair in person, had been counsel to one of the parties.[11] The arbitrator had been appointed eight times in two years by the same law firm.[12]

19. The SCC did not remove an arbitrator for lack of impartiality in the following situations. The arbitrator was a former partner in the law firm now representing one of the parties.[13] The arbitrator worked for a company that had several times worked for one of the parties.[14] The arbitrator was the chief judge of the Court of First Instance in the city where one of the parties had its registered office.[15] The arbitrator's cousin was a board member of the parent company of one of the parties.[16] The arbitrator had been a client of the law firm representing one of the parties.[17] The arbitrator had been an arbitrator in other arbitrations related to the arbitration in question.[18] The arbitrator had been counsel in an arbitration where the chair's spouse had been opposing counsel.[19]

20. In SCC arbitrations the parties are also free to agree that the arbitrators should have certain qualifications. According to Article 15(1) a party may challenge an arbitrator 'if he/she does not possess qualifications agreed by the parties'.

III. DISCLOSURE

A. General

21. Section 9 requires an individual who is approached for appointment as arbitrator to disclose all circumstances that under sections 7 and 8 might prevent that person from serving as arbitrator. Section 9 further requires an arbitrator to inform the parties and the other arbitrators as soon as all arbitrators are appointed and thereafter during

9. It has been suggested that SCC determinations may be stricter than corresponding determinations by the courts; Wallin, Skiljemannajäv grundat på flera uppdrag från samma part eller advokatbyrå, JT 2004/05, 449.
10. Overviews of SCC determinations have been made in the following articles available at the SCC website: Johansson, M., SAR 1999:2, 175; Öhrström, M., SAR 2002:1 35; Magnusson, A. & Larsson, H., SAR 2004:2, 47; Jung, H., SIAR 2008:1, 1; Lindström, N., published on the SCC website.
11. SCC case (0[illegible]/2005).
12. SCC case (1[illegible]/2004).
13. SCC case (0[illegible]/2006).
14. SCC case (0[illegible]/2006).
15. SCC case (6[illegible]/1999).
16. SCC case (8[illegible]/2000).
17. SCC case (7[illegible]/2003).
18. SCC case (1[illegible]/2003).
19. SCC case (0[illegible]/2010).

the arbitration as soon as the arbitrator becomes aware of a new circumstance of the same kind.[20]

22. The duty of disclosure under section 9 does not expressly cover circumstances other than those stated in sections 7 and 8. This means that the duty of disclosure under section 9 does not cover qualifications that the parties have agreed for the arbitrators or one of them, in addition to the requirements under those two sections.

23. Nevertheless, a duty of disclosure regarding qualifications that the parties have agreed may still exist, though not under section 9. Suppose that the arbitration agreement requires that the party-appointed arbitrators should be authorized public accountants (Sw. *auktoriserade revisorer*), but that one party appoints a person who is only an approved public accountant (Sw. *godkänd revisor*). This person would have a duty (assuming awareness of the qualification agreement between the parties) to disclose the fact that he or she is not an authorized public accountant, a duty in the sense that that individual may, for failing to disclose this fact, not be entitled to remuneration for serving as arbitrator or may even be liable in damages.

24. This duty of disclosure could also be explained in terms of contract, on the assumption that the relationship between the parties and the arbitrator is subject to a contractual analysis (this issue is briefly treated in part VI. F). An arbitrator's main duty is to administer justice between the parties, typically by rendering an arbitral award binding on them. An arbitrator who lacks a qualification agreed by the parties is unable to perform his or her main duty. Under ordinary contractual principles a party to a contract would of course have a duty to disclose their inability to perform.

25. The *travaux préparatoires* state that if it is doubtful whether a certain circumstance is disqualifying, the fact that the arbitrator has suppressed the circumstance, i.e., intentionally not disclosed it, may be the additional factor that causes the question to be answered in the affirmative.[21] In *Korsnäs*,[22] the Supreme Court said (at p. 329) that that statement seems to concern clearly borderline cases where the issue of disqualification is particularly difficult to assess, which the Court found the specific case not to be. Though the Supreme Court did not develop its view on situations that would be 'clearly borderline cases' or give any examples of such, it may be noted that the Court took the word 'suppressed' in the *travaux* at face value; it may be inferred that 'suppression' would therefore require the arbitrator's awareness of the relevant circumstance and of its potential for disqualification as well as the arbitrator's

20. The Act does not explicitly oblige an arbitrator to inform the parties of these circumstances concerning a fellow arbitrator. On this issue, see Heuman, L., *Arbitration Law of Sweden: Practice and Procedure* 232 (Juris Publg. 2003) and Schöldström, P., *The Arbitrator's Mandate* 325 (Jure Förlag AB 1998).
21. Govt. bill 1998/99:35 p. 219.
22. *Korsnäs AB v. AB Fortum Värme samägt med Stockholms stad*, judgment by the Supreme Court made on 9 Jun. 2010 in case no T 156-09, NJA 2010 p. 317. See n. 4.

deliberate decision not to disclose it precisely because of its potential for disqualification.[23]

B. SCC Arbitration

26. Arbitrators also have a duty of disclosure under Article 14(2)-(3) of the SCC Rules. This is a duty to disclose, before appointment and during the arbitration, any circumstances that may give rise to justifiable doubts as to the arbitrator's impartiality or independence. Article 14(2)-(3) also describes how disclosure should be made.

27. The SCC Rules do not expressly place a duty on the arbitrator to make disclosure regarding qualifications that the parties have agreed. Nevertheless, such a duty may also exist in SCC arbitration for the reasons discussed above. There is in fact a stronger case for the existence of that duty in SCC arbitrations than in ad hoc arbitrations under the Act since Article 14(1) provides that a party may challenge an arbitrator 'if he/she does not possess qualifications agreed by the parties'.

28. Arbitrators in SCC arbitrations must, under Article 14(2), submit to the SCC 'a signed statement of impartiality and independence disclosing any circumstances which may give rise to justifiable doubts as to that person's impartiality or independence.' The SCC sends the statement to the parties and the other arbitrators. The statement is invariably in a form that the SCC sends to the arbitrators for them to fill in, sign and return to the SCC. The form requires the arbitrator to confirm acceptance of appointment, of availability[24] and of impartiality and independence. The form has two alternatives for the latter. The first is an unqualified statement that the arbitrator is not aware of any circumstances giving rise to justifiable doubts as to the arbitrator's impartiality or independence. The second alternative is that the arbitrator confirms impartiality and independence, but also discloses certain circumstances that may give rise to justifiable doubts as to the arbitrator's impartiality or independence.

IV. REMOVAL OF ARBITRATOR

A. Introduction

29. The Act and the SCC Rules use several terms – such as discharge and release from appointment – for what in the following will be called 'removal' of the arbitrator. It is suggested that regardless of the term used, the legal consequence of removal is always

23. *Korsnäs AB v. AB Fortum Värme samägt med Stockholms stad*, decision by the Svea Court of Appeal made on 7 Dec. 2006 in case no T 5044-04; the Svea Court of Appeal has held that an omission by the arbitrator to disclose relevant circumstances did not in itself constitute lack of impartiality.

24. Confirmation of availability is a rather new feature in the form. The arbitrator is required to confirm that 'I can and will dispose the time necessary in order for the case to be settled in the most expeditious and practicable manner possible.' By ticking this box in the form, the arbitrator also confirms awareness of the duties to establish a timetable promptly and to make an award within the applicable time limit.

one and the same: taking away from the arbitrator the power to affect the legal position of the parties *inter se*.

B. Removal by Parties Jointly

30. Though this is not stated expressly in the Act, it is quite clear that the parties jointly can remove an arbitrator for any reason or indeed no reason at all[25] or, in other words, take away from the arbitrator the power to affect the legal position of the parties *inter se*.[26] Precisely because the parties jointly can remove an arbitrator, it must be the case that an agreement between the parties themselves to remove an arbitrator is sufficient in itself for the removal to occur, even if the arbitrator removed is informed of the removal only later.

31. Joint removal of an arbitrator by the parties may take the form of one party's challenge of the arbitrator, which is accepted or agreed by the other party.

C. Removal Otherwise

32. The Act expressly only deals with removal of an arbitrator for two reasons: lack of impartiality (section 10) and delay (section 17). Thus the Act does not expressly deal with removal of an arbitrator for lack either of general qualifications under section 7 or of additional qualifications agreed by the parties.

1. Removal for Lack of Impartiality

33. It follows from section 10(1) that the arbitral tribunal decides on a request that an arbitrator be removed for lack of impartiality under section 8, unless the parties have agreed that a third party should do so. This means the whole arbitral tribunal, including the challenged arbitrator.[27] A sole arbitrator would thus have to decide a request for his or her own removal.

34. Although several arguments could be advanced against this mechanism, and indeed were raised during the drafting of the Act,[28] it does not seem to have created difficulties in practice.

35. The Act does not expressly state to whom a request for removal should be addressed. Since section 10(1) provides that the 'challenge shall be adjudicated by the arbitrators', it may be inferred that the arbitral tribunal is the proper addressee of a challenge. However, to be on the safe side – and because the other party may agree to the challenge, which would constitute a joint removal – it is advisable to send the

25. See, for example, Govt. bill 1998/99:35 p. 100 and 222; Schöldström, P., *The Arbitrator's Mandate*, 146.
26. Schöldström, P., *The Arbitrator's Mandate*, 333.
27. Govt. bill 1998/99:35 p. 219.
28. Govt. bill 1998/99:35 p. 86–87.

request to the other party as well; it would seem that this is indeed the invariable practice.

36. The request should, as it is termed in section 10(1) 'be presented' within fifteen days. The words 'be presented' means that the request must have been received by the addressee, not merely issued by the requesting party, at the relevant moment in time.

37. Time starts to run on the day that the challenging party became aware both of the appointment of the arbitrator and of the existence of the circumstance alleged to bias the arbitrator (section 10(1)). Time stops running at midnight fifteen days later. Thus if time starts running on a Sunday, time is up at midnight Monday two weeks later.

38. If the challenge is successful, the arbitral tribunal's decision stands; it cannot be appealed (section 10(2)). Then it has been determined that the challenged arbitrator does not (any longer) have the power to affect the legal position of the parties *inter se*. The term used in section 8(2) is that the arbitrator is 'discharged' (the literal translation of the Swedish term is that the arbitrator is 'severed from his task'.)

39. If the challenge is not successful, then the arbitral tribunal's decision can be brought before the court (section 10(3)). This 'appeal' must take the form of an application to the relevant District Court, naming the counterparty in the arbitration as respondent, requesting that the arbitrator 'be removed from his post' as it is worded in (the English translation of) section 10(3). It should be noted that, as is expressly provided in section 10(3), the basis for such an application can be that the arbitral tribunal either has dismissed the challenge for having been made too late (i.e., made after fifteen days) or has denied it on substantive grounds, for example, that the circumstance alleged to constitute bias does not do so according to the arbitral tribunal.

40. An application to the District Court must be made within thirty days from and including the day when the applicant party received the arbitral tribunal's decision on the challenge (section 10(3)).

41. Section 10(3) expressly states that the arbitral tribunal may continue the arbitral proceedings while the District Court is handling the application. The tribunal should of course invite the parties to state their views on this matter before continuing or staying the arbitral proceedings.

42. According to section 44(3) of the Act, the District Court's decision to remove an arbitrator for lack of impartiality may not be appealed. By contrast, the Court's decision not to remove an arbitrator for lack of impartiality may be appealed under general rules (section 39 of the Court Assistance Act[29]).

2. *Removal for Delay*

43. Section 17 enables the District Court, on party application, to remove an arbitrator for delaying the arbitration and at the same time also appoint a replacement arbitrator.

29. (*Sw: Lag (1996:242) om domstolsärenden*).

The *travaux préparatoires* state that it is sufficient for removal that the arbitrator has delayed the arbitration, and that the applicant party would not be required to establish that the arbitrator has been negligent or deliberately obstructed the arbitration.[30] This means that the standard would be objective. The court would thus ask what a prudent arbitrator would have done in the relevant situation, on the basis of the material and arguments put forward by the parties, and then determine whether or not the arbitrator in question has or has not met that standard. In so doing the court may be expected to bear in mind that section 21 requires arbitrators to handle the dispute in a 'speedy manner'.

44. It seems that the courts have not yet had to decide an application under section 17. This does not necessarily indicate that the section is without practical importance. It is surely a disincentive for arbitrators to be slow.

3. *Removal for Lack of a General Qualification or One Agreed by Parties*

45. The Act does not expressly provide a mechanism for removal of an arbitrator who is alleged to lack either a general qualification under section 7 or a qualification agreed by the parties.

46. It may nevertheless be possible to 'remove' an arbitrator lacking such a qualification. The method could be as follows.[31] If a party or another 'appointor' has appointed an arbitrator lacking a general qualification under section 7 or a qualification agreed by the parties, typically in the arbitration agreement, then that appointment should not qualify as an appointment under the Act. If this is so, then the consequences of appointing that person are those stated in the Act for failure to appoint, to the extent the parties have not agreed otherwise as permitted by the Act. Among these further consequences is the jurisdiction of the District Court to appoint an arbitrator under section 14(3). If the respondent in that case (i.e., the party who the applicant claims has failed to appoint) alleges that the person does have the general or agreed qualification in question or argues that the consequence of a lack thereof does not in law amount to a failure to appoint, then the District Court will have to try these allegations as issues incidental to the main issue of appointment.

D. SCC Arbitration

47. The parties can also jointly remove an arbitrator where a third party has appointed the arbitrator.[32]

48. Since the SCC Rules do not provide otherwise, the parties may also jointly remove an arbitrator in SCC arbitrations. They may achieve this result if one party challenges

30. Govt. bill 1998/99:35 p. 96.
31. It has been argued that this method is not available; Heuman, L., *Arbitration Law of Sweden: Practice and Procedure*, 208.
32. Govt. bill 1998/99:35 p. 100 and 222.

the arbitrator and the other party agrees to the challenge; then the arbitrator must, as expressed in Article 15(4), 'resign'. Read literally, this means that the arbitrator continues to be an arbitrator until they resign. However, the better view would be that the arbitrator ceases to be an arbitrator (i.e., is deprived of the power as arbitrator to affect the legal position of the parties *inter se*) as soon as the SCC receives the agreement to the challenge so that no act of resignation by the arbitrator is required. Steps may however be required before the arbitrator is deprived of that power, namely that the SCC under Article 16(1)(i) accepts the resignation and then releases the arbitrator from their appointment.

49. As noted above, section 10(1) allows the parties to agree that a third party should decide on a request that an arbitrator be removed for lack of impartiality under section 8. In section 11 it is further stated that the parties may agree that an arbitral institution should finally decide such a request. In SCC arbitration such an agreement has been made through the medium of the SCC Rules, Article 15 (Challenge to arbitrators) and Article 16 (Release from appointment). Article 15(4) expressly states that the SCC makes the 'final decision' on the challenge.

50. In essence, Articles 15 and 16 provide that a challenge for lack of impartiality and independence as well as lack of qualifications agreed by the parties should be made in writing to the SCC within fifteen days (from when the circumstances giving rise to the challenge became known to the challenging party) and that the SCC must release an arbitrator from appointment if the challenge is sustained.

51. Section 17 allows the parties to agree that an arbitral institution should finally decide a request for removal of an arbitrator for delay. According to Article 16(1) the SCC must release an arbitrator from appointment where the arbitrator is prevented from adequately fulfilling their functions; this wording covers delay. Under Article 16(2) the SCC must also give the parties and the arbitrators an opportunity to submit comments before taking a decision.

52. In contrast to Article 15(4), it is not expressly stated in Article 16 that a decision by the SCC to 'release an arbitrator from appointment' under Article 16, notably for delay, is to be 'final'. It is therefore arguable that the parties have not agreed, within the meaning of section 17, that the SCC should finally decide a request for removal of an arbitrator for delay.[33] If this is so, parties may file an application to the District Court under section 17, as if the SCC's decision not to grant the request for removal for delay had not been taken.

53. As opposed to the Act, the SCC Rules do provide a mechanism for the removal during the arbitration of an appointed arbitrator who lacks qualifications agreed by the parties. Article 15(1) states that a party may challenge an arbitrator 'if he/she does not possess qualifications agreed by the parties'. This decision is however not final in the sense of section 11 of the Act.

33. See also Madsen, F., *Skiljeförfarande i Sverige* (2d ed., 2009), 136-137.

V. APPOINTMENT OF ARBITRATOR

A. Introduction

54. The appointment of an arbitrator is an act that gives a person – alone as a sole arbitrator or together with other persons appointed as arbitrators – power to affect the legal position of the parties *inter se*, in practice to render an arbitral award binding on them.

55. It is quite clear that the decisive element of each party's appointment is (the issue of) a notice by the appointing party to the other party of the name of the person that is appointed.[34] 'Appointment' within the meaning of the Act is thus one party's message to the other that a certain individual is appointed as arbitrator. The idea underlying the provision in section 14(2) of the Act is that, once such notice has been given, the notifying party 'may not revoke the appointment without the consent of the other party'. This means that an appointment in theory does not require that the appointee has agreed to the appointment, though in practice this is no doubt always so. It should be observed that it is the *issue* of the notice of appointment that counts, not the receipt of the notice by the other party. However, in most cases this may be expected to be of academic interest only, since the notice of appointment usually forms part of the request for arbitration as provided in section 19(2) and part of the answer to the request, respectively.

B. Number of Arbitrators and Manner of Appointment

56. The basic rule, stated in section 12(1), is that the parties may decide the number of arbitrators and the manner of their appointment. Section 12(2) then provides that if the parties have not agreed otherwise, sections 13–16 apply. Section 12(3) is dealt with below.

57. The fallback provision in section 13 is that there should be three arbitrators and that each party should appoint one arbitrator and then those two so appointed will appoint the third arbitrator. This is probably also the most common situation in practice.

58. For situations where each party is to appoint one arbitrator, section 14(1) provides, in practical terms, the following. When the respondent has received a request for arbitration that meets the requirements for a request under section 19, then the respondent must appoint an arbitrator within thirty days from receipt of that request, the appointment to be made by written notice to the claimant. If the respondent does not do so, the District Court will appoint an arbitrator on the claimant's application (section 14(3)).

34. For a detailed and comparative analysis of the issue of appointment, see Schöldström, P., *The Arbitrator's Mandate*, 221-247.

59. Where an arbitrator is not appointed in time by party-appointed arbitrators, by a third party or by the parties jointly, the District Court will on application appoint the arbitrator (section 15).

60. Replacement appointment is dealt with in section 16. The main rule is that where an arbitrator resigns or is removed, the District Court will on application appoint a new arbitrator. However, an exception exists for situations where the circumstances preventing the resigned or removed arbitrator from serving arose after the appointment. In these situations the original 'appointor' should make the replacement appointment. The idea behind the main rule is to prevent – typically – the respondent from disrupting the arbitration by appointing an arbitrator who will not serve.[35] Disruptive motives are thought not to be in play where the arbitrator cannot serve because of events happening after appointment, which explains the exception.[36]

61. Section 12(3) gives the District Court general jurisdiction also to appoint arbitrators in other situations than those covered by sections 14–17, on two cumulative conditions: that the parties have agreed to give the Court this jurisdiction and that one of them applies for the appointment.

62. One matter of some practical importance must finally be mentioned. Section 18 provides that, where the District Court is to appoint an arbitrator under section 12(3) or sections 14–17, the Court may dismiss the request for appointment for lack of legal foundation only if the lack is manifest. The concrete result intended by the provision is the following.[37] The Court should decline to appoint an arbitrator only where the respondent has managed to make it abundantly clear that the arbitration agreement asserted by the applicant as the basis for the application for appointment is either invalid or inapplicable. This intention reflects the legislator's ambition to get arbitrations going by helping to establish the arbitral tribunal. Another provision reflecting the same ambition is section 44(3), according to which the Court's decision *to appoint* an arbitrator may not be appealed; but the Court's decision *not to appoint* an arbitrator may be appealed under general rules (section 39 of the Court Assistance Act).

C. SCC Arbitration

63. The basic rule is that the parties may agree on the number of arbitrators (Article 12). The Article goes on to provide, in effect, that where the parties have not so agreed, the SCC decides whether there will be three arbitrators or a sole arbitrator. In reaching its decision the SCC will take into account such factors as the complexity of the case and the amount in dispute.

64. Details about how arbitrators are to be appointed in different situations, if the parties have not agreed otherwise, are set out in Article 13. Article 13(3) may be said

35. Govt. bill 1998/99:35 p. 94–95.
36. This is implied in the part of the *travaux préparatoires* dealing with this matter; Govt. bill 1998/99:35 p. 94–95.
37. Govt. bill 1998/99:35 p. 96–97.

to cater for the typical situation with three arbitrators; each party is to appoint one arbitrator and – in contrast to the mechanism in the Act where those two arbitrators are to appoint the third arbitrator – the SCC is to appoint the chair of the arbitral tribunal.

65. Besides, in SCC arbitration it should be the case that the appointee's consent to appointment is not in theory necessary for an appointment to have been made, though consent at least from the arbitrator appointed by the SCC will in practice always have been obtained by the SCC. Two things may be noted. First, that Article 2(vi) requires a Request for Arbitration to include the name of the arbitrator appointed by the Claimant. Second, that Article 5(1)(v) requires an Answer to include the name of the arbitrator appointed by the Respondent.

66. A party's appointment should – in keeping with the fallback rule in section 14(2), from which there is no deviation in the SCC Rules – be irrevocable once the SCC has received the party's notice of appointment, whether as a part of the Request for Arbitration or the Answer or as a separate communication to the SCC.

D. Multi-party Situations

67. The Act caters expressly only for classic two-party arbitration. Some of the Act's provisions may nevertheless be possible to apply to other kinds of arbitrations, but it seems difficult to state with any certainty precisely how the courts would apply these provisions in different multi-party settings. This territory is largely uncharted in Swedish arbitration law. The following is restricted to a few remarks on the issue of appointment of arbitrators in multi-party situations.

68. One provision in the Act in particular has been drafted with multi-party situations in mind, namely section 12(3).[38] This gives the District Court general jurisdiction also to appoint arbitrators in situations other than those covered by sections 14–17, provided that the parties have so agreed and that one of them applies to the District Court for appointment under that section. The Court would thus be able to appoint, for example, a sole arbitrator or a whole three-person arbitral tribunal if the arbitration clause in a multi-party contract provides that the Court should do so.

69. That appointment would satisfy requirements that follow from the French *Dutco* decision.[39] This was an ICC arbitration where one member of a consortium had made claims in an ICC arbitration against two other members. The ICC Rules then in force required the two respondents jointly to appoint an arbitrator. When they did not do so the ICC Court appointed an arbitrator in their stead, and an arbitral award was subsequently rendered. The French Cour de Cassation held that it violated the principle of equality of the parties that the claimant had had its choice of arbitrator, but the respondents not. The Court therefore set aside the arbitral award.

38. Govt. bill 1998/99:35 p. 221.
39. *Siemens AG and BKMI Industrieanlagen GmbH v. Dutco Construction Company Pvt.*, judgment by the Cour de Cassation, Première chambre civile, made on 7 Jan. 1992, 1992 Rev. Arb. 470.

70. Some Swedish cases may be said to be broadly in line with the concept of equality of the parties as laid down in the *Dutco* decision. The main issue in these cases was whether the arbitration clause was a bar to litigation in court in view of how the arbitrators were to be appointed under the clause. One is *Rita Urhelyi v. Arbetsmarknadens Försäkringsaktiebolag*,[40] where an arbitration clause was held not to be a bar to litigation in court because it entitled one of the parties to appoint the majority of the arbitrators. Another case is *Christer J.* et al. *v. Svenska kommunalarbetareförbundet*,[41] where the arbitration clause provided for five arbitrators. The Supreme Court held that the arbitration clause did not bar litigation in court because the fifth arbitrator might come to be appointed by a body that had already asserted its view on the fundamental issue in dispute between the parties. Yet another case is *Bostadsrättsföreningen Mossviolen 1 v. Folkhem Försäljnings AB*.[42] The Supreme Court held that the reality of the situation was that the claimant had contracted out of its right to appoint an arbitrator and, to put it bluntly, had done so while effectively being controlled by the respondent. The Supreme Court held that that arbitration clause did not bar litigation in court.[43]

71. The SCC Rules have a provision designed for appointment of arbitrators in multi-party situations.[44] This is Article 13(4), which is to the effect that the SCC will appoint the whole arbitral tribunal where there are multiple claimants or respondents and either side fails jointly to appoint an arbitrator.

VI. PARTICULAR ISSUES

A. Rights and Duties of Arbitrator

72. The following deals with the arbitrator's rights and duties as a supplier of services to the parties. A complete coverage of this area of the law is not intended; the ambition is to deal with some matters that are or may be important in practice.[45]

---

40. *Rita Urhelyi v. Arbetsmarkandens Försäkringsaktiebolag*, decision by the Supreme Court made on 26 Jun. 1987 in case no Ö1790-84, NJA 1974 p. 573. See also Govt. bill 1998/99:35 p. 90 where it is stated that the Act is not intended to change the holding in the case.
41. *Christer J.* et al. *v. Svenska Kommunalarbetarförbundet*, decision by the Supreme Court made on 29 Dec. 1982 in case no Ö 1028/81, NJA 1982 p. 853.
42. *Bostadsrättsföreningen Mossviolen 1 v. Folkhem Försäljnings AB*, decision by the Supreme Court made on 6 Mar. 1992 in case no Ö 1653-89, NJA 1992 p. 143.
43. However, the respondent succeeded in 'saving' the arbitration clause as a bar to litigation by making a commitment before the Court to the effect that the claimant was free and unrestricted in its appointment of arbitrator. But for this commitment the Court would have found that the arbitration clause did not bar litigation in court.
44. Magnusson, A., Shaughnessy, P., *The 2007 Arbitration Rules of the Arbitration Institute of the Stockholm Chamber of Commerce*, 3 Stockholm Intl. Arbitration Rev. (2006).
45. For more complete coverage on a comparative basis, see Schöldström, P., *The Arbitrator's Mandate*, 3[illegible]1-372.

1. *Rights of Arbitrator: Remuneration*

73. The starting point is that the arbitrator and both parties (all parties in a multi-party situation) may agree the remuneration of the arbitrator. Failing agreement, the rule is that the parties are jointly and severally liable to the arbitrator for reasonable compensation for work and expenses (section 37). The rule has one exception, which is designed for the case where the respondent has successfully alleged that the arbitration agreement invoked by the claimant does not give the arbitral tribunal jurisdiction.[46] The exception is embodied in section 37(1) second sentence, according to which the respondent is only liable in exceptional circumstances to remunerate the arbitrators where the arbitral tribunal dismisses a claim for lack of jurisdiction. In those cases the arbitrator thus has a claim only on the claimant.

74. Section 39(1) provides that an agreement regarding compensation to the arbitrators that is not entered into with the parties jointly is void, the reason of course being that a fee agreement between the arbitrator and only one of the parties would not happily accord with the arbitrator's position effectively as a judge between the parties, or in other words would intrude on the arbitrator's impartiality and independence.

a. Level

75. As noted above the arbitrator is entitled to reasonable remuneration for work and expenses. In the last resort the court will determine the reasonableness of an arbitrator's remuneration, but these cases are very rare. It follows from the Supreme Court's decision in the *NEMU* case that reasonableness is to be understood as the market value of the services rendered as arbitrator.[47] In that case the Supreme Court held that the character (difficulty) and amount of work (time) put in are fundamental in assessing reasonableness. The Supreme Court also put some weight on the fact that the arbitrators in the case were not only highly qualified in general, but also specially qualified in the subject matter of the arbitrated dispute.[48]

76. In practice, the chair of the arbitral tribunal is usually considered to be entitled to more remuneration than the party-appointed arbitrators.[49] This is to reflect that the chair usually puts in more work to manage the proceedings and draft the award.

---

46. Govt. bill 1998/99:35 p. 163. See also Schöldström, P., *The Arbitrator's Mandate*, 363 with further references.
47. *NEMU Mitt i Sverige AB v. Skanska Mitt AB*, judgment by the Supreme Court made on 22 Oct. 1998 in case no T 105-98, NJA 1998 p. 574.
48. See Schöldström, P., *Skiljemäns arvoden – NJA 1998 s. 574*, JT 1998/99, 692. and Edlund, L., *Om ersättning till skiljemän*, JT 1998/99, 1036.
49. Compare the Appendix to the SCC Rules, according to which co-arbitrators are entitled to 60% of the chair's remuneration.

b. *Maturity*

77. Failing agreement, it must be the case that the arbitrator's remuneration falls due to be paid when the award is rendered, because by so doing the arbitrators complete their performance. However, the Act contains no explicit provision to that effect, nor is there any case law. The lack of an explicit provision does not seem to have caused practical problems.

c. *Advance*

78. The Act recognizes the long established practice of arbitrators in Sweden to request and receive an advance on their remuneration as security for their forthcoming claims. Section 38(1) provides that the arbitrators may request security for their compensation (except if the parties have agreed otherwise in, as stated in section 39(1), a 'manner that is binding on the arbitrators').

79. Section 38(2) makes a distinction between remuneration for work and compensation for expenses when it comes to drawing on the advance: arbitrators may draw on the advance during the arbitration to recover compensation for expenses, but not to cover remuneration for work. They may draw on the advance to cover remuneration for work only when their final award, with determination of their remuneration, has become enforceable, i.e., after three months. However, it is quite common for the arbitrators to request and receive permission from the parties to draw on the advance to cover remuneration for work as soon as the award is rendered.

d. *Fixing*

80. Section 37(2) provides that in their final award the arbitrators may order the parties to pay them compensation and that the compensation will be stated separately for each arbitrator. If no party brings an action in court against the arbitrators concerning that part of the award within three months (under section 41(1)), then that part of the award may be executed against the parties or one of them on the application of the arbitrators. The practical effect is thus that, if no such action is brought, the 'compensation part' of the dispositive part of the arbitral award is transformed from an invoice to the parties to an order that may be executed against the parties or one of them by the enforcement authorities on the application of the arbitrators.[50] There seem to be no examples of such applications. What usually happens is that the arbitrators satisfy their claims on the parties by drawing on the advance that the parties have paid.

50. For an account of the background of this mechanism, see Schöldström, P., *The Arbitrator's Mandate*, 149–150.

2. *Enforcing Rights of Arbitrator*

a. *Seeking Payment*

81. It is beyond doubt that an arbitrator can bring an action in court against the parties, or one of them, to recover payment for serving as arbitrator.[51] However, it appears that such an action has not been brought for many decades, the explanation being, once again, that arbitrators usually satisfy their claims for remuneration out of the advance. Arbitrators who use the possibility in section 37(2) to order the parties in the award to pay compensation do not need to bring an action in court because that order is equivalent to a court judgment that may be executed against the parties or one of them.

b. *Withholding Performance*

82. Section 40 provides that arbitrators may not withhold the award pending payment of compensation. The practical importance of this provision is virtually none, since it only embraces completed awards. Arbitrators would not withhold the award within the meaning of this section if the only thing left to do was for them to sign the award. Nor does this section prevent arbitrators from requesting (additional) *security* for compensation.[52]

c. *Termination*

83. Arbitrators can of course terminate their appointment (resign), in the sense that they declare that they will not perform their main duty to administer justice between the parties.

d. *Damages*

84. It is not clear whether the parties may be liable in damages to the arbitrator. On the assumption that ordinary contractual principles apply, these would suggest that, for example, the parties would be liable in damages if the arbitrator has at their request set aside time for a hearing that the arbitrator cannot fill with other remunerative work because the parties settle just before the hearing. Though it is not unusual that parties settle just before the hearing, such liability claims by arbitrators do not seem ever to have been made; one reason is probably that most arbitrators have little difficulty filling the time not needed for the hearing with other remunerative work. Arbitrations that are settled just before the hearing will usually lead to discussions between the arbitrators and the parties about adequate remuneration to the former. The end result

51. See, for example, Schöldström, P., *The Arbitrator's Mandate*, 156.
52. The *travaux préparatoires* hint at this possibility; SOU 1994:81 p. 300. See also Schöldström, P., *The Arbitrator's Mandate*, 364–365.

can be that the remuneration eventually agreed includes an element of compensation for time that cannot be filled with remunerative work.

3. *Duties of Arbitrator*

a. *Main Duty*

85. The arbitrator's main duty is to administer justice between the parties. Section 21 starts by providing that the 'arbitrators shall handle the dispute in an impartial, practical, and speedy manner'. The section goes on to provide that the arbitrators must also 'act in accordance with the decisions of the parties insofar as there is no impediment to so doing'.

86. This provision thus states the service that the arbitrator is to supply to the parties, although it does not do so in detail.

b. *Other Duties*

87. The following three specific duties may be mentioned briefly.

88. The arbitrator has a duty of disclosure under section 9 as described above.

89. Under section 31 arbitrators have a duty to make their award in writing and sign it.

90. If the arbitrators, as is most often the case, have requested and received an advance on their remuneration from the parties or one of them, the arbitrators have a duty to render account for the advance and, of course, pay back any balance.

4. *Enforcing Duties of Arbitrator*

91. Specific performance is not available to enforce the arbitrator's main duty to administer justice between the parties.[53]

92. However, specific performance should be available, for example, for return of documentary evidence submitted to the arbitral tribunal in the original.

93. Liability in damages of the arbitrators to the parties is a matter that has been discussed,[54] but not produced any case law. A non-Swedish case deserves brief mention in this context. This is from the Supreme Court of Finland.[55] The Court found that the chair of an arbitral tribunal had failed to disclose circumstances that were likely to give rise to justifiable doubts as to his impartiality and independence, as the Finnish Arbitration Act also obliges arbitrators to do. The arbitral award in question

53. See Schöldström, P., *The Arbitrator's Mandate*, 332 with further references.
54. See Schöldström, P., *The Arbitrator's Mandate*, 158 and 331-343.
55. Judgment by the Supreme Court of Finland made on 31 Jan. 2005, KKO:2005:14.

had been set aside because the chair was considered not impartial due to those circumstances. The Supreme Court held that the failure to disclose was negligent and that the chair was liable, in contract, for costs wasted in the arbitration. In later proceedings at first instance the damages to be paid by the chair were assessed at about eighty thousand euro. It is quite possible that Swedish courts would have come to the same conclusion under Swedish law.[56]

a. Reduction of Remuneration

94. Reduction of remuneration is available in the sense that determining the reasonableness of an arbitrator's remuneration may be influenced by poor performance by the arbitrator.

5. SCC Arbitration

a. Remuneration of Arbitrator

95. The remuneration due to the arbitrator basically depends on the amount in dispute in accordance with a table set out in an Appendix to the SCC Rules.[57] The Appendix states that in a three-member arbitral tribunal the co-arbitrators will receive 60% of the fee of the chair. The Appendix also states that deviations from fees according to the table may be decided by the SCC in exceptional circumstances. The SCC determines remuneration as a part of the costs of the arbitration (Article 43, which refers to the Appendix). That determination may, as held in *Soyak*,[58] be appealed in the sense that the parties (or one of them) in an action against the arbitrator for reduction of remuneration, are entitled to have the fee assessed in substance. The SCC's determination may however be expected to stand up in court unless the SCC has quite clearly miscalculated the remuneration or some other mistake has clearly occurred in the SCC's determination.[59]

---

56. If arbitrators are liable in damages under Swedish law, one old provision may protect them. This is ch. 18 s. 9 of the Book of Commerce, which provides that if a person has supplied certain services to a principal and rendered an account for them, then a liability claim by the principal on the service supplier must be brought – in the form of an action in a court of law –within one year; otherwise the claim is lost. It is strongly arguable that an arbitrator would qualify as a service supplier within the meaning of this provision. In addition, an arbitrator would typically render an account within the meaning of the provision by rendering an arbitral award that includes a payment order under s. 37(2) together with a covering letter that renders an account for advances held by the arbitrators. See however Lindskog, 389.
57. Appendix III, Schedule of Costs.
58. *Soyak International Construction & Investment Inc. v. Werner Melis, Kaj Hobér and Steffen Kraus*, decision by the Supreme Court made on 3 Dec. 2008 in case no Ö 4227-06, NJA 2008 p. 1118.
59. Case report and observations by Schöldstrom, P. and Öhrström, M. in SIAR 2008:3, 226.

b. *Exclusion of Liability*

96. Article 48 provides that neither 'the SCC nor the arbitrator(s) are liable to any party for any act or omission in connection with the arbitration unless such act or omission constitutes wilful misconduct or gross negligence.' This exclusion clause may be expected to take effect according to its explicit wording, i.e., as a regular contractual exclusion clause, even if the contractual matrix that a SCC arbitration produces – between the arbitrators, the parties and the SCC – has not been worked out in detail.[60]

B. Arbitrator as Witness in Other Proceedings and as Subject of Discovery

97. Under Swedish law the duty to testify under oath in a court of law – especially in civil proceedings such as proceedings to set aside an arbitral award – is extensive by international standards. The main rule is laid down in Chapter 36 section 1(1) of the Code of Judicial Procedure,[61] which flatly states that 'anyone who is not a party to the case may be heard as a witness'. There are a few narrow exceptions to the main rule. None of them apply to arbitrators as such.[62] The practical effect is that arbitrators may be called upon to testify in cases for setting aside arbitral awards that they have rendered. This is not only of academic interest; it happens now and then that arbitrators are summoned to court to testify and that they do so.[63]

98. A related issue is whether arbitrators may be subjects of discovery, i.e., be ordered by the court to hand over their material in the arbitration concerned. The Court of Appeal case *Soyak International Construction & Investment Inc. v. Hochtief AG*[64] was about setting aside an arbitral award. The claimant requested the Court to order the three arbitrators to hand over all their material in the arbitration, such as notes, memoranda, minutes from their deliberations and drafts of the award. The claimant's stated purpose was to prove with this material that in the arbitration the arbitrators had not taken proper account of the claimant's case. The Court denied the request for reasons that may be described as follows: the order would not happily accord with fundamental notions of the proper functioning of judicial deliberations, which require integrity and secrecy. In other words, the Court recognized that arbitrators must be

60. For discussion see Schöldström, P., *Contractual Relations in Institutional Arbitration*, in *Between East and West: Essays in Honour of Ulf Franke* 451 (Hobér, K. et al. eds., JurisNet 2010).
61. (*Sw: Rättegångsbalk (1942:740)*).
62. Arbitrators who are members of the bar (Sw. *advokater*) may be able to invoke the exception regarding attorney-client privilege in ch. 36 s. 5(1) of the Code of Judicial Procedure.
63. One example is *Partrederiet för M/S Red Sea v. Götaverken Sölvesborg AB*, decision by the Supreme Court made on 13 Jul. 1990 in case no T 80-89, NJA 1990 p. 419, where the chair of the three-member arbitral tribunal testified about whether one of the parties in the arbitration had withdrawn its claim in the arbitration. Another example is *Korsnäs AB v. AB Fortum Värme samägt med Stockholms stad*, judgment by the Supreme Court made on 9 Jun. 2010 in case no T 156-09, NJA 2010 p. 317. This was a case for setting aside an arbitral award for lack of arbitrator impartiality where the arbitrator concerned testified; the award was not set aside.
64. *Soyak International Construction & Investment Inc. v. Hochtief AG*, decision by Svea Court of Appeal made on 13 Jan. 2006 in case no T 6398-03, RH 2007:50.

able to deliberate freely, as do judges, without fear of having the deliberations exposed afterwards.

C. Secretary to Arbitral Tribunal

1. General

99. Secretaries to arbitral tribunals have for many decades been a familiar feature in Swedish arbitration. Many well-known Swedish arbitrators have started out as secretaries to arbitral tribunals. The almost invariable practice has been for the tribunal to engage a secretary only after having received the parties' permission to do so. Today this is the invariable practice.

100. One argument that may be raised against secretaries is that they add to the cost of the arbitration. The counter-argument is that that is not necessarily so since the secretary does things that the arbitrators or one of them, notably the chair, would otherwise have to do. An unreported first instance case supports the counter-argument.[65] This was a case for reduction of the remuneration of the chair of the arbitral tribunal, who among his expenses had included remuneration to the secretary (appointed with the parties' approval). The secretary's remuneration was slightly lower than the chair's and slightly higher than the remuneration to the other two arbitrators. The action was not successful. The Court held that the secretary had carried out work that otherwise would have had to be carried out by the arbitrators, that the 'delegation of work that had taken place had been expedient and rational from an economic point of view' and that 'this division of labour had resulted in a substantial saving of costs'.

2. SCC Arbitration

101. The SCC's 'Arbitrator's Guidelines' state that the SCC must be informed by the arbitrators if they wish to appoint a secretary, that the SCC then asks the parties if they agree and that a secretary may not be appointed if any party disagrees. The Guidelines also state that the fee of the secretary shall be borne by the Arbitral Tribunal and additional expenses that the secretary has had shall be borne by the parties.[66]

65. *Intermatic Aktiebolag v. R. Håkansson*, judgment by the Halmstad District Court made on 5 Dec. 1983 in case no T 271/83 (unreported), Nr DT 504.
66. The SCC's 'Arbitrator's Guidelines' are available at http://www.sccinstitute.se/filearchive/3/33332/Guidelines%202010_March.pdf.

CHAPTER 7
Applicable Law

Christer Danielsson

I. APPLICABLE LAW

1. When discussing applicable law in arbitral proceedings, we are faced with at least three different questions: (i) Which law will apply to the arbitral proceedings as such? (ii) Which substantive law will apply to the merits of the case? and (iii) Which law will apply to the arbitration agreement between the parties? These questions will be dealt with separately below, along with the issue whether the *jura novit curia* principle is applicable in arbitration proceedings taking place in Sweden.

A. *Lex Arbitri*

2. The law governing the arbitral proceedings as such, or the *lex arbitri*, has been described as 'a body of rules which sets a standard external to the arbitration agreement, and the wishes of the parties, for the conduct of the arbitration'.[1] No arbitration takes place in a legal void, and the *lex arbitri* is the underlying law governing the existence and the conduct of the arbitral proceedings as such.

3. Although the scope of the *lex arbitri* in different jurisdictions may vary, it is typically expected to deal with things that include the following:

- whether a dispute is arbitrable or not capable of being referred to arbitration;
- equal treatment of the parties;
- interim measures of protection, and court assistance if required;
- rules on the finality and challenge of an award.

1. See Blackaby et al., *Redfern and Hunter, On International Arbitration* 175 (5th ed., Oxford U. Press 2009).

4. The prevailing view in theory and practice internationally is that the law of the place, or the seat, of arbitration will govern the proceedings, and Sweden is no exception. Section 46 of the Swedish Arbitration Act (Sw: *Lag (1999:116) om skiljeförfarande*) (the Act) states:

> This Act shall apply to arbitral proceedings which take place in Sweden notwithstanding that the dispute has an international connection.

5. This means that Swedish arbitration law, primarily the Act and case law relevant to it, will be applicable to all arbitral proceedings seated in Sweden, whether administered by the SCC or another institution, or conducted ad hoc.[2] This is true regardless of whether arbitration takes place in Sweden as a result of a choice by the parties, or as determined by the arbitral tribunal pursuant to section 22 of the Act or the SCC Board under section 20 of the Rules of Arbitration of the Arbitration Institute of the Stockholm Chamber of Commerce (SCC Rules). Section 46 of the Act means that the parties cannot agree in general that arbitral proceedings in Sweden must follow for example German, Spanish, or Swiss arbitration law. Such an agreement would violate the Act and should not be given effect by the arbitrators.[3]

6. The Act is, however, largely non-mandatory in nature (see below) and gives parties autonomy and freedom to agree on other solutions. For example, if they so wish they may agree that institutional frameworks will apply such as the SCC Rules or the IBA Rules on the Taking of Evidence in International Commercial Arbitration (IBA Rules). This has been expressed as follows in the Government bill which introduced the Act:

> It follows from [section 46] that the Act shall always apply to arbitral proceedings taking place in Sweden. This means that parties cannot generally agree that an arbitration taking place in Sweden shall follow foreign law as far as the proceedings as such are concerned. The parties are not, however, precluded from agreeing on other rules with respect to issues where the Act is not mandatory, which may of course be based on foreign law.[4]

7. Which provisions of the Act, then, are non-mandatory and may be replaced with rules from foreign jurisdictions? Some of them expressly have this character. For example, sections 13–16 regarding appointment and replacement of arbitrators are stated to apply only where the parties have not agreed otherwise. Another example is section 42 concerning the tribunal's power to rule on liability for costs. Many provisions, however, have no such label as to their mandatory or non-mandatory character. The general view seems to be that, as a starting point, it is possible for the

2. The place or seat of arbitration is a technical term which has little or nothing to do with the actual geographical location of hearings or other meetings in the proceedings, see Sec 20 of the SCC Rules, Govt. bill 1998/99:35 p 225; cf. Lindskog, Skiljeförfarande, 1080 et seq.
3. It cannot be ruled out that a foreign court – in a country whose arbitration law has been chosen by the parties as applicable to the proceedings – may take a different view, maintaining that the parties have an unlimited right to agree on applicable arbitration law. This could lead to procedural complications, although in practice agreements to apply foreign arbitration law to proceedings taking place in Sweden are very rare, Heuman, *Arbitration Law of Sweden: Practice and Procedure* 669 (Juris Publg. Inc. 2003).
4. Govt. bill 1998/99:35 p. 244.

parties to derogate from such provisions, but that the scope of party freedom must be determined taking into account several circumstances, such as the nature of the provision in question, the derogation sought by the parties and the point in time when the derogation is made.[5] A general conclusion as to the mandatory or non-mandatory character of a specific provision is therefore difficult to draw in the abstract.

8. The Act contains rules that give parties recourse to Swedish public courts in certain matters. These rules will form part of the *lex arbitri* and apply to all arbitrations taking place in Sweden. One such rule is the provision concerning the right to challenge a final award before a Swedish court (section 34 of the Act). Additionally, before a final award has been given, a party has the right under section 2 of the Act to turn to a public court if they wish to challenge the validity of an arbitration agreement or the competence of the tribunal. The Swedish Supreme Court has established, in a case between an English entity and the Russian Federation, that non-Swedish parties have this right if the proceedings take place in Sweden, even if the dispute has no other connection to Sweden. Sweden as the place of arbitration, as agreed by the parties, was deemed the sole relevant factor when determining that the Swedish court had jurisdiction under section 2 of the Act.[6]

B. Law Applicable to the Merits of the Case

9. Commercial contracts sometimes set out the rights and obligations of the parties in such detail that no relevant law will have to be applied by the arbitrators when they build their award. The outcome of the dispute will turn on the facts and evidence alone. Normally, however, at least some legal rules will have to be applied. Laws in different nations of course differ and it is therefore essential to know what law applies to the

5. *Ibid.*, p. 44. Madsen, *Commercial Arbitration in Sweden* 344 (3d ed., Oxford U. Press 2006), referring to a statement by the Swedish Law Council, says that it is 'unclear' which provisions of the Act are mandatory; according to the Council on Legislation, a provision can be tentatively assumed to be mandatory unless otherwise stated. As pointed out by Lindskog (Skiljeförfarande, 75 et seq.) and Heuman (Heuman, *Arbitration Law of Sweden*, 255 n. 26), the view of the Law Council has not been expressly accepted by the Government; cf. Hobér, *International Commercial Arbitration in Sweden* 36 (Oxford U. Press 2011), who asserts that 'most of the provisions' of the Act are non-mandatory, giving parties ample room to agree on other rules.

6. *RosInvestCo UK Ltd v. The Russian Federation*, decision by the Supreme Court made on 12 Nov. 2010 in case no Ö 2301-09, NJA 2010 p. 508. The Supreme Court judgment means that the much criticised ruling by the Svea Court of Appeal in the Titan case (*Titan Corporation v. Alcatel CIT SA*, decision by the Svea Court of Appeal made on 28 Feb. 2008 in case no T 1038-05, RH 2005:1) is no longer of any relevance; cf. Patricia Shaugnessy in SIAR 2005:2, 264 et seq., Christer Söderlund, *ibid.*, 275 et seq., and Hans Bagner in Festskrift till Lars Heuman, 15 et seq. In *Titan*, the Svea Court of Appeal declined jurisdiction over a challenge motion on the basis that the dispute did not have sufficient connection to Sweden, despite the parties having named Stockholm as the place of arbitration and Stockholm being identified in the award as the place where the award was rendered. It has been argued that the principle laid down in NJA 2010 p. 508, i.e., that the place of arbitration is the sole relevant factor when determining jurisdiction, should also apply where the place of arbitration has been decided by the arbitral tribunal or by an institution such as the SCC, see Heuman, Svensk domsrätt på skiljedomsrättens område, in JT 2010/11, 948 et seq., at 959.

contract in question. This law is often referred to as the 'proper law of the contract', the 'governing law', or *lex contractus*.

10. In international arbitration, a whole range of issues may also arise that are outside the scope of the *lex contractus*. This may be the case with issues concerning, for example, legal capacity to enter into agreements and the right to represent legal entities. These and other issues may have to be determined by a different system of law than the law governing the contract itself. The question of applicable law therefore requires careful attention by the arbitral tribunal.

11. The principle of party autonomy is fundamental in Swedish arbitration law. The Act has no provision regarding the law applicable to the merits of the case. When introducing the Act, the Government left the matter outside the statute, but it is clear that the parties are entitled to agree on the applicable substantive law.[7] This principle is also reflected in the SCC Rules. Article 22(1) states that the arbitral tribunal decides the merits of the dispute on the basis of the law(s) or rules of law agreed upon by the parties. If the parties have not made any such agreement, the tribunal applies the law or rules of law which it considers most appropriate.

12. These two situations will be discussed separately below.

1. Applicable Law Agreed by the Parties

13. The starting point in all international arbitration is that the laws of all different jurisdictions have the same value, and that none of them has privileged status over any other law. The primary allegiance of the arbitrators is to the agreement between the parties. If the parties have decided the applicable law, the arbitrators are bound by this choice.

14. The parties may of course have made such a choice already when they concluded their original contract. Many contracts have a clause stating that the contract is subject to and governed by, for example, the law of the country of the seller, or some other law considered relevant by the parties. The parties may also exercise their freedom to choose the applicable law at a later point in time, when a dispute has occurred, and even during the arbitral proceedings, although this may of course lead to practical complications.

15. The fact that the choice of the parties is binding means that if the arbitrators apply different law(s) or rules than determined by the parties, the award may be challenged and set aside since the arbitrators have exceeded their mandate.[8]

16. Article 22(2) of the SCC Rules provides that any designation by the parties of the law of a given jurisdiction will be taken to refer to the substantive law of that country and not to its conflict of law rules. For example, if Swedish law is designated in a

7. See for example Heuman, *Arbitration Law of Sweden*, 683.
8. However, the award may not, of course, be set aside on the grounds that the arbitrators have followed the parties' choice of law but incorrectly applied the law chosen.

contract, then Swedish substantive law will apply in a dispute regarding that contract, and not whatever other law that would have been pointed out by Swedish conflict of law rules. This means that any chance of so called *renvoi* is excluded, in line with the view of most private international law systems.

17. The agreement may point to the law of the country of one of the parties, or to a third neutral country. There is no requirement that the law chosen has any connection to either party. In many international contracts, the law of a third country, for example Swedish, English or Swiss law, is chosen precisely for the reason of neutrality.

18. There is also no requirement that a particular national law is designated. Article 22 of the SCC Rules speaks about 'law(s) or rules of law'. This gives parties room to designate, for example, a combination of rules from two or more systems of law as applicable, or use other language referring to 'general principles of law', 'public international law', 'Lex Mercatoria' or similar. The practical effect of references of this kind may however be difficult for the parties to predict.[9] A national system of law has the advantage of being a complete legal system, designed to give an answer to any legal question, and of being an existing and known system which enables reasonably accurate interpretation by experienced practitioners.[10]

19. According to Article 22(3) of the SCC Rules, the arbitrators may decide the dispute *ex aequo et bono* or as *amiable compositeur* only if the parties have expressly authorized them to do so. It is very unusual that parties grant arbitrators such discretion. But if they do, the tribunal is free to decide the case without the application of, at least, non binding legal rules that would otherwise have applied. The prevailing view is that mandatory legal rules applicable to the case may not, however, be disregarded by the tribunal.[11]

20. When parties have included a choice of law clause in their contract, or in a separate agreement, the task of the arbitrators to determine applicable law is simple and straightforward. The task gets more difficult when one of the parties argues that a choice of law agreement has been concluded tacitly or implicitly. According to the 1980 Rome Convention, the parties' choice should either be express or demonstrated with reasonable certainty by the terms of the contract or the circumstances of the case. According to the Rome I Regulation, the choice should be made expressly or clearly demonstrated by the terms of the contract or the circumstances of the case.[12]

21. In exceptional circumstances, the mere initiating of arbitral proceedings as such can be taken to constitute an agreement to a specific choice of law. In one example, the

9. See for example Hobér, *International Commercial Arbitration in Sweden*, 42 et seq.
10. Blackaby et al., *Redfern and Hunter, On International Arbitration*, 199.
11. A specific question is whether such authorization would also have *procedural effect*, so as to make arbitrators not bound by claims, facts and circumstances strictly as submitted by the parties. In the *travaux préparatoires* to the Act, it was suggested that there is such effect (Govt. bill 1998/99 35 p. 141, 145).
12. Article 3 of the Rome Convention on the Law Applicable to Contractual Obligations, Art. 3 of Regulation (EC) No 593/2008 of 17 Jun. 2008 on the law applicable to contractual obligations (Rome I).

arbitral tribunal found that the claimant had accepted a reference to Swedish law as applicable to the merits of the case simply by initiating arbitration under an arbitration clause in the general terms and conditions of the respondent.[13] The arbitration clause in question included a reference to substantive law stating that in case of arbitration 'the laws of Sweden shall govern the matter regulated by the agreement'. The tribunal concluded that the claimant by its conduct, including initiating arbitration by referring to the arbitration clause, had agreed to comply with the terms and conditions of the arbitration clause as a whole – i.e., not only the part referring the dispute to arbitration, but also the language pointing to Swedish law as applicable to the merits.

22. Sometimes a contract may have unclear or contradictory choice of law provisions. The tribunal will then have to interpret the contract provisions with a view to determining the intention of the parties. In doing so, they will consider factors like the wording of the provisions and the contractual context in which they appear.[14]

23. As concerns Swedish law and international sales, it may be noted that Sweden has acceded to the United Nations Convention on Contracts for the International Sale of Goods (CISG). The substantive provisions of the CISG have been incorporated into Swedish law by the 1987 Swedish Act on International Sales. If a dispute concerns an international sales transaction as defined in the CISG, and the parties have chosen Swedish substantive law to apply, then the relevant articles of the CISG as incorporated by the 1987 Swedish Act will apply.[15]

2. *Applicable Law Determined by the Tribunal*

24. How will applicable law be determined when the parties have not used their autonomy and left the question undecided? For many years, the dominating view required arbitrators to go through a conflict of laws system to find the applicable law, a form of indirect method. The suggestion was that the conflict of law rules of the place of arbitration must be applied as an instrument pointing to the substantive law that would apply to the merits of the case. As for ad hoc proceedings taking place in Sweden, it has been suggested that applicable law in the absence of a party agreement will normally be decided based on Swedish conflict of law rules.[16] This principle exists in some other legal systems as well but has been abandoned elsewhere and has been called 'increasingly anachronistic.'[17]

25. Section 22 of the SCC Rules reflects the more modern view, stating that in the absence of party agreement the arbitral tribunal applies the law or rules of law which it considers to be most appropriate.[18] This is the so called 'direct choice' method, or

13. SCC Case No. 33/2007, commented by Åstenius & Björk in SIAR 2009:1, p. 147 et seq.
14. Hobér, *International Commercial Arbitration in Sweden*, 47.
15. (*Sw: Lag (1987:822) om internationella köp*), as amended in 2012.
16. Lindskog, Skiljeförfarande, 1109 et seq. See for a contrasting opinion, Hobér, *International Commercial Arbitration in Sweden*, 34.
17. Blabkaby et al., *Redfern and Hunter, On International Arbitration*, 236.
18. Cf Art. 35(1) of the UNCITRAL Arbitration Rules, adopted 2010 (UNCITRAL Rules).

voie directe, which means that the tribunal chooses the law applicable without reference to any conflict of law rules. The thinking behind the method is that if arbitrators can be trusted to decide a dispute, they can presumably also be trusted to determine the set of rules which will guide them in their decision. Additionally, the parties may have chosen the location for the proceedings for practical and other reasons, and not out of a preference for the conflict of law rules of that country, and therefore no reason exists to insist that those rules should be used.

26. When using the *voie directe* method, arbitrators will typically consider such factors as: (i) the domicile of the parties, (ii) the place where the contract was concluded, (iii) the contents of the contract, and (iv) the agreed seat of the arbitration. It has been argued that the discretion granted to the tribunal should not be used to give unpredictable and surprising results. The arbitral tribunal should use normative reasoning and point to a system of law that has some kind of relevant connection to the dispute from a legal perspective.[19]

27. Under the SCC Rules, then, the tribunal is not bound by Swedish conflict of laws rules and should see itself as free to disregard those rules. This is not to say that the end result will never be the same as if conflict of laws rules had been applied. These rules can often be expected to serve as a point of reference for arbitrators in Sweden even when the *voie directe* method is applied. Some of these conflicts of law rules will therefore be briefly touched upon.

28. Sweden is a party to both the 1980 Rome Convention and the Rome I Regulation. The Rome Convention still applies in Sweden to contracts entered into between 1 July 1998 and 17 December 2009 and will therefore continue to be relevant in the future. The Rome I Regulation, based largely on the Rome Convention, applies to contracts entered into after 17 December 2009.

29. Party autonomy is the starting point under both the Rome Convention and the Rome I Regulation. For situations where the parties have made no such choice, Article 4 of the Rome I Regulation gives a number of fixed rules for different types of contract obligations, some of which include:[20]

- a contract for the sale of goods (or the provision of services) shall be governed by the law of the country where the seller (or the service provider) has his habitual residence;
- a contract relating to a right in rem in immovable property or to a tenancy of immovable property shall be governed by the law of the country where the property is situated;[21]
- a franchise contract shall be governed by the law of the country where the franchisee has his habitual residence;

19. Lindskog, Skiljeförfarande, 1109 n. 43.
20. Article 4(1).
21. An exception applies to short term leases for private use.

- a distribution contract shall be governed by the law of the country where the distributor has his habitual residence.

30. Where a contract is not covered by any of the type of situations regulated in Article 4, the contract is governed by the law of the country where the party required to effect the characteristic performance of the contract has its habitual residence.[22]

31. Where the issue is not determined by either of the rules mentioned, the contract is governed by the law of the country with which it is most closely connected.[23] This rule is similar to the principle traditionally referred to in Sweden in situations where there are no specific choices of law rules to turn to. According to this principle, the applicable law is that of the jurisdiction where the contract in question has its centre of gravity.

32. The Rome I Regulation expressly states that it does not affect treaties already entered into.[24] This means that under Swedish conflict of law rules, the Swedish 1964 Act on the Law Applicable to International Sale of Goods[25] will still apply, since it is based on the 1955 Hague Convention.[26] The 1964 Act provides that the law of the place where the seller is domiciled when it receives the order will apply in the absence of a choice by the parties. If the order has been received at a permanent place of business of the seller, the law of that place is applied.

33. It can be argued whether it is reasonable to apply the 1964 Act when two non-Swedish parties have agreed to arbitrate in Sweden and where neither party, or only one of them, comes from a country which has ratified the 1955 Hague Convention. As mentioned, the direct choice method under section 22 of the SCC Rules gives arbitrators space to disregard Swedish conflict of law rules and find a different solution considered more appropriate in such a case, as well as in other situations.

3. *Restrictions on Party Autonomy*

34. Although arbitration is consensual in nature and governed by the will of the parties, there is no avoiding the fact that there are rules and principles that restrict party autonomy. These may be in the form of mandatory rules that, under certain circumstances, will be observed by the tribunal regardless of the choice of applicable law by the parties.

35. Mandatory rules are rules that 'cannot be derogated from by way of Contract'.[27] These can be in fields of for example labour law, consumer protection law, currency regulations or national laws governing the trade in arms. The general view is that arbitrators must apply mandatory rules that exist in the *lex contractus* as chosen by the parties, unless the parties have expressly excluded those mandatory rules from

22. Article 4(2).
23. Article 4(4).
24. Article 25.
25. (*Sw: Lag (1964:528) om tillämplig lag beträffande internationella köp av lösa saker*).
26. The Hague Convention of 15 Jun. 1955 on the Law Applicable to International Sales of Goods.
27. Article 3(3) of the Rome Convention.

application. For example, if the parties have simply stated that 'this contract is governed by Swedish law', the arbitrators must apply the mandatory rules of Swedish law. This will normally be the case when the *lex contractus* is determined by the arbitral tribunal in the absence of party agreement.[28]

36. In this context, competition rules have attracted particular attention and debate. Are these rules mandatory and should therefore always be applied by arbitrators, or are parties free to exclude for example EU competition rules, so as to avoid the effect of a particular clause in their contract being considered void under EU law? A widespread view is that these rules must always be applied and cannot be set aside by the parties by choosing some other law as applicable law.[29] According to this view, EU law would always apply to the extent relevant given the facts of the case, regardless of whether the parties have chosen for example Australian law as applicable.

37. A different question is whether the arbitral tribunal must consider EU competition law aspects ex officio or only if the issue is raised by at least one of the parties. The former position has been argued by some with reference to the *Eco Swiss* case, where the European Court of Justice held that an arbitral award failing to uphold EU law may be annulled by a national court as being in violation of *ordre public*.[30] The prevailing view among arbitrators in Sweden has been said to be that arbitrators, despite the *Eco Swiss* case, are not obligated to apply such rules unless the issue is raised by one of the parties.[31]

38. Sometimes the application of mandatory rules of laws other than the *lex contractus* may come into question.[32] This seems to require, first, that the substance of the dispute has some evident connection with that particular jurisdiction. Second, the mandatory rules in question would have to be considered to safeguard some strong and purportedly legitimate interest of that country. The willingness of arbitrators to look outside the *lex contractus* for mandatory rules will also depend on whether the *lex contractus* has been chosen by the parties or determined by the tribunal.[33]

39. Finally, principles forming part of public policy may also have to be considered by the arbitrators and have an impact on party autonomy. Where the parties have chosen the *lex contractus*, national public policy aspects of that law will normally be considered by the arbitrators unless the parties have clearly expressed otherwise. Outside the

---

28. However, views seem to differ on the procedural matter as to whether the arbitrators must apply such mandatory rules whether or not invoked by the parties, see Hobér, *International Commercial Arbitration in Sweden*, 53 et seq.
29. *Ibid.*, 54; cf. Art. 3 of the 1980 Rome Convention, stipulating that mandatory rules of a country cannot be contracted out of when all elements relevant to the situation are connected with that country.
30. *Eco Swiss China Time v. Benetton International*, ruling by European Court of Justice in case no C-126/97, 1999, ECR I-3055.
31. Hobér, *International Commercial Arbitration in Sweden*, 54, Lindskog, Skiljeförfarande, 241; this was the position of the Swedish Government when the Act was introduced and the Eco Swiss case was still pending, see Govt.bill 1998/99:35 p. 58.
32. Cf. Art. 7(1) of the Rome Convention and Art. 9(3) of the Rome I Regulation.
33. See Hobér, *International Commercial Arbitration in Sweden*, 54 et seq., saying that arbitral practice in this area 'presents a rather mixed picture'.

lex contractus, arbitrators are under no obligation to respect national policy aspects. However, in Sweden as in most other States there is general agreement that contract provisions concerning bribery and corruption are invalid on the grounds that they violate international public policy. The same is typically true with clauses aimed at facilitating for example drug trafficking, violation of human rights, or religious or sexual discrimination.[34]

4. *The Scope of Lex Contractus*

40. Although the *lex contractus* is often the focus when applicable law is considered, many important issues fall outside party autonomy and *lex contractus* and follow other choice of law principles.[35]

41. One such exception is the group of issues which will typically be governed by the personal law, the *lex corporationis*, of the party in question. *Lex corporationis* is most often the law of the place where the legal entity is registered or where the board of the entity has its seat. Issues governed by the *lex corporationis* include the following:

- Questions concerning corporate identity, such as whether the entity has been validly established, liquidated or otherwise dissolved, or whether two or more entities have merged or de-merged.
- Questions regarding who has the right to represent the entity in question and, for example, enter into agreements on its behalf.
- Other corporate issues such as voting and shareholders' rights, dividend policies, rules regarding the transfer or collateralization of shares, and others.[36]

42. Another exception to party autonomy and the *lex contractus* is real property. Questions with regard to real estate – both rights and obligations of the parties and in relation to third parties – will typically be governed by the law of the jurisdiction where the property is located (*lex rei sitae*). *Lex rei sitae* will also govern relations between one of the parties and third parties when it comes to movable property. For example, rights of the buyer in the property as against the creditors of the seller are governed by the law of the jurisdiction in which the goods sold are located at the time of execution of the contract.[37]

43. Issues concerning agency, that is, whether an agent is able to bind a principal in relation to a third party, normally fall outside the scope of *lex contractus*. It has been suggested that the law governing the internal relationship between principal and agent

34. *Ibid.*, 58.
35. See Art. 1 of the Rome Convention and the Rome I Regulation for areas excluded from their scope.
36. Tension may arise concerning these and similar issues between the *lex corporationis* and some other law designated in a *shareholders agreement* between the parties, see Hobér, *International Commercial Arbitration in Sweden*, 80.
37. *Ibid.*, 83.

is the *lex contractus* of the arrangement between the two, whereas the external relationship between the agent and third parties is mostly governed by the law of the country where the agent performs activities.[38]

44. Tort typically falls outside party autonomy. The prevailing view is that issues concerning tort are governed by the law of the place where the alleged tort was committed (the *lex loci delicti commissi*). This is also the main rule under the Rome II Regulation, which applies as part of Swedish conflict of law rules as of January 2009.[39]

45. The classification of rules or concepts has become less of a challenge with increased international harmonization. At least in the commercial field, most legal concepts are classified in a similar way in most jurisdictions (with, for example, statute of limitations treated as a substantive issue rather than as a procedural one). Should the issue arise when the parties have chosen the applicable law themselves, the arbitrators are likely also to apply the classification rules of that law, if and to the extent necessary. However, when arbitrators in Sweden apply Swedish conflict of laws rules, they are also expected to apply Swedish classifications rules.[40]

5. *Jura Novit Curia*

46. In proceedings before Swedish courts, the *jura novit curia* principle applies. This principle, Latin for 'the judge knows the law', means that judges apply the legal rule that they find appropriate in relation to the facts invoked by the parties regardless of whether the parties have referred to that rule or not.[41] The principle means not only that the court may apply the legal rule it finds appropriate but also that it is under an obligation to do so.[42] In other words, it is the right and the duty of judges to make an independent legal qualification of the facts put before them. In the words of Hobér, 'the judge is the ultimate high priest of the law'.[43]

47. Statutory support for the *jura novit curia* principle is a provision in the Code of Judicial Procedure[44] (Chapter 35 section 2) according to which it is not necessary to bring evidence with respect to the content of the law. The Swedish Supreme Court has restated and applied the principle in several cases.[45]

---

38. *Ibid.*, 81.
39. Regulation (EC) No 864/2007 of 11 Jul. 2007 on the law applicable to non-contractual obligations (Rome II); the regulation contains exceptions to the main rule which will not be dealt with here.
40. Hobér, *International Commercial Arbitration in Sweden*, 85 et seq.
41. However, the judge may not base a ruling on any legally relevant facts (Sw. 'rättsfakta') other than those invoked by the claimant or the respondent, as the case may be, and also may not go beyond the claim submitted by the claimant.
42. Lindskog, Skiljeförfarande, 713.
43. Hobér, *International Commercial Arbitration in Sweden*, 213.
44. *(Sw: Rättegångsbalk (1942:740))*
45. See for example *Anne-Marie Q v. Lars Q*, judgment by the Swedish Supreme Court made on 27 Oct. 1989 in case no. T 109/89, NJA 1989 p. 614, *B.R. v. Auto-West*, judgment by the Supreme Court made on 8 Feb. 1993 in case no T 279-90, NJA 1993 p. 13 and *Sydkraft v. Skandia*, judgment by the Supreme Court made on 14 Oct. 1999 in case no Ö 5176-98, NJA 1999 p. 629.

48. The Act is silent on the topic of the applicability of the *jura novit curia* principle in arbitration proceedings (as are the SCC Rules). However, the issue is addressed in the *travaux préparatoires* to the act. In the *travaux préparatoires* to the Act, the Government states that it must be assumed that 'for the time being' the *jura novit curia* principle is also adhered to in arbitration proceedings, 'at least in domestic disputes'.[46] It is added that this means that an arbitration award cannot successfully be challenged on the basis that the arbitrators have applied a legal rule not referred to by the parties in their pleadings.[47]

49. In respect of arbitration proceedings involving only Swedish parties, this position is widely recognized in the legal literature. Lindskog states unequivocally that the *jura novit curia* principle applies in such arbitration proceedings, as does Heuman.[48] However, in disputes where one party or both are non-Swedish, the position is less clear.[49] This is indicated already in the *travaux préparatoires*. As noted, the Government's statement in respect of the applicability of the *jura novit curia* principle is made with reference to 'domestic disputes', adding that if the dispute involves foreign parties it must be taken into account that the *jura novit curia* principle may not be recognized to the same extent in their home jurisdictions.[50]

50. Lindskog, for his part, states that it is possible that the *jura novit curia* principle 'needs to be modified' in arbitration proceedings with an international element.[51] In the mid-nineties, Gotthard Calissendorff, a leading Swedish arbitrator in his day, called into question whether the principle should be applied at all in arbitration proceedings, especially in proceedings involving non-Swedish parties.[52] Hobér, writing in 2011, takes the same position: 'It may be called into question whether the principle of *iura novit curia* is applicable to arbitrations. Arguably, this is not the case, at least not where the parties, or at least one of them, are foreign ...'[53] Hobér refers to an award from 2000 by the Svea Court of Appeal in which the court upheld an arbitral award where the arbitrators had applied legal rules not relied on by the parties.[54] Both parties, as well as counsel and the arbitrators, were Swedish. Hobér notes that it remains to be addressed

46. Madsen notes that the Government, by using the expression 'for the time being', has indicated that the position might change, Madsen, *Om principen jura novit curia vid skiljeförfaranden*, *JT* 2010/11, 485 et seq., at 496.
47. Govt. bill 1998/99:35 p. 145 et seq.
48. Lindskog, Skiljeförfarande, 713, and Heuman, *Arbitration Law of Sweden*, 378. Kleineman is of the same opinion, *Principen jura novit curia – särskilt i skiljeförfaranden*, in Vänbok till Bertil Södermark, 93 et seq. However, Hobér and to some extent Madsen advocates against applying the principle in domestic proceedings; see below.
49. Madsen notes that it is widely recognized that the *jura novit curia* principle applies in domestic arbitration proceedings, whilst it is less clear whether there is any room for the principle in international arbitration proceedings conducted in Sweden; Madsen, *Om principen jura novit curia vid skiljeförfaranden*, 486.
50. Govt. bill 1998/99:35 p. 146.
51. Lindskog, Skiljeförfarande, 714.
52. Calissendorff, *Jura novit curia i internationella skiljeförfaranden i Sverige*, JT 1995-96, 147 et seq.
53. Hobér, *International Commercial Arbitration in Sweden*, 257.
54. *Gustafson v. Länsförsäkringar*, judgment by the Svea Court of Appeal made on 18 May 2000 in case no T 8090-99. See observations on the award by Martin Wallin in SIAR 2003:1, 263 et seq.

by a court whether the outcome would be the same in a non-domestic case. In his opinion, that is 'unlikely'.[55] The main reason for Hobér's scepticism toward applying the *jura novit curia* principle in arbitration proceedings is that the outcome of the case may come as a complete surprise to both parties, a consequence that in his opinion would be difficult to reconcile with the fundamental principle that arbitration is consensual in nature and with the philosophy that the parties are the masters of the procedure.[56]

51. The latter is taken as the starting point in Madsen's analysis.[57] He notes that unlike in court proceedings, the parties can agree that the arbitrators may not apply legal rules other than those relied on by the parties. If so, use of other rules will result in the award being set aside on the grounds that the arbitrators have exceeded their mandate. However, even when no such agreement is in place, Madsen advocates that the *jura novit curia* principle be applied restrictively, especially in international arbitration proceedings. In his opinion, arbitrators in international proceedings should not use any legal rule the application of which would come as a surprise to the parties. In this context, Madsen refers to recommendations adopted by the ILA at a conference on the contents of the applicable law in international commercial arbitration.[58] Pursuant to those recommendations, the arbitrators 'should primarily receive information about the contents of the applicable law from the parties' and '[i]n general ... should not introduce legal issues – propositions of law that may bear on the outcome of the dispute – that the parties have not raised' (Recommendations 5 and 6). According to Madsen, it can be assumed that arbitrators in international proceedings will seek guidance in the ILA recommendations, noting that this would mean a considerable modification of the *jura novit curia* principle as applied by Swedish courts.[59]

52. Kleineman recognizes that the *jura novit curia* principle needs to be somewhat modified in international arbitration proceedings. He distinguishes between the right and the duty of arbitrators to apply other legal rules than those brought up by the parties. His conclusion is that arbitrators have the right to apply such rules but unlike in domestic proceedings they are not under any obligation to do so.[60]

53. Finnish arbitration law, and Finnish legal culture in general, is similar to that in Sweden. Therefore it is worth noting that in a 2008 judgment the Finnish Supreme Court chose not to set aside an award rendered in international arbitration proceedings governed by Finnish law despite the fact that the tribunal had applied a legal rule not

---

Wallin concludes that 'the effect of the judgment is that the *jura novit curia* principle in arbitration proceedings involving Swedish parties has been strengthened'.

55. Hobér, *International Commercial Arbitration in Sweden*, 317.
56. *Ibid.*, 213.
57. Madsen, *Om principen jura novit curia vid skiljeförfaranden*, 485 et seq.
58. ILA Rio de Janeiro Conference (2008) International Commercial Arbitration, Final Report Ascertaining the Contents of the Applicable Law in International Commercial Arbitration.
59. Madsen, *Om principen jura novit curia vid skiljeförfaranden*, 501 et seq.
60. Kleineman, *Principen jura novit curia – särskilt i skiljeförfaranden*, i Vänbok till Bertil Södermark, 123.

referred to by the parties and not brought to their attention by the arbitrators.[61] A commentator notes that the Supreme Court affirms that 'the arbitrators are not restricted to the point of law pleaded by the parties', concluding that 'once the facts have been presented to the tribunal, it is free to ascribe to these facts whatever legal basis it deems fit for its decision, whether pleaded by the parties or not'.[62] In other words, what the Supreme Court did was to accept the application of the *jura novit curia* principle despite the proceedings being truly international, with neither party being Finnish.

54. If and when the *jura novit curia* principle does apply and arbitrators therefore have a right and a duty to apply the appropriate legal rules when the parties do not refer to those rules, it is widely recognized that arbitrators should seek to act so as to avoid surprise effects.[63] Thus, preceding adoption of the Act, the legislative committee stated that if arbitrators find that a legal rule not referred to by the parties may be applicable, then the parties should be alerted to the existence of that rule.[64] Madsen writes that the parties should be given the opportunity to comment on legal rules which the tribunal considers applying.[65] Hobér states that arbitrators should ascertain that the parties are 'properly informed of how and which laws and legal principles might be applied by the arbitrators in order to avoid surprises once the award is rendered'.[66] Lindskog writes that arbitrators should in an appropriate manner make the parties aware of legal rules under consideration by the tribunal, though adding that arbitrators should not bring up any rule that requires invoking new facts and circumstances for its successful application.[67] Kleineman advocates a more restrained approach:

> [A] tribunal should be very careful with bringing up new legal pathways in the later stages of arbitration proceedings. If they do so, this can easily be looked upon as the tribunal wishing to point out new directions to one of the parties, resulting in protests, requests that the hearing be postponed and claims of partiality on the part of the tribunal'.[68]

55. If the tribunal applies a rule without bringing it up with the parties, this may in Lindskog's opinion constitute a violation of the tribunal's case management duties and result in the award being set aside.[69] Wallin for his part notes that 'it is still an open question whether an award from an international arbitration procedure in Sweden can

61. *Werfen Austria GmbH v. Polar Electro Europé BV, Zug branch*, decision by the Finnish Supreme Court made on 2 July 2008 in case no S2006/716, translation in SIAR 2008:3, 259 et seq. Neither of the parties was Finnish.
62. Observations by Sophie Nappert in SIAR 2008:3, 283 et seq., at 284.
63. Govt. bill 1998/99:35 p. 146, Nordenson, *Materiell processledning i skiljeförfarande*, JT 1993/94, 217 (the tribunal should conduct a dialogue with the parties in order to get their view of the legal issues), and Heuman, *Arbitration Law of Sweden*, 324.
64. SOU 1994:81, 150.
65. Madsen, *Om principen jura novit curia vid skiljeförfaranden*, JT 2010-11, 503.
66. Hobér, *International Commercial Arbitration in Sweden*, 317.
67. Lindskog, Skiljeförfarande, 611.
68. Kleineman, *Principen jura novit curia – särskilt i skiljeförfaranden*, i Vänbok till Bertil Södermark, p. 121.
69. Lindskog, Skiljeförfarande, 903.

be challenged on the grounds of lack of procedural guidance from the arbitrators'.[70] It can be noted that in the award mentioned above the Finnish Supreme Court did not find that the tribunal's failure to bring to the attention of the parties the rule which it applied constituted a procedural error which would result in the arbitration award being set aside.

56. Of course practical problems may arise if arbitrators are under an obligation never to apply a legal rule without providing the parties the opportunity to comment on the applicability of the rule. What to do, for example, if the arbitrators themselves do not realize the relevance of the rule until after the case has been closed? Should they then reopen the case and ask for the parties views on the rule they are contemplating applying? Or should they refrain from applying the rule, resulting in a different outcome of the dispute?

57. To sum up, it is widely recognized that arbitrators in domestic proceedings should adhere to the *jura novit curia* principle, whilst the opposite position dominates when it comes to international proceedings.[71] And when there is a right and a duty to apply legal rules not referred to by the parties, arbitrators should seek to give the parties an opportunity to comment on rules that they contemplate using.

C. Law Governing the Arbitration Agreement

58. The arbitration agreement as such lies at the centre of many disputes, the parties arguing opposite positions on questions like: Has an arbitration agreement been entered into? Has the arbitration agreement been transferred to a third party? Is the matter in dispute arbitrable at all? Have the arbitral proceedings been initiated correctly and in compliance with the arbitration agreement?

59. To resolve these and other similar issues, the question of applicable law must first be answered. The doctrine of separability means that different laws can apply to the arbitration agreement and the disputed main contract. And the choice of law clause in the main contract, if any, does not automatically extend to the arbitration agreement.

60. For arbitrations taking place in Sweden, section 48 of the Act deals with this issue. As a starting point, it states that the law agreed upon by the parties governs the arbitration agreement. According to the *travaux préparatoires* to the Act, the choice of the parties must explicitly point to the arbitration agreement – a general choice of law

70. Wallin, SIAR 2003:1, 272. As for domestic proceedings, Wallin concludes that there is 'limited scope' for challenging an award based on failure to bring up the existence of a rule which is applicable to the facts and circumstances invoked. See also Nordenson, *Materiell processledning i skiljeförfarande*, 218 et seq.

71. Needless to say, if a distinction is to be made between 'domestic' and 'international' proceedings, it can be discussed where to draw the line. Should the *jura novit curia* principle apply only when both parties, counsel and all arbitrators are Swedish? What if both parties are Swedish and one counsel is Swedish but the other counsel, say, English? And what if the parties are Swedish but one or more of the arbitrators are non-Swedish? etc.

clause is not enough.[72] Such an explicit choice of law with respect to the arbitration agreement is rare in practice. The subsidiary rule of section 48 of the Act may therefore be more important.

61. Where there is no choice of law by the parties, section 48 provides that the law of the place of arbitration governs the arbitration agreement – provided that the parties have agreed on that place of arbitration in their arbitration clause. If there is no such choice as to the place of arbitration, the *travaux préparatoires* suggest that the issue will be determined by Swedish conflict of law rules.[73] Such an approach would call for some kind of centre of gravity test being used, since no international conventions or other specific rules exist on the subject.[74] Such a test may turn out inconclusive, since a centre of gravity may be difficult to find for an arbitration agreement. Different solutions are possible here. One alternative is to let the place of arbitration be decisive, even if it has not been agreed by the parties but decided by for example by the Board of the SCC under sections 9 and 20 of the SCC Rules.[75]

62. In its second paragraph, section 48 states that the rule above does not apply to the issue whether a party was authorized to enter into an arbitration agreement or was duly represented. These issues are normally determined by the personal law (*lex corporationis*) of the party in question, as determined in accordance with Swedish conflict of law rules.[76]

63. This principle was applied for example in a 2007 SCC arbitration, where one question was whether two companies C and E had the authority to bind two other companies A and B to an arbitration agreement. One side argued that this issue should be resolved in accordance with the laws of the United Arab Emirates, which was the law governing the disputed main contract in question. The tribunal found that the *lex contractus* did not cover the question of validity of the arbitration agreement. Instead, with reference to section 48 of the Act, the tribunal found that the laws of Yemen and the People's Republic of China, respectively, as *lex corporationis*, were to determine the question of whether the necessary authority existed.[77]

72. Govt. bill 1998/99:35, p. 193.
73. *Ibid.*, 245.
74. The Rome Convention and the Rome I Regulation exclude arbitration agreements from their scope of application.
75. For cases under s. 48 of the Act, see for example Hobér, *International Commercial Arbitration in Sweden*, 88.
76. Govt. bill 1998/99:35, p. 245.
77. SCC Case No. 30/2003, referenced in SIAR 2009:1, 89 et seq.

CHAPTER 8

The Proceedings

Stefan Brocker & Kristoffer Löf*

I. INTRODUCTION

1. This chapter will deal with the conduct of an arbitration in Sweden, from its commencement to its termination. In principle, two sets of rules apply to the conduct of arbitral proceedings in Sweden.

2. First are the rules of the Swedish Arbitration Act (Sw: *Lag (1999:116) om skiljeförfarande*) (the Act), some of which are mandatory. Second, where no such mandatory rules are applicable to the situation at hand, resort should be had to the parties' agreement as to conduct of the arbitration. Such agreement is most commonly found in the arbitration agreement, including the institutional rules specified therein, if any.

3. Beyond this, the arbitral tribunal is free to decide the most appropriate way of conducting the arbitration, within the limitations that follow from the overriding procedural principles of party autonomy and due process.

4. Generally speaking, the principle of party autonomy entails that it is for the parties to decide on the appropriate procedure and the arbitral tribunal must, as a general rule,[1] abide by the parties' joint instructions. If the parties come to no agreement, it is for the arbitral tribunal to determine the conduct of the proceedings, within the confines of the requirement of due process. Due process, in turn, is manifested in

* Much like a legal brief prepared in an international arbitration, this contribution is the result of a teamwork. The authors are in debt to Marcus Berglie, Maria Bouvin, Azadeh Razani, Helena Sjöholm and Oskar Wrede, all associates at Mannheimer Swartling, for their assistance with and research for this contribution. Any views expressed and mistakes and omissions made in this contribution are, however, attributable solely to the authors.

1. See s. 21 of the Act, under which the arbitral tribunal should 'act in accordance with the decisions of the parties insofar as there is no impediment to so doing'.

requirements of equal treatment of the parties and that each party should be afforded a reasonable opportunity to present its case.

5. This chapter will address the mandatory rules that the arbitral tribunal must comply with in order not to make the award susceptible to successful challenges for excess of mandate or for failure to observe due process. As for institutional rules, this chapter will address the solutions provided for by the Rules of Arbitration of the Arbitration Institute of the Stockholm Chamber of Commerce (SCC Rules) with respect to the issues discussed. Although many international arbitrations in Sweden are conducted under the ICC and the UNCITRAL Rules, and indeed under other rules, those rules will not, with a few exceptions, be discussed here. However, irrespective of which set of rules apply, the interrelationship between the Act and institutional rules is generally the same. Most of what is said here will therefore also have a bearing on arbitrations conducted under rules other than the SCC Rules.

6. This chapter will also attempt to describe a 'typical' international arbitration in Sweden, from the viewpoint of what can be conceived of as 'best practice'. Taking a bird's eye perspective, a typical international arbitration may be said to encompass the following general steps, all of which will be discussed in further detail below:

(i) The arbitration is commenced by filing a request for arbitration, including the claimant's appointment of an arbitrator. The respondent submits its answer to the request for arbitration, in which the respondent appoints an arbitrator. If it is an ad hoc arbitration, the appointed arbitrators select a third arbitrator who is appointed as the chairperson. If it is an SCC arbitration, the SCC normally appoints the chairperson, following which the file is transferred to the arbitral tribunal.

(ii) When the arbitral tribunal has been constituted and is in receipt of the file, the parties and the arbitral tribunal fix a timetable and set basic rules for the arbitration.

(iii) The written phase of the arbitration then commences. The claimant submits its statement of claim, specifying its case, which is followed by the respondent's statement of defence, as well as any counterclaim. These two submissions are then followed by one or several additional submissions by each party. Written witness statements and expert reports are also submitted in this phase.

(iv) During the written phase of the proceedings, the arbitral tribunal may also have to decide on procedural issues, such as its jurisdiction, amended claims, production of documents or applicable law. Separate hearings can be held in order to hear the parties' arguments in respect of parts of the case determined in separate awards, or on various procedural matters determined in procedural orders.

(v) Following a possible pre-hearing conference, a hearing is held where the witnesses and experts are heard and the parties' respective cases are orally presented.

(vi) In some arbitrations, post-hearing briefs are submitted by each party.

(vii) Cost submissions are made.
(viii) The award is rendered.

7. The steps set out above are more or less closely followed in most international arbitrations in Sweden. However, as will be seen in this chapter, the parties and the arbitral tribunal have great flexibility in organizing an arbitration in Sweden in the manner that best fits the efficient resolution of the case at hand.

II. COMMENCEMENT OF ARBITRATION

A. Request for Arbitration

1. *Introduction*

8. Arbitral proceedings are formally commenced when the claimant requests initiation of arbitration.[2] This is made by filing a 'request for arbitration'. A request for arbitration must fulfil the formal requirements of the Act, unless the parties have agreed that other requirements are to apply. These other requirements, that deviate from or supplement the rules of the Act, are often found in institutional rules. Institutional rules are binding on the parties if they have referred to them in the arbitration agreement or if the rules have otherwise been adopted by the parties.

2. *Requirements under the Act*

9. A request for arbitration becomes effective – and the arbitration thus commences – when a party receives from the other party a written communication which meets the requirements of being a request for arbitration.[3] This rule is non-mandatory and the parties may agree that arbitration is to be initiated in other ways.[4]

10. Under the Act, the request for arbitration must contain:

(i) An express and unconditional request for arbitration.
(ii) A statement of the issue which is covered by the arbitration agreement and which is to be resolved by the arbitrators.
(iii) A statement of the party's choice of arbitrator, where the party is required to appoint one. If the dispute under the parties' arbitration agreement is to be resolved by a sole arbitrator, the claimant need not make a statement of its choice of arbitrator in the request for arbitration.

---

2. The date of commencement of arbitration can be significant. In situations where it is required by law or contract that a party must bring an action within a certain period in order not to lose its right to bring a claim, the decisive date for determining whether such an action has been brought is the date of commencement of arbitration (see s. 45 of the Act).
3. Section 19 of the Act.
4. Govt. bill 1998/99:35, 224. It should be noted that applicable institutional rules can provide that the arbitration is commenced on another date than the date which follows from the Act, normally on the date when the institution has received the request for arbitration.

11. A request for arbitration that does not fulfil these requirements is of no effect and will not constitute a valid request for arbitration under the Act.[5] Consequently, no arbitration will be considered to have commenced. In this situation, the proceedings will not commence until the respondent receives supplementary information that completes the request for arbitration.

12. However, if the other party accepts a defective request by appointing its arbitrator, or otherwise responds to the request for arbitration in a manner that implies acceptance of commencement of the arbitration, the arbitration will be considered to have commenced despite the defect.[6]

13. As mentioned above, a request for arbitration must be in writing.[7] There is no requirement that it must be signed. A submission by fax,[8] and likely also by e-mail,[9] is sufficient, provided that the sender can prove that the respondent has actually received it (see further below, regarding requirements on service of notices). The claimant's fax activity report or e-mail is not sufficient to prove that the respondent received the request.[10]

14. Two exceptions exist to the requirement that a request for arbitration must be in writing. If a written arbitration agreement has been entered into concerning an existing dispute and the agreement includes a clear statement of the issue in dispute, no need arises to notify the opposing party in writing of the issue in dispute.[11] Similarly, no written notification is required when the parties in the presence of the arbitral tribunal enter into a new or expanded arbitration agreement on issues they want the arbitral tribunal to determine. In the latter case, no need arises for a new request for arbitration to be made in order for the proceeding to be seen as having commenced with respect to the new issue and for the arbitral tribunal to resolve the dispute.[12]

15. The requirements on a request for arbitration will be addressed further in the following.

5. Govt. bill 1998/99:35, 103 et seq.
6. Govt. bill 1998/99:35, 224, and SOU 1994:81, 274.
7. Section 19 of the Act.
8. Govt. bill 1998/99:35, 221 and SOU 1994:81, 270. See also *Kenneth O v. Motor Union Assuransfirma AB*, decision by the Supreme Court on 23 Jun. 1993 in case no Ö 2317-91, NJA 1993 p. 308.
9. See Lindskog, 615, and Heuman, *Arbitration Law of Sweden: Practice and Procedure* 306 (Juris Publg. Inc. 2003). See also Englund, 133–139.
10. *F.D.* (application for restoration), decision by the Supreme Court on 24 Mar. 2010 in case no Ö 3626-08, NJA 2010 p. 165.
11. Govt. bill 1998/99:35, 101.
12. Govt. bill 1998/99:35, 101 and SOU 1994:81, 133. See also *C. G. Ohlssons v. C. Bergström and J. S. L. Lindberg*, decision by the Supreme Court on 18 Oct. 1911, NJA 1911 p. 499, and *Kenneth O v. Motor Union Assuransfirma AB*, decision by the Supreme Court on 23 Jun. 1993 in case no Ö 2317-91, NJA 1993 p. 308.

a. Requirement of an Express and Unconditional Request for Arbitration

16. The first requirement for a valid request for arbitration is that it contains an express and unconditional request for arbitration.[13] This requirement is based on the notion that, in view of the important legal consequences of filing a request for arbitration, it must be clear to the respondent whether and when a request has been made.

17. A proposal to arbitrate or an expression of intent to initiate arbitration do not constitute express and unconditional requests for arbitration.[14] Nor does a notification that a party will request arbitration if payment is not received by a certain date or if the dispute is not resolved before a certain date, qualify as a request for arbitration.[15]

b. Requirement of a Statement of the Disputed Issue

18. The second requirement for a valid request for arbitration is that it must include a statement of the issue covered by the arbitration agreement which is to be resolved by the arbitral tribunal.[16] The purpose of this rule is to set a preliminary framework for the proceedings and to enable the respondent to appoint an arbitrator based on this information.

19. Requests for relief do not need to be included in the request for arbitration. Under section 23 of the Act, the claimant may present the relief sought at a later stage of the proceedings. Nor does the matter in dispute have to be described exhaustively or in detail in the request for arbitration and the claimant is not required to state legal grounds for its claims. In practice, however, the request for arbitration usually includes a preliminary statement of the relief sought.

20. It has been debated whether it is sufficient to indicate the abstract nature of the issue to be determined by the arbitral tribunal, or whether a party should describe the issue in concrete terms.[17] In practice, it is seldom an issue whether the disputed matter has been described in sufficient detail, because parties tend to describe the actual dispute in the request for arbitration, rather than to refer to abstract concepts. It seems clear, however, that a request for arbitration regarding 'this dispute' or 'with reference

13. Section 19 of the Act.
14. See Lindskog, 616, and Heuman, *Arbitration Law of Sweden: Practice and Procedure*, 299. See also *Rättviks ångsågsaktiebolag v. Aktiebolaget Hälsinge träexport*, decision by the Supreme Court on 27 May 1921, NJA 1921 p. 253. In this case, a party had terminated an agreement due to breach of contract by the opposing party. The opposing party protested against the termination in a letter in which it stated that the wrongful termination constituted a breach of contract, demanded that the dispute be referred to arbitration and reserved its right to compensation for all damages incurred. After further correspondence between the parties, the opposing party finally sent a letter stating that it requested arbitration. This first letter was not considered sufficient in order to serve as a request for arbitration. A valid request for arbitration was considered to have been made in the second letter.
15. Cars, 93, and Heuman, *Arbitration Law of Sweden: Practice and Procedure*, 299.
16. Section 19 of the Act.
17. See Cars, 93–94, Heuman, *Arbitration Law of Sweden: Practice and Procedure*, 300–302, and Lindskog, 617.

to the arbitration clause' in a particular contract cannot be accepted as a request for arbitration because, in that case, the matter in dispute is not indicated at all. The same applies if a request for arbitration merely refers to a question regarding 'compensation' or 'damages'. Such a request needs to be supplemented so as to provide the opposing party with a basis for its choice of arbitrator as well as an approximate idea of the matter to be decided by the arbitrators.[18] The opposing party must also be able to ascertain whether the dispute is covered by a valid and applicable arbitration agreement and whether it is arbitrable. It has been suggested that the respondent should also be able to ascertain whether a statute of limitation or contractual time bars apply to the claim.[19]

21. Facts, legal grounds and arguments presented in the request for arbitration may be substantially developed in the course of the proceedings before the arbitral tribunal. Moreover, the Act enables the claimant to subsequently introduce new claims, as well as for the respondent to present counterclaims (Article 23). Accordingly, the description of the dispute contained in the request for arbitration is preliminary. Only to a limited extent does it provide the framework for the arbitration.

c. *Requirement of a Statement on Choice of Arbitrator*

22. The third requirement for a valid request for arbitration is that it includes a statement of the requesting party's choice of arbitrator (if the party is required under the arbitration agreement to appoint one).[20] Failure to do so means that the claimant has not made a request for arbitration within the meaning of the Act.[21]

23. The purpose of this requirement is to expedite the proceedings. Since a claimant has a better knowledge of the dispute than the opposing party, the claimant should appoint an arbitrator before the respondent.[22]

24. If the arbitration agreement provides that the parties are jointly to appoint the arbitrator(s), it is not necessary for the claimant to suggest an arbitrator in the request for arbitration.[23]

25. If the arbitration agreement provides that the dispute is to be decided by three arbitrators, but the claimant nevertheless prefers a less expensive route with a sole arbitrator, the claimant should still appoint an arbitrator and seek the opposing party's

---

18. Heuman, *Arbitration Law of Sweden: Practice and Procedure*, 301. See also *Fredriksson v. Smålandsstenars vatten- och sanitära förening*, decision by the Supreme Court made on 10 Mar. 1955, NJA 1955 p. 224. In this case, the claimant first sent a letter to the opposing party setting out the details of the claim. After the claim was contested by the opposing party, the claimant sent a request for arbitration without repeating the details of the issue. The request for arbitration was considered valid in this case.
19. See Finn Madsen, *Commercial Arbitration in Sweden* 136 (2d ed., Oxford University Press 2006).
20. Section 19 of the Act.
21. Govt. bill 1998/99:35, 103–104.
22. Govt. bill 1998/99:35, 102, and SOU 1994:81, 134–135.
23. Govt. bill 1998/99:35, 224, and SOU 1994:81, 136.

consent to having the dispute decided by a sole arbitrator.[24] Thus, the claimant should not omit to nominate an arbitrator in the request for arbitration.

26. The appointed arbitrator is presumed to have accepted the mandate.[25] However, this has not been understood to mean that a request for arbitration becomes inoperative if the presumption is not satisfied.[26] The Act requires the request for arbitration to be unconditional, but is silent as to whether the choice of arbitrator must be made without conditions. In our view, this means that the request for arbitration as such must not be conditional upon the appointed arbitrator accepting the nomination. However, the choice of arbitrator may be conditional upon the appointed arbitrator's acceptance of the nomination, with the request for arbitration still being valid.[27]

d. *Withdrawal of Request for Arbitration*

27. There is no provision under the Act addressing the situation where a request for arbitration is withdrawn. However, it has been suggested that withdrawal should be possible in accordance with general legal principles, provided that a notification of withdrawal is received by the opposing party by the latest at the same time as the party takes notice of the request.[28]

28. The effect of a withdrawal before the arbitral tribunal is constituted, but after the opposing party has taken notice of the request, is unclear. According to one commentator, there is probably no right to withdraw the request in this situation.[29] An arbitral tribunal should thus be constituted if the opposing party nominates its arbitrator.[30] This would also be in line with the provision in section 28 of the Act, under which the arbitral tribunal is to dismiss a claim that is withdrawn unless the opposing party requests a ruling on the issue. A respondent thus has a right to require final adjudication of a claim that the claimant has referred to arbitration, even if the claimant withdraws the claim.

24. Govt. bill 1998/99:35, 224, and SOU 1994:81, 274.
25. Govt. bill 1998/99:35, 224, and SOU 1994:81, 274.
26. See Madsen, *Commercial Arbitration in Sweden* 138 (2d ed., Oxford University Press 2006).
27. Other views have been discussed in Heuman, *Arbitration Law of Sweden: Practice and Procedure*, 306, and Lindskog, 618, the latter stating that a conditional choice of arbitrator should be invalid. If that view were to be accepted, the request should in any event become operative as soon as the claimant makes its choice of arbitrator unconditional or appoints another person as arbitrator; see Heuman, *Arbitration Law of Sweden: Practice and Procedure*, 306.
28. See Ch. 1 s. [illegible] of the Contracts Act, and Lindskog, 622.
29. Lindskog, 623.
30. Section 14(2) of the Act provides that a party's notification of its choice of arbitrator cannot be withdrawn without the consent of the opposing party. According to Lindskog, 623, this should mean that an opposing party can see to it that an arbitral tribunal is constituted by nominating its arbitrator.

3. *Requirements on Request for Arbitration under the SCC Rules*

29. As mentioned in the preceding section, the rules set forth in the Act with respect to commencement of arbitration are non-mandatory. The parties are thus free to agree on how arbitration is to be commenced. Accordingly, if the parties' arbitration agreement refers to institutional arbitration under the SCC Rules, the requirements laid down by those rules take precedence over the fall-back rules of the Act.

30. Under Article 4 of the SCC Rules, the arbitration is commenced on the date when the SCC receives the request for arbitration. Accordingly, as opposed to what is the case under the Act, the date when the *respondent* receives the request for arbitration is of no relevance under the SCC Rules in this respect.

31. Article 2 of the SCC Rules sets out the requirements for a valid request for arbitration. The request must include:

(i) Details of the parties and their counsel.
(ii) A summary of the dispute.
(iii) A preliminary statement of the relief sought by the claimant.
(iv) A copy or description of the arbitration agreement or clause under which the dispute is to be settled.
(v) Comments on the number of arbitrators and the seat of arbitration.
(vi) If applicable, details of the arbitrator appointed by the claimant.

32. Upon filing the request for arbitration, the claimant has to pay the registration fee in accordance with Article 3 and Appendix III of the SCC Rules. If the claimant fails to pay the registration fee after having received a reminder from the SCC, the request for arbitration will be dismissed (Articles 3(2) and 10(ii)).Evidence of payment should preferably be enclosed with the request, thereby expediting the proceedings.[31]

33. Similar to the Act, the SCC Rules allow the respondent to accept a defective request for arbitration. Consequently, Article 31 states that a party who has failed to object without delay to a defective request will be considered to have waived the right to object to such failure. However, if the deficiency is substantial, the SCC will ask the claimant to supplement its request.

34. In the same manner as the Act, the SCC Rules do not require the claimant to set out in detail the issues to which the dispute relates. The claimant will have the opportunity to fully develop its case before the arbitral tribunal at a later stage (see Article 24 of the SCC Rules). A short summary of the background to the dispute is therefore sufficient.

35. The nature and complexity of the dispute is of relevance for the number of arbitrators to be appointed (if not agreed on in the arbitration agreement). The complexity of the dispute may also have an impact on the amount of the advance on costs to be deposited.[32]

31. Öhrström, 122.
32. Öhrström, 118.

36. In contrast to the Act, the SCC Rules require a preliminary statement of the relief sought to be included in the request for arbitration.[33] However, the statement of relief is only preliminary until a statement of claim is submitted to the arbitral tribunal.[34] Preliminary details of relief are necessary in order for the SCC to determine the amount of the advance on costs to be paid.[35]

37. Absent the parties' agreement, the SCC will decide on the number of arbitrators in accordance with Article 12 of the SCC Rules. The main rule is that the arbitral tribunal is to consist of three arbitrators.

38. The parties are free to comment on the appropriate procedure, including on the nomination and qualifications of the arbitrator(s) to be appointed by the SCC.[36]

39. A request for arbitration is normally accompanied by a power of attorney for counsel for the claimant. If a power of attorney is not submitted, that failure is not considered a bar to continuation of the proceedings at the SCC. It is the duty of the arbitral tribunal to make sure that necessary authorization is in place.[37]

4. *Service of Request for Arbitration*

40. A party is considered to have received the request for arbitration when that party is notified of the request and has been given the opportunity to read it. It is therefore of great importance that the claimant obtains some reliable form of written evidence showing that the respondent (through an authorized person) has actually received the request for arbitration. The importance of securing evidence of service should be stressed, since the sender has the burden of proof in this respect.[38]

---

33. The Act only requires a statement on the disputed issue that is covered by the arbitration agreement, which issue is to be resolved by the arbitral tribunal, see s. 19(2) of the Act.
34. Article 24 of the SCC Rules.
35. If the amount of the claim is subsequently increased or decreased, the deposit may be adjusted accordingly. If the claim is declaratory, the claimant will be asked to estimate the value of the dispute so as to enable the SCC to determine the advance on costs payable. Such an indication of the value of the dispute may be included in the request for arbitration. However, if not included, this does not result in an invalid request.
36. Öhrström, 120.
37. Öhrström, 121–122. The claimant usually also submits registration certificate and other relevant documents if the parties are corporate entities. See also Lindskog, 582–583. Lindskog is of the view that the arbitral tribunal has no obligation to verify whether the parties have authorized representatives. However, since the parties are responsible for payment of the arbitrators' fee, it is in the interest of the arbitral tribunal to make sure that the parties are legally represented.
38. Heuman, 'Delgivning av påkallelseskrift i skiljeförfarande', 461. The Service of Documents Act and the alternative forms of service of process set out in the act are not applicable to arbitral proceedings; see *Christine L v. Sven A*, decision by the Supreme Court on 26 May 1999 in case no Ö 3715-9[illegible], NJA 1999 p. 300, where the Supreme Court applied a provision regarding the authorized recipient of the Swedish Service of Documents Act by analogy. In this case, an award had been delivered by registered mail and the recipient had signed the delivery acknowledgement although a messenger authorized by the recipient physically received the document. Personal service was considered to have been effected. See also *E. O. & Henry Trading AB v. ICA Handlarnas AB*, decision by the Supreme Court on 12 Dec. 2001 in case no

41. The Act does not set out formal requirements with respect to service of a request for arbitration. However, the Supreme Court has clarified that the Swedish Service of Documents Act is not applicable to arbitral proceedings, but that service of the request for arbitration must be effected personally.[39] It is therefore of great importance for the claimant to make sure that the opposing party actually receives the request for arbitration and to secure proof thereof.

42. If the request for arbitration is transmitted by fax, the sender's activity report has been found to be insufficient evidence as to whether the fax transmission has resulted in a corresponding printout from the addressee's fax transceiver.[40] Therefore, the general view is that the sender should always request confirmation by an authorized representative that the recipient has received the message.[41]

43. E-mails are sometimes used for transmitting notices. It is not clear how this should be treated. Technically, it is possible to obtain a delivery notice and also an acknowledgement of the recipient reading an e-mail. However, e-mails can be received and read by other persons than intended. It has therefore been suggested that such acknowledgement may not suffice as evidence of service.[42]

44. It is common that commercial agreements include 'notices provisions'.[43] Case law suggests that it is not sufficient to comply with such a notice provision in order to have achieved proper service of a request for arbitration if there is no evidence that the request has actually been received by an authorized representative of the opposing party.[44] One view is that, even if complying with the notice provision, the claimant must at least check public records in order to verify the accuracy of the address stated in the provision.[45]

Ö 4237-99, NJA 2001 p. 855, and *AB Akron-Maskiner v. N. G. G*, decision by the Supreme Court on 27 Jun. 2002 in case no Ö 3631-01, NJA 2002 p. 377.

39. *Scanax Aktiebolag v. Svensk Filmtjänst Aktiebolag*, decision by the Supreme Court made on 25 May 1996 in case no Ö 5023/94, NJA 1996 p. 330. See also Lars Heuman in JT 1996/97, 459-464. In *Jan A v. John D*, judgment by the Supreme Court made on 19 Jun. 1993 in case no T 296/89, NJA 1993 p. 252, a request for arbitration had first been received by counsel for the claimant and, after several months, by the claimant personally. With reference to the circumstances of the case, the Supreme Court held that the request for arbitration had been made at the later date when the claimant had received the request personally.
40. *Kenneth O v. Motor Union Assuransfirma AB*, decision by the Supreme Court on 23 Jun. 1993 in case no Ö 2317-91, NJA 1993 p. 308.
41. Seipel, 374–376, and Heuman, *Arbitration Law of Sweden: Practice and Procedure*, 306 et seq.
42. Hobér, *International Commercial Arbitration in Sweden*, 208.
43. A notices provision in an agreement states how (e-mail, letter or fax) and to whom notices may validly be sent under the agreement.
44. In *Lenmorniiproekt OAO v. Arne Larsson Partner Leasing AB*, decision by the Supreme Court on 16 Apr. 2010 in case no Ö 13-09, NJA 2010 p. 219, enforcement in Sweden of a Russian arbitral award was refused by the Supreme Court because the party against which the award was invoked had not been given proper notice of the arbitration. In this case the request for arbitration had been sent to the designated address for sending notices to the respondent under the main contract. But the respondent had changed its address, officially registered its new address with the Swedish Companies Registration Office and moved offices before the arbitration was initiated and had not participated in any stage of the arbitration.
45. See discussion in Hobér, *International Commercial Arbitration in Sweden*, 208. See also Lindskog, 88.

45. Applying the SCC Rules avoids the uncertainty of establishing the exact time of the respondent's receipt of the request. Once the request for arbitration has been received and accepted by the SCC, the arbitration is considered to have commenced and the SCC assumes responsibility for serving the request for arbitration on the respondent.

46. The requirements of the SCC Rules for proper service of documents are relatively low. In principle, it is sufficient to send a request for arbitration by fax to a number provided by the claimant. However, in practice, the SCC makes great efforts in order to ensure that the respondent actually receives the request for arbitration. Service is considered to have been achieved when reasonable efforts have been made to reach the respondent.[46]

47. Article 8 of the SCC Rules provides that any notice or communication from the SCC is to be sent to the last known address of the addressee. Delivery can be either by courier or registered mail, fax, e-mail or other means of communication that provides a record of sending. Further, it is stated that a notice will be considered to have been received by the addressee on the date it would normally have been received given the chosen means of communication. The same rules apply to the arbitral tribunal's communications to the parties (Article 33 of the SCC Rules).

B. Answer to Request for Arbitration and Constitution of the Arbitral Tribunal

48. The Act provides that, if the claimant has appointed its arbitrator in the request for arbitration, the respondent must notify the claimant of its choice of arbitrator within thirty days as from the date of service of the request for arbitration.[47] The two arbitrators thus appointed then appoint the chairperson of the arbitral tribunal,[48] at which point the arbitral tribunal is constituted.

49. Apart from the requirement to appoint an arbitrator within thirty days, the Act is silent with respect to how the respondent is to answer the request for arbitration. In practice, however, the respondent's choice of arbitrator is usually made in a written answer to the request for arbitration. The answer may also set out a brief response to the request for arbitration, including the respondent's position with respect to the claim, and other information, such as contact details of counsel. Thus, although not provided for in the Act, the answer to the request for arbitration in ad hoc proceedings is often similar to an answer submitted in accordance with the more detailed requirements of the SCC Rules, which will be discussed in the following.

46. Öhrström, 127 and 133.
47. Section 14 of the Act. If the respondent fails to appoint its arbitrator within thirty days, the arbitrator will, upon the claimant's application, be appointed by the district court of competent jurisdiction; see s. 13(3) of the Act.
48. Section 13 of the Act. Should the two party-appointed arbitrators fail to appoint a chairperson within thirty days, any of the parties may, under s. 14 of the Act, apply to the district court that the court appoint the chairperson.

50. Under Article 5 of the SCC Rules, the Secretariat of the SCC sends the respondent a copy of the request for arbitration (and documents attached). The Secretariat also sets a time limit within which the respondent must submit an answer to the SCC. Usually the respondent is given two weeks to submit its answer.[49] The respondent's answer must include:

(i) objections concerning the existence, validity or applicability of the arbitration agreement; however, failure to raise objections does not preclude the respondent from subsequently raising objections at any time up to and including submission of the statement of defence;
(ii) an admission or denial of the relief sought in the request for arbitration;
(iii) a preliminary statement of counterclaims or set-offs;
(iv) comments on the number of arbitrators and the seat of arbitration; and
(v) if applicable, details of the arbitrator appointed by the respondent.

51. The Secretariat sends the respondent's answer to the claimant and the claimant is given the opportunity to comment on the answer. Under Article 5(3) of the SCC Rules, failure by a respondent to submit an answer will not prevent the arbitration from proceeding. Under the SCC Rules, the Board of the SCC appoints the chairperson unless the parties have agreed otherwise (Article 13 of the SCC Rules).

52. Under the SCC Rules, once the arbitral tribunal has been appointed and the advance on costs has been paid, the case will be referred to the arbitral tribunal.

III. MULTIPARTY ARBITRATIONS

A. Introductory Remarks

53. Arbitrations that involve more than two parties are referred to as 'multiparty arbitrations'.[50] Multiparty arbitration appears to be increasingly common.[51]

54. Multiparty arbitration can take many different forms. The most straightforward example is when the request for arbitration already names several parties, all of which are parties to the contract in dispute and, thus, are parties to the same arbitration agreement. Multiparty situations may also occur when there are several contracts, each of which has a bearing on the issues in dispute (e.g., this is often the case with large construction contracts).[52] Sometimes more than two parties are involved in the

49. Öhrström, 127.
50. See Voser, 346.
51. See Born, *International Arbitration Cases and Materials* 877 (Aspen Publishers 2011): 'Although empirical evidence is limited, it appears that a significant and increasing number of international arbitrations involve multiparty disputes, with roughly a third of all ICC arbitrations involving multiple parties'. Although there are no official SCC statistics, the authors of this contribution have been informed that roughly every fifth SCC arbitration registered in 2010 and 2011 (up to October) involves multiple parties.
52. See Hobér, *International Commercial Arbitration in Sweden*, 149. See also Blackaby et al., *Redfern and Hunter on International Arbitration* 150–152 (5th ed., Oxford U. Press 2009).

arbitration from the outset of the arbitral proceedings, i.e., they are named in the request for arbitration, and sometimes additional parties are joined after the arbitration has commenced.[53]

55. Many advantages are often associated with having all issues related to a dispute dealt with in the same arbitration, rather than in separate arbitrations. Not only does this save time and costs, it also avoids the risk of conflicting decisions in respect of the same issues of facts or law or both. In national court proceedings, it is generally possible to consolidate separate proceedings, or to join additional parties, and often a number of mechanisms are available to achieve that.[54] However, in arbitration this is more complicated, sometimes even impossible, since the arbitral process is based on a contractual undertaking between the relevant parties.[55]

56. This section examines some of the issues relating to multiparty arbitrations, namely consolidation, joinder and intervention. Another important issue is the question how to appoint arbitrators in multiparty situations. This latter issue will not be discussed here.

B. Consolidation, Joinder and Intervention

1. Introduction

57. The concepts of consolidation, joinder and intervention are connected and the terms are sometimes used interchangeably. In this contribution, the term 'consolidation' is used as it is most commonly used, i.e., to describe when two arbitral proceedings are merged into one proceeding. The term 'joinder' is often used to reflect a situation where a party to an ongoing arbitration requests that a third party be joined to the arbitration. The term 'intervention' is typically used for situations where a third contracting party wishes to join a pending arbitration. This is also how the terms 'joinder' and 'intervention' will be used here, although, admittedly, 'joinder' is regularly used to describe both those concepts.

58. Under Swedish arbitration law, it is not possible to join additional parties to an ongoing arbitration or to consolidate different arbitrations, absent an agreement to that effect between all parties affected. Such agreement may be found in the arbitration agreement or consent may be given when the question arises.

59. This approach is in line with Article V(1)(d) of the Convention on the Recognition and Enforcement of Foreign Arbitral Awards, 1958 (New York Convention) which allows refusal to recognize and enforce arbitral awards where '[t]he composition of the arbitral authority, or the arbitral procedure was not in accordance with the agreement

53. See Voser, 348–349.
54. See Born, *International Arbitration Cases and Materials*, 877.
55. See Blackaby et al., 150 and Hobér, *International Commercial Arbitration in Sweden*, 149.

of the parties'. By allowing a request for joinder or consolidation without an unambiguous agreement between the parties, an arbitral tribunal alters the parties' agreement as regards both the 'composition of the arbitral authority' and the 'arbitral procedure', thus jeopardizing recognition and enforceability of any future award.[56]

2. *Consolidation*

60. The Act does not include provisions dealing with consolidation of arbitral proceedings.[57] Observing the fundamental arbitral principle of party autonomy, the legislator has left it to the parties to agree, if they should want consolidation to be possible.

61. Unlike the Act, the SCC Rules contain a provision providing for consolidation. Article 11 of the SCC Rules provides as follows:

> If arbitration is commenced concerning a legal relationship in respect of which an arbitration between the same parties is already pending under these Rules, the Board may, at the request of a party, decide to consolidate the new claims with the pending proceedings. Such decision may only be made after consulting the parties and the Arbitral Tribunal.[58]

62. Article 11 addresses the situation where an arbitration is initiated and – before an arbitral tribunal has been constituted – one of the parties requests the arbitration to be consolidated with an already pending arbitration. Accordingly, Article 11 does not provide for consolidation of two ongoing arbitrations which both have arbitral tribunals in place. A number of further requirements must be met in order for the SCC Board to be able to grant a request for consolidation under Article 11.

63. First, as indicated above, a party must request consolidation.

64. Second, the new arbitration must be between the same parties as the original arbitration.

65. Third, the new arbitration must concern the same legal relationship as the original arbitration. The new arbitration may have been initiated under the same arbitration agreement as the original arbitration,[59] or the new arbitration may have been initiated under another arbitration agreement, found in another contract between the parties.[60]

---

56. See Born, *International Commercial Arbitration*, 2074: 'In the context of recognizing arbitral awards, Art. V(1)(d) of the Convention provides for the non-recognition of awards that are rendered following arbitral proceedings where *consolidation, joinder, or intervention* was ordered, notwithstanding an arbitration agreement that did not permit such actions'. (Emphasis added.)
57. The provisions of the Code of Judicial Procedure (*Sw: Rättegångsbalk* (*1942:740*)) on consolidation of separate court proceedings, or joinder of related claims, are not applicable to arbitral proceedings.
58. Article 11 of the SCC Rules.
59. In such case, the claim could just as well have been made in the original arbitration (provided that the new claim would be considered a permitted amendment under Art. 25 of the SCC Rules).
60. Such a claim could not always have been made in the original arbitration, since the arbitral tribunal derives its jurisdiction only from the arbitration agreement under which it has been

If the two arbitrations relate to the same contract, they may often be presumed to concern the same legal relationship. However, if the claims made in the two arbitrations are under different contracts, it is not always easy to determine whether the claims concern the same legal relationship. The fact that the parties chose to enter into two contracts rather than one might imply that the parties themselves were of the view that there were two different legal relationships. Examples of where different contracts may be said to concern the same legal relationship are often found in large infrastructure projects. Other examples include when the parties have entered into a letter of intent and, subsequently, a share purchase agreement, or when they have entered into a loan agreement and then a separate pledge agreement as security for the loan. They may also have entered into a series of similar contracts, for example for recurring supply of a certain product. Whether or not the contracts in question concern the same legal relationship is ultimately something for the SCC Board to decide.

66. Fourth, the new arbitration must be initiated under the same rules as the original arbitration. Accordingly, an arbitration under the SCC Rules may not be consolidated with an arbitration under the SCC Rules for Expedited Arbitration.[61]

67. It should also be noted that the SCC Rules do not give the arbitral tribunal the authority to consolidate proceedings. Only the SCC Board is invested with such authority.

3. *Joinder and Intervention*

68. A core question widely debated in the arbitration community is whether to accept joinder or intervention of additional parties to an ongoing arbitration.[62] Neither the Act nor the SCC Rules address the issue of joining (whether by intervention or joinder) additional parties to an already ongoing arbitration.

69. It has been suggested that, as a matter of principle, from the moment an arbitration has commenced a third party may only be joined to the arbitration 'in case this is authorized by the relevant arbitration rules and the applicable procedural law. When they are silent, such joinder is not possible without the consent of all parties involved'.[63]

constituted. In practice, however, such a new claim as here discussed – a claim relating to the 'same legal relationship' as the original claim – would, arguably, also be covered by the arbitration agreement in the original arbitration. The reason for this is that most arbitration agreements are wide in scope. They often cover 'any' dispute arising 'out of or in connection with' the agreement in which they are included. Hence, in most situations covered by Art. 11 of the SCC Rules, the claim could just as well have been made in the original arbitration, either directly, as a counter-claim or as an amendment of the case under Art. 25 of the SCC Rules.

61. See Öhrström, 144.
62. See Roos, 219.
63. See Hanotiau, 176.

70. This principle has its foundation in the New York Convention provisions with respect to party autonomy,[64] which principles are reflected in the Act. As such, the principle also applies to international arbitrations in Sweden. Accordingly, joinder and intervention require consent of all parties affected: of those joined and of those already parties to the arbitration. This was illustrated in a reported SCC case from 2001.[65] The SCC Board was asked to order joinder. The SCC Board held that, under Swedish law and the SCC rules, joinder was not to be allowed. This finding was also repeated by the sole arbitrator in a procedural order and in the final award, which stated that '[a] third party may be brought into the proceedings only by agreement to that effect between the parties already in the proceedings and the third party, provided that the grounds for a claim against the third party is based on the arbitration agreement.'[66]

71. In conclusion, if the Act and/or the SCC Rules apply to the dispute in question, joinder or intervention of an additional party will only be possible if an arbitration agreement is in place between the joining or intervening party and the parties in the arbitration, and they all consent to the joinder or intervention.[67] Such consent may be given in the arbitration agreement or in the arbitration rules referred to in that agreement, or it may be given by the parties when the issue arises.

4. *Drafting the Arbitration Agreement to Allow for Joinder and Intervention*

72. As discussed above, the Swedish legislator has determined that it is for the users of arbitration to decide if and how they want to provide for joinder and intervention in arbitration. The SCC has come to the same conclusion in its rules.

73. When there are multiple parties to a transaction, careful consideration should be given to drafting the arbitration clause in order to allow – or to not allow – joinder and intervention. This applies irrespective of whether the institutional rules referred to provide for joinder and intervention. If the parties wish joinder and intervention to be possible, guidance may be found in the IBA Guidelines on Conflicts of Interest in International Arbitration for Drafting International Arbitration Clauses.

74. Careful analysis of the contract in question, and of the various party constellations and claim structures that may arise, ought to be carried out before adopting rules providing for intervention and joinder. If it is desired that multiparty arbitration be possible with respect to claims arising under two or more different contracts, it should be emphasized that additional considerations need to be made so as to allow not only for multiparty arbitration, but also for multi-contract arbitration.

---

64. See, for example, Art. V(1)(d) of the New York Convention.
65. *X v. Y Holdings AG and Y AG*, arbitral award rendered in SCC case no 9/2001, Stockholm Arbitration Report 2002, 125–133.
66. *X v. Y Holdings AG and Y AG*, arbitral award rendered in SCC case no 9/2001, Stockholm Arbitration Report 2002, 125.
67. See Hanotiau, 165–167.

IV. CONDUCT OF PROCEEDINGS

A. Introduction

75. As alluded to in the introduction to this chapter, there are in principle two sets of rules that will decide the conduct of arbitral proceedings in Sweden. First, we have the mandatory rules in the Act. Second, where no such mandatory rules exist, there is the arbitration agreement including institutional rules specified therein, such as the SCC Rules.

76. The Act contains few mandatory rules on procedure, whilst the SCC Rules provide an outline only of the various steps to be taken, but not a comprehensive set of procedural rules. Instead, the arbitral procedure is to a great extent set by the parties' agreements and by directions from the arbitral tribunal having regard to the overriding procedural principles of equal treatment of the parties and the parties' right to present their cases.

77. As a matter of principle, an arbitration in Sweden is to be conducted independently of the Code of Judicial Procedure.[68] However, the Code contains general procedural principles which could serve as non-mandatory guidance to the arbitral tribunal when procedural issues are to be determined in relation to which the Act and other applicable rules are silent and there is no set arbitral practice to rely on.[69]

1. *Party Autonomy and Due Process*

78. The principle of party autonomy is one of the cornerstones of Swedish arbitration. Under section 21 of the Act, the arbitral tribunal should, in its handling of the dispute 'act in accordance with the decisions of the parties insofar as there is no impediment to do so'.[70] In short, this means that the parties' joint instructions regarding procedure must be complied with unless they violate Swedish public policy/mandatory rules or if they cannot reasonably be carried out.[71]

68. (*Sw: Rättegångsbalk* (*1942:740*)).Govt. bill 1998/99: 35, 47 and SOU 1994:81, p. 74.
69. Case law that predates the Act provides various examples of the Code of Judicial Procedure influencing arbitrations. In *Bertil B. v. AB Bonnierföretagen*, decision by the Supreme Court made on 2 Jun. 1989 in case no Ö 502-88, NJA 1989 p. 247, the Supreme Court declared that it was natural to seek guidance in the Code of Judicial Procedure with respect to legal costs in arbitrations See also *Esselte AB v. Allmänna Pensionsfonden*, decision by the Supreme Court made on 3 Apr. 2008 in case no T 5685/96, NJA 1998 p. 189, where the Supreme Court found that the principles of res judicata in civil proceedings apply to arbitrations unless there are strong reasons to the contrary. The Code of Judicial Procedure may also be of indirect importance insofar as Swedish lawyers engaging in arbitral proceedings are accustomed to its governing principles, see e.g., Hobér, *International Commercial Arbitration in Sweden*, 199.
70. Cf. Art. 19(1) of the SCC Rules: 'Subject to these Rules and any agreement between the parties, the Arbitral Tribunal may conduct the arbitration in such manner as it considers appropriate.'
71. Govt. bill 1998/99:35, 110. See also Madsen, *Commercial Arbitration in Sweden* 154 (2d ed., Oxford University Press 2006).

79. The principle of equal treatment of the parties is another fundamental principle governing arbitrations in Sweden.[72] The principle is recognized in section 21 of the Act, which provides that the arbitrators should handle the dispute in an 'impartial, practical and speedy manner', although it has been held that the principle of equal treatment has wider implications than the requirement of impartiality.[73] The principle of equal treatment means that the parties should be offered the same procedural rights and duties so that each party will be given an opportunity, to the extent necessary, to present its case orally or in writing.[74] For example, the arbitral tribunal may not determine that only one party may request production of documents, present evidence or otherwise present its case, or that only one party must comply with the timetable set for the arbitration. However, this requirement of equal treatment should not be interpreted to mean, for example, that only because one party's request for production of documents has been granted, the other party's request must also be granted. Nor does it require that the parties necessarily are afforded the exact same amount of time to present their respective case at the hearing.

80. The due process requirements underpinning the principle of equal treatment sometimes override the principle of party autonomy. An agreement between the parties which gives only one party a procedural benefit or which deprives one party of a procedural right it has under the Act may be held invalid.[75]

81. Party autonomy and due process further entail that each party must be given an opportunity to comment on what has been submitted by the other party. This rule is peremptory, as a party cannot in advance waive its right to present its case.[76] It is doubtful whether the parties may validly conclude an agreement to that effect during the proceedings.[77]

72. See, for instance, Lindskog, 578, Heuman, *Arbitration Law of Sweden: Practice and Procedure*, 260 and Carbonneau, 8.
73. Lindskog, 579.
74. Section 24(1) of the Act. Art. 19(2) of the SCC Rules comprises the requirement of impartiality as well as the principle of equal treatment and the right for the parties to present their respective cases: 'In all cases, the Arbitral Tribunal shall conduct the arbitration in an impartial, practical and expeditious manner, giving each party an equal and reasonable opportunity to present its case.'
75. Heuman, *Arbitration Law of Sweden: Practice and Procedure*, 260 and Blackaby et al., *Redfern and Hunter on International Arbitration*, 366.
76. Govt. bill 1998/99:35, 227 and 311.
77. See Heuman, *Arbitration Law of Sweden: Practice and Procedure*, 257 and Blackaby et al., *Redfern and Hunter on International Arbitration*, 366. See also *Dentirol v. SwissCo*, decision by the Court of Appeal for Western Sweden made on 30 Sep. 2005 in case no T 4805-03, where the arbitral tribunal had permitted the filing of additional written submissions in excess of the number stipulated in the SCC Rules for Expedited Arbitrations. The Court of Appeal placed the burden on the challenging party to prove that the arbitral tribunal had had reason not to allow the additional submissions, and noted that the challenging party had failed to discharge that burden.

2. *Powers of the Arbitral Tribunal*

82. It follows from the above that, absent binding instructions from the parties, arbitrators have broad discretion to decide the most appropriate way to conduct the proceedings within the confines of the governing principles of equal treatment of the parties and their right to plead their cases.[78] Before doing so the arbitrators should allow the parties to present a view on procedural matters.

83. The arbitral tribunal's determinations with respect to procedure are often made in the form of procedural orders. As to their legal status, procedural orders and other procedural determinations are categorized as decisions within the meaning of section 27(3) of the Act (see further in section VIII).

84. Grave procedural errors may constitute grounds for challenge. As described in detail elsewhere in this book, section 34(1)(6) of the Act provides that an award may be wholly or partially set aside if an irregularity occurred in the course of the proceedings and it is probable that the irregularity influenced the outcome of the case. However, under section 34(2) a party is not entitled to rely on a procedural error which the party, through participation in the proceedings without objection, may be considered to have waived.[79] This rule applies to procedural decisions that violate procedural rules or principles as well as to instances where the arbitral tribunal has disregarded an agreement between the parties.[80]

85. The Act does not specify at which point in time a party must object to the decision in question. In this regard, it has been suggested that Swedish proceedings would in most cases follow Article 4 of the UNCITRAL Model Law on International Commercial Arbitration 1985. With amendments as adopted in 2006 (Model Law), which provides that an objection should be made 'without undue delay'.[81] What constitutes undue delay may vary depending on the circumstances in the particular situation, e.g., on the nature of the decision or omission by the arbitral tribunal. An alternative is that the arbitral tribunal inform the parties at an early stage that any protest must be made within a certain period as from the relevant decision.[82]

---

78. See Sekolec and Eliasson, 214–215.
79. The *travaux préparatoires* to the Act do not explain the purpose of the rule, which also exists under the Model Law, but the corresponding documents in relation to the old Arbitration Act of 1929 indicate that one important function was to prevent a party from being able to speculate on the outcome of the arbitral proceedings, see NJA II 1929 p. 49. It has been suggested that the rule serves an even more important corrective purpose since it may enable the arbitrators to correct the effects of wrongful procedural decisions, see Heuman, *Arbitration Law of Sweden: Practice and Procedure*, 271 and Lindskog, 973. See also *Globe Nuclear Services and Supply GNSS, Limited v. AO Techsnabexport*, decision by the Svea Court of Appeal on 18 Dec. 2009 in case no T 5383-07. In this case the court found that a party had not objected to the arbitral tribunal's handling of the case. The party was therefore prevented from challenging the arbitral award in this regard.
80. See Heuman, *Arbitration Law of Sweden: Practice and Procedure*, 270–71.
81. See Heuman, *Arbitration Law of Sweden: Practice and Procedure*, 276.
82. See Heuman, *Arbitration Law of Sweden: Practice and Procedure*, 276.

B. Organizing the Proceedings

86. Once the arbitral tribunal has been formed, various matters need to be dealt with at the very outset, such as the schedule for filing written submissions, and the form and sequence in which they must be filed, evidentiary matters, dates for procedural meetings, preparatory hearings and the merits hearing, fees, the language of the proceedings, the seat of arbitration, and confidentiality.[83] Commonly, the arbitral tribunal initiates a telephone conference or summons the parties to a case management meeting for the purpose of resolving these matters.[84] Normally, the chairperson of the arbitral tribunal manages the proceedings.

C. Preliminary Issues

87. Quite often issues emerge at an early stage of the proceedings which may need to be dealt with as preliminary issues in the sense that they are to be resolved before the arbitral tribunal examines the substance of the claims. Examples are the seat of arbitration, the arbitral tribunal's jurisdiction, applicable law and whether the proceedings should be bifurcated into a liability phase and a quantum phase.

88. Under the Act, the arbitral tribunal is to decide the seat of arbitration, if no such agreement exists between the parties,[85] whilst under the SCC Rules the SCC Board is to determine the seat unless agreed upon by the parties.[86] It is not uncommon that the seat of arbitration has been determined by the parties in the arbitration agreement.

89. Absent the parties' agreement, it is for the arbitral tribunal to decide when and in what form the issue of applicable law should be decided. The arbitral tribunal should determine the applicable law in a decision early in the proceedings, so that the parties know which law or rules will apply to the case that they are to present.

90. Under section 29 of the Act, '[a] part of the dispute, or a certain issue which is of significance to the resolution of the dispute, may be decided through a separate award, unless opposed by both parties'. Accordingly, the arbitral tribunal may raise the question of bifurcation *sua sponte*, although it is of course more likely that the initiative comes from one of the parties. If both parties agree that a separate award should be rendered on, for example, liability or on an issue of law, the arbitral tribunal is bound to follow the parties' agreement.[87] If the parties disagree in this regard, the arbitral tribunal must conduct a careful analysis of the issues involved and the potential consequences before deciding on bifurcation.

83. In SCC proceedings, the arbitral tribunal is required to promptly consult with the parties with a view to establishing a provisional timetable for the conduct of the arbitration and to send the provisional timetable to the parties and the Secretariat, see Art. 23 of the SCC Rules.
84. See also Blackaby et al., *Redfern and Hunter on International Arbitration*, 371 and Sutton et al., 222.
85. Section 22 of the Act. See also Heuman, *Arbitration Law of Sweden: Practice and Procedure*, 707–711.
86. Article 20 of the SCC Rules.
87. Govt. bill 1998/99:35, 132.

91. Another example of a preliminary issue that may have to be decided by the arbitral tribunal at an early stage is the question of the arbitral tribunal's jurisdiction. The Act does not contain specific provision as to when during the proceedings the arbitral tribunal should rule on its own jurisdiction. Depending on the circumstances of the case there may be reason for an arbitral tribunal to deal with this issue before it proceeds to the merits of the case.

D. Interim Measures

92. Unless the parties have agreed otherwise, the arbitral tribunal may, at the request of a party, order the other party to undertake a certain interim measure to secure the claim which is to be adjudicated in the dispute.[88] The arbitral tribunal is afforded extensive possibilities to decide on the particular measure to be undertaken in order, for instance, to secure evidence.[89]

93. In most jurisdictions,[90] an arbitral tribunal's decisions in this respect are not enforceable. However, the parties are bound by such decisions as amongst themselves and a party's failure to comply with a decision may be ascribed importance by the arbitral tribunal in other respects, for example when it comes to determining liability for loss caused or when calculating damages.[91]

E. Written Submissions

1. *Introduction*

94. Once the arbitral tribunal has been constituted and is in receipt of the file, and the basic rules of the procedure have been set, the arbitration typically continues with exchange of written submissions. The primary purpose of the first exchange of written submissions (the statement of claim and the statement of defence), is to define the issues to be determined by the arbitral tribunal and to set the framework for the dispute. In virtually all arbitrations, the first exchange of submissions is followed by at least one further round of submissions: the claimant's 'reply' and the respondent's 'rejoinder'.

88. See s. 25(4) of the Act and Art. 32 of the SCC Rules.
89. Govt. bill 1998/99:35, 229. According to Heuman, there is nothing to prevent the arbitral tribunal from requesting the voluntary participation of a third party in this regard, see Heuman, *Arbitration Law of Sweden: Practice and Procedure*, 333.
90. Under the Model Law, the main rule is that an interim measure issued by an arbitral tribunal should be recognized as binding and, unless otherwise provided by the arbitral tribunal, enforced upon application to the competent court, irrespective of the country in which it was issued, Art. 17H(1). Legislation based on the Model Law with the 2006 amendments has been enacted in Australia, Brunei, Hong Kong, Costa Rica, Georgia, Ireland, Mauritius, New Zealand, Peru, Rwanda, Slovenia and the State of Florida (see www.UNCITRAL.org).
91. SOU 1994:81, 102 and 285. See also Govt. bill 1998/99:35, 74.

95. Submission of the statement of claim and the statement of defence is expressly provided for in Article 24 of the SCC Rules and indirectly provided for under section 23 of the Act. Apart from these provisions, there are no rules with respect to the written submissions to be made by the parties. The requirements that apply with respect to the statements of claim and defence, respectively, will be discussed below.

2. *Statement of Claim*

96. Section 23 of the Act sets forth the minimum requirements for the claimant's statement of claim and the respondent's statement of defence, if not otherwise agreed between the parties. The statement of claim must contain the claimant's prayers for relief in respect of the issue stated in the request for arbitration and the material facts invoked in support. Failing this, the arbitral tribunal should order the claimant to remedy deficiencies.

97. The Act does not require the claimant to file or even identify evidence, whether oral or documentary, together with the statement of claim. In domestic arbitrations in Sweden, which may be more or less influenced by practices before Swedish courts, it is therefore sometimes seen that evidence is submitted and specified only towards the end of the written phase of the proceedings. In international arbitrations in Sweden, however, it is commonly agreed by the parties or determined in a first procedural order issued by the arbitral tribunal that all evidence, including witness statements, relied on by the claimant in support of the allegations in the statement of claim are to be referenced in and submitted together with the statement of claim. This is also the default rule under the SCC Rules, under which the documents on which the claimant relies are to be submitted together with the statement of claim (see below). In the authors' experience, much is gained in terms of time and the number of briefs can be kept to a minimum, if this 'front-loaded' procedure is adopted, rather than having a procedure where the evidentiary situation is not known until shortly before the hearing.

98. Article 24 of the SCC Rules provides that a statement of claim should be submitted by the claimant within a period set by the arbitral tribunal. The statement of claim must include the following (if not already submitted):

(i) the specific relief sought;
(ii) the material circumstances on which the claimant relies; and
(iii) the documents on which the claimant relies.

3. *Statement of Defence*

99. Under the Act, the respondent is to state its position in relation to the claimant's prayers for relief and state the facts supporting its own position within the time set by the arbitral tribunal. Thus, the statement of defence should contain an acceptance or denial of the claimant's prayers for relief. In addition, the statement of defence normally contains admission or denial of facts relied upon by the claimant.[92] If the respondent wishes to object to the jurisdiction of the arbitral tribunal, that objection must, as a general rule, be included in the statement of defence. Failing this, the objection may be considered to have been waived.

100. Article 24 of the SCC Rules provides that a statement of defence should be submitted by the respondent within a period set by the arbitral tribunal. The statement of defence must include the following (if not already submitted):

(i) objections concerning the existence, validity or applicability of the arbitration agreement;
(ii) a statement whether, and to what extent, the respondent admits or denies the relief sought by the claimant;
(iii) the material circumstances on which the respondent relies;
(iv) any counterclaim or set-off claim and the grounds on which it is based; and
(v) the documents on which the respondent relies.

4. *Request for Relief*

101. The scope of the arbitral tribunal's jurisdiction is set by the arbitration agreement and supplemented by agreements or admissions made by the parties during the course of the proceedings. The prayers for relief (and any counterclaim filed by the respondent) also define the limits of the arbitral tribunal's mandate and are therefore of fundamental importance to the outcome of the proceedings. Besides, the prayers for relief have decisive implications for the res judicata effect of the award and the *lis pendens* effect of the proceedings.

102. There are no explicit requirements as to how the request for relief should be formulated. An arbitral tribunal has the power to order performance, either of a specific action or payment of monies, and to grant injunctive and declaratory relief, if either of the parties so requests. Declaratory claims seeking to establish the existence of a certain fact or an alleged interpretation of a contract may also be granted by the arbitral tribunal. But again, since the request for relief to some extent defines the limits of the arbitral tribunal's mandate, it has to be specified to such a degree that there is no doubt how the award is to be phrased if the relief is granted. The parties must explicitly and unequivocally state what they wish the arbitrators to decide. An undefined request for 'appropriate relief' or similar is not sufficient.

103. The arbitral tribunal has the power to dismiss a request for relief that is not sufficiently specific and clear.[93] Before doing so, however, the arbitral tribunal has an obligation to seek clarification in respect of requests for relief that are not sufficiently

92. Section 23 of the Act.
93. Lindskog, 681.

specific and clear. Failure to do so may constitute a procedural error and subject the award to challenge.[94]

5. *Facts Relied on in Support of Request for Relief*

104. In both domestic and international arbitrations in Sweden, the parties are expected to make the factual allegations they intend to rely upon in support of requests for relief. The arbitral tribunal is bound by the factual allegations made by the parties. The arbitral tribunal may thus not grant a request for relief on the basis of facts not relied on by the parties.[95]

6. *Amendment and Withdrawal of Claim*

105. Under section 23 of the Act and Article 25 of the SCC Rules, the claimant may submit new requests for relief and the respondent its own request for relief (counterclaim or set-off claim).[96] However, two conditions must be fulfilled. First, the claims must fall within the scope of the arbitration agreement. Second, adjudication of those claims must not be considered inappropriate by the arbitral tribunal. It is thus within the discretion of the arbitral tribunal, taking into consideration the time at which the new claim is submitted and other circumstances, to decide if a new claim should be allowed. According to the *travaux préparatoires*, the presumption is that the arbitral tribunal should be generous in allowing a new claim as long as the claim falls within the scope of the arbitration agreement.[97] However, the timing of the claim is of fundamental importance to consider, since late introduction of claims must not be allowed to be used as a means to obstruct the proceedings.[98] Subject to the same conditions, each party may amend or supplement previously presented claims and introduce new facts in support of its case. The right to amend or supplement a claim

---

94. Hobér, *International Commercial Arbitration in Sweden*, 215 and Lindskog, 681.
95. The requirement to specify the facts relied upon was interpreted strictly in a domestic challenge case before the Svea Court of Appeal in *Systembolaget AB v. V&S Vin & Sprit AB*, judgment by Svea Court of Appeal made on 1 Dec. 2009 in case no T 4548-08. In this case, Systembolaget AB requested an arbitral award to be set aside and maintained that the arbitral tribunal had exceeded the scope of its mandate by basing its ruling on facts that, in Systembolaget AB's view, had not been relied on by V&S Vin & Sprit AB. The Svea Court of Appeal granted the challenge and set aside the arbitral award in its entirety. The ruling, which is based on a strict application of domestic procedural rules, has been criticized and should not be considered to express any general rule that is applicable in international arbitration.
96. It should be noted that the SCC Rules set a time limit for amendments of claims. Claims may only be adjusted prior to close of proceedings under Art. 34 of the SCC Rules. The proceedings are to be declared closed by the arbitral tribunal when the parties have had a reasonable opportunity to present their cases. However, in exceptional circumstances and prior to making the final award, the proceedings may be reopened by the arbitral tribunal on its own motion or on request by a party.
97. Govt. bill 1998/99:35, 108 and 226. An arbitral tribunal's decision to dismiss a new claim can be a ground for challenge, see Lindskog, 684.
98. Govt. bill 1998/99:35, 226.

under section 23 of the Act is not mandatory and the parties may thus agree to disregard or amend that section.

106. In the view of the authors, an arbitral tribunal in an arbitration in Sweden should only dismiss a new or amended claim if allowing it would have a material adverse effect on the proceedings. When deciding this issue the arbitral tribunal needs to consider a number of factors. Two important aspects are time and cost-efficiency. Permitting amended claims may delay the proceedings. However, several different issues may be subject to dispute which are related to each other and if the underlying facts are the same then it might ultimately be more cost efficient to have these issues adjudicated in the same arbitral proceeding. Another factor to be considered by the arbitral tribunal is whether the award will result in res judicata for the dismissed claim if it is brought separately in subsequent proceedings.[99]

107. It should be noted that the parties in an arbitration may enter into a valid arbitration agreement orally or by conduct (including by omission to object). This implies that if a party submits a claim that is not covered by the arbitration agreement, that claim may, nevertheless, be tried by the arbitral tribunal if the opposing party fails to raise a jurisdictional objection. In that case, the original arbitration agreement is considered to have been extended to cover the new claim as well.[100]

108. If a delay in the proceedings has been caused by a party due to amendment of, or supplement to, a claim being allowed, this may have an impact on allocation of costs among the parties.[101]

109. If a party withdraws a claim, the arbitral tribunal should dismiss (without prejudice) that part of the dispute unless the opposing party requests a ruling on the withdrawn claim (section 28 of the Act). The party's entitlement to a ruling exists to prevent the opposing party from initiating new arbitration proceedings concerning the same claim.[102]

99. See Govt. bill 1998/99:35, 227.
100. Govt. bill 1998/99:35, 109 and 226.
101. Govt. bill 1998/99:35, 109 and 227.
102. See *Håkan Hedenstierna v. Handelshögskolan i Stockholm*, decision by the Supreme Court on 30 Nov. 2010 in case no T 3258-09, NJA 2010 p. 600. In this case, the claimant had initiated arbitration regarding certain claims in 2004. One claim was later withdrawn by the claimant without reason. The respondent did not request a ruling on the withdrawn claim and the arbitration proceeded on the remaining claims and an arbitral award was rendered in 2006. About six months later, the claimant initiated a new arbitration regarding the same claim that had previously been withdrawn in the first arbitration. The respondent objected and asserted that the arbitration agreement was no longer valid regarding the claim. The arbitral tribunal agreed with the respondent and dismissed the claim. However, the tribunal's decision was reversed by the Svea Court of Appeal. The Svea Court of Appeal reasoned that, since the respondent did not use its right to request a ruling on the withdrawn claim, the claimant was at liberty to raise that claim again. As to the validity of the arbitration agreement, mere withdrawal of a claim was not considered enough to alter or terminate the arbitration agreement. The court therefore found that the arbitration agreement was still valid between the parties. The Supreme Court came to the same ruling as the Svea Court of Appeal.

F. Hearings

1. *General*

110. Upon a party's request and provided that the parties have not agreed otherwise, at least one hearing will be held prior to determination of an issue referred to the arbitral tribunal for resolution.[103] A party's right to a hearing is absolute in the sense that a request for a hearing may not be denied by the arbitral tribunal, save for the – arguably rare – cases where the parties have already agreed that no hearings are to be held during the arbitration.[104]

111. The right to a hearing does not extend to other issues than those substantive matters which have been referred to the arbitral tribunal for adjudication.[105] In other words, the right to a hearing applies to issues relevant to the merits of the case. Consequently, a party cannot require the arbitral tribunal to arrange a hearing solely to deal with, for example, questions pertaining to case administration.[106]

112. In certain circumstances, the parties may lose their right to a hearing due to their own inaction. The *travaux préparatoires* to the Act explain that the arbitral tribunal can order the parties to request a hearing within a certain period. Should both parties fail to do so before the given deadline, they will be considered to have impliedly waived their right to a hearing.[107] However, considering the great importance attached to the right to a hearing in Swedish legal tradition, the arbitral tribunal should be wary of drawing conclusions solely based on the parties' failure to request a hearing within a stipulated period. Before considering denying a party a hearing on the grounds that the party has missed a deadline for requesting a hearing, the arbitral tribunal must be confident that the deadline imposed was not unreasonable and that the party has had adequate time to consider whether a hearing is necessary. If this is not the case, the decision not to have a hearing may be considered a violation of due process, subjecting the resulting award to the risk of being set aside in a subsequent challenge proceeding.

113. In practice, the absolute majority of arbitrations involve at least one hearing, during which the parties are allowed to present their legal arguments and evidence – and to challenge the other party's evidence. This hearing is often referred to as the 'main hearing', the 'final hearing' or the 'merits hearing'. It is also sometimes referred

103. Section 24(1) of the Act, which also provides that '[t]he arbitrators shall afford the parties, to the extent necessary, an opportunity to present their cases in writing and orally'. The same principle is expressed in Art. 27(1) of the SCC Rules, under which a hearing 'shall be held if requested by a party, or if deemed appropriate by the Arbitral Tribunal.'
104. Govt. bill 1998/99:35, 112 and 227. See also Hobér, *International Commercial Arbitration in Sweden*, 250 and Lindskog, 703.
105. Govt. bill 1998/99:35, 112. See also e.g., Lindskog, 701 et seq.
106. Such a hearing shall, however, be arranged by joint request from both parties, in accordance with the principle of party autonomy, or if the arbitral tribunal otherwise considers it appropriate, in accordance with the principle that the arbitral tribunal determines the conduct of the proceedings. See also Lindskog, 674.
107. Govt. bill 1998/99:35, 227. See also Madsen, *Commercial Arbitration in Sweden* 212 et seq. (3d ed., Oxford University Press 2007).

to as the 'evidentiary hearing'.[108] Although the proceedings, as a matter of principle, may be organized so that the evidence is taken at a separate hearing and counsel's oral submissions are delivered at another hearing (as is often done, for example, in France), in most arbitrations in Sweden the hearing is not used strictly for the purpose of presenting the evidence, but also for counsel to argue the case. For this reason, this contribution uses the term 'merits hearing', to distinguish the hearing from hearings on procedural and jurisdictional issues (hearings which may also involve taking evidence and which, thus, may be evidentiary hearings).

114. Depending on the complexity of the case before the arbitral tribunal, the merits hearing is preceded by other forms of hearing, as will be discussed below.

115. The arbitral tribunal has considerable flexibility in determining the place of hearings. Unless the parties have agreed otherwise, the arbitral tribunal may in principle decide to hold meetings and hearings in a different place or country than the seat of arbitration.[109] Notwithstanding the flexibility granted to the arbitral tribunal in this respect, it should always set the time, date and place for hearings in consultation with the parties.[110]

2. *Procedural Meetings*

116. As soon as the arbitral tribunal has been constituted, a meeting or, perhaps more commonly, a telephone conference is often arranged with the parties. This meeting is sometimes referred to as a 'scheduling conference' or a 'directions hearing'.

108. See, for example, the IBA Rules on the Taking of Evidence in International Arbitration 2010 (IBA Rules).

109. Section 22 of the Act. See also Govt. bill 1998/99:35, 113 et seq. The same applies under Art. 20(2) of the SCC Rules, which provides: 'The Arbitral Tribunal may, after consultation with the parties, conduct hearings at any place which it considers appropriate.' In a much-criticized case concerning the challenge of an arbitral award (*Titan Corporation v. Alcatel CIT SA*, decision by the Svea Court of Appeal made on 28 Feb. 2008 in case no T 1038-05, RH 2005:1), the Svea Court of Appeal ruled that the arbitration in question lacked connection to Sweden due to the fact, amongst others, that no meetings had been held in Sweden. Despite the fact that the place of arbitration was Sweden, the Court therefore refused to try the challenge. The parties then settled and the case was therefore never tried by the Supreme Court. The Titan ruling has generally been viewed as incorrect. In 2011, in its ruling in the case *RosInvestCO v. The Russian Federation*, decision by the Supreme Court made on 12 Nov. 2010 in case no Ö 2301-09, NJA 2010 p. 508, the Supreme Court removed the doubts created by the *Titan* case, stating that: 'where the parties have agreed that the proceedings shall take place in Sweden, it lacks importance [for the purposes of Swedish courts' jurisdiction] that the parties or the arbitrators have chosen to locate meetings in a different country, that the arbitrators are not Swedish, that they have performed their work in a different country, or that the dispute concerns an agreement that otherwise has no connection to Sweden.' (Our translation.) Accordingly, if Sweden is the place of arbitration, meetings and hearings may be held outside of Sweden, without Swedish courts' jurisdiction being affected.

110. Under Art. 27(2) of the SCC Rules, it is an explicit requirement that the arbitral tribunal consults with the parties before making any decisions in these respects. Although not expressly provided for, the same requirement must be understood to apply under the Act. If the parties are in disagreement with respect to where to hold the hearing, it is submitted that the arbitral tribunal as the default location should order the hearing to take place at the place of arbitration, unless compelling practical considerations point at another hearing location.

117. The primary purpose of this first meeting between the arbitral tribunal and the parties is to discuss and, if possible, agree the timetable for the proceedings. The SCC Rules require that the arbitral tribunal promptly consult with the parties with a view to setting a provisional timetable for the arbitration.[111] Although it is not a legal requirement, it is advisable also in ad hoc arbitrations under the Act to fix the timetable for the entire arbitration at the outset of the proceedings. In less complex matters, this may be done through e-mail correspondence rather than at a meeting.

118. Another important purpose of the first meeting is to discuss the rules that are to apply to conduct of the proceedings. As discussed above, the Act, as well as the major institutional rules, provides no details with respect to conduct of the proceedings. Instead, it is for the parties and the arbitral tribunal to adopt detailed rules which they see fit the case. These detailed rules for the proceedings may be discussed and adopted at the outset of the arbitration, or the arbitral tribunal may resolve issues later, as they arise. The Act and the SCC Rules do not require Terms of Reference or detailed procedural orders to be adopted by the arbitral tribunal. The first procedural order issued by the arbitral tribunal may therefore be limited to including a timetable for the parties' written submissions. In practice, however, it is advisable already in the first procedural order to address procedural issues which can be expected to arise later on in the proceedings. There are several reasons for this. It is generally easier to agree on procedural issues in the abstract at the beginning of the arbitration, rather than when the issues have arisen and the parties have already taken their positions. It also saves time if as many issues as possible are sorted out early and all at once, instead of being argued in separate correspondence before the arbitral tribunal at a later stage. And importantly, it provides for a fair proceeding if all parties involved - counsel, arbitrators, party representatives - share common ground with respect to the rules that are to apply. This is particularly important if the parties, their counsel or the arbitrators come from different legal backgrounds. It may in these instances be helpful to sort out early, for example, if, how and when production of documents may be requested, whether and how witness statements should be used, how documentary evidence is to be presented, what cut-off dates apply for new evidence and for demonstrative exhibits, and how to proceed with examination of witnesses at the hearing.

119. As mentioned in section IV.C above, the arbitral tribunal should also at this point raise and determine issues regarding applicable law and, if it is an ad hoc arbitration under the Act, the seat of the arbitration, if these issues have not already been agreed upon.[112]

---

111. Article 23 of the SCC Rules.

112. Absent the parties' agreement, the arbitral tribunal determines the seat of arbitration under s. 22 of the Act. If it is a SCC arbitration, however, the seat of arbitration is determined by the SCC Board, under Art. 20(1) of the SCC Rules. Irrespective of the seat of arbitration, hearings and meetings may be conducted at other places than the seat of arbitration; see s. 22(2) of the Act and Art. 20(2) of the SCC Rules. The seat of arbitration is thus fictional but is of importance because it determines which district court and Court of Appeal has jurisdiction to try actions concerning, for example, challenges to and appointment of arbitrators, as well as challenges and other proceedings against the award and the authority of the arbitral tribunal.

120. As indicated above, the first procedural meeting typically results in a procedural decision by the arbitral tribunal, taking the form of a 'first procedural order'. The written phase of the arbitration then proceeds in accordance with that first procedural order. Unless issues arise that require intermittent meetings, the next occasion for the arbitral tribunal and the parties to meet is often at a 'pre-hearing conference', usually by telephone.

121. In international arbitrations in Sweden, the pre-hearing conference generally deals with practical and procedural issues that need to be arranged or settled before the hearing. These may be issues relating to booking the hearing venue and arranging court reporters and interpreters, or how to schedule witnesses for appearance at the hearing. The case as such is normally not discussed in detail at this meeting, although certain clarifications may be sought, for example, with respect to the relief sought.

122. In domestic Swedish arbitrations, as well as in international arbitrations with Swedish arbitrators and counsel, the pre-hearing conference can sometimes have a somewhat different purpose. In addition to sorting out practical and procedural issues, the meeting is used to clarify the parties' respective cases, including prayers for relief and facts, legal arguments and evidence relied upon.[113] In these cases, the meeting is often referred to as a 'preparatory hearing'.[114] This meeting may be useful for the arbitrators' and the parties' understanding of what factual and legal issues are in dispute, so as to focus the merits hearing on contentious issues. However, if non-Swedish parties or counsel are involved in the arbitration, it is submitted that a preparatory hearing of this kind should be arranged only after the arbitral tribunal has explained in detail what it wants to achieve with the meeting and what it expects from the parties.

123. As an alternative to arranging a preparatory hearing of the kind described immediately above, the arbitral tribunal may issue a 'case summary' for the parties to comment on in writing.[115] The case summary is essentially a draft of the background sections of the final arbitral award. It thus includes the procedural background as well as the factual background to the dispute, to the extent the facts are not contentious. It also sets out the issues in dispute and the parties' respective factual account and arguments in relation to each such issue. The case summary leaves blank the arbitral tribunal's reasons and the operative part of the award – the *dispositif* – which obviously should not exist, let alone be presented, even in draft format before the arbitral tribunal has heard all evidence and the parties have concluded their respective arguments. Although primarily used in domestic Swedish arbitrations, case summaries are sometimes also seen in international arbitrations in Sweden. Just as the preparatory

113. See e.g., Madsen, *Commercial Arbitration in Sweden* 212 (3d ed., Oxford University Press 2007) and Hobér, *International Commercial Arbitration in Sweden*, 245.
114. The preparatory hearing in this sense has its equivalent in Swedish court proceedings. This is the reason why it is often seen in domestic Swedish arbitrations.
115. As is the case with 'preparatory meetings', this practice stems from domestic arbitrations. The Swedish word then used for the case summary is *recit* and, because of this, the case summary is sometimes referred to as a 'recital' in international arbitrations in Sweden.

hearing, if used correctly the case summary can serve to focus the hearing on the issues in dispute, since the parties have received confirmation from the arbitral tribunal that it has correctly understood what those issues are. At the same time, the case summary allows the parties to ascertain that all their arguments have been read and correctly understood by the arbitral tribunal.

3. *Jurisdictional Hearings*

124. In cases where the respondent challenges the arbitral tribunal's jurisdiction (or competence), and the arbitral tribunal decides to bifurcate the proceedings to resolve the jurisdictional objections separately before proceeding to the merits of the case, it may be necessary to hold a jurisdictional hearing. Just as a merits hearing, a jurisdictional hearing is preceded by written submissions as well as procedural meetings as described above. At the jurisdictional hearing, witnesses and experts, relevant to the issue of jurisdiction, may be heard, typically in accordance with the format of a merits hearing. Should the arbitral tribunal subsequently rule that it has jurisdiction, another scheduling meeting is normally arranged, setting out the timetable for the remainder of the arbitration. The parties then exchange written submissions on the merits of the case, followed by a pre-hearing conference and, finally, the hearing on the merits.

125. A decision to bifurcate the proceedings into a separate jurisdictional phase inevitably leads to delays if the arbitral tribunal finds that is has jurisdiction. The procedural steps set out above then need to be taken twice. It may therefore often be more economical, with regard to both time and costs, to hear the jurisdictional objections together with the case on the merits, at the merits hearing.

4. *Merits Hearing*

126. In most arbitrations conducted under Swedish arbitration law, the proceedings before the arbitral tribunal are concluded by a merits hearing. During the merits hearing, the parties are given the opportunity to present their respective cases by giving an oral account of their prayers for relief, factual and legal arguments, as well as presenting written and oral evidence. In accordance with the principle of party autonomy, the parties may of course agree that the merits hearing be more limited in scope. For instance, the parties can decide that the merits hearing should be devoted only to examination of witnesses and experts and that the parties' arguments will be made by written submissions to the arbitral tribunal. Similarly, unless the parties agree otherwise, the arbitral tribunal may give directions limiting the scope of the merits hearing. However, it is important for the arbitral tribunal to allow each party sufficient opportunity to elaborate on those parts of its case that the party regards as important and to highlight certain content in the written evidence. Although a party's right to argue its case orally is absolute, there is no right for a party to do so for an indefinite period. Within the confines provided by the principles of procedural equality and the parties' right to a reasonable opportunity to present their cases, the arbitral tribunal may, for example, impose time limits for oral arguments.

127. The aim under Swedish legal tradition is to hold the merits hearing for a continuous period without prolonged intermissions.[116] In complex arbitrations, the arbitral tribunal may foresee that the merits hearing will last for several weeks and experience severe difficulties in scheduling a merits hearing without prolonged intermissions. In these cases, the solution is often to divide the merits hearing into a number of shorter hearings. Although not very common, is also conceivable to hear all evidence at one hearing and then after some days or weeks hear the oral closing arguments (which may also be preceded or followed by post-hearing briefs). However, the arbitral tribunal should be wary of splitting up the hearings so that one party is treated more favourably than the other party. For instance, it has been suggested that it would be inappropriate to divide the hearing so that the claimant presents evidence at one hearing and the respondent at a later one.[117]

128. There is no provision in the Act or the SCC Rules that regulates the conduct of a hearing, leaving great leeway for the arbitral tribunal and the parties to set up a tailor-made schedule for the merits hearing. Despite this, a distinct pattern or structure exists for merits hearings which is more or less closely followed in most arbitrations under Swedish law.

129. The merits hearing is thus typically initiated by the parties' opening statements. In this first stage of the hearing, each party – beginning with the claimant, unless otherwise agreed[118] – gives an account of its prayers for relief as well as the material facts and legal arguments relied upon in support. The central written evidence relied upon by the party is also presented and commented upon. However, there is no requirement that a document must be exhibited or referred to at the hearing in order for it to be relied upon as evidence. It suffices that the document has been filed with the written submissions. The arbitrators can be presumed to have considered all documents submitted to them before the merits hearing. The opening statements can therefore be held relatively concisely.[119]

130. In giving their opening statements, the parties' counsel should thus try to summarize the most important parts of the written material already submitted to the arbitrators in a clear and logical manner in order to give the arbitral tribunal 'a good, coherently positive predisposition towards the party's claim.'[120]

131. It is rather often difficult for counsel orally to describe certain elements of the case, such as complex technical details. In these situations, counsel can use technical aids, display sketches, photographs, films and the like to explain the relevant circumstances for the arbitral tribunal. Importantly, however, in order to allow the other party

116. Heuman, *Arbitration Law of Sweden: Practice and Procedure*, 476.
117. *Ibid.*
118. Hobér, *International Commercial Arbitration in Sweden*, 251.
119. *Ibid.*
120. Heuman, *Arbitration Law of Sweden: Practice and Procedure*, 477.

to prepare its case without the risk of surprises, no new evidence and no new factual allegations are expected to be made or presented at the hearing. If, for example, a picture is used during the opening statement to describe a company structure, the information in that picture should already be in the case file, albeit in writing and not previously depicted in that way.[121]

132. The parties' opening statements are followed by examination of witnesses and experts. In virtually all international arbitrations, the parties submit written witness statements prior to the merits hearing. In these cases, the international trend appears to be towards not allowing real examinations-in-chief of the witnesses. Instead, written statements stand in lieu of examination-in-chief and oral testimonies are limited to cross-examination and, possibly, re-direct examination.[122] With respect to party-appointed experts who have submitted expert opinions on legal, technical, economic and other issues, the trend also seems to be to limit examination-in-chief and focus on cross-examination. However, experts are typically allowed at least some time to explain their expert reports, which are often complex.

133. When hearing witnesses, the usual order is to start with the claimant's witnesses and proceed with the respondent's witnesses, but alterations to this order are often seen if the case is better presented in other ways.[123]

134. The final stage of the merits hearing generally consists of the parties' closing arguments. In delivering their closing arguments, the parties are expected to argue their cases from a legal as well as a factual perspective. The parties are also expected to give their view on how the arbitral tribunal is to assess the written and oral evidence presented during the merits hearing or earlier in the proceedings. Unless otherwise agreed, the claimant should start with its closing argument. This general principle applies even in situations where the claimant does not have the burden of proof.[124]

135. Unless post-hearing briefs are to be exchanged or the proceedings for some other reason are set to continue after the merits hearing, it is preferable that the arbitral tribunal ends the merits hearing by declaring the arbitral proceedings closed and

121. Such pictures, PowerPoint slides etc., used to explain and demonstrate facts already in the case, are referred to as 'demonstrative exhibits'. It is advisable that the arbitral tribunal, already in its first procedural order, sets a date for the parties to exchange demonstrative exhibits intended to be used at the hearing, preferably a few days before the hearing starts. In this way, the parties will have time to review the demonstratives so as to ascertain that no new information is included, and to object if new information is found to be included, thus avoiding time-consuming arguments over this at the merits hearing.
122. Hobér, *International Commercial Arbitration in Sweden*, 251.
123. For example, it may be that some witnesses from each side testify on the same subject matter. It may then benefit the arbitral tribunal to hear those witnesses consecutively. It is also common that all experts are heard in one block, starting with the claimant's experts, after the factual witnesses from both sides have been heard. Examination of experts will then be concentrated in time, which facilitates the experts sitting in during the other experts' examinations. Sometimes, the arbitral tribunal may also want to ask questions to the experts of both sides simultaneously, after they have given their evidence (a so-called experts' conference, which can take a number of different expressions).
124. Heuman, *Arbitration Law of Sweden: Practice and Procedure*, 478.

explaining that it will not consider further submissions from the parties. This declaration – which must be made before the award is rendered under the SCC Rules, but which is not a requirement under the Act[125] –clarifies that the arbitral tribunal wishes no further input. It also reinforces the arbitrators' ability to stave off belated and unsolicited submissions from the parties.

5. *Post-hearing Briefs*

136. In complex arbitrations where the merits hearing has lasted for many days or weeks, it may be difficult for the parties to present their respective cases orally at the end of the merits hearing. In these cases, it is common – at least from an international perspective – for the closing arguments to be presented after the merits hearing in the form of post-hearing briefs. This approach enables the parties to review the transcript from the hearing and carefully analyse all evidence.[126] It also enables the arbitrators to ask the parties to comment on particular legal or factual issues. Besides, in cases where the merits hearing is concluded with oral closing arguments, post-hearing briefs may be used as a complement.

137. There are no provisions in the Act or in the SCC Rules specifically dealing with post-hearing briefs. It is therefore up to the parties and the arbitral tribunal to determine the approach they see fit. The most common approach to submission of post-hearing briefs is that both parties submit their briefs simultaneously on a date either agreed between them or ordered by the arbitral tribunal. These first post-hearing briefs are sometimes followed, after a short period, by rebuttal post-hearing briefs, also filed simultaneously. The rebuttal briefs are typically limited to comments on errors and new arguments in the other party's first brief. It is also common for arbitral tribunals to limit the number of pages allowed in the post-hearing and rebuttal post-hearing briefs, respectively.

G. Conduct of Proceedings When One Party Is Absent

138. A basic principle of Swedish arbitration is that each party should be given a reasonable opportunity to present its case. The rule is expressly set out in section 24 of the Act and in Article 19(2) of the SCC Rules. Section 24 also provides for the right of each party to receive all material submitted to the arbitral tribunal by the opposing party or other party. A party is also entitled to a hearing prior to determination of an issue referred to the arbitral tribunal, if it so requests and unless otherwise agreed between the parties.

139. Instances occur, however, when one party is inactive or entirely absent in the proceedings. The Act and the SCC Rules provide tools to deal with attempts to obstruct the proceedings, including how to proceed with an entirely absent respondent.

125. Article 34 of the SCC Rules.
126. See Hobér, *International Commercial Arbitration in Sweden*, 250 et seq.

140. Section 24(3) of the Act provides that, if a party fails without valid cause to appear at a hearing or otherwise to comply with an order of the arbitral tribunal, this does not prevent continuation of the proceedings and resolution of the dispute on the basis of existing materials.

141. Similarly, Article 30 of the SCC Rules provides directions in case a party defaults in presenting its case. If the claimant fails to submit a statement of claim in accordance with Article 24 of the SCC rules and cannot show good cause for its failure, the arbitral tribunal will terminate the proceedings (provided that the respondent has not filed a counterclaim). If the respondent has filed a counterclaim, the arbitration will proceed only as regards the counterclaim.[127]

142. In other cases, if a party fails without good cause to submit a statement of defence or other written submission in accordance with Article 24, or if it fails to appear at a hearing or otherwise to avail itself of the opportunity to present its case, the arbitral tribunal may proceed with the arbitration and make an award. The SCC Rules thus accord with the Act in this respect. These rules entail that the arbitral tribunal is authorized to proceed ex parte if a party fails without justification to appear or to plead its case.

143. The arbitral tribunal cannot render a 'default judgment' based exclusively on the failure of a party to appear or to participate in the arbitration. Nor can it dismiss the case due to a party's inaction.[128] The arbitral tribunal must examine the case on the merits based on the entirety of the evidence presented, notwithstanding that one party is absent. A party's inaction does not entail an implied admission of the facts invoked by the opposing party. Thus, facts and arguments in favour of the absent party must objectively be taken into account by the arbitral tribunal, but without introducing new facts or evidence.[129]

144. If the absent party shows 'valid cause' or 'good cause' for its failure to submit a statement or to appear at a hearing, that party will be given a new opportunity to do so. Such cause could, for example, be that the respondent has not been duly notified about the ongoing arbitration. A misunderstanding may also be accepted as valid cause if there is no reason to assume that the party is trying to obstruct the proceedings.[130]

127. Öhrström, 204.
128. Govt. bill 1998/99:35, 112. Cf. Lindskog, 708.
129. Hobér, *International Commercial Arbitration in Sweden*, 205 and 265; Lindskog, 711–712; Heuman, *Arbitration Law of Sweden: Practice and Procedure*, 404 et seq.; Madsen, *Commercial Arbitration in Sweden* 172 (2d ed., Oxford University Press 2006) and Cars, 113–115.
130. Govt. bill 1998/99:35, 112. The requirement for a 'valid cause' depends on the actual circumstances. Guidance can be found in Ch. 32 s. 8 of the Swedish Code of Judicial Procedure regarding 'legal excuse'. Under the Swedish Code of Judicial Procedure, legal excuse mainly exists when a person is impeded from doing what is required by reason of a breakdown in general modes of communication, sickness or another circumstance that he did not have reason to anticipate. However, the requirement for 'valid cause' should not be as strict as 'legal excuse' that is applicable in court proceedings. See Lindskog, 709; Heuman, *Arbitration Law of Sweden: Practice and Procedure*, 398 et seq. and Hobér, *Party Substitution under Swedish Arbitration Law*, 48 et seq., regarding 'valid cause'.

145. Even in proceedings with one party absent, the arbitral tribunal should aim at maintaining the adversarial principle.[131] The arbitral tribunal should thus keep the inactive party informed and all submissions and all summonses to hearings should be communicated to that party with an opportunity to comment.

146. If new submissions are made at the final hearing, it is for the arbitral tribunal to decide whether the absent party should be given the opportunity to comment on them.[132] However, the arbitral tribunal has no obligation to proactively safeguard the interests of an absent party.[133] In other words, the adversarial principle applies and the fact that one party is absent does not turn the arbitration into an inquisitorial proceeding.

147. In rendering an award when one party is absent, the arbitral tribunal must ensure that the non-active party has been given an opportunity to present its case and to submit comments on the arguments and evidence submitted by the opposing party. It has been proposed that the arbitral tribunal explains in the award the measures that have been taken in order to enable the absent party to present its case.[134]

V. EVIDENCE

A. Introduction

148. Clearly, presentation of evidence is crucial to the outcome of virtually every dispute.[135] Evidence is everything that supports the facts and allegations presented by the parties and is thus supposed to assist the arbitral tribunal in determining issues of fact and disputed issues of experts' opinions.[136] According to section 25(1) of the Act, the parties are responsible for presenting and introducing evidence. Thus, the arbitrators are not to conduct a factual investigation of their own volition. The arbitrators

131. Govt. bill 1998/99:35, 112–113, and Heuman, *Arbitration Law of Sweden: Practice and Procedure*, 387.
132. It is debated how strictly the adversarial principle should be upheld in the case of new arguments being submitted at the final hearing. According to Lindskog, there is scope for the arbitral tribunal's discretion in this regard. It should not be necessary to communicate arguments that are considered not to be critical to the outcome of the dispute. However, a new claim, new evidence or new factual allegations should always be communicated to the absent party and the party should be given the opportunity to comment on the claim. See Govt. bill 1998/99:35, 113; Cars, 115; Lindskog, 712; and Heuman, *Arbitration Law of Sweden: Practice and Procedure*, 385-390.
133. Nordenson, 219–220. See also Lindskog, 712.
134. Hobér, *International Commercial Arbitration in Sweden*, 265.
135. It has been estimated that the eventual outcomes in perhaps 60% to 70% of international arbitrations probably turn on the facts rather than application of relevant principles of law, whereas a good proportion of the remainder turn on a combination of facts and law, see Blackaby et al., 384.
136. Issues of fact and opinion are not always easily distinguishable. As an example, the content of foreign law applicable in international arbitrations in Sweden is normally treated as an issue of fact. But since interpretation of law is often the crux of the matter, the parties may want to rely on different expert opinions and/or the writings of legal authorities, see Hobér, *International Commercial Arbitration in Sweden*, 220.

may, however, appoint experts unless both parties object (see further section V.C.3 below).

149. The IBA Rules on the Taking of Evidence in International Commercial Arbitration (IBA Rules)[137] contain provisions regarding presentation of documents, factual and expert witnesses and inspections, as well as conduct of evidentiary hearings. The IBA Rules are not directly applicable to arbitrations in Sweden unless the parties so agree, but they may nevertheless serve as guidelines for the parties and the arbitrators as in many respects they reflect 'best practice' in international arbitration.[138] Accordingly, one party's objection to the applicability of the IBA Rules does not prohibit the arbitrators from turning to them for guidance on certain issues, in the same way as the arbitral tribunal, in its discretion, may seek guidance from other sources when the parties cannot agree on how to resolve a certain procedural issue and where no mandatory rules apply to the situation at hand.

150. The IBA Rules are designed for use in conjunction with, and adopted together with, institutional, ad hoc or other rules or procedures governing international arbitrations. According to the Committee of the International Bar Association's Legal Practice Division, the IBA Rules reflect procedures in use in many different legal systems, which make them particularly useful when the parties come from different legal cultures.[139] In our experience, the IBA Rules provide a number of helpful clarifications and innovations for the process of taking evidence, amounting to a valuable toolbox for an efficient procedure.[140] In fact, international arbitrations taking place in Sweden are often guided by the IBA Rules.

151. In Swedish arbitral proceedings, the admissibility, relevance, materiality and weight of evidence is for the arbitral tribunal to determine and the parties are, in principle, free to present almost any kind of document, witness, statement or occurrence in order to prove their case. Accordingly, there is nothing preventing a party from submitting e.g., evidence obtained illegally or wrongfully or hearsay evidence.[141] Lawyers from common-law jurisdictions participating in arbitrations in Sweden should thus be aware that reliance cannot successfully be placed on technical rules concerning admissibility of evidence.

152. Section 25(2) of the Act identifies two instances where the arbitral tribunal may refuse to admit evidence. First, evidence may be rejected if it is 'manifestly irrelevant to the case', for instance because previously submitted evidence is considered sufficient. Since it may be difficult for the arbitral tribunal fully to assess evidentiary

137. International Bar Association's 2nd edition 1999 of its Rules adopted by a resolution of the IBA Council on 29 May 2010.

138. In practice, it is probably more common that the parties agree to use the IBA Rules as guidelines as opposed to making them directly applicable, see Hobér, *International Commercial Arbitration in Sweden*, 221.

139. See Tawil and Gill, 2.

140. See further Brocker, *The New IBA Rules on the Taking of Evidence in International Arbitration – From a Cost-Efficiency Perspective*, 8, http:// www.sccinstitute.se.

141. This basic tenet is also authoritative in civil and criminal proceedings in Sweden.

relevance beforehand, this option is sparsely exercised in practice.[142] Second, the arbitral tribunal may refuse to admit evidence where 'such refusal is justified having regard to the time at which the evidence is offered'. If the arbitral tribunal has issued a so-called preclusion order, i.e., ordered a party to submit its evidence by a certain date, the party should only be allowed to submit additional evidence after that date under specific circumstances.[143] However, this rule is also applicable where there is no explicit cut-off date for submission of new evidence, if a party wishes to introduce new evidence at a late stage of the proceedings.[144] The tribunal will then have to consider whether there is a risk that the proceedings will be delayed if the new evidence is accepted and if the new evidence was presented late with a view to surprising the other party.[145] If a late request to submit additional evidence is prompted by evidence introduced by the other party, it may be reasonable to admit the new evidence.[146]

B. Documentary Evidence

1. *Reliance on Documents*

153. Documents play a fundamental role in international arbitrations, as most commercial disputes to some extent concern interpretation of contracts and related documentation. Moreover, arbitrators generally accord greater evidentiary weight to documents than to witness testimony.[147] Witnesses may forget or have false recollections of certain events. They may also feel inclined, without lying or omitting crucial facts, to adapt their testimony in favour of the party who introduced them, whether or not they have an interest in the outcome of the dispute. It is therefore understandable that arbitrators prefer as far as possible to place reliance on documentary evidence.

154. As described in section V.A above, any kind of document may be relied on as evidence in arbitral proceedings in Sweden. The parties and the arbitral tribunal normally agree at an early stage how and when documents are to be presented. The common practice is for the parties to submit the documentary evidence they rely on together with their respective memorials.[148] Typically, the arbitral tribunal, after having consulted with the parties, will decide on a 'cut-off date' after which no new documents can be introduced.

155. Under Article 26(2) of the SCC Rules, the arbitral tribunal may require a party to identify separately the documentary evidence it intends to rely on and specify the

142. Cf. Hobér, *International Commercial Arbitration in Sweden*, 222.
143. Govt. bill 1998/99:35, 228.
144. Govt. bill 1998/99:35, 228. It is not uncommon that a party attempts to introduce new evidence at or immediately prior to the final hearing.
145. Cf. Madsen, *Commercial Arbitration in Sweden* 178 (2d ed., Oxford University Press 2006) and Hobér, *International Commercial Arbitration in Sweden*, 223.
146. Cf. Heuman, *Arbitration Law of Sweden: Practice and Procedure*, 427.
147. Cf. Blackaby et al., *Redfern and Hunter on International Arbitration*, 389; Hobér, *International Commercial Arbitration in Sweden*, 224; and Heuman, *Arbitration Law of Sweden: Practice and Procedure*, 445.
148. See, for instance, Derains, 88.

circumstances intended to be proved by that evidence. In our experience, arbitral tribunals rarely exercise this option in international arbitrations taking place in Sweden.[149] Rather, the practice is that the parties refer to the written evidence in connection with the factual allegations in the submissions.

2. *Production of Documents*

156. There is no duty of 'disclosure' or 'discovery' in Swedish law, but the arbitral tribunal may – upon a motion of a party – order a party to produce documents. Absent specific rules, the arbitral tribunal has wide discretion – within the confines of the general procedural principles of the Act – to set the conditions for document production. However, in international arbitrations taking place in Sweden, the IBA Rules commonly serve as guidelines for the arbitral tribunal and the parties.[150]

157. If the parties have not agreed on specific rules to be applied with respect to document production and if the IBA Rules for some reason are not considered as a source of guidance, Swedish arbitrators sometimes turn to the Code of Judicial Procedure for guidance.[151] This means, *inter alia*, that the tribunal may reject a request if the document in question appears to be immaterial or if evidence can be obtained by different means and at a lesser cost. Swedish procedural law takes the approach that a requested document must be of potential relevance in relation to a contested issue in the dispute, which issue is relevant to the case. In other words, the IBA Rules and the Code of Judicial Procedure set out largely similar requirements. A party who wishes to obtain a document which is in the possession of its opponent should submit to the arbitral tribunal a request for production, including an explanation as to why the document is relevant to the case.[152] In order for the arbitrators to be able to assess whether or not a document is immaterial, the document must be sufficiently identified. If several documents are requested, it may be acceptable that the party refers to specific categories, such as invoices or letters covering a certain period and containing certain information.[153] However, it may be difficult to assess the relevance of certain evidence at an early stage of the proceedings.

158. The IBA Rules set a relatively high threshold for document production. In the previous version of the IBA Rules, a Request to Produce should contain a description of

---

149. In Swedish civil proceedings, the parties are required to specify the circumstances which they intend to prove with respect to both documentary evidence and witnesses (so-called *evidentiary themes*) in a 'statement of evidence' often submitted late in the written phase of the proceedings.

150. Brocker, *Discovery in International Arbitration – The Swedish Approach*, 2 Stockholm Arbitration Report 22 (2001). See also Hobér, *International Commercial Arbitration in Sweden*, 225 and Heuman, *Arbitration Law of Sweden: Practice and Procedure*, 448. It may be noted that under s. 15 of the old Arbitration Act of 1929, this power was explicitly given to arbitrators.

151. Hobér, *International Commercial Arbitration in Sweden*, 226.

152. Brocker, *Discovery in International Arbitration – The Swedish Approach*, 2 Stockholm Arbitration Report 22 (2001).

153. Brocker, *Discovery in International Arbitration – The Swedish Approach*, 2 Stockholm Arbitration Report (SAR) 23 (2001).

how the documents requested were 'relevant and material to the outcome of the case'. Although a seemingly insignificant amendment, the 2010 version requires that the document be relevant to the case and material to its outcome.[154] In the view of the authors, this two-pronged nature of the standard should mean that the arbitral tribunal must engage in a prima facie analysis of the request and determine, first, whether the documents sought are relevant to substantiate a party's factual allegation and, second, whether such factual allegation, if proven, will realistically affect the outcome of the case. The arbitral tribunal may find that the documents requested are relevant to substantiate a certain factual allegation, but if the allegation prima facie will have no effect on the outcome of the case, the request should be denied.[155]

159. The IBA Rules do not address the issue of timing. Since fishing expeditions are not generally allowed, and each request must be tied to a contentious factual allegation in the case, it is often advisable to postpone filing document requests to the second stage of arbitration when the arbitral tribunal is typically better informed of the case, and, thus, in a better position to determine whether a requested document is relevant to the case and material to its outcome.[156]

160. An otherwise sufficient request to produce may be denied on the basis that the content of the document qualifies as trade secrets or contains privileged information.[157]

161. As in international arbitrations in general, it is often agreed in international arbitrations in Sweden to use so-called Redfern Schedules for document requests.[158] A Redfern Schedule is a table which contains the following four columns: (1) identification of document(s) or categories of documents requested; (2) short presentation of the reasons for each request; (3) summary of objections by the other party to production of the document(s) requested;[159] and (4) the arbitral tribunal's decision on each request. The parties discuss the requests between them by exchanging updated versions of the Redfern Schedule, which is then submitted to the arbitrators for decision if the parties are not able to agree with respect to every request. This procedure helps the tribunal make an informed decision promptly and efficiently.[160]

162. In Swedish arbitrations, no sanctions are available to the arbitrators, should a party fail to voluntarily comply with an order for production of documents issued by

154. Article 3.3(b) of the IBA Rules.
155. See Brocker, *The New IBA Rules on the Taking of Evidence in International Arbitration – From a Cost-Efficiency Perspective*, 5–6.
156. See Brocker, *The New IBA Rules on the Taking of Evidence in International Arbitration – From a Cost-Efficiency Perspective*, 6.
157. It is generally held that the rules of privilege contained in the Code of Judicial Procedure are analogously applicable in this regard.
158. In the authors' experience, the use of Redfern Schedules has become so widespread that many procedural orders in international arbitrations in Sweden merely refer to 'Redfern Schedules' without offering much more guidance as to their contents. See also Hobér, *International Commercial Arbitration in Sweden*, 228.
159. It may be noted that, since for practical reasons the table is only suitable for providing a summary of objections, the objections are often also set out in a letter, referred to in the Redfern Schedule and explaining the objections in more detail.
160. See Derains, 90. Cf. Blackaby et al., *Redfern and Hunter on International Arbitration*, 396.

the arbitral tribunal.[161] Under section 26 of the Act, a party may seek the arbitral tribunal's consent to apply to the district court for an enforceable document production order. The arbitral tribunal should grant such an application if it finds that the documents requested may be relevant as evidence. If approved by the arbitral tribunal, the district court will grant the application if it is considered 'lawful'.

C. Witnesses and Experts

1. *General Remarks*

163. The practice in international arbitrations in Sweden is that the parties submit written witness statements which they refer to in connection with the factual allegations in the submissions.[162] In domestic Swedish arbitral proceedings, however, written witness statements are still relatively uncommon.[163] In those proceedings, the parties usually submit so-called statements of evidence, which are documents outlining the written and oral evidence on which the parties wish to rely and what they intend to prove with each document or witness. This statement of evidence must detail, with respect to each witness, what the witness will testify to and what allegations are intended to be proven by the testimony.

164. The parties are free to agree on the form of witness testimony. As indicated above, it may be submitted in the form of a written witness statement or through examination of the witness at the merits hearing, or both. If witness statements are used, the normal practice is for statements to stand in lieu of the examination-in-chief, which will save time at the hearing. A party should always be entitled to cross-examine a witness whose testimony is presented by way of a written witness statement. If the witness is not present for cross-examination, despite having been asked to appear, the arbitral tribunal should normally not attach significant evidentiary weight to the witness statement, or dismiss it altogether.

161. Regarding the arbitral tribunal's right to draw negative inferences from a party's failure to comply with an order.

162. The use of written witness statements is explicitly recognized in Art. 28(2) of the SCC Rules. Moreover, Art. 4(5) of the IBA Rules provides widely accepted guidelines as to the contents and form of witness statements. For a commentary on the IBA Rules, with criticism in some respects, see Brocker, 'The New IBA Rules on the Taking of Evidence in International Arbitration – from a cost-efficiency perspective', available at http://www.sccinstitute.se.

163. See Hobér, *International Commercial Arbitration in Sweden*, 234. This may change, however, in light of the fact that the Code of Judicial Procedure was recently amended to the effect that witness statements are now generally accepted if both parties agree and the court does not consider this to be manifestly inappropriate, see Ch. 36, s. 14(2). Under the old regime, which was in place for more than sixty years, witness statements were only allowed in certain specified situations.

2. *Witnesses*

165. There are no restrictions as to who may testify in arbitral proceedings. Consequently, party representatives may appear to give testimony in the same way as witnesses not formally affiliated with a party.[164] It is for the arbitrators to take issues of party affiliation or otherwise into account when assessing the evidentiary weight to be given to testimony.

166. The Act contains no rules on evidentiary privilege. Absent the parties' agreement, it will therefore be for the arbitral tribunal to determine which privilege regime will apply. It has been suggested that the provisions of the Code of Judicial Procedure may be applied by analogy in this regard.[165] Some privileges under the Code of Judicial Procedure are absolute whereas others may be set aside under certain circumstances. For instance, an attorney may be heard as a witness concerning matters entrusted to him in the performance of his assignment only if the party concerned (usually the client) consents.[166] A witness may also refuse to give testimony that would involve disclosure of a trade secret, but that privilege is not upheld if 'extraordinary reason' exists to examine the witness on the subject.[167] However, the rules of the Code of Judicial Procedure offer little guidance in situations where the parties and the witnesses are from different jurisdictions, with different privilege regimes. It has therefore been suggested that the privileges of the country of domicile of the witness may be invoked in addition to the Swedish provisions.[168] Arguably, however, that could lead to unequal treatment of the parties, since the parties may come under different privilege protection. In the authors' experience, arbitral tribunals are sometimes seen resolving this by determining a common privilege regime in a procedural order, which regime may be inspired by the rules of several jurisdictions and applicable to all parties and witnesses involved.

167. As described in the previous section, written witness statements are commonplace in international arbitrations. The general rule is that a witness or expert on whose testimony a party seeks to rely must attend the hearing for cross-examination unless otherwise agreed by the parties.[169] Since the idea is that written witness statements replace oral direct examination, it will generally be for the party not relying on the witness to decide whether the witness is to appear at the hearing.[170]

164. However, arbitral tribunals in Sweden tend to distinguish between party representatives and witnesses insofar as only the former are entitled to be present during the entire hearing, i.e., also before they testify, see Hobér, *International Commercial Arbitration in Sweden*, 229. Cf. Heuman, *Arbitration Law of Sweden: Practice and Procedure*, 435.
165. Cf. Govt. Bill 1998/99:35, 116–117, see also Hobér, *International Commercial Arbitration in Sweden*, 227–228 and Heuman, *Arbitration Law of Sweden: Practice and Procedure*, 450.
166. Chapter 36 s. 5 of the Code of Judicial Procedure.
167. Chapter 36 s. 6 of the Code of Judicial Procedure.
168. Heuman, *Skiljemannarätt*, 463.
169. See Art. 28(3) of the SCC Rules and Art. 8(1) of the IBA Rules.
170. Blackaby et al., *Redfern and Hunter on International Arbitration*, 403.

168. The parties' responsibility under the Act to present evidence includes a responsibility to ensure that witnesses are present at the hearing.[171] Should a witness fail to attend the hearing, the consequences have to be assessed in each individual case.[172] The absence of a witness will normally not give grounds for postponement of the hearing, although this may be an alternative if the witness is crucial for one of the parties and that party is able to demonstrate that the witness had valid reason/lawful excuse for not appearing. If possible, however, the arbitrators ought to try to have the witness testify by means of video or telephone conferencing or, alternatively, schedule a separate session for examination of that witness.

169. In Swedish arbitrations, it is generally accepted that party representatives meet with the party's witnesses to interview and prepare them before they give oral testimony at a hearing.[173] The same view is adopted by the IBA Rules, which provide that '[i]t shall not be improper for a Party, its officers, employees, legal advisors or other representatives to interview its witnesses and to discuss their prospective testimony with them'.[174] Indeed, it is often necessary for counsel to meet with witnesses during the preparatory stage in order to assess the relevance of their testimony as well as their general credibility and, not least, to prepare the witness statement.

170. Arbitrators are not empowered to administer oaths.[175] Witnesses cannot therefore testify under oath before an arbitral tribunal. However, under 26(1) of the Act, a tribunal may consent to witnesses being heard under oath before a competent District Court. Under Article 8(4) of the IBA Rules:

> [a] witness of fact providing testimony shall first affirm, in a manner determined appropriate by the Arbitral Tribunal, that he or she commits to tell the truth or, in the case of an expert witness, his or her genuine belief in the opinions to be expressed at the Evidentiary Hearing. If the witness has submitted a Witness Statement or an Expert Report, the witness shall confirm it.

This provision is an expression of common practice in international arbitrations.

171. The party who has called a witness usually starts the examination and the other party is then offered the opportunity to cross-examine the witness. In Swedish judicial procedure, leading questions may not be asked during direct examination of a witness.[176] The Act does not contain such a restriction, but it is part of set arbitral practice that the same principle also applies to arbitral proceedings in Sweden.[177] In

171. See Hobér, *International Commercial Arbitration in Sweden*, 229.
172. SOU 1994:81, 146–147, and Govt. bill 1998/99:35, 115.
173. See, for instance, Lundblad, 332, and Hobér, *International Commercial Arbitration in Sweden*, 230.
174. Article 4(3) of the IBA Rules.
175. See s. 25(3) of the Act.
176. See ch. 36, s. 17 of the Code of Judicial Procedure.
177. See Hobér, *International Commercial Arbitration in Sweden*, 232 and Lundblad, 337. Cf. Heuman, *Arbitration Law of Sweden: Practice and Procedure*, 438. Art. 8(2) of the IBA Rules stipulates that questions to a witness during direct and re-direct testimony may not be 'unreasonably leading'.

reality, however, the chairperson of a tribunal may be hesitant to intervene against leading questioning.[178] In any event, it may be assumed that the evidentiary weight of testimony will be lower if it was largely induced by leading questions.[179] If the witness has submitted a written statement, direct examination will normally be limited to a few introductory questions before the witness is handed over for cross-examination by opposing counsel.

172. Occasionally, a party is able to extract new relevant evidence from cross-examination. However, this function must be considered incidental, as the main objective of cross-examination is rather to weaken the other party's case and to reinforce facts favourable to the client's case.[180] Typically, the cross-examiner will attempt to expose flaws or inconsistencies in direct testimony/written witness statement in order to undermine the credibility of the witness.

173. The first question a party, or rather its counsel, needs to ask in this regard is whether cross-examination is necessary in the first place. In many cases, this question is to be answered in the negative, as the potential risks often outweigh the potential gains.[181] The fact that a party chooses not to cross-examine the other party's witnesses is not to be interpreted as an acceptance of such testimony. There are other – often more efficient – ways than cross-examination to challenge testimony, for example by referring to documentary evidence.

174. Cross-examination in international arbitration is an area where differences in legal culture may be particularly apparent. If one were to generalize, common-law lawyers opt to cross-examine more often than their continental colleagues and their examinations tend to be longer. The common-law approach to cross-examination is also typically more intense, in a way sometimes perceived as aggressive by arbitral tribunals not accustomed to the practice.

175. When the cross-examination is finished, the other party is afforded the opportunity to conduct re-direct examination. The purpose of re-direct examination is, essentially, to remedy potential damage caused by cross-examination. Accordingly, a party is not supposed to ask questions aimed at supplementing direct examination or other questions unrelated to issues discussed in cross-examination. Leading questions are usually not permitted in re-direct examinations.[182]

176. The arbitral tribunal may ask questions which the arbitrators consider relevant to the issues before them. In Swedish arbitrations this mandate is often exercised with caution, with the arbitrators focusing mostly on clarifying issues genuinely unclear to them. Good reasons exist for this approach. First, the arbitrators should not 'invent' new allegations or give rise to presentation of new allegations. Second, the arbitral tribunal should avoid creating an appearance of bias.

---

178. Lundblad 337.
179. See Heuman, *Arbitration Law of Sweden: Practice and Procedure*, 438.
180. See Lundblad, 338 and Hobér, *International Commercial Arbitration in Sweden*, 232.
181. Cf. Hobér *International Commercial Arbitration in Sweden*, 233.
182. Hobér, *International Commercial Arbitration in Sweden*, 234.

3. *Experts*

177. International commercial arbitrations often involve advanced technical issues or complicated quantifications of damages claims. Since most arbitrators are lawyers, they may need the assistance of experts to resolve the dispute in these cases. Experts may be appointed either by the parties, by the tribunal or by a neutral third party, for instance an arbitral institution. The fact that section 25 of the Act allows the arbitral tribunal to appoint its own expert(s) is an exception to the fundamental principle that the parties present the evidence. However, if both parties object, the arbitral tribunal cannot appoint its own expert(s). In practice, experts are rarely appointed by tribunals in Swedish arbitrations. There are no requirements as to who may appear as an expert witness. The rules and procedure usually applied to submission of expert evidence are in all material respects similar to those applied to submission of witness testimony.

178. If each party appoints its own expert, which is by far the most commonly adopted method,[183] the evidence presented will almost invariably be conflicting with respect to crucial issues. The arbitral tribunal will then find itself in the difficult position of having to evaluate the respective expert testimony, both of which are founded on experience foreign in kind to their own. In addition, party-appointed experts have often been accused of submitting reports based on different facts and assumptions, which would make the tribunal's task virtually impossible.[184] However, some guidance as to how to deal with this problem has been provided in the 2010 amendments to the IBA Rules. Article 5(4) of the IBA Rules provides that the arbitral tribunal, in its discretion, may order party-appointed experts who will submit, or who have submitted, expert reports on the same or related issues to meet and confer on such issues and to report remaining areas of disagreement and the reasons for such disagreement.

179. Critics have asserted that party-appointed experts all too often act as 'hired guns' on behalf of the party who engages them.[185] An attempt to address this problem has also been made in the new IBA Rules.[186] Under Article 5(2)(c) of the IBA Rules, the expert report must contain a statement of the expert's independence not only from the parties, but also from their legal advisors and the arbitral tribunal.

180. Whether appointed by a party or by the arbitral tribunal, an expert will present its findings in an expert report. Like witnesses in general, experts are subjected to cross-examination at the hearing unless otherwise agreed by the parties.

183. See Blackaby et al., *Redfern and Hunter on International Arbitration*, 408.
184. See Brocker, *The New IBA Rules on the Taking of Evidence in International Arbitration – From a Cost-Efficiency Perspective*, 8, http://www.sccinstitute.se.
185. See Brocker, *The New IBA Rules on the Taking of Evidence in International Arbitration – From a Cost-Efficiency Perspective*, 8, http://www.sccinstitute.se.
186. See comments in Brocker, *The New IBA Rules on the Taking of Evidence in International Arbitration – From a Cost-Efficiency Perspective*, 8, http://www.sccinstitute.se.

D. Inspection of Subject Matter of Dispute

181. At the request of a party, the arbitral tribunal may inspect the subject matter of the dispute. This method is mainly used in construction disputes or disputes concerning process plants or similar property. It normally takes the form of a site inspection. However, inspections have become increasingly uncommon in modern arbitrations, since models, photographs, drawings or video recordings may often be used to fulfil the same purpose.[187]

182. Inspection is a recognized method of presenting evidence. If used, the parties and their representatives can attend any inspection. The arbitrators, in consultation with the parties, set the timing and arrangements for the inspection, including how observations made during the inspection are to be recorded.[188]

E. Evaluation of Evidence and Burden of Proof

183. The Act contains no rules on how the arbitrators are to analyse and assess evidence presented by the parties. Accordingly, arbitrations in Sweden are based on the principle that arbitrators are free to evaluate evidence in any way they consider appropriate. The principle of free evaluation of evidence also governs Swedish judicial procedure.

184. Despite the discretion afforded to the arbitrators when it comes to evaluating evidence, some general observations may be made. As alluded to in section V.B.1 above, arbitrators tend to attach greater weight to documents than to oral testimony. Moreover, witnesses with a clear interest in the outcome of the case and witnesses who appear to have been overly prepared by counsel will generally be regarded with more scepticism than those who come across as 'truly independent'.[189]

185. If a party fails to comply with an order issued by the arbitral tribunal, the tribunal may draw negative (adverse) inferences from such failure. Although the Act is silent on this issue, statements in the *travaux préparatoires* indicate that the arbitral tribunal has a general right to draw conclusions of this type.[190] A clear-cut example is that a party has questioned the authenticity of a copy of a document and the opponent fails to present the original, despite being ordered to do so by the arbitral tribunal. In many instances, however, it is less clear what type of inferences the arbitral tribunal may draw from failure to comply with an order.[191] Both the SCC Rules[192] and the IBA

187. See Blackaby et al., *Redfern and Hunter on International Arbitration*, 411.
188. Cf. Art. 7 of the IBA Rules. See also Hobér, *International Commercial Arbitration in Sweden*, 237.
189. Cf. Hober, *International Commercial Arbitration in Sweden*, 237 and Blackaby et al., *Redfern and Hunter on International Arbitration*, 389.
190. SOU 1994:81, 285, and Govt. bill 1998/99:35, 74. See also Heuman, *Arbitration Law of Sweden: Practice and Procedure*, 405.
191. Nilsson, *Negative Inferences: An Arbitral Tribunal's Powers to Draw Adverse Conclusions from a Party's Failure to Comply with the Tribunal's Orders*, in *Between East and West: Essays in honour of Ulf Franke* 362–363 (Hobér et al. eds., JurisNet 2010).
192. Article 30(3) of the SCC Rules.

Rules[193] recognize the right to draw negative inferences, although neither provides guidance as to the evidentiary weight of failure or the precise nature of the inference. It has been suggested that the practical importance of this right is limited since few arbitrators would be prepared to decide a case solely on the basis of a negative inference.[194]

186. Whilst the evaluation of evidence is viewed as a procedural matter governed by the *lex arbitri*, the burden of proof is viewed as a matter governed by the substantive law applicable to the agreement (the *lex contractus*).[195] It has been said, however, that international arbitral tribunals almost invariably apply the principle that each party is to prove the facts upon which it relies in support of its case (unless a certain proposition is so notorious or obvious that no proof is necessary).[196] This principle is explicitly stated in the UNCITRAL Rules, which provide that '[e]ach party shall have the burden of proving the facts relied on to support his claim or defence'.[197] However, the burden of proof may shift depending on the facts and circumstances of the individual case and the arguments relied on by the parties.[198] In Swedish civil procedure, the claimant often has the burden of proving the facts upon which it relies, but the burden of proof may also be imposed on the party for whom it is easiest to secure certain evidence.[199]

187. There are no general rules that set the standard of proof required to convince an arbitral tribunal. Naturally, the tribunal may be inclined to require a higher degree of proof with respect to more serious allegations, e.g., of misconduct or criminal activity. Under normal circumstances, however, the required standard ought to be that of the 'balance of probability'.

F. Court Assistance with Respect to Evidence

188. An arbitral tribunal in Sweden is not empowered to administer oaths, nor is it empowered to impose conditional fines or take other coercive measures against a party or a third party who refuses to be examined or to produce documents. However, as mentioned in section V.B.2 above, Swedish arbitration law allows for the courts to provide assistance in this regard.[200] Section 26 of the Act provides for a procedure involving two steps. A party who wishes to receive court assistance must first request

193. Article 9(5) of the IBA Rules.
194. Hobér, *International Commercial Arbitration in Sweden*, 238.
195. See Art. 18(1) of the Rome I Regulation (Regulation (EC) No 593/2008 of the European Parliament and of the Council of 17 Jun. 2008 on the Laws Applicable to Contractual Obligations) and Art. 14(1) of the 1980 Rome Convention on the Laws Applicable to Contractual Obligations, which has been incorporated into Swedish law. See also SOU 1994:81, 153, and Hobér, *International Commercial Arbitration in Sweden*, 238.
196. Blackaby et al., *Redfern and Hunter on International Arbitration*, 387.
197. Article 24(1) of the UNCITRAL Rules.
198. Hobér, *International Commercial Arbitration in Sweden*, 238.
199. See, for instance, case *Elektrobyrån AB v. BTH Bygg AB*, decision by the Supreme Court made on 27 Mar. 2001 in case no T 5001-98, NJA 2001 p. 177, where the Supreme Court ruled that a party who asserts that a fixed price was agreed for a construction project has the burden of proving this assertion.
200. Section 26 of the Act.

permission from the arbitral tribunal,[201] which is to approve the request if it considers the measure to be 'justified having regard to the evidence in the case'. According to the *travaux préparatoires*, the examination or document requested must be of significance as evidence.[202] This implies that the measures must be capable of affecting the outcome of the case.[203] In other words, the evidence must, prima facie, be of relevance to a factual allegation which, if proven, would affect the outcome of the case. As to examinations of witnesses, experts or a party, the party seeking court assistance must also explain why the relevant person should be heard under oath or truth affirmation and not just before the arbitrators at an evidentiary hearing in the arbitration. If the party refers to credibility reasons and provides at least some support in this regard, it has been suggested that the arbitral tribunal should be rather generous in its assessment.[204] However, if the benefits are not obvious, it is submitted that considerations as to time and costs often outweigh the need to have a witness heard under oath.

189. Under section 25(2) of the Act, the arbitral tribunal may also refuse to give its consent, if the request is considered to have been made too late in the proceedings.

190. Once the arbitral tribunal has approved the request, the party may apply to the District Court. The approval of the arbitral tribunal must be submitted together with the application to the court. Unless the arbitral tribunal has indicated another court, the application is to be considered by the Stockholm District Court.[205]

191. The District Court will grant the application if 'the measure may lawfully be taken'. This means that the court should assess whether Swedish procedural law allows the court to order the measure in question. For instance, a requested document must be sufficiently identified for an order to be enforceable.[206] Moreover, the rules on privilege in the Code of Judicial Procedure may prevent the court from ordering a witness to testify or a document to be disclosed. Moreover, it is not uncommon that the other party objects that the documents requested contain trade secrets.[207] A party may

201. There is some uncertainty as to whether the parties can agree that the District Court is to assist with taking evidence at a party's request without the arbitrators' consent being required, see Heuman, *Arbitration Law of Sweden: Practice and Procedure*, 458.
202. Govt. bill 1998/99:35, 118.
203. See Hobér *International Commercial Arbitration in Sweden*, 240. Cf. Madsen, *Commercial Arbitration in Sweden* 186 (2d ed., Oxford University Press 2006) and Heuman, *Arbitration Law of Sweden: Practice and Procedure*, 459 et seq. See also Art. 26(3) of the SCC Rules, which provides that the arbitral tribunal may order a party to produce documents or other evidence which may be *relevant to the outcome of the case*.
204. SOU 1994:81, 149, and Govt. bill 1998/99:35, 118.
205. See ss. 26 and 44(2) of the Act.
206. See, for instance, *Karin F. v. Sparbanken Sverige AB*, decision by the Supreme Court made on 23 Oct. 1998 in case no Ö 3507-96, NJA 1998 p. 590 (II), where the respondent requested that the claimant be ordered to disclose 'all written documentation' in relation to certain credits that were relevant in the case. The Supreme Court found that the documents were not sufficiently specified, nor were they identifiable in the sense that the party had explained which factual allegation the documents were intended to prove.
207. Trade secrets are defined in s. 1 of the Trade Secrets Act *(Sw: Lag (1990:409) om skydd för företagshemligheter)*. In the Code of Judicial Procedure, the term 'professional secrets' is used. However, the Supreme Court has concluded that the two terms have essentially the same

only be ordered to disclose documents that include trade secrets if there are extraordinary reasons for such disclosure.[208]

192. The District Court's examination is thus limited to issues of lawfulness. Accordingly, it is not for the court to examine whether the measure could be considered justified, but the court is to accept the arbitral tribunal's assessment of the evidentiary relevance in this respect.[209]

193. If the documents contain trade secrets, the situation is somewhat more complex. As mentioned above, an order to disclose trade secrets is only lawful if there are 'extraordinary reasons' for such disclosure. In order to determine whether such reasons exist, the court's lawfulness test must establish whether the evidentiary value of the document in question may be expected to be so high as to outweigh the interest of a party not to have its trade secrets disclosed. The Supreme Court made clear in *Euroflon Tekniska Produkter AB v.Flexiboys i Motala AB* (the 'Flexiboys case'[210]) that, also in such a situation, the starting point is that the court is to accept the arbitral tribunal's assessment of evidentiary value.[211] However, if the arbitral tribunal has not provided details as to the evidentiary value of the documents in question, the court is to make its own assessment of evidentiary value, so as to enable the court to weigh the interest of the evidence being disclosed, against the interest of the protection of trade secrets. This is thus an exception from the rule that it is ordinarily (if no trade secrets objection is made) for the arbitral tribunal to assess whether the measure is justified.[212]

194. The question whether Swedish courts have jurisdiction when an application under s. 26 of the Act is directed against a foreign party is not explicitly addressed in the Act. However, in *RosInvestCo v. Russian Federation*,[213] a case that concerned a dispute as to whether the arbitral tribunal had jurisdiction, the Supreme Court concluded that, for Swedish courts to have jurisdiction, it is sufficient that the parties have agreed that arbitral proceedings are to take place in Sweden. The ruling of the Supreme Court has

---

meaning, see *Sparbanken Sverige AB v. Marcus A.* et al., decision by the Supreme Court made on 6 Jun. 1995 in case no Ö 4372-94, NJA 1995 p. 347.

208. When assessing whether there is extraordinary reason for disclosure, the court weighs the interests between the evidentiary value of the trade secret and its economic value and considers the likelihood of damage in case of disclosure, see Fitger, The Code of Judicial Procedure, commentary to ch. 36, s. 6.
209. See Govt. bill 1998/99:35, 229.
210. *Euroflon Tekniska Produkter AB* v. *Flexiboys i Motala AB*, decision by the Supreme Court made on 10 May 2012 in case no Ö 1590-11, NJA 2012 p. 289.
211. Flexiboys case, para. 17 of the decision.
212. Before the law was clarified by the Flexiboys case, the courts of appeal had rendered a number of somewhat conflicting decisions on the issue. In a ruling of 9 Mar. 2011 (*Yara International ASA v. Joint Stock Company Acron*, decision by the Svea Court of Appeal made on 9 Mar. 2011 incase no Ö 8181-10), the Svea Court of Appeal found that there was extraordinary reason for disclosure of documents that contained trade secrets, with reference to, e.g., that the requested documents (and thus, presumably, the trade secrets) were relatively old and that the amount claimed in the arbitration was substantial. It may be questioned whether a substantial amount in dispute, in and of itself, should make it easier to obtain production of documents containing trade secrets. The case did not come under the Supreme Court's review.
213. *RosInvestCO v. The Russian Federation*, decision by the Supreme Court made on 12 Nov. 2010 in case no Ö 2301-09, NJA 2010 p. 508.

also been relied on by the Swedish courts in proceedings initiated under section 26 of the Act.[214]

195. Further, in many international arbitrations in Sweden the documents requested are located abroad and witnesses are domiciled in other countries. Even in these situations, Swedish courts may assist in ordering the measures in question.[215] However, if an order by a Swedish court is not enforceable in the country where the witness or document is located, it may not be worthwhile applying under section 26 of the Act.[216]

VI. CONFIDENTIALITY

196. It is often said that parties, when faced with a dispute, consider the perceived 'confidentiality' of arbitration as an important factor in favouring their choice. Despite this, the Act contains no provisions regarding the confidentiality of arbitral proceedings. This notwithstanding, it is generally accepted that arbitral proceedings are private in the sense that arbitral proceedings take place *in camera*, unless the parties have agreed otherwise. In other words, no third parties can attend hearings in arbitral proceedings without the consent of the parties to the arbitration.[217] This is also the principle adopted by the SCC Rules.[218]

A. Parties

197. As indicated above, the Act contains no provisions regarding the parties' duty of confidentiality in arbitration. The same is true for the SCC Rules. However, the Supreme Court judgment in the so-called Bulbank case[219] provides significant guidance as to the role of confidentiality in arbitral proceedings under Swedish law in general, and the parties' duty of confidentiality in particular. The case was determined under the 1929 Arbitration Act, but the Supreme Court made clear that the conclusions were also applicable to the 1999 Act. The facts of the case are rather instructive.

---

214. See, for instance *Yara International ASA v. Joint Stock Company Acron*, decision by the Svea Court of Appeal made on 9 Mar. 2011 incase no Ö 8181-10.
215. See the ruling of the Svea Court of Appeal in *Yara International ASA v. Joint Stock Company Acron*, decision by the Svea Court of Appeal made on 9 Mar. 2011 incase no Ö 8181-10.
216. See Hober, *International Commercial Arbitration in Sweden*, 239, who submits that this is probably an important reason why such applications are rare in international arbitrations taking place in Sweden.
217. See Heuman, *Skiljemannarätt*, 30. In the case *Foreign Trade Bank Ltd (Bulbank) v. A.I Trade Finance Inc (AIT)*, decision by the Supreme Court made on 27 October 2000 in case no T 1881-99, NJA 2000 p. 538 (the 'Bulbank case'), the Supreme Court stated that arbitrations (in general) are of a private nature and that third parties do not have the right to attend arbitration hearings.
218. Article 27(3) of the SCC Rules thus provides that hearings should be held in private, unless otherwise agreed by the parties.
219. *Bulgarian Foreign Trade Bank Ltd (Bulbank) v. A.I Trade Finance Inc (AIT)*,decision by the Supreme Court made on 27 Oct. 2000 in case no T 1881-99, NJA 2000 p. 538.

198. In the course of ongoing arbitral proceedings between Bulbank and AIT, representatives of AIT sent a copy of a decision by the arbitral tribunal on the validity of the arbitration agreement to an award reporting service in the United States, *Mealey's International Arbitration Report*, where it was published. When Bulbank became aware of the publication, it wrote to AIT and to the arbitral tribunal, stating that the publication was a material breach of the arbitration agreement. Bulbank purported to revoke the arbitration agreement with immediate effect and requested the arbitral tribunal to declare the arbitration agreement invalid on this ground. Bulbank did not succeed in its request. Subsequently, an arbitral award on the merits was rendered against Bulbank. Bulbank challenged the award.

199. The question before the Supreme Court was whether AIT was bound by a duty of confidentiality under the arbitration agreement. As a point of departure, the Supreme Court accepted that arbitral proceedings are private and that third parties have no right to attend hearings or take part in submissions in the arbitral proceedings. The Supreme Court went on to clarify that arbitral tribunals and counsel, due to their assignments, are obliged to be discreet. Confidentiality may also apply to their instructions under the ethical rules of their profession. However, any conclusions regarding the parties' duty of confidentiality could not be drawn from such circumstances. The Supreme Court found that the generally prevailing view in Sweden was that in arbitration, the duty of confidentiality does not apply without a separate agreement to that effect. The Supreme Court also reviewed foreign law and found that there was no clear position in other countries that could shed light upon the Swedish law position. Against this background, the Supreme Court concluded that there is no implied duty of confidentiality for the parties under the arbitration agreement.

200. In summary, the Bulbank case establishes that a duty of confidentiality for parties is neither a legal obligation that follows from the very nature of arbitration as a means of dispute resolution, nor an implied condition that can be inferred implicitly from all arbitration agreements. Accordingly, parties that consider confidentiality of arbitral proceedings to be of importance are well advised to expressly agree to confidentiality. This should preferably be done by way of a specific sub-clause in the parties' arbitration agreement (or a separate agreement that explicitly refers to the arbitration agreement) which clearly stipulates the scope and duration of and sanctions for the parties' confidentiality undertakings.[220]

220. A confidentiality provision in the main agreement in which the arbitration clause is included may in principle be interpreted as covering an arbitration arising out of the agreement. However, since such provisions are often broadly worded, it is in many cases difficult to delineate the exact scope of the parties' confidentiality undertakings with respect to arbitration proceedings. See further Jarvin, 'Sekretess i svenska och internationella skiljeförfaranden', 152, and Magnusson, 'Avtal om sekretess i skiljeförfarande', 169.

B. Arbitrators

201. Under Article 46 of the SCC Rules, the SCC and the arbitral tribunal are obliged to maintain confidentiality with respect to the arbitration and to the award, unless otherwise agreed by the parties. The SCC and the arbitral tribunal could be liable to compensate the parties if they breach this duty of confidentiality.

202. The Act contains no provision corresponding to Article 46 of the SCC Rules. However, the prevailing opinion among Swedish authors has long been that arbitrators have a duty of confidentiality by virtue of their assignment.[221] This view was confirmed in the Bulbank case where the Supreme Court held that:[222]

> There also appears to be an in principle unanimous view that arbitrators, because of the assignment with which they have been entrusted, must observe discretion in the arbitral proceedings, which applies even if an arbitrator has been appointed by a court. Counsel for a party should probably be regarded as having a similar obligation to his principal based on the assignment given.

203. This duty of loyalty also applies after the arbitrators' mandate is terminated. An arbitrator who violated the duty of confidentiality could be liable to pay damages to the parties.[223] However, according to Supreme Court case law, an arbitrator who is called as a witness to testify in challenge proceedings cannot refuse to answer questions regarding the arbitral tribunal's deliberations if this is relevant to the case.[224]

204. Since an arbitrator is regarded as being appointed by both parties, consent to reveal information relating to the arbitration must be given by both parties.[225]

C. Counsel

205. In the same way as for arbitrators, counsel in arbitral proceedings have traditionally been considered to be bound by a duty of confidentiality in relation to the arbitral process. This view was adopted by the Supreme Court in the Bulbank case. However, as reflected in the Supreme Court statement quoted in paragraph 265 above, the duty of confidentiality for counsel only applies in favour of the client. Accordingly, counsel

221. This opinion is given in a number of statements in the legal literature as well as in *travaux préparatories*, see for example SOU 1995:65, 185, Jarvin, 'Sekretess i svenska och internationella skiljeförfaranden', 152 and Heuman, *Arbitration Law of Sweden: Practice and Procedure*, 14, and Cars, 73.

222. Excerpt from quotation from the Supreme Court, translated and given in Stockholm Arbitration Report 2000:2, Judgment of the Supreme Court of Sweden rendered in 2000 in Case N T 1881-99: the Bulbank Case p. 144. It has however been discussed whether the Bulbank case has changed this opinion (or whether such opinion has been prevailing at all), see Heuman, *Tystnadsplikt och underlåtenhet att ställa säkerhet i skiljetvist*, 669.

223. See Cars, 110.

224. *Partrederiet för M/S Red Sea v. Götaverken Sölvesborg Aktiebolag*, decision by the Supreme Court made on 13 Jul. 1990 in case no T 80-89, NJA 1990 p. 419.

225. See SOU 1994:81, 195, and discussion in Heuman, *Arbitration Law of Sweden: Practice and Procedure*, 17.

may reveal information regarding the arbitration if their client has consented to that disclosure.

D. Witnesses and Experts

206. Witnesses and experts testifying in arbitral proceedings are not bound by a duty of confidentiality, absent a separate agreement to that effect.

VII. COSTS

A. Costs in Arbitration

1. *Introduction*

207. Costs arising from an arbitration can be divided into four main categories: (i) fees of the arbitral tribunal; (ii) registration and administration fees of the arbitral institution[226] (if applicable); (iii) expenses of the arbitral tribunal and the arbitral institution (if applicable); and (iv) the costs incurred by each party (including fees for legal representation).[227] Questions regarding the scope, allocation and determination of costs will be addressed in the following.

2. *Fees of the Arbitral Tribunal*

208. In arbitrations under the SCC Rules, the fee to the chairperson of the arbitral tribunal or to a sole arbitrator is to be set and based on the amount in dispute, in accordance with a fixed schedule of fees.[228] Within each bracket of amounts in dispute, the schedule of fees sets out two fee amounts – a minimum fee and a maximum fee. Fees are normally decided at the median level.[229] The level of fees is ultimately decided by the specific circumstances of the case. These circumstances might be, for example, the complexity of the subject matter of the dispute, the number of parties involved and other procedural aspects of the case such as length of proceedings.[230] In exceptional circumstances, the board of the SCC may, under Article 2(4) in Appendix III of the SCC Rules, deviate from the amounts set in the schedule of fees. Where the amount in dispute cannot be ascertained (which is sometimes the case when declaratory relief is

226. The provisions regarding costs in the Act are non-mandatory. Accordingly, if the parties have agreed on the SCC Rules, the SCC Rules take precedence over the Act in case the two sets of regulations do not correspond.
227. The presentation in this section follows the enumeration of arbitration costs in Art. 43 (1) of the SCC Rules, i.e.: (i) the fees of the arbitral tribunal, (ii) the administrative fee, and (iii) the expenses of the arbitral tribunal and the SCC. Thereafter the costs of each party are discussed.
228. See Art. 2 (1) in Appendix III Schedule of Costs of the SCC Rules.
229. See Magnusson, 56.
230. *Ibid*.

sought, the value of which may be difficult to assess), the board of the SCC will set the fees of the arbitral tribunal, taking all relevant circumstances into account.[231]

209. In ad hoc arbitrations under the Act, the fees of the arbitral tribunal are set by the arbitral tribunal itself, subject to any agreement entered into with the parties. Section 37 of the Act provides that the arbitral tribunal is to receive 'reasonable compensation' for its work and expenses. The provision is non-mandatory and may, under section 39 of the Act, be altered or waived by the parties' agreement. An agreement that institutional rules apply is in effect an agreement that the Act's provision in section 37 on fees to arbitrators does not apply. Instead the parties agree to be bound by the decision on fees made by the arbitral institution.

210. The expression 'reasonable compensation' is not further elucidated in the provision in the Act. However, the question of reasonable compensation was considered in the Supreme Court case *NEMU Mitt i SverigeAB (NEMU) v. Jan H, Gunnar B and Bo N (the arbitrators)*.[232] In this case, NEMU claimed that the compensation to the arbitral tribunal, which was set by the arbitral tribunal in the arbitral award, should be reduced to a certain amount. The arbitrators contested the claim on the basis that their compensation was reasonable. The Supreme Court did not reduce the compensation payable to the arbitrators. The Supreme Court concluded that the basis for the arbitrators' compensation should be the time spent and, consequently, the arbitrators should keep notes regarding measures taken and time spent on these measures.[233] With respect to the hourly rates to apply, the Supreme Court took into consideration that the arbitrators were highly qualified and had special competence in the field in question.[234] The Supreme Court also stated that the question of reasonable compensation should further be decided by looking at what is normally paid for similar assignments, i.e., compensation should be assessed on the basis of commercial principles. In principle, an attorney who is engaged as an arbitrator has the right to obtain compensation for the assignment as arbitrator on the same principles as other assignments, i.e., assignments in their capacity as an attorney. The Supreme Court also made it clear that when the parties appoint distinguished business lawyers or highly qualified specialist lawyers as arbitrators, they have to expect remuneration at a level normally charged by such lawyers (as long as not otherwise agreed).[235]

211. Notably, the Supreme Court also stated that the fact that the arbitration costs were disproportionally high compared with the value in dispute did not motivate

231. Article 2(3) in Appendix III of the SCC Rules.
232. *NEMU Mitt i Sverige AB v. Jan H, Gunnar B and Bo N (the arbitrators)*, decision by the Supreme Court made on 22 Oct. 1998 in case no T 105-98, NJA 1998 p. 574.
233. However, the Supreme Court declared that such notes were no prerequisite for the right to compensation.
234. *NEMU Mitt i Sverige AB v. Jan H, Gunnar B and Bo N (the arbitrators)*, decision by the Supreme Court made on 22 Oct. 1998 in case no T 105-98, NJA 1998 p. 574, p. 580.
235. *NEMU Mitt i Sverige AB v. Jan H, Gunnar B and Bo N (the arbitrators)*, decision by the Supreme Court made on 22 Oct. 1998 in case no T 105-98, NJA 1998 p. 574, p. 580, 579 et seq.

reducing the compensation to the arbitrators.[236] The high costs could essentially be attributed to the parties' way of pleading the case. This statement by the Supreme Court has been construed in different ways. On the one hand, the statement has been construed to suggest that, although the amount in dispute has no 'direct bearing on the assessment of what is reasonable compensation... the arbitrators should ensure that the costs of the arbitral proceedings are commensurate with the value of the subject matter'.[237] On the other hand, the statement has been construed to mean that the relation between the arbitration costs and the value in dispute should not affect assessment of reasonable compensation, at least not necessarily.[238]

212. As mentioned above, the parties may jointly enter into an agreement with the arbitrators regarding arbitrators' compensation.[239] An agreement between the parties to which the arbitrators are not parties is only binding in relation to the arbitrators if the agreement was known to and understood by the arbitrators when they accepted the assignment.[240]

213. The arbitral tribunal's fees, as set in the final award, may be challenged (or 'appealed') separately by a party, to the District Court under section 41 of the Act, without challenging the award proper. In *Soyak v. WM* et al., the Supreme Court found that this right to appeal also applied to fees of the arbitral tribunal that had been set by an arbitral institution.[241] The Supreme Court ruling has been described as controversial and criticized for interfering with the autonomy of the institutional arbitral process.[242] However, the Supreme Court concluded that section 41 of the Act gives a party a procedural right to appeal the decision on fees, even in cases where the fees have been set by an arbitral institution. In the authors' view, any other outcome would have been surprising because the wording of the mandatory statutory provision in question leaves no room for another interpretation. Importantly, although acknowledging the procedural right to appeal, the Supreme Court did not assess whether the challenging party had substantive rights to have the decision on fees amended. The Supreme Court remitted the case back to the District Court in this respect. The case subsequently settled, without this substantive issue being assessed by the District Court. In our view, the District Court ought to have found that, although there was a procedural right for the party to challenge the fees under section 41 of the Act, the challenge could not

236. *NEMU Mitt i Sverige AB v. Jan H, Gunnar B and Bo N (the arbitrators)*, decision by the Supreme Court made on 22 Oct. 1998 in case no T 105-98, NJA 1998 p. 574, p. 580, 581.
237. See Heuman, *Arbitration Law of Sweden: Practice and Procedure*, 552.
238. See Schöldström, 693.
239. Section 39 of the Act. It may also be noted that an arbitrator who receives, or agrees to receive, compensation from only one of the parties, may be disqualified under s. 8(4) of the Act; see discussion in Hobér, *International Commercial Arbitration in Sweden*, 173.
240. SOU 1994:81, 299, Govt. bill 1998/99:35, 240, and Kvart and Olsson, 141.
241. *Soyak International Construction & Investment Inc. v. Werner Melis, Kaj Hobér and Steffen Kraus*, decision by the Supreme Court made on 3 Dec. 2008 in case no Ö 4227-06, NJA 2008 p. 1118.
242. See Ramberg and Lazareff.

succeed on the merits, since fees set by an arbitral institution are binding upon the parties.[243]

3. *Administrative Fee*

214. If the dispute is to be settled in accordance with the SCC Rules, an administrative fee, which is set in accordance with a certain schedule based on the amount in dispute,[244] is also payable.

215. The administrative fee includes a registration fee payable by the claimant upon filing the request for arbitration.[245] If the registration fee is not paid upon filing the request for arbitration, the secretariat of the SCC will set a period within which the claimant must, at the risk of dismissal, pay the fee. The registration fee is non-refundable.

4. *Expenses of the Arbitral Tribunal and the SCC*

216. Under the Act, the parties reimburse reasonable expenses of the arbitral tribunal.[246] The same applies under the SCC Rules, under which expenses of the SCC are also to be reimbursed.[247]

217. Reimbursable expenses of the arbitral tribunal are, according to SCC practice, compensation for travel and accommodation, and costs of premises and technical equipment which the arbitral tribunal has arranged for in connection with the arbitral proceedings. When staying at a place other than their place of practice, the arbitrators are also entitled to a *per diem* allowance.[248] The expenses of the arbitral tribunal may also include the fees and expenses of an expert appointed by the arbitral tribunal (under Article 29 of the SCC Rules).[249]

---

243. The parties to the arbitration agreement had agreed, by referring to institutional rules, that substantive fee decisions were to be made by an arbitral institution, the decisions of which the parties had agreed to be bound by. As mentioned above, s. 39 of the Act provides that such an agreement is valid and that determination of fees by the arbitral institution supersedes the Act's provision regarding 'reasonable fees' in s. 37. The substantive provision in s. 37 is thus non-mandatory and possible to waive by agreement, under s. 39. At the same time, the procedural right to appeal under s. 41 is, somewhat incoherently, not covered by s. 39.
244. In the same way as determination of fees to the arbitral tribunal, the amount in dispute should (according to Art. 3(2) of the SCC Rules) be the aggregated value of all claims, counterclaims and set-offs. Where the amount in dispute cannot be ascertained, the board of the SCC determines the administrative fee taking all relevant circumstances into account. According to Art. 3([illegible]) in Appendix III to the SCC Rules the board may, in exceptional circumstances, deviate from the amounts set out in the schedule.
245. See Art. 3 (1) of the SCC Rules. The registration fee amounts to Euro (EUR) 1.500, according to Art. 1([illegible]) in Appendix III to the SCC Rules.
246. Section 37 of the Act.
247. Article 43 (1) and (6).
248. See Madsen, *Commercial Arbitration in Sweden* 312 (3d ed., Oxford University Press 2007).
249. Article 4 in Appendix III to the SCC Rules.

218. Before taking measures that could lead to considerable costs, the arbitral tribunal should obtain consent from the parties. Such measures could be hiring an interpreter or renting hearing premises. The arbitral tribunal should of course carefully consider objections and the reasons for these by the party concerned. However, if the arbitral tribunal considers it necessary to take the measure in question, it has been suggested that 'the arbitration agreement can be deemed to include an acceptance by the parties of the arbitral tribunal involving them in joint and several liability for costs'.[250]

5. *Costs of the Parties*

219. In addition to the fees and expenses of the arbitral tribunal and, when applicable, the arbitral institution, the parties, of course, have costs of their own. The most significant cost item is usually the parties' costs for legal representation. The cost of retaining experts to present their opinions on various issues is often also significant.

220. Upon the request of a party, the arbitral tribunal may order a party to compensate the other party for costs incurred, including its costs for legal representation.[251] Neither the Act nor the SCC Rules provide guidance as to what kind of costs of the parties are reimbursable. However, in *Bonnierföretagen v. Bertil B*, the Supreme Court found that, unless the parties have agreed on another way of determining costs, it is natural for an arbitral tribunal to seek guidance in the provisions of the Code of Judicial Procedure.[252] The judgment predates the 1999 Arbitration Act, under which the principles of the Code of Judicial Procedure are not relevant in arbitrations. However, the principles of the Code with respect to reimbursable costs for legal representation are largely in accordance with what may be perceived as a general arbitral practice. The Supreme Court judgment is therefore still of some relevance.

221. Under the Code of Judicial Procedure, compensation for litigation costs is fully to cover reasonable costs of preparation and presentation of the case, including fees for legal representation. Further, compensation is also payable for the time and effort expended by the party by reason of the litigation.

222. In *Sala International AB v. Alliance Assurance Co Ltd among others*, the Supreme Court made clear that determining compensable costs for legal representation should not primarily be based on time spent.[253] Instead, such determination is to take into account the nature and magnitude of the case as well as the care and expertise with which the work has been carried out by counsel. When assessing the nature of the case, the complexity of the substantive and legal circumstances as well as the degree of

250. See Heuman, *Arbitration Law of Sweden: Practice and Procedure*, 554 et seq.
251. Section 42 of the Act and Art. 43 of the SCC Rules.
252. *Bertil B. v. AB Bonnierföretagen*, decision by the Supreme Court made on 2 Jun. 1989 in case no Ö 502-88, NJA 1989 p. 247.
253. *Sala International AB v. Alliance Assurance Co Ltd among others*, decision by the Supreme Court made on 29 Dec. 1997 in case no Ö 75-96, NJA 1997 p. 854.

specialist knowledge required by counsel should be considered.[254] As regards the magnitude of the case, the length of the case in terms of time and the work required by counsel may be considered.[255] Further, the amount in dispute and the importance of the outcome of the case for the party should be taken into consideration.

223. Amounts awarded as compensation for costs may, if a party so requests, include interest under the Interest Act,[256] running from the date of the award until payment is made. Since the right to receive interest on arbitration costs is a procedural right, the Interest Act applies in this respect when Swedish law governs the arbitration, irrespective of whether another law applies to the merits of the case.

B. Advance on Costs[257]

224. The arbitral tribunal's right to compensation normally does not arise until the arbitration has come to an end and the final award is rendered. In order for the arbitral tribunal to secure payment from the parties, the Act and the SCC Rules contain provisions enabling the arbitral tribunal and the SCC, as applicable, to request advance payments for costs.[258] In ad hoc arbitrations, the parties may agree, with binding effect on the arbitrators, that the provisions on advances for costs shall not apply.[259]

225. Under the SCC Rules, the board of the SCC sets the amount to be paid by the parties as an advance on costs. This amount should correspond to the estimated amount of the costs of the entire arbitration.[260] The advance on costs is set by adding together the preliminary fees to the arbitral tribunal according to the schedule of fees (see 1.2 above), the administrative fee to the SCC (as preliminarily decided), a predefined amount to cover expenses and an amount to cover value added tax (if applicable).[261] When deciding the advance on costs, the principle is that no additional deposits should be needed.[262] However, if the amount in dispute changes or if other circumstances arise, so as significantly to change the size or character of the case, the fees could be re-calculated. In that case the advance on costs should also be re-calculated.[263]

226. Under section 38 of the Act, the arbitral tribunal may request security for its compensation (including arbitrator fees and expenses). This security often takes the

254. See Madsen, *Commercial Arbitration in Sweden* 327 (3d ed., Oxford University Press 2007).
255. See Madsen, *Commercial Arbitration in Sweden* 327 (3d ed., Oxford University Press 2007).
256. (*Sw: Räntelag (1975:635)*).
257. In the Act, the term 'security' is used. In the following the term 'advance on costs'(which is used in the SCC Rules) will be used both in relation to the SCC Rules and the Act.
258. See s 38 of the Act and Art. 45 of the SCC Rules.
259. Section 39 of the Act. The provision in the SCC Rules applies if the parties have agreed to apply the rules, without excluding the provision on advance on costs.
260. Article 45(2) of the SCC Rules.
261. Cf. Art. 43(1) of the SCC Rules and Magnusson, 56.
262. See Magnusson, 56.
263. See Magnusson, 56.

form of an advance on costs to be paid as a deposit. The Act contains no provisions on how the advance on costs should be calculated. The arbitral tribunal may therefore set the amount more freely than the SCC. However, the provision on advance on costs is non-mandatory for the arbitral tribunal. The arbitral tribunal is of course free to decide not to request an advance on costs from the parties.

227. Where proceedings concern different individual claims, counterclaims and set-offs, the arbitral tribunal may fix separate advances on costs for each individual claim. In that case each party pays an advance on costs corresponding to its claim.[264] One purpose of this rule is that it may prevent a respondent from presenting an unfounded counterclaim in order to force the claimant to pay a higher advance on costs.[265]

228. An advance on costs may be requested at the beginning of the proceedings, which is the normal procedure, or later during the proceedings.[266] If the advance on costs already furnished is found not to be sufficient, the arbitral tribunal may require an additional advance on costs from the parties during the proceedings.[267] Where the requested advance on costs is not provided by either of the parties, the arbitral tribunal may terminate the proceedings, in whole or in part (corresponding to the individual claim for which the advance on costs has not been paid).[268]

229. A request for advance on costs is to be addressed to both parties, for each to pay half of the total amount.[269] If a party fails to provide its share of the requested advance on costs within the period specified by the arbitral tribunal, the opposing party may provide the entire advance on costs.[270] Moreover, a party that does not pay the advance on costs is considered to have waived its right to invoke the arbitration agreement as a bar to judicial proceedings in court.[271]

230. In *3S Swedish Special Supplier AB v. Sky Park AB*, the Supreme Court addressed the question whether a party who had also paid the other party's advance on costs

---

264. Section 38(1) of the Act only mentions that the arbitrators may fix separate security for individual cases. Art. 45(3) in the SCC Rules is more exhaustive stating that '[w]here counterclaims or set-offs are submitted, the [b]oard may decide that each of the parties shall pay advances on costs corresponding to its claim'.
265. SOU 1994:81, 198, and Heuman, *Arbitration Law of Sweden: Practice and Procedure*, 565.
266. SOU 1994:81, 199, and Madsen, *Commercial Arbitration in Sweden* 314 (3d ed., Oxford University Press 2007).
267. Under Art. 45(3) of the SCC Rules, such additional advance during the course of the arbitration requires a request from the arbitral tribunal to the board of the SCC, which may order the parties to pay additional advances. In arbitrations under the Act, the arbitral tribunal's right to request security for costs is found in s. 38(1) of the Act. This provision entitles the arbitral tribunal to request security at any time during the arbitral proceeding; see Heuman, *Arbitration Law of Sweden: Practice and Procedure*, 564.
268. Section 38(1) of the Act. The same applies under Art. 45(4) in the SCC Rules, pursuant to which, however, the words 'shall terminate' are used. If one of the parties does not pay its part of the advance on costs, the arbitral tribunal should first give the other party an opportunity to pay that part of the advance on costs.
269. Article 45(3) of the SCC Rules. The Act does not contain such an explicit provision, but the corresponding provisions should also apply under the Act. See Kvart and Olsson, 143.
270. Section 38(1) of the Act.
271. See Madsen, *Commercial Arbitration in Sweden* 316 f (3d ed., Oxford University Press 2007) referring to s. 5(3) of the Act.

could seek payment from the other party of that other party's share in court when the arbitration was still ongoing.[272] In the arbitration, Sky Park AB had declared that it had no intention of paying its part of the amount requested. 3S Swedish Special Supplier AB therefore paid the entire advance on costs. The Supreme Court stated that the parties, unless otherwise agreed, are jointly and severally liable for compensation to the arbitral tribunal. The Court further stated that a party who has paid the entire advance on costs has a right to claim compensation from the counterparty for the counterparty's share. However, it is not until the arbitration is finally settled that final liability for payment between the parties can be determined. Thus, there is no right to recourse for a paid advance on costs while the arbitration is still ongoing. Conversely, under the SCC Rules, if one party makes the required payment, the arbitral tribunal may, at the request of that party, make a separate award for reimbursement of the payment; see Article 45(4) of the SCC Rules.

231. As an exception to the general rule of equal payment between the parties, the parties may agree that one of the parties is to pay the entire or most of the compensation for the arbitration costs. Agreements of this kind are common in employment contracts, such as agreements between a company and its managing director or other executives, where the company typically bears the entire cost of the arbitration. A request for advance on costs should in that case be proportional to the agreement.[273]

232. Under section 38(2) of the Act, the arbitral tribunal may decide during the arbitration to release a portion of the advance on costs in order to cover its expenses. However, the advance on costs may not, without the parties' approval, be used to cover compensation for the arbitrators' work. This may be done only after the arbitrators' compensation has been decided in a final award and the parties have failed to fulfil their payment obligations in accordance with that award.[274] In the great majority of cases, the advance security is a monetary deposit (rather than, for example, a bank guarantee). The arbitrators can set-off their compensation against the paid-in advance on costs. It appears to be appropriate that, in connection therewith, the arbitral tribunal send a final statement of account to the parties.[275] Under Article 45(5) of the SCC Rules, the board may '[a]t any stage during the arbitration or after the Award has been made draw on the Advance on Costs to cover the Costs of the Arbitration', i.e., including fees for the arbitrators' work.

233. A decision to request an advance on costs from the parties or to release the advance on costs must be made by the arbitrators collectively. Thus, one of several arbitrators is not authorized to make that decision alone.[276] If only one of the parties

272. *Swedish Special Supplier AB v. Sky Park AB*, decision by the Supreme Court made on 29 Dec. 2009 in case no T 5119-99, NJA 2000 p. 773.
273. See Kvart and Olsson, 143.
274. Section 38(2) of the Act.
275. See Madsen, *Commercial Arbitration in Sweden* 317 (3d ed., Oxford University Press 2007).
276. SOU 1994:81, 298, Govt. bill 1998/99:35, 240, and Heuman, *Arbitration Law of Sweden: Practice and Procedure*, 561.

has provided the entire advance on costs, the same party may also solely consent to release of the advance on costs by the arbitral tribunal[277] (see more below).

C. Final Allocation of Costs between the Parties

234. Under the Act and the SCC Rules, the parties are jointly and severally liable to pay reasonable compensation to the arbitral tribunal for work and expenses.[278]

235. However, one exception exists to this general rule of joint and several liability. Where the arbitral tribunal has determined in the award that it lacks jurisdiction to determine the dispute, the respondent is liable for payment only insofar as required due to special circumstances.[279] For example, if the respondent's negligence has increased the costs, the respondent should be liable for those costs, notwithstanding the exception.[280]

236. Upon a request from a party and although the parties are jointly liable to compensate the arbitral tribunal, the arbitral tribunal may order one party to compensate the other party for arbitration costs. The arbitral tribunal may also order a party to compensate the costs incurred by the other party itself, including that party's costs of legal representation. When allocating costs between the parties, the main rule is that costs follow the event and, accordingly, that the losing party bears all costs including costs reasonably incurred by the winning party.[281]

237. It is not always easy to determine which of the parties 'won' a case for the purpose of allocating costs. An arbitration usually involves several contentious issues and several prayers for relief, some of which may be granted and others denied. In the authors' view, the arbitral tribunal should allocate the costs between the parties taking into account the time and effort spent during the proceedings with respect to the contentious issues in question (if that is possible to assess). If, for example, the greater part of the parties' submissions concerned the issue of liability and only little effort was spent on arguing quantum, it would usually be correct to view the claimant as the successful party if liability was established, even if the full quantum amount sought by the claimant was not awarded. To assist the arbitral tribunal in this exercise, the parties may, in their cost submissions, summarize their respective views on how the total time spent was divided amongst the main contentious issues in the case.

277. Section 39(2) of the Act.
278. Section 37 of the Act, and Art. 43(6) of the SCC Rules.
279. Section 37, second sentence, of the Act.
280. See Heuman, *Arbitration Law of Sweden: Practice and Procedure*, 557.
281. This is expressly provided for in Art. 43 of the SCC Rules, under which the allocation of costs is to be made with 'regard to the outcome of the case and other relevant circumstances'. Although not expressly provided for under the Act, the principle that costs follow the event is the general principle under Swedish law, codified in the Code of Judicial Procedure (ch. 18, s. 1). The principle is also applied in ad hocarbitrations in Sweden, unless the parties have agreed otherwise.

238. The arbitral tribunal may also use its discretionary powers to allocate costs to sanction an obstructing party.[282] In these cases, for the sanction to have any effect, it is advisable that the arbitral tribunal already make clear during the proceedings that obstruction may influence the arbitral tribunal's decision with respect to allocation of costs. For example, this may be made clear in the first procedural order.

VIII. THE AWARD

A. Categories of Awards

1. Distinguishing between an 'Award' and a 'Decision'

239. The Act distinguishes between 'awards' and 'decisions' (or 'orders'). Under section 27(1) of the Act, a determination of the substantive issues in an arbitration – i.e., the merits of the case – is to be made in an 'award'. This applies irrespective of whether the entire matter in dispute or only a part of it is decided.

240. Section 27(1) of the Act further provides that a decision by which the arbitral tribunal terminates the proceedings without ruling on the issues that have been referred to it is also to be made in the form an award.

241. It does not matter how the arbitral tribunal designates its decision. If the decision is, in fact, an award, because: (i) it includes a determination on the merits or (ii) it terminates the proceedings, it will be treated as an award by Swedish courts. Similarly, it does not matter if a finding that the arbitral tribunal has jurisdiction is designated, for example, 'partial award on jurisdiction'. This finding does not dispose of the merits of the case and since it does not result in termination of the proceedings, it is, as a matter of Swedish law, a decision.[283]

242. Pursuant to the definition in section 27(3) of the Act, decisions are determinations that neither include a ruling on the merits of a case nor terminate the proceedings as a whole. A determination of a procedural issue which does not imply that the proceedings are to be terminated is thus to be considered as a decision.

243. It follows from the foregoing that a separate decision on jurisdiction is to be styled differently depending on the outcome of the jurisdictional issue. When an arbitral tribunal finds that it lacks jurisdiction and thus terminates the arbitral proceedings on that basis, this is to be done in the form of an award. This award can be reviewed by

282. In an arbitration under the SCC Rules, this right to use the cost allocation as a sanction must be understood to follow from the wording of Art. 43 that the arbitral tribunal is to have regard to 'other relevant circumstances'.

283. See e.g., *Joint Stock Company Acron v. Yara International ASA*, decision by the Svea Court of Appeal made on 12 Apr. 2010 in case no Ö 9250-09, RH 2010:75. In this case, the arbitral tribunal found, after a jurisdictional hearing, that it had jurisdiction. To this effect, the arbitral tribunal rendered a 'Partial Award on Jurisdiction'. The respondent in the arbitration brought a challenge against the partial award. The court explained that, although styled 'Partial Award on Jurisdiction', it was in fact a procedural decision. As such, it could not be challenged.

a competent court by way of an appeal under section 36 of the Act. Conversely, should the arbitral tribunal find that it has jurisdiction, the determination will take the form of a decision. As further explained below, such a decision is not binding.[284] Recourse against it is only possible in connection with a challenge of the final award under section 34 of the Act.[285]

244. Unless the parties have agreed otherwise, an award is final and binding. Decisions, in contrast, do not acquire legal force and are thus not enforceable and are not binding on the arbitral tribunal.[286] Consequently, decisions may – at least as a general rule – be amended by the arbitral tribunal at any stage of the proceedings.[287] This does not mean, however, that it is always appropriate for an arbitral tribunal to deviate from a decision that it has taken earlier in the proceedings. The parties necessarily adapt to the procedural decisions made by the arbitral tribunal and should not need to re-argue each issue covered by those decisions in the event that the arbitral tribunal were to reconsider its decision.[288] Moreover, if a procedural decision has been accepted by both parties, for example by signing terms of reference that include the decision, the decision ought also, at least in principle, to be considered binding on the arbitral tribunal and on the parties as an effect of the principle of party autonomy. Consequently, in order for the arbitral tribunal to deviate from that decision, both parties should agree to the deviation.

245. The arbitral tribunal can also determine that certain categories of decisions, e.g., on matters of jurisdiction, should be binding. Such a determination does not elevate the decisions in question to awards according to the Act, but nevertheless implies that the decisions become binding on the parties and the arbitrators during the arbitral proceedings.[289]

2. *Final Award*

246. An arbitration in Sweden is always concluded through rendering an award.[290] This final award – which may be preceded by one or multiple separate awards – either

284. See s. 2(2) of the Act.
285. Govt. bill 1998/99:35, 77 and 124. Notwithstanding this, it is possible to achieve a court review of the arbitrators' jurisdiction *during* the arbitral proceedings, namely by bringing an action under s. 2 of the Act, requesting declaratory relief to the effect that the arbitral tribunal lacks jurisdiction or competence to adjudicate the dispute. See further *RosInvest Co UK Ltd v. The Russian Federation*, decision by the Supreme Court made on 12 November 2010 in case no Ö 2301-09, NJA 2010 p. 508.
286. Govt. bill 1998/99:35, 124. See also Heuman, *Arbitration Law of Sweden: Practice and Procedure*, 525; Lindskog, 810; and Madsen, *Commercial Arbitration in Sweden* 238 (3d ed., Oxford University Press 2007).
287. As Lindskog notes, a decision whereby an arbitrator is removed on the grounds of bias under s. 10 of the Act cannot be changed by the arbitral tribunal. The reason for this is not, however, that the decision acquires legal force, but rather that the decision is of an irreversible nature. See Lindskog, 810. See also Govt. bill 1998/99:35, 124.
288. To this effect, see also Heuman, *Arbitration Law of Sweden: Practice and Procedure*, 525.
289. *Ibid.*
290. Section 27(1) and (3) of the Act. Also provided for in Art. 39 of the SCC Rules.

determines the substantive issues referred to the arbitral tribunal, i.e., the merits of the case, or terminates the arbitration without a ruling on the merits.[291] The latter may occur in a number of different scenarios, such as when the parties have settled, the arbitral tribunal concludes that it lacks jurisdiction or that the dispute should be dismissed on the basis of lis pendens or res judicata. Other examples where a final award is rendered without a ruling on the merits are when the claimant withdraws its claim and where the proceedings are terminated because the parties have failed to provide security for costs pursuant to section 38(1) of the Act.

247. Final awards that do not contain a ruling on the merits may be appealed to the competent court of jurisdiction, in accordance with section 36 of the Act. Most often, such an appeal is made when a party is dissatisfied with a finding by the arbitral tribunal that it lacks jurisdiction to hear the case.

248. Final awards that do contain a ruling on the merits may not be appealed in accordance with section 36 of the Act. The only recourse available against awards rendered on the merits is to rely on the limited grounds available to set aside the award pursuant to sections 33 and 34 of the Act.

3. *Separate Awards*

249. The arbitral tribunal may decide part of the dispute or a certain issue that is relevant for final resolution of the dispute in a separate award, unless both parties object.[292] Separate awards – which are subject to the same formal requirements as other types of award – are final in nature and, *mutatis mutandis*, acquire the same legal effects as final awards, including being enforceable and recognizable.

250. Although the term used in the Act and the SCC Rules is 'separate award',[293] in practice, these awards are sometimes referred to as e.g., 'partial awards', 'interim awards', or 'interlocutory awards'. However, irrespective of the designation of the award, if it is an award on the merits of the case, but not the final award, the provisions of the Act (and the SCC Rules) addressing separate awards apply.

251. Somewhat simplistically, separate awards may be divided into two categories: (1) separate awards that finally dispose of one of several claims in a case (dispositive separate awards), and (2) separate awards on issues that are determinative of, but do

291. Final awards without any ruling on the merits may contain decisions in respect of the arbitrators' compensation and the allocation of costs between the parties. See e.g., Madsen, *Commercial Arbitration in Sweden* 236 (3d ed., Oxford University Press 2007).
292. Section 29(1) of the Act and Art. 38 of the SCC Rules. Unlike s. 29(1) of the Act, Art. 38 of the SCC Rules does not contain the provison 'unless both parties object thereto'. Needless to say, however this also applies under the SCC Rules, as a function of the principle of party autonomy.
293. The Swedish term used in the Act is *särskild skiljedom*.

not dispose of, resolution of the main claim(s) in the case (determinative separate awards).[294]

252. A dispositive separate award is typically enforceable.[295] A practical example of a situation in which such a separate award may be rendered is where a party, in whole or in part, has admitted one of several prayers for relief.[296] A dispositive separate award may also be an appropriate tool to adjudicate a relatively uncomplicated claim that is not interconnected with other claims in the dispute and which can be assessed relatively easily on the basis of a limited amount of immediately available evidence. Under Article 45(4) of the SCC Rules, the arbitral tribunal may also, upon a party's request, make a separate award for reimbursement of costs, in cases where one party refuses to pay its share of the advance on costs and the other party has thus paid the entire advance.

253. As a limitation on the arbitral tribunal's freedom to render separate awards, the Act provides that a claim invoked as a defence by way of set-off must be adjudicated in the same award as the main claim, against which set-off is sought.[297] In effect, this limitation implies that a dispositive separate award cannot preclude the opposing party from raising a set-off claim.[298]

254. A determinative separate award does not typically adjudicate any of the prayers for relief, but rather serves to determine an issue which is preliminary to the main issue, so as to make the remainder of the arbitration less complex. This kind of separate award is only declaratory and, thus, cannot normally be enforced. For example, there may be an argument over the existence or meaning of a certain contractual provision. If the provision exists, extensive evidence will be required in order to establish breach, whilst if it does not exist, no further argument or evidence is required. In this situation, it may save time and costs first to determine as a preliminary issue whether the provision exists. The most common situation in which a determinative separate award is rendered is probably where the arbitral tribunal has ordered the arbitration to be bifurcated into a liability phase and a quantum phase. The separate award will in these instances deal with the issue of liability, i.e., whether the respondent is, as such, liable in damages. Only if the arbitral tribunal reaches a finding of liability will it proceed to assess the 'quantum', i.e., the damages to be awarded in the final award. A determinative separate award may, as a further example, be appropriate if there is an objection

294. A simpler way of describing the two different kinds of separate awards could be to call them 'partial awards' and 'interim awards'. In this contribution, however, we refer to them as 'dispositive separate awards' and 'determinative separate awards' in order not to confuse 'interim awards' with orders on interim measures. As discussed below, such orders are sometimes referred to as 'interim awards' or 'awards on interim measures'.

295. See Heuman, *Arbitration Law of Sweden: Practice and Procedure*, 527 and Lindskog, 829. The enforceability of an award requires, of course, that the claim is such that enforcement can be sought. If the award provides merely for declaratory relief it cannot, with a few exceptions that will not be discussed here, be enforced.

296. Cf. s. 29(2) of the Act.

297. Section 29(1) of the Act.

298. See Madsen, *Commercial Arbitration in Sweden* 244 (3d ed., Oxford University Press 2007).

that a particular claim is time-barred.[299] In complex cases, the proceedings may sometimes be divided into several phases, each concluded by a separate award. However, as discussed in section IV.F.3 above, bifurcated proceedings may result in delays and increased costs. The possibility to bifurcate proceedings should therefore be used with caution and only if there are clear benefits in doing so.

255. A determinative separate award acquires legal force and is binding. Accordingly, it binds the arbitral tribunal, or any subsequent arbitral tribunal adjudicating issues pertaining to the same legal relationship between the same parties. Consequently, the final award must not deviate from the ultimate finding of the determinative separate award. However, this applies only to the operative part of the award, not to the reasons. In the final award and if justified, the arbitral tribunal may thus diverge from the reasons stated in a separate award,[300] for example with respect to how certain evidence has been assessed or with respect to how certain findings are to be legally qualified.

256. All separate awards can be challenged in accordance with the rules that apply for final awards. In this connection, it should be underlined that the period for bringing such an action starts to run upon receipt of the separate award and not upon receipt of the final award.[301] Therefore, in most cases, it is necessary for the dissatisfied party to initiate challenge proceedings against a separate award before the final award has been rendered and thus before the arbitration has been terminated.

257. When a separate award is challenged by one of the parties before the final award has been rendered, the arbitral tribunal may decide, at its discretion, whether to continue or stay the arbitral proceedings pending the outcome of the challenge proceedings.[302] However, the arbitral tribunal should be wary of its general obligation to conduct the proceedings in a practical and expeditious manner.[303] We would submit that exceptional circumstances should exist in order for an arbitral tribunal to accept that the arbitration be delayed merely because one of the parties does not agree with, and challenges, a separate award rendered by the arbitral tribunal. Such exceptional circumstances could be that the arbitral tribunal realizes that it has committed a grave procedural error in the separate award and, consequently, that a real risk arises that the separate award will be set aside.

299. Govt. bill 1998/99:35, 131.
300. See e.g., Heuman, *Arbitration Law of Sweden: Practice and Procedure*, 533 and Hobér, *International Commercial Arbitration in Sweden*, 263.
301. Govt. bill 1998/99:35, 236.
302. See e.g., Hobér, *International Commercial Arbitration in Sweden*, 262.
303. Section 21 of the Act, and Art. 19(2) of the SCC Rules.

4. *Consent Awards*

258. At the request of the parties, the arbitral tribunal may record a settlement reached by the parties in an award.[304] Such a consent award on agreed terms is subject to the same formal requirements and has the same legal effects as other types of award.

259. In practice, a settlement is often recorded in a consent award so that the arbitral tribunal notes in the award that the parties have agreed to settle the dispute and then refers to an appendix to the award, where the settlement agreement is found. In other instances, the parties do not want the entire settlement agreement to be appended. They then instruct the arbitral tribunal what terms are to be included in the consent award, for example, that the respondent is to pay a certain amount to the claimant, failing which certain interest is to accrue.

260. The parties can request that the arbitral tribunal record their agreement in a consent award at any time until the arbitral tribunal renders its final award.[305] The parties' rationale for seeking confirmation of a settlement reached in a consent award is typically that an award – in contrast to a settlement agreement – is enforceable and recognizable under the New York Convention.

261. As indicated above, both section 27(2) of the Act and Article 39(1) of the SCC Rules use the word 'may': '... the Arbitral Tribunal may... record the settlement in the form of a consent award.' The wording suggests that it is within the arbitral tribunal's discretion to decide whether or not to issue a consent award. The *travaux préparatoires* to the Act clarify that there is no unconditional obligation incumbent upon an arbitral tribunal to issue a consent award at the parties' request.[306] However, considering the fundamental principle of party autonomy, the number of situations in which it can be considered justifiable for an arbitral tribunal to refuse such a request is very limited. In essence, an arbitral tribunal should only deny a joint request from the parties if the arbitrators can foresee that the consent award would become invalid, for example on the basis that it violates public policy or that it would include determination of a non-arbitrable issue.[307]

5. *Default Awards*

262. As discussed in section IV.G above, a party's failure without valid cause to appear at a hearing or otherwise to comply with an order of the arbitral tribunal does not prevent the arbitral tribunal from proceeding with the arbitration.[308] In other words,

304. Section 27(2) of the Act, and Art. 39(1) of the SCC Rules.
305. It is thus possible for the parties to reach a settlement and have it confirmed in a consent award even after the point in time when the proceedings have been formally closed. See Hobér, *International Commercial Arbitration in Sweden*, 264.
306. Govt. bill 1998/99:35, 133.
307. See s. 33 of the Act and Govt. bill 1998/99:35, 133. See also Hobér, *International Commercial Arbitration in Sweden*, 265.
308. Section 32 of the Act, and Art. 30(2) of the SCC Rules.

non-appearance or non-participation of a party does not ultimately prevent the arbitral tribunal from rendering an award on the merits of the case.

263. However, it is not possible for the arbitral tribunal to issue a default award. Even if one party refuses to participate in the arbitration, the award must be based on an assessment on the merits of what has been submitted to the arbitral tribunal.[309]

264. In proceedings where one party chooses to remain passive without valid cause, the arbitral tribunal should ensure that the non-active party is given sufficient opportunity to present its case before the award is rendered. In order to minimize the risk of the award being invalid or challengeable, it is also advisable for the arbitral tribunal to include a detailed description of those efforts in the award.[310]

6. *Interim Orders*

265. The arbitral tribunal may order interim measures, such as freezing orders and injunctions, necessary to secure the claim that is the subject of the arbitration.[311] These orders are sometimes referred to as 'interim awards' or 'awards on interim measures' and, notably, the SCC Rules provide that an interim measure may take the form of 'an order or an award'.[312] However, if the measure in question is 'interim' and, thus, does not finally dispose of the merits of the case, the measure is really a 'decision' within the meaning of the Act. In arbitrations taking place in Sweden, it is therefore more appropriate to designate rulings on security measures as 'decisions' or, as is more commonly the case, 'orders'.[313]

B. Requirements as to Form of Awards

1. *Statutory Requirements*

266. Pursuant to the principle of party autonomy, the parties to an arbitration agreement are in essence at liberty to agree on the formal requirements of the award to be rendered by the arbitral tribunal. This freedom is limited only by certain statutory minimum requirements, laid down in section 31 of the Act.

309. Section 24(3) of the Act.
310. Hobér, *International Commercial Arbitration in Sweden*, 265.
311. Section 25(4) of the Act.
312. Article 32(3) of the SCC Rules.
313. There may of course be situations where, even if the arbitration is seated in Sweden, it is appropriate to designate an order on interim measures as an award, for example for reasons of enforceability of the order in another jurisdiction.

267. Requirements as to the form of the award are as follows:[314]

(a) The award should be in writing.
(b) The award should be signed[315] by the arbitrators. As a main rule, all arbitrators should sign the award. It is sufficient, however, that a majority of the arbitrators sign the award, provided that the reason(s) why not all the arbitrators have signed the award are stated in the award.[316] Another deviation from the main rule is that the parties may agree that the chairperson of the arbitral tribunal alone will sign the award.[317] This is often a practical solution to avoid delay in issuing the award when the arbitrators reside in different countries.
(c) The award should state the place of arbitration. This information is of significance since the place of arbitration determines, amongst other things, which Swedish court is competent to try an action against the award under sections 33 (invalidity), 34 (challenge), 36 (termination of proceedings without a ruling on the merits) and 41 (compensation to the arbitrators) of the Act.
(d) The award should state the date upon which the award is made.

268. An award that does not fulfil the statutory requirements with regard to written form and signing, i.e., items (a)–(b) above is invalid.[318] However, deficiencies pertaining to written form and signing – and thus the validity of the award – can be rectified by amending the award under section 35 of the Act.

269. The requirements to state the place of arbitration and the date when the award was made, i.e., items (c)–(d), are not sanctioned in the sense that failure to observe either or both of these requirements leads to invalidity of the award.[319] Since this kind of error cannot lead to invalidity of the award, it can only be attacked by way of a challenge to the award under section 34 of the Act on the basis that a procedural error has been committed. However, for such a challenge to succeed, the error in question must be found probably to have influenced the outcome of the case.[320] It may therefore

314. Cf. Art. 36 of the SCC Rules.
315. It is sufficient that the arbitrators sign the last page of the award. There is no obligation for the arbitrators to indicate the place and date of signing. It should also be noted that the award does not have to be signed at the place of arbitration. See Govt. bill 1998/99:35, 232 and 242; Heuman, *Arbitration Law of Sweden: Practice and Procedure*, 501; and Hobér, *International Commercial Arbitration in Sweden*, 266.
316. Section 31(1) of the Act.
317. Govt. bill 1998/99:35, 232. See also Madsen, *Commercial Arbitration in Sweden* 258 (3d ed., Oxford University Press 2007). In this connection, it is noteworthy that s. 31(1) of the Act does not authorize the parties to instruct any other arbitrator than the chairperson to sign the award.
318. Section 33(1), item 3, of the Act.
319. Govt. bill 1998/99:35, 232.
320. Section 34(1), item 6, of the Act.

be ruled out that an award could be successfully challenged on the basis that it omits the place of arbitration or the date upon which it is made, or both.[321]

270. In cases where the award lacks an indication of the place of arbitration, Swedish jurisdiction for challenge proceedings is not automatically ruled out. Pursuant to the *travaux préparatoires* to the Act, a party may in these circumstances initiate challenge proceedings with the Court of Appeal at the place which ought to have been specified in the award.[322] Should it not be possible to determine that location, e.g., due to the arbitration agreement being silent in respect of the place of arbitration and the proceedings having been held in a number of different locations, the parties are always entitled to challenge the award before the Svea Court of Appeal.[323]

271. In addition to the above requirements, some types of award must contain instructions with respect to how to seek recourse against them, as follows:

(i) An award whereby the arbitrators have concluded the proceedings without ruling on the issues submitted to them – i.e., a final award without a ruling on the merits – must contain clear instructions to the parties as to how to appeal the award.[324]
(ii) An award that includes an order to the parties to pay compensation to the arbitrators must instruct the parties how to bring an action against the award in this respect, i.e., how to challenge costs separately.[325]

272. In every arbitration under the SCC Rules, the SCC supplies the arbitrators with a copy of the 'Arbitrator's Guidelines to the Rules of the Arbitration Institute of the Stockholm Chamber of Commerce'. These guidelines include an SCC Model Award.[326]

2. *More on Content of the Award*

273. Awards typically encompass an account of the procedural background of the arbitration, including the identity of the parties and a description of the dispute to be adjudicated. It is also advisable that the arbitral tribunal – as part of the procedural background – explain the circumstances that give the arbitral tribunal jurisdiction. In this regard, the *travaux préparatoires* to the Act hold that for evidentiary reasons it is sensible – although not a mandatory requirement – that the award reproduce the

321. The *travaux préparatoires* explain that the requirements in s. 31(2) of the Act – as opposed to the requirements concerning written form and signing – are 'unsanctioned'. See Govt. bill 1998/99:35, 232. See also Hobér, *International Commercial Arbitration in Sweden*, 266.
322. Govt. bill 1998/99:35, 242. See also Heuman, *Arbitration Law of Sweden: Practice and Procedure*, 513 and Hobér, *International Commercial Arbitration in Sweden*, 266.
323. Section 43(1) of the Act.
324. Section 36(1) *in fine* of the Act.
325. Section 41(1) of the Act. In this connection, it should be noted that the Supreme Court has ruled that s. 41 of the Act is also applicable when an arbitral institution has made the decision on compensation to the arbitrators. See discussion about *Soyak International Construction & Investment Inc. v. Werner Melis, Kaj Hobér and Steffen Kraus*, decision by the Supreme Court made on [illegible] Dec. 2008 in case no Ö 4227-06, NJA 2008 p. 1118 in s. VII.A.2 above.
326. The guidelines are available at the SCC web site (http://www.sccinstitute.com).

applicable arbitration agreement.[327] Finally, the procedural background commonly includes a chronology of the parties' submissions and the procedural decisions taken by the arbitral tribunal.

274. The award should also specify the parties' respective prayers for relief and the legal grounds invoked in support. Typically, this part of the award also includes a summary of the arguments, facts and evidence relied upon by each of the parties.

275. As will be discussed in the following section, the background description and the parties' respective arguments are commonly followed by the arbitral tribunal's discussion, setting out the reasons for the award. However, the length, structure and style of the reasons vary, depending on the nature of the dispute and the individual preferences of the arbitrators (and, in some cases, the parties and their counsel).[328]

276. Finally, the award must include a clear dispositive ruling in relation to each prayer for relief. This operative part of the award – the dispositive section or the *dispositif* – is of crucial importance for enforceability of the award and for determination of its res judicata effect.

3. *Reasons*

277. The Act contains no requirement to the effect that the arbitral tribunal must state its reasons for the award (but, as discussed below, the arbitration agreement or institutional rules, or both, may contain such a requirement). According to the *travaux préparatoires* to the Act, the rationale for not requiring the arbitral tribunal to provide reasons includes: (i) that the costs of arbitration can be kept low, (ii) that the dispute can be settled more expediently, and (iii) that the number of challenge proceedings relating to the arbitrators' reasons can be kept down.[329] The fact that the award in an arbitration under the Act lacks reasons or that the reasons provided are too brief, contain contradictions or are otherwise flawed, are thus not grounds for challenging the award.[330] In practice, however, including in ad hoc arbitrations under the Act, it is extremely uncommon that an arbitral tribunal delivers an award without providing the reasons upon which the award is based.[331]

327. Govt. bill 1998/99:35, 232.
328. See e.g., Hobér, *International Commercial Arbitration in Sweden*, 270.
329. See Govt. bill 1998/99:35, 135. With respect to challenge proceedings, the legislator has thus accepted that, with very scarce reasons, it is more difficult to prove what errors the arbitral tribunal has committed in reaching its conclusions and, consequently, an un-reasoned award may be more difficult to challenge. It may be noted that the ability to check and control what the arbitral tribunal has done is *the very reason* for a requirement that the award is to be reasoned. However, the Swedish legislator and, as will be discussed below, the Supreme Court, have laid emphasis on ensuring the finality of the award, rather than on facilitating challenges to it.
330. See e.g., Heuman, *Arbitration Law of Sweden: Practice and Procedure*, 498.
331. See e.g., Govt. bill 1998/99:35, 135; Lindskog, 776 et seq. and Hobér, *International Commercial Arbitration in Sweden*, 267.

278. Unlike the Act, the SCC Rules require the arbitral tribunal to state the reasons upon which the award is based, unless the parties have agreed otherwise.[332] This is in line with most other institutional rules and the UNCITRAL Rules.[333] Accordingly, if the parties have referred to such rules in the arbitration agreement, the award is to contain reasons. As an exception to this, the SCC Rules for Expedited Arbitration, which are gaining increased popularity for international arbitrations as well,[334] do not require the arbitral tribunal to provide reasons unless a party so requests.[335]

279. When the arbitration agreement refers to the SCC Rules, or the parties have otherwise agreed that the award is to contain reasons, the question arises what the consequences are if the arbitral tribunal fails to provide reasons. May lack of reasons in the award or other flaws pertaining to reasons amount to a successful ground for challenge of the award?

280. This question was addressed in *Soyak International Construction & Investment Inc v. Hochtief AG.*[336] In this case, the Supreme Court had to consider whether an arbitral tribunal had fulfilled its obligation to provide reasons under an arbitration agreement that referred to the SCC rules. The plaintiff submitted that the reasons in the award were incomplete and inconsistent and that this constituted a violation of Article 36(1) of the SCC Rules. In turn, the Supreme Court underlined that, in the context of challenge proceedings, the value of obtaining complete and well-articulated reasons for an award must be balanced against the interest in the finality of the award. Moreover, it must be taken into account that challenge proceedings should only concern procedural irregularities and not amount to a review of the arbitral tribunal's determinations on the merits. In judging whether the arbitral tribunal had complied with the requirement to render a reasoned award, the courts will by necessity have difficulty in distinguishing between, on the one hand, the sufficiency of the reasons provided from a purely procedural viewpoint, and, on the other hand, the quality of the reasons given in relation to the merits of the case. Under these circumstances, the Supreme Court concluded that only a total lack of reasons, or reasons of such poor nature that they must be considered equivalent to non-existing, can constitute a procedural irregularity of such severity that the award can be successfully challenged.[337] In the case before it,

332. Article 36(1) of the SCC Rules.
333. See e.g., Art. 25(2) of the Rules of Arbitration of the International Chamber of Commerce (ICC Rules), Art. 26(1) of the Arbitration Rules of the London Court of International Arbitration (LCIA Rules), and Art. 31(2) of the Model Law.
334. Ragnwaldh, *Need for Speed – An Expert's View on Fast Track Arbitration*, Com. Dispute Res. 41 (March 2012).
335. Article 35(1) of the SCC Rules for Expedited Arbitration 2010.
336. *Soyak International Construction & Investment Inc v. Hochtief AG*, decision by the Supreme Court made on 31 Mar. 2009 in case no T 4387-07, NJA 2009 p. 128.
337. In more detail, the Supreme Court concluded that a total lack of reasons, or reasons of such poor nature that they must be considered equivalent to non-existing, constitutes an irregularity in the course of the proceedings of such severe nature that it will be presumed that it has influenced the outcome of the case (cf. s. 34(1), item 6, of the Act). It is also noteworthy that the Supreme Court emphasized that a violation of an instruction to include reasons in the award is to be classified as a procedural irregularity and not an excess of mandate (cf. s. 34(1), item 2, of the Act).

the Supreme Court found that the arbitral tribunal had in fact described what it considered to be established with respect to every disputed issue. Accordingly, the challenge to the award was rejected.

4. *Dissenting Opinions*

281. Neither the Act, nor the SCC Rules, address dissenting opinions of arbitrators.[338] However, it is generally held that under Swedish arbitration law, an arbitrator is entitled - albeit not obliged - to declare their view on matters adjudicated by attaching a dissenting opinion to the award.[339]

282. The above implies that it is within the arbitrator's discretion to decide whether their dissenting opinion should be communicated to the parties via an appendix to the award or completely left out of the award. In the former case, i.e., when an arbitrator chooses to disclose their dissenting opinion to the parties, the dissenter is expected to provide their reasons for dissent with the majority.[340] However, in providing those reasons the dissenting arbitrator should take into account the confidentiality of deliberations and be wary of disclosing statements made under discussions not covered by the reasons provided by the majority.[341] The dissenting arbitrator should typically focus on explaining the basis of their own opinion, rather than passing strictures on and thereby undermining the majority reasoning.[342] It has also been submitted that a dissenting arbitrator under certain circumstances should limit the

338. A previous version of the SCC Rules contained a provision explicitly stating that a dissenting opinion *may* be included in the award. This provision was considered by the SCC to be redundant and was excluded from future versions of the SCC Rules solely on this basis. The fact that the SCC Rules currently in force do not encompass an express provision on dissenting opinions should thus not be interpreted as an indication that the SCC has intended any change in respect of the admissibility of disclosing an arbitrator's dissenting opinion in awards made under the SCC Rules. See Öhrström, 216.

339. See e.g., Hobér, *International Commercial Arbitration in Sweden*, 271. Heuman takes a slightly different view from Hobér in this respect, saying that it is not 'altogether clear whether an arbitrator is unconditionally entitled to declare a dissenting opinion or whether the majority may forbid him to do so', but concludes that 'Swedish legal tradition suggests if anything that the dissenting arbitrator is entitled to have his opinion appended to the award.' See Heuman, *Arbitration Law of Sweden: Practice and Procedure*, 500.

340. See e.g., Madsen, *Commercial Arbitration in Sweden* 260 (3d ed., Oxford University Press 2007) and Hobér, *International Commercial Arbitration in Sweden*, 271. Cf. Lindskog, who argues that although preferable, there is no absolute obligation incumbent upon an arbitrator to provide the reasons for his dissenting opinion. See Lindskog, 774.

341. Cf. Heuman, *Arbitration Law of Sweden: Practice and Procedure*, 499. On the confidentiality of deliberations.

342. This does not mean that the dissenting arbitrator should under all circumstances refrain from criticizing the majority. For example, a dissenting opinion may serve the useful purpose of shedding light on a severe procedural flaw committed by the majority. However, it is imperative that a dissenting arbitrator uses their opinion responsibly and does not - whether intentionally or not - invite the losing party to initiate an improper challenge to the award. See Heuman, *Arbitration Law of Sweden: Practice and Procedure*, 500, and Madsen, *Commercial Arbitration in Sweden* 260 (3d ed., Oxford University Press 2007).

scope of their reasons in order not to incur unnecessary costs on the parties to the arbitration.[343]

283. In practice, it is common that the dissenting arbitrator signs the award along with the majority and makes a note next to his signature that informs recipients of the award that their dissenting opinion is set out in an appendix to the award. In other, arguably less frequent cases, the dissenting arbitrator abstains from signing the award and self-limits to referring to the dissenting opinion attached to the award.[344]

284. Finally, it should be emphasized that although an arbitrator – as a matter of principle – is entitled to declare to the parties' dissent with the majority, an error committed by the arbitral tribunal with respect to drafting or disclosure, or both, of the dissenting opinion, does not render the award invalid or challengeable.[345]

C. Decision-Making of the Arbitral Tribunal: Deliberations and Voting

1. *Governing Principles*

285. The Act lays down few formal requirements for the arbitral tribunal's decision-making process. The purpose of the Act's provisions on the decision-making process is merely to provide minimum requirements necessary to ensure enforceability of the award.[346]

286. First, unless the parties have agreed otherwise,[347] the arbitral tribunal is under a duty to base its award on the applicable law. However, the practical importance of this so-called duty to apply the law is limited by the fact that the award cannot be challenged with reference to an incorrect determination of the merits.[348] Accordingly, incorrect application of the law is not a ground for challenge.

287. Second, the arbitral tribunal must limit its determination to the issues referred to it by the parties for determination. The arbitral tribunal may therefore not go beyond the parties' respective prayers for relief. Should the arbitral tribunal act in breach of this principle, and thus rule *ultra petita*, the award is challengeable under section 34 of the Act.[349]

---

343. See e.g., Lindskog, 774.
344. Cf. s. 31(3) of the Act. If the dissenting arbitrator does not sign the award and no indication as to the reason for this is given in the award, it can be questioned whether the award fulfils the mandatory requirement pertaining to signing the award set out in s. 31(1) of the Act. See Hobér, *International Commercial Arbitration in Sweden*, 271.
345. See e.g., Heuman, *Arbitration Law of Sweden: Practice and Procedure*, 500 and Lindskog, 774.
346. Govt. bill 1998/99:35, 134.
347. The principle of party autonomy allows the parties to agree that the arbitrators should decide the dispute as *amiable compositeur* or *ex aequo et bono*. See s. 21 of the Act and Govt. bill 1998/99:35, 122. See also e.g., Hobér, *International Commercial Arbitration in Sweden*, 256.
348. See Hobér, *International Commercial Arbitration in Sweden*, 256.
349. See Madsen, *Commercial Arbitration in Sweden* 279 (3d ed., Oxford University Press 2007) and Hobér, *International Commercial Arbitration in Sweden*, 257.

288. Third, the arbitral tribunal cannot base its award on other facts than those invoked by the parties. Deviation from this principle may amount to a procedural error that can form the basis for challenge proceedings against the award under section 34 of the Act.

289. Fourth and finally, the arbitral tribunal is under an obligation to consider all claims submitted to it. Should the arbitral tribunal inadvertently fail to deal with a particular claim in the final award, the arbitral tribunal can supplement the award under section 32 of the Act within a certain time frame. If supplementation is not made in due time, the ruling *infra petita* may constitute a procedural error of such nature that the award can be successfully challenged under section 34 of the Act,[350] or appealed under section 36 of the Act.

2. *Deliberations*

290. The arbitral tribunal's deliberations typically commence after the final hearing and may be held with the arbitrators physically present or e.g., by teleconferencing, via video link or by written correspondence.[351]

291. Amongst the few provisions of the Act dealing with deliberations, section 30 is pivotal. This provision provides that an arbitrator's failure to take part in deliberations without valid cause does not prevent the other arbitrators from deciding the matter.[352] Two important conclusions can be drawn from this rule.

292. First, all arbitrators must be given the opportunity to participate at all stages of the deliberations.[353] This implies that deliberations as a general rule should not be carried out in the absence of one of the arbitrators. It also implies that each arbitrator must be allowed to state their point of view on the matters referred to the arbitral tribunal.[354] This requirement must be strictly upheld in relation to contentious issues.[355] However, the arbitrator's individual right to participate in the deliberations is not unconditional. Should the contentious issues have been duly discussed between all arbitrators and two arbitrators agree on how to decide the matter, they may decide by majority vote that the deliberations are to be considered closed,[356] and then – in order

350. See Hobér, *International Commercial Arbitration in Sweden*, 257.
351. See Heuman, *Arbitration Law of Sweden: Practice and Procedure*, 484.
352. A provision of similar purport can be found in Art. 36(5) of the SCC Rules.
353. Govt. bill 1998/99:35, 231.
354. See Heuman, *Arbitration Law of Sweden: Practice and Procedure*, 488.
355. *Åsbacka Trävaruaktiebolag v. E Hedberg*, decision by the Supreme Court made on 20 November 1924, NJA 1924 p. 569. If the chairperson consults only one arbitrator before describing – what they jointly perceive as – non-contentious issues in a draft award, the losing party cannot have the award set aside if the third arbitrator omits to raise objections or demand further deliberations because of issues regarded as non-contentious by the two other arbitrators.
356. *Moelven Valåsens Sågverk AB v. Mikko V*, decision by the Supreme Court made on 1 Jan. 1996 in case no SÖ 47, NJA 1996 C 21.

not to delay the proceedings further – decide the case without admitting the presence of a dissenting arbitrator for drafting the reasons.[357]

293. It does not matter who appointed the arbitrator; all arbitrators have the same duty to remain impartial and independent throughout the proceedings – including in the deliberations– and to consider the arguments of all parties involved.

294. Second, if an arbitrator is absent from the deliberations without a valid cause, the other arbitrators may still hold deliberations and decide on the issues referred to them by the parties.[358] In that situation, the arbitrators who are present in the deliberations constitute the arbitral tribunal.[359] The possibility to hold deliberations in the absence of one of the arbitrators is intended to prevent obstruction by one of the party-appointed arbitrators and should be used restrictively.[360] The other arbitrators may only proceed with deliberations in the absence of the third arbitrator if the absent arbitrator has been given due notice of the deliberations and has failed to present a valid cause for absence. The term 'valid cause' is to be construed as any situation or event that prevents the arbitrator from participating in the deliberations, e.g., sickness.[361] Should deliberations be held and the case be decided in the absence of an arbitrator that has presented such a valid cause, the award could be set aside.[362]

295. The deliberations are confidential and the arbitrators may not – either before, or after the award has been rendered – reveal matters discussed during deliberations or other information relating to deliberations. The confidentiality of the deliberations applies not only in relation to third parties, but also vis-à-vis the parties and their counsel. Consequently, neither the parties nor any of their representatives may be present during deliberations. If one of the parties claims that a procedural error occurred relating to the conduct of deliberations, the chairperson may, however, prove the party wrong by disclosing brief information of a procedural nature concerning the conduct of deliberations. Furthermore, confidentiality does not prevent an arbitrator from revealing relevant information about the deliberations, if ordered to testify in court proceedings concerning a challenge to the relevant award.[363]

296. It has been suggested that an expert engaged by the arbitral tribunal may be allowed to attend the deliberations to give opinions, under the strict condition that the expert does not add new facts to the case.[364] Another view, which the authors subscribe to, is that an arbitral tribunal ought to be careful in communication with its appointed expert. Preferably, the arbitral tribunal should discuss and agree with the

357. See Heuman, *ArbitrationLaw of Sweden: Practice and Procedure*, 485. See also the Svea Court of Appeal award *The Czech republic v. CME Czech Republic BV*, decision by the Svea Court of Appeal made on 15 May 2003 in case no T 8735- 01, RH 2003:55, regarding alleged exclusion of an arbitrator from the deliberations.
358. Govt. bill 1998/99:35, 128 et seq.
359. See Lindskog, 842.
360. See Lindskog, 840.
361. Govt. bill 1998/99:35, 231.
362. See Heuman, *Arbitration Law of Sweden: Practice and Procedure*, 490–493.
363. See Heuman, *Arbitration Law of Sweden: Practice and Procedure*, 486 et seq.
364. See Heuman, *Arbitration Law of Sweden: Practice and Procedure*, 493 et seq.

parties how it is to interact with the expert and, failing such agreement, communication with the expert should take place in the presence of the parties.[365]

3. *Voting*

297. If the arbitrators cannot reach a unanimous decision, the issue is resolved by majority voting.[366] If no majority can be reached, both the Act and the SCC Rules provide – in contrast to the Model Law – that the chairperson of the arbitral tribunal shall have the decisive vote.[367] The risk of a hung arbitral tribunal is thereby avoided.

298. The Act is silent with respect to how to determine 'voting themes' as well as to the voting procedure, leaving these issues to the discretion of the arbitrators.[368] As a general rule, however, the vote concerns the dispositive section of the award, which in turn is essentially determined by the prayers for relief, irrespective of the arbitrators' individual reasons for the award.[369] Should a disagreement arise on how voting is to be conducted, the majority – or, as a last resort, the chairperson – decides.[370]

299. An arbitrator who has lost a vote on an issue – whether in a decision or in a separate award –is still expected to participate in subsequent decisions and vote in a loyal manner, bound by the majority's, or the chairperson's, previous decision.[371]

365. One way of doing this is for the arbitral tribunal to instruct its expert in writing, after having invited the parties to comment on the instructions. The expert's findings should then also be reported in writing, with a possibility for the parties to comment on the report and to challenge the findings of the tribunal-appointed expert at the merits hearing.
366. Govt. bill 1998/99:35, 128.
367. See s. 30(2) of the Act and Art. 35(1) of the SCC Rules. The Act is based on the assumption that the arbitral tribunal consists of three arbitrators. If the number of arbitrators were five, a literal interpretation of s. 30(2) of the Act might have undesirable effects. Assume that two party-appointed arbitrators are of one opinion and two of another opinion, whilst the chairperson is of a third opinion; in such a situation, no majority can be reached. A literal interpretation of s. 30(2) of the Act would in this situation lead to the chairperson's minority opinion deciding the dispute. This is, for obvious reasons, not desirable. Similar to the opinion expressed by Lindskog, see Lindskog, 847, s. 30(2) of the Act should therefore, in the given context and for reasons of efficiency, be considered to provide that the chairperson has the casting vote in deciding between the two alternatives proffered by the four co-arbitrators.
368. Govt. bill 1998/99:35, 128. See also Heuman, *Arbitration Law of Sweden: Practice and Procedure*, 495 et seq.
369. *Frida Charlotta Wall v. Försäkringsaktiebolaget Fylgia*, decision by the Supreme Court made on 11 Nov. 1918, NJA 1918 p. 478.
370. Govt. bill 1998/99:35, 128. See also Heuman, *Arbitration Law of Sweden: Practice and Procedure*, 495 et seq. and Hobér, *International Commercial Arbitration in Sweden*, 258. Lindskog, however, appears to be of a different opinion, suggesting that the 'voting theme' is indicated by the Act as the dispositive section of the award and that it may not be changed by the arbitrators. See Lindskog, 844 et seq.
371. See Hobér, *International Commercial Arbitration in Sweden*, 258 and Heuman, *Arbitration Law of Sweden: Practice and Procedure*, 496.

D. Rendering the Award

1. *Time Limit for Rendering Award*

300. The Act does not specify a certain period within which the award must be made by the arbitral tribunal (i.e., an 'award period'). In other words, no statutory time limit exists for rendering the award.

301. The SCC Rules set a six-month award period.[372] The period starts to run on the date when the arbitration is referred to the arbitral tribunal. Upon a reasoned request from the arbitral tribunal, or if otherwise considered necessary, the SCC Board may extend the award period.[373] Thus no automatic extension of the award period occurs.[374] However, the SCC monitors the award period and assists the arbitrators by notifying them if the end of the period is approaching without an award having been rendered.[375]

302. Awards rendered after expiry of the relevant award period are not invalid, but can be challenged and set aside on the basis of section 34(2) of the Act. Should no such challenge proceedings be initiated within the three-month period for challenge proceedings under section 34(2) of the Act, the error is considered to have been waived.

2. *Delivery of Award*

303. The Act assumes that the arbitral tribunal will make a written award to be transmitted to the parties. Pursuant to section 31(3) of the Act, the award should be delivered to the parties immediately after it has been rendered. Although not expressly stated in the Act, this obligation is incumbent upon the arbitral tribunal, and is usually arranged for by the chairperson.[376] Under the SCC Rules, the arbitral tribunal is also to deliver the award to the parties.[377]

304. It is sufficient that the award is delivered by mail or courier, since the Act does not require formal service of the award.[378] If the award is served through the legal representatives of the parties, the chairperson should verify that the representatives' powers of attorney do not exclude authorization in this respect.[379] There are no legal requirements that the award be deposited, approved or registered with a court or other

372. Article 37 of the SCC Rules.
373. An extension that exceeds two months is normally not granted, unless both parties agree or exceptional circumstances prevail. See Öhrström, 222.
374. Notwithstanding this fact, the SCC has on a few occasions – where the arbitral tribunal has failed to respond to reminders from the Institute or to otherwise make it clear that it is informed of the deadline for rendering the award – chosen to extend the award period ex officio. See Öhrström, 223.
375. *Ibid.*
376. See Lindskog, 861.
377. Article 36(4) of the SCC Rules.
378. Govt. bill 1998/99:35, 232 et seq.
379. See Heuman, *Arbitration Law of Sweden: Practice and Procedure*, 509.

authority. However, in arbitrations under the SCC Rules, one original of the award should be sent to the SCC Secretariat for archiving.[380]

305. It is in the winning party's interest that the award is promptly delivered to the parties since the time limits for challenging the award under section 34(3), section 36 and correction, interpretation or additional award under section 32 of the Act, start to run when the award is served. It is also in the arbitrators' interest that the award is delivered as soon as possible, as the time limit to challenge compensation payable to the arbitrators, under section 41(1) of the Act, is counted from when the parties receive the award.[381]

306. The award is served when it reaches a party and the party knows that the document served is an arbitral award.[382] However, a party does not have to read the award for the time limits to start running.[383] The arbitral tribunal should try to make sure that the parties receive the award simultaneously.[384] If the award is sent by ordinary mail, it may be advisable that the arbitrators also send it by fax or e-mail so as to avoid one party receiving the award before the other party.[385]

307. To avoid uncertainty as to calculation of the periods for challenge, the chairperson should obtain written confirmation that the parties have received the award. When this proof is considered necessary, the award should be sent by courier with receipt or registered mail with a receipt. In most cases, the signed receipt in combination with testimony as to the content of the package will constitute sufficient evidence.

3. *Refusal to Render Award*

308. According to section 40 of the Act, the arbitrators may not refuse to render or withhold the award pending payment of compensation due to them. The fact that the arbitral tribunal may require security from the parties has been considered sufficient to protect the arbitrators' interests in this respect.[386] However, the provision is non-mandatory. In principle, the arbitrators may therefore agree with the parties to have a lien over the award.[387] In practice, agreements to that effect are rarely if ever entered into.

---

380. Article 36(4) of the SCC Rules. See also Öhrström, 219.
381. See Madsen, *Commercial Arbitration in Sweden* 260 (3d ed., Oxford University Press 2007).
382. See *E.O.* et al *v. ICA Handlarnas AB*, decision by the Supreme Court made on 12 Dec. 2001 in case no Ö 4237-99, NJA 2001 p. 855. See also Heuman, *Arbitration Law of Sweden: Practice and Procedure*, 509.
383. *Ibid.*
384. See Öhrström, 218.
385. See Lindskog, 861 et seq.
386. Govt. bill 1998/99:35, 164. See also Madsen, *Commercial Arbitration in Sweden* 322 (3d ed., Oxford University Press 2007).
387. Govt. bill 1998/99:35, 241.

309. As discussed in section VII.B above, under the SCC Rules, the parties must pay an advance on costs – sufficient to cover the arbitrators' fees as well.[388] This is why the question of lien over the award does not arise.

E. Correcting, Interpreting and Supplementing Award

1. General

310. The mandate of the arbitral tribunal is completed upon rendering the award.[389] Therefore, the general rule is that the arbitral tribunal cannot change the final award once rendered. However, exceptions to this rule exist. In order to avoid unnecessary and costly involvement of courts, the arbitral tribunal may under certain circumstances correct, amend and/or interpret the award after it has been rendered.[390]

311. The authority of the arbitral tribunal to correct and amend arbitral awards is limited to obvious inaccuracies, such as typographical or computational mistakes.[391] The arbitrators may also supplement an award if they have inadvertently failed to decide on an issue that should have been settled in the award.[392] The arbitrators' authority to correct and amend does not entail a right to correct inaccuracies brought to the arbitral tribunal's attention and that can be traced back to the arbitral tribunal's assessment of the case, such as mistakes in the application of law or failure to properly consider certain evidence.[393] The correction or amendment should thus not require new substantive considerations by the arbitrators.[394]

312. Under the Act, the arbitral tribunal has authority to correct and supplement the award of its own volition, i.e., without a request from a party.[395] In contrast, the SCC Rules only permit the arbitrators to correct – but not to supplement – the award of their

388. Cf. Öhrström, 218.
389. Section 27(4) of the Act.
390. Section 32 of the Act and Arts 41-42 of the SCC Rules. It follows explicitly from s. 27(4) of the Act that the arbitrators' mandate also covers correction, supplementation and interpretation of the award, notwithstanding that the mandate is formally completed with rendering the award.
391. Section 32 of the Act. See also Govt. bill 1998/99:35, 136, and Madsen, *Commercial Arbitration in Sweden* 263 (3d ed., Oxford University Press 2007). Art. 41(1) of the SCC Rules states explicitly what kind of corrections and supplements may be made: 'Within 30 days of receiving the award, a party may, upon notice to the other party, request that the Arbitral Tribunal correct any clerical, typographical or computational errors in the award, or provide an interpretation of a specific point or part of the award.'
392. Govt. bill 1998/99:35, 136. Under Art. 42 of the SCC Rules, such a correction is to be made in the form of an additional award.
393. See Heuman, *Arbitration Law of Sweden: Practice and Procedure*, 543.
394. Lindskog, 868.
395. If the arbitral tribunal chooses to correct or amend the award on its own volition, the arbitrators should carefully explain the purpose of and reasons for the correction or supplementation. See Govt. bill 1998/99:35, 233.

own volition.[396] Neither the Act, nor the SCC Rules, allow the arbitral tribunal to interpret an arbitral award without a request by any of the parties.[397]

313. Section 32 of the Act is non-mandatory on the arbitral tribunal. The arbitral tribunal is thus under no obligation to correct, supplement or interpret awards, even if requested by both parties.[398] Under Articles 41 and 42 of the SCC Rules, the arbitral tribunal may only deny a party's request in this respect, if it considers the request not to be justified. The arbitrators must afford the parties the opportunity to comment on any measure under section 32 of the Act that the arbitral tribunal intends to take, before a final decision is made.[399]

314. With respect to supplements to the award (under the Act) or rendering an additional award (under the SCC Rules), unlike a correction of the award, these measures do not entail a change in the award delivered but merely a supplementation. A supplement can, for example, be made when an interest claim has been overlooked or when the award fails to state how the responsibility to pay the arbitrators' remuneration is to be allocated between the parties.[400]

315. The award cannot be supplemented if the arbitrators have decided deliberately not to rule on a certain issue, since the authority to supplement covers only flaws or shortcomings in the award caused by an oversight or a mistake.[401] In cases where the arbitral tribunal has deliberately not ruled on a certain issue, the arbitrators' decision to leave out an issue from the award may constitute a procedural irregularity.[402] The party affected by the irregularity may then challenge the award under section 34 of the Act, rather than request an additional award. Alternatively, the award may be appealable under section 36 of the Act, if the arbitral tribunal has terminated the proceedings without addressing all issues referred to it for determination.

316. If a party has failed to properly raise an issue, present a claim or invoke certain evidence during the course of the arbitration, an amendment cannot be made. In this situation, it is not the arbitral tribunal that has overlooked the issue.[403]

317. With respect to interpretation of the award in an arbitration under the Act,[404] the arbitral tribunal may only clarify the dispositive section, i.e., the operative part of the

396. See Art. 41(2) of the SCC Rules.
397. See Madsen, *Commercial Arbitration in Sweden* 263 (3d ed., Oxford University Press 2007) and Hobér, *International Commercial Arbitration in Sweden*, 291.
398. Govt. bill 1998/99:35, 137. See also Madsen, *Commercial Arbitration in Sweden* 263 (ed ed., Oxford University Press 2007). Similarly, Arts 41–42 of the SCC Rules stipulate that the arbitral tribunal need only correct, amend or interpret the award if the arbitrators consider that the request for such a measure is 'justified'.
399. Section 32(3) of the Act. Cf. Arts 41(1) and 42 of the SCC Rules.
400. See Lindskog, 872.
401. See Hobér, *International Commercial Arbitration in Sweden*, 289 and Heuman, *Arbitration Law of Sweden: Practice and Procedure*, 545.
402. *Ibid.*
403. See Heuman, *Arbitration Law of Sweden: Practice and Procedure*, 545.
404. Govt. bill 1998/99:35, 137 and 233.

award. It cannot interpret the reasons, even if the reasons given in the award are vague in part or in full.[405]

318. Unlike the Act, the SCC Rules do not limit the scope of interpretation to the operative part of the award. Article 42 of the SCC Rules refers to a 'specific point or part of the award'.[406] However, in order for a request for interpretation to be justified, which is a requirement for the request to be entertained, it should in most cases need to concern the operative part of the award.

2. *Time Limitations*

319. Proceedings under section 32 of the Act and Articles 41 and 42 of the SCC Rules must be carried out promptly. To this end, those provisions set out the following time limitations:

(i) Should the arbitrators of their own volition wish to correct or supplement the award, they must do so within thirty days of the date of issuing the award.[407]
(ii) A party requesting a correction, supplement or interpretation of the award must do so within thirty days of the day of receipt of the award.[408]
(iii) After having received a timely request from a party, the arbitral tribunal must correct or interpret the award within thirty days, and supplement the award within sixty days, from receipt of the request.[409]

320. During the time limits thus set, the arbitrators are unimpeded from correcting, supplementing or interpreting the award, irrespective of the expiry of any time limits for delivery of the award that the parties may have otherwise agreed upon.[410] Moreover, the arbitrators may correct, supplement or interpret an award even though the winning party has applied for enforcement of the award and even if an enforcement order has been issued.[411] The arbitral tribunal cannot order a stay of execution due to a request for correction.[412]

321. Since the arbitral tribunal is not entitled to extend the time limits under the Act, and since the SCC Board may only grant extensions of time for rendering additional awards – not for corrections–the arbitral tribunal may occasionally have to refrain from correcting, supplementing or interpreting the award. This situation may arise when, for example, the arbitral tribunal considers it necessary to enable the other party to

405. This follows from the wording of s. 32(1), last sentence, of the Act. See further Hobér, *International Commercial Arbitration in Sweden*, 290.
406. See Hobér, *International Commercial Arbitration in Sweden*, 291.
407. Section 32(1) of the Act, and Art. 41(2) of the SCC Rules.
408. Section 32(1) of the Act, and Art. 41(1) of the SCC Rules.
409. Section 32(1) of the Act, and Art. 41(1) and 42 of the SCC Rules. Under Art. 42 of the SCC Rules, the SCC Board may grant extensions of the arbitral tribunal's respite to issue an additional award.
410. Govt. bill 1998/99:35, 233.
411. See Heuman, *Arbitration Law of Sweden: Practice and Procedure*, 539.
412. *Ibid*.

comment on a request for correction before a correction can be made and this cannot be done before the relevant time limit expires.[413]

3. *Additional Remuneration to Arbitral Tribunal for Correcting, Supplementing or Interpreting Award?*

322. The Act and the SCC Rules are silent with respect to whether the arbitral tribunal is authorized to order the parties to pay additional remuneration to the arbitrators for correcting, amending or interpreting the award.

323. Decisions whereby the arbitral tribunal corrects, supplements or issues an interpretation of the award are formally part of the final award.[414] Since the Act entitles the arbitral tribunal to decide on the compensation due to the arbitrators in the final award, it has been suggested that the arbitral tribunal must also be considered competent to award themselves additional remuneration for correcting, supplementing or interpreting the award.[415] If this were not the case, arbitrators might be unwilling to correct, supplement or interpret an award, even though such a measure would be justified.[416] If correction, supplement or interpretation is a consequence of negligence on the part of the arbitral tribunal, it has been suggested that the arbitrators should refrain from awarding themselves additional remuneration for the additional work resulting from their own error.[417]

324. In SCC arbitrations, where the arbitral tribunal's remuneration is based on the amount in dispute and, thus, not strictly on the actual time spent on the case, the situation is somewhat different than in arbitrations under the Act. The remuneration set in the final award should in SCC arbitrations probably be viewed as also including compensation for subsequent work relating to correcting, supplementing and interpreting the award.

F. Legal Effects of Award

1. *Enforceability*

325. An immediate effect of rendering the award is that the award becomes enforceable unless declaratory in nature, in which case it becomes recognizable.

---

413. See Heuman, *Arbitration Law of Sweden: Practice and Procedure*, 541 et seq.
414. Govt. bill 1998/99:35, 233. For practical reasons, however, a new document is usually drafted and issued by the arbitrators. See Hobér, *International Commercial Arbitration in Sweden*, 288. The same formal requirements apply with respect to such a document, as with respect to the award proper; see Art. 41(3) of the SCC Rules. In other words, it must be signed, state the place of arbitration etc.
415. See Heuman, *Arbitration Law of Sweden: Practice and Procedure*, 542.
416. *Ibid.*
417. See e.g., Hobér, *International Commercial Arbitration in Sweden*, 288 and Heuman, *Arbitration Law of Sweden: Practice and Procedure*, 542.

2. *Res Judicata*

326. An award rendered has legal force – or, in other words, res judicata effect – according to principles of Swedish civil procedural law.[418] In concise terms, the res judicata effect implies that a court or arbitral tribunal may not review the matter on the merits after it has been decided in a final award, but must instead, if subsequently seized with the same matter, dismiss it. Furthermore, it means that issues decided in the final award are binding in future disputes between the same parties – be it in court or arbitration – where the same issues are of incidental or preliminary character.[419]

327. The general rule is that the principle of res judicata is to be applied in the same manner in arbitration as it is applied in civil procedure under the Code of Judicial Procedure.[420] However, the Swedish Supreme Court has made it clear that this will not be the case if, due to the distinctive features of arbitration, strong reasons exist to depart from the civil procedure doctrine of res judicata.[421] Differences between civil procedure and arbitration must therefore be considered when assessing the case at hand, and in case of such differences, it must be assessed whether reasons exist to depart from the res judicata doctrine of civil procedural law.[422]

328. Under civil procedure doctrine, the res judicata effect generally only extends to the parties to the dispute. The award will only have legal effects and bind third parties under exceptional, well-defined, circumstances, such as where a third party would have been bound by a party's disposition of the legal relationship in dispute.[423]

329. The res judicata effect of the award applies to those legal consequences considered in the dispute, as well as alternative legal consequences that are economically equivalent to those in the dispute. Thus, new requests for relief that merely differ quantitatively from claims already adjudicated become res judicata and should be dismissed in future disputes.[424]

330. All alternative factual bases, legal grounds and possible objections to the relief sought are precluded by the award.[425] However, facts that occur after the award and which thus could not be relied upon in the arbitration, constitute *facta supervenientia* and may be invoked as facts in support of or in defence against a claim in future

418. *Aktiebolaget Skånska Cementgjuteriet v. Motoraktiebolaget I Karlstad*, decision by the Supreme Court made on 30 Dec. 1953, NJA 1953 p. 751, and *Esselte AB v. Allmänna Pensionsfonden*, decision by the Supreme Court made on 3 Apr. 2008 in case no T 5685/96, NJA 1998 p. 189
419. See e.g., Hobér, *International Commercial Arbitration in Sweden*, 279, and Heuman, *Arbitration Law of Sweden: Practice and Procedure*, 536.
420. See the Svea Court of Appeal ruling in the case *The Czech republic v. CME Czech Republic BV*, decision by the Svea Court of Appeal made on 15 May 2003 in case no T 8735- 01, RH 2003:55, and *Esselte AB v. Allmänna Pensionsfonden*, decision by the Supreme Court made on 3 Apr. 2008 in case no T 5685/96, NJA 1998 p. 189.
421. *Esselte AB v. Allmänna Pensionsfonden*, decision by the Supreme Court made on 3 Apr. 2008 in case no T 5685/96, NJA 1998 p. 189.
422. See Heuman, *Arbitration Law of Sweden: Practice and Procedure*, 385.
423. Ekelöf, Bylund & Edelstam, 230 et seq.
424. See Fitger, 17:41-17:47.
425. Ekelöf, Bylund & Edelstam, 192-197.

disputes.[426] The res judicata effects of an arbitral award extend only to questions covered by the arbitration agreement. Consequently, issues outside the competence of the arbitral tribunal are not precluded by the award.[427]

331. The award's reasons do not acquire res judicata effect, but may nevertheless be of critical importance in interpreting and understanding the legal effect of the award.[428]

3. *Other Effects of Award*

332. As mentioned above, the mandate of the arbitrators is considered terminated when the final award has been rendered.[429] Nevertheless, the arbitrators still possess authority to:

(i) correct, supplement and interpret the award under section 32 of the Act;[430] and
(ii) resume the arbitral proceedings after a remission order by a court during challenge proceedings, in order for the arbitral tribunal to eliminate a ground for setting aside or invalidating an award.[431]

333. Another effect of the award is that periods for certain time limits start to run, namely:

(i) the thirty-day period for the parties to request, and for the arbitral tribunal to decide, to correct, supplement or interpret the award under section 32 of the Act;[432]
(ii) the three-month period to initiate challenge proceedings under section 34 of the Act; and
(iii) the three-month period to bring action against the award regarding payment of compensation to the arbitrators under section 41 of the Act.

334. For the parties in the arbitration, these periods start to run on the day upon which the party receives the award. No formal service of the award is required under the Act, but the day of service may have to be proved in order to decide when the periods have commenced. The periods relevant to the arbitrators start running on the day when the award is rendered.[433]

426. Ekelöf, Bylund, and Edelstam, 200 et seq.
427. See also Heuman, *Arbitration Law of Sweden: Practice and Procedure*, 358.
428. See Hobér, *International Commercial Arbitration in Sweden*, 282.
429. Section 27(4) of the Act.
430. Cf. Art. 41 of the SCC Rules.
431. Section 35 of the Act.
432. Under the SCC Rules, the time limit for a party to request correction or interpretation of an award, and for the arbitral tribunal to correct or interpret an award on its own motion, is thirty days. In turn, the time limit for the parties to request an additional award is thirty days. See Arts 42-43 of the SCC Rules.
433. See Hobér, *International Commercial Arbitration in Sweden*, 277.

CHAPTER 9

Recourse to the Courts against an Arbitral Award

Gisela Knuts

I. INTRODUCTION

1. Finality of awards is a core principle in international arbitration. Nevertheless, state courts as a rule exercise some degree of control over arbitration proceedings with a seat in their country. This is a natural consequence of the fact that the state recognizes and enforces arbitration agreements as well as awards issued on the basis of such arbitration agreements. The incorporation of rules on invalidity and setting aside strikes a balance between ensuring finality of awards and the possibility of annulment in case of procedural irregularities.[1] The possibility of review by state courts safeguards certain key procedural standards such as objectivity, fairness and justice.[2]

2. An award cannot be reviewed by a court on the merits. Rather, under Swedish law an award can only be challenged on procedural grounds, such as due process. Thus, procedural defects must be distinguished from substantive ones. The distinction is relevant when assessing which awards could be declared invalid or set aside by Swedish courts and when considering an arbitral tribunal's authority to correct the award.[3] An award is binding even if the arbitral tribunal has manifestly disregarded the law or grossly misjudged the merits.[4] In legal doctrine, a general distinction has been

1. Filip De Ly, *Comment: Comparative Observations on Arbitral Awards and Setting Aside*, in *The Swedish Arbitration Act of 1999, Five Years On – A Critical Review of Strengths and Weaknesses*, 511–513 (Lars Heuman & Sigvard Jarvin eds., JurisNet 2006); Lars Heuman. *Arbitration Law of Sweden: Practice and Procedure* 572 (Juris Publishing Inc. 2003).
2. Kaj Hobér, *International Commercial Arbitration in Sweden* 294 (Oxford Univeristy Press 2011).
3. Lars Heuman, *Arbitration Law of Sweden: Practice and procedure*, 573, 586–587.
4. Fredrik Andersson et al., *Arbitration in Sweden* 164 (Jure L. Books 2011).

made between substantive and procedural defects, with substantive defects being misinterpretations of rules of substantive law – such as wrongly imposing the burden of proof on a party or misinterpreting conflict-of-laws rules or substantive clauses in the main contract – whereas procedural defects would be a wrongful refusal to admit evidence or the arbitrators having decided an issue that was res judicata or lis pendens.[5]

3. Different jurisdictions deal differently with invalidity, setting aside and their inherent procedural aspects. Most provisions dealing with invalidity and setting aside in the Swedish Arbitration Act (Sw: *Lag (1999:116) om skiljeförfarande*) (the Act) conform to the UNCITRAL Model Law on International Commercial Arbitration 1985 with amendments as adopted in 2006 (Model Law) and most foreign laws.

4. The Act distinguishes between invalid and challengeable awards. Awards under section 33 of the Act are invalid *ab initio* and the issue of invalidity should be examined by a court of its own motion, if the award is brought before it by the courts, while challengeable awards must be challenged in accordance with the conditions in section 34 of the Act.

5. The Act provides the parties with a right to appeal an award in which the arbitral tribunal has not ruled on the issues submitted to it. This rule can be found in section 36 and can be used, e.g., in situations where the arbitral tribunal has rendered a final award declining jurisdiction. This could be an important remedy in disputes where litigation in the respondent's jurisdiction is an unrealistic option for the claimant.[6]

II. RECOURSE TO THE COURTS: INVALIDITY AND SETTING ASIDE UNDER SWEDISH LAW

6. The finality of arbitration awards is the cornerstone of the rules regarding invalidity and setting aside of awards under Swedish law. In contrast to litigation, an arbitration award cannot be set aside on its merits. When choosing arbitration, the parties waive the right to challenge the award on the merits. Instead, the award can only be challenged on formal grounds.[7] Awards cannot be retried or amended.[8]

7. As the principle of finality of awards is one of the cornerstones of Swedish arbitration law, this is also reflected in the assessment of whether an irregularity is substantive or procedural. It follows from the principle of finality of awards that an

5. Lars Heuman, *Arbitration Law of Sweden: Practice and Procedure*, 573.
6. Kaj Hobér, *International Commercial Arbitration in Sweden*, 351.
7. SOU 1994:81 'Ny lag om skiljeförfarande' 169 (Fritzes, 1994), Govt. bill 1998/99:35, 'Ny lag om skiljeförfarande' 139 (Stockholm, 1998), Finn Madsen, *Commercial Arbitration in Sweden – A Commentary on the Arbitration Act (1999:116) and the Rules of the Arbitration Institute of the Stockholm Chamber of Commerce* 244–245 (Jure Förlag AB 2004); Lars Heuman, *Arbitration Law of Sweden: Practice and Procedure*, 571.
8. Finn Madsen, *Commercial Arbitration in Sweden – A Commentary on the Arbitration Act (1999:116) and the Rules of the Arbitration Institute of the Stockholm Chamber of Commerce* 245 (Jure Förlag AB 2004), see also *Gun M v. skiljenämnden*, decision by the Supreme Court made on 27 Nov. 1986 in case no Ö 1123-86, NJA 1986 p. 620.

award cannot be set aside based on a substantive irregularity, whereas procedural irregularities under certain circumstances may lead to an award being set aside.

8. The distinction between substantive and procedural defects was a key issue in *TBB Tekniska Byggnadsbyrån (bankruptcy estate) v. Byggnadsstyrelsen,*[9] in which the claimant alleged that the arbitral tribunal had founded the award on the wrongful assumption that the claimant had drafted and provided an agreement; thus the arbitral tribunal had failed to duly handle the case as it should have ensured that this question was properly elucidated. The Supreme Court found that the arbitral tribunal had considered which of the parties had drafted the agreement in its evaluation of the evidence presented in the case, which is a part of the substantive assessment of a dispute. Consequently, the court found that no procedural irregularities were present and upheld the award. The case could be interpreted as reflecting the Swedish courts' tendency to uphold arbitration awards in situations where the distinction between substantive and procedural irregularities is vague.

9. As a general principle, courts should not review procedural irregularities based on how the courts would have handled the procedure; rather, courts should grant arbitrators flexibility to conduct the proceedings at their own discretion.[10] Hence, the courts should respect the arbitrators' discretion, provided that no instruction from the parties, procedural rule of the Act or basic principle of due process is infringed. As such, minor procedural irregularities or errors should not be considered.[11]

10. This standpoint is supported by *Paul J v. Reprotype Aktiebolag,*[12] where the Supreme Court focused on whether procedural rules had been disregarded to a significant extent. This requirement implies that procedural irregularities must have involved a degree of seriousness in order for the award to be set aside.[13] This way of reasoning is further reflected in section 34(1)(6) of the Act, stipulating that procedural irregularities of a kind that has not been explicitly referred to in the other grounds for challenges in section 34, can only constitute grounds for setting aside an award if the irregularities have affected the outcome of the case. However, even though no other grounds for challenge explicitly require effect on the outcome of the case, it has been suggested that the courts would disregard errors of a more trivial nature.[14] The assessment of whether a procedural error is of such a serious nature that the arbitral award may successfully be challenged is dependent on the circumstances in each individual case.

9. *TBB Tekniska Byggnadsbyrån (bankruptcy estate) v. Byggnadsstyrelsen*, decision by the Supreme Court made on 27 Nov. 1973, NJA 1973 p. 740.
10. See e.g., Lars Heuman, *Arbitration Law of Sweden: Practice and Procedure*, 575.
11. Lars Heuman, *Arbitration Law of Sweden: Practice and Procedure*, 575–576.
12. *Paul J v. Reprotype Aktiebolag*, decision by the Supreme Court made on 24 Oct. 1975, NJA 1975 p. 536. See also Lars Heuman, *Arbitration Law of Sweden: Practice and Procedure*, 576.
13. Kaj Hobér *International Commercial Arbitration in Sweden*, 296.
14. Lars Heuman, *Arbitration Law of Sweden: Practice and Procedure*, 576.

A. Invalidity of the Award

1. In General

11. Section 33 of the Act exhaustively lists the grounds for invalidity of an award. The grounds listed in section 33 are considered so serious that they result in an arbitral award being invalid, based on considerations of public interest and the interests of third parties. As further explained below, section 33 should be interpreted and applied restrictively.[15] This approach is further reflected in case law as no arbitral award has been declared invalid under section 33, though there are cases where corrections made to an arbitral award under section 32 of the Act are invalid since it was not signed by all arbitrators.[16]

12. The grounds for invalidity in section 33 protect a public interest and are, as such, mandatory and cannot be waived.[17] Thus, if the court finds that one of the grounds for invalidity in section 33 is present, it cannot refuse to declare the award invalid.[18] In this sense, the Act differs from the Model Law, where the corresponding grounds for challenge are conditional, i.e., the courts *may* set aside an award which conflicts with, e.g., public policy.[19]

13. An award that is invalid according to section 33 is invalid in itself without any need for a party to take action. The Act also differs in this respect from the Model Law, in which the grounds for invalidity render the award not void, but voidable.[20] Although there is no need for a party to take action, it is often in practice necessary to initiate court proceedings to obtain a confirmation of invalidity. Such action may be necessary to prevent the prevailing party from enforcing the award under the Convention on the Recognition and Enforcement of Foreign Arbitral Awards, 1958 (New York Convention).[21] Court proceedings to confirm invalidity are not in themselves sufficient to prevent enforcement of the award. However, the Court of Appeal may stay enforcement of the award, which is rare. If enforcement of the award is sought abroad, it is for the court seized with an action for recognition and enforcement to determine the relevance of the Court of Appeal's decision to stay enforcement.

---

15. See Govt. bill 1998/99:35, 'Ny lag om skiljeförfarande', 141 et seq.
16. See e.g., *Wirgin Advokatbyrå Handelsbolag v. If Skadeförsäkringar AB*, judgment by the Svea Court of Appeal made on 12 Sep. 2005 in case no T 4390-04, an arbitral award was declared partly invalid.
17. Stefan Lindskog, *Skiljeförfarande – En kommentar* 900 (Norstedts Juridik AB 2005).
18. SOU 1994:81 'Ny lag om skiljeförfarande', 290; Govt. bill 1998/99:35, 235; Lars Heuman, *Arbitration Law of Sweden: Practice and Procedure*, 575.
19. See David St. John Sutton, *Ch. 23: Swedish Awards: Proper Form, Validity and Recourse*, in *The Swedish Arbitration Act of 1999, Five Years On – A Critical Review of Strengths and Weaknesses*, 494–495.
20. See David St. John Sutton, *Ch. 23: Swedish Awards: Proper Form, Validity and Recourse*, 496–497.
21. Kaj Hobér, *International Commercial Arbitration in Sweden*, 294.

14. Since the award is invalid in itself, a party may participate in the arbitration proceedings without protesting or reserving the right to challenge the award after the proceedings have ended, and may then initiate an action for declaration of invalidity afterwards. There is no time limit for filing an action for invalidity.[22] In this respect as well, the Act differs from the Model Law, as the latter provides a three-month time limit for all recourse against arbitral awards.[23]

15. The absence of a time limit for an action for declaration of invalidity can mean that an award could be declared invalid decades after it has been issued. Because of such concerns, and to ensure finality of arbitral awards, the list of grounds for invalidity in section 33 is exhaustive and should be applied restrictively.[24]

2. *Section 33 Item 1: Lack of Arbitrability*

16. According to section 33 item 1, an award is invalid if it includes determination of an issue that may not be decided by arbitrators under Swedish law, i.e., disputes that are not capable of out-of-court settlement.[25] The arbitrability requirement is based on the fact that the parties may not attain by arbitration a legal position which they could not achieve by mutual agreement. This also means that if a claim would be illegal or constitute a *pactum turpe* the dispute cannot be settled by arbitration because the remedies are not sanctioned by law.[26] Thus, the concept of arbitrability can be referred to as a public policy limitation on arbitration. Therefore, it is difficult to distinguish between arbitrability and public policy.[27]

17. Reasons for non-arbitrability can be public or third-party interests. The Act does not specify which disputes are arbitrable, but guidance is found in Swedish substantive law. It is noteworthy that the mere existence of mandatory provisions in civil law, consumer law, tenancy law or labour law does not in itself render all disputes in that field non-arbitrable.

18. In a 2009 case,[28] the claimant argued that an arbitral award was invalid because it dealt with matters that could not be handled in arbitration, as the arbitral tribunal had decided questions relating to criminal law. The Svea Court of Appeal rejected the plea because it found that the arbitral tribunal had assessed questions relating to Swedish contract law and not criminal law.

22. Lars Heuman, *Arbitration Law of Sweden: Practice and Procedure*, 572.
23. Section 34(3) of the Model Law.
24. Cf. Govt. bill 1998/99:35, 'Ny lag om skiljeförfarande', 139 et seq.
25. Cf. s. 1 of the Act.
26. Fredrik Andersson et al., *Arbitration in Sweden*, 60.
27. Kaj Hobér, *International Commercial Arbitration in Sweden*, 302–303.
28. *Globe Nuclear Services and Supply GNSS, Limited v. AO Techsnabexport*, decision by the Svea Court of Appeal made on 18 Dec. 2009 in case no T 5883-07.

3. *Section 33 Item 2: Public Policy*

19. In section 33 item 2, public policy, or *ordre public,* is listed as grounds for invalidity, stating that an award is invalid if the award or the manner in which it arose is clearly incompatible with the basic principles of the Swedish legal system. This ground for invalidity ensures that arbitral awards violating fundamental principles of Swedish law can be declared invalid.

20. The concept of *ordre public* is interpreted narrowly, covering only fundamental legal principles of either a substantive or a procedural nature.[29] Although breach of public policy is a common basis for a claim of invalidity under section 33, the Swedish Courts of Appeal have never declared an arbitral award invalid based on a breach of public policy.[30] Coherent with this, the Svea Court of Appeal stated in 2005 that a violation of EU competition law can only lead to an annulment in '*obvious cases*'.[31]

21. The *travaux préparatoires* made clear that a breach of public policy only exists when there has been a breach of a legal standard of *particular importance* and that only *highly offensive* events are covered by the provision.[32] These statements serve to emphasize that the threshold is quite high for an award to be deemed incompatible with public policy. An example of the courts' restrictive application of section 33 is a case from the Svea Court of Appeal where the court rejected an action for invalidity under section 33 item 2 since it was not *obvious* that the agreement upon which the claimant based its claim was an element in a third party tax evasion.[33]

22. A distinction can be made between procedural public policy and substantive public policy. Invalidity for breach of procedural public policy follows if the award is based on forged evidence or other procedural documents, and the forgery has affected the award.[34] To invalidate an award, the evidence must presumably be wilfully forged by or with the consent of one of the parties, and it must be clear that the document was decisive for the outcome of the case. Thus, false testimony from a witness will not suffice to render an award invalid. Violations of procedural public policy could further occur in situations where one of the parties has appointed all arbitrators, even if the appointment procedure is stipulated in the arbitration agreement.[35]

23. Violations of substantive public policy relate mainly to claims based on gambling or criminal acts, or contracts that are illegal under Swedish substantive law. If an arbitral award obliges someone to do something prohibited by law, it is invalid based

---

29. Bengt Olsson & Johan Kvart, *Lagen om skiljeförfarande – En kommentar* 136–137 (Norstedts Juridik AB 2000).
30. Kaj Hobér, *International Commercial Arbitration in Sweden*, 303.
31. *Latvian Republic v. JSC Latvijas Gaze*, decision by the Svea Court of Appeal made on 4 May 2005 in case no T 6730-03.
32. Govt. bill 1998/99:35, 'Ny lag om skiljeförfarande', 141–142.
33. *Sea Carriers Inc. and Frontline Ltd v. Blad Foundation*, decision by the Svea Court of Appeal made on 16 Sep. 2002 in case no T 6588-01-79.
34. Stefan Lindskog, *Skiljeförfarande – En kommentar*, 907–908.
35. Kaj Hobér, *International Commercial Arbitration in Sweden*, 304.

on public policy.[36] Invalidity may also follow when an award is so punitive that it cannot be tolerated.[37]

24. Invalidity of an award was assessed in a case from 2002. In that case, the claimant sought to have an award declared invalid because the arbitral tribunal had decided an issue which was later found to constitute tax fraud.[38] The Svea Court of Appeal found that while a court may refuse to deal with claims that are not accepted by the legal system and thus invalid according to civil law, the Supreme Court had stated in an earlier case that such refusal required that the content of the agreement be inappropriate or unfair and that this should be obvious either from the grounds for the claim or from the assessment of the case. Further, according to the Supreme Court, for a court to refuse to assess a claim, it also had to be clear that the agreement in question was invalid and lacked legal effect due to its involving a breach of law or morality.[39] The Svea Court of Appeal did not find that these rather strict conditions were met in the case.[40]

25. In a 2009 case,[41] the claimant argued among other things that the arbitral award was invalid because of its punitive character. The claimant argued that the award had resulted in him having to reimburse compensation received from the Swedish Social Insurance Authorities. The Svea Court of Appeal did not declare the award invalid.

26. According to European Court of Justice practice, a breach of EU competition law constitutes a breach of public policy.[42] Thus, an award incompatible with EU competition law is invalid under section 33 item 2. This was affirmed by the Court of Appeal for Western Sweden in a 2003 case.[43] In the challenge proceedings, the losing party argued that the arbitral award was contrary to mandatory EU law, and should be declared invalid. The Court of Appeal acknowledged that a breach of public policy can occur not only if fundamental principles of Swedish law have been overlooked, but also when a breach of EU law occurs, as EU law is an integral part of the Swedish legal

---

36. Bengt Olsson & Johan Kvart, *Lagen om skiljeförfarande – En kommentar*, 136–137.
37. Kaj Hobér, *International Commercial Arbitration in Sweden*, 306.
38. *Sea Carriers Inc. and Frontline Ltd v. Blad Foundation*, decision by the Svea Court of Appeal made on 16 Sep. 2002 in case no T 6588-01-79.
39. *Brattebergs Sågverk AB (bankruptcy estate) v. Mullsjö Maskinförsäljning AB*, decision by the Supreme Court made on 27 May 1992 in case no Ö 809-91, NJA 1992 p. 299.
40. *Sea Carriers Inc. and Frontline Ltd v. Blad Foundation*, decision by the Svea Court of Appeal made on 16 Sep. 2002 in case no T 6588-01-79.
41. *Richard Larsson v. Rynninge IK*, decision by the Svea Court of Appeal made on 28 Aug. 2009 in case no T 1548-08.
42. See *Eco Swiss China Time v. Benetton International*, ruling by European Court of Justice in case no C-126/97, 1999, ECR I-3055, see also 'Judgments rendered by the District Court of The Hague on 2[illegible] May 2004 in (1) case GK/RK 2002-979 and 2003-1617 and by the Court of Appeal of The Hague on 24 March 2005 in (2) case 04/694 and 04/695 (*Marketing Displays International Inc. v. VR Van Raalte Reclame B.V.*). Observations by Diederik de Groot, Stockholm Intl. Arbitration Rev. 201–229 (2006:2), Pierre Heizmann & Jacob Grierson, *SNF v Cytec Industrie: National Courts within the EC Apply Different Standards to Review International Awards Allegedly Contrary to Art. 81 EC*, Stockholm Intl. Arbitration Rev. 39–49 (2007:2).
43. *Dirland Telecom S.A v. Viking Telecom AB (publ)*, decision by the Court of Appeal for Western Sweden made on 29 Dec. 2003 in case no T 4366-02. Commented in Stockholm Arbitration Report, 2004:2, published by the SCC.

system. However, section 33 item 2 only applies to breaches of fundamental principles of EU law. In this case, a declaration of invalidity was sought on the basis that an award was incompatible with an EU directive and a decision by the Council of the European Union. The Court of Appeal found that the EU law in question did not express a fundamental principle that constituted public policy. The award was therefore not declared invalid.

27. In a subsequent 2005 case,[44] an agreement between a Latvian company and the Latvian Republic obligated the Latvian Republic not to regulate gas prices, except in relation to domestic end-consumers. However, the Latvian Republic considered the exception to include all categories of consumers in Latvia and regulated gas prices accordingly. The Latvian company initiated arbitral proceedings in Sweden. The arbitral tribunal found that the Latvian Republic had not performed its obligations under the agreement and therefore ordered it to compensate the Latvian company. The Latvian Republic challenged the award and alleged it to be invalid according to section 33. The Latvian Republic alleged that compensation from the state to the Latvian company would constitute state aid and thus constitute a breach of public policy, i.e., EU law.

28. The Svea Court of Appeal found that compensation to the Latvian company did not constitute state aid. The Court also clarified that even if the compensation had constituted illegal state aid, the award might not be in breach of Swedish public policy. The Latvian Republic further alleged that the arbitral award constituted a breach of public policy because it set aside a decision from the Latvian Energy Authorities. On this claim, the Svea Court of Appeal held that the award did not set aside the Latvian Energy Authorities' mandate. The Court also emphasized that even if the Authorities' mandate would have been set aside, the award would still not have constituted a breach of Swedish public policy. The case highlights the Court of Appeal's strict interpretation of the concept of public policy.

4. *Section 33 Item 3: Defect in Form*

29. The mandatory requirements for arbitral awards can be found in section 31(1) of the Act. For an award to be valid under the Act, it must be made in writing and signed by the arbitrators. These requirements provide legal safeguards for the parties. Consequently, section 33 item 3 of the Act contains a reference to these requirements, stating that an award is invalid unless it fulfils the formal requirements of section 31 item 1.

44. *Latvian Republic v. JSC Latvijas Gaze*, decision by the Svea Court of Appeal made on 4 May 2005 in case no T 6730-03.

30. In older case law, the Supreme Court strictly maintained the formal requirements and declared an award invalid for lack of signatures.[45] Today, some scholars are of the opinion that the formal requirements should not be interpreted as strictly.[46] Instead, commentators suggest that an award with defects in form could be corrected by the arbitrators according to section 32.[47]

5. *Section 33(2): Partial Invalidity*

31. An arbitral award can be declared invalid only in part.[48] An example of partial invalidity is if the arbitrators have decided both on issues that are arbitrable and on issues that are not. In such cases the court may declare an award partially invalid if the decisions that are invalid can be distinguished from the rest of the award.[49]

B. Grounds for Setting Aside the Award

1. *In General*

32. The grounds for setting aside an arbitral award can be found in section 34 of the Act. The purpose of section 34 is to ensure the observance of procedural safeguards in the course of the arbitration. This section illustrates the balance between ensuring the finality of an arbitration award and the possibility of annulling an award in case of irregularities.[50] In contrast to invalidity of the award under section 33, section 34 includes a time bar in its second and third paragraphs. Further, in contrast to the grounds for invalidity, section 34 does not protect public or third party interests.[51]

33. Section 34 is exclusive, meaning that an award can only be set aside if challenged under this section.[52] An award may be set aside in full or in part. Only those parts that are tainted by error may be set aside. However, as case law shows,[53] it may sometimes be difficult to determine which parts of the award are affected and which are not. It is conceivable that a challenged part is an integral part of the award, and that therefore

45. Lars Heuman, *Arbitration Law of Sweden: Practice and Procedure*, 502 see also *N. Hobro v. Paulistroms bruks AB (bankruptcy estate)*, decision by the Supreme Court made on 5 Jun. 1912, NJA 1912 p. 263.
46. Åke Hassler & Thorsten Cars, *Skiljeförfarande* 134, n. 17 (Norstedts Juridik AB 1989).
47. Lars Heuman, *Arbitration Law of Sweden: Practice and Procedure*, 502.
48. Stefan Lindskog, *Skiljeförfarande – En kommentar* 909 (Norstedts Juridik AB 2005).
49. Lars Heuman, *Arbitration Law of Sweden: Practice and Procedure*, 577.
50. SOU 1994:81, Ny lag om skiljeförfarande, 169, Prop 1998/99:35, 139 and Lars Heuman, *Arbitration Law of Sweden: Practice and Procedure*, 572.
51. Finn Madsen, *Commercial Arbitration in Sweden – A Commentary on the Arbitration Act (1999:116) and the Rules of the Arbitration Institute of the Stockholm Chamber of Commerce*, 245.
52. Finn Madsen, *Commercial Arbitration in Sweden – A Commentary on the Arbitration Act (1999:116) and the Rules of the Arbitration Institute of the Stockholm Chamber of Commerce*, 244–245.
53. *Premiepensionsmyndigheten v. CSC Sverige AB*, decision by the Svea Court of Appeal made on 11 May 2004 in case no T 11006-02.

the award cannot suitably be sustained. In such a case, the Court may decide also to set aside other parts of the award than those directly tainted by error.[54] Nevertheless, even if the conditions are met, the court has no mandate to decide ex officio whether to set aside an award. Instead, a challenge must first be brought by a party.

34. The Act contains no provision concerning the burden of proof. The general principle is that the applicant has the burden of proving his claim in a challenge action. There are, however, exceptions. The parties may, for example, be deemed to have agreed to allocate the burden of proof differently.[55]

2. Section 34 Item 1: Dispute Not Covered by a Valid Agreement between the Parties

35. Under section 34 item 1, an award may be challenged if the arbitration agreement is invalid. The same section also covers situations where the arbitration agreement is valid but not applicable to the situation in question.[56] The section does not, however, remove the award's validity.[57] If, under an applicable foreign law, a lack of arbitrability exists, this does not make the award invalid, but it does make the award open to challenge. With reference to the doctrine of separability, an award may not be challenged by claiming that the whole contract is invalid; instead, the invalidity claim must pertain to the arbitration agreement.

3. Section 34 Item 2: Excess of Mandate

36. Under section 34 item 2, an award should be set aside if it has been made after the expiry of the period agreed by the parties.[58] The rule does not consider whether the outcome was affected by the delay or whether the losing party, as a consequence, experienced additional loss.

37. It is the parties, not the arbitrators, who are entitled to extend the time limit for delivering an award. However, in accordance with most institutional rules, an arbitration institute may extend the time limit if requested by a party or the tribunal, sometimes even ex officio. The parties can exclude this option, but they must do so by clear wording in the arbitration agreement. If a time limit is extended by an arbitration

54. Stefan Lindskog, *Skiljeförfarande – En kommentar*, 992–993; Finn Madsen, *Commercial Arbitration in Sweden – A Commentary on the Arbitration Act (1999:116) and the Rules of the Arbitration Institute of the Stockholm Chamber of Commerce*, 245, see also *Dödsboet (estate), Ida J. and E. T. v. H.S. and H.K.*, decision by the Supreme Court made on 26 Aug. 1941, NJA 1941 p. 468.
55. Lars Heuman, *Arbitration Law of Sweden: Practice and Procedure*, 578–579.
56. Finn Madsen, *Commercial Arbitration in Sweden – A Commentary on the Arbitration Act (1999:116) and the Rules of the Arbitration Institute of the Stockholm Chamber of Commerce*, 246.
57. SOU 1994:81 'Ny lag om skiljeförfarande', 174, Govt. bill 1998/99:35, 'Ny lag om skiljeförfarande', 142.
58. SOU 1994:81 'Ny lag om skiljeförfarande', 177, Govt. bill 1998/99:35, 'Ny lag om skiljeförfarande' (Stockholm, 1998), 146.

institute, a party who wants to retain its right to challenge the award based on the time extension not being made in due course must protest during the proceedings.[59]

38. An award can also be set aside if 'the arbitrators have otherwise exceeded their mandate'. The arbitrators' mandate can be defined as the parties' joint request, which means that the arbitrators' mandate is limited by the arbitration agreement. Further, the arbitrators' mandate is shaped by subsequent agreements and arrangements, understandings, instructions, or conduct by the parties.[60]

39. The arbitrators may be deemed to have exceeded their mandate if they violate the instructions of the parties or if they render an award relating to an issue other than those referred to them. The arbitrators are also deemed to have exceeded their mandate when basing an award on facts or grounds not invoked by a party.[61]

40. Awarding the prevailing party more than it claimed is another example of excess of mandate.[62] However, if the arbitrators grant a party damages including indirect loss, despite such compensation being excluded in the parties' contract, this is considered an error of substance and thus does not constitute a ground for challenge.[63] Another example of when arbitrators are held not to have exceeded their mandate is when they decide a claim that has been filed after expiry of the time limit stated in the contract.[64]

41. In assessing whether the arbitrators have exceeded their mandate, case law draws a distinction between applying legal grounds not pleaded by a party and interpretation within the frame of the arbitrators' evaluation of evidence, the latter falling within the arbitrators' mandate.[65]

42. Challenge proceedings based on alleged excess of mandate seldom lead to awards being set aside.[66] Even so, in a case from 2009,[67] the Svea Court of Appeal set aside an award which was based on a fact that had not been invoked by either party. The Svea Court of Appeal stressed that the parties had approved the narrative part of the award before the award was rendered, and thereby approved the account of the claims and

59. Lars Heuman, *Arbitration Law of Sweden: Practice and Procedure*, 614.
60. Kaj Hobér, *International Commercial Arbitration in Sweden*, 320–321, e.g., when the choice of law is unclear and/or difficult to apply, see *JSC Aeroflot Russian Airlines v. Russo International Venture Inc and MGM Production Group Inc*, decision by the Svea Court of Appeal made on 21 Feb. 2005 in case no T 1164-03; see also (322) *The Czech Republic v. CME Czech Republic BV*, decision by the Svea Court of Appeal made on 15 May 2003 in case no T 8735-01, RH 2003:55.
61. Kaj Hober, *International Commercial Arbitration in Sweden*, 312, 313, 315 (see *Systembolaget AB v. V&S Vin & Sprit AB*, judgment by Svea Court of Appeal made on 1 Dec. 2009 in case no T 4548-08), where the court seems to have applied such a principle *e contrario*); Lars Heuman, *Arbitration Law of Sweden: Practice and Procedure*, 249.
62. Kaj Hober, *International Commercial Arbitration in Sweden*, 313.
63. Kaj Hober, *International Commercial Arbitration in Sweden*, 320 and Lars Heuman, *Arbitration Law of Sweden: Practice and Procedure*, 610–611.
64. Kaj Hober, *International Commercial Arbitration in Sweden*, 320.
65. *Matthias Kjellberg v. Proffice AB*, decision by the Svea Court of Appeal made on 20 Mar. 2008 in case no T 5398-05.
66. Gary B. Born, *International Commercial Arbitration* 2607 (vol. II, Kluwer Law International 2009).
67. *Systembolaget AB v. V&S Vin& Sprit AB*, judgment by Svea Court of Appeal made on 1 Dec. 2009 in case no T 4548-08.

facts of the case. The Svea Court of Appeal interpreted the narrative part of the award and found that although the relevant fact had indeed been invoked, it had been invoked only in relation to a different aspect of the case. Therefore, the Court found that the award was based on a circumstance not invoked by the parties, and that therefore the arbitrators had exceeded their mandate. The award was set aside. It should be noted that the case was a domestic arbitration. It has been argued that the court's reasoning might have been different if the same questions had arisen in an international arbitration.

43. In *Soyak International Construction & Investment Inc v. Hochtief AG*,[68] the Supreme Court assessed the question of excess of mandate in an arbitration under the Rules of Arbitration of the Arbitration Institute of the Stockholm Chamber of Commerce (SCC Rules). In contrast to the Act, the SCC rules require the tribunal to state the reasons upon which the award is based. A party challenged the award claiming lack of reasoning and that the findings were incomplete or contradictory. The Supreme Court stated that excess of mandate as grounds for challenge mainly concerns cases where the arbitrators have considered matters that were not invoked, or where the arbitrators consider certain matters in violation of the parties' instructions. The Supreme Court stated that an award based upon deficient reasoning can be contrary to the rule of law, and thus constitute a procedural irregularity. However, the Supreme Court stressed that only reasoning so deficient that it could be considered equivalent to nonexistent reasoning would constitute grounds for challenge. In the case under discussion, the arbitral tribunal had neglected to state its reasoning on the evaluation of evidence, but this neglect was not severe enough for the award to be set aside.

44. An arbitral award should be set aside if the arbitrators have deviated from the arbitration agreement by applying a national law other than that chosen by the parties.[69] However, case law indicates that where an arbitration agreement contains conflicting provisions, the arbitrators do not exceed their mandate when choosing which provision to apply.[70] In one case, this issue was considered in relation to choice-of-law clauses. The Court of Appeal applied a pragmatic approach to the arbitrators' power to choose the applicable law, implying that it would take a wilful disregard of the applicable law for the arbitrators to have exceeded their mandate.[71] In a similar case, the claimant claimed that the arbitral tribunal had based its decision on a general fairness assessment instead of on the applicable law. The Court of Appeal

---

68. *Soyak International Construction & Investment Inc v. Hochtief AG*, judgment of the Supreme Court made on 31 Mar. 2009 in case no T 4387-07, NJA 2009 p. 128 (See the section about Appeal against Arbitrators Compensation).
69. Lars Heuman, *Arbitration Law of Sweden: Practice and Procedure*, 603; Kaj Hobér, *International Commercial Arbitration in Sweden*, 319 et seq. regarding the distinction between limitation on mandate and merits of the case.
70. See *JSC Aeroflot Russian Airlines v. Russo International Venture Incand MGM Production Group Inc*, decision by the Svea Court of Appeal made on 21 Feb. 2005 in case no T 1164-03 (*The Czech republic v. CME Czech Republic BV*, decision by the Svea Court of Appeal made on 15 May 2003 in case no T 8735-01, RH 2003:55).
71. *JSC Aeroflot Russian Airlines v. Russo International Venture Incand MGM Production Group Inc*, decision by the Svea Court of Appeal made on 21 Feb. 2005 in case no T 1164-03.

concluded that the arbitral tribunal had acted in accordance with the choice-of-law clause and stressed that each legal statement in an award need not be derived from a specific rule of law in order for the arbitrators to have complied with the parties' choice-of-law.[72]

45. Further, as stated above, an award may only be challenged on formal grounds, meaning that it may not be set aside due to wrongful application of substantive law. It may be very difficult to determine whether the arbitrators have failed to apply the chosen substantive law or if they have simply applied the chosen substantive law incorrectly. The distinction is important because the latter does not constitute an excess of mandate.[73] In *Aeroflot*[74] the main question was whether the arbitral tribunal had exceeded its mandate when deciding which law to apply. The Court stated that an arbitral tribunal exceeds its mandate if it wilfully neglects a choice-of-law clause. However, an incorrect interpretation of a choice-of-law clause must be attributed to the substantive assessment, which falls outside the scope of section 34.

46. In *Soyak International Construction & Investment Inc v. Hochtief AG*, the Supreme Court stated that not every violation of the parties' chosen procedural rules is considered an excess of mandate; instead section 34 item 6 may apply.[75] The difference is important because the latter provision imposes an additional causal requirement, i.e., that the procedural irregularity in question must have influenced the outcome of the case. However, in some cases an implied causal requirement may exist, i.e., since an award can be set aside in whole or in part, those parts of an award unaffected by the excess of mandate may not be set aside through challenge.[76] Some scholars have suggested that a causal requirement should be incorporated when it is obvious that the excess of mandate did not influence the outcome.[77] In *Perstorp Aktiebolag v. Silver Lining Finance SA (bankruptcy estate)*,[78] the Svea Court of Appeal applied such a requirement. In that case, the Svea Court of Appeal reasoned that the arbitrators had not exceeded their mandate because the disputed facts had not affected the outcome of the case.

72. *The Czech Republic v. CME Czech Republic BV*, decision by the Svea Court of Appeal made on 15 May 2003 in case no T 8735-01, RH 2003:55.
73. Kaj Hobér, *International Commercial Arbitration in Sweden*, 321, e.g., when the choice of law is unclear and/or difficult to apply, see *JSC Aeroflot Russian Airlines v. Russo International Venture Incand MGM Production Group Inc*, decision by the Svea Court of Appeal made on 21 Feb. 2005 in case no T 1164-03; see also (322) *The Czech republic v. CME Czech Republic BV*, decision by the Svea Court of Appeal made on 15 May 2003 in case no T 8735-01, RH 2003:55.
74. *JSC Aeroflot Russian Airlines v. Russo International Venture Incand MGM Production Group Inc*, decision by the Svea Court of Appeal made on 21 Feb. 2005 in case no T 1164-03.
75. *Soyak International Construction & Investment Inc v. Hochtief AG*, judgment of the Supreme Court made on 31 Mar. 2009 in case no T 4387-07, NJA 2009 p. 128.
76. Lars Heuman, *Arbitration Law of Sweden: Practice and Procedure*, 595; Kaj Hobér, *International Commercial Arbitration in Sweden*, 324 (*Systembolaget AB v. V&S Vin & Sprit AB*, judgment by Svea Court of Appeal made on 1 December 2009 in case no T 4548-08, where the court seems to have accepted that some form of causal requirement did exist.)
77. Stefan Lindskog, *Skiljeförfarande – En kommentar*, 936–937 and Kaj Hobér, *International Commercial Arbitration in Sweden*, 324.
78. *Perstorp Aktiebolag v. Silver Lining Finance SA (bancruptcy estate)*, decision by the Svea Court of Appeal made on 31 Aug. 2011 in case no T 4050-10.

4. *Section 34 Item 3: The Arbitral Proceedings Took Place in Sweden, Contrary to Section 47*

47. In many arbitration proceedings, one or both of the parties are foreign. If so, and if the parties have agreed to arbitrate in a jurisdiction other than Sweden, the award may be challenged in accordance with section 34 item 3 of the Act and set aside if the arbitrators, notwithstanding the parties' agreement, decide to conduct the arbitration in Sweden.[79] This basis for challenge is supported by the general principle that Swedish courts or other public authorities should not contribute to an arbitration taking place in Sweden when the parties have not so agreed.[80] Accordingly, section 47 of the Act states that the arbitral proceedings shall take place in Sweden if it is so stated in the arbitration agreement. In accordance with section 47(2) of the Act, this is also the case where one party is domiciled in Sweden or otherwise subject to the jurisdiction of the Swedish courts, and the arbitration agreement provides no other jurisdiction. According to section 47(3) of the Act, arbitration proceedings conducted under the Act may only take place in Sweden under the conditions outlined in that section.

5. *Section 34 Item 4: An Arbitrator Has Been Appointed Contrary to the Agreement between the Parties or the Act*

48. Arbitration clauses may provide certain qualifications for the arbitrators, and sometimes persons with certain qualifications are expressly excluded in the arbitration clause.[81] For example, the arbitration clause may provide that the arbitrator must be a judge or a technical expert. It is not possible for arbitrators to cure the lack of qualification by acquiring it after the arbitration.[82] Any provisions regarding arbitrators' qualifications must be acknowledged by the person or body that is chosen by a party to appoint an arbitrator.[83]

49. In cases where a party questions the qualifications of an appointed arbitrator, the matter cannot be decided while the proceedings are in progress. Instead, the party should make the requisite objection and reserve the right to challenge the award after it has been made.[84]

50. If the requirements are expressed in vague terms, the principle of *in dubio pro validate* comes into play, meaning that in case of doubt an award should be upheld.

---

79. Lars Heuman, *Arbitration Law of Sweden: Practice and Procedure*, 615.
80. Govt. bill 1998/99:35, 'Ny lag om skiljeförfarande', 189 and Kaj Hobér, *International Commercial Arbitration in Sweden* 325 (Oxford University Press 2011).
81. SOU 1994:81 'Ny lag om skiljeförfarande', 178, 291, Govt. bill 1998/99:35, 'Ny lag om skiljeförfarande', 235, 146; Lars Heuman, *Arbitration Law of Sweden: Practice and Procedure*, 616.
82. Kaj Hobér, *International Commercial Arbitration in Sweden*, 326.
83. Lars Heuman, *Arbitration Law of Sweden: Practice and Procedure*, 616. It should be noted that in SCC arbitrations, the Board can release an arbitrator from appointment if the arbitrator does not possess the qualifications agreed by the parties, see Art. 15 of the Rules of the Arbitration Institute of the Stockholm Chamber of Commerce.
84. Lars Heuman, *Arbitration Law of Sweden: Practice and Procedure*, 616.

Provisions excluding certain categories of people as arbitrators may be considered to include an agreement that enlarges the grounds for disqualification. If an arbitrator is appointed by an unauthorized person or body, the award should be set aside.

6. *Section 34 Item 5: The Arbitrators Lack Legal Capacity or There Are Grounds for Disqualification*

51. Section 34 item 5 refers to the requirements in sections 7 and 8 of the Act, stating that an arbitrator must possess full legal capacity and be impartial.[85] Section 34 item 5 is seldom relied upon in setting aside proceedings. Instead issues concerning disqualification are usually decided during the arbitration. Section 10 of the Act provides that a party must challenge an arbitrator within fifteen days from when the party became aware of the appointment and the existence of the circumstances that enable disqualification. In accordance with section 34, a party who has participated in the proceeding without raising an objection will be deemed to have waived such objection. Section 11 of the Act states that the parties may agree that a request referred to in section 10 shall be conclusively determined by an arbitration institution.

52. An award may only be set aside based on this section when the party became aware of the grounds for disqualification after the arbitration proceedings. However, even if the challenge of an arbitrator was decided during the proceedings, new grounds for disqualification may subsequently arise. Such new information, combined with pre-existing grounds, may result in the award being set aside.

53. Even if no single circumstance in itself is enough to constitute grounds for disqualification, a combination of different circumstances may be sufficient. Notably, the arbitrators' assessment of substantive or procedural matters cannot serve as an argument for one or more of them being disqualified. Likewise, wrongful decisions on the merits do not constitute grounds for setting aside an award. Only in cases where the arbitrators have made several serious and obvious errors during the proceedings, and where they have clearly favoured one party in the award, may the award be set aside.[86]

54. In 2001, the Svea Court of Appeal examined the question whether two of the arbitrators should be disqualified due to simultaneously having been involved in a case relevant to that particular arbitration.[87] The Svea Court of Appeal stated that when comparing the two proceedings, the key issue was what the parties had invoked, i.e., what the arbitrators could try, and not what the arbitrators had actually tried. For the similarities between the proceedings to disqualify an arbitrator, they must be able to lead to corresponding assessments. The Svea Court of Appeal did not find the similarities between the two proceedings such that they would have resulted in

85. Kaj Hobér, *International Commercial Arbitration in Sweden*, 326. Regarding s. 8 see *Ingela C. v. Kommunernas Försäkringsaktiebolag*, judgment by the Supreme Court made on 17 Dec. 1981 in case no T 303-81, NJA 1981 p. 1205.
86. Lars Heuman, *Arbitration Law of Sweden: Practice and Procedure*, 621–622.
87. *Återförsäkringsaktiebolaget Patria v. Trygg-Hansa försäkringsaktiebolag*, decision by the Svea Court of Appeal made on 15 Nov. 2001 in case no T 677-99.

disqualification. However, the Svea Court of Appeal stressed the importance of the objectivity and impartiality of arbitrators.

55. The Court of Appeal further stressed that according to the practice of the European Court of Human Rights, a party's doubts about an arbitrator's impartiality is grounds for disqualification if the doubts are objectively justified. For this reason and in light of the high standards that must be required of an arbitrator, the Court held that one of the two arbitrators did not meet the requirements on impartiality or independence as set out by the Act since he had not informed the parties of the relevant circumstances. However, the Court of Appeal found that the right to invoke disqualification had been precluded, and the award was therefore not set aside.

56. In another case, the Court of Appeal considered it insufficient for disqualification that an arbitrator had worked for the same employer as one of the parties, given that it was clear that there had been no joint interests or loyalty relationships between the arbitrator and the party that could undermine confidence in the arbitrator's impartiality.[88]

57. In *A. Jilkén v. Ericsson AB*, the Supreme Court disqualified an arbitrator based on the relationship between one of the parties and the law firm to which the arbitrator was tied as a consultant.[89] The arbitrator had a part time assignment as Senior Legal Advisor for a law firm that represented one of the parties in legal matters, and had not disclosed this fact to the parties in the arbitration. The Supreme Court stated that the ties between the arbitrator and the law firm were not strong (as the arbitrator's business did not form an integrated part of the law firm's business and as he had not had any direct contact with the party). Nevertheless, the arbitrator had used the law firm's stationary in his correspondence with the parties in the arbitration. Also, under the Code of Conduct of the Swedish Bar Association, the arbitrator would have been barred from taking on any assignments as counsel for a counterparty to the party in question. The Supreme Court stressed the existence of an important commercial bond between the law firm and the party, and also a bond of loyalty and mutual interest which could undermine confidence in the impartiality of the arbitrator.

58. In its assessment, the Supreme Court relied upon rules from arbitration institutes such as the ICC and the SCC and the IBA Guidelines on Conflicts of Interest in International Arbitration (IBA Guidelines) and stressed that international standards can serve as an important point of reference in challenge proceedings. The Supreme Court found that both SCC practice and the IBA Guidelines supported the assessment that the ties between a party and the law firm in which an arbitrator acted as legal advisor could undermine confidence in the arbitrator. Thus, the Supreme Court set aside the award.

---

88. *Mariestads kommun v. GE Capital Equipment Finance Aktiebolag*, decision by the Svea Court of Appeal made on 19 Feb. 2004 in case no T 7627-01.
89. *A. Jilkén v. Ericsson AB*, judgment by the Supreme Court made on 19 Nov. 2007 in case no T 2448-96, NJA 2007 p. 841.

59. Some much debated Swedish case law relating to disqualification of arbitrators concerns repeat appointments, i.e., where an arbitrator has been appointed multiple times by the same party, or where information that might result in disqualification has not been disclosed to the opposing party.[90]

60. The issue of how many times a law firm may appoint the same arbitrator without disqualifying the arbitrator was assessed in *Korsnäs AB v. AB Fortum Värme samägt med Stockholms stad*.[91] The Supreme Court took several factors into account, e.g., the number of appointments, whether they had been made by the same lawyer, and the complexity of the appointments. The Supreme Court finally made an overall assessment of the circumstances in the specific case. In the assessment, the Supreme Court stressed the importance of distinguishing between appointments as party-appointed arbitrator and as chair. A chair is normally not appointed by a party; hence, appointments as chair cannot be taken into account in an assessment of connections between the arbitrator and the law firm. The Supreme Court found that the arbitrator's appointments came from the law firm in question in only some 10% of his appointments during the past ten years. Thus, the Supreme Court found no reason for disqualification.

61. Both repeat appointments and failure to disclose information were discussed in a 2006 case before the Svea Court of Appeal.[92] In the case, the claimant requested that the Court of Appeal set aside an award because the arbitrator appointed by the other party had been appointed by that same party before and had failed to disclose this, despite having had the opportunity to do so. The Court stated that the mere fact that an arbitrator has had several mandates from the same client does not imply that the person is disqualified as an arbitrator. The Court stated that the arbitrator in question should have informed the parties about his relevant previous appointments as arbitrator. However, the Court did not find the arbitrator's negligence to be severe enough for the award to be set aside.

62. In the above-mentioned cases, *Korsnäs AB v. AB Fortum Värme samägt med Stockholms stad* and *A. Jilkén v. Ericsson AB* the Supreme Court also provided some guidance on the implications of failure to disclose information that may give rise to doubts as to the arbitrator's impartiality. The Supreme Court's reasoning in these cases may imply that failure to disclose such circumstances does not constitute independent grounds for challenge, even though failure to disclose did have an impact on the decision by the Supreme Court to set aside the award in *A. Jilkén v. Ericsson AB*. The

90. Fredrik Andersson et al., *Arbitration in Sweden*, 86, 90; *Korsnäs AB v. AB Fortum Värme samägt med Stockholms stad*, judgment by the Supreme Court made on 9 Jun. 2010 in case no T 156-09, NJA 2010 p. 317; *A. Jilkén v. Ericsson AB*, judgment by the Supreme Court made on 19 Nov. 2007 in case no T 2448-96, NJA 2007 p. 841; *Rapla Invest AB (bankruptcy estate) v. TNK Trade Limited*, decision by the Svea Court of Appeal made on 7 Dec. 2006 in case no T 5044-04.

91. *Korsnäs AB v. AB Fortum Värme samägt med Stockholms stad*, judgment by the Supreme Court made on 9 Jun. 2010 in case no T 156-09, NJA 2010 p. 317.

92. *Rapla Invest AB (bankruptcy estate) v. TNK Trade Limited*, decision by the Svea Court of Appeal made on 7 Dec. 2006 in case no T 5044-04.

Supreme Court's approach on disclosure conforms to international case law as well as the IBA Guidelines on Conflicts of Interest in International Arbitration.

7. *Section 34 Item 6: Other Procedural Irregularities*

63. Section 34 item 6, also referred to as '*the general clause*', stipulates that for an award to be set aside on this ground: (1) the arbitrators must have committed a procedural irregularity, (2) the party challenging the award shall not negligently have caused the irregularity, and (3) it must be likely that the irregularity has affected the outcome (the so-called causal requirement).

64. It has been acknowledged that the word '*otherwise*' in section 34 item 6 suggests that this point is subsidiary to the other grounds for challenge.[93] In *Soyak International Construction & Investment Inc. v. Hochtief AG,*[94] the Supreme Court expressed the view that section 34 item 2 deals with the scope of the arbitrators' assessment of the merits of the case, while section 34 item 6 addresses instructions as to how the proceedings are to be conducted.[95] The party contemplating challenging an award must not forget the additional causal requirement provided under section 34 item 6.[96] The principles of res judicata and *jura novit curia* are two good examples illustrating the difficulties of distinguishing situations challengeable using section 34 item 2 from those covered by section 34 item 6. Disregarding the res judicata principle was previously deemed to constitute an excess of mandate but is now considered a procedural irregularity. It is likely that an award based on legal arguments not invoked by any party can be challenged using either section 34 item 2 or section 34 item 6.[97]

65. Regarding the principle of res judicata, unless the respondent neglects to object by raising the defence of res judicata, the award cannot be set aside on such grounds.[98] As for the principle of *jura novit curia*, as long as the parties do not agree differently, the

93. Kaj Hobér, *International Commercial Arbitration in Sweden*, 328.
94. *Soyak International Construction & Investment Inc v. Hochtief AG*, judgment of the Supreme Court made on 31 March 2009 in case no T 4387-07, NJA 2009 p. 128.
95. Kaj Hobér, *International Commercial Arbitration in Sweden*, 336; see also *E. A. v. Försäkringsaktiebolaget Fylgia and Brand- och livförsäkringsaktiebolaget*, decision by the Supreme Court made on 27 Feb. 1937, NJA 1937 p. 120.
96. Lars Heuman, *Arbitration Law of Sweden: Practice and Procedure*, 595, 623.
97. Kaj Hobér, *International Commercial Arbitration in Sweden*, 317–319 (*Esselte AB v. Allmänna Pensionsfonden*, decision by the Supreme Court made on 3 Apr. 2008 in case no T 5685-96, NJA 1998 p. 189); Lars Heuman, *Arbitration Law of Sweden: Practice and Procedure*, 606 (*Aktiebolaget Skånska Cementgjuteriet v. Motoraktiebolaget i Karlstad*, decision by the Supreme Court made on 30 Dec. 1953, NJA 1953 p. 751).
98. Kaj Hobér, *International Commercial Arbitration in Sweden*, 335–336. See *Esselte AB v. Allmänna Pensionsfonden*, decision by the Supreme Court made on 3 Apr. 2008 in case no T 5685-96, NJA 1998 p. 189, which defines the principle of res judicata as a procedural irregularity covered by s. 34(1) item 6. As for application of lis pendens and res judicata in international arbitration see *The Czech republic v. CME Czech Republic BV*, decision by the Svea Court of Appeal made on 15 May 2003 in case no T 8735-01, RH 2003:55. The application seems to be the same as in domestic arbitration.

principle would seem to apply in domestic arbitration proceedings.[99] In international arbitration, nevertheless, the principle would not seem to apply as rigorously as in court litigation in Sweden.[100] It must be considered that in many countries, e.g., common-law countries, the principle of *jura novit curia* is not applied, and that applying the principle in international arbitration therefore could have undesirable or unexpected consequences. A strict application of the principle might result in the dispute being decided based on legal rules or concepts that the parties have not invoked. Unless the parties are provided with sufficient opportunity to present their case as regards application of provisions not invoked, the tribunal risks violating due process.

66. As mentioned above, if a procedural irregularity is the product of wrongful application of substantive law, the award may not be challenged. Such situations may be difficult to distinguish from challengeable procedural irregularities. For example, erroneous evaluation of evidence is a substantive misjudgment, while incorrectly refusing to accept evidence is considered a procedural irregularity.[101]

67. Some procedural irregularities are less serious than others, and not all procedural irregularities constitute grounds for challenge.[102] Due to the principle of protecting the finality of the award, only obvious violations may result in setting aside an award. A fundamental principle, the violation of which may constitute grounds for setting aside an award, is that the procedure is adversarial. Another fundamental principle is that the parties must be given due opportunity to present their case. Having said this, the tribunal is nevertheless allowed to dismiss evidence if it is manifestly irrelevant. Such a decision is not challengeable if based on the arbitrators' assessment of the merits of the case.[103]

68. In contrast to section 34 item 2, section 34 item 6 requires that the party has not negligently caused the irregularity. The rationale behind this requirement is that the party at fault should not benefit from its own mistake.[104] However, this should be distinguished from situations where negligent actions by one party result in the arbitrators exceeding their mandate. If a party has not expressed itself clearly, resulting in the arbitrator understanding the party's acts incorrectly, the award cannot be set

99. Finn Madsen, *Commercial Arbitration in Sweden – A Commentary on the Arbitration Act (1999:116) and the Rules of the Arbitration Institute of the Stockholm Chamber of Commerce*, 250.
100. SOU 1994:81 'Ny lag om skiljeförfarande', 177; Govt. bill 1998/99:35, 'Ny lag om skiljeförfarande', 145.
101. Kaj Hobér, *International Commercial Arbitration in Sweden*, 329.
102. Lars Heuman, *Arbitration Law of Sweden: Practice and Procedure*, 582.
103. Kaj Hobér, *International Commercial Arbitration in Sweden*, 330. (Regarding whether to set aside an award because a party has not been given the opportunity fully to plead its case and to submit evidence, see *Gunnar Jansson v. The Estate of Oscar Jansson*, decision by the Supreme Court made on 2 Jun. 1965, NJA 1965 p. 384. See also *Paul J v. Reprotype Aktiebolag*, decision by the Supreme Court made on 24 Oct. 1975, NJA 1975 p. 536.
104. SOU 1994:81 'Ny lag om skiljeförfarande', 180; Govt. bill 1998/99:35, 'Ny lag om skiljeförfarande' 148.

aside on those grounds.[105] Also, according to the *travaux préparatoires*, falsified evidence – such as a witness giving perjured testimony – does not in itself make the award challengeable.[106]

8. *Section 34(2): Waiver*

69. Section 34(2) provides for a passivity rule, obliging the parties to object to circumstances otherwise deemed to have been waived by their participation. Thus, in order to retain the right to challenge an award, a party must not participate in the arbitral proceedings without objecting that the arbitration agreement is invalid or does not govern the issue raised.[107] To retain its right to challenge an award, a party must object to every individual decision by the arbitrators. However, objections based on circumstances of which a party was unaware, and should not have been aware of, are not deemed to have been waived by mere participation.[108]

70. Furthermore, under section 34(2) a party's appointment of an arbitrator shall not be regarded as acceptance of the arbitrators' jurisdiction. However, in combination with other circumstances, a party's appointment of an arbitrator may constitute a waiver.[109] In such situations the party must object in order not to forfeit the right to challenge the award. The situation can also be viewed in relation to section 10 of the Act, pursuant to which a party forfeits its right to challenge an award for lack of impartiality if the party disregards the time limit for challenging an arbitrator.

9. *Section 34(3): Time Limit*

71. Section 34(3) contains a three-month time limit for bringing a challenge. The time limit starts when the award is delivered to the parties in its entirety, and the time limit

105. Finn Madsen, *Commercial Arbitration in Sweden – A Commentary on the Arbitration Act (1999:116) and the Rules of the Arbitration Institute of the Stockholm Chamber of Commerce*, 255 and *Partrederiet för M/S Red Sea v. Götaverken Sölvwirginesborg AB*, decision by the Supreme Court made on 13 Jul. 1990 in case no T 80-89, NJA 1990 p. 419.
106. Govt. bill 1998/99:35, 'Ny lag om skiljeförfarande', 150; Finn Madsen, *Commercial Arbitration in Sweden – A Commentary on the Arbitration Act (1999:116) and the Rules of the Arbitration Institute of the Stockholm Chamber of Commerce*, 255.
107. Finn Madsen, *Commercial Arbitration in Sweden – A Commentary on the Arbitration Act (1999:116) and the Rules of the Arbitration Institute of the Stockholm Chamber of Commerce*, 247.
108. Finn Madsen, *Commercial Arbitration in Sweden – A Commentary on the Arbitration Act (1999:116) and the Rules of the Arbitration Institute of the Stockholm Chamber of Commerce*, 257–258 (see n. 773).
109. SOU 1994:81 'Ny lag om skiljeförfarande', 291–292; Govt. bill 1998/99:35, 'Ny lag om skiljeförfarande', 236; Finn Madsen, *Commercial Arbitration in Sweden – A Commentary on the Arbitration Act (1999:116) and the Rules of the Arbitration Institute of the Stockholm Chamber of Commerce*, 258.

cannot be extended.[110] However, the court does not ex officio assess whether the time limit has been exceeded.

72. Furthermore, the provision provides that after the time limit has expired, the party may not invoke new grounds in support of its action. This limitation refers to so-called legal grounds under Swedish procedural law rather than those grounds listed in section 34.[111] A new ground refers to a dispositive fact not invoked which, if it exists, constitutes a ground for challenge. However, according to the *travaux préparatoires*, a party is entitled to adjust its claim within the same grounds for challenge. This concerns certain sets of facts within the same specific context. However, the party should not be allowed to invoke a completely different ground.[112] The current limitation also applies to new circumstances not known to the challenging party before the time limit expired.[113]

III. RECOURSE TO THE COURTS: OTHER LIMITATIONS ON THE FINALITY OF ARBITRAL AWARDS

73. Apart from the rules in sections 33 and 34 mentioned above, a party has access to judicial review in certain other circumstances. First, stay of proceedings under section 35 will be discussed. Thereafter, the conditions on which a party may appeal a final award declining jurisdiction under section 36 or appeal the decision on arbitrator compensation under section 41 will be explained below. Finally, the possibility for foreign parties to waive the right to challenge an award by means of an exclusion agreement under section 51 will be examined.

A. Cure of Defects

1. Section 35 of the Act: The Possibility for the Court of Appeal to Stay the Proceedings

74. Under section 35, the Court of Appeal may, upon a party's request, stay the invalidity or setting aside of proceedings to give the arbitrators the opportunity to resume the arbitral proceedings or to take such other action that in the arbitral tribunal's opinion will eliminate the grounds for invalidity or setting aside.

75. The conditions for a stay of the proceedings are that one of the parties has requested the stay and the court finds the challenge to the award to be substantiated,

110. Finn Madsen, *Commercial Arbitration in Sweden – A Commentary on the Arbitration Act (1999:116) and the Rules of the Arbitration Institute of the Stockholm Chamber of Commerce*, 259 (see references to cases in n. 777); Kaj Hobér, *International Commercial Arbitration in Sweden*, 310.

111. Kaj Hobér, *International Commercial Arbitration in Sweden*, 310.

112. Govt. bill 1998/99:35, 'Ny lag om skiljeförfarande', 149–150.

113. Finn Madsen, *Commercial Arbitration in Sweden – A Commentary on the Arbitration Act (1999:116) and the Rules of the Arbitration Institute of the Stockholm Chamber of Commerce*, 260.

or that both parties have requested the stay. Section 35 is discretionary and the court may decline to grant a stay notwithstanding the conditions for a stay being met.[114] Even if both parties request remission it is still within the court's discretion whether or not to grant the request. A decision by the court to remit the award to the arbitrators is not subject to appeal.[115]

76. Remission of a dispute to the arbitrators will result in a new arbitral award in most cases, even if the arbitrators do not change the outcome of the dispute. This follows from the renewed arbitration proceedings resulting in additional costs.[116]

77. Section 35(2) states that if the arbitrators render a new award, a party may challenge it within the time determined by the court, without filing a new action, insofar as the challenge relates to the resumed arbitration proceedings or to amendments made to the first award.

78. Where the arbitration agreement contains a time limit for rendering the award, the court should be able to stay the proceedings and allow the tribunal to revisit the case as long as the original award was rendered within the time limit. Nevertheless, the court should still make an independent assessment considering the purpose and the length of the original time limit set by the parties and the time that may be expected to remedy the award.[117]

79. Section 35, which is modelled on Article 34(4) of the Model Law, complements section 32, which enables the arbitrators to correct, supplement, and interpret the award in case of any obvious inaccuracy within a specified period after rendering the award.[118] Section 35 makes it possible to prevent more drastic consequences – invalidity and setting aside – in situations where a procedural defect can be remedied by the arbitrators. Still, section 35 seems to have played a very limited role in practice as there is yet no case law regarding the section.

B. Appeal of Award Declining Jurisdiction

1. *In General*

80. Section 36 provides a party with the possibility of appeal if the arbitral tribunal has terminated the proceedings without ruling on the issues submitted to it. Under section 36 the award may be amended by the Court of Appeal, and it is for the Court of Appeal to determine whether the procedural issues have been correctly assessed by the arbitral

114. Finn Madsen, *Commercial Arbitration in Sweden – A Commentary on the Arbitration Act (1999:116) and the Rules of the Arbitration Institute of the Stockholm Chamber of Commerce*, 262.
115. Govt. bill 1998/99:35, 'Ny lag om skiljeförfarande', 154, 237.
116. Govt. bill 1998/99:35, 'Ny lag om skiljeförfarande', 237.
117. Govt. bill 1998/99:35, 'Ny lag om skiljeförfarande', 237.
118. Finn Madsen, *Commercial Arbitration in Sweden – A Commentary on the Arbitration Act (1999:116) and the Rules of the Arbitration Institute of the Stockholm Chamber of Commerce*, 261.

tribunal.[119] The decision by the Court of Appeal may be appealed to the Supreme Court if the Court of Appeal grants leave to appeal.

81. On international comparison, there are few provisions equivalent to section 36 of the Act. For example, there is no similar provision in the Model Law. This may seem somewhat surprising, as section 36 creates a possibility to appeal awards declining jurisdiction. Section 36 thus constitutes a valuable addition to the parties' toolbox. The question whether or not the arbitral tribunal has jurisdiction over a certain dispute is of high importance in many international arbitration proceedings. Often, the question of jurisdiction is in dispute between the parties, and it is for the arbitral tribunal to determine whether or not it has jurisdiction. Under most arbitration laws, the tribunal's decision declining jurisdiction becomes final, and the party invoking the tribunal's jurisdiction has no alternative but to litigate in the home jurisdiction of its counterparty. More often than not, this is not a desirable option.

82. Section 36 of the Act, nevertheless, provides the party invoking jurisdiction with the possibility to appeal the tribunal's decision declining jurisdiction to the Swedish courts. The tribunal's decision declining jurisdiction may thus be revisited by the Swedish courts, which may come to a different conclusion from the tribunal. If the tribunal's jurisdiction is confirmed by the court, the parties must subject themselves to the jurisdiction of an arbitral tribunal and the arbitration proceedings will continue.

2. *Section 36(1): Appeal of Award Declining Jurisdiction*

83. Section 36(1) only applies to awards. If an issue has been determined within the proceedings, such determination constitutes a decision and not an award. For example, if a party has pleaded that the arbitral tribunal has no jurisdiction but the arbitral tribunal rejects the plea, the tribunal confirms its jurisdiction in a decision, not an award.[120] The tribunal's decision is not binding and may therefore be revisited.[121] Nevertheless, in the opposite situation, when the arbitral tribunal finds that it lacks jurisdiction, it dismisses the case by means of an award (and not a decision). This follows from section 27(1) of the Act which stipulates that any decision by the arbitral tribunal terminating the proceedings without a ruling on the merits shall be in the form of an award.

84. There are two ways in which an arbitral tribunal can conclude a case without ruling on the merits. The first is by rendering an award whereby the dispute is written off. The reasons for writing off a dispute may be: (i) a withdrawal by one or more of the parties, (ii) that the arbitration agreement is no longer in force, (iii) that the time for the arbitral tribunal to deliver its award has expired, (iv) that a party has not provided the

119. SOU 1994:81 'Ny lag om skiljeförfarande', 295; Govt. bill 1998/99:35, 'Ny lag om skiljeförfarande', 238; and Lars Heuman, *Arbitration Law of Sweden: Practice and Procedure*, 522.

120. Lars Heuman, *Arbitration Law of Sweden: Practice and Procedure*, 522.

121. SOU 1994:81 'Ny lag om skiljeförfarande', 156; Govt. bill 1998/99:35, 'Ny lag om skiljeförfarande', 24.

requested security for compensation or (v) that the matter is res judicata or lis pendens.[122]

85. The second way for an arbitral tribunal to conclude a case without ruling on the merits is by rendering an award whereby the dispute is dismissed. A case may be dismissed when the arbitrators conclude that they lack jurisdiction, e.g., when no binding arbitration agreement applies to the case in question. Other grounds for dismissal can be lack of legal capacity or lack of arbitrability.[123]

86. Section 36(1) also requires that the arbitration proceedings have come to an end. The proceedings end when the arbitrators have signed the written award (sections 27 and 31). In *Alucoal Holdings Limited v. JSC Novukuznetsk Aluminium Plant*,[124] the Court of Appeal dismissed an appeal because the arbitral tribunal had not terminated the proceedings. In the arbitration proceedings one of the parties had invoked several arbitration agreements in support of the tribunal's jurisdiction. This action did not constitute additional arbitration proceedings. Thus, even though the arbitral tribunal had rendered an award on some of the issues in dispute, the Court of Appeal found that there were still issues left to decide. The arbitration proceedings had therefore not come to an end. The Court of Appeal's assessment was supported by lack of clear instructions on how to appeal the award. Such instructions are required under section 36(1), which stipulates that an award must contain '*clear instructions*' on the actions required by a party who wishes to appeal the award.

87. Section 36(1) further stipulates that an award in which the arbitral tribunal does not rule on the merits may be appealed within three months. If no appeal of the award declining jurisdiction is made within the time limit, the award is binding upon a subsequent arbitral tribunal or court. The award thus makes the issue res judicata.[125] The three-month time limit starts from the date on which the party received the award. If the award has been corrected, supplemented or interpreted according to section 32, the time limit starts from the date on which the party received the award in its final wording.

88. In practice, awards declining jurisdiction are appealed more frequently than awards on the merits.[126] In a number of cases, the appeal of an award-declining jurisdiction resulted in the award being reversed. One example is a 2004 case, where the Court of Appeal found that the arbitral tribunal should not have dismissed the case because the claimant was entitled to arbitration proceedings under the law.[127] Similarly, the award was reversed in a 2005 case where the Court of Appeal found that the

122. Govt. bill 1998/99:35, 'Ny lag om skiljeförfarande', 230.
123. Lars Heuman, *Arbitration Law of Sweden: Practice and Procedure*, 521.
124. *Alucoal Holdings Limited v. JSC Novukuznetsk Aluminium Plant*, decision by the Svea Court of Appeal made on 17 Feb. 2004 in case no T 3226-03.
125. Kaj Hobér, *International Commercial Arbitration in Sweden*, 348–349.
126. Kaj Hobér, *International Commercial Arbitration in Sweden*, 349, Jernej Sekolec & Nils Eliasson, *Ch. 9: The UNCITRAL Model Law on Arbitration and the Swedish Arbitration Akt: A Comparison*, 241.
127. *Tjänstemannaförbundet HTF v. M 7 Borås ideell förening (bankruptcy estate)*, decision by the Svea Court of Appeal made on 28 Jun. 2004 in case no T 1342-03.

arbitral tribunal had misjudged its jurisdiction and dismissal of the case was due to the arbitral tribunal having applied the wrong national law.[128]

89. Naturally, there have also been numerous unsuccessful appeals of awards declining jurisdiction. For example, the Court of Appeal dismissed an appeal in a 2009 case.[129] The Court of Appeal found that the arbitral tribunal had correctly found itself to lack jurisdiction. In the request for arbitration, the claimant had made the case conditional upon an oral hearing in the proceedings. It followed that the arbitral tribunal lacked jurisdiction, because a request for arbitration must be unconditional.

90. The Court of Appeal also agreed with a tribunal's ruling in a 2007 case and upheld the award. In this case the Court of Appeal performed a thorough assessment of jurisdiction. The claimant claimed that he was entitled to stock options in a company. The employment agreement in question included an arbitration clause, and the issue was whether certain stock options were covered by the arbitration clause in that employment agreement. After interpreting the contract, the Court of Appeal concluded that the stock options were not covered by the arbitration clause and, therefore, no binding arbitration agreement had been concluded. Hence, the tribunal's award declining jurisdiction was upheld.[130]

91. The Court of Appeal is not entitled to rule on the merits of the case when hearing an appeal under section 36. As with all challenges to awards, the court's review is limited to procedural issues. Thus, the court may review the substantive basis for the tribunal's decision to terminate the arbitration but it may not rule on the merits. It is thus only the substance of the jurisdictional or other procedural issue that caused termination of proceedings that will be reviewed by the court.[131]

92. In *Josef Broberg v. Norsk Hydro ASA*,[132] the claimant appealed an arbitral award under section 36 alleging that the arbitral tribunal had omitted to consider all of the claims submitted to it, and that an award on the substantive issues had thus not been issued. The Court of Appeal found that the arbitral tribunal had addressed and rejected the claims submitted to it. Thus, the arbitral tribunal had decided on the substantive issues in dispute. Consequently, the award could not be appealed under section 36.

93. The Court of Appeal reached the same conclusion in a subsequent investment arbitration case.[133] In that case, the arbitral tribunal had dismissed a case for lack of an

128. *OAO Arkhangelskoe Geologodobychnoe Predpriyatie v. Archangel Diamond Corporation*, judgment by the Svea Court of Appeal made on 15 Nov. 2005 in case no T 2277-04.
129. *Johan Forsgren v. AFA Trygghetsförsäkringsaktiebolag*, decision by the Svea Court of Appeal made on 1[illegible] Mar. 2009 in case no T 5004-08.
130. *Nicolas Persson v. Onetwocom AB*, judgment by the Svea Court of Appeal made on 21 Feb. 2007 in case no T 6726-05.
131. Finn Madsen, *Commercial Arbitration in Sweden – A Commentary on the Arbitration Act (1999:116) and the Rules of the Arbitration Institute of the Stockholm Chamber of Commerce*, 267; Kaj Hobér, *International Commercial Arbitration in Sweden*, 350.
132. *Josef Broberg v. Norsk Hydro ASA*, decision by the Svea Court of Appeal made on 4 February 2004 in case no T 1747-03.
133. *William Nagel v. Czech Republic*, decision by the Svea Court of Appeal made on 30 May 2005 in case no T 9059-03.

arbitration agreement. The arbitration agreement relied upon in the proceedings required that an investment had been made for someone to be considered a party. To reach its decision, the arbitral tribunal had to determine if a particular matter should be qualified as an 'investment' or not. The arbitral tribunal found that the conditions of an investment were not met and dismissed the case. The Court of Appeal found that the arbitral tribunal's decision to dismiss the case was closely connected to the merits of the case. Thus, the arbitral tribunal had ruled on the merits of the case and the award could not be appealed under section 36. In a comparable case from 2008,[134] the arbitral tribunal found that it lacked jurisdiction since the claimant had not made an 'investment'. The arbitral award was appealed under section 36. The Supreme Court found that the arbitral tribunal had omitted to apply the doctrine of assertion, i.e., the tribunal should have assumed that the circumstances referred to by the claimant were correct, which the Supreme Court found would have meant that the arbitral tribunal had jurisdiction. Hence, the Supreme Court reversed the arbitral award.

94. The Court of Appeal may revise the award. The Court of Appeal, however, has no right to order the arbitral tribunal to resume the proceedings. If dealing with an award in which the arbitral tribunal has declined jurisdiction for lack of a binding arbitration agreement, a binding judgment from the Court of Appeal will be decisive for whether a binding and applicable arbitration agreement covers the issues in dispute.[135] Accordingly, the court's judgment in this respect becomes res judicata.

95. A reversed award does not automatically result in new arbitral proceedings. In order to resume the proceedings the claimant must file a new request for arbitration.[136] The initiation of new proceedings raises the question whether the same arbitral tribunal is still mandated to decide the case on the merits, or whether a new arbitral tribunal should be constituted. The tribunal's mandate is, according to the Act, completed when the tribunal has delivered a final award. Hence, it may be inferred that a new arbitral tribunal should be constituted. This issue has, however, not yet been decided by the Supreme Court.

3. *Section 36(2): Appeal on Costs of Award Declining Jurisdiction*

96. According to section 36(2), an award in which the arbitral tribunal does not decide on the issues submitted to it can also be appealed with respect to allocation of costs. The appeal does not require a party to challenge or appeal the award in itself. However, such action for review of the costs allocation can be brought only if the arbitration proceedings were terminated by an award declining jurisdiction, and thus not if the proceedings were terminated without a ruling on the merits for other reasons, e.g.,

134. *Petrobart Limited v. The Kyrgyz Republic*, judgment by the Supreme Court made on 28 Mar. 2008 in case no T 2113-06, NJA 2008 p. 406.
135. Govt. bill 1998/99:35, 'Ny lag om skiljeförfarande', 238.
136. Govt. bill 1998/99:35, 'Ny lag om skiljeförfarande', 230–231.

withdrawal.[137] The costs allocation in a situation of withdrawal may only be challenged by an action to set aside the award under section 34.[138]

97. A question of allocation of the arbitration costs under section 36(2) of the Act was determined by the Supreme Court in the case *H.H. v. Handelshögskolan.*[139] The arbitration proceedings had been conducted in two parts. In the first proceedings, one of the parties had withdrawn a claim. In the next proceedings, the party pleaded the same claim that it had previously withdrawn. This time the arbitral tribunal declined jurisdiction. The award was appealed under section 36, and the Supreme Court found that the arbitral tribunal had jurisdiction and thus granted the appeal. The claimant had also appealed the allocation of costs under section 36(2). The Supreme Court annulled the tribunal's decision on costs. However, the Supreme Court declined jurisdiction on the question of costs allocation in the award. As there was a binding arbitration agreement between the parties, the allocation of costs was to be determined by the tribunal. Accordingly, the Supreme Court remitted this question to the tribunal.

C. Appeal against Arbitrator's Compensation

98. Unlike under many other arbitration laws, the tribunal may determine its own remuneration under the Act. For reasons of balance, the parties may appeal the tribunal's decision on compensation to a court of law. Further, because a decision on the tribunal's compensation needs only be a majority decision, section 41 also enables an arbitrator to appeal the tribunal's majority decision on compensation. Section 41 further stipulates that the award must include clear instructions on the actions to be taken by a party that wishes to appeal an award on costs. Nevertheless, lack of instructions does not constitute grounds for setting aside the award.[140]

99. A party (or an arbitrator) who wishes to appeal an award on the tribunal's compensation may bring an action in the District Court. The action must be brought within three months from the date upon which the party received the award, or as regards an arbitrator, within three months from delivery of the award. If the award has been corrected, supplemented, or interpreted in accordance with section 32 of the Act, the action must be brought within three months from the date when the party received the award in its final wording, or as regards an arbitrator, within three months from the date when the award was delivered in its final wording.

100. A party may only appeal the tribunal's decision on compensation as to the amount of the tribunal's fees and expenses. Allocation of those fees and expenses as between the parties to the tribunal may be reviewed only in the course of proceedings

137. Kaj Hobér, *International Commercial Arbitration in Sweden*, 350.
138. Govt. bill 1998/99:35, 'Ny lag om skiljeförfarande', 155.
139. *H.H. v. Handelshögskolan*, judgment by the Supreme Court made on 30 Nov. 2010 in case no T 3258-09, NJA 2010 p. 600.
140. Kaj Hobér, *International Commercial Arbitration in Sweden*, 177.

to set aside the award which, however, presupposes that the arbitrators have committed a procedural error.

The scope of the District Court's review when the tribunal's compensation is appealed is not limited to procedural irregularities. Upon request by a party, the court may consider, for example, whether the tribunal's compensation is unreasonable considering the time dedicated to the assignment and the complexity of the case.[141] If only one party files proceedings, the reduction of the tribunal's compensation also applies in favour of the other party according to section 41(2) of the Act.[142]

In *Soyak International Construction and Investment Inc. v. Hobér, Kraus and Melis*,[143] the Supreme Court examined section 41. In appealing the tribunal's compensation, Soyak requested that the compensation be reduced. The issue before the Supreme Court was whether Soyak could submit an appeal on the tribunal's compensation, as the decision on costs had been made by the SCC under the SCC Rules, and not by the tribunal itself. The Supreme Court held that a party has not forfeited its right to appeal under section 41 only because the tribunal's compensation had been determined by an arbitral institution, since the parties were ordered to pay the tribunal's compensation in the dispositive part of the award. Hence, the SCC's cost decision was enforceable under section 37. According to the Supreme Court, section 41 applies to all decisions on compensation that are included in the dispositive part of the award, provided that the whole decision on compensation is included explicitly or by a clear reference. It is noteworthy that the Supreme Court's decision merely concerned the question whether the claimant had standing to appeal the decision on costs. The Supreme Court did not, however, assess the question whether the tribunal's compensation was reasonable in substance.

101. The importance of the case is probably limited in practice. Although a decision by an institution may be appealed under section 41, the parties have accepted the related fee structure when agreeing to a certain set of institutional rules. As regards the SCC, the formula for determining the tribunal's fees is described in the Rules and is thus transparent and foreseeable.[144]

102. Appeals against the tribunal's compensation are rare and the Soyak case has not – nor can it be expected to – increase the number of appeals. One reason for the scarce number of appeals may be that the chances of prevailing are considered small. In addition, tribunals seated in Sweden are considered fairly cost-conscious. At least,

141. Lars Heuman, *Arbitration Law of Sweden: Practice and Procedure*, 566–567; Kaj Hobér, *International Commercial Arbitration in Sweden*, 178.
142. SOU 1994:81 'Ny lag om skiljeförfarande', 202; Govt. bill 1998/99:35, 'Ny lag om skiljeförfarande', 168.
143. *Soyak International Construction & Investment Inc. v. Werner Melis, Kaj Hobér and Steffen Kraus*, decision by the Supreme Court made on 3 Dec. 2008 in case no Ö 4227-06, NJA 2008 p. 1118.
144. For an overview of how costs are determined by the SCC, see Marie Öhrström, *The 'Soyak' Case – Judicial Terrorism or Justified Cost Control?*, Stockholm International Arbitration Review 252 et seq. (2008).

section 41 reduces the risk of tribunals overcompensating themselves when deciding on their compensation.[145]

D. Exclusion Agreements

103. Under section 51 of the Act, the parties may enter into an exclusion agreement, i.e., a waiver of the right to challenge an award. An exclusion agreement is valid between parties in a strictly commercial relationship who are not domiciled and do not have their place of business in Sweden.[146] An exclusion agreement must be made in writing and must expressly refer to the parties' waiver of the right to challenge an award.[147] By way of an exclusion agreement the parties may waive the right to invoke any or all challenge grounds under section 34.[148] If one or both of the parties are domiciled or have their place of business in Sweden an exclusion agreement will not be valid.

104. As set forth in section 51, the parties may only waive the right to challenge the award under section 34 by way of an exclusion agreement. The right to claim invalidity of the award under section 33 cannot be waived.[149] Whether the same applies to the right of appeal under section 36 is unsettled.[150]

IV. PROCEDURAL ASPECTS

105. Under section 43, actions for invalidity and challenges to awards must be brought in the Court of Appeal. If the arbitral award does not state the place of the arbitration, the Svea Court of Appeal in Stockholm is the competent court. An appeal against the arbitrators' compensation is brought in the relevant District Court.

106. The main rule is that a challenge action can only be tried by one-instance in order to limit costs and to promote consistent application of the Act.[151] The Court of Appeal's decision may only be appealed to the Supreme Court if the Court of Appeal grants leave to appeal. According to section 43(2), the Court may grant leave to appeal to the Supreme Court if the case involves an important precedent. In practice, the Court of Appeal seldom grants such a right to appeal.[152] In this respect, the Act is stricter than

145. Marie Öhrström, *The 'Soyak' Case – Judicial Terrorism or Justified Cost Control?*, 257.
146. Where none of the parties is domiciled or has its place of business in Sweden, such parties may in a commercial relationship through an express, written agreement exclude or limit application of the grounds for setting aside an award as set forth in s. 34. An award which is subject to such an agreement will be recognized and enforced in Sweden in accordance with the rules applicable to a foreign award.
147. Lars Heuman, *Arbitration Law of Sweden: Practice and Procedure*, 716.
148. Kaj Hobér, *International Commercial Arbitration in Sweden*, 344.
149. Stefan Lindskog, *Skiljeförfarande: En kommentar*, 1204.
150. Stefan Lindskog, *Skiljeförfarande: En kommentar*, 1211.
151. Govt. bill 1998/99:35, 'Ny lag om skiljeförfarande', 171; Lars Heuman, *Arbitration Law of Sweden: Practice and Procedure*, 574.
152. Hans Bagner, *The Swedish Challenge Procedure*, in *Festskrift till Lars Heuman* 22 (Jan Kleineman et al. eds., Jure Förlag AB 2008).

the Model Law,[153] as under the Model Law an appeal against a challenge decision by a court is not conditional on leave to appeal being granted.[154] In recent years the Courts of Appeal seem to have granted leave to appeal to the Supreme Court somewhat more often than in previous years. Nevertheless, the general rule remains that awards are set aside only in exceptional cases.

107. The Swedish one-instance model promotes quick termination at limited expense.[155] To maintain the objective that setting aside proceedings are to be resolved quickly and at limited cost, leave to appeal should not be granted routinely.[156] The Courts of Appeal regularly emphasize the importance of finality when hearing challenges of arbitral awards.

108. As explained above, Swedish courts tend to uphold arbitral awards.[157] Even so, the losing party may bring a challenge action to delay enforcement of the award or to force a settlement. A challenge action does not automatically stay execution of the award; execution is stayed only if the Court of Appeal deems this appropriate.[158] Even if the court does not stay execution of the award, a challenge action – whether frivolous or not – will cause the opposing party additional costs. In this context, it is good to note that as a general rule, the loser pays principle prevails in Sweden as regards actions before national courts.

153. In this respect, the Act also differs from general Swedish procedural law, as it is the Court of Appeal itself, not the Supreme Court, that decides whether to grant leave to appeal.
154. See Jernej Sekolec & Nils Eliasson, *Ch. 9: The UNCITRAL Model Law on Arbitration and the Swedish Arbitration Akt: A Comparison*, 239.
155. Lars Heuman, *Arbitration Law of Sweden: Practice and Procedure*, 574.
156. Filip De Ly, *Comment: Comparative Observations on Arbitral Awards and Setting Aside*, 511–513.
157. Lars Heuman, *Arbitration Law of Sweden: Practice and Procedure*, 574.
158. Such reason can be that the Court of Appeal finds reasonable grounds for the challenge action, which the applicant needs to prove, see *Götaverken Arendal AB v. General National Maritime Transport Company*, decision by the Supreme Court made on 13 Aug. 1979, NJA 1979 p. 527; *Forenede Cresco v. Datema*, decision by the Supreme Court made on 23 Nov. 1992 in case no Ö 3659-92, NJA 1992 p. 733 and *Société Planavergne S.A. v. K.B. i Stockholm AB*, decision by the Supreme Court made on 30 Sep. 2003 in case no Ö 3390-01, NJA 2003 p. 379.

CHAPTER 10

Application of the New York Convention by Swedish Courts

Pontus Ewerlöf

I. A BRIEF BACKGROUND

1. Arbitration has long been an attractive tool for commercial dispute resolution, yet recognition and enforcement of awards, from an international standpoint, were initially restricted only to those countries in which they had been rendered. In the 1920s, the League of Nations adopted two treaties, namely the Geneva Protocol on Arbitration Clauses (1923) and the Geneva Convention on the Execution of Foreign Arbitral Awards (1927), so that arbitral awards became internationally enforceable (albeit only among the contracting member States). However, by the 1950s, there was some dissatisfaction with the Geneva treaties and in 1953 the ICC presented a report and a preliminary draft convention,[1] which, with some modifications, was subsequently adopted by the United Nations on 10 June 1958. The Convention on the Recognition and Enforcement of Foreign Arbitral Awards, 1958 (the New York Convention), saw the light of day.

2. The 1958 New York Convention is, and has been since its entry into force, a key instrument in international arbitration, effectively harmonizing the international scene on recognition and enforcement of foreign arbitral awards.[2] At present, no less than

1. The ICC International Court of Arbitration Bulletin Vol. 9/No. 1 – May 1998, *Report and Preliminary Draft Convention adopted by the Committee on International Commercial Arbitration, 13 March 1953, ICC Publication no 174*, 7–9.
2. It has been suggested that, after more than fifty years in existence, the New York Convention is in need of modernization, see e.g., van den Berg, *50 Years of the New York Convention*, ICCA International Arbitration Conference, 2008, 649 et seq. The main reason for revision summarized by van den Berg is that a number of provisions are outdated, unclear or missing and thus insufficient to support maintenance of the object and purpose of the New York Convention in

148 countries are contracting members of the New York Convention. Sweden ratified the New York Convention on 28 January 1972.[3] In addition to the New York Convention, the UNCITRAL Arbitration Rules, adopted 2010 (UNCITRAL Rules) and the UNCITRAL Model Law on International Commercial Arbitration 1985, with amendments as adopted in 2006 (Model Law), have been largely influential in international arbitration practice.

3. This chapter elaborates on the Swedish perspective on recognition and enforcement of arbitral awards, having regard to the influence and applicability of the New York Convention. First, a concise summation is provided of the Swedish legal framework and the distinction between foreign and domestic awards. Second, the procedure for enforcement of Swedish arbitral awards is summarized, followed by a thorough analysis of the steps in enforcing foreign arbitral awards and the grounds for refusal that may be invoked. The chapter concludes with a brief review of how Swedish courts in practice deal with recognition and enforcement of foreign arbitral awards.

4. The issue of sovereign immunity in relation to execution of arbitral awards against property or assets belonging to foreign States is touched upon only briefly. Neither the New York Convention nor the Swedish Arbitration Act *(Sw: Lag (1999:116) om skiljeförfarande)* (the Act) deals with this issue. However, it should be noted that a plea of sovereign immunity by a State, which is a party to an arbitration agreement, may certainly lead to potential problems, not only in the arbitration, but also at the stage of enforcement of the arbitral award.[4]

II. THE SWEDISH LEGAL FRAMEWORK ON THE RECOGNITION AND ENFORCEMENT OF ARBITRAL AWARDS

5. Sweden ratified the New York Convention in 1972 without either the 'reciprocity' reservation or the 'commercial nature' reservation available to the signatories. Accordingly, all foreign arbitral awards are enforceable in Sweden, irrespective of where they are rendered and whether they are of a commercial nature or not. The provisions of the New York Convention have been incorporated into the Act. Since the New York Convention is not incorporated by reference, but transformed into Swedish law through specific statutory provisions, the implementation of Article V of the New York Convention in the Act demonstrates slight variations from the wording of the New York

---

the future. The submitted need for, or even more significant, the prospects of a revision of the New York Convention is controversial. The main argument against such a revision is that it would be impossible to have all of the signatories to the New York Convention agreeing on suggested amendments. For a further discussion in this respect, see Gaillard *50 Years of the New York Convention*, ICCA International Arbitration Conference, 2008, 689 et seq., and Lamm, *ibid.*, 697 et seq.

3. The New York Arbitration Convention, http://www.newyorkconvention.org/contracting-states, (accessed 9 Apr. 2013) and Govt. bill 1998/99:35, p. 37.

4. For a thorough discussion in this respect, see Hobér, *International Commercial Arbitration in Sweden* 10 et seq. (Oxford U. Press 2011) describing, *inter alia*, the UN Convention on Jurisdictional Immunities of States and Their Property, adopted by the UN General Assembly in 2004.

Convention.[5] These variations notwithstanding, the Swedish Supreme Court has always stressed the importance of respecting the objective and purpose of the New York Convention and the Foreign Arbitration Agreements and Arbitral Awards Act (1929 Act)[6] and, subsequently, the Act.[7] In *Société Planavergne SA v. KB i Stockholm AB*, the Supreme Court concluded that the Swedish provisions on enforcement of foreign arbitral awards should be interpreted in light of 'the general efforts to facilitate enforcement which [is] the main objective of the [New York] Convention'.[8] The difference between the wording of the Act and the New York Convention is thus not intended to produce any substantive difference in practice (see further discussion in this respect in section V.B below). Accordingly, it is safe to assume that parties relying on Article V of the New York Convention for recognition and enforcement of an arbitral award in Sweden can expect the courts to apply foreseeable and internationally established principles on procedural due process, arbitrability and public policy.[9]

6. The generally arbitration-friendly approach of Swedish courts implies that the provisions of the New York Convention are to be seen as a minimum requirement. Hence, it may be argued that the New York Convention does not necessarily prevent the Swedish courts from enforcing foreign arbitral awards, which would not be recognized by courts in another contracting State.[10] It has been held in legal literature that if a foreign arbitral award is invalidated in the State of its origin for reasons totally unacceptable from a Swedish point of view, this would not be an impediment to enforcement in Sweden, notwithstanding that the award lacks legal force in the State of its origin.[11] However, it has been held that, although the New York Convention does

5. Hobér, *International Commercial Arbitration in Sweden*, 358–359.
6. (*Sw: Lag (1929:147) om utländska skiljeavtal och skiljedomar*). The former Swedish arbitration act of 1929 was divided between the Arbitration Act 1929 (*Sw: Lag (1929:145) om skiljemän*) (applicable to domestic arbitrations) and the 1929 Foreign Arbitration Agreements and Arbitral Awards Act (applicable to foreign arbitrations).
7. Hobér, *International Commercial Arbitration in Sweden*, 359, and Andersson, et al., *Arbitration in Sweden* 184 (Jure Förlag AB 2011).
8. See also the case of *Götaverken Arendal AB v. General National Maritime Transport Company*, decision by the Supreme Court made on 13 August 1979, NJA 1979 p. 527 where the Supreme Court, in applying the 1929 Act, referred to 'the overall objective of the New York Convention to facilitate enforcement'. An unofficial English translation of the judgment is to be found, *inter alia*, in *VI Yearbook of Commercial Arbitration*, 1981, 237–242. Since the 1929 Act was also based on Art. V of the New York Convention, case law under the 1929 Act may also be relevant under the Act.
9. Hobér, *International Commercial Arbitration in Sweden*, 359. See also Lindskog, *Skiljeförfarande – En kommentar* 1165 (Norstedts Juridik AB 2012).
10. See Art. II of the New York Convention, which requires enforcement jurisdictions to allow applicants to rely on treaties and laws that are more favourable than the New York Convention itself.
11. Lindskog, *Skiljeförfarande – En kommentar*, 1146 and 1149. Lindskog refers to this as a kind of inversed *ordre public*, applicable e.g., in cases where an arbitrator has been disqualified because of gender, sexual preferences, ethnicity or because the arbitrator has an 'undesired' political persuasion. See the Amsterdam Court of Appeal decision on 28 Apr. 2009 in *Yukos Capital S.A.R.L. v. OAO Rosneft*, No. 200.005.269/01, further discussed by Bachand, *When – If Ever – Should Failure to Challenge an Award before the Courts of the Seat Amount to a Waiver of New York Convention Defences* in *Between East and West: Essays in Honour of Ulf Franke* 10–11 (Hobér et al. ed. 2010).

not oblige courts to refuse enforcement even if a ground set out in Article V is established, courts of contracting States must exercise a certain measure of restraint from enforcing foreign arbitral awards where an opposing party furnishes proof of a ground for refusal as contained in Article V(1) of the New York Convention, or that one of the circumstances set out in Article V(2) of the New York Convention exists.[12]

7. Under the Act, there is a distinction between domestic (Swedish) and foreign arbitral awards with respect to their recognition and enforcement.[13] This distinction is retained from the 1929 Act.

8. The principles on recognition and enforcement of foreign arbitral awards are set out in sections 52–60 of the Act. The general rule, stated in section 53 of the Act, is that foreign arbitral awards, which are based on an arbitration agreement, are to be recognized and enforced in Sweden. Exceptions from the general rule, i.e., grounds for refusal, are contained in subsequent sections 54 and 55 of the Act, and the procedure of *exequatur* is set out in sections 56–60 of the Act.

9. In contrast, Swedish arbitral awards are, with some minor exceptions, treated in the same manner as judgments of Swedish courts with respect to their enforcement. This implies, *inter alia*, that Swedish arbitral awards will not have to undergo any procedure of *exequatur* in order to be enforceable in Sweden. Instead, the Swedish Enforcement Code is directly applicable to such awards.

III. THE DISTINCTION BETWEEN FOREIGN AND DOMESTIC AWARDS

10. The significance of whether an award is to be considered domestic or foreign is quite substantial since, as touched upon previously, a domestic award (as opposed to a foreign award) is not required to undergo a procedure of *exequatur*. This is also the purpose of section 52 of the Act, namely, to divide arbitral awards into two categories (i.e., domestic or foreign), in effect categorizing arbitral awards either as directly recognizable and enforceable[14] (domestic awards), or as awards which require a certain examination prior to their recognition and enforcement (foreign awards).[15] Foreign awards are enforced in accordance with the New York Convention, as incorporated into the Act, and the views expressed in the New York Convention are thus in principle decisive.[16] To this end, examination of foreign arbitral awards is mainly focused on whether grounds exist for refusal as set out in sections 54 and 55 of the Act. However, prior to any such examination, the nationality of the arbitral award

12. See Möller, *Discretion Pursuant to Art. V of the New York Convention*, in *Between East and West: Essays in Honour of Ulf Franke* 331 (Hobér et al. ed., 2010).
13. See, e.g., the Model Law, which deals with all awards rendered in international commercial arbitration in a uniform manner irrespective of where they were made.
14. See, however, s. IV below with respect to the summary review of Swedish arbitral awards performed by the Enforcement Authority prior to enforcement.
15. Lindskog, *Skiljeförfarande – En kommentar*, 1142.
16. *Ibid.*, 1231.

must inevitably be determined. This is the gateway to recognition and enforcement of a foreign award.

11. The first determinative prerequisite for a foreign arbitral award, as set out in section 52(1) of the Act, is that it is made abroad. Conversely, all arbitral awards made in Sweden are regarded as Swedish arbitral awards, notwithstanding the nationality of the parties and the arbitral tribunal. Swedish law thus applies a territorial test when determining the nationality of the arbitral award.[17] In conjunction with that, section 52(2) of the Act states that an award is considered to have been made in the country where the place of arbitration is situated. Pursuant to section 22 of the Act, it is primarily the parties who determine the place of arbitration, failing which, the arbitrators determine the place of arbitration.

12. As to what is to be understood as the place of arbitration, the *travaux préparatoires* to the Act state that the determining factor is where the arbitral proceedings have taken place. Consequently, an award made in arbitral proceedings in Sweden would be considered as domestic.[18] Inversely, an award made in arbitral proceedings abroad would be considered as foreign. The *travaux préparatoires* to the Act continue that even if the parties have agreed that the arbitral proceedings are to take place in a locality outside of Sweden, but part of the arbitral proceedings have taken place in Sweden, then the arbitral award is still considered as foreign.[19]

13. Although section 52 of the Act is seemingly clear and unambiguous, the provision has previously given rise to certain interpretative difficulties. It has been held that, in order for a Swedish court to accept the place of arbitration agreed upon by the parties, or otherwise determined by the arbitrators, at least a 'tangible connection' to that place must exist, e.g., that at least part of the arbitral proceedings takes place there, or that one of the parties, or the arbitrators, are of the nationality of that place, or similar.[20]

17. The Act is thus based on the same principles as, e.g., Art. 1(2) of the Model Law and Art. I(1) of the New York Convention. See also Govt. bill 1998/99:35, p. 198, Madsen, *Commercial Arbitration in Sweden* 369 (Oxford U. Press 2007), and Heuman, *Arbitration Law of Sweden: Practice and Procedure* 722 (Juris Publg. Inc. 2003).
18. See Govt. bill 1998/99:35, p. 198, and Madsen, *Commercial Arbitration in Sweden*, 369.
19. See Govt. bill 1998/99:35, pp. 113 et seq. and 198. See also Madsen, *Commercial Arbitration in Sweden*, 370, and Heuman, *Arbitration Law of Sweden: Practice and Procedure*, 722.
20. See Govt. bill 1998/99:35, p. 113 et seq., and *Titan Corporation v. Alcatel CITSA*, decision by the Svea Court of Appeal made on 28 Feb. 2008 in case no T 1038-05, RH 2005:1. In this respect, it should first be noted that, pursuant to s. 22 of the Act, the arbitrators may hold hearings and meetings elsewhere than the agreed or determined place of arbitration. Reference to the place of arbitration as being a geographical place for the arbitral proceedings thus gives limited guidance in interpreting what is considered as the 'place' of arbitration. Second, it may be questioned if there is any (deliberate) discrepancy between the first and the second para. of s. 52 of the Act, i.e., that the arbitral award may be rendered elsewhere than the agreed or determined place of arbitration. For a thorough discussion on this matter, see Lindskog, *Skiljeförfarande - En kommentar*, 1153 et seq., and n .6. See the English House of Lords case *Hiscox v. Outhwaite* [1991] 1 W.L.R. 545 (decided in 1991) and commented on by e.g., Bagner, *Recognition and Enforcement of Foreign Arbitral Awards – A Global Commentary on the New York Convention* 22–23 (Kronke et al. ed. 2010). The ruling of the House of Lords in this case was effectively reversed by legislation with the enactment of the English Arbitration Act 1996 (s. 53).

14. However, recent developments in the field of international arbitration challenge the view set out in the *travaux préparatoires,*[21] in legal literature[22] and lower court instances,[23] i.e., that arbitral proceedings must, in some way, be connected with the venue chosen. This 'old' view has lost its relevance in light of the Supreme Court decision in *RosInvestCo UK Ltd v. The Russian Federation*. In that decision, the Supreme Court concluded that, where the parties have agreed upon Sweden as the place for the arbitral proceedings, it is irrelevant that the parties or the arbitrators have chosen to locate meetings in other States, that the arbitrators are not Swedish, that the arbitrators have chosen to undertake work in another State or that the dispute relates to an agreement with no connection to Sweden; the place of arbitration would still be considered to be Sweden and the arbitral award would therefore be Swedish.[24] The described development is elucidated by the fact that the word 'place' is now often exchanged, or exchangeable, for the word 'seat'.[25] There now seems to be a well-established principle among Swedish and international arbitrators that the designation of the place (or seat) of arbitral proceedings is not a geographic, concrete, or tangible connection to a designated place; rather, it is a legal fiction.[26]

15. It should be borne in mind that the place (or seat) of arbitration also plays an important role in determining the *lex arbitri*, i.e., the law of the State that should govern the arbitral proceedings and the courts of the State that are competent to assist in the arbitration and to control the lawfulness of the arbitration and the award. Since the place (or seat) of arbitration is determinative for the *lex arbitri*, it may be held that an arbitral award would be considered as foreign if the arbitral proceedings are subject to

21. See SOU 1994:81 pp. 145 and 275, and Govt. bill 1998/99:35, p. 113 et seq.
22. See e.g., Heuman, *Arbitration Law of Sweden: Practice and Procedure*, 711.
23. *Titan Corporation v. Alcatel CITSA*, decision by the Svea Court of Appeal made on 28 Feb. 2008 in case no T 1038-05, RH 2005:1.
24. *RosInvestCoUK Ltd v. The Russian Federation*, decision by the Supreme Court made on 12 Nov. 2010 in case no Ö 2301-09, NJA 2010 p. 508. The conclusions of the Supreme Court should be seen in light of the heavily criticized previous decision by the Svea Court of Appeal in the Titan case (n. 23 above).
25. See e.g., Art. 20 of the SCC Rules, Art. 16 of the Swiss Rules of International Arbitration (Swiss Rules), Art. 16 of the Arbitration Rules of the London Court of International Arbitration (LCIA) and ss. 53 and 100 of the 1996 English Arbitration Act. Support can also be drawn from the stance taken by most modern institutional arbitration rules – see e.g., Art. 18(2) and (3) of the Rules of Arbitration of the International Chamber of Commerce (ICC Rules), Art. 13(2) of the AAA Rules, Art and Art. 39(b) of the WIPO Arbitration Rules (WIPO Rules). In *Himpurna California Energy Ltd (Bermuda) v. Republic of Indonesia*(2000) 25 YCA 111, para. 73 (Interim Award, UNCITRAL, 1999), the arbitral tribunal felt it necessary to move the hearing from Jakarta to The Hague as a result of an injunction ordered by the courts of Jakarta enjoining the arbitral proceedings and imposing a fine of USD 1 million per day for any breach of the injunction. See also *PT Garuda Indonesia v. Birgen Air*[2002] 1 SLR 393 (CA). See *RosInvestCO UK Ltd v. The Russian Federation*, decision by the Supreme Court made on 12 Nov. 2010 in case no Ö 2301-09, NJA 2010 p. 508.
26. Shaughnessy, *The 2007 Arbitration Rules of the Arbitration Institute of the Stockholm Chamber of Commerce*, 2 Stockholm Intl. Arbitration Rev. 267 (2005). See also Redfern & Hunter, *Law and Practice of International Arbitration* 181 (5th ed., Oxford U. Press 2009), wherein it is held that 'the place of arbitration is not merely a matter of geography. It is the territorial link between the arbitration itself and the law of the place in which that arbitration is legally situated.'

a legal system other than the Swedish legal system.[27] Inversely, an award issued abroad with arbitral proceedings subject to Swedish law may be considered as domestic.[28] Although slightly different from the view seemingly conceived by the legislator,[29] a reasonable interpretation of the concept of 'place' of arbitration under section 52 of the Act may thus be that, if the law of one State governs the arbitral proceedings, the 'place' of arbitration is considered to be in that State.[30]

16. When the place of arbitration can be determined, other points of connection (such as where the arbitral award was signed) have no significance as to the nationality of the award. However, in cases where the place of arbitration cannot be determined (i.e., the law of which State the arbitral proceedings are subject to may not be determined), the *travaux préparatoires* to the Act, as well as legal literature, suggest a presumption that the locality of the arbitral proceedings stated in the arbitral award should determine the nationality of the award, unless particular circumstances point to another locality. However, the suggested presumption should not be held as indisputable, although the party alleging that the place (or rather, seat) is another than that stated in the arbitral award carries the burden of proof for that statement.[31] If no other points of connection may be determined, it has been suggested in legal literature that the place where the award was signed (or, if that place may not be determined, the place where the chairman signed the award) may be decisive.[32]

17. It should be mentioned that the discussion regarding arbitral awards characterized as 'a-national' or 'floating', in the sense that they are detached from all national arbitration laws, has no bearing on enforceability of the award in Sweden. Under Swedish law, the territorial test applies with respect to the nationality of an arbitral award. Put differently; every arbitral award that is not rendered, or deemed to have been rendered in Sweden is a foreign award and therefore enforceable as such under the Act.[33]

---

27. See Govt. Bill 1998/99:35, p. 198, and Lindskog, *Skiljeförfarande – En kommentar*, 1145 and 1154.
28. Lindskog, *Skiljeförfarande – En kommentar*, 1154, n. 7.
29. See Govt. Bill 1998/99:35, p. 198.
30. See Lindskog, *Skiljeförfarande - En kommentar*, 1154 et seq., in particular n. 11 where Lindskog suggests that the point of departure is, that determining the place of arbitration is all about securing necessary control of law and order and thus that the relevant fact must be under which legal system the arbitral proceedings have been subjected. See also, *ibid.*, 1167, n. 20. Note that some jurisdictions, e.g., Switzerland, allow the parties to agree to make the arbitral proceedings subject to the procedural law of another State than the place for arbitration. This, however, is not the case under Swedish law since s. 46 of the Act explicitly sets forth that the Act should be applied to arbitral proceedings taking place in Sweden.
31. See Govt. Bill 1998/99:35 pp. 199 and 225; Lindskog, *Skiljeförfarande – En kommentar*, 1155 and n. 15; Madsen, *Commercial Arbitration in Sweden*, 370; and Heuman, *Arbitration Law of Sweden: Practice and Procedure*, 711 and 722.
32. Lindskog, *Skiljeförfarande – En kommentar*, 1156. However, see Heuman, *Arbitration Law of Sweden: Practice and Procedure*, 722 who states that the place where the arbitrators signed the award has no bearing on the question whether the award is foreign.
33. Hobér, *International Commercial Arbitration in Sweden*, 357, n. 4 and 37–38.

IV. ENFORCEMENT OF SWEDISH ARBITRAL AWARDS

A. Enforcement in Sweden

18. A Swedish arbitral award is enforceable with respect to all obligations imposed on the opposing party by the arbitral tribunal. This includes payment liability for monetary claims, as well as any specific performance imposed on the opposing party. In addition, recovery of costs and fees ordered by the arbitral tribunal is enforceable.[34]

19. In most cases, enforcement of Swedish arbitral awards will be unproblematic. The Swedish Enforcement Code applies and only minor differences exist between enforcement of Swedish court judgments and Swedish arbitral awards. One of these differences is that, unlike Swedish court judgments, Swedish arbitral awards are subject to a summary review prior to their execution. Swedish arbitral awards are thus not immediately enforceable. In addition, the opposing party should always be given an opportunity to state its case concerning enforcement prior to execution of the award. The latter may entail problems if enforcing the award is a matter of urgency, e.g., because the opposing party is taking measures to evade enforcement, *inter alia*, by moving or withdrawing property. The applicant is then referred to bring an action to a district court in accordance with the provisions for security measures under the Code of Judicial Procedure.[35]

20. The grounds on which the Enforcement Authority may refuse execution of a Swedish arbitral award are few and restrictively applied. The Enforcement Authority may refuse execution only where: (i) the arbitral award does not meet the requirements of written form and signature under section 31(1) of the Act, or (ii) the arbitration agreement foresees a right to challenge the award on the merits and the time for that challenge has not yet expired.[36] Moreover, if there is reason to believe that an award may be invalid and no litigation in relation thereto is pending, the Enforcement Authority should direct the party seeking enforcement to initiate court proceedings regarding the validity of the award within a month.[37] It should be noted that the scope for declaring an award invalid is very limited under section 33 of the Act. After such court proceedings are initiated, it is for the court to decide on enforcement.[38] If the party seeking enforcement fails to initiate court proceedings within the stipulated time, enforcement proceedings are to be cancelled by the court.[39]

21. The respondent in the enforcement proceedings before the Enforcement Authority cannot prevent enforcement by invoking grounds for setting aside an award under section 34 of the Act. These grounds can only be determined within the framework of challenge proceedings before the competent court.

---

34. See Andersson, et al., *Arbitration in Sweden*, 147 and 183.
35. (*Sw: Rättegångsbalk* (*1942:740*)). See Ch. 15 of the Code of Judicial Procedure.
36. Chapter 3, s. 15 of the Enforcement Code.
37. Chapter 3, s. 16 of the Enforcement Code.
38. Chapter 3, s. 18 of the Enforcement Code.
39. Chapter 3, s. 18 of the Enforcement Code.

B. Enforcement Abroad

22. Enforcing Swedish arbitral awards abroad is a matter entirely for the laws of the enforcing State. Since Sweden has ratified the New York Convention without reservation, the reciprocity requirements should not bar Swedish awards from being enforced abroad.[40] Rather, the prospects of enforcement of arbitral awards rendered in Sweden are very favourable in courts of a contracting party to the New York Convention.[41] For example, U.S. courts have confirmed national policy strongly favouring arbitration under the New York Convention and have also acknowledged that arbitration clauses are afforded special deference in light of federal policy favouring arbitration, which has led U.S. courts to refer disputes to the SCC on several occasions. Moreover, U.S. courts are also very likely to enforce awards rendered under the SCC Rules.[42]

23. It may also be mentioned that, due to the 1977 recommendation of the Chamber of Commerce and Industry of the USSR and the American Arbitration Association, the SCC Rules have long since been, and remain, a preferable choice of rules of arbitration between U.S. and Russian (previously Soviet) companies, with the SCC as the appointing authority.[43] Notably, several higher courts in Russia, Belarus, Kazakhstan and Ukraine have supported recognition and enforcement of arbitral awards made under the SCC Rules by acknowledging, *inter alia*; the legal effect and finality of an SCC award; the right to apply for enforcement of an SCC award despite an agreement for voluntary performance; SCC jurisdiction over civil law relationships; SCC jurisdiction, in the absence of a party's objection to it, over the matter in dispute; appointment and jurisdiction of the SCC by way of interpretation of the arbitration clause; the effects of receipt and responses to notices of commencement of SCC arbitral proceedings; and the limits of a (Russian) court to revise an SCC award in enforcement proceedings.[44]

40. Hobér, *International Commercial Arbitration in Sweden*, 356 et seq. and Hobér, *Enforcement of Arbitral Awards*, 1 Stockholm Arbitration Report 74 (1999).
41. Hobér, *Enforcement of Arbitral Awards*, 1 Stockholm Arbitration Report 74 (1999) and Vesselinovitch, *Enforcement of SCC and Russian Arbitration Awards in the United States Courts: An Overview*, 2 Stockholm Arbitration Report 38 (2003).
42. Vesselinovitch, *Enforcement of SCC and Russian Arbitration Awards in the United States Courts: An Overview*, 2 Stockholm Arbitration Report 42 et seq. (2003).
43. See Khvalei, *Enforcement of SCC Arbitral Awards in CIS Countries: Reflections on Arbitration History* in *Between East and West: Essays in Honour of Ulf Franke* 269 (Hobér et al. eds., 2010).
44. For an in-depth review of enforcement case law in this respect, see Khvalei, Benedictsson, *Recognition and Enforcement of Foreign Arbitral Awards in the Russian Federation*, 1 Stockholm Intl. Arbitration Rev. 23–48 (2005) and Khvalei, *Enforcement of SCC Arbitral Awards in CIS Countries: Reflections on Arbitration History*, in *Between East and West: Essays in Honour of Ulf Franke*, 269–289. See also the SCC unofficial translations of the ruling of the Supreme Court of Ukraine on 24 Nov. 2010, *RosUkrEnergo AG v. NJSC 'Naftogaz of Ukraine'*, the ruling of the Supreme Court of Ukraine on 31 Aug. 2011, *Evertrade v. Kherson Sea Commercial Port* and the decision of the Federal Commercial Court of Saint Petersburg on 10 Mar. 2011, *Odfjell SE v. Proizvodstvennoye obyedineniye 'Severnoye mashinostroitelnoye predpriyatiye'*, *Arbitration Institute of the Stockholm Chamber of Commerce Library, Court Decisions*, SCC, Web, http://www.sccinstitute.com/library/domar-2.aspx (accessed 6 Feb. 2012)

24. On this topic, it must also be noted that, since Sweden has generous rules regarding the validity of arbitration agreements, e.g., recognizing arbitration agreements which are not in writing, it would generally be difficult to prevent enforcement of an award on the basis of such an agreement (where Swedish law applies to the arbitration agreement)[45] by invoking invalidity of the agreement.[46] Entering into an arbitration agreement is no different from entering into any other agreement under Swedish law. In light thereof, an arbitration agreement is considered valid if: the contracting parties are legally qualified to conclude the arbitration agreement; the arbitration agreement has not been tainted by e.g., duress, fraud, undue influence, mistake, or other circumstance which may make the arbitration agreement void pursuant to the ordinary rules of contract law; it is clear that the parties have agreed on arbitration, and that the arbitration agreement is related to the particular legal relationship; and that the subject matter of the dispute is capable of settlement by way of arbitration.[47]

V. ENFORCEMENT OF FOREIGN ARBITRAL AWARDS

A. Recognition and Enforcement of Foreign Arbitral Awards

25. When determining an award as foreign, subsequent issues of recognition and enforcement arise. To this end, section 53 of the Act raises a presumption that an award should be recognized and enforced if it is based on an arbitration agreement, unless a ground for refusal set out in section 54 or 55 of the Act exists.[48] A distinction exists between recognition on the one hand, and enforcement on the other. Recognition is merely a matter of recognizing the arbitral award as having legal effect, i.e., acknowledging the award's legal force and thereby concurrently granting it precedential effect to prospective subsequent rulings, after which enforcement may be sought separately. Moreover, it entails res judicata for claims based on the issue ruled upon.[49] Enforcement, however, entails that the award is considered as a final and binding judgment of a Swedish court,[50] effectively authorizing the Enforcement Authority to carry out enforcement.

26. Section 53 of the Act is largely in concurrence with Articles II and III of the New York Convention, though with the significant difference that there is no requirement

45. On the issue of determining the law applicable to the arbitration agreement under Swedish law, see section V.B.1 below.
46. See Hobér, *International Commercial Arbitration in Sweden*, 356 et seq. and Hobér, *Enforcement of Arbitral Awards*, 1 Stockholm Arbitration Report 74 (1999).
47. See Hobér, *International Commercial Arbitration in Sweden*, 91 et seq.
48. See s. 53 of the Act and the Supreme Court judgment *Lenmorniiproekt OAO v. Arne Larsson & Partners AB*, decision of the Supreme Court made on 16 Apr. 2010 in case no Ö 13-09, NJA 2010 p. 219.
49. Lindskog, *Skiljeförfarande – En kommentar*, 1160; Madsen, *Commercial Arbitration in Sweden*, 372 et seq. and Hobér, *International Commercial Arbitration in Sweden*, 358. See also Lindskog, *Skiljeförfarande – En kommentar*, 1160, where Lindskog suggests that the scope of legal effect should be determined by the law applicable to the arbitral award.
50. Madsen, *Commercial Arbitration in Sweden*, 373.

that the arbitral agreement be in writing.[51] In this respect, however, it is held that section 53 of the Act is not applicable to statutory arbitration since recognition and enforcement thereunder requires an (arbitration) 'agreement'. Rather, with respect to awards rendered in statutory arbitration it is likely that these will be treated in the same manner as foreign court judgments.[52] Moreover, no limitations exist as to nationality of an award, and Sweden has not made any reservations to the New York Convention with regard to restricting the application of the New York Convention solely to arbitral awards made in other contracting States or solely to disputes arising from commercial relationships.[53]

27. To enforce a foreign arbitral award, the award must undergo the procedure of *exequatur* set out in sections 56–60 of the Act. In that procedure, the grounds for refusal set out in sections 54 and 55 are tried. However, the distinction between recognition and enforcement should again be noted. Recognition of a foreign award (which will not automatically lead to enforcement of the award) does not require a procedure of *exequatur*. Instead, it is for the court or arbitral tribunal, in the proceedings to which the issue of recognition has arisen, to apply sections 52–60 of the Act (particularly the issue of grounds for refusal set out in sections 54 and 55). Hence, it is solely in enforcement of a foreign arbitral award that the procedure of *exequatur* has to be initiated.[54] In this context, it should also be mentioned that enforcement of a foreign award cannot be sought against a third party.[55]

28. The procedure of *exequatur* is initiated by lodging an application for enforcement of a foreign arbitral award with the Svea Court of Appeal.[56] Thus, the Svea Court of Appeal is the exclusive forum for the procedure of *exequatur*. It may be noted that, as a rule, the proceedings are limited to submissions in writing. The procedure of *exequatur* implicitly contains the issue of recognition, although it focuses on the issue

51. Lindskog, *Skiljeförfarande – En kommentar*, 1142. See Art. 7, Option I(3) of the Model Law, as adopted in 2006, which provides that '[A]n arbitration agreement is in writing if its content is recorded in any form, whether or not the arbitration agreement or contract has been concluded orally, by conduct, or by other means'.
52. Lindskog, *Skiljeförfarande – En kommentar*, 1158, Madsen, *Commercial Arbitration in Sweden*, 373 and Heuman, *Arbitration Law of Sweden: Practice and Procedure*, 722.
53. Lindskog, *Skiljeförfarande – En kommentar*, 1158, Madsen, *Commercial Arbitration in Sweden*, 373, n. 9 and Heuman, *Arbitration Law of Sweden: Practice and Procedure*, 718.
54. See s. 56 of the Act, 'An application for the *enforcement* of a foreign award shall be lodged with the Svea Court of Appeal.' (emphasis added). See also Lindskog, *Skiljeförfarande – En kommentar*, 1143, 1160, 1164 and 1184, and Madsen, *Commercial Arbitration in Sweden*, 386.
55. See *The estate of Juan Aramendía Rosas v. NCC International AB.* decision by the Svea Court of Appeal made on 16 Apr. 2012 in case no Ö 8038-10. In this case, the respondent to the arbitral proceedings was a branch of a Norwegian subsidiary of NCC International AB. However, the Norwegian subsidiary had been liquidated in 2006. The Svea Court of Appeal stated that, to enable enforcement of the arbitral award against the respondent to enforcement proceedings (in this case, NCC International AB), the applicant must show that the respondent to the enforcement proceedings has assumed the obligations under the arbitral award and thus is the proper party to the enforcement proceedings. The court found that the applicant failed in this respect. Consequently, the court dismissed the application for enforcement. The judgment of the court has been appealed to the Supreme Court.
56. See s. 56 of the Act.

of whether grounds exist for refusal to enforce the foreign award.[57] A consequence of an award being recognized is that the arbitral award, as mentioned above, gains legal effect,[58] i.e., the award is executable, it may be invoked in other proceedings and it constitutes res judicata. However, if grounds for refusal set out in sections 54 and 55 of the Act exist, the foreign award will not be granted legal effect.[59]

29. The application for enforcement is required to contain the arbitral award in the original, or a certified copy thereof, appended to the application. However, the Act does not require that the original arbitration agreement, or a duly certified copy thereof, is provided to the court (as opposed to Article IV of the New York Convention). This is probably the case since, in principle, oral arbitration agreements are accepted as valid. However, if a party contests that an arbitration agreement exists, the invoking party must provide evidence of the agreement's existence (which, of course, poses difficulties in any case where the agreement is not in writing).[60] With regard to the authenticity of the required award, its translation and the existence of an arbitration agreement, Swedish procedural rules are likely to apply.[61] It may be noted that the documents do not have to be authenticated.[62]

30. Furthermore, a certified translation of the entire award into Swedish must be submitted, unless the Svea Court of Appeal decides otherwise. It is within the Svea Court of Appeal's discretion to assess whether it can sufficiently comprehend the contents of a foreign award drafted in a foreign language. A certified translation is seldom required if the arbitral award is drafted in Danish or Norwegian. With respect to arbitral awards drafted in English, it has been held in the *travaux préparatoires* and in legal literature that such awards may also be accepted without translation.[63] However, there is no firm practice in this respect and it should therefore be emphasized that this issue is dealt with by the court on a case-by-case basis.[64] Moreover, in any event Swedish procedural law requires submissions and statements in court to be drafted and presented in Swedish. Hence, should a party be required to prove the existence of an arbitration agreement, the Svea Court of Appeal would likely require a translation of the agreement.

57. See ss 54 and 55 of the Act, with explicit reference to 'recognition', as well as 'enforcement'.
58. Lindskog, *Skiljeförfarande – En kommentar*, 1160 and Madsen, *Commercial Arbitration in Sweden*, 372 et seq. See also Heuman, *Arbitration Law of Sweden: Practice and Procedure*, 719 et seq.
59. Lindskog, *Skiljeförfarande – En kommentar*, 1183.
60. See s. 58 of the Act, Govt. bill 1998/99:35, p. 203, and Govt. bill 1971:131, p. 41; Madsen, *Commercial Arbitration in Sweden*, 373 and 375 and Heuman, *Arbitration Law of Sweden: Practice and Procedure*, 744.
61. Madsen, *Commercial Arbitration in Sweden*, 387 et seq.
62. Madsen, *Commercial Arbitration in Sweden*, 387.
63. See Govt. bill 1998/99:35, pp. 203 and 247 et seq.; Lindskog, *Skiljeförfarande – En kommentar*, 1184; Madsen, *Commercial Arbitration in Sweden*, 387 et seq.; and Heuman, *Arbitration Law of Sweden: Practice and Procedure*, 743.
64. See, however, *Pamer GmbH v. Gert Wolfgang Benkert*, decision by the Supreme Court made on 9 Jun. 2011 in case no Ö 5970-09, NJA 2011 p. 345, with regard to translation of court rulings in enforcement proceedings under the Brussels I Regulation, wherein the Supreme Court stated that in most cases documents in English would be acceptable.

31. The application should be handled swiftly and often enough, as previously mentioned, the court's decision could be based on the documents alone without a hearing.[65] It may be mentioned that, pursuant to section 58 of the Act, the court may postpone its decision on enforcement pending the outcome of challenge proceedings or when the opposing party has requested a stay of enforcement proceedings. In these situations, the court may order (upon request by the applicant) that the opposing party provides sufficient security. It should, however, be emphasized that parallel challenge proceedings will not as a rule postpone enforcement proceedings unless the opposing party shows that the challenge is likely to succeed.[66] It is safe to say that a postponement in enforcement proceedings is reluctantly granted, in light of the courts' explicit aspiration to facilitate enforcement of arbitral awards.[67]

B. Grounds for Refusing Recognition and Enforcement of a Foreign Award

32. The grounds for refusal set out in section 54 of the Act correspond to Article V(1) of the New York Convention.[68] As evident from the Supreme Court's statements in *Götaverken*[69] and *Société Planavergne*[70] referred to above, the overall objective of the New York Convention, i.e., to facilitate enforcement, will be loyally pursued by Swedish courts. Accordingly, interpretations of section 54 of the Act should pay great attention to Article V of the New York Convention, as well as international case law surrounding it.[71] As set forth in section 54 of the Act, recognition and enforcement of a foreign award 'shall' be refused if grounds for refusal exist. This may be compared with the New York Convention and the Model Law, which both provide a measure of discretion for the courts in stating that a foreign award 'may' be refused recognition and enforcement if there are grounds for refusal.[72]

33. There are slightly different views among legal scholars and practitioners on what significance the difference in wording between section 54 of the Act and Article V of the New York Convention would have in practice. First of all, although the New York

65. Andersson, et al., *Arbitration in Sweden*, 186.
66. *Ibid.*, 187 and Supreme Court decisions in *Forenede Cresco v. Datema*, decision by the Supreme Court made on 23 Nov. 1992 in case no Ö 3659-92, NJA 1992 p. 733 and *The Republic of Latvia v. SwembaltAB*, decision by the Supreme Court made on 18 Dec. 2002 in case no Ö 4303-02, NJA 2002 C 62.
67. See *Götaverken Arendal AB v. General National Maritime Transport Company*, decision by the Supreme Court made on 13 Aug. 1979, NJA 1979 p. 527 and *Société Planavergne S.A. v. K.B. i Stockholm AB*, decision by the Supreme Court made on 30 Sep. 2003 in case no Ö 3390-01, NJA 2003 p. 379.
68. Heuman *Arbitration Law of Sweden: Practice and Procedure*, 720 and Andersson, et al., *Arbitration in Sweden*, 184.
69. *Götaverken Arendal AB v. General National Maritime Transport Company*, decision by the Supreme Court made on 13 Aug. 1979, NJA 1979 p. 527.
70. *Société Planavergne S.A. v. K.B. i Stockholm AB*, decision by the Supreme Court made on 30 Sep. 2003 in case no Ö 3390-01, NJA 2003 p. 379.
71. Lindskog, *Skiljeförfarande – En kommentar*, 1165.
72. See Art. V(1) of the New York Convention and Art. 36 of the Model Law; Kronke, H., et al. eds., *Recognition and Enforcement of Foreign Arbitral Awards – A Global Commentary on the New York Convention*, 308 et seq. and Madsen, *Commercial Arbitration in Sweden*, 375.

Convention undisputedly[73] leaves some discretion to the courts of the State where recognition and enforcement is sought, it has been held that such discretion is narrow and would be unlikely to be exercised where the award was subject to a fundamental or structural defect.[74] Second, it may be argued that section 54 of the Act, notwithstanding its wording, would still leave narrow room for Swedish courts not to refuse recognition and enforcement of an award if it is reasonably clear that the relevant error had no effect on the outcome of the case.[75] It has been held that it would be too formalistic to attach weight to an error without real importance, and Swedish courts would usually be pragmatic in dealing with matters of this kind.[76] Consequently, with the restrictive application of the discretion available under the New York Convention and the possible opening for a pragmatic application of section 54 of the Act by Swedish courts, in practice, the difference in wording between the Act and the New York Convention would as a rule not imply any critical differences in the possibilities to enforce an award.[77]

34. Under the Act, there is no time limitation for claiming that grounds for refusal exist.[78] However, it has been discussed whether the inactivity of a party may constitute a waiver of New York Convention defences. There seems to be a common understanding that most objections under Article V(1)(a), (b), (c) and (d) are waivable.[79] A party who has participated in arbitral proceedings and fails to raise objections to errors during those proceedings cannot, as a rule, later rely on those errors as an objection to enforcement of an award. This approach is in line with section 34(2) of the Act, which states that a party is deemed to have waived grounds for challenging an arbitral award,

73. See, however, the French official translation of the New York Convention, where this discretion is not evident from the wording of Art. V(1) – 'la reconnaissance et l'exécution de la sentence ne seront refuses … que si …'. The apparent difference between the English and French texts is discussed by Paulsson, *May or Must under the New York Convention: An Exercise in Syntax and Linguistics*, in 14 Arbitration Intl., 227 et seq (1998).
74. See e.g., Möller, *Discretion Pursuant to Art. V of the New York Convention* in *Between East and West: Essays in Honour of Ulf Franke*, 332 and 341 – Möller states that the best view seems to be that the discretion under Art. V of the New York Convention should primarily be exercised only in cases where the right to rely on a certain ground for refusal has been lost because of a waiver. See also *Dardana Ltd v. Yukos oil Co.* [2002] 1. Lloyd's Report 225 (Q.B.) [8], *Kanoria v. Guinness* [2006] 1.Lloyd's Report 701 (Q.B.) [25] [26], and *Dallah v. Ministry of Religious Affairs, Government of Pakistan* [2009] EWCA Civ 755 [58] [79].
75. See e.g., Danelius, *Application of the New York Convention in Swedish Courts*, 2 Stockholm Arbitration Report, 44 (2004), and Andersson, et al., *Arbitration in Sweden*, 185.
76. Danelius, *The Application of the New York Convention in Swedish Courts*, 2 Stockholm Arbitration Report 44 (2004). See Hobér, '*Sista striden mellan internationalister och territorialister – Berättelsen om Hillmarton och Chromalloy*' in *Festskrift till Ulf K. Nordenson*, 209-211(Jure AB, 1999), who found it difficult to apply this pragmatic view in light of the discussions in the *travaux préparatoires* to the Act. However, Hobér now seems to have adopted the more pragmatic view in Hobér, *International Commercial Arbitration in Sweden*, 359.
77. See *Société Planavergne S.A. v. K.B. i Stockholm AB*, decision by the Supreme Court made on 30 Sep. 2003 in case no Ö 3390-01, NJA 2003 p. 379 discussed in s. II above.
78. In this respect, it should also be noted that neither the New York Convention, nor the Act contain any statute of limitations as to enforcement proceedings. In Sweden, the general limitation period of ten years will thus apply.
79. See e.g., Möller, *Discretion Pursuant to Art. V of the New York Convention* in *Between East and West: Essays in Honour of Ulf Franke*, 331–332 and Born, *International Commercial Arbitration*, 2760 et seq.

inter alia, by participating in the arbitral proceedings without raising objection to errors, which may constitute a ground for challenging the award. There seems to be no valid reason why such a waiver should not also apply to proceedings for recognition and enforcement under the Act.

35. More controversial is the proposition that failure to challenge – or failure to succeed in a challenge to – an award before the courts of the seat of arbitration amounts to a waiver of New York Convention defences.[80] In brief, the acceptance or non-acceptance of such a proposition is dependent on how the legal order of the seat and its courts are treated, as well as what implications may be drawn from the parties' choice of seat. A distinction is drawn between the territorial approach, on the one hand, and the delocalized approach, on the other hand.[81] Under the territorial approach, which is said to be the most widely accepted approach, the seat anchors the arbitration to the legal order of the State in which it takes place. This implies that there is no room for the courts of the State where enforcement is sought, at their own discretion, to disregard a decision of e.g. annulment of an award by a court at the seat of arbitration. In contrast, under the delocalized approach, the choice of seat of arbitration is deemed to be more for the sake of convenience and the arbitrators operate in an international forum detached from any particular national forum and guided only by the agreement. Hence, the enforcing authority should be free to ignore decisions of the court at the seat of the arbitration. If one adopts the idea that the parties' agreement on a particular seat for the arbitral proceedings reflects their intention to give 'exclusive' power to make decisions relating to the validity of the award, this may have extraterritorial effects. In that case, an unsuccessful party in challenge proceedings (or a party who renounces challenge proceedings) should be precluded from relying on grounds, in subsequent enforcement proceedings, that it could have raised before the courts of the seat.[82] There are, however, objections to this proposition, primarily based on the notion that some defences may not be the subject of advance waivers, e.g., public policy-based defences to the validity of an award.[83]

80. For further discussion, see Bachand, *When – If Ever – Should Failure to Challenge an Award before the Courts of the Seat Amount to a Waiver of New York Convention Defences*, in *Between East and West: Essays in Honour of Ulf Franke* 1-18 (Hobér et al. eds., JurisNet LLC, 2010), Möller, *Discretion Pursuant to Art. V of the New York Convention*in *Between East and West: Essays in Honour of Ulf Franke*, 332–333, and Born, *International Commercial Arbitration* 2760–2763 (Kluwer L. Intl. 2009), with case law references.

81. See *Recognition and Enforcement of Foreign Arbitral Awards – A Global Commentary on the New York Convention* 324 et seq (Kronke et al. eds., Wolters Kluwer 2010). See Bachand, *When – If Ever – Should Failure to Challenge an Award before the Courts of the Seat Amount to a Waiver of New York Convention Defences*, in *Between East and West: Essays in Honour of Ulf Franke* 6–11 (Hobér, et al. eds., 2010), discussing Gaillard's distinction between 'monolocalisation', on the one hand, and 'multilocalisation' and a 'transnational' view, on the other hand. See also, Hobér, '*Sista striden mellan internationalister och territorialister – Berättelsen om Hillmarton och Chromalloy*' in *Festskrift till Ulf K. Nordenson*, 195-211.

82. Bachand, *When – If Ever – Should Failure to Challenge an Award before the Courts of the Seat Amount to a Waiver of New York Convention Defences*, in *Between East and West: Essays in Honour of Ulf Franke* 17–18 (Hobér, et al. eds., 2010).

83. *Ibid.*, 18. - Bachand also discusses the situation where the parties in fact have not chosen the seat, but, e.g., an arbitration institute has determined the seat, due to lack of agreement between the parties, p. 13, and where the unsuccessful respondent contends that it never was

36. A court can only take into consideration grounds under section 54, which have been invoked by a party.[84] It is the party against which the award has been invoked who must, in turn, invoke and prove grounds for refusal.[85] The respondent to enforcement proceedings must prove that enforcement would have been refused in the applicable jurisdiction.[86] The provision should be read in light of the general effort to facilitate enforcement of foreign awards expressed in the New York Convention,[87] and the rules on grounds for refusing enforcement are often restrictively interpreted.[88]

37. Section 54 of the Act is divided into five grounds for refusal, namely:

(i) that the parties to the arbitration agreement, pursuant to the law applicable to them, lacked capacity to enter into the agreement or were not properly represented, or that the arbitration agreement was not valid under the law to which the parties have subjected it, or failing any indication thereon, under the law of the country where the award was made;
(ii) that the party against whom the award is invoked was not given proper notice of appointment of the arbitrator or of the arbitration proceedings, or was otherwise unable to present his case;
(iii) that the award deals with a dispute not contemplated by, or not falling within, the terms of submission to arbitration, or contains decisions on matters which are beyond the scope of the arbitration agreement, provided that, if the decision on a matter which falls within the mandate can be separated from those which fall outside the mandate, that part of the award

under a duty to arbitrate with the claimant, because of lack of an arbitration agreement or invalidity thereof, pp. 15–16. See also Born, *International Commercial Arbitration*, 2761, and Möller, *Discretion Pursuant to Art. V of the New York Convention*, in *Between East and West: Essays in Honour of Ulf Franke* 338–339 (Hobér, et al. eds., 2010).

84. Lindskog, *Skiljeförfarande – En kommentar*, 1165 and 1175.
85. Madsen, *Commercial Arbitration in Sweden*, 375; Lindskog, *Skiljeförfarande – En kommentar*, 1173; and Hobér, *International Commercial Arbitration in Sweden*, 360. There is an exception to this main rule, viz., if a party denies that it has entered into an arbitration agreement with the party seeking enforcement, the latter must prove in the enforcement proceedings that there was a valid arbitration agreement, see s. 58 of the Act. Cf *Société Planavergne S.A. v. K.B. i Stockholm AB*, decision by the Supreme Court made on 30 Sep. 2003 in case no Ö 3390-01, NJA 2003 p. 379, where the Supreme Court found that the burden of proof may shift back to the party refusing enforcement even in this case.
86. See *Forenede Cresco v. Datema*, decision by the Supreme Court made on 23 Nov. 1992 in case no Ö 3659-92, NJA 1992 p. 733 and Lindskog, *Skiljeförfarande – En kommentar*, 1174, discussing the formerly applied evidentiary requirements under the 1929 Act, where Swedish courts were required to conduct a prognosis of the outcome of enforcement proceedings in the competent foreign court.
87. See Supreme Court judgments *Lenmorniiproekt OAO v. Arne Larsson & Partners AB*, decision of the Supreme Court made on 16 Apr. 2010 in case no Ö 13-09, NJA 2010 p. 219, *Société Planavergne S.A. v. K.B. i Stockholm AB*, decision by the Supreme Court made on 30 Sep. 2003 in case no Ö 3390-01, NJA 2003 p. 379, *Götaverken Arendal AB v. General National Maritime Transport Company*, decision by the Supreme Court made on 13 Aug. 1979, NJA 1979 p. 527 and *Forenede Cresco v. Datema*, decision by the Supreme Court made on 23 Nov. 1992 in case no Ö 3659-92, NJA 1992 p. 733; Madsen, *Commercial Arbitration in Sweden*, 375 and Heuman, *Arbitration Law of Sweden: Practice and Procedure*, 720.
88. Heuman, *Arbitration Law of Sweden: Practice and Procedure*, 720.

which contains decisions on matters falling within the mandate may be recognized and enforced;

(iv) that the composition of the arbitral tribunal, or the arbitral procedure, was not in accordance with the agreement between the parties or, failing such agreement, was not in accordance with the law of the country where the arbitration took place; or

(v) that the award has not yet become binding on the parties, or has been set aside or suspended by a competent authority of the country in which, or under the law of which, the award was made.

1. *Incapacity, Lack of Representation and Invalidity of the Arbitration Agreement*

38. The first ground for refusal, set out in section 54(1) of the Act, concerns different situations where a party is not bound by the arbitration agreement on which the arbitral award is based, i.e., either due to: (i) lack of capacity to enter into an arbitration agreement or insufficient representation or misrepresentation when entering into the arbitration agreement, or (ii) invalidity of the arbitration agreement. The provision largely corresponds to Article V(1)(a) of the New York Convention.[89]

39. Determining a contracting party's capacity to enter into an arbitration agreement, or whether he has been duly represented when entering into the arbitration agreement, will likely be tried in light of personal law in accordance with the conflict of law rules in Swedish international private law.[90] Under Swedish choice of law rules, the capacity of a company would normally be determined under the law of the country in which the company is incorporated (*lex corporationis*).[91] It may here be noted that, if the arbitration agreement was entered into without the necessary capacity or representation, there is no impediment to subsequent ratification of the arbitration agreement, consequently healing the incapacity.[92] The issue of potential immunity from enforcement of States, and state-owned companies, is discussed separately in section VII below.

40. With regard to invalidity, an arbitration agreement may be invalid for a number of reasons. If, e.g., there is a requirement in the foreign legal system that an arbitration agreement has to be in written form (which is not the case in Sweden)[93] to be binding

89. Govt. bill 1971:131, p. 35 and Heuman, *Arbitration Law of Sweden: Practice and Procedure*, 728. See Hobér, *International Arbitration in Sweden*, 361 et seq.
90. Govt. bill 1998/99:35, pp. 191, 194 and 245, and Lindskog, *Skiljeförfarande – En kommentar*, 1167.
91. Andersson, et al., *Arbitration in Sweden*, 37.
92. See Govt. bill 1971:131, p. 39 and Madsen, *Commercial Arbitration in Sweden*, 377, n. 19.
93. Art. V(1)(a) of the New York Convention refers to Art. II, which in turn states that the arbitration agreement has to be in writing and signed by the parties. However, Art. VII.1 grants the right to Contracting States to provide more lenient rules in their national law (a so-called more favourable provision). Therefore, Swedish law is not contradictory to the New York

upon the parties, and there is no such written agreement, the arbitration agreement would be considered non-binding. Another issue may be lack of arbitrability under the applicable legal system, or whether the arbitration agreement was entered into under threat or similar conditions.[94]

41. The validity of the arbitration agreement would be adjudicated under the law applicable to the arbitration agreement. The applicable law is primarily determined by the parties' agreement on the law applicable to the arbitration agreement. The choice of law need not be explicit, although it has to concern the arbitration agreement.[95] It may be noted that the issue of whether an agreement on the applicable legal system with regard to the arbitration agreement has been reached is likely to be adjudicated under Swedish law.[96] Failing an agreement on applicable law, the validity of the arbitration agreement will be tried under the law of the country to which the parties have agreed, or the arbitral institution or arbitral tribunal has decided, as the seat of the arbitration, i.e., the *lex arbitri*.[97] Only when there are no indications as to choice of law will the law of the country where the award was made be applicable.[98]

42. If the parties are both of the same nationality, and the dispute is not of an international character, it may (absent other decisive indications) be assumed that the parties intended that the proceedings should be held in their native country.[99]

2. *Violation of Due Process*

43. The second ground for refusal, set out in section 54(2) of the Act, concerns the issue of due process. If the party against whom the award is invoked was not given proper notice of the appointment of the arbitrator(s), or of the arbitration proceedings, or was otherwise unable to present their case, the award will not be recognized and enforced. The provision corresponds to Article V(1)(b) of the New York Convention.[100]

44. The provision aims to safeguard that the parties to the arbitration have had a reasonable opportunity to participate in the arbitral proceedings and to state their case,

Convention. It may also be noted that it is not likely that a party may directly rely on the provisions of the New York Convention, as Sweden conforms to a dualistic approach with regard to implementing international law. See Madsen, *Commercial Arbitration in Sweden*, 378 et seq., and n. 25, and Heuman, *Arbitration Law of Sweden: Practice and Procedure*, 729 et seq.

94. See Govt. bill 1998/99:35, pp. 192 and 245 and Madsen, *Commercial Arbitration in Sweden*, 378 et seq.
95. See Govt. bill 1998/99:35, p. 193.
96. Lindskog, *Skiljeförfarande – En kommentar*, 1167, n. 18.
97. Andersson, et al., *Arbitration in Sweden*, 37.
98. See s. 54(1) of the Act, Govt. bill 1998/99:35, p. 191; Heuman, *Arbitration Law of Sweden: Practice and Procedure*, 721 and 729; and Lindskog, *Skiljeförfarande – En kommentar*, 1167.
99. Govt. bill 1998/99:35, p. 193.
100. Govt. bill 1971:131, p. 35 and Heuman, *Arbitration Law of Sweden: Practice and Procedure*, 730.

i.e., to maintain the adversarial principle.[101] It has been argued that the rule of due process is an international provision.[102] However, national courts have on occasion looked at national law for guidance, although noting that a transgression of national law may not necessarily be a transgression of the New York Convention.[103] The provision will in any case be interpreted restrictively.[104] Neither the Act, nor the New York Convention explicitly address the issue of applicable law with regard to assessing whether a party has been able to present their case. It may, however, be assumed that it is the law applicable to the arbitral proceedings that is primarily applicable to such issues.[105]

45. To this end, an overall assessment should be made, taking into consideration the circumstances at hand. Of particular significance may be to what extent the respondent to the enforcement proceedings has adequately attempted to protect its interest.[106] The Supreme Court stated in *F.W. Flosbach & Cie v. Normans skogs- och sågverksaktiebolag,*[107] albeit obiter dictum, that a party who has not received all the written documentation provided to the arbitral tribunal cannot be deemed to have been given a (reasonably) fair opportunity to state their case, i.e., the principle of due process has been violated.

46. Furthermore, procedural time limits (e.g., time limits to appoint arbitrators imposed by arbitration institutes) of one to two weeks are likely to be acceptable from a due process perspective.[108] In addition, it has been argued in legal literature that, if a party has not been adequately informed of the appointment of arbitrators, or the arbitration as such, it may be the case that the arbitral award cannot be deemed to exist at all, *inter alia,* due to the arbitrators' lack of mandate.[109]

47. In *Lenmorniiproekt OAO v. A.L. & Partner Leasing AB,* the Supreme Court stated, with reference to the *travaux préparatoires,* that it is for the party against whom the arbitral award has been invoked to show that the invoking party (i.e., the party who

101. Heuman, *Arbitration Law of Sweden: Practice and Procedure,* 730.
102. *Ibid.,* 731.
103. *Ibid.,* 731, and Madsen, *Commercial Arbitration in Sweden,* 379, n. 26.
104. Heuman, *Arbitration Law of Sweden: Practice and Procedure,* 731.
105. Madsen, *Commercial Arbitration in Sweden,* 380. It may be noted that in *Société Planavergne S.A. v. KB. i Stockholm AB,* decision by the Supreme Court made on 30 Sep. 2003 in case no Ö 3390-01 NJA 2003 p. 379, the Supreme Court relied on the arbitral tribunal's statement in the arbitral award with regard to the issue of due process. The arbitral award stated that the parties had been sent a notice by registered mail, summoning them to the final hearing. As the respondent had not objected to this fact, nor were there any other reasons to believe that the respondent had not had adequate means to participate in the proceedings, the Supreme Court found no reason to refuse enforcement of the arbitral award.
106. Lindskog, *Skiljeförfarande – En kommentar,* 1168.
107. *F.W. Flosbach & Cie v. Normans skogs- och sågverksaktiebolag,* NJA 1953 p. 407.
108. See Heuman, *Arbitration Law of Sweden: Practice and Procedure,* 732.
109. Lindskog, *Skiljeförfarande – En kommentar,* 733 et seq. and 1167, n. 20.

requested arbitration) has not adequately notified the respondent of the arbitral proceedings.[110] The evidentiary requirements should be set rather low.

48. The New York Convention does not require notices to be served in accordance with formal rules applicable to civil proceedings.[111] Although the Swedish Service of Documents Act is thus not applicable to arbitral proceedings, the rules specifying the persons who are entitled to accept service on behalf of a Swedish corporation would likely provide some guidance also with respect to arbitral proceedings.[112] It should be noted that it is not a ground for refusal that the respondent has not received the arbitral award prior to the enforcement proceedings, or that the arbitral award was signed for by an unauthorized representative.[113] Furthermore, a party's failure to plead their case, despite receiving notices of hearings and communicated submissions and other documents, does not constitute grounds for refusal.[114]

49. On the issue of 'proper' notice, the Supreme Court in *Lenmorniiproekt OAO v. A.L. & Partner Leasing AB* concluded (noting the lack of guidance from the New York Convention in this respect) that notice requirements with regard to commencement documents (i.e., the request for arbitration) must be held strict. The Supreme Court continued that in light of due process, it cannot be accepted that an arbitral award be recognized and enforced against a party who was not notified of the arbitral proceedings or who was not even aware of the arbitral proceedings. With regard to such notices, as a matter of principle a requirement must be upheld that such a notice has reached the respondent. Whether or not there is a contractual obligation to inform a counterparty of one's current address would most likely have no significance on this issue.[115] If there is no indication in the arbitral award, or any indication by other means, that the respondent has received the notice, or if the respondent (in a recognition and enforcement procedure) can present an investigation which raises considerable doubt as to whether the claimant has properly notified the respondent, it may generally be considered that grounds for refusal exist. The Supreme Court stated, however, that

110. See s. 3 of the Supreme Court judgment *Lenmorniiproekt OAO v. Arne Larsson & Partners AB*, decision of the Supreme Court made on 16 Apr. 2010 in case no Ö 13-09, NJA 2010 p. 219 and Govt. bill 1971:131, p. 39. See also Heuman, *Arbitration Law of Sweden: Practice and Procedure*, 732.

111. Heuman, *Arbitration Law of Sweden: Practice and Procedure*, 732.

112. See *Christine L. v. Sven A.*, decision by the Supreme Court made on 26 May 1999 in case no Ö 3715-97, NJA 1999 p. 300 and Hobér, *International Commercial Arbitration in Sweden*, 209–210.

113. Heuman, *Arbitration Law of Sweden: Practice and Procedure*, 732. See s. 34(3) of the Act regarding challenge proceedings where the time limit for initiating such proceedings depends on when the arbitral award was actually served on the party.

114. Heuman, *Arbitration Law of Sweden: Practice and Procedure*, 733.

115. See *Lenmorniiproekt OAO v. Arne Larsson & Partners AB*, decision of the Supreme Court made on 16 Apr. 2010 in case no Ö 13-09, NJA 2010 p. 219, s. 8. Although the Supreme Court did not make any general and principled statements regarding the effectiveness of a 'notice clause', the statements clearly indicate that, brought to a head, the requirements for notification of a request for arbitration are higher than just to comply with the 'notice clause' of a contract. See also Hobér, *International Commercial Arbitration in Sweden*, 208–209, and Lindskog, *Skiljeförfarande – En kommentar*, 81 et seq.

if the respondent, despite insufficient notice, still managed to present their case, this issue may be considered differently.[116]

50. In the case cited above, the arbitral tribunal concluded (in the award) that the respondent had received the claimant's request for arbitration by way of it being sent to an address which was stated both in the request for arbitration, as well as in the parties' agreement, as being that of the respondent. A subpoena had also been sent to the address (although it was returned stating that no such addressee existed at that address). However, the respondent had in fact moved to a different address prior to initiation of the arbitral proceedings and no documents pertaining to the arbitration had reached any representative of the respondent. Moreover, the respondent had not taken part in the arbitral proceedings. Hence, the Supreme Court, after making an overall assessment of the notion of due process, concluded that the respondent in the enforcement proceedings had not been duly notified of the arbitral proceedings. Consequently the award was not to be recognized or enforced.[117]

51. The Supreme Court judgment shows that, since it arguably would not be sufficient to rely on contractually agreed notice requirements, the parties have a significant interest in ensuring that the opposing party duly receives (i.e., to the correct and current address) any notices sent, and particularly documents which initiate arbitral proceedings. Moreover, it is in the parties' (as well as the arbitral tribunal's) interest to verify the identity of the recipient. In addition, the arbitral tribunal must ensure that the award states that the opposing party has been duly notified of the request for arbitration.[118] It may also be noted that the Supreme Court has opened the possibility to present an investigation, which raises 'considerable doubt' as to whether the claimant properly notified the respondent of the request for arbitration. This entails a slight shift in evidentiary requirements, from 'proving' that grounds for refusal exist to 'considerable doubt' (at least with regard to notice requirements for documents pertaining to commencement of arbitral proceedings). However, the Supreme Court

116. *Lenmorniiproekt OAO v. Arne Larsson & Partners AB*, decision of the Supreme Court made on 16 Apr. 2010 in case no Ö 13-09, NJA 2010 p. 219, s. 9.

117. *Ibid.*, s. 10.

118. See the conclusions of Tude & Scherp, case report on the Supreme Court's decision in *Lenmorniiproekt OAO v. Arne Larsson & Partners AB* made on 16 Apr. 2010 in case no Ö 13-09, NJA 2010 p. 219, 2 Stockholm Intl. Arbitration Rev. 138 (2009). See also Govt. bill 1971:131, p. 39, which states that if there is no reference whatsoever in the arbitral award that the respondent has been notified of the arbitral proceedings, the respondent to the enforcement proceedings must be deemed to have met its evidentiary requirements. In *Richard E v. Monimpex*, decision by the Supreme Court in 1993 in case no SÖ 174, NJA 1993 C 56, the Svea Court of Appeal found that, in light of the fact that the arbitral award stated that the respondent had been notified, the respondent had not shown that he had not had the opportunity to state his case. The Supreme Court did not overturn the Court of Appeal judgment (see also *Tommy Klatzko v Konsult AB v. Pevaeche SA*, decision by the Supreme Court made in 1989 in case no SÖ 66, NJA 1989 C 22.) It may be noted that the Supreme Court might rule differently today in light of the judgment in *Lenmorniiproekt OAO v. Arne Larsson & Partners AB*, decision of the Supreme Court made on 16 Apr. 2010 in case no Ö 13-09, NJA 2010 p. 219.

emphasizes that it is another matter if the respondent still manages to state their case, consequently somewhat limiting the assessment of 'considerable doubt'.[119]

3. *Arbitrators Exceeding their Mandate*

52. The third ground for refusal, set out in section 54(3) of the Act, concerns arbitrators exceeding their mandate, i.e., the mandate contained in the parties' arbitration agreement and their dispositions in the proceedings.[120] The provision corresponds to Article V(1)(c) of the New York Convention.[121] If the arbitral award deals with a dispute not contemplated by, or not falling within, the terms of the submission to arbitration, or contains decisions on matters which are beyond the scope of the submission to arbitration, those decisions should not be recognized and enforced.[122] The provision should be interpreted so that if the arbitral tribunal deals with issues beyond the terms of procedure outlined for the arbitral tribunal, there is a ground for refusal.[123] It should be noted that an arbitral tribunal's omission to address a party's prayer for relief and its underlying issues may also constitute an excess of mandate.[124] The provision encompasses not only awards, which have exceeded the request for arbitration but also awards which differ from, or exceed, the claims or submissions of a party, or other predefined limits to adjudication of the dispute.[125] However, the provision is interpreted restrictively and there is a clear tendency of courts to construe procedural actions of the parties in such a way that there is no excess of mandate.[126]

53. The arbitral award may also be refused in part, if such a decision may be separated from those decisions which fall within the mandate. Consequently, a part of the award, which falls within the terms, or scope, of the submission to arbitration should be

---

119. See Tude & Scherp case report on the Supreme Court's decision in *Lenmorniiproekt OAO v. Arne Larsson & Partners AB* made on 16 Apr. 2010 in case no Ö 13-09, NJA 2010 p. 219, Stockholm Intl. Arbitration Rev. 137 (2009).
120. Lindskog, *Skiljeförfarande – En kommentar*, 1168.
121. Govt. bill 1971:131, p. 35.
122. See s. 54(3) of the Act, Art. V(1)(c) of the New York Convention, Heuman, *Arbitration Law of Sweden: Practice and Procedure*, 735; Madsen, *Commercial Arbitration in Sweden*, 380 et seq. and Hobér, *International Commercial Arbitration in Sweden*, 364.
123. Lindskog, *Skiljeförfarande – En kommentar*, 1169 and Heuman, *Arbitration Law of Sweden: Practice and Procedure*, 735 et seq.
124. Hobér, *International Commercial Arbitration in Sweden*, 313 et seq. See, however, Lindskog, *Skiljeförfarande – En kommentar*, 1168, n. 27, who asserts that the provision does not apply to an arbitral tribunal's omission to consider a prayer for relief. Rather, s. 54(4) of the Act would apply in such cases.
125. Heuman, *Arbitration Law of Sweden: Practice and Procedure*, 735, and *Götaverken Arendal AB v. General National Maritime Transport Company*, decision by the Supreme Court made on 13 Aug. 1979, NJA 1979 p. 527.
126. Heuman, *Arbitration Law of Sweden: Practice and Procedure*, 736.

recognized and enforced.[127] Moreover, the enforcement proceedings must not create opportunities to review the award on the merits.[128]

54. Applicable law with regard to exceeding the mandate contained in the arbitration agreement is likely to be the law applicable to the arbitration agreement, i.e., primarily the law to which the parties have agreed, or, failing such an agreement, the law of the country in which the arbitral proceedings are held.[129] Applicable law with regard to exceeding the mandate due to the parties' dispositions during the proceedings is likely to be tried under the law applicable to the arbitral proceedings.[130]

4. *Irregularity in the Composition of the Arbitral Tribunal or the Arbitral Procedure*

55. The fourth ground for refusal, set out in section 54(4) of the Act, concerns the situation where the appointment and composition of the arbitral tribunal, or the arbitral procedure, was not in accordance with the agreement of the parties, or, failing such an agreement, was not in accordance with the law of the country where the arbitration took place.[131] The provision corresponds to Article V(1)(d) of the New York Convention. The provision aims at two situations, *viz.*, first where there have been irregularities with regard to appointment of arbitrators or the composition of the arbitral tribunal, and second where there have been irregularities in procedure.[132]

56. Section 54(4) of the Act provides a choice of law rule. Assessments of whether there are grounds for refusal is based on the parties' agreement, and, failing such an agreement, the law of the country in which the arbitration took place. In this respect, the place of arbitration is understood as the legal system applicable to the arbitration. The actual locality of the arbitral proceedings is not relevant in this respect (see further section III above).[133] With respect to the appointment of the arbitral tribunal, the provision generally aims at the choice of arbitrators, as well as lack of qualifications in respect to the requirements set for the arbitration. As regards the composition of the arbitral tribunal, the provision mainly regards the number of arbitrators.[134] With

127. Lindskog, *Skiljeförfarande – En kommentar*, 1169, Heuman, *Arbitration Law of Sweden: Practice and Procedure*, 737 et seq., and Madsen, *Commercial Arbitration in Sweden*, 381.
128. Heuman, *Arbitration Law of Sweden: Practice and Procedure*, 737.
129. Lindskog, *Skiljeförfarande – En kommentar*, 1169, Heuman, *Arbitration Law of Sweden: Practice and Procedure*, 736, and Madsen, *Commercial Arbitration in Sweden*, 381, n. 31.
130. Lindskog, *Skiljeförfarande – En kommentar*, 1169 and n. 25. See Heuman, *Arbitration Law of Sweden: Practice and Procedure*, 736, where Heuman suggests that, in cases where the respondent alleges that the arbitral tribunal has exceeded the request for arbitration or a party's claim, an autonomous interpretation is most likely preferable to applying *lex arbitri* – a conclusion which Lindskog does not agree with (see Lindskog, *Skiljeförfarande – En kommentar*, 1169, n. 25).
131. See s. 54(4) of the Act, and Madsen, *Commercial Arbitration in Sweden*, 381.
132. Govt. Bill 1971:131, p. 35 and Heuman, *Arbitration Law of Sweden: Practice and Procedure*, 2003, 738.
133. Lindskog, *Skiljeförfarande – En kommentar*, 1170 et seq.
134. *Ibid.*, 1170.

respect to incorrect arbitral proceedings, the provision aims at deviations from the parties' agreement or the law of the applicable legal system.[135]

57. In assessing conformity of the appointment or composition of the arbitral tribunal, or the arbitral proceedings, the court primarily examines whether any deviation has occurred from what the parties agreed, including institutional rules made applicable by the parties.[136] However, the situation may arise where the parties' agreement contradicts mandatory law of the applicable legal system. In those cases, it is suggested that mandatory law will supersede the parties' agreement and that the arbitral tribunal should conform to mandatory law. There are likely no grounds to refuse enforcement of an award where the arbitral tribunal has conformed to mandatory law.[137] Inversely, where the parties agree that the arbitration agreement will apply, knowingly in contradiction to mandatory law, it has been held in legal literature that the award should not be enforced, since the award may successfully be challenged in the legal system where it was made.[138]

5. *Non-binding Arbitral Awards*

58. The fifth ground for refusal, set out in section 54(5) of the Act, concerns the situation where the arbitral award has not yet become binding on the parties, or has been set aside or suspended by a competent authority of the country in which, or under the law of which, the award was made.[139] The provision corresponds to Article V(1)(e) of the New York Convention.[140] In turn, it is for the party against whom the award has been invoked to invoke and show grounds for refusal in this respect.[141] It should be noted that the party seeking enforcement does not have to show that the award is also enforceable in the country where it was made (i.e., there is no requirement of a double *exequatur* procedure).[142]

59. It has been held that the issue of whether the arbitral award is binding upon the parties is determined by the law applicable to the arbitral proceedings.[143] The issue of when the arbitral award becomes binding upon the parties is determined by the law

135. See, however, the High Court of Justice, Queen's Bench Division Commercial Court judgment in *Tongyuan (USA) International Trading Group (China) v. Uni-Clan Ltd*, ICCA Yearbook Commercial Arbitration, 2001, 886–893, where enforcement of the award was not refused although the arbitral proceedings had taken place at a different locality than that set in the arbitration agreement, because the party had had no interest in participating in the arbitral proceedings.
136. Heuman, *Arbitration Law of Sweden: Practice and Procedure*, 738.
137. Lindskog, *Skiljeförfarande – En kommentar*, 1170 and n. 37. However, see also Heuman, *Arbitration Law of Sweden: Practice and Procedure*, 738 et seq. who states that enforcement may be refused on account of the arbitral tribunal not having respected the agreement between the parties.
138. Lindskog, *Skiljeförfarande – En kommentar*, 1170, n. 37.
139. See s. 54(5) of the Act, and Lindskog, *Skiljeförfarande – En kommentar*, 1171 et seq.
140. Govt. bill 1971:131, p. 35, and Govt. bill 1998/99:35, pp. 200 and 247.
141. Lindskog, *Skiljeförfarande – En kommentar*, 1173 et seq.
142. Govt. bill 1998/99:35, p. 200.
143. Madsen, *Commercial Arbitration in Sweden*, 381, n. 33.

governing the arbitral award.[144] It is likely that Swedish conflict of law rules will apply in determining which legal system governs the arbitral award.[145] Generally, an award is binding upon the parties as soon as it cannot be reviewed on its merits, even if it is still open to nullification or challenge proceedings.[146] This concept of 'binding', as used in the New York Convention, was accepted by the Supreme Court in *Götaverken Arendal AB (Sweden) v. General National Maritime Transport Company (Libya)*. Accordingly, challenge proceedings or other recourses against the award are of no significance in this respect.[147]

60. Furthermore, enforcement of an award may be refused if the award has been set aside or suspended by a competent authority of the country in which, or under the law of which, the award was made. It is likely that Swedish law will be applied in respect of determining where the award was made.[148] An award set aside by a competent authority in the country where the arbitral award was made will not be enforced in Sweden.[149] In order to prevent recognition and enforcement, the award must in fact have been set aside; a pending application for setting aside the award will not suffice.[150] As mentioned above, actions against an award are of no significance in determining whether an award is binding upon the parties. In addition, the setting aside, or suspension, of an arbitral award must be made by a competent authority after a special examination. Thus, an automatic suspension of the award's enforceability, due to a party bringing an action against it, does not constitute a suspension as set out in section 54(5) of the Act.[151]

144. Govt. bill 1998/99:35, p. 200, and Madsen, *Commercial Arbitration in Sweden*, 2007, 383.
145. Lindskog, *Skiljeförfarande – En kommentar*, 1171 and n. 40.
146. Hobér, *International Commercial Arbitration in Sweden*, 366 and Kronke, et al. eds., *Recognition and Enforcement of Foreign Arbitral Awards – A Global Commentary on the New York Convention*, 311 et seq., where the concept of 'binding' awards is elaborated.
147. See Govt. bill 1971:131, pp. 13 and 69 et seq., Govt. bill 1998:99:35, p. 200, *Götaverken Arendal AB v. General National Maritime Transport Company*, decision by the Supreme Court made on 13 Aug. 1979, NJA 1979 p. 527; Lindskog, *Skiljeförfarande – En kommentar*, 1171 et seq., and Heuman, *Arbitration Law of Sweden: Practice and Procedure*, 2003, 723.
148. Lindskog, *Skiljeförfarande – En kommentar*, 1171.
149. Govt. bill 1971:131, p. 34, Madsen, *Commercial Arbitration in Sweden*, 382, and n. 34. See, however, the discussion in s. II, para. 6, *supra*.
150. Hobér, *International Commercial Arbitration in Sweden*, 367, n. 34.
151. See Govt. bill 1998/99:35, p. 202, *Götaverken Arendal AB v. General National Maritime Transport Company*, decision by the Supreme Court made on 13 Aug. 1979, NJA 1979 p. 527, Madsen, *Commercial Arbitration in Sweden*, 2007, 382, n. 35 et seq., and Heuman, *Arbitration Law of Sweden: Practice and Procedure*, 726. See also *Forenede Cresco v. Datema*, decision by the Supreme Court made on 23 Nov. 1992 in case no Ö 3659-92, NJA 1992 p. 733 (in applying the old 1929 Act) which upheld the notion that enforcement of an award cannot be refused unless it has been set aside in the foreign state, or at least that that outcome is probably in the ruling of a challenge proceeding in that country. See also, however, Lindskog, *Skiljeförfarande – En kommentar*, 1172, n. 48, who suggests that automatic suspension of enforcement of an award is likely to be based on certain protective interests of the foreign legal system. With automatic suspension there is no need for a special examination by a competent authority. This entails that the Swedish order (that an automatic suspension does not constitute a suspension under s. 54(5) of the Act (and the New York Convention)) has the effect that protection from enforcement of the award is in fact weakened, contrary to the purposes of the suspension in the foreign legal system.

6. *Arbitrability and Public Policy*

61. The grounds for refusal set out in section 55 of the Act concern the case where the arbitral award includes determination of an issue which, under Swedish law, may not be decided by arbitrators (i.e., the issue is non-arbitrable), or that recognition and enforcement of the award would be clearly incompatible with the basic principles of the Swedish legal system (i.e., in violation of public policy).[152] Section 55 of the Act corresponds to Article V(2) of the New York Convention.[153] The grounds for refusal contained in section 55 are considered by the court on its own motion, i.e., ex officio, and should be interpreted in light of the New York Convention and the international case law surrounding it. However, as the provision regards mandatory Swedish law and Swedish public policy, international influence is largely restricted, although it has been held that an international perspective should be applied rather than a Swedish perspective.[154]

62. With regard to the first ground for refusal in section 55(1) of the Act, the main rule is that the issue of arbitrability should be determined in light of Swedish law. As such, arbitrability under Swedish law generally requires that the issue may be settled amicably out of court.[155] Consequently, the fact that an issue is non-arbitrable under a foreign legal system does not constitute grounds for refusal under section 55 of the Act, even where the foreign legal system applies to the arbitration agreement, as well as the issue, which the award concerns.[156]

63. This notwithstanding, it is submitted that, even in cases where the arbitral award conflicts with Swedish mandatory provisions (so that the issue may not be settled through arbitration), it may still be recognized and enforced if the issue may be settled through arbitration under the applicable foreign legal system. This would, however, be conditional upon the foreign legal system being recognized as a legal system of a certain standard, and that the applicable legal system was not chosen with the intent of circumventing Swedish mandatory law.[157]

64. The second ground for refusal in section 55(2) of the Act, i.e., incompatibility with Swedish public policy, should only apply in particularly offensive cases.[158] The content of public policy does not lend itself to be defined in an absolute manner.[159] Although an issue is determined as arbitrable as such, there are issues which public courts generally

152. See s. 55 of the Act, and Lindskog, *Skiljeförfarande – En kommentar,* 1177 et seq.
153. Govt. bill 1971:131, p. 35, SOU 1994:81, p. 237 et seq., Govt. bill 1998/99:35, p. 199, and Lindskog, *Skiljeförfarande – En kommentar,* 1177.
154. Lindskog, *Skiljeförfarande – En kommentar,* 1178, Heuman, *Arbitration Law of Sweden: Practice and Procedure,* 740 et seq.; Heuman & Millqvist, *Journal of International Arbitration,* vol. 20, 493 (Kluwer L. Intl. 2003) and Andersson, et al., *Arbitration in Sweden,* 186.
155. See s. 1(1) first sentence of the Act and Lindskog, *Skiljeförfarande – En kommentar,* 222, 844and 1178.
156. Lindskog, *Skiljeförfarande – En kommentar,* 844 and 1178.
157. *Ibid.,* 845, n. 25, and 1178 et seq.
158. Govt. bill 1998/99:35, pp. 142 and 234, Lindskog, *Skiljeförfarande – En kommentar,* 1180.
159. See Govt. bill 1998/99:35, p. 49.

will not deal with. Primarily, unacceptable claims would include claims based on, e.g., gambling or criminal acts, such as an order to pay an agreed upon bribe (so-called *pactum turpe*-cases),[160] arbitral awards which order a party to perform certain unlawful acts, or where the arbitral award has a penal character. Furthermore, a foreign arbitral award, which, under the foreign legal system, is enforceable against a third party, or has been awarded only for appearances, may violate Swedish public policy.[161] Moreover, arbitral awards which arbitrators have rendered with disregard to mandatory law (of profound significance) that aims to protect third party interests or the public interest[162] may be considered incompatible with Swedish public policy.[163] In addition, and in light of the above, awards, which conflict with Swedish or EU competition law are likely to be considered incompatible with Swedish public policy.[164]

65. Arbitral awards to this end, and their recognition and enforcement, would be considered incompatible with Swedish public policy.[165] In addition, it is likely that section 55(2) of the Act also covers arbitral proceedings, which are clearly incompatible with Swedish public policy. It should, however, be noted that arbitrators' assessments of the issue in dispute cannot be challenged by reference to section 55 of the Act.[166]

66. Public policy covers not only principles of substantive law, but also procedural law.[167] There may be issues of due process, such as improper appointment of arbitrators, which are covered by section 55(2) of the Act. If, e.g., one party appointed the arbitrators single-handedly, the proceedings may be considered incompatible with

160. See Judge Lagergren's famous award from 1963, published in full text; see Wetter, *Issues of Corruption before International Arbitral Tribunals: The Authentic Text and True Meaning of Judge Gunnar Lagergren's Award in ICC Case No 1110*, Arbitration Intl. 277–294 (1994). See also Heuér, *International Arbitration in Sweden*, 59 and 117, who notes that a modern approach to Judge Lagergren's conclusion that a contract including bribes was non-arbitrable is that an allegation of bribery and corruption does not deprive an arbitral tribunal of its jurisdiction because the issue is non-arbitrable. Rather, arbitral tribunals today generally should try such claims on the merits and reject them because they violate international public policy.
161. Lindskog, *Skiljeförfarande – En kommentar*, 1180, Heuman & Millqvist, *Journal of International Arbitration*, 494 and *Robert Grizila v. Johnny Letth (bankruptcy estate)*, judgment by the Supreme Court made on 23 Oct. 2002 in case no Ö 2309-02, NJA 2002 C 45.
162. Lindskog, *Skiljeförfarande – En kommentar*, 847.
163. Govt. bill 1998/99:35, p. 141 et seq., Lindskog, *Skiljeförfarande – En kommentar*, 846 et seq., and Madsen, *Commercial Arbitration in Sweden*, 270 et seq.
164. See Govt. bill 1998/99:35, p. 58 et seq., and Madsen, *Commercial Arbitration in Sweden*, 2007 271, and n. 15. See also *Eco Swiss China Time v. Benetton International*, ruling by European Court of Justice in case no C-126/97, 1999, ECRI-3055, and Dhunér, *EC Competition Law and National Arbitration Procedure*, Stockholm Arbitration Report 24–32 (2000).
165. Govt. bill 1998/99:35, p. 141, and Madsen, *Commercial Arbitration in Sweden*, 270.
166. Lindskog, *Skiljeförfarande – En kommentar*, 1181. However, Lindskog does indicate that in certain exceptional cases the arbitrators' wrongful application of law is of such gravity that the award would be declared invalid due to its incompatibility with Swedish public policy, see Lindskog, *Skiljeförfarande – En kommentar*, 846 et seq. and 1181.
167. Govt bill 1998/99:35, p. 141 et seq., Lindskog, *Skiljeförfarande – En kommentar*, 845 et seq., and Madsen, *Commercial Arbitration in Sweden*, 270.

fundamental legal certainty, and therefore incompatible with Swedish public policy.[168] Moreover, arbitral awards rendered due to criminal acts, such as threats against or bribery of an arbitrator, may be considered to fall within the concept of public policy.[169] It has also been suggested that awards rendered on the basis of false evidence or false witness statements may be considered incompatible with Swedish public policy.[170]

67. Section 55(2) of the Act has successfully been applied only once, namely in *Robert Grizila v. Johnny Letth (bankruptcy estate)*. In April 2001, Johnny Letth was sentenced to prison in Sweden for bank fraud and forgery. Concurrently, goods were impounded by the police and subsequently levied to satisfy claims by Johnny Letth's creditors. Johnny Letth objected to the levy, claiming that the goods had been pledged, by way of a title-transfer security transaction under German law, to his brother Robert Grizila. However, the District Court, in upholding and with reference to the decision of the Enforcement Authority, found it more than likely that the goods in question had been acquired with money he had gained through criminal activities (as had been asserted by the District Court and the Court of Appeal in the earlier criminal proceedings). In September 2001, Johnny Letth was declared bankrupt.

68. During the spring of 2002, Johnny Letth's brother Robert Grizila submitted an arbitral award to the Svea Court of Appeal and applied for its enforcement. Allegedly, the two brothers had entered into a commission agency contract in Slovenia in August 2000, pursuant to which Johnny Letth was to procure a car, two mobile phones, a digital camera and a floor-heating device on behalf of Robert Grizila. In August 2001, an award covering the car, mobile phones and the digital camera was rendered in Ljubljana, Slovenia, and the respondent Johnny Letth was found liable for rent for the lease of certain premises and damages for breach of contract.

69. The Svea Court of Appeal refused to recognize the award on grounds of public policy and concluded that it could be questioned whether the award reflected a true

168. Lindskog, *Skiljeförfarande – En kommentar*, 848 et seq. See also Heuman & Millqvist, *Journal of International Arbitration*, 494, who note that some countries, which require a substantiated violation of public policy, may enforce awards where the parties have agreed that only one of the parties appoints all of the arbitrators, as long as no procedural principles have been contravened, e.g., by only appointing three strictly impartial persons.

169. Govt. bill 1998/99:35, p. 141 et seq., Lindskog, *Skiljeförfarande – En kommentar*, 848 et seq., and Madsen, *Commercial Arbitration in Sweden*, 270 et seq.

170. The situation was discussed in the *travaux préparatoires* to the Act in the context of petitions for reversal of arbitral awards. Reference was made to the Model Law and the New York Convention, in which it was found that the concept of *ordre public* encompasses false evidence as grounds for invalidity. However, it was decided that no such explicit reference should be included in the Swedish bill, see Govt. bill 1998/99:35, p. 150 et seq. Lindskog argues, despite these considerations in the *travaux préparatoires*, that the provision should not be interpreted so as to exclude false evidence from the scope of s. 55(2) of the Act. Rather, Lindskog argues that it is up to the courts to decide in which cases false evidence may be so offensive that the arbitral award should not be upheld, see Lindskog, *Skiljeförfarande – En kommentar*, 850 and n. 56. Heuman and Millqvist, however, argue that awards based on false evidence should not be considered in violation of national or international public policy, as Swedish legislators considered the issue and refrained from introducing it in legislation, see *Journal of International Arbitration*, 494 et seq. See Madsen, *Commercial Arbitration in Sweden*, 272, and n. 19.

legal relationship between the parties. Reference was made, *inter alia,* to the fact that the parties were brothers, that the property in question was subject to another legal proceeding (i.e. the claims of Johnny Letth's creditors in his bankruptcy), in which it had been alleged that a security transfer had taken place, whereas the arbitral award was based on a commission agency agreement without reference to any alleged security transfer, and that two somewhat differing awards had been submitted by the applicant in the enforcement proceedings. Furthermore, no explanation seems to have been given during the enforcement proceedings as to why a dispute had arisen between the brothers, nor how it led to arbitral proceedings. Rather, the Svea Court of Appeal appears to have denied recognition and enforcement of the award as it had reason to believe that the award constituted a fictitious document created to deceive the bankruptcy estate of Johnny Letth. Upon appeal, the Supreme Court upheld the decision of the Svea Court of Appeal.[171]

VI. SEPARATE, PARTIAL AND INTERIM AWARDS

70. In complex matters, arbitral tribunals sometime render separate awards on a specific part of the dispute or on a certain issue in the dispute. The term separate award is used in e.g. section 29 of the Act, Article 38 of the SCC Rules, Article 34(1) of the UNCITRAL Rules and Article 26.7 of the LCIA Rules. The term 'separate award' is interchangeable with the term 'partial award', which is also often used. Unfortunately, these terms have sometimes been confused with the term 'interim award'. The difference between an 'interim' award, on the one hand, and a 'separate' or 'partial' award, however, is that an interim award is not a definite adjudication of a matter in dispute but is subject to subsequent review by the arbitral tribunal. By contrast, a separate or partial award is a final ruling on parts of the dispute.

71. The New York Convention does not expressly address any of the above types of award. However, as a rule, separate or partial awards are enforceable under the New York Convention, whereas true interim awards are not.

72. In reality, many 'interim' awards are in fact 'separate' or 'partial' awards. When determining whether an award should be deemed 'interim' or 'separate/partial', the term used by the arbitral tribunal is not decisive. Instead, the court in which recognition and enforcement is sought must make its own determination based on the contents of the award. That determination may sometimes be difficult. For example, under Article 45(4) of the SCC Rules, at the request of the claimant, an arbitral tribunal may render a separate award for reimbursement of part of the advance on costs paid by the claimant on behalf of the respondent subsequent to the respondent's failure to pay its share in accordance with the decision of the SCC Board. Since the final allocation of costs between the parties is to be decided by the arbitral tribunal in the final award, it

171. See *Robert Grizila v. Johnny Letth (bankruptcy estate),* judgment by the Supreme Court made on 23 Oct. 2002 in case no Ö 2309-02, NJA 2002 C 45 and the in-depth account and analysis of the case by Heuman & Millqvist in *Journal of International Arbitration,* 497–506, and Hobér, *International Arbitration in Sweden,* 371 et seq.

may be argued that such a separate award in fact is an interim award. This notwithstanding, the Svea Court of Appeal has found that such an award is enforceable and may form the basis for an application for bankruptcy.[172] It may be put in question whether such an award may also be recognized and enforced abroad under the New York Convention.[173] However, the question remains undetermined.

73. Whereas separate or partial awards are generally enforceable under the Act and the New York Convention, interim awards on security measures are, as a rule, not enforceable under Swedish law. The *travaux préparatoires* to the Act provide that only courts should be able to decide on enforceable security measures.[174]

VII. STATE IMMUNITY FROM ENFORCEMENT

74. It is generally held that a State is not entitled to plead immunity from *jurisdiction* once it has agreed to submit a dispute to arbitration, e.g., as a signatory to an agreement with an arbitration clause included.[175] By such an agreement, the State is deemed to have waived the immunity from jurisdiction defence. However, the issue of state immunity from enforcement of an arbitral award may imply more difficulties. Internationally, there is, in fact, considerable disagreement as to the absolute nature of the immunity granted to States under the New York Convention for enforcement purposes.[176]

75. In a fairly recent decision,[177] the Supreme Court stated that state immunity from jurisdiction is accepted more and more restrictively. It is now held that state immunity only applies to sovereign acts by a State. A State's commercial acts or acts under private law are, in light of the restrictive immunity theory, exempt from the right to immunity from other States' jurisdiction. The Supreme Court noted that, in Western Europe, it is commonly held that immunity from enforcement covers state property, which is used for state purposes. However, enforcement against state property is acceptable if the property is used, or intended to be used, for commercial purposes, even in cases where the State has not rescinded its right to immunity.[178] The Supreme Court concluded that

172. *Consafe ITAB v. Auto Connect Sweden AB*, judgment by Svea Court of Appeal made on 11 Mar. 2009 in case no Ö 280-09.

173. See Govt. bill 1998/99:35, p. 124.

174. Govt. bill 1998/99:35, p. 73. Note that an emergency arbitrator appointed in accordance with the SCC Rules (Appendix II) is to make an emergency decision (not an award) on interim measures. Such a decision would be treated in the same manner as decisions on interim measures made by the tribunal in the ordinary course of arbitral proceedings and are not enforceable under Swedish law.

175. Hobér, *International Commercial Arbitration in Sweden*, 26.

176. Kronke, et al. eds., *Recognition and Enforcement of Foreign Arbitral Awards – A Global Commentary on the New York Convention*, 27, elaborating the distinction between the capacity of the State *iure gestionis* and *iure imperii*. See also, Hobér, *International Commercial Arbitration in Sweden*, 31.

177. *Sedelmayer v. The Russian Federation*, judgment by the Supreme Court made on 1 Jul. 2011 in case no Ö 170-10, NJA 2011 p. 475.

178. *Sedelmayer v. The Russian Federation*, judgment by the Supreme Court made on 1 Jul. 2011 in case no Ö 170-10, NJA 2011 p. 475. s. 9.

immunity from enforcement may be invoked with regard to property used in a State's official functions, although it should be noted that state-owned non-commercial property is not automatically covered by immunity. If the purpose of possession of property is of a qualified nature (e.g., if the property is used in the State's official representation or other similar acts of an official nature, or if the property is covered by Article 21 of the 2004 UN Convention on Jurisdictional Immunities of States and Their Property) it will be covered by state immunity.[179] It should, however, be noted that the scope of state immunity does not coincide with the scope of diplomatic immunity. Hence, if the property is predominantly used for other purposes (than state official purposes) which are of a commercial nature or otherwise of a non-official nature, or both, the property may be subject to enforcement (even though the property is in part used for official purposes). In such cases, the different purposes must be considered collectively and an assessment made whether they are of a qualified nature, thus covered by state immunity from enforcement.[180] The Supreme Court explicitly stated that real estate which is used in part for diplomatic functions, will generally be covered by state immunity from enforcement.[181] In the case at hand, however, the Supreme Court found that the real estate was not primarily used for state official activities, and thus that the purpose of the use of the real estate was not sufficiently of such qualified nature that it should enjoy immunity from enforcement.[182]

VIII. ENFORCEMENT OF ICSID AWARDS

76. The Convention on the Settlement of Investment Disputes between States and Nationals of Other States (ICSID Convention – also known as the Washington Convention) is ratified by Sweden and implemented in Swedish law by virtue of a separate act.[183] Arbitral awards rendered in investment disputes under the ICSID Convention concerning payment liability are directly enforceable in the same manner as a Swedish court judgment. Accordingly, an ICSID award need not undergo the procedure of *exequatur* as described in section V.A above.[184]

IX. A GENERAL OVERVIEW OF SWEDISH COURT PRACTICE

77. Sweden has long enjoyed an excellent reputation as a venue for arbitration. Sweden has a modern arbitration law and a very well-functioning legal system. A long tradition of arbitration practice gives it the foundation to offer not just reliable, but also a responsive, arbitration service.[185] This is also reflected when it comes to recognition and enforcement of foreign arbitral awards.

179. *Ibid.*, s. 14.
180. *Ibid.*, s. 16.
181. *Ibid.*, s. 15.
182. *Ibid.*, s. 23.
183. *Sw.* Lag (1966:735) *om erkännande och verkställighet av skiljedomar i vissa internationella investeringstvister.*
184. Andersson et al., *Arbitration in Sweden*, 187.
185. Madsen, *Commercial Arbitration in Sweden*, xiv.

78. Prior to the enactment of the Act in 1999, recognition and enforcement of foreign arbitral awards was governed by the 1929 Act. However, since Article V of the New York Convention was also applicable under the 1929 Act, case law prior to the enactment of the Act may also be relevant under the Act.

79. Normally, recognition and enforcement of a foreign arbitral award is only a matter of formalities. Court practice shows that there are very few cases in which recognition and enforcement has been rejected.[186] Most cases are determined within four to six months from the date of the application, i.e., including the time for serving the application on the respondent. In addition, in the limited number of cases appealed to the Supreme Court, the Svea Court of Appeal's decision has been upheld in almost all, if not in fact all, cases.

80. This notwithstanding, some notable features are evident from case law in relation to recognition and enforcement of foreign arbitral awards under the Act, which should be mentioned.

81. First, very few arbitral awards are subject to recognition and enforcement proceedings at all. In fact, the number of these cases is less than five annually. This should be compared to the total annual number of international arbitrations pending where the award could potentially be recognized and enforced in Sweden. However, statistics on those arbitrations would give limited guidance. Several of the arbitrations are ad hoc proceedings, which would not be covered by any statistics. In addition, it may be the case that foreign parties with no direct link to Sweden still have assets in Sweden and that recognition and enforcement are therefore sought there.

82. Second, and somewhat surprisingly, the defences raised by respondents against applications for recognition and enforcement of foreign arbitral awards are seldom applicable, i.e., they are not based on the grounds for refusing recognition and enforcement under sections 54 and 55 of the Act. The reason for this is difficult to understand. However, in a notable number of cases, the respondent has no legal representation, which possibly affects its chances to successfully plead its case. In this respect, it must be noted that the enumeration of grounds for such refusal in sections 54 and 55 of the Act is exhaustive.[187] Defences such as that the respondent has already discharged its obligations under the arbitral award, or that the respondent has a set-off

186. An international comparison shows that the 'failure rate', i.e., cases where enforcement of an award under the New York Convention has been refused by the court, is about 10%, see Brady in *50 Years of the New York Convention*, ICCA International Arbitration Conference, 2008, 709. Although the 'failure rate' seemingly is higher internationally than in Swedish courts, it is still evident that the New York Convention is an effective instrument which well serves its purpose. See also the compilation of enforcement decisions of the Svea Court of Appeal, in the appended compilation of enforcement decisions of the Svea Court of Appeal.

187. See, e.g., *Fløjstrup v. Madsen*, decision by the Supreme Court made on 6 May 2008 in case no Ö 543-08, NJA 2008 N 32, where the Supreme Court found that the fact that a party had been incorrectly indicated in the award did not constitute a ground for refusing enforcement of the award.

claim, are not grounds for refusal. Such defences may, and should, instead be raised in the subsequent execution phase with the Enforcement Authority.[188]

83. Third, out of the very few applications submitted to the Svea Court of Appeal, a striking number of these is withdrawn by the applicant before adjudication and are thus written off by the court. The reasons for these withdrawals are not stated, but a good guess is that the respondent has voluntarily discharged its obligations under the arbitral award or that the parties have settled the case before the end of the proceedings before the court.

84. The conclusion of these features may be that in most cases a party with a Swedish connection accepts an arbitral award and acts in accordance therewith. If not, facing poor odds of being successful in refusing recognition and enforcement of the arbitral award under the Act, many parties seem to believe that court proceedings should be avoided and therefore discharge their obligations under the arbitral award once the application for recognition and enforcement is submitted. In any event, the statistics show that the Act (and accordingly the New York Convention) is effective in that most recognition and enforcement proceedings are avoided in the first place. In those cases, which are adjudicated, the arbitral award will be recognized and enforced almost without exception.

85. Also worth mentioning in this respect are the somewhat similar proceedings for recognition and enforcement of foreign judgments laid down in the Brussels I Regulation,[189] which is applicable to EU Member States. In *Hilcourt (Docklands) Limited (UK) v. TeliaSonera AB (Sweden)*,[190] the Svea Court of Appeal declared that a decision by the English High Court of Justice, Chancery Division, was enforceable in Sweden in accordance with the Brussels I Regulation. However, the somewhat controversial issue in the case was that the decision by the High Court of Justice concerned recognition and enforcement of an arbitral award between the parties previously rendered in London. It may thus be argued that the parties may circumvent proceedings for recognition and enforcement set out in the Act, and thereby the New York Convention, by having an arbitral award declared enforceable in domestic proceedings (within the EU) and subsequently relying on the Brussels I Regulation instead of the Act.

188. See *Förlagsgrupp Superdruk (previously Publishing Group 'Expres' Ltd.) v. Solna Offset AB*, decision by the Svea Court of Appeal made on 19 Apr. 2012 in case no Ö 4963-11, where the court stated that the counterclaim invoked by the respondent did not constitute a hindrance to a declaration of enforceability, and pointed out that such claims may instead be considered in the execution process.

189. Council Regulation (EC) No 44/2001 of 22 Dec. 2000 on jurisdiction and the recognition and enforcement of judgments in civil and commercial matters. Note that a revised Brussels I Regulation has been adopted on 12 Dec. 2012, in which recital 12 attempts to further clarify the scope of the regulation with regard to arbitration. The new Brussels I Regulation shall apply from 10 Jan. 2015 and the Swedish government has appointed a committee to assess the need for legislation and draft a government bill for the implementation of the new Brussels I Regulation. The committee shall present its report on 13 Sep. 2013.

190. *Hilcourt (Docklands) Limited (UK) v. TeliaSonera AB (Sweden)*, decision by the Supreme Court made on 22 Sep. 2005 in case no Ö 3417-05, NJA 2005 p. 642.

86. Since the definition of a judgment in Article 32 of the Brussels I Regulation includes any judgment given by a court or tribunal of a Member State, whatever the judgment may be called, including a decree, order, decision or writ of execution, there seems to be no controversy in this respect in accepting the Svea Court of Appeal's decision. However, it has been submitted that this should not be acceptable as a matter of principle.[191] Such a position is prudent and easy to agree with, primarily because the opposite would open the possibility to circumvent the Act, and thus the New York Convention, when it comes to recognition and enforcement of foreign (albeit EU) arbitral awards. This notwithstanding, it is difficult to find support for such a position. The scope of the exception for 'arbitration' set out in Article 1.2(d) of the Brussels I Regulation is somewhat unclear. In *Marc Rich*,[192] the European Court of Justice addressed the interpretation of this article, and stated that preliminary issues (*in casu*, the appointment of an arbitrator and the validity of an arbitration agreement) are covered by the exception in Article 1.2(d).[193] In addition, it has been held that the exception applies to certain supporting (or ancillary) functions to the arbitral proceedings, such as e.g., adjudication of an arbitrator's alleged bias, challenge or invalidity of arbitral awards, and taking evidence and/or discovery.[194] There seems to be no support, however, for the proposition that the exception in Article 1.2(d) would also cover recognition and enforcement of an arbitral award.[195] Such an action is not a preliminary or otherwise supporting function to an imminent or pending arbitration.

87. Unfortunately, *Hilcourt (Docklands) Limited (UK) v. TeliaSonera AB*[196] *(Sweden)* before the Supreme Court was based on an extraordinary judicial remedy (miscarriage of justice) only and thus did not include substantive issues, e.g., whether or not the Brussels I Regulation applies in relation to recognition and enforcement of decisions on arbitral awards. In practice, however, one may question if this possibly available route would imply inconvenience for the respondent (or for that matter advantage for the applicant), since statistics show that, almost without exception, a foreign arbitral award would be recognized and enforced under the Act anyway.

191. See Lindskog, *Skiljeförfarande – En kommentar*, 1147 and n. 28, who seems to believe that this alternative route should not be accepted. Lindskog has previously held that it is only in cases where the arbitral award has formed the basis for a fully developed judgment by the foreign court, i.e. not in a procedure of exequatur, where the foreign judgment may be enforced in accordance with the Brussels I Regulation. See also, Pålsson, *Skiljeförfarande och Bryssel/Luganokonventionerna*, in *Svensk Juristtidning*, 1994, 1-22 (in particular 15-17).

192. *Marc Rich & CoAG v. Società Italiana Impianti*, European Court of Justice ruling in SPA (C-190/89), [1991] ECR1-3855.

193. See *RosInvestCO UK Ltd v. The Russian Federation*, decision by the Supreme Court made on 12 Nov. 2010 in case no Ö 2301-09, NJA 2010 p. 508, where the Supreme Court did not grant leave to appeal with respect to the scope of Art. 1.2(d) of the Brussels I Regulation, though noting that the exception clearly also covers a claim for declaratory relief in relation to the jurisdiction (*in casu* whether a valid arbitration agreement existed) of the arbitral tribunal.

194. See, however, Schlosser, *The 1968 Brussels Convention and Arbitration*, 227–242, where Schlosser submits that the Brussels I Regulation applies to all court proceedings in relation to arbitral proceedings.

195. *Ibid.* See also *supra* n. 189, with regard to the revised Brussels I Regulation.

196. *Hilcourt (Docklands) Limited (UK) v. TeliaSonera AB (Sweden)*, decision by the Supreme Court made on 22 Sep. 2005 in case no Ö 3417-05, NJA 2005 p. 642.

Compilation of enforcement decisions of the Svea Court of Appeal (2000-2012)

Case No.	Applicant/Respondent	Filing Date	Decision Date	Outcome	Appellate Case No.
Ö 4232-00	*Group 4 Securities BV v. Rajiv Mehta*	00-06-14	00-10-31	Enforced	
Ö 4859-00	*American Pacific corporation v. Sydsvensk Produktutveckling AB bankruptcy estate*	00-07-05	01-03-21	Enforced	
Ö 4645-99	*Société Planavergne SA v. K.B. i Stockholm AB*	99-06-17	01-09-07	Partially enforced*	NJA 2003 p. 379
Ö 6039-01	*Oy HD-Consult v. Johnny Letth*	01-08-22	01-10-10	Enforced	
Ö 3221-02	*Robert Grizila v. Johnny Letth bankruptcy estate*	02-03-08	02-05-31	Denied*	NJA 2002 C 45
Ö 6498-01	*Odfjell Seachemm AS v. Windsor Chemicals Europe AB*	01-09-20	02-06-11	Enforced	
Ö 5684-02	*Sunnywood Group Ltd v. Joakim Andersson*	02-05-24	02-09-26	Enforced	
Ö 7182-01	*SwemBalt Aktiebolag v. Republic of Latvia*	01-10-19	02-10-29	Enforced*	NJA 2002 C 62
Ö 9153-02	*Norske Skog Flooring Holding AS v. Välinge Aluminium AB*	02-10-21	03-01-03	Withdrawn	
Ö 5959-03	*Frigo Navigation Ltd v. Mediteranska Plovidba DD*	03-07-30	03-08-27	Withdrawn	
Ö 2235-04	*Mekajohtotiet Oy et al. v. Bo Andersson*	04-03-18	04-04-01	Withdrawn	
Ö 7159-04	*Ekpac International Ltd v. RM Rocade AB*	04-09-14	04-11-11	Withdrawn	
Ö 9735-04	*Orbis Spólka Akcyjna A v. Prenad International AB*	04-12-15	05-06-10	Withdrawn	

Case No.	Applicant/Respondent	Filing Date	Decision Date	Outcome	Appellate Case No.
Ö 2321-05	*Sparebanken Nord Norge v. Per-Gunnar Svendsen*	05-03-29	05-09-28	Enforced	
Ö 2262-07	*Marian Janowski et al. v. Appelkvist Fryseri AB*	07-03-02	07-11-19	Withdrawn	
Ö 3501-07	*Jens Madsen et al. v. Finn Bjarne Fløjstrup*	07-05-07	07-12-28	Enforced*	NJA 2008 N 32
Ö 8421-07	*A/S Bolderaja v. Bo Andrén AB*	07-11-22	08-06-18	Withdrawn	
Ö 1661-08	*Fabryka Wyrobów Lnianych Swiebodzice Sp. z.o.o.v. Carabaque International AB*	08-02-28	08-10-08	Enforced*	NJA 2009 N 9
Ö 1438-07	*Lenmorniiproekt OAO v. A.L. & Partner Leasing*	07-02-23	08-12-04	Dismissed*	NJA 2010 p. 219
Ö 7186-08	*Fabryka Wyrobów Lnianych Swiebodzice Sp. z.o.o.v. Carabaque International AB*	08-09-15	08-12-22	Dismissed, lis pendens	
Ö 10174-08	*Vista USA, LLC v. Combex AB*	08-12-29	09-02-11	Enforced	
Ö 1475-09	*Helsingør Boligeselskab afdelning 12, Blicherparken v. Morneon Fasad AB*	09-02-18	09-06-24	Withdrawn (upon appeal)	
Ö 9368-09	*Eagle Navigation Ltd v. MD Shipping Line AB*	09-11-27	10-03-30	Enforced	
Ö 7456-10	*Crestcom v. Hans Jakobsson*	10-09-20	11-01-10	Enforced	
Ö 7503-10	*Tecwill Oy v. Kilanda Fastigheter och Maskiner KB*	10-09-21	11-05-10	Enforced	
Ö 3171-10	*Commisimpex SA v. The Democratic Republic of the Kongo*	10-04-15	12-02-10	Enforced	
Ö 8038-10	*The estate of Juan Aramendía Rosas v. NCC International AB*	10-10-08	12-04-16	Dismissed	Appealed, 12-05-09

Case No.	Applicant/Respondent	Filing Date	Decision Date	Outcome	Appellate Case No.
Ö 4963-11	*Förlagsgrupp Superdruk (previously Publishing Group 'Expres' Ltd.) v. Solna Offset AB*	11-06-10	12-04-19	Enforced	
Ö 5300-12	*Subway International B.V. v. Amir Bozaghian*	12-06-13	(Pending)		
Ö 511-13	*Solna Offset AB v Publishing Group*	13-01-11	(Pending)		

* The Svea Court of Appeal's decision was upheld by the Supreme Court.

APPENDIX I

THE SWEDISH ARBITRATION ACT OF 1999*

(SFS 1999:116) Entered into force on 1 April 1999

THE ARBITRATION AGREEMENT

Section 1

Disputes concerning matters in respect of which the parties may reach a settlement may, by agreement, be referred to one or several arbitrators for resolution. Such an agreement may relate to future disputes pertaining to a legal relationship specified in the agreement. The dispute may concern the existence of a particular fact.

The parties may authorize the arbitrators to fill gaps in agreements, in addition to interpreting agreements.

Arbitrators may rule on the civil law effects of competition law as between the parties.

Section 2

The arbitrators may rule on their own jurisdiction to decide the dispute. The aforesaid shall not prevent a court from determining such a question at the request of a party. The arbitrators may continue the arbitral proceedings pending the determination by the court.

Notwithstanding the fact that the arbitrators have determined, in a decision rendered during the proceedings, that they have jurisdiction to resolve the dispute, such decision is not binding. The provisions of sections 34 and 36 shall apply in respect of an action to challenge an arbitral award which includes a decision in respect of jurisdiction.

* Translated by Professor Kaj Hobér, Partner, Mannheimer Swartling, Stockholm.

Section 3

Where the validity of an arbitration agreement which constitutes part of another agreement is to be determined in conjunction with the determination of the jurisdiction of the arbitrators, the arbitration agreement shall be deemed to constitute a separate agreement.

Section 4

A court may not, over an objection of a party, rule on an issue which, pursuant to an arbitration agreement, is to be decided by arbitrators.

A party must invoke an arbitration agreement on the first occasion that a party pleads his case on the merits in the court. The invocation of an arbitration agreement raised on a later occasion shall have no effect unless the party had a legal excuse and invoked the excuse as soon as it ceased to exist. An objection based on an arbitration agreement shall be taken into consideration notwithstanding the fact that the party who makes the objection has allowed an issue which is covered by the arbitration agreement to be determined by the Debt Enforcement Authority in a case administered in an expedited collection procedure.

Whilst a dispute is pending before arbitrators or prior thereto, a court may, irrespective of the arbitration agreement, issue such decisions in respect of security measures as the court is lawfully authorized to issue.

Section 5

A party shall forfeit his right to rely on the arbitration agreement as a bar to court proceedings where the party:

- has opposed a request for arbitration;
- fails to appoint an arbitrator in due time; or
- fails, in due time, to provide his share of the requested security for the compensation to the arbitrators.

Section 6

Where a dispute between a business enterprise and a consumer concerns goods, services, or any other products supplied principally for private use, an arbitration agreement may not be relied on where it was entered into prior to the dispute. However, such agreements shall apply with respect to rental or lease relationships where, by virtue of the agreements, a regional rent tribunal or a regional tenancies tribunal is appointed as the arbitral tribunal and where the provisions of chapter 8, section 28 or chapter 12, section 66 of the Real Estate Code do not stipulate otherwise.

The first paragraph shall not apply where the dispute concerns an agreement between an insurer and a policyholder regarding insurance based on a collective agreement or group agreement, and which representatives of the group handle. Nor shall the first paragraph apply where the international obligations of Sweden provide otherwise.

THE ARBITRATORS

Section 7

Any person who enjoys full legal capacity in regard to his actions and his property may act as arbitrator.

Section 8

An arbitrator shall be impartial.

At the request of a party, an arbitrator shall be discharged if there exists any circumstance which may diminish confidence in the arbitrator's impartiality. Such a circumstance shall always be deemed to exist:

- where the arbitrator or a person closely associated with him is a party, or otherwise may expect considerable benefit or detriment, as a result of the outcome of the dispute;
- where the arbitrator or a person closely associated with him is the director of a company or any other association which is a party, or otherwise represents a party or any other person who may expect considerable benefit or detriment as a result of the outcome of the dispute;
- where the arbitrator has taken a position in the dispute, as an expert or otherwise, or has assisted a party in the preparation or conduct of his case in the dispute; or
- where the arbitrator has received or demanded compensation in violation of section 39, second paragraph.

Section 9

A person who is asked to accept an appointment as arbitrator shall immediately disclose all circumstances which, pursuant to sections 7 or 8, may be deemed to prevent him from serving as arbitrator. An arbitrator shall inform the parties and the other arbitrators of such circumstances as soon as all arbitrators have been appointed and thereafter in the course of the arbitral proceedings as soon as he has learned of any new circumstance.

Section 10

A request to discharge an arbitrator due to a circumstance set forth in section 8 shall be presented within fifteen days from the date on which the party became aware both of the appointment of the arbitrator and of the existence of the circumstance. The request is to be tried by the arbitrators, unless the parties have decided that it is to be tried by someone else.

If the request is granted, the decision is not subject to appeal.

A party who is dissatisfied with a decision denying a request, or dismissing a request on the grounds that it was not timely filed, may file an application with the District Court that the arbitrator be discharged. The application must be submitted within thirty days from the date on which the party received the decision. The arbitrators may continue the arbitral proceedings pending the determination of the District Court.

Section 11

The parties may agree that a request referred to in section 10, first paragraph, is to be conclusively tried by an arbitration institution.

Section 12

The parties may determine the number of arbitrators and the manner in which they are to be appointed.

Sections 13-16 shall apply unless the parties have agreed otherwise.

Where the parties have so agreed, and where any of the parties so requests, the District Court shall also appoint arbitrators in situations other than those stated in sections 14-17.

Section 13

The arbitrators shall be three in number. Each party shall appoint one arbitrator, and the arbitrators so appointed shall appoint the third.

Section 14

Where each party is required to appoint an arbitrator and one party has notified the opposing party of his choice of arbitrator in a request for arbitration pursuant to section 19, the other party must, within thirty days of receipt of the notice, notify the first party in writing in respect of his choice of arbitrator.

A party who, in this manner, has notified the other party of his choice of arbitrator may not revoke the appointment without the consent of the other party.

If the other party fails to appoint an arbitrator within the stipulated period of time, the District Court shall appoint an arbitrator at the request of the first party.

Section 15

Where an arbitrator is to be appointed by other arbitrators, but they fail to do so within thirty days from the date on which the last arbitrator was appointed, the District Court shall appoint the arbitrator at the request of a party.

Where an arbitrator is to be appointed by someone other than a party or arbitrators, but such is not done within thirty days of the date when a party desiring the appointment of an arbitrator requested that the person responsible for the appointment make such appointment, the District Court shall, at the request of a party, appoint the arbitrator. The same shall apply where an arbitrator is to be appointed by the parties jointly, but they have failed to agree within thirty days from the date on which the question was raised, through receipt by one party of a notice from the other party.

Section 16

Where an arbitrator resigns or is discharged, the District Court shall, at the request of a party, appoint a new arbitrator. Where the arbitrator cannot fulfil his duties due to circumstances which have arisen subsequent to his appointment, the person who was originally required to make the appointment shall, instead, appoint a new arbitrator. Sections 14 and 15 apply with respect to such an appointment. The period of time within which a new arbitrator shall also be appointed, for the party who requested arbitration, is thirty days to be calculated, with respect to all parties, from the date when the person who is to appoint the arbitrator became aware thereof.

Section 17

Where an arbitrator has delayed the proceedings, the District Court shall, at the request of a party, discharge the arbitrator and appoint another arbitrator. The parties may decide that an arbitration institution shall instead, finally determine such a request.

Section 18

Where a party has requested that the District Court appoint an arbitrator pursuant to section 12, third paragraph or sections 14-17, the Court may reject the request on the ground that arbitration is manifestly not legally permissible.

THE PROCEEDINGS

Section 19

Unless otherwise agreed by the parties, the arbitral proceedings are initiated when a party receives a request for arbitration in accordance with the second paragraph hereof.

A request for arbitration must be in writing and must include:

- an express and unconditional request for arbitration;
- a statement of the issue which is covered by the arbitration agreement and which is to be resolved by the arbitrators; and
- a statement of the party's choice of arbitrator where the party is required to appoint an arbitrator.

Section 20

Where the arbitral tribunal is composed of more than one arbitrator, one of them shall be appointed chairman. Unless the parties or the arbitrators have decided otherwise, the chairman shall be the arbitrator appointed by the other arbitrators or by the District Court, instead of such arbitrators.

Section 21

The arbitrators shall handle the dispute in an impartial, practical, and speedy manner. In so doing, they shall act in accordance with the decisions of the parties insofar as there is no impediment to do so.

Section 22

The parties shall determine the place of arbitration. Where this is not the case, the arbitrators shall determine the place of arbitration.

The arbitrators may hold hearings and meetings elsewhere in Sweden, or abroad, unless otherwise determined by the parties.

Section 23

Within the period of time determined by the arbitrators, the claimant shall state his prayers for relief in respect of the issue stated in the request for arbitration, as well as the circumstances relied on by the party in support thereof. Thereafter, within the period of time determined by the arbitrators, the respondent shall state his position in relation to the prayers for relief and the circumstances relied on by the respondent in support thereof.

The claimant may submit new prayers for relief, and the respondent his own prayers for relief, provided that the prayers for relief fall within the scope of the arbitration agreement and, taking into consideration the time at which they are submitted or other circumstances, the arbitrators do not consider it inappropriate to try such prayers for relief. Subject to the same conditions, each party may, during the proceedings, amend or supplement previously presented prayers for relief and may rely on new circumstances in support of his case.

The first and second paragraphs hereof shall not apply where the parties have decided otherwise.

Section 24

The arbitrators shall afford the parties an opportunity to present their respective cases in writing or orally, to the extent necessary. Where a party so requests, and provided that the parties have not otherwise agreed, an oral hearing shall be held prior to the determination of an issue referred to the arbitrators for resolution.

A party shall be given an opportunity to review all documents and all other materials pertaining to the dispute which are supplied to the arbitrators by the other party or by another person.

Where one of the parties, without valid cause, fails to appear at a hearing or otherwise fails to comply with an order of the arbitrators, such failure shall not prevent the proceedings from continuing, nor a resolution of the dispute on the basis of the existing materials.

Section 25

The parties shall supply the evidence. The arbitrators may, however, appoint experts, unless both parties are opposed thereto.

The arbitrators may refuse to admit evidence that is offered where such evidence is manifestly irrelevant to the case or where such refusal is justified having regard to the time at which the evidence is offered.

The arbitrators may not administer oaths or truth affirmations. Nor may they impose conditional fines or otherwise order compulsory measures with a view to obtaining requested evidence.

Unless the parties have agreed otherwise, the arbitrators may, at the request of a party, decide that, during the proceedings, the other party must undertake a certain interim measure to secure the claim which is to be tried by the arbitrators. The arbitrators may order that the party requesting the interim measure must provide reasonable security for the damage which may be incurred by the other party as a result of the interim measure.

Section 26

Where a party wishes a witness or an expert to testify under oath, or a party to be examined under truth affirmation, that party may, after obtaining the consent of the arbitrators, submit an application to such effect to the District Court. The aforementioned shall apply where a party wishes that a party or other person be ordered to produce as evidence a document or an object. If the arbitrators consider that the measure is justified having regard to the evidence in the case, they shall approve the request. Where such measure may lawfully be taken, the District Court shall grant the application

The provisions of the Code of Judicial Procedure shall apply with respect to a measure referred to in the first paragraph. The arbitrators shall be summoned to hear the testimony of a witness, an expert, or a party, and shall be afforded the opportunity to ask questions. The absence of an arbitrator from such hearing shall not prevent the hearing from taking place.

THE ARBITRAL AWARD

Section 27

The issues which have been referred to the arbitrators shall be decided in an arbitral award. Where the arbitrators terminate the arbitral proceedings without deciding such issues, this shall also be made in an arbitral award.

Where the parties enter into a settlement agreement, the arbitrators may, at the request of the parties, confirm the settlement agreement in an arbitral award.

Other determinations, which are not included in an arbitral award, are referred to as decisions.

The mandate of the arbitrators shall be deemed to be completed when they have rendered a final arbitral award, unless otherwise provided in sections 32 or 35.

Section 28

Where a party withdraws a prayer for relief, the arbitrators shall dismiss that part of the dispute, unless the other party requests that the arbitrators rule on the prayer for relief.

Section 29

A part of the dispute, or a certain issue which is of significance to the resolution of the dispute, may be decided in a separate arbitral award, unless both parties object thereto. However, a claim relied on by way of set-off shall be tried in the same award as the main claim.

Where a party has admitted a prayer for relief, in whole or in part, a separate arbitral award may be rendered in respect of that which has been admitted.

Section 30

Where an arbitrator fails, without valid cause, to participate in the determination of an issue by the arbitral tribunal, such failure will not prevent the other arbitrators from deciding the issue.

Unless the parties have decided otherwise, the opinion agreed upon by the majority of the arbitrators participating in the determination of the dispute shall be the opinion of the arbitral tribunal. If no majority is attained for any opinion, the opinion of the chairman shall prevail.

Section 31

An arbitral award shall be made in writing and be signed by the arbitrators. It is sufficient that the award is signed by a majority of the arbitrators, provided that the reason why all of the arbitrators have not signed the arbitral award is noted therein. The parties may decide that the chairman of the arbitral tribunal alone shall sign the arbitral award.

The arbitral award shall state the place of arbitration and the date when the award is made.

The arbitral award shall be delivered to the parties immediately.

Section 32

If the arbitrators find that an arbitral award contains an obvious inaccuracy as a consequence of a typographical error, error in computation, or other similar error by the arbitrators, or any another person, or if the arbitrators by oversight have failed to decide an issue which should have been dealt with in the arbitral award, they may, within thirty days of the date of the rendering of the arbitral award, decide to correct or supplement the arbitral award. They may also correct or supplement an arbitral award, or interpret the operative part of an arbitral award, where any of the parties so requests within thirty days of receipt of the award by that party.

Where, at the request of any of the parties, the arbitrators decide to correct an arbitral award or interpret the operative part of an arbitral award, such an act shall take place within thirty days from the date of receipt, by the arbitrators, of the party's request. Where the arbitrators decide to supplement the award, such an act shall take place within sixty days.

Before the arbitrators take any decision pursuant to this section, the parties should be afforded an opportunity to express their views with respect to the measure.

INVALIDITY OF ARBITRAL AWARDS AND SETTING ASIDE ARBITRAL AWARDS

Section 33

An arbitral award is invalid:

- if it includes determination of an issue which, in accordance with Swedish law, may not be decided by arbitrators;
- if the arbitral award, or the manner in which the award arose, is manifestly incompatible with the fundamental principles of Swedish law; or
- if the arbitral award does not fulfil the requirements with regard to written form and signing pursuant to section 31, first paragraph.

The invalidity may apply to a certain part of the award.

Section 34

An arbitral award which may not be challenged in accordance with section 36 shall, following a challenge, be wholly or partially set aside at the request of a party:

- if it is not covered by a valid arbitration agreement between the parties;

- if the arbitrators have rendered the award after the expiration of the period of time decided by the parties, or where the arbitrators have otherwise exceeded their mandate;
- if arbitral proceedings, according to section 47, should not have taken place in Sweden;
- if an arbitrator has been appointed in conflict with the agreement between the parties, or with this Act;
- if an arbitrator was disqualified due to any circumstance set forth in sections 7 or 8; or
- if otherwise, through no fault of the party, an irregularity has occurred in the course of the proceedings which probably has influenced the outcome of the case.

A party shall not be entitled to rely on a circumstance which he, by participating in the proceedings without objection, or otherwise, may be deemed to have waived. A party shall not be regarded as having accepted the jurisdiction of the arbitrators to determine the issue referred to arbitration solely by having appointed an arbitrator. It follows from sections 10 and 11 that a party may lose the right in accordance with the first paragraph, sub-section 5 to rely on a circumstance set forth in section 8.

An action must be brought within three months from the date when the party received the arbitral award or, where correction, supplementation, or interpretation has taken place pursuant to section 32, within a period of three months from the date when the party received the arbitral award in its final wording. Following the expiration of the time limit, a party may not invoke a new ground in support of his action to challenge the arbitral award.

Section 35

A court may stay proceedings concerning the invalidity or setting aside of an arbitral award for a certain period of time in order to provide the arbitrators with an opportunity to resume the arbitral proceedings or to take some other measure which, in the opinion of the arbitrators, will eliminate the ground for the invalidity or setting aside:

- provided the court finds that the claim in the case is to be accepted and either of the parties requests a stay; or
- both parties request a stay.

Where the arbitrators render a new arbitral award, a party may, within the period of time determined by the court and without submitting a writ of summons, challenge the arbitral award to the extent that the challenge is caused by the resumed arbitral proceedings or by an amendment to the first arbitral award (SFS 2000:180).

Section 36

An award whereby the arbitrators have concluded the proceedings without ruling on the issues submitted to them for resolution may be changed, in whole or in part, at the application of a party. Such action must be brought within three months from the date when the party received the award or, where correction, supplementation, or interpretation has taken place in accordance with section 32, within a period of three months from when the party received the arbitral award in its final wording. The arbitral award shall contain clear instructions as to what must be done by a party who wishes to challenge the award.

An action in accordance with the first paragraph which only concerns an issue referred to in section 42 is permissible where the arbitral award means that the arbitrators have considered themselves to lack jurisdiction to try the dispute. Where the arbitral award means something else, a party who desires to attack the decision may do so by challenging the arbitral award in accordance with the provisions of section 34.

ARBITRATION COSTS

Section 37

The parties shall be jointly and severally liable to pay reasonable compensation to the arbitrators for work and expenses. However, where the arbitrators have stated in the arbitral award that they lack jurisdiction to try the dispute, the party that did not request arbitration shall be liable to pay only to the extent that special circumstances so require.

In a final arbitral award, the arbitrators may order the parties to pay compensation to them, together with interest from the date occurring one month following the date of the rendering of the arbitral award. The compensation shall be stated separately for each arbitrator.

Section 38

The arbitrators may request security for the compensation. They may fix separate security amounts for individual prayers for relief. Where a party fails to provide its share of the requested security within the period of time determined by the arbitrators, the other party may provide the entire security. Where the requested security is not provided, the arbitrators may terminate the proceedings, in whole or in part.

During the proceedings, the arbitrators may decide to use the security to cover expenses. Following the determination of the arbitrators' compensation in a final arbitral award and where such part of the award has become enforceable, the arbitrators may pay themselves from the security, in the event that the parties fail to fulfil their payment obligations in accordance with the award. The entitlement to the security also includes income from the property.

Section 39

The provisions of sections 37 and 38 shall apply unless otherwise jointly decided by the parties in a manner that is binding on the arbitrators.

An agreement regarding compensation to the arbitrators that is not entered into with the parties jointly is void. Where one of the parties has provided the entire security, such party alone may, however, consent to the realisation of the security by the arbitrators to cover compensation for work performed.

Section 40

The arbitrators may not withhold the arbitral award pending the payment of the compensation due to them.

Section 41

A party or an arbitrator may bring an action in the District Court against the arbitral award regarding the payment of compensation to the arbitrators. Such action must be brought within three months from the date when the party received the award and, in the case of an arbitrator, within the same period of time as of the rendering of the arbitral award. Where correction, supplementation, or interpretation has taken place in accordance with section 32, the action must be brought by a party within three months from the date when the party received the arbitral award in its final wording and, in the case of an arbitrator, within the same period of time as from the date when the arbitral award was rendered in its final wording. The arbitral award shall contain clear instructions as to what must be done by a party who wishes to bring an action against the award in this respect.

A judgment pursuant to which the compensation to an arbitrator is reduced shall apply also to a party who did not bring the action.

Section 42

Unless otherwise agreed by the parties, the arbitrators may, at the request of a party, order the other party to pay compensation for the party's costs and determine the manner in which the compensation to the arbitrators is finally to be allocated as between the parties. The order of the arbitrators may also include interest, if a party has so requested.

FORA AND TIME PERIODS

Section 43

An action against an arbitral award pursuant to sections 33, 34, and 36 shall be considered by the Court of Appeal within whose district the arbitral proceedings were held. Where the place of arbitration is not stated in the arbitral award, the action may be brought before the Svea Court of Appeal.

The decision of the Court of Appeal may not be appealed. The Court of Appeal may, however, grant leave to appeal the decision where it is of importance, as a matter of precedent, that the appeal be considered by the Supreme Court.

An action regarding compensation to an arbitrator shall be considered by the District Court at the place of arbitration. Where the place of arbitration is not stated in the arbitral award, the action may be brought before the Stockholm District Court.

Section 44

Applications to appoint or discharge an arbitrator shall be heard by the District Court at the place where one of the parties is domiciled or by the District Court at the place of arbitration. The application may also be heard by the Stockholm District Court. Where possible the opposing party shall be afforded the opportunity to express his opinion on the application before it is granted. Where the application concerns the removal of an arbitrator, the arbitrator should also be heard.

Applications concerning the taking of evidence in accordance with section 26 shall be heard by the District Court determined by the arbitrators. In the absence of such decision, the application shall be heard by the Stockholm District Court.

Where the District Court has granted an application to appoint or remove an arbitrator, such decision may not be appealed. Nor may a determination of the District Court in accordance with section 10, third paragraph otherwise be appealed.

Section 45

Where, according to law or by agreement, an action by a party must be brought within a certain period of time, but the action is covered by an arbitration agreement, the party must request arbitration in accordance with section 19 within the stated period of time.

Where arbitration has been requested in due time but the arbitral proceedings are terminated without a final and binding determination of the issue which was submitted to the arbitrators, and this is not due to the fault of the party, the action shall be deemed to have been instituted in due time where a party requests arbitration or institutes court proceedings within thirty days of receipt of the arbitral award, or where the arbitral award has been set aside or declared invalid or an action against the award in accordance with section 36 has been dismissed, from the time when such judgment becomes final.

INTERNATIONAL MATTERS

Section 46

This Act shall apply to arbitral proceedings which take place in Sweden notwithstanding the fact that the dispute has an international connection.

Section 47

Arbitral proceedings in accordance with this Act may be commenced in Sweden, where the arbitration agreement provides that the proceedings shall take place in Sweden, or where the arbitrators or an arbitration institution pursuant to the agreement have determined that the proceedings shall take place in Sweden, or the opposing party otherwise consents thereto.

Arbitral proceedings in accordance with this Act may also be commenced in Sweden against a party which is domiciled in Sweden or is otherwise subject to the jurisdiction of Swedish courts with regard to the matter in dispute, unless the arbitration agreement provides that the proceedings shall take place abroad.

In other cases, arbitral proceedings in accordance with this Act may not take place in Sweden.

Section 48

Where an arbitration agreement has an international connection, the law agreed upon by the parties shall govern the agreement. Where the parties have not reached such an agreement, the arbitration agreement shall be governed by the law of the country in which, by virtue of the agreement the proceedings have taken place or shall take place.

The first paragraph shall not apply to the issue of whether a party was authorized to enter into an arbitration agreement or was duly represented.

Section 49

Where foreign law is applicable to the arbitration agreement, section 4 shall apply to issues which are covered by the agreement, except when:

- in accordance with the applicable law, the agreement is invalid, inoperative, or incapable of being performed; or
- in accordance with Swedish law, the dispute may not be determined by arbitrators.

That a court has jurisdiction to issue such decisions regarding security measures as the court is authorized to issue in accordance with law, notwithstanding the arbitration agreement, is set forth in section 4, third paragraph.

Section 50

The provisions of sections 26 and 44 regarding the taking of evidence during arbitral proceedings in Sweden shall also apply in respect of arbitral proceedings which take place abroad, where the proceedings are based on an arbitration agreement and, pursuant to Swedish law, the issues which are referred to the arbitrators may be resolved by the arbitrators.

Section 51

Where none of the parties is domiciled or has its place of business in Sweden, such parties may in a commercial relationship in an express written agreement exclude or limit the application of the grounds for setting aside an arbitral award set forth in section 34.

An arbitral award which is subject to such an agreement shall be recognised and enforced in Sweden in accordance with the rules applicable to a foreign arbitral award.

RECOGNITION AND ENFORCEMENT OF FOREIGN ARBITRAL AWARDS

Section 52

An arbitral award made abroad shall be deemed to be a foreign arbitral award.

For purposes of applying this Act, an arbitral award shall be deemed to have been made in the country where the place of arbitration is situated.

Section 53

Unless otherwise provided for in sections 54-60, a foreign arbitral award which is based on an arbitration agreement shall be recognised and enforced in Sweden.

Section 54

A foreign arbitral award shall not be recognised and enforced in Sweden where the party against whom the award is invoked proves:

- that the parties to the arbitration agreement, pursuant to the law applicable to them, lacked capacity to enter into the agreement or were not duly represented, or that the arbitration agreement is invalid under the law to which the parties have subjected it or, failing any indication thereon, under the law of the country where the award was made;
- that the party against whom the award is invoked was not given proper notice of the appointment of the arbitrator or of the arbitration proceedings, or was otherwise unable to present his case;
- that the award deals with a dispute not contemplated by, or not falling within, the terms of the submission to arbitration, or contains decisions on matters which are beyond the scope of the arbitration agreement, provided that, if the decision on a matter which falls within the mandate can be separated from those which fall outside the mandate, that part of the award which contains decisions on matters falling within the mandate may be recognised and enforced;
- that the appointment of the arbitral tribunal, or its composition or the arbitral procedure, was not in accordance with the agreement of the parties or, failing

such agreement, was not in accordance with the law of the country where the arbitration took place; or
- that the arbitral award has not yet become binding on the parties, or has been set aside or suspended by a competent authority of the country in which, or under the law of which, the arbitral award was made.

Section 55

Recognition and enforcement of a foreign arbitral award shall also be refused where the court finds:

- that the arbitral award includes determination of an issue which, in accordance with Swedish law, may not be decided by arbitrators; or
- that it would be manifestly incompatible with the fundamental principles of Swedish law to recognise and enforce the arbitral award.

Section 56

An application for the enforcement of a foreign arbitral award shall be lodged with the Svea Court of Appeal.

The original arbitral award or a certified copy of the arbitral award must be appended to the application. Unless the Court of Appeal decides otherwise, a certified translation into the Swedish language of the entire award must also be submitted.

Section 57

An application for enforcement shall not be granted unless the opposing party has been afforded an opportunity to express his opinion on the application.

Section 58

Where the opposing party objects that an arbitration agreement was not entered into, the applicant must submit the arbitration agreement in an original or a certified copy and, unless otherwise decided by the Court of Appeal, must submit a certified translation into the Swedish language, or otherwise prove that an arbitration agreement was entered into.

Where the opposing party objects that a request has been made to set aside the arbitral award or a motion for a stay of execution has been submitted to the competent authority referred to in section 54, sub-section 5, the Court of Appeal may postpone its decision and, at the request of the applicant, order the other party to provide reasonable security in default of which enforcement might otherwise be ordered.

Section 59

Where the Court of Appeal grants the application, the arbitral award shall be enforced as a final and binding judgment of a Swedish court, unless otherwise determined by the Supreme Court following an appeal of the decision of the Court of Appeal.

Section 60

Where a security measure has been granted in accordance with chapter 15 of the Code of Judicial Procedure, a request for arbitration abroad which might result in an arbitral award which is recognised and may be enforced in Sweden shall, in conjunction with the application of section 7 of the same chapter, be equated with the commencement of an action.
Where an application for the enforcement of a foreign arbitral award has been made, it is for the Court of Appeal to examine a request for a security measure or a request to set aside such decision.

This Act shall enter into force on 1 April 1999, at which time the Arbitration Act (SFS 1929:145) and the Foreign Arbitration Agreements and Awards Act (SFS 1929:147) shall be repealed.

The previous Act shall apply to arbitral proceedings which have been commenced prior to the entry into force or, with respect to enforcement of a foreign arbitral award, if the application for enforcement was made prior to the entry into force.

Where an arbitration agreement has been concluded prior to the entry into force, the provisions of section 18, second paragraph, section 21, first paragraph, sub-section 1, and section 26, second and third paragraphs of the Arbitration Act (SFS 1929:145) shall apply, in so far as the period of time within which the award shall be rendered is concerned, to proceedings that are commenced within two years from the date of the entry into force of the new Act.

In the circumstances set forth in sub-sections 2 and 3, the parties may agree that only the new Act shall apply.

If statutes or other legislation refer to the Arbitration Act (SFS 1929:145), the new Act shall be applied instead.

APPENDIX II

ARBITRATION RULES OF THE ARBITRATION INSTITUTE OF THE STOCKHOLM CHAMBER OF COMMERCE

Adopted by the Stockholm Chamber of Commerce and in force as of 1 January 2010*

Under any arbitration agreement referring to the Arbitration Rules of the Arbitration Institute of the Stockholm Chamber of Commerce (the "Arbitration Rules") the parties shall be deemed to have agreed that the following rules, or such amended rules, in force on the date of the commencement of the arbitration, or the filing of an application for the appointment of an Emergency Arbitrator, shall be applied unless otherwise agreed by the parties.

---

*. *The English text prevails over other language versions*

Article 1 About the SCC

The Arbitration Institute of the Stockholm Chamber of Commerce (the "SCC") is the body responsible for the administration of disputes in accordance with the "SCC Rules"; the Arbitration Rules of the Arbitration Institute of the Stockholm Chamber of Commerce (the "Arbitration Rules") and the Rules for Expedited Arbitrations of the Stockholm Chamber of Commerce (the "Rules for Expedited Arbitrations"), and other procedures or rules agreed upon by the parties. The SCC is composed of a board of directors (the "Board") and a secretariat (the "Secretariat"). Detailed provisions regarding the organisation of the SCC are set out in Appendix I.

Commencement of proceedings

Article 2 Request for Arbitration

A Request for Arbitration shall include:

- (i) a statement of the names, addresses, telephone and facsimile numbers and e-mail addresses of the parties and their counsel;
- (ii) a summary of the dispute;
- (iii) a preliminary statement of the relief sought by the Claimant;
- (iv) a copy or description of the arbitration agreement or clause under which the dispute is to be settled;
- (v) comments on the number of arbitrators and the seat of arbitration; and
- (vi) if applicable, the name, address, telephone number, facsimile number and e-mail address of the arbitrator appointed by the Claimant.

Article 3 Registration Fee

- (1) Upon filing the Request for Arbitration, the Claimant shall pay a Registration Fee. The amount of the Registration Fee shall be determined in accordance with the Schedule of Costs (Appendix III) in force on the date when the Request for Arbitration is filed.
- (2) If the Registration Fee is not paid upon filing the Request for Arbitration, the Secretariat shall set a time period with in which the Claimant shall pay the Registration Fee. If the Registration Fee is not paid within this time period, the Secretariat shall dismiss the Request for Arbitration.

Article 4 Commencement of arbitration

Arbitration is commenced on the date when the SCC receives the Request for Arbitration.

Article 5 Answer

(1) The Secretariat shall send a copy of the Request for Arbitration and the documents attached thereto to the Respondent. The Secretariat shall set a time period within which the Respondent shall submit an Answer to the SCC. The Answer shall include:

(i) any objections concerning the existence, validity or applicability of the arbitration agreement; however, failure to raise any objections shall not preclude the Respondent from subsequently raising such objections at any time up to and including the submission of the Statement of Defence;
(ii) an admission or denial of the relief sought in the Request for Arbitration;
(iii) a preliminary statement of any counterclaims or set-offs;
(iv) comments on the number of arbitrators and the seat of arbitration; and
(v) if applicable, the name, address, telephone number, facsimile number and e-mail address of the arbitrator appointed by the Respondent.

(2) The Secretariat shall send a copy of the Answer to the Claimant. The Claimant shall be given an opportunity to submit comments on the Answer.
(3) Failure by the Respondent to submit an Answer shall not prevent the arbitration from proceeding.

Article 6 Request for further details

The Board may request further details from either party regarding any of their written submissions to the SCC. If the Claimant fails to comply with a request for further details, the Board may dismiss the case. If the Respondent fails to comply with a request for further details regarding its counterclaim or set-off, the Board may dismiss the counterclaim or set-off. Failure by the Respondent to otherwise comply with a request for further details shall not prevent the arbitration from proceeding.

Article 7 Time periods

The Board may, on application by either party or on its own motion, extend any time period which has been set for a party to comply with a particular direction.

Article 8 Notices

(1) Any notice or other communication from the Secretariat or the Board shall be delivered to the last known address of the addressee.
(2) Any notice or other communication shall be delivered by courier or registered mail, facsimile transmission, e-mail or any other means of communication that provides a record of the sending thereof.
(3) A notice or communication sent in accordance with paragraph (2) shall be deemed to have been received by the addressee on the date it would normally have been received given the chosen means of communication.

Article 9 Decisions by the Board

When necessary the Board shall:

(i) decide whether the SCC manifestly lacks jurisdiction over the dispute pursuant to Article 10 (i);
(ii) decide whether to consolidate cases pursuant to Article 11;
(iii) decide the number of arbitrators pursuant to Article 12;
(iv) make any appointment of arbitrators pursuant to Article 13;
(v) decide the seat of arbitration pursuant to Article 20; and
(vi) determine the Advance on Costs pursuant to Article 45.

Article 10 Dismissal

The Board shall dismiss a case, in whole or in part, if:

(i) the SCC manifestly lacks jurisdiction over the dispute; or
(ii) the Advance on Costs is not paid pursuant to Article 45.

Article 11 Consolidation

If arbitration is commenced concerning a legal relationship in respect of which an arbitration between the same parties is already pending under these Rules, the Board may, at the request of a party, decide to consolidate the new claims with the pending proceedings. Such decision may only be made after consulting the parties and the Arbitral Tribunal.

Composition of the Arbitral Tribunal

Article 12 Number of arbitrators

The parties may agree on the number of arbitrators. Where the parties have not agreed on the number of arbitrators, the Arbitral Tribunal shall consist of three arbitrators, unless the Board, taking into account the complexity of the case, the amount in dispute or other circumstances, decides that the dispute is to be decided by a sole arbitrator.

Article 13 Appointment of arbitrators

(1) The parties may agree on a different procedure for appointment of the Arbitral Tribunal than as provided under this Article. In such cases, if the Arbitral Tribunal has not been appointed within the time period agreed by the parties or, where the parties have not agreed on a time period, within the time period set by the Board, the appointment shall be made pursuant to paragraphs (2)-(6).

(2) Where the Arbitral Tribunal is to consist of a sole arbitrator, the parties shall be given 10 days within which to jointly appoint the arbitrator. If the parties fail to make the appointment within this time period, the arbitrator shall be appointed by the Board.
(3) Where the Arbitral Tribunal is to consist of more than one arbitrator, each party shall appoint an equal number of arbitrators and the Chairperson shall be appointed by the Board. Where a party fails to appoint arbitrator(s) within the stipulated time period, the Board shall make the appointment.
(4) Where there are multiple Claimants or Respondents and the Arbitral Tribunal is to consist of more than one arbitrator, the multiple Claimants, jointly, and the multiple Respondents, jointly, shall appoint an equal number of arbitrators. If either side fails to make such joint appointment, the Board shall appoint the entire Arbitral Tribunal.
(5) If the parties are of different nationalities, the sole arbitrator or the Chairperson of the Arbitral Tribunal shall be of a different nationality than the parties, unless the parties have agreed otherwise or unless otherwise deemed appropriate by the Board.
(6) When appointing arbitrators, the Board shall consider the nature and circumstances of the dispute, the applicable law, the seat and language of the arbitration and the nationality of the parties.

Article 14 Impartiality and independence

(1) Every arbitrator must be impartial and independent.
(2) Before being appointed as arbitrator, a person shall disclose any circumstances which may give rise to justifiable doubts as to his/her impartiality or independence. If the person is appointed as arbitrator, he/she shall submit to the Secretariat a signed statement of impartiality and in dependence disclosing any circumstances which may give rise to justifiable doubts as to that person's impartiality or independence. The Secretariat shall send a copy of the statement of impartiality and independence to the parties and the other arbitrators.
(3) An arbitrator shall immediately inform the parties and the other arbitrators in writing where any circumstances referred to in paragraph (2) arise during the course of the arbitration.

Article 15 Challenge to arbitrators

(1) A party may challenge any arbitrator if circumstances exist which give rise to justifiable doubts as to the arbitrator's impartiality or independence or if he/she does not possess qualifications agreed by the parties. A party may challenge an arbitrator whom it has appointed or in whose appointment it has participated, only for reasons of which it becomes aware after the appointment was made.

(2) A challenge to an arbitrator shall be made by submitting a written statement to the Secretariat setting forth the reasons for the challenge within 15 days from when the circumstances giving rise to the challenge became known to the party. Failure by a party to challenge an arbitrator within the stipulated time period constitutes a waiver of the right to make the challenge.

(3) The Secretariat shall notify the parties and the arbitrators of the challenge and give them an opportunity to submit comments on the challenge.

(4) If the other party agrees to the challenge, the arbitrator shall resign. In all other cases, the Board shall make the final decision on the challenge.

Article 16 Release from appointment

(1) The Board shall release an arbitrator from appointment where:

(i) the Board accepts the resignation of an arbitrator;
(ii) a challenge to the arbitrator under Article 15 is sustained; or
(iii) the arbitrator is otherwise prevented from fulfilling his/her duties or fails to perform his/her functions in an adequate manner.

(2) Before the Board releases an arbitrator, the Secretariat may give the parties and the arbitrators an opportunity to submit comments.

Article 17 Replacement of arbitrators

(1) The Board shall appoint a new arbitrator where an arbitrator has been released from his/her appointment pursuant to Article 16, or where an arbitrator has died. If the arbitrator being replaced was appointed by a party, that party shall appoint the new arbitrator, unless otherwise deemed appropriate by the Board.

(2) Where the Arbitral Tribunal consists of three or more arbitrators, the Board may decide that the remaining ar bitrators shall proceed with the arbitration. In making its decision, the Board shall take into account the stage of the arbitration and other relevant circumstances. Before making such decision, the parties and the arbitrators shall be given an opportunity to submit comments.

(3) Where an arbitrator has been replaced, the newly composed Arbitral Tribunal shall decide whether and to what extent the proceedings are to be repeated.

The proceedings before the Arbitral Tribunal

Article 18 Referral to the Arbitral Tribunal

When the Arbitral Tribunal has been appointed and the Advance on Costs has been paid, the Secretariat shall refer the case to the Arbitral Tribunal.

Article 19 Conduct of the arbitration

(1) Subject to these Rules and any agreement between the parties, the Arbitral Tribunal may conduct the arbitration in such manner as it considers appropriate.
(2) In all cases, the Arbitral Tribunal shall conduct the arbitration in an impartial, practical and expeditious manner, giving each party an equal and reasonable opportunity to present its case.

Article 20 Seat of arbitration

(1) Unless agreed upon by the parties, the Board shall decide the seat of arbitration.
(2) The Arbitral Tribunal may, after consultation with the parties, conduct hearings at any place which it considers appropriate. The Arbitral Tribunal may meet and deliberate at any place which it considers appropriate. If any hearing, meeting, or deliberation is held elsewhere than at the seat of arbitration, the arbitration shall be deemed to have taken place at the seat of arbitration.
(3) The award shall be deemed to have been made at the seat of arbitration.

Article 21 Language

(1) Unless agreed upon by the parties, the Arbitral Tribunal shall determine the language(s) of the arbitration. In so determining, the Arbitral Tribunal shall have due regard to all relevant circumstances and shall give the parties an opportunity to submit comments.
(2) The Arbitral Tribunal may request that any documents submitted in languages other than the language(s) of the arbitration be accompanied by a translation into the language(s) of the arbitration.

Article 22 Applicable law

(1) The Arbitral Tribunal shall decide the merits of the dispute on the basis of the law(s) or rules of law agreed upon by the parties. In the absence of such agreement, the Arbitral Tribunal shall apply the law or rules of law which it considers to be most appropriate.

(2) Any designation made by the parties of the law of a given state shall be deemed to refer to the substantive law of that state and not to its conflict of laws rules.

(3) The Arbitral Tribunal shall decide the dispute *ex aequo et bono or as amiable compositeur* only if the parties have expressly authorised it to do so.

Article 23 Provisional timetable

After the referral of the case to the Arbitral Tribunal, the Arbitral Tribunal shall promptly consult with the parties with a view to establishing a provisional timetable for the conduct of the arbitration. The Arbitral Tribunal shall send a copy of the provisional timetable to the parties and to the Secretariat.

Article 24 Written submissions

(1) The Claimant shall, within the period of time determined by the Arbitral Tribunal, submit a Statement of Claim which shall include, unless previously submitted:

(i) the specific relief sought
(ii) the material circumstances on which the Claimant relies; and
(iii) the documents on which the Claimant relies.

(2) The Respondent shall, within the period of time determined by the Arbitral Tribunal, submit a Statement of Defence which shall include, unless previously submitted:

(i) any objections concerning the existence, validity or applicability of the arbitration agreement;
(ii) a statement whether, and to what extent, the Respondent admits or denies the relief sought by the Claimant;
(iii) the material circumstances on which the Respondent relies;
(iv) any counterclaim or set-off and the grounds on which it is based; and
(v) the documents on which the Respondent relies.

(3) The Arbitral Tribunal may order the parties to submit additional written submissions.

Article 25 Amendments

At any time prior to the close of proceedings pursuant to Article 34, a party may amend or supplement its claim, counterclaim, defence or set-off provided its case, as amended or supplemented, is still comprised by the arbitration agreement, unless the Arbitral Tribunal considers it inappropriate to allow such amendment or supplement having regard to the delay in making it, the prejudice to the other party or any other circumstances.

Article 26 Evidence

(1) The admissibility, relevance, materiality and weight of evidence shall be for the Arbitral Tribunal to determine.

(2) The Arbitral Tribunal may order a party to identify the documentary evidence it intends to rely on and specify the circumstances intended to be proved by such evidence.

(3) At the request of a party, the Arbitral Tribunal may order a party to produce any documents or other evidence which may be relevant to the outcome of the case.

Article 27 Hearings

(1) A hearing shall be held if requested by a party, or if deemed appropriate by the Arbitral Tribunal.

(2) The Arbitral Tribunal shall, in consultation with the parties, determine the date, time and location of any hearing and shall provide the parties with reasonable notice thereof.

(3) Unless otherwise agreed by the parties, hearings will be held in private.

Article 28 Witnesses

(1) In advance of any hearing, the Arbitral Tribunal may order the parties to identify each witness or expert they intend to call and specify the circumstances intended to be proved by each testimony.

(2) The testimony of witnesses or party-appointed experts may be submitted in the form of signed statements.

(3) Any witness or expert, on whose testimony a party seeks to rely, shall attend a hearing for examination, unless otherwise agreed by the parties.

Article 29 Experts appointed by the Arbitral Tribunal

(1) After consultation with the parties, the Arbitral Tribunal may appoint one or more experts to report to it on specific issues set out by the Arbitral Tribunal in writing.

(2) Upon receipt of a report from an expert appointed by the Arbitral Tribunal, the Arbitral Tribunal shall send a copy of the report to the parties and shall give the parties an opportunity to submit written comments on the report.

(3) Upon the request of a party, the parties shall be given an opportunity to examine any expert appointed by the Arbitral Tribunal at a hearing.

Article 30 Default

(1) If the Claimant, without showing good cause, fails to submit a Statement of Claim in accordance with Article 24, the Arbitral Tribunal shall terminate the proceedings provided the Respondent has not filed a counterclaim.
(2) If a party, without showing good cause, fails to submit a Statement of Defence or other written statement in accordance with Article 24, or fails to appear at a hearing, or otherwise fails to avail itself of the opportunity to present its case, the Arbitral Tribunal may proceed with the arbitration and make an award.
(3) If a party without good cause fails to comply with any provision of, or requirement under, these Rules or any procedural order given by the Arbitral Tribunal, the Arbitral Tribunal may draw such inferences as it considers appropriate.

Article 31 Waiver

A party, who during the arbitration fails to object without delay to any failure to comply with the arbitration agreement, these Rules or other rules applicable to the proceedings, shall be deemed to have waived the right to object to such failure.

Article 32 Interim measures

(1) The Arbitral Tribunal may, at the request of a party, grant any interim measures it deems appropriate.
(2) The Arbitral Tribunal may order the party requesting an interim measure to provide appropriate security in connection with the measure.
(3) An interim measure shall take the form of an order or an award.
(4) Provisions with respect to interim measures requested before arbitration has been commenced or a case has been referred to an Arbitral Tribunal are set out in Appendix II.
(5) A request for interim measures made by a party to a judicial authority is not incompatible with the arbitration agreement or with these Rules.

Article 33 Communications from the Arbitral Tribunal

Article 8 shall apply to communications from the Arbitral Tribunal.

Article 34 Close of proceedings

The Arbitral Tribunal shall declare the proceedings closed when it is satisfied that the parties have had a reasonable opportunity to present their cases. In exceptional circumstances, prior to the making of the final award, the Arbitral Tribunal may reopen the proceedings on its own motion, or upon the application of a party.

Awards and decisions

Article 35 Awards and decisions

(1) When the Arbitral Tribunal consists of more than one arbitrator, any award or other decision of the Arbitral Tribunal shall be made by a majority of the arbitrators or, failing a majority, by the Chairperson.
(2) The Arbitral Tribunal may decide that the Chairperson alone may make procedural rulings.

Article 36 Making of awards

(1) The Arbitral Tribunal shall make its award in writing, and, unless otherwise agreed by the parties, shall state the reasons upon which the award is based.
(2) An award shall include the date of the award and the seat of arbitration in accordance with Article 20.
(3) An award shall be signed by the arbitrators. If an arbitrator fails to sign an award, the signatures of the majority of the arbitrators or, failing a majority, of the Chairperson shall be sufficient, provided that the reason for the omission of the signature is stated in the award.
(4) The Arbitral Tribunal shall deliver a copy of the award to each of the parties and to the SCC without delay.
(5) If any arbitrator fails without valid cause to participate in the deliberations of the Arbitral Tribunal on an issue, such failure will not preclude a decision being made by the other arbitrators.

Article 37 Time limit for final award

The final award shall be made not later than six months from the date upon which the arbitration was referred to the Arbitral Tribunal pursuant to Article 18. The Board may extend this time limit upon a reasoned request from the Arbitral Tribunal or if otherwise deemed necessary.

Article 38 Separate award

The Arbitral Tribunal may decide a separate issue or part of the dispute in a separate award.

Article 39 Settlement or other grounds for termination of the arbitration

(1) If the parties reach a settlement before the final award is made, the Arbitral Tribunal may, upon the request of both parties, record the settlement in the form of a consent award.

(2) If the arbitration for any other reason is terminated before the final award is made, the Arbitral Tribunal shall issue an award recording the termination.

Article 40 Effect of an award

An award shall be final and binding on the parties when rendered. By agreeing to arbitration under these Rules, the parties undertake to carry out any award without delay.

Article 41 Correction and interpretation of an award

(1) Within 30 days of receiving an award, a party may, upon notice to the other party, request that the Arbitral Tribunal correct any clerical, typographical or computational errors in the award, or provide an interpretation of a specific point or part of the award. If the Arbitral Tribunal considers the request justified, it shall make the correction or provide the interpretation within 30 days of receiving the request.

(2) The Arbitral Tribunal may correct any error of the type referred to in paragraph (1) above on its own motion within 30 days of the date of an award.

(3) Any correction or interpretation of an award shall be in writing and shall comply with the requirements of Article 36.

Article 42 Additional award

Within 30 days of receiving an award, a party may, upon notice to the other party, request the Arbitral Tribunal to make an additional award on claims presented in the arbitration but not determined in the award. If the Arbitral Tribunal considers the request justified, it shall make the additional award within 60 days of receipt of the request. When deemed necessary, the Board may extend this 60 day time limit.

Costs of the Arbitration

Article 43 Costs of the Arbitration

(1) The Costs of the Arbitration consist of:

(i) the Fees of the Arbitral Tribunal;
(ii) the Administrative Fee; and
(iii) the expenses of the Arbitral Tribunal and the SCC.

(2) Before making the final award, the Arbitral Tribunal shall request the Board to finally determine the Costs of the Arbitration. The Board shall finally determine the Costs of the Arbitration in accordance with the Schedule of

Costs (Appendix III) in force on the date of commencement of the arbitration pursuant to Article 4.

(3) If the arbitration is terminated before the final award is made pursuant to Article 39, the Board shall finally determine the Costs of the Arbitration having regard to when the arbitration terminates, the work performed by the Arbitral Tribunal and other relevant circumstances.

(4) The Arbitral Tribunal shall include in the final award the Costs of the Arbitration as finally determined by the Board and specify the individual fees and expenses of each member of the Arbitral Tribunal and the SCC.

(5) Unless otherwise agreed by the parties, the Arbitral Tribunal shall, at the request of a party, apportion the Costs of the Arbitration between the parties, having regard to the outcome of the case and other relevant circumstances.

(6) The parties are jointly and severally liable to the arbitrator(s) and to the SCC for the Costs of the Arbitration.

Article 44 Costs incurred by a party

Unless otherwise agreed by the parties, the Arbitral Tribunal may in the final award upon the request of a party, order one party to pay any reasonable costs incurred by another party, including costs for legal representation, having regard to the outcome of the case and other relevant circumstances.

Article 45 Advance on Costs

(1) The Board shall determine an amount to be paid by the parties as an Advance on Costs.

(2) The Advance on Costs shall correspond to the estimated amount of the Costs of Arbitration pursuant to Article 43(1).

(3) Each party shall pay half of the Advance on Costs, unless separate advances are determined. Where counterclaims or set-offs are submitted, the Board may decide that each of the parties shall pay the advances on costs corresponding to its claim. Upon a request from the Arbitral Tribunal or if otherwise deemed necessary, the Board may order parties to pay additional advances during the course of the arbitration.

(4) If a party fails to make a required payment, the Secretariat shall give the other party an opportunity to do so within a specified period of time. If the required payment is not made, the Board shall dismiss the case in whole or in part. If the other party makes the required payment, the Arbitral Tribunal may, at the request of such party, make a separate award for reimbursement of the payment.

(5) At any stage during the arbitration or after the Award has been made, the Board may draw on the Advance on Costs to cover the Costs of the Arbitration.

(6) The Board may decide that part of the Advance on Costs may be provided in the form of a bank guarantee or other form of security.

General rules

Article 46 Confidentiality

Unless otherwise agreed by the parties, the SCC and the Arbitral Tribunal shall maintain the confidentiality of the arbitration and the award.

Article 47 Enforcement

In all matters not expressly provided for in these Rules, the SCC, the Arbitral Tribunal and the parties shall act in the spirit of these Rules and shall make every reasonable effort to ensure that all awards are legally enforceable.

Article 48 Exclusion of liability

Neither the SCC nor the arbitrator(s) are liable to any party for any act or omission in connection with the arbitration unless such act or omission constitutes wilful misconduct or gross negligence.

APPENDIX I
ORGANISATION

Article 1 About the SCC

The Arbitration Institute of the Stockholm Chamber of Commerce (the "SCC") is a body providing administrative services in relation to the settlement of disputes. The SCC is part of the Stockholm Chamber of Commerce, but is independent in exercising its functions in the administration of disputes. The SCC is composed of a board of directors (the "Board") and a secretariat (the "Secretariat").

Article 2 Function of the SCC

The SCC does not itself decide disputes. The function of the SCC is to:

(i) administer domestic and international disputes in accordance with the SCC Rules and other procedures or rules agreed upon by the parties; and
(ii) provide information concerning arbitration and mediation matters.

Article 3 The Board

The Board shall be composed of one chairperson, a maximum of three vice-chairpersons and a maximum of 12 additional members. The Board shall include both Swedish and non-Swedish nationals.

Article 4 Appointment of the Board

The Board shall be appointed by the Board of Directors of the Stockholm Chamber of Commerce (the "Board of Directors"). The members of the Board shall be appointed for a period of three years and are eligible for re-appointment in their respective capacities for one further three year period only, unless exceptional circumstances apply.

Article 5 Removal of a member of the Board

In exceptional circumstances, the Board of Directors may remove a member of the Board. If a member resigns or is removed during a term of office, the Board of Directors shall appoint a new member for the remainder of the term.

Article 6 Function of the Board

The function of the Board is to take the decisions required of the SCC in administering disputes under the SCC Rules and any other rules or procedures agreed upon by the parties. Such decisions include decisions on the jurisdiction of the SCC, determination of advances on costs, appointment of arbitrators, decisions upon challenges to arbitrators, removal of arbitrators and the fixing of arbitration costs.

Article 7 Decisions by the Board

Two members of the Board form a quorum. If a majority is not attained, the Chairperson has the casting vote. The Chairperson or a Vice Chairperson may to take decisions on behalf of the Board in urgent matters. A committee of the Board may be appointed to take certain decisions on behalf of the Board. The Board may delegate decisions to the Secretariat, including decisions on advances on costs, extension of time for rendering an award, dismissal for non-payment of registration fee, release of arbitrators and fixing of arbitration costs. Decisions by the Board are final.

Article 8 The Secretariat

The Secretariat acts under the direction of a Secretary General. The Secretariat carries out the functions assigned to it under the SCC Rules. The Secretariat may also take decisions delegated to it by the Board.

Article 9 Procedures

The SCC shall maintain the confidentiality of the arbitration and the award and shall deal with the arbitration in an impartial, practical and expeditious manner.

APPENDIX II
EMERGENCY ARBITRATOR

Article 1 Emergency Arbitrator

(1) A party may apply for the appointment of an Emergency Arbitrator until the case has been referred to an Arbitral Tribunal pursuant to Article 18 of the Arbitration Rules.

(2) The powers of the Emergency Arbitrator shall be those set out in Article 32 (l)-(3) of the Arbitration Rules. Such powers terminate when the case has been referred to an Arbitral Tribunal pursuant to Article 18 of the Arbitration Rules or when an emergency decision ceases to be binding according to Article 9 (4) of this Appendix.

Article 2 Application for the appointment of an Emergency Arbitrator

An application for the appointment of an Emergency Arbitrator shall include:

(i) a statement of the names and addresses, telephone and facsimile numbers and e-mail addresses of the parties and their counsel;
(ii) a summary of the dispute;
(iii) a statement of the interim relief sought and the reasons therefor;
(iv) a copy or description of the arbitration agreement or clause on the basis of which the dispute is to be settled;
(v) comments on the seat of the emergency proceedings, the applicable law(s) and the language(s) of the proceedings; and
(vi) proof of payment of the costs for the emergency proceedings pursuant to Article 10 (l)-(2) of this Appendix.

Article 3 Notice

As soon as an application for the appointment of an Emergency Arbitrator has been received, the Secretariat shall send the application to the other party.

Article 4 Appointment of the Emergency Arbitrator

(1) The Board shall seek to appoint an Emergency Arbitrator within 24 hours of receipt of the application for the appointment of an Emergency Arbitrator.

(2) An Emergency Arbitrator shall not be appointed if the SCC manifestly lacks jurisdiction over the dispute.

(3) Article 15 of the Arbitration Rules applies except that a challenge must be made within 24 hours from when the circumstances giving rise to the challenge of an Emergency Arbitrator became known to the party.

(4) An Emergency Arbitrator may not act as an arbitrator in any future arbitration relating to the dispute, unless otherwise agreed by the parties.

Article 5 Seat of the emergency proceedings

The seat of the emergency proceedings shall be that which has been agreed upon by the parties as the seat of the arbitration. If the seat of the arbitration has not been agreed by the parties, the Board shall determine the seat of the emergency proceedings.

Article 6 Referral to the Emergency Arbitrator

Once an Emergency Arbitrator has been appointed, the Secretariat shall promptly refer the application to the Emergency Arbitrator.

Article 7 Conduct of the emergency proceedings

Article 19 of the Arbitration Rules shall apply to the emergency proceedings, taking into account the urgency inherent in such proceedings.

Article 8 Emergency decisions on interim measures

(1) Any emergency decision on interim measures shall be made not later than 5 days from the date upon which the application was referred to the Emergency Arbitrator pursuant to Article 6 of this Appendix. The Board may extend this time limit upon a reasoned request from the Emergency Arbitrator, or if otherwise deemed necessary.

(2) Any emergency decision on interim measures shall:

  (i) be made in writing;
  (ii) state the date when it was made, the seat of the emergency proceedings and the reasons upon which the decision is based; and
  (iii) be signed by the Emergency Arbitrator.

(3) The Emergency Arbitrator shall promptly deliver a copy of the emergency decision to each of the parties and to the SCC.

Article 9 Binding effect of emergency decisions

(1) An emergency decision shall be binding on the parties when rendered.

(2) The emergency decision may be amended or revoked by the Emergency Arbitrator upon a reasoned request by a party.

(3) By agreeing to arbitration under the Arbitration Rules, the parties undertake to comply with any emergency decision without delay.

(4) The emergency decision ceases to be binding if:

  (i) the Emergency Arbitrator or an Arbitral Tribunal so decides;

(ii) an Arbitral Tribunal makes a final award;
(iii) arbitration is not commenced within 30 days from the date of the emergency decision; or
(iv) the case is not referred to an Arbitral Tribunal within 90 days from the date of the emergency decision.

(5) An Arbitral Tribunal is not bound by the decision(s) and reasons of the Emergency Arbitrator.

Article 10 Costs of the emergency proceedings

(1) The party applying for the appointment of an Emergency Arbitrator shall pay the costs of the emergency proceedings upon filing the application.
(2) The costs of the emergency proceedings include:

(i) the fee of the Emergency Arbitrator which amounts to EUR 12,000; and
(ii) the application fee which amounts to EUR 3,000.

(3) Upon a request from the Emergency Arbitrator or if otherwise deemed appropriate, the Board may decide to increase or reduce the costs having regard to the nature of the case, the work performed by the Emergency Arbitrator and the SCC, and other relevant circumstances.
(4) If payment of the costs of the emergency proceedings is not made in due time, the Secretariat shall dismiss the application.
(5) At the request of a party, the costs of the emergency proceedings may be apportioned between the parties by an Arbitral Tribunal in a final award.

APPENDIX III
SCHEDULE OF COSTS

Arbitration Costs

Article 1 Registration Fee

(1) The Registration Fee referred to in Article 3 of the Arbitration Rules amounts to EUR 1 500.
(2) The Registration Fee is non-refundable and constitutes a part of the Administrative Fee in Article 3 below. The Registration Fee shall be credited to the Advance on Costs to be paid by the Claimant pursuant to Article 45 of the Arbitration Rules.

Article 2 Fees of the Arbitral Tribunal

(1) The Board shall determine the fee of a Chairperson or sole arbitrator based on the amount in dispute in accordance with the table below.
(2) Co-arbitrators shall each receive 60 per cent of the fee of the Chairperson. After consultation with the Arbitral Tribunal, the Board may decide that a different percentage shall apply.
(3) The amount in dispute shall be the aggregate value of all claims, counterclaims and set-offs. Where the amount in dispute cannot be ascertained, the Board shall determine the Fees of the Arbitral Tribunal taking all relevant circumstances into account.
(4) In exceptional circumstances, the Board may deviate from the amounts set out in the table.

Article 3 Administrative Fee

(1) The Administrative Fee shall be determined in accordance with the table below.
(2) The amount in dispute shall be the aggregate value of all claims, counterclaims and set-offs. Where the amount in dispute cannot be ascertained, the Board shall determine the Administrative Fee taking all relevant circumstances into account.
(3) In exceptional circumstances, the Board may deviate from the amounts set out in the table.

Article 4 Expenses

In addition to the Fees of the arbitrator(s) and the Administrative Fee, the Board shall fix an amount to cover any reasonable expenses incurred by the arbitrator(s) and the

SCC. The expenses of the arbitrator(s) may include the fee and expenses of any expert appointed by the Arbitral Tribunal pursuant to Article 29 of the Arbitration Rules.

ARBITRATORS' FEES

Amount in dispute (EUR)	**Fee of the Chairman/Sole Arbitrator (EUR)**	
	Minimum	**Maximum**
to 25 000	**2 500**	**5 500**
from 25 001 to 50 000	**2 500** + 2 % on the amount above 25 000	**5 500** + 14 % on the amount above 25 000
from 50 001 to 100 000	**3 000** + 2 % on the amount above 50 000	**9 000** + 4 %on the amount above 50 000
from 100 001 to 500 000	**4 000** + 1 % on the amount above 100 000	**11 000** + 5 % on the amount above 100 000
from 500 001 to 1000 000	**8 000** + 0,8 % on the amount above 500 000	**31 000** + 2,4 % on the amount above 500 000
from 1000 001 to 2 000 000	**12 000** + 0,5 % on the amount above 1000 000	**43 000** + 2,5 % on the amount above 1000 000
from 2 000 001 to 5 000 000	**17 000** + 0,2% on the amount above 2 000 000	**68 000** + 0,8 % on the amount above 2 000 000
from 5 000 001 to 10 000 000	**23 000** + 0,1 % on the amount above 5 000 000	**92 000** + 0,68 % on the amount above 5 000 000
from 10 000 001 to 50 000 000	**28 000** + 0,03 % on the amount above 10 000 000	**126 000** + 0,15 % on the amount above 10 000 000
from 50 000 001 to 75 000 000	**40 000** + 0,02 % on the amount above 50 000 000	**186 000** + 0,16 % on the amount above 50 000 000
from 75 000 001 to 100 000 000	**45 000** + 0,012 % on the amount above 75 000 000	**226 000** + 0,02 % on the amount above 75 000 000
from 100 000 001	To be determined by the Board	To be determined by the Board

The Costs of the Arbitration may easily be calculated at www.sccinstitute. com

ADMINISTRATIVE FEE

Amount in dispute (EUR)	Administrative Fee (EUR)
Up to 25 000	**1 500**
from 25 001 to 50 000	**1 500** + 4 % on the amount above 25 000
from 50 001 to 100 000	**2 500** + 2 % on the amount above 50 000
from 100 001 to 500 000	**3 500** + 1,6 % on the amount above 100 000
from 500 001 to 1000 000	**9 900** + 0,8 % on the amount above 500 000
from 1000 001 to 2 000 000	**13 900** + 0,5 % on the amount above 1 000 000
from 2 000 001 to 5 000 000	**18 900** + 0,1 % on the amount above 2 000 000
from 5 000 001 to 10 000 000	**21 900** + 0,14 % on the amount above 5 000 000
from 10 000 001 to 50 000 000	**28 900** + 0,02 % on the amount above 10 000 000
from 50 000 001 to 75 000 000	**36 900** + 0,02 % on the amount above 50 000 000
from 75 000 001	**41 900** + 0,01 % on the amount above 75 000 000
	Maximum 60 000

The Costs of the Arbitration may easily be calculated at www.sccinstitute. com

Appendix III

RULES FOR EXPEDITED ARBITRATIONS OF THE ARBITRATION INSTITUTE OF THE STOCKHOLM CHAMBER OF COMMERCE

Adopted by the Stockholm Chamber of Commerce and in force as of 1 January 2010*

Under any arbitration agreement referring to the Rules for Expedited Arbitrations of the Arbitration Institute of the Stockholm Chamber of Commerce (the "Rules for Expedited Arbitrations") the parties shall be deemed to have agreed that the following rules, or such amended rules, in force on the date of the commencement of the arbitration, or the filing of an application for the appointment of an Emergency Arbitrator, shall be applied unless otherwise agreed by the parties.

* *The English text prevails over other language versions*

Article 1 About the SCC

The Arbitration Institute of the Stockholm Chamber of Commerce (the "SCC") is the body responsible for the administration of disputes in accordance with the "SCC Rules"; the Arbitration Rules of the Arbitration Institute of the Stockholm Chamber of Commerce (the "Arbitration Rules") and the Rules for Expedited Arbitrations of the Stockholm Chamber of Commerce (the "Rules for Expedited Arbitrations"), and other procedures or rules agreed upon by the parties. The SCC is composed of a board of directors (the "Board") and a secretariat (the "Secretariat"). Detailed provisions regarding the organisation of the SCC are set out in Appendix I.

Commencement of proceedings

Article 2 Request for Arbitration

A Request for Arbitration shall include:

(i) a statement of the names, addresses, telephone and facsimile numbers and e-mail addresses of the parties and their counsel;
(ii) a summary of the dispute;
(iii) a preliminary statement of the relief sought by the Claimant;
(iv) a copy or description of the arbitration agreement or clause under which the dispute is to be settled; and
(v) comments on the seat of arbitration.

Article 3 Registration Fee

(1) Upon filing the Request for Arbitration, the Claimant shall pay a Registration Fee. The amount of the Registration Fee shall be determined in accordance with the Schedule of Costs (Appendix III) in force on the date when the Request for Arbitration is filed.
(2) If the Registration Fee is not paid upon filing the Request for Arbitration, the Secretariat shall set a time period within which the Claimant shall pay the Registration Fee. If the Registration Fee is not paid within this time period, the Secretariat shall dismiss the Request for Arbitration.

Article 4 Commencement of arbitration

Arbitration is commenced on the date when the SCC receives the Request for Arbitration.

Article 5 Answer

(1) The Secretariat shall send a copy of the Request for Arbitration and the documents attached thereto to the Respondent. The Secretariat shall set a

time period within which the Respondent shall submit an Answer to the SCC. The Answer shall include:

(i) any objections concerning the existence, validity or applicability of the arbitration agreement; however, failure to raise any objections shall not preclude the Respondent from subsequently raising such objections at any time up to and including the submission of the Statement of Defence;
(ii) an admission or denial of the relief sought in the Request for Arbitration;
(iii) a preliminary statement of any counterclaims or set-offs; and
(iv) comments on the seat of arbitration.

(2) The Secretariat shall send a copy of the Answer to the Claimant. The Claimant shall be given an opportunity to submit comments on the Answer.
(3) Failure by the Respondent to submit an Answer shall not prevent the arbitration from proceeding.

Article 6 Request for further details

The Board may request further details from either party regarding any of their written submissions to the SCC. If the Claimant fails to comply with a request for further details, the Board may dismiss the case. If the Respondent fails to comply with a request for further details regarding its counterclaim or set-off, the Board may dismiss the counterclaim or set-off. Failure by the Respondent to otherwise comply with a request for further details shall not prevent the arbitration from proceeding.

Article 7 Time periods

The Board may, on application by either party or on its own motion, extend any time period which has been set for a party to comply with a particular direction.

Article 8 Notices

(1) Any notice or other communication from the Secretariat or the Board shall be delivered to the last known address of the addressee.
(2) Any notice or other communication shall be delivered by courier or registered mail, facsimile transmission, e-mail or any other means of communication that provides a record of the sending thereof.
(3) A notice or communication sent in accordance with paragraph (2) shall be deemed to have been received by the addressee on the date it would normally have been received given the chosen means of communication.

Article 9 Decisions by the Board

When necessary the Board shall:

(i) decide whether the SCC manifestly lacks jurisdiction over the dispute pursuant to Article 10 (i);
(ii) decide whether to consolidate cases pursuant to Article 11;
(iii) make any appointment of arbitrator pursuant to Article 13;
(iv) decide the seat of arbitration pursuant to Article 20; and
(v) determine the Advance on Costs pursuant to Article 44.

Article 10 Dismissal

The Board shall dismiss a case, in whole or in part, if:

(i) the SCC manifestly lacks jurisdiction over the dispute; or
(ii) the Advance on Costs is not paid pursuant to Article 44.

Article 11 Consolidation

If arbitration is commenced concerning a legal relationship in respect of which an arbitration between the same parties is already pending under these Rules, the Board may, at the request of a party, decide to consolidate the new claims with the pending proceedings. Such decision may only be made after consulting the parties and the Arbitrator.

The Arbitrator

Article 12 Number of Arbitrators

The arbitration shall be decided by a sole Arbitrator.

Article 13 Appointment of Arbitrator

(1) The parties may agree on a different procedure for appointment of the Arbitrator than as provided under this Article. In such cases, if the Arbitrator has not been appointed within the time period agreed by the parties or, where the parties have not agreed on a time period, within the time period set by the Board, the appointment shall be made pursuant to paragraphs (2)–(4).
(2) The parties shall be given 10 days within which to jointly appoint the Arbitrator. If the parties fail to make the appointment within this time period, the Arbitrator shall be appointed by the Board.
(3) If the parties are of different nationalities, the Arbitrator shall be of a different nationality than the parties, unless the parties have agreed otherwise or unless otherwise deemed appropriate by the Board.
(4) When appointing Arbitrator, the Board shall consider the nature and circumstances of the dispute, the applicable law, the seat and language of the arbitration and the nationality of the parties.

Article 14 Impartiality and independence

(1) The Arbitrator must be impartial and independent.

(2) Before being appointed as Arbitrator, a person shall disclose any circumstances which may give rise to justifiable doubts as to his/her impartiality or independence. If the person is appointed as Arbitrator, he/she shall submit to the Secretariat a signed statement of impartiality and independence disclosing any circumstances which may give rise to justifiable doubts as to that person's impartiality or independence. The Secretariat shall send a copy of the statement of impartiality and independence to the parties.

(3) The Arbitrator shall immediately inform the parties in writing where any circumstances referred to in paragraph (2) arise during the course of the arbitration.

Article 15 Challenge to Arbitrator

(1) A party may challenge the Arbitrator if circumstances exist which give rise to justifiable doubts as to the Arbitrator's impartiality or independence or if he/she does not possess qualifications agreed by the parties.

(2) A challenge to the Arbitrator shall be made by submitting a written statement to the Secretariat setting forth the reasons for the challenge within 15 days from when the circumstances giving rise to the challenge became known to the party. Failure by a party to challenge the Arbitrator within the stipulated time period constitutes a waiver of the right to make the challenge.

(3) The Secretariat shall notify the parties and the Arbitrator of the challenge and give them an opportunity to submit comments on the challenge.

(4) If the other party agrees to the challenge, the Arbitrator shall resign. In all other cases, the Board shall make the final decision on the challenge.

Article 16 Release from appointment

(1) The Board shall release the Arbitrator from appointment where:

(i) the Board accepts the resignation of the Arbitrator;
(ii) a challenge to the Arbitrator under Article 15 is sustained; or
(iii) the Arbitrator is otherwise prevented from fulfilling his/her duties or fails to perform his/her functions in an adequate manner.

(2) Before the Board releases an arbitrator, the Secretariat may give the parties and the Arbitrator an opportunity to submit comments.

Article 17 Replacement of Arbitrator

(1) The Board shall appoint a new Arbitrator where the Arbitrator has been released from his/her appointment pursuant to Article 16, or where the Arbitrator has died.
(2) Where the Arbitrator has been replaced, the new Arbitrator shall decide whether and to what extent the proceedings are to be repeated.

The proceedings before the Arbitrator

Article 18 Referral to the Arbitrator

When the Arbitrator has been appointed and the Advance on Costs has been paid, the Secretariat shall refer the case to the Arbitrator.

Article 19 Conduct of the arbitration

(1) Subject to these Rules and any agreement between the parties, the Arbitrator may conduct the arbitration in such manner as the Arbitrator considers appropriate.
(2) In all cases, the Arbitrator shall conduct the arbitration in an impartial, practical and expeditious manner, giving each party an equal and reasonable opportunity to present its case.
(3) The following shall apply to the proceedings, unless the Arbitrator, for special reasons, decides otherwise:

    (i) in addition to the Statement of Claim and the Statement of Defence, the parties each may only submit one written statement, including statements of evidence;
    (ii) the statements must be brief; and
    (iii) the time limits within which the documents shall be submitted may not exceed 10 working days.

(4) The Arbitrator may order a party to finally state its claims for relief and the facts relied on as grounds thereof, and the evidence on which the party relies. At the expiration of the time period for such statement, the party may not amend its claim for relief nor adduce additional facts or evidence, unless the Arbitrator, for special reasons, so permits.

Article 20 Seat of arbitration

(1) Unless agreed upon by the parties, the Board shall decide the seat of arbitration.
(2) The Arbitrator may, after consultation with the parties, conduct hearings at any place which the Arbitrator considers appropriate. If any hearing or

meeting is held elsewhere than at the seat of arbitration, the arbitration shall be deemed to have taken place at the seat of arbitration.

(3) The award shall be deemed to have been made at the seat of arbitration.

Article 21 Language

(1) Unless agreed upon by the parties, the Arbitrator shall determine the language(s) of the arbitration. In so determining, the Arbitrator shall have due regard to all relevant circumstances and shall give the parties an opportunity to submit comments.

(2) The Arbitrator may request that any documents submitted in languages other than the language(s) of the arbitration be accompanied by a translation into the language(s) of the arbitration.

Article 22 Applicable law

(1) The Arbitrator shall decide the merits of the dispute on the basis of the law(s) or rules of law agreed upon by the parties. In the absence of such agreement, the Arbitrator shall apply the law or rules of law which the Arbitrator considers to be most appropriate.

(2) Any designation made by the parties of the law of a given state shall be deemed to refer to the substantive law of that state and not to its conflict of laws rules.

(3) The Arbitrator shall decide the dispute *ex aequo et bono* or as *amiable compositeur* only if the parties have expressly authorised the Arbitrator to do so.

Article 23 Timetable

After the referral of the case to the Arbitrator, the Arbitrator shall promptly establish a timetable for the conduct of the arbitration. The Arbitrator shall send a copy of the timetable to the parties and to the Secretariat.

Article 24 Written submissions

(1) The Claimant shall, within the period of time determined by the Arbitrator, submit a Statement of Claim which shall include, unless previously submitted:

(i) the specific relief sought;
(ii) the material circumstances on which the Claimant relies; and
(iii) the documents on which the Claimant relies.

(2) The Respondent shall, within the period of time determined by the Arbitrator, submit a Statement of Defence which shall include, unless previously submitted:

(i) any objections concerning the existence, validity or applicability of the arbitration agreement;
(ii) a statement whether, and to what extent, the Respondent admits or denies the relief sought by the Claimant;
(iii) the material circumstances on which the Respondent relies;
(iv) any counterclaim or set-off and the grounds on which it is based; and
(v) the documents on which the Respondent relies.

(3) The Arbitrator may order the parties to submit additional written submissions.

Article 25 Amendments

At any time prior to the close of proceedings pursuant to Article 34, a party may amend or supplement its claim, counterclaim, defence or set-off provided its case, as amended or supplemented, is still comprised by the arbitration agreement, unless the Arbitrator considers it inappropriate to allow such amendment or supplement having regard to the delay in making it, the prejudice to the other party or any other circumstances.

Article 26 Evidence

(1) The admissibility, relevance, materiality and weight of evidence shall be for the Arbitrator to determine.
(2) The Arbitrator may order a party to identify the documentary evidence it intends to rely on and specify the circumstances intended to be proved by such evidence.
(3) At the request of a party, the Arbitrator may order a party to produce any documents or other evidence which may be relevant to the outcome of the case.

Article 27 Hearings

(1) A hearing shall be held if requested by a party and if deemed necessary by the Arbitrator.
(2) The Arbitrator shall, in consultation with the parties, determine the date, time and location of any hearing and shall provide the parties with reasonable notice thereof.
(3) Unless otherwise agreed by the parties, hearings will be held in private.

Article 28 Witnesses

(1) In advance of any hearing, the Arbitrator may order the parties to identify each witness or expert they intend to call and specify the circumstances intended to be proved by each testimony.
(2) The testimony of witnesses or party-appointed experts may be submitted in the form of signed statements.
(3) Any witness or expert, on whose testimony a party seeks to rely, shall attend a hearing for examination, unless otherwise agreed by the parties.

Article 29 Experts appointed by the Arbitrator

(1) After consultation with the parties, the Arbitrator may appoint one or more experts to report to the Arbitrator on specific issues set out by the Arbitrator in writing.
(2) Upon receipt of a report from an expert appointed by the Arbitrator, the Arbitrator shall send a copy of the report to the parties and shall give the parties an opportunity to submit written comments on the report.
(3) Upon the request of a party, the parties shall be given an opportunity to examine any expert appointed by the Arbitrator at a hearing.

Article 30 Default

(1) If the Claimant, without showing good cause, fails to submit a Statement of Claim in accordance with Article 24, the Arbitrator shall terminate the proceedings provided the Respondent has not filed a counterclaim.
(2) If a party, without showing good cause, fails to submit a Statement of Defence or other written statement in accordance with Article 24, or fails to appear at a hearing, or otherwise fails to avail itself of the opportunity to present its case, the Arbitrator may proceed with the arbitration and make an award.
(3) If a party without good cause fails to comply with any provision of, or requirement under, these Rules or any procedural order given by the Arbitrator, the Arbitrator may draw such inferences as it considers appropriate.

Article 31 Waiver

A party, who during the arbitration fails to object without delay to any failure to comply with the arbitration agreement, these Rules or other rules applicable to the proceedings, shall be deemed to have waived the right to object to such failure.

Article 32 Interim measures

(1) The Arbitrator may, at the request of a party, grant any interim measures the Arbitrator deems appropriate.
(2) The Arbitrator may order the party requesting an interim measure to provide appropriate security in connection with the measure.
(3) An interim measure shall take the form of an order or an award.
(4) Provisions with respect to interim measures requested before arbitration has been commenced or a case has been referred to an Arbitrator are set out in Appendix II.
(5) A request for interim measures made by a party to a judicial authority is not incompatible with the arbitration agreement or with these Rules.

Article 33 Communications from the Arbitrator

Article 8 shall apply to communications from the Arbitrator.

Article 34 Close of proceedings

The Arbitrator shall declare the proceedings closed when the Arbitrator is satisfied that the parties have had a reasonable opportunity to present their cases. In exceptional circumstances, prior to the making of the final award, the Arbitrator may reopen the proceedings on the Arbitrator's own motion, or upon the application of a party.

Awards and decisions

Article 35 Making of awards

(1) The Arbitrator shall make the award in writing and sign the award. A party may request a reasoned award no later than at the closing statement.
(2) An award shall include the date of the award and the seat of arbitration in accordance with Article 20.
(3) The Arbitrator shall deliver a copy of the award to each of the parties and to the SCC without delay.

Article 36 Time limit for final award

The final award shall be made not later than three months from the date upon which the arbitration was referred to the Arbitrator pursuant to Article 18. The Board may extend this time limit upon a reasoned request from the Arbitrator, or if otherwise deemed necessary.

Article 37 Separate award

The Arbitrator may decide a separate issue or part of the dispute in a separate award.

Article 38 Settlement or other grounds for termination of the arbitration

(1) If the parties reach a settlement before the final award is made, the Arbitrator may, upon the request of both parties, record the settlement in the form of a consent award.
(2) If the arbitration for any other reason is terminated before the final award is made, the Arbitrator shall issue an award recording the termination.

Article 39 Effect of an award

An award shall be final and binding on the parties when rendered. By agreeing to arbitration under these Rules, the parties undertake to carry out any award without delay.

Article 40 Correction and interpretation of an award

(1) Within 30 days of receiving an award, a party may, upon notice to the other party, request that the Arbitrator correct any clerical, typographical or computational errors in the award, or provide an interpretation of a specific point or part of the award. If the Arbitrator considers the request justified, the Arbitrator shall make the correction or provide the interpretation within 30 days of receiving the request.
(2) The Arbitrator may correct any error of the type referred to in paragraph (1) above on the Arbitrator's own motion within 30 days of the date of an award.
(3) Any correction or interpretation of an award shall be in writing and shall comply with the requirements of Article 35.

Article 41 Additional award

Within 30 days of receiving an award, a party may, upon notice to the other party, request the Arbitrator to make an additional award on claims presented in the arbitration but not determined in the award. If the Arbitrator considers the request justified, the Arbitrator shall make the additional award within 30 days of receipt of the request. When deemed necessary, the Board may extend this 30 day time limit.

Costs of the Arbitration

Article 42 Costs of the Arbitration

(1) The Costs of the Arbitration consist of:

(i) the Fee of the Arbitrator;
(ii) the Administrative Fee; and
(iii) the expenses of the Arbitrator and the SCC.

(2) Before making the final award, the Arbitrator shall request the Board to finally determine the Costs of the Arbitration. The Board shall finally determine the Costs of the Arbitration in accordance with the Schedule of Costs (Appendix III) in force on the date of commencement of the arbitration pursuant to Article 4.
(3) If the arbitration is terminated before the final award is made pursuant to Article 38, the Board shall finally determine the Costs of the Arbitration having regard to when the arbitration terminates, the work performed by the Arbitrator and other relevant circumstances. The Arbitrator shall include in the final award the Costs of the Arbitration as finally determined by the Board and specify the fees and expenses of the Arbitrator and the SCC.
(4) Unless otherwise agreed by the parties, the Arbitrator shall, at the request of a party, apportion the Costs of the Arbitration between the parties, having regard to the outcome of the case and other relevant circumstances.
(5) The parties are jointly and severally liable to the Arbitrator and to the SCC for the Costs of the Arbitration.

Article 43 Costs incurred by a party

Unless otherwise agreed by the parties, the Arbitrator may in the final award, upon the request of a party, order one party to pay any reasonable costs incurred by another party, including costs for legal representation, having regard to the outcome of the case and other relevant circumstances.

Article 44 Advance on Costs

(1) The Board shall determine an amount to be paid by the parties as an Advance on Costs.
(2) The Advance on Costs shall correspond to the estimated amount of the Costs of Arbitration pursuant to Article 42 (1).
(3) Each party shall pay half of the Advance on Costs, unless separate advances are determined. Where counterclaims or set-offs are submitted, the Board may decide that each of the parties shall pay the advances on costs corresponding to its claim. Upon a request from the Arbitrator or if otherwise deemed

necessary, the Board may order parties to pay additional advances during the course of the arbitration.

(4) If a party fails to make a required payment, the Secretariat shall give the other party an opportunity to do so within a specified period of time. If the required payment is not made, the Board shall dismiss the case in whole or in part. If the other party makes the required payment, the Arbitrator may, at the request of such party, make a separate award for reimbursement of the payment.

(5) At any stage during the arbitration or after the Award has been made, the Board may draw on the Advance on Costs to cover the Costs of the Arbitration.

(6) The Board may decide that part of the Advance on Costs may be provided in the form of a bank guarantee or other form of security.

General rules

Article 45 Confidentiality

Unless otherwise agreed by the parties, the SCC and the Arbitrator shall maintain the confidentiality of the arbitration and the award.

Article 46 Enforcement

In all matters not expressly provided for in these Rules, the SCC, the Arbitrator and the parties shall act in the spirit of these Rules and shall make every reasonable effort to ensure that all awards are legally enforceable.

Article 47 Exclusion of liability

Neither the SCC nor the arbitrator are liable to any party for any act or omission in connection with the arbitration unless such act or omission constitutes wilful misconduct or gross negligence.

APPENDIX I
ORGANISATION

Article 1 About the SCC

The Arbitration Institute of the Stockholm Chamber of Commerce (the "SCC") is a body providing administrative services in relation to the settlement of disputes. The SCC is part of the Stockholm Chamber of Commerce, but is independent in exercising its functions in the administration of disputes. The SCC is composed of a board of directors (the "Board") and a secretariat (the "Secretariat").

Article 2 Function of the SCC

The SCC does not itself decide disputes. The function of the SCC is to:

(i) administer domestic and international disputes in accordance with the SCC Rules and other procedures or rules agreed upon by the parties; and
(ii) provide information concerning arbitration and mediation matters.

Article 3 The Board

The Board shall be composed of one chairperson, a maximum of three vice-chairpersons and a maximum of 12 additional members. The Board includes both Swedish and non-Swedish nationals.

Article 4 Appointment of the Board

The Board shall be appointed by the Board of Directors of the Stockholm Chamber of Commerce (the "Board of Directors"). The members of the Board shall be appointed for a period of three years and are eligible for re-appointment in their respective capacities for one further three year period only, unless exceptional circumstances apply.

Article 5 Removal of a member of the Board

In exceptional circumstances, the Board of Directors may remove a member of the Board. If a member resigns or is removed during a term of office, the Board of Directors shall appoint a new member for the remainder of the term.

Article 6 Function of the Board

The function of the Board is to take the decisions required of the SCC in administering disputes under the SCC Rules and any other rules or procedures agreed upon by the parties. Such decisions include decisions on the jurisdiction of the SCC, determination of advances on costs, appointment of arbitrators, decisions upon challenges to arbitrators, removal of arbitrators and the fixing of arbitration costs.

Article 7 Decisions by the Board

Two members of the Board form a quorum. If a majority is not attained, the Chairperson has the casting vote. The Chairperson or a Vice Chairperson may take decisions on behalf of the Board in urgent matters. A committee of the Board may be appointed to take certain decisions on behalf of the Board. The Board may delegate decisions to the Secretariat, including decisions on advances on costs, extension of time for rendering an award, dismissal for non-payment of registration fee, release of arbitrators and fixing of arbitration costs. Decisions by the Board are final.

Article 8 The Secretariat

The Secretariat acts under the direction of a Secretary General. The Secretariat carries out the functions assigned to it under the SCC Rules. The Secretariat may also take decisions delegated to it by the Board.

Article 9 Procedures

The SCC shall maintain the confidentiality of the arbitration and the award and shall deal with the arbitration in an impartial, practical and expeditious manner.

APPENDIX II
EMERGENCY ARBITRATOR

Article 1 Emergency Arbitrator

(1) A party may apply for the appointment of an Emergency Arbitrator until the case has been referred to the Arbitrator pursuant to Article 18 of the Rules for Expedited Arbitrations.

(2) The powers of the Emergency Arbitrator shall be those set out in Article 32 (1)–(3) of the Rules for Expedited Arbitrations. Such powers terminate when the case has been referred to the Arbitrator pursuant to Article 18 of the Rules for Expedited Arbitrations or when an emergency decision ceases to be binding according to Article 9 (4) of this Appendix.

Article 2 Application for the appointment of an Emergency Arbitrator

An application for the appointment of an Emergency Arbitrator shall include:

(i) a statement of the names and addresses, telephone and facsimile numbers and e-mail addresses of the parties and their counsel;
(ii) a summary of the dispute;
(iii) a statement of the interim relief sought and the reasons therefor;
(iv) a copy or description of the arbitration agreement or clause on the basis of which the dispute is to be settled;
(v) comments on the seat of the emergency proceedings, the applicable law(s) and the language(s) of the proceedings; and
(vi) proof of payment of the costs for the emergency proceedings pursuant to Article 10 (1)–(2) of this Appendix.

Article 3 Notice

As soon as an application for the appointment of an Emergency Arbitrator has been received, the Secretariat shall send the application to the other party.

Article 4 Appointment of the Emergency Arbitrator

(1) The Board shall seek to appoint an Emergency Arbitrator within 24 hours of receipt of the application for the appointment of an Emergency Arbitrator.

(2) An Emergency Arbitrator shall not be appointed if the SCC manifestly lacks jurisdiction over the dispute.

(3) Article 15 of the Rules for Expedited Arbitrations applies except that a challenge must be made within 24 hours from when the circumstances giving rise to the challenge of an Emergency Arbitrator became known to the party.

(4) An Emergency Arbitrator may not act as an arbitrator in any future arbitration relating to the dispute, unless otherwise agreed by the parties.

Article 5 Seat of the emergency proceedings

The seat of the emergency proceedings shall be that which has been agreed upon by the parties as the seat of the arbitration. If the seat of the arbitration has not been agreed by the parties, the Board shall determine the seat of the emergency proceedings.

Article 6 Referral to the Emergency Arbitrator

Once an Emergency Arbitrator has been appointed, the Secretariat shall promptly refer the application to the Emergency Arbitrator.

Article 7 Conduct of the emergency proceedings

Article 19 of the Rules for Expedited Arbitrations shall apply to the emergency proceedings, taking into account the urgency inherent in such proceedings.

Article 8 Emergency decisions on interim measures

(1) Any emergency decision on interim measures shall be made not later than 5 days from the date upon which the application was referred to the Emergency Arbitrator pursuant to Article 6 of this Appendix. The Board may extend this time limit upon a reasoned request from the Emergency Arbitrator, or if otherwise deemed necessary.

(2) Any emergency decision on interim measures shall:

(i) be made in writing;
(ii) state the date when it was made, the seat of the emergency proceedings and the reasons upon which the decision is based; and
(iii) be signed by the Emergency Arbitrator.

(3) The Emergency Arbitrator shall promptly deliver a copy of the emergency decision to each of the parties and to the SCC.

Article 9 Binding effect of emergency decisions

(1) An emergency decision shall be binding on the parties when rendered.
(2) The emergency decision may be amended or revoked by the Emergency Arbitrator upon a reasoned request by a party.
(3) By agreeing to arbitration under the Rules for Expedited Arbitrations, the parties undertake to comply with any emergency decision without delay.
(4) The emergency decision ceases to be binding if:

(i) the Emergency Arbitrator or an Arbitrator so decides;

(ii) an Arbitrator makes a final award;
(iii) arbitration is not commenced within 30 days from the date of the emergency decision; or
(iv) the case is not referred to an Arbitrator within 90 days from the date of the emergency decision.

(5) An Arbitrator is not bound by the decision(s) and reasons of the Emergency Arbitrator.

Article 10 Costs of the emergency proceedings

(1) The party applying for the appointment of an Emergency Arbitrator shall pay the costs of the emergency proceedings upon filing the application.
(2) The costs of the emergency proceedings include:

(i) the fee of the Emergency Arbitrator which amounts to EUR 6,000; and
(ii) the application fee which amounts to EUR 1,500.

(3) Upon a request from the Emergency Arbitrator or if otherwise deemed appropriate, the Board may decide to increase or reduce the costs having regard to the nature of the case, the work performed by the Emergency Arbitrator and the SCC, and other relevant circumstances.
(4) If payment of the costs of the emergency proceedings is not made in due time, the Secretariat shall dismiss the application.
(5) At the request of a party, the costs of the emergency proceedings may be apportioned between the parties by an Arbitrator in a final award.

APPENDIX III
SCHEDULE OF COSTS

Arbitration Costs

Article 1 Registration Fee

(1) The Registration Fee referred to in Article 3 of the the Rules for Expedited Arbitrations amounts to EUR 1 000.

(2) The Registration Fee is non-refundable and constitutes a part of the Administrative Fee in Article 3 below. The Registration Fee shall be credited to the Advance on Costs to be paid by the Claimant pursuant to Article 44 of the Rules for Expedited Arbitrations.

Article 2 Fee of the Arbitrator

(1) The Board shall determine the Fee of the Arbitrator based on the amount in dispute in accordance with the table below.

(2) The amount in dispute shall be the aggregate value of all claims, counterclaims and set-offs. Where the amount in dispute cannot be ascertained, the Board shall determine the Fee of the Arbitrator taking all relevant circumstances into account.

(3) In exceptional circumstances, the Board may deviate from the amounts set out in the table.

Article 3 Administrative Fee

(1) The Administrative Fee shall be determined in accordance with the table below.

(2) The amount in dispute shall be the aggregate value of all claims, counterclaims and set-offs. Where the amount in dispute cannot be ascertained, the Board shall determine the Administrative Fee taking all relevant circumstances into account.

(3) In exceptional circumstances, the Board may deviate from the amounts set out in the table.

Article 4 Expenses

In addition to the Fee of the Arbitrator and the Administrative Fee, the Board shall fix an amount to cover any reasonable expenses incurred by the Arbitrator and the SCC. The expenses of the Arbitrator may include the fee and expenses of any expert appointed by the Arbitrator pursuant to Article 29 of the Rules for Expedited Arbitrations.

ARBITRATORS' FEES

Amount in dispute (EUR)	**Arbitrator's Fee (EUR)**	
	Minimum	**Maximum**
to 25 000	**2 000**	**4 000**
from 25 001 to 50 000	**2 200** + 2% of the amount above 25 000	**4 000** + 6% of the amount above 25 000
from 50 001 to 100 000	**2 500** + 0,01% of the amount above 50 000	**5 500** + 4% of the amount above 50 000
from 100 001 to 500 000	**2 500** + 1,5% of the amount above 100 000	**7 500** + 1% of the amount above 100 000
from 500 001 to 1 000 000	**5 000** + 0,8% of the amount above 500 000	**11 500** + 2,2% of the amount above 500 000
from 1 000 001 to 2 000 000	**9 000** + 0,3% of the amount above 1 000 000	**13 500** + 2% of the amount above 1 000 000
from 2 000 001 to 5 000 000	**13 000** + 0,05% of the amount above 2 000 000	**33 500** + 0,05% of the amount above 2 000 000
from 5 000 001 to 10 000 000	**17 000** + 0,07% of the amount above 5 000 000	**35 000** + 0,3% of the amount above 5 000 000
from 10 000 001 to 50 000 000	**21 000** + 0,03% of the amount above 10 000 000	**50 000** + 0,02% of the amount above 10 000 000
from 50 000 001 to 75 000 000	**31 000** + 0,05% of the amount above 50 000 000	**58 000** + 0,04% of the amount above 50 000 000
from 75 000 001	**35 000** + 0,02% of the amount above 75 000 000	**68 000** + 0,04% of the amount above 75 000 000

The Costs of the Arbitration may easily be calculated at www.sccinstitute.com

ADMINISTRATIVE FEE

Amount in dispute (EUR)	**Administrative Fee (EUR)**
to 25 000	**1 500**
from 25 001 to 50 000	**1 500**
from 50 001 to 100 000	**1 500** + 2% of the amount above 50 000
from 100 001 to 500 000	**2 200** + 0,5% of the amount above 100 000
from 500 001 to 1 000 000	**4 500** + 0,7% of the amount above 500 000
from 1 000 001 to 2 000 000	**8 000** + 0,2% of the amount above 1 000 000
from 2 000 001 to 5 000 000	**10 000** + 0,1% of the amount above 2 000 000
from 5 000 001 to 10 000 000	**13 000** + 0,08% of the amount above 5 000 000
from 10 000 001 to 50 000 000	**17 000** + 0,01% of the amount above 10 000 000
	Maximum 30 000

The Costs of the Arbitration may easily be calculated at www.sccinstitute. com

Bibliography

Literature

Adlercreutz, *Avtalsrätt I*, 12th ed., Lund: Juristförlaget i Lund 2002.

Adlercreutz, *Avtalsrätt II*, 5th ed., Lund: Juristförlaget i Lund 2001.

Andersson, Isaksson, Johansson & Nilsson, *Arbitration in Sweden*, Stockholm: Jure Förlag AB 2011.

Arbitration in Sweden, published by the Stockholm Chamber of Commerce, Stockholm: Norstedts 1977.

Bernitz, *Standardavtalsrätt*, 7th ed., Stockholm: Norstedts Juridik 2008.

Blackaby, et al., *Redfern and Hunter on International Arbitration*, 5th ed., Oxford: Oxford University Press 2009.

Bogdan, *Concise Introduction to EU Private International Law*, Groningen: Europa Law Publishing 2006.

Born, *International Arbitration Cases and Material*, New York: Aspen Publishers 2011.

Born, *International Commercial Arbitration*, 3rd ed., Austin: Kluwer Law International 2009.

Carbonneau, *The Law and Practice of Arbitration*, 3rd ed., New York: JurisNet 2009.

Cars, *Lagen om Skiljeförfarande – En kommentar*, Stockholm: Fakta Info Direkt Sweden AB 1999.

Daele, *The Challenge and Disqualification of International Arbitrators*, Alphen aan den Rijn: Kluwer Law International 2012.

Derains, 'Towards Greater Efficiency in Document Production before Arbitral Tribunals – A Continental Viewpoint', in *International Court of Arbitration Bulletin 2006 Special Bulletin, Document Production in International Arbitration* No. 676 (2006): 83.

Dillén, *Bidrag till läran om skiljeavtalet*, Stockholm: AB Gustaf Larssons Bokhandels förlag 1933.

Ekelöf, Bylund & Edelstam, *Rättegång Tredje häftet*, 7th ed., Stockholm: Norstedts Juridik AB 2006.

Fitger, *Rättegångsbalken*, Stockholm: Norstedts Juridik AB 1984.

Grönfors, *Avtalslagen*, 3rd ed., Norstedts Juridik AB 1995.

Hanotiau, *Complex Arbitrations: Multiparty, Multicontract, Multi-issue and Class Actions*, The Hague: Kluwer Law International 2006.

Hassler & Cars, *Skiljeförfarande*, 2nd ed., Stockholm: Norstedts Juridik AB 1989.

Heuman, *Current Issues in Swedish Arbitration*, Kluwer Juristförlaget 1990.

Heuman, *Arbitration Law of Sweden: Practice and Procedure*, New York: Juris Publishing, Inc. 2003.

Heuman, *Skiljemannarätt*, Stockholm: Norstedts Juridik 1999.

Hobér, *Investment Arbitration in Eastern Europe: In Search for a Definition of Expropriation*, New York: JurisNet 2007.

Hobér, *International Commercial Arbitration in Sweden*, Oxford: Oxford University Press 2011.

Karlgren, *Passivitet – en köprättslig och allmänt avtalsrättslig studie*, Stockholm: P.A. Norstedts & Söners Förlag 1965.

Kronke et al. (ed.), *Recognition and Enforcement of Foreign Arbitral Awards – A Global Commentary on the New York Convention*, Wolters Kluwer 2010.

Kvart & Olsson, *Tvistlösning genom skiljeförfarande: en handledning till lagen om skiljeförfarande*, 2nd ed., Stockholm: Norstedts Juridik AB 2007.

Lehrberg, *Avtalsrättens grundelement*, 2nd ed., Uppsala: The Institute for Bank and Business Law 2006.

Lindskog, *Skiljeförfarande: En kommentar*, Stockholm: Norstedts Juridik AB 2005.

Lindskog, *Skiljeförfarande: En kommentar*, 2nd ed., Stockholm: Norstedts Juridik AB 2012.

Madsen, *Commercial Arbitration in Sweden*, Oxford: Oxford University Press 2006.

Madsen, *Skiljeförfarande I Sverige – En kommentar till lagen (1999:116) om skiljeförfarande och till reglerna för Stockholms Handelskammares Skiljedomsinstitut*, 2nd ed., Stockholm: Jure Förlag AB 2009.

Nordh, *Processens ram i tvistemål*, 2nd ed., Uppsala: Iustus 2006.

Olsson & Kvart, *Lagen om skiljeförfarande – En kommentar*, Stockholm: Norstedts Juridik AB 2000.

Ramberg & Ramberg, *Allmän avtalsrätt*, 7th ed., Stockholm: Norstedts Juridik AB 2007.

Reed, Paulson & Blackaby, *Guide to ICSID Arbitration*, 2nd ed., Kluwer Law International 2011.

Schreuer et al., *The ICSID Convention – A Commentary*, Cambridge: Cambridge University Press 2009.

Schöldström, *The Arbitrator's Mandate – A Comparative Study of Relationships in Commercial Arbitration under the Laws of England, Germany, Sweden and Switzerland*, Stockholm: Jure Förlag AB 1998.

Sheppard, *Arbitrator Independence in ICSID Arbitration in International Investment Law for the 21st Century*, Oxford: Oxford University Press 2009.

Sutton, Gill & Gearing, *Russell on Arbitration*, 23rd ed., London: Sweet & Maxwell 2007.

van den Berg, et al. (eds), *50 Years of the New York Convention, ICCA International Arbitration Conference*, Wolters Kluwer 2009.

Westberg, *Det Provisoriska Rättsskyddet i Tvistemål, Bok 1*, Lund: Juristförlaget i Lund 2004.

Öhrström, *Stockholms Handelskammares Skiljedomsinstitut: En handbok och regelkommentar för skiljeförfaranden*, Stockholm: Norstedts Juridik AB 2009.

Travaux Préparatoires

Government Bill 1998/99:35 *Ny lag om skiljeförfarande.*
SOU 1994:81 *Ny lag om skiljeförfarande.*
SOU 1995:65 *Näringslivets tvistlösning.*
NJA II 1929 p 49.
NJA II 1887 No. 4 *Lagarne om skiljemän samt angående förändrad lydelse af 46 § utsökningslagen.*

International Travaux Préparatoires

ICC International Court of Arbitration Bulletin Vol. 9/No. 1 – May 1998, *Report and Preliminary Draft Convention adopted by the Committee on International Commercial Arbitration, 13 March 1953, ICC Publication No. 174.*

Articles

Bagner, 'The Swedish Challenge Procedure' in *Festskrift till Lars Heuman*, ed. Kleineman, Westberg & Carlsson, Stockholm: Jure Förlag AB 2008.
Bagner, *International Arbitration Court Decisions*, New York: Juris 2008.
Brocker, 'Discovery in International Arbitration – The Swedish Approach', *Stockholm Arbitration Report 2001:2.*
Calissendorff, 'Jura novit curia i internationella skiljeförfaranden i Sverige', in *Juridisk Tidskrift 1995/96 No. 1 (1996).*
Capper, *SCC Arbitral Awards 2004–2009*, ed. Jarvin & Magnusson, New York: Juris 2011.
Danelius, 'The Application of the New York Convention in Swedish Courts', *Stockholm Arbitration Report 2004:2.*
de Groot, 'Judgments Rendered by the District Court of The Hague on 27 May 2004 in (1) case GK/RK 2002-979 and 2003-1617 and by the Court of Appeal of The Hague on 24 March 2005 in (2) case 04/694 and 04/695 (Marketing Displays International Inc. V. VR Van Raalte Reclame B.V.). Observations by Diederik de Groot', in *Stockholm International Arbitration Review 2006:2.*
de Ly, 'Comment: Comparative Observations on Arbitral Awards and Setting Aside', in *The Swedish Arbitration Act of 1999, Five Years On – A Critical Review of Strengths and Weaknesses*, ed. Heuman & Jarvin, New York: JurisNet 2006.
Dhunér, "EC Competition Law and National Arbitration Procedure', in *Stockholm Arbitration Report 2000:1.*
Dhunér, *SCC Arbitral Awards 2004–2009*, ed. Jarvin & Magnusson, New York: Juris 2011.
Edlund, 'Om ersättning till skiljemän', in *Juridisk Tidskrift 1998/99 No. 1 (1999).*

Eliasson, 'Investor-State Arbitration and Chinese Investors', in *Contemporary Asia Arbitration Journal*, Vol. 2, No. 2 (November 2009).

Eliasson, 'Investment Treaty Protection of Chinese Natural Resources Investments' in *Transnational Dispute Management*, Vol. 7, No. 4 (December 2010).

Eliasson, 'Investment Arbitration and Hong Kong', in *Arbitration in Hong Kong: A Practical Guide*, 2nd ed., London: Sweet & Maxwell 2011.

Eliasson, 'Chinese Investment Treaties: Jurisdictional Aspects', in *Foreign Investment and Dispute Resolution Law and Practice in Asia*, ed. Bath & Nottage, London: Routledge 2011.

Englund, 'Användande av e-post vid underrättelser enligt lagen om skiljeförfarande', in *Juridisk Tidskrift No. 1 2009/10 (2010).*

Farren, *SCC Arbitral Awards 2004–2009*, ed. Jarvin & Magnusson, New York: Juris 2011.

Gernandt, 'Ulf Franke - Thirty-Five Years and Afterwards', in *Between East and West: Essays in Honour of Ulf Franke*, ed. Hobér, Magnusson & Öhrström, New York: Juris 2010.

Goldberg & Blanke, *SCC Arbitral Awards 2004–2009*, ed. Jarvin & Magnusson, New York: Juris 2011.

Heitzmann & Grierson. 'SNF v Cytec Industrie: National Courts within the EC Apply Different Standards to Review International Awards Allegedly Contrary to Article 81 EC'. *Stockholm International Arbitration Review 2007:2.*

Heuman, 'Delgivning av påkallelseskrift i skiljeförfarande', in *Juridisk Tidskrift* No. 2 1996/97 (1997).

Heuman, 'Tystnadsplikt och underlåtenhet att ställa säkerhet i skiljetvist', in *Juridisk Tidskrift* No. 3 2000/01 (2001).

Heuman, 'Omfattar skiljedomens rättskraft i entreprenadtvister icke bedömda ersättningskrav?', in *Juridisk Tidskrift No. 5 1992/93* (1993).

Heuman & Millqvist, *Journal of International Arbitration*, Vol. 20, Issue 5, Kluwer Law International 2003.

Heuman, 'Svensk domsrätt på skiljedomsrättens område', in *Juridisk Tidskrift No. 4 2010/11* (2011).

Hobér, 'Party Substitution under Swedish Arbitration Law', in *Swedish and International Arbitration 1983*, Yearbook of the Arbitration Institute of the Stockholm Chamber of Commerce, ed. Franke, Stockholm: the Arbitration Institute of the Stockholm Chamber of Commerce 1983.

Hobér, 'In Search for the Centre of Gravity. Applicable Law in International Arbitrations in Sweden', in *Swedish and International Arbitration*, 1994.

Hobér, 'Enforcement of Arbitral Awards', in *Stockholm Arbitration Report 1999:1.*

Hobér, 'Sista striden mellan internationalister och territorialister? - berättelsen om Hilmarton och Chromalloy', in *Festskrift till Ulf K. Nordenson*, Stockholm: Jure Förlag AB 1999.

Hobér, 'The Energy Charter Treaty: An Overview', in *Journal of World Investment & Trade*, Vol. 8, No. 3 (June 2007).

Hobér, 'The Energy Charter Treaty – Awards Rendered', in *Dispute Resolution International*, Vol. 1, No. 1 (June 2007).

Hobér, 'State Responsibility and Attribution', in *The Oxford Handbook of International Investment Law*, ed. Muchlinski, Ortino & Schreuer, Oxford: Oxford University Press 2008.

Hobér, 'Investment Arbitration and the Energy Charter Treaty' in *Journal of International Dispute Settlement*, Vol. 1, No. 1 (February 2010).

Hobér & Eliasson, 'Review of Investment Treaty Awards by Municipal Courts' in *Arbitration under International Investment Agreements*, ed. Yannaca-Small, Oxford: Oxford University Press 2010.

Håstad, 'Om underlåtenhet av Yngve Skarin och Bertil Bengtsson att ta ställning till översänt kontrakt respektive inlämnad seminarieuppsats. En civil- och processrättslig kommentar till NJA 1962 s. 276', in *Festskrift till Bertil Bengtsson*, Stockholm: Nerenius & Santérus Förlag 1993.

Jarvin, 'Sekretess i svenska och internationella skiljeförfaranden', in *Juridisk Tidskrift No. 1 1996/97* (1997).

Johansson, 'Decisions by the Arbitration Institute of the Stockholm Chamber of Commerce regarding challenge of arbitrators', in *Stockholm Arbitration Report* 1999:2.

Jung, 'SCC Practice: Challenges to Arbitrators, SCC Board Decisions 2005-2007', in *Stockholm International Arbitration Review 2008:1.*

Khvalei & Benedictsson, 'Recognition and Enforcement of Foreign Arbitral Awards in the Russian Federation', in *Stockholm International Arbitration Review 2005:1.*

Kleineman, 'Principen jura novit curia – särskilt i skiljeförfaranden', in *Vänbok till Bertil Södermark*, ed. Lars Göthlin, Stockholm: Norstedts Juridik AB 2009.

Liebscher, 'Observations to Danish Maritime and Commercial Court Decision 2003 in case S-22-01', in *International Arbitration Court Decisions*, 3rd ed., New York: Juris 2008.

Lundblad, 'Något om vittnesbeviset i domstol och skiljeförfarande', in *Festskrift till Jan Sandström*, ed. Ramberg, et al., Stockholm: Nerenius & Santérus Förlag AB 1997.

Madsen, 'Interim Measures – The Frontier of International Arbitration', in *Festskrift till Lars Heuman*, Stockholm: Jure Förlag 2008.

Madsen, 'Om principen jura novit curia vid skiljeförfaranden', in *Juridisk Tidskrift No. 2 2010/11* (2011).

Magnusson, 'The Practice of the Arbitration Institute of the Stockholm Chamber of Commerce – an Inside View', in *Stockholm Arbitration Report 2001:2.*

Magnusson, 'Avtal om sekretess i skiljeförfarande', in *Juridisk Tidskrift No. 1 2002/03* (2003).

Magnusson, 'Prima facie decisions on Jurisdiction', in *Stockholm Arbitration Report 2000:2.*

Magnusson & Larsson, 'Recent Practice of the Arbitration Institute of the Stockholm Chamber of Commerce: Prima Facie Decisions on Jurisdiction and Challenges of Arbitrators', in *Stockholm Arbitration Report 2004:2.*

Magnusson & Shaughnessy, 'The 2007 Arbitration Rules of the Arbitration Institute of the Stockholm Chamber of Commerce', in *Stockholm International Arbitration Review 2006:3.*

Mohammar & Isaksson, 'Några reflektioner kring handläggningen av mål om klander enligt lagen om skiljeförfarande', in *Vänbok till Bertil Södermark*, ed. Göthlin et al., Stockholm: Norstedts Juridik AB 2009.

Moholitny, *International Arbitration Court Decisions*, New York: Juris 2008.

Nappert, 'Observations to Finnish Supreme Court Decision 2 July 2008 in Case No S2006/716', in *Stockholm International Arbitration Review 2008:3.*

Nilsson, Bo G.H., 'Negative Inferences: An Arbitral Tribunal's Powers to Draw Adverse Conclusions from a Party's Failure to Comply with the Tribunal's Orders', in *Between East and West: Essays in honour of Ulf Franke*, ed. Hobér, Magnusson & Öhrström, New York: JurisNet 2010.

Nordenson, 'Materiell processledning i skiljeförfarande', in *Juridisk Tidskrift* No. *1 1993/94.*

O'Connor, Gatenby & Menin, 'Observations to Final Arbitral Award rendered in 2003 in SCC case 24/2002', in *Stockholm Arbitration Report 2004:2.*

Paulsson, *Arbitration International*, Vol. 14, No. 2, Kluwer Law International 1998.

Permyakova, 'Denial of Jurisdiction: Form, Consequences and Review under the Model Law, National Arbitration Laws and Case Law', in *Stockholm International Arbitration Review 2007:1.*

di Pietro, 'Observations to the Swedish Svea Court of Appeal Decision 15 June 2005 132', in *Stockholm International Arbitration Review 2005:2.*

Puhakka & Pråhl, *SCC Arbitral Awards 2004–2009*, New York: Juris 2011.

Pålsson, 'Skiljeförfarande och Bryssel/Luganokoncentionerna', in *Svensk Juristtidning* 1994.

Ramberg, 'Inkorporering av standardavtal', in *Juridisk Tidskrift No. 3 2007/08* (2008).

Ragnwaldh, 'Need for Speed - An Expert's View on Fast Track Arbitration', in *Commercial Dispute Resolution*, March 2012.

Ramberg & Lazareff, 'Challenging Arbitrators' Fees Determined by Arbitration Institutions', in *Between East and West: Essays in Honour of Ulf Franke*, ed. Hobér, Magnusson & Öhrström, New York: JurisNet 2010.

Ramsjö & Strömberg, 'Manifest Lack of Jurisdiction? A Selection of Decisions of the Arbitration Institute of the Stockholm Chamber of Commerce concerning the Prima Facie Existence of an Arbitration Agreement (2005-2009)', in *Stockholm International Arbitration Review 2009:2.*

Rau, '"Separability" in the United States Supreme Court', in *Stockholm International Arbitration Review 2006:1.*

Reldén, 'Krav på denunitaton för bundenhet av skiljeklausul vid singularsuccession', in *Juridisk Tidskrift No. 4 2003/04* (2004).

Reldén & Nilsson, 'Olycksfall i arbetet eller en skiljedomsovänlig praxis? - Kommentarer om svensk domsrätt vid klander av skiljedom', in *Juridisk Tidskrift No. 4 2005/06* (2006).

Reldén & Nilsson, 'Incorporation and Passivity: Entering into Arbitration Agreements under Swedish law', in *Between East and West: Essays in honour of Ulf Franke*, ed. Hobér, Magnusson & Öhrström, New York: JurisNet 2010.

Roos, 'Multi-party Arbitration and Rule-Making: Same Issues, Contrasting Approaches', in *50 Years of the New York Convention: ICCA International Arbitration Conference*, ICCA Congress Series, 2009 Dublin Vol. 14, ed. van den Berg, The Hague: Kluwer Law International 2009.

Rubins, *International Arbitration Court Decisions*, ed. Jarvin & Magnusson, New York: Juris 2008.

Runesson, 'The Arbitration Agreement as a Matter of Swedish Contract Law', in *The Swedish Arbitration Act of 1999, Five Years On: A Critical Review of Strengths and Weaknesses*, ed. Heuman & Jarvin, New York: JurisNet 2006.

Schlosser, *Arbitration International*, Vol. 7, No. 3 (1991).

Schöldström, 'Skiljemäns arvoden – NJA 1998 s. 574', in *Juridisk Tidskrift No. 3 1998/99* (1999).

Schöldström, 'Arbitrator Fees in Institutional Arbitration Subject to Substantive Review in Court', in *Stockholm International Arbitration Review 2008:3*.

Schöldström, 'Contractual Relations in Institutional Arbitration', in *Between East and West: Essays in Honour of Ulf Franke*, ed. Hobér, Magnusson & Öhrström, New York: JurisNet 2010.

Schöldström, 'Påståendedoktrinen och skiljeförfarande', in *Juridisk Tidskrift No. 1 2008/09* (2008).

Schöldström, *International Arbitration Court Decisions*, ed. Jarvin & Magnusson, New York: Juris 2008.

Schöldström, *SCC Arbitral Awards 2004–2009*, ed. Jarvin & Magnusson, New York: Juris 2011

Seipel, 'Telefaxad vadeinlaga', in *Juridisk Tidskrift No. 2 1993/94* (1994).

Sekolec & Eliasson, 'The UNCITRAL Model Law on Arbitration and the Swedish Arbitration Act: A Comparison', in *The Swedish Arbitration Act of 1999, Five Years On: A Critical Review of Strengths and Weaknesses*, ed. Heuman & Jarvin, New York: JurisNet 2006.

Shaughnessy, 'Observations to Svea Court of Appeal Case No. T 1038–05' in *Stockholm International Arbitration Review 2005:2*.

Shaughnessy, 'The New SCC Emergency Arbitrator Rules', in *Between East and West: Essays in Honour of Ulf Franke*, ed. Hobér, Magnusson & Öhrström, New York: JurisNet 2010.

Shaughnessy, 'Pre-Arbitral Urgent Relief, The New SCC Emergency Arbitrator Rules' in *Journal of International Arbitration*, Vol. 27, No. 4 (August 2010).

Sinclair, 'ICSID arbitration: how long does it take?', in *Global Arbitration Review*, Vol. 4, No. 5 (October 2009).

Smit, 'Observations to Case No. G20010379', in *Stockholm International Arbitration Review 2005:1*.

St. John Sutton, 'Chapter 23: Swedish Awards: Proper Form, Validity and Recourse', in *The Swedish Arbitration Act of 1999, Five Years On – A Critical Review of Strengths and Weaknesses*, ed. Heuman & Jarvin, New York: JurisNet, 2006.

Stoltysinski & Olechowski, *International Arbitration Court Decisions*, New York: Juris 2008.

Söderlund, 'Observations to Svea Court of Appeal Case No. T 1038–05' in *Stockholm International Arbitration Review 2005:2.*

Tude & Scherp, *Stockholm International Arbitration Review 2009:2.*

Udris & Kacevska, *International Arbitration Court Decisions*, New York: Juris 2008.

Walker, 'Final Arbitration Award Rendered in 2000 in Case 108/1997: Majority Award Arbitrator Dissenting in Part–Observations', in *Stockholm Arbitration Report 2001:1.*

Wallin, 'Observations to Svea Court of Appeal, Case No T 8090-99', in *Stockholm Arbitration Report 2003:1.*

van den Berg, A.J., *ICCA Yearbook Commercial Arbitration,* Volume XXVI-2001, Kluwer Law International, 2001.

Voser, 'Multi-party Disputes and Joinder of Third Parties', in *50 Years of the New York Convention: ICCA International Arbitration Conference*, ICCA Congress Series, 2009 Dublin Vol. 14, ed. van den Berg, The Hague: Kluwer Law International 2009.

Welamson, '*Anmälan av P-O. Bolding, Skiljedom*', in *Svensk Juristtidning 1964.*

Vesselinovitch, 'Enforcement of SCC and Russian Arbitration Awards in the United States Courts: An Overview', in *Stockholm Arbitration Report 2003:2.*

Wetter, *Arbitration International,* Vol. 10, No. 3, 1994, Kluwer Law International 1994.

Wiwen-Nilsson, *International Arbitration Court Decisions,* 3rd ed., New York: Juris 2008.

Wälde, 'Investment Arbitration under the Energy Charter Treaty – From Dispute Settlement to Treaty Implementation', in *Arbitration International,* Vol. 12, No. 4, 1996.

Zykin & Landrove, 'Obeservations to SCC Case No. 12/2002', in *SCC Arbitral Awards 2004–2009*, New York: Juris 2011.

Zettermarck & Reldén, 'Bör lagen om skiljeförfarande internationaliseras', in *Vänbok till Bertil Södermark*, ed. Göthlin et al., Stockholm: Norstedts Juridik AB 2009.

Åhman, *International Arbitration Court Decisions*, New York: Juris 2008.

Åstenius & Björk, 'Observations to SCC Case No. 33/2007', in *Stockholm International Arbitration Review 2009:1.*

Öhrström, 'Decisions by the SCC Institute regarding Challenge of Arbitrators', in *Stockholm Arbitration Report 2002:1.*

Öhrström, 'The "Soyak" Case – Judicial Terrorism or Justified Cost Control?', in *Stockholm International Arbitration Review 2008:3.*

Other Material

Brocker, 'The New IBA Rules on the Taking of Evidence in International Arbitration – from a cost-efficiency perspective', paper given at a conference arranged by the Swedish Arbitration Association (Stockholm, 27 January 2011), available at http://www.sccinstitute.com/library/articles.aspx

Lindström, 'Challenges to Arbitrators – Decisions by the SCC Board during 2006–2010', available at http://www.sccinstitute.com.

UNCITRAL Report of Working Group II (Arbitration and Conciliation) on the Work of its Fiftieth Session New York, 9–13 February 2009, A/CN.9/669 (March 9 2009).

Eliasson, *10 Years of Energy Charter Treaty Arbitration*, Conference Report presented at the joint ICSID, SCC and ECT Secretariat Conference '10 years of Energy Charter Treaty Arbitration' (6 June 2011), available at http://www.sccinstitute.com/filearchive/4/41105/Report%20Ten%20Years%20of%20ECT%20Arbitration,%2030%20June%202011.pdf.

Lundstedt, *SCC Practice: Emergency Arbitrator Decisions Rendered in 2010*, available at http://www.sccinstitute.com/filearchive/4/41504/Emergency%20arbitration%20final.pdf (last visited 13 November 2011).

Tawil & Gill, Foreword to the 2010 IBA Rules on the Taking of Evidence in International Arbitration (29 May 2010).

Investment Arbitration Reporter, *Interview: Author of Forthcoming Study on Arbitrator Disqualification Explains Why ICSID Arbitrators Are So Difficult to Unseat* (8 June 2011), available at http://www.iareporter.com/articles/20110608.

How to Access Swedish Legal Authorities

Introduction

This book cites a vast number of Swedish legal authorities. The Swedish arbitration community has endeavoured to make Swedish legal authorities in the field of arbitration law available to a non-Swedish audience. This section provides an overview of where those authorities can be found.

Statutes

Many Swedish statutes have been translated into English by the Swedish Government Offices and are available online free of charge. Currently these translations can be accessed at http://www.government.se/sb/d/3288.

The Swedish Arbitration Act is available in nine languages other than Swedish, including Russian and Chinese, at the SCC website (www.sccinstitute.com/library.aspx). The SCC website also contains certain important Swedish private law statutes in Russian and Chinese. The materials on the SCC website are available free of charge.

Case Law

Swedish case law in arbitration matters is frequently translated into English. Many such translations are available at the Swedish Arbitration Portal (http://www.arbitration.sccinstitute.com/Swedish-Arbitration-Portal/)

Swedish cases in English translation have also been published in the Stockholm Arbitration Report (Juris Publishing) and the Stockholm International Arbitration Report (JurisNet).

Table of Cases

I. NATIONAL COURT DECISIONS

A. Sweden

1. Supreme Court

2. *Court of Appeal*

3. District Court

The Russian Federation v. Sedelmayer, 12 December 2002, Stockholm District Court, T 6-583-98, 36, 41, 47, 48

4. Labour Court

Byggnadsfirman J. Karlsson v. Svenska Byggnadsträarbetareförbundets avdelning nr 89 et al., 1931, AD 1931 no. 64, 53

Göran Holmqvist v. Fritidsbolaget M.C.B. AB, 1 July 1977, AD 1977 no. 112 (A 122-1977), 63, 67

B. France

Cf. Poiré v. Tripier, Cour de Cassation, mixed chamber, 11 February 2003, reprinted in 19(3) Arbitration International 368, 54

Siemens AG and BKMI Industrieanlagen GmbH v. Dutco Construction Company Pvt., Cour de Cassation, Première chambre civile, 7 January 1992, 1992 Rev. Arb. 470, 128

C. Finland

Judgment by the Supreme Court of Finland, 31 January 2005, KKO 2005:14, 133

Decision by the Supreme Court of Finland, 2 July 2008 in case no S2006/716, translation in SIAR 2008:3, 259 et seq., 150

D. England

Hiscox v. Outhwaite [1991] 1 W.L.R. 545, House of Lords (1991), 271

Tongyuan (USA) International Trading Group (China) v. Uni-Clan Ltd, High Court of Justice, Queen's Bench Division Commercial Court, 19 January, 2001, published in ICCA Yearbook Commercial Arbitration, Volume XXVI-2001, p. 886–893, 290

Dardana Ltd v. Yukos oil Co. [2002] 1. Lloyd's Report 225 (Q.B.) (21 March 2001), 290

Ecuador v. Occidental Exploration and Production Company (non-justiciability), Judgment, [2005] EWHC 774 (Comm), 29 April 2005, 37 *Occidental Exploration and Production Company v. Ecuador* (non-justiciability), Judgment of the Court of Appeal, [2005] EWCA Civ 1116, 9 September 2005, paras. 57–58, 37

Ecuador v. Occidental Exploration and Production Company, Judgment, [2006] EWHC 345 (Comm), 2 March 2006, para. 7, 49

Czech Republic v. European Media Ventures SA, Judgment, [2007] EWHC 285 (Comm), 5 December 2007, 49

Kanoria v. Guinness [2006] 1. Lloyd's Report 701 (Q.B.) (21 February 2006), 280

Dallah v. Ministry of Religious Affairs, Government of Pakistan [2009] EWCA Civ 755 (20 July 2009), 280

E. The Netherlands

Yukos Capital S.A.R.L. v. OAO Rosneft, Amsterdam Court of Appeal, (28 April 2009), 269

F. Russia

G. Ukraine

H. Canada

II. ARBITRAL AWARDS AND ORDERS

A. ICC

B. SCC

C. Other Arbitral Awards

III. EU

Index

S